WEATHER DATA HANDBOOK

For HVAC and Cooling Equipment Design

 Ecodyne Cooling Products Division

McGraw-Hill Book Company

New York St. Louis San Francisco Auckland Bogotá
Hamburg Johannesburg London Madrid Mexico
Montreal New Delhi Panama Paris São Paulo
Singapore Sydney Tokyo Toronto

To all those people,
including the many engineers and architects,
who find a repeated need for reliable
weather data.

Library of Congress Cataloging in Publication Data

Ecodyne Corporation.   Weather Data Handbook.

Edition of 1958 by Fluor Products Company published under title: Evaluated weather data for cooling equipment design.
Includes indexes.
1. Air conditioning—Climatic factors. 2. Heating—Climatic factors. 3. Cooling towers—Climatic factors. I. Fluor Products Company. Evaluated weather data for cooling equipment design. II. Title.
TH7687.5.E26   1980   697'.002   79-27370
ISBN 0-07-018960-9

1 2 3 4 5 6 7 8 9 0   HDHD   8 9 8 7 6 5 4 3 2 1 0

TABLE OF CONTENTS

TABLE OF CONTENTS

INDEX TO FIGURES

INDEX TO TABLES

PREFACE

The successful design of atmospheric heat exchange equipment is dependent upon sufficient knowledge of weather data to make adequate predictions of the conditions to be encountered during the operating life of the equipment. Reliable hourly weather information spanning a sufficient period to establish dependable frequency of occurrence levels supplies a base for reliable design calculations.

The data contained in this book represents detailed tabulations of wet bulb temperature frequencies for the summer months, tabulations in three frequency categories for winter and summer conditions and tabulations of various weather parameters useful in estimating performance for wet/dry and natural draft cooling towers and other applications.

In addition to the vast amount of new material appearing herein, this edition also contains material from the 1958 version, *Evaluated Weather Data for Cooling Equipment Design*, and Addendum No. 1, 1964, which are no longer in print.

Acknowledgment and thanks are extended to all who have helped make this project possible. Loren W. Crow, Consulting Meteorologist, Denver, Colorado, served as technical liaison agent between the Ecodyne Cooling Products Division of Ecodyne Corporation and the National Climatic Center of the United States Department of Commerce. He also carried out the analysis for, and presentation of, the tabulated data.

The efforts of many other people were necessary to process the data for this project. Personnel at Ecodyne who have contributed their time in the planning, preparation and editing of this book include James Klein, Gordon Wistrom, John Ovard and Norman Dolan. Special acknowledgment is due Mr. Grady McKay, Chief of Automatic Data Processing Service Division at the National Climatic Center, and to Mr. Ray Barr, Project Supervisor. Acknowledgment is also due to Mr. Oscar Richard, Chief, Engineering Meteorology Section, United States Air Force Environmental Technical Applications Center, Scott Air Force Base, Illinois.

The complete summaries from which this compilation material are developed are available from the Ecodyne Cooling Products Division of Ecodyne Corporation for use if a particular design problem should require more detailed or specific analysis.

Yale Abrams

FOREWORD

The transfer of heat in large quantities is essential to many industrial processes, most forms of power generation and the heating and cooling of large buildings and building complexes. Proper design of heating and cooling equipment is primarily a function of the weather conditions prevalent in the immediate geographical location. Over-design is an expensive waste while under-design will result in failure to meet the needs of the affected project.

Some of the most efficient heat exchange equipment develops lower temperatures through the evaporation of water. The comparatively low cost of water, even with chemical treatment to avoid corrosion, offers economic advantages for rapid cooling from beginning temperatures in excess of 100°F to temperatures which approach the current wet bulb temperature of the atmosphere. Water is in this favorable position since its evaporation into the atmosphere causes cooling due to the latent heat of evaporization to temperatures below the actual (dry bulb) temperature of the surrounding air.

The same principle is at work when a thermometer bulb covered with a wetted wick is subjected to rapid air movement. This "wet bulb" temperature is, along with the "dry bulb" temperature, a measure of the dryness of the air. On a psychrometric chart, the intersection of any dry bulb and wet bulb line locates a state point for which the actual amount of moisture can be read.

In addition, most psychrometric charts have relative humidity and specific volume lines from which these respective quantities can be determined. It is important to note that lines of constant enthalpy (heat content) are very nearly parallel to the wet bulb lines. This means, of course, that all air and water vapor mixtures with the same wet bulb temperatures have approximately the same enthalpy. The wet bulb temperature is therefore taken as the most important temperature criterion in evaporative cooling processes.

This ability of air to cool water to a temperature approaching the air's wet bulb temperature is utilized in modern cooling towers. Streams of water are sprayed or allowed to splash within a structure, usually containing air and water baffles called filling or packing, through which large quantities of air are moved. Extremely large areas of contact between the air and the water can be achieved by this spraying and splashing of the water into the air and by the forming of sheets of water on the packing.

The cooling of the water as it passes through the tower depends not only on the wet bulb of the air entering the tower but also on the quantity of air moved. The quantity of air moved is dependent on the size of the tower, the power consumption of the motors, the efficiencies of the gears and the fans, the resistance of packing to air movement and the specific volume of the air as it reaches the fan.

The most important single environmental factor affecting the performance of a cooling tower is the wet bulb temperature of the air entering the intakes. A designer knowing the wet bulb temperature that can be expected in a particular locality can design a tower to cool the required quantity of water to the temperature desired, providing, of course, that this temperature is not lower than the wet bulb temperature itself. Since the wet bulb temperature varies from hour to hour, from day to day, and from year to year, the choice of a so-called "design wet bulb" is one requiring mature judgment and reliable information.

As availability of water or cost of water delivered to the point of use increases, opportunities develop for use of combinations which include both wet and dry cooling. Liquids which have very high temperatures moved through metal heat exchangers can lose large quantities of heat through the dry process. Probably the most common example of this cooling process is shown by the use of radiators on automobiles. When additional heat must still be removed, a second stage of evaporative cooling can produce the still lower temperatures that may be required. Thus, the analysis of various combinations of wet/dry cooling towers is of growing concern in many industrial heat exchange problems.

Sets of dry bulb and wet bulb temperature frequencies can also assist engineers in selecting appropriate equipment for space heating problems and for calculating energy consumption estimates.

The first four parts in this book relate primarily to the summer months of June–September, which contain most of the critical hours for applications of evaporative cooling equipment. Frequencies of winter temperature data, particularly dry bulb temperature, are included in Part 5 as they relate to heating problems. Sets of annual weather data are presented for use in calculations related to combined wet/dry cooling tower applications.

Although the data presented in this book cover many locations, the selection of proper design temperature values will generally be for some other location. Design estimates made by direct transposition of data from the nearest city or tower to the point of installation may produce erroneous results. For major installations involving large expenditures of money or critical temperature balance, further detailed studies are recommended.

Section 1: MAN AND WEATHER

In man's endeavor to adapt his living habits and industrial processes to his physical environment, primary consideration must be given to an adequate evaluation of the physical environment itself. Consideration of an area's climate is both elementary and essential to the design of buildings. Design engineers who utilize the earth's atmosphere as a heat source or heat sink, either in an industrial process or in comfort air conditioning, must also have pertinent weather information.

The atmosphere at any point on the globe is subject to considerable variation, and within the general science of meteorology man has observed these changes and recorded certain measurements of atmospheric phenomena. The condition and behavior of the atmosphere constitutes weather, while the average weather of a locality is generally referred to as climate.

For many purposes the average weather for a given period of time is more important than the weather on a particular day or at a particular hour. On the other hand, it is important that a designer know the total number of hours that certain extreme conditions are expected to occur during the given period of time.

Section 2: PERTINENT DESIGN VALUES

The efficiency of evaporative cooling equipment reaches its greatest test during the summer months. The critical weather element affecting cooling tower efficiency is wet bulb temperature.

Hourly observations have been considered during the four summer months of June, July, August and September. The total number of hours during these four months is 2,928. In treating this period as the primary summer period, the number of hours that any wet bulb temperature will be equaled or exceeded are reported as percent of the total hours in this four-month period.

If a given wet bulb temperature is equaled or exceeded for 29 hours during this period, it can be said that that point in the total wet bulb temperature scale is at the 1% level — down from the top — of the total four-month summer period. Conversely, 99% of all hours are below that temperature. Since all the highest wet bulb temperature values occur during this four-month period, the 1% value would be, in reality, one-third of 1% for the entire annual population of hours. Similarly, the 15% level of the four summer months would be, in effect, the 5% level for the entire annual population of hours.

The expected summer wet bulb temperatures for the 1%, 5%, 15% and 50% levels are tabulated by stations in this manual. One iso-line map for the 1% level is also presented.

It is generally poor planning to design evaporative cooling equipment for the one single hour when an extreme condition might occur during the total life of the equipment because unnecessary expense would be involved for *all* the other hours when atmospheric conditions were less than that extreme.

By contrast, if the design engineer chooses values which are too low, the equipment will be undersized for a good many hours of operation and may produce critical situations in industrial processes. Thus, except for very extreme or unusual circumstances, it is his responsibility to design somewhat below the all-time extreme of heat and moisture, yet give reasonable assurance that the equipment will accomplish its required assignment during a high percentage of its operating lifetime.

Because there is variation in the daily, monthly and annual weather patterns at any geographical location, no single day, month, or year can be used to describe exactly what can be expected on some other day, month or year in the future.

The information reported in this manual is based on millions of individual hourly observations from several hundred separate geographic locations. These data have been carefully evaluated and are presented in summary form. The complete tabulations of hourly records from which the summaries have been made are on file at Ecodyne. These data can be used when special analyses are desired.

Wind data were analyzed in order to prepare a map containing the predominant wind velocity and direction coincident with the summer season high wet bulb temperatures. The wind direction is also presented to the closest 10° azimuth in tabular form.

The 5% level of summer dry bulb temperatures was determined and the results presented in table and iso-line map form.

FIGURE 1
DIRECTORY MAP
United States official weather stations
from which hourly weather observations have been utilized in the preparation of this manual.

OFFICIAL WEATHER STATIONS

ECODYNE Ecodyne Cooling
Products Division

Section 3: SOURCES OF DATA

Hourly data, collected 24 hours per day, 365 days per year by trained observers at many of the nation's airports, are processed by computer to yield percentile levels based upon several years of historical data from which the average yearly pattern is developed.

In addition to the hourly observations made at National Weather Service observation stations, generally located at civilian airports, there are hourly weather observations made at military stations. The data base from which either summer or annual hourly data have been tabulated for frequency levels exceeds 250 separate locations.

For stations for which actual hourly data are not available, estimates of such data have been made using a technique developed during 1962 and 1963 by Loren W. Crow for the American Society of Heating, Refrigeration and Air-Conditioning Engineers, Inc., (ASHRAE) as Research Project 23 (RP-23) whereby reliable estimates of the hourly data are calculated from recorded daily maximum and minimum temperatures.

The Third Edition of "Recommended Outdoor Design Temperatures for Southern California, Arizona and Nevada," published by the Southern California Chapter of ASHRAE in March, 1964, was used as reference material for many stations in those three states.

Wind data coincident with extreme temperatures have been extracted from a study made by the Arctic Meteorological Research Group, McGill University, for Headquarters Quartermaster Research and Engineering Command, United States Army.

The ten-year reference period for most of the hourly data covered in this manual were taken from the ten years 1948 through 1957. The largest portion of data were produced at the National Weather Records Center in Asheville, North Carolina. Canadian data were obtained from the Air Service Branch of the Department of Transport. The data from the Mexican stations were obtained from the Mexican Government Observatory in Mexico City.

Most of the data presented in part 12 is reprinted from AFM 88-29, TM 5-785, NAVFAC P-89, *Facility Design and Planning Engineering Weather Data*, Departments of the Air Force, the Army, and the Navy, 1 July 1979.

Section 4: WEATHER STATIONS

Data for the weather stations contained in this book have been tabulated on three levels. On the first level, stations having detailed tabulations of wet bulb frequencies by 1°F intervals for the summer months June-September are included. The geographic location of these stations is presented in Figs. 1, 2, and 3. In Table 1 the names of these stations begin at the full left hand margin. These same stations carry latitudinal and longitudinal positions and the span of years from which those frequency data were tabulated.

The second level includes all of the stations in the first level plus other cities and towns from which design data in three distinct frequency categories have been developed for winter and summer conditions. Slightly more than 1,000 locations throughout the United States are included here and their locations are shown on the state maps in Part 6. The identifying names of the additional stations on this level beyond those included in the first level are indented in the Table 1 list.

On the final level are stations for which data have been tabulated relating various weather parameters useful in developing estimates of operational performance characteristics of wet/dry and natural draft cooling towers as well as other applications. The 91 stations in this category are identified in Table 1 with an asterisk at the end of each name. All stations on this level are included on the second level and some are also included on the first level. Wet bulb tabulations on this third level of data are in 2°F intervals for the full 12 months of the year. The reference time period of hourly weather data used to develop this level was 1949-58, which matches a high fraction of the time periods used to develop the frequency data for the four summer months in the first level.

TABLE I

DIRECTORY OF WEATHER STATIONS
Type, Elevation, Latitude, Longitude, Period of Recording

KEY TO TYPE OF STATION

Code	Agency	Type
WSAP	National Weather Service	Airport
FAA	Federal Aeronautics Administration	Airport
AFB	United States Air Force	Air Force Base
NAS	United States Navy	Naval Air Station
MCAS	United States Marine Corps	Marine Corps Air Station
WSCO	National Weather Service	City Office
DOT	Canadian Department of Transport	Airport
FWC	United States Navy	Fleet Weather Central
AB	United States Air Force	Air Base
AP	Commercial Airline, U.S. Army, etc.	Airport
MGO	Mexican Government Observatory	

Station	Type	Elev. (ft.)	Lat. Deg	Lat. Min	Long. Deg	Long. Min	Period of Recording (Inclusive)
ALABAMA							
Alexander City		660					
Andalusia		260					
Anniston	WSAP	599	N33	35	W 85	51	1948-54
Auburn		730					
Birmingham*	WSAP	630	N33	34	W 86	45	35-39,48-57
Brewton		85					
Citronello		331					
Decatur		580					
Demopolis		100					
Dothan	FAA	321	N31	14	W 85	26	49-54
Eufaula		207					
Evergreen	FAA	257	N31	25	W 87	2	50-54
Florence (Muscle Shoals)	FAA	562	N34	45	W 87	37	49-54
Gadsden		570					
Greenville		444					
Haleyville		947					
Huntsville	WSAP	619					
Jasper		525					
Mobile*	WSAP	217	N30	41	W 88	14	35-39,48-57
Mobile	WSCO	119					
Montgomery	WSAP	195	N32	18	W 86	24	48-57
Ozark		380					
Selma (Craig)	AFB	207					
Talladega		565					
Thomasville		405					
Troy		580					
Tuscaloosa	FAA	170ᵣ	N33	14	W 87	37	49-54
ALASKA							
Anchorage	WSAP	90					
Anchorage (Elmendorf)	AFB	258	N63	15	W149	48	49-57
Barrow		22					
Bethel	WSAP	125					
Cordova	WSAP	41					
Fairbanks	WSAP	436					
Fairbanks (Ladd)	AFB	484	N76	50	W147	37	49-56
Juneau	WSAP	17					
Kodiak		21					
Kotzebue	WSAP	10					
Nome	WSAP	13					
ARIZONA							
Ajo		1763					
Casa Grande		1405					
Douglas	FAA	4076	N31	28	W109	36	49-54
Flagstaff	WSAP	6973	N35	8	W111	40	50-56
Fort Huachuca	AP	4664					
Gila Bend	FAA	853	N32	34	W112	43	49-54
Globe		3540					
Kingman	AP	3446	N35	15	W113	57	35-39
Luke	AFB	1087					
Nogales		3800					
Page		4270					
Phoenix*	WSAP	1112	N33	26	W112	2	35-39,48-57
Prescott	WSAP	5014	N34	39	W112	26	48-57
Safford		2990					
Tucson*	WSAP	2558	N32	8	W110	57	35-39,48-57
Williams	AFB	1351					
Winslow	WSAP	4880	N35	1	W110	44	35-39,48-57
Yuma	FAA	199	N32	40	W114	36	49-56
ARKANSAS							
Arkadelphia		200					
Batesville		277					
Blytheville	AFB	264					
Brinkley		205					
Camden		116					
El Dorado	FAA	252	N33	13	W 92	48	50-54
Fayetteville	FAA	1253	N36	0	W 94	10	50-54
Fort Smith	WSAP	449	N35	20	W 94	22	49-57
Harrison		1150					
Hot Springs Nat. Pk.		710					
Jacksonville (Little Rock)	AFB	337					
Jonesboro		345					
Little Rock*	WSAP	265	N34	44	W 92	14	35-39,49-57
Pine Bluff	FAA	204	N34	10	W 91	56	49-54
Russelville		360					
Texarkana	WSAP	361	N33	27	W 94	0	49-54
Walnut Ridge	FAA	275	N36	8	W 90	56	49-54
CALIFORNIA							
Arcata	FAA	217	N40	59	W124	6	50-56
Auburn		1297					
Bakersfield*	WSAP	494	N35	25	W119	3	35-39,48-57
Banning	AP	2349					
Barstow	AP	2142					
Bishop	WSAP	4108					
Blythe*	FAA	395	N33	37	W114	43	49-54
Burbank	WSAP	699	N34	12	W118	22	35-39,48-57
Chico		205					
Coalinga		676					
Concord		195					
Covina		575					
Crescent City	FAA	50	N41	47	W124	14	50-54
Daggett	FAA	1929	N34	52	W116	47	35-39,49-56
Downey		116					
El Cajon		525					
El Centro	NAS	-30	N32	49	W115	40	48-56
El Toro	MCAS	380	N33	40	W117	44	48-56
Escondido		660					
Eureka	WSAP	203					
Fairfield (Travis)	AFB	72					
Fresno	WSAP	326	N36	43	W119	49	35-39,48-57
Indio		11					
Laguna Beach		35					
Livermore		545					
Lompoc (Vandenburg)	AFB	552					
Long Beach	WSAP	34	N33	49	W118	9	49-56
Los Angeles*	WSAP	122	N33	56	W118	23	48-57
Los Angeles	WSCO	312					
Mather	AFB	92					
McClellan	AFB	86					
Merced (Castle)	AFB	178	N37	22	W120	34	49-56
Modesto		91					
Montague	FAA	2635	N41	46	W122	28	50-54
Monterey		38					
Napa		16					
Needles	FAA	913	N34	46	W114	38	49-54
Oakland	WSAP	3	N37	44	W122	12	35-39,48-57
Oceanside		30					
Ontario		995					
Oxnard	AFB	43					
Palmdale	FAA	2517	N34	38	W118	5	49-54
Palm Springs		411					
Pasadena		864					
Petaluma		27					
Red Bluff	WSAP	344	N40	9	W122	15	48-57
Redding	WSAP	495	N40	35	W122	24	35-39
Redlands		1318					
Richmond		55					
Riverside (March)	AFB	1511	N33	54	W117	15	49-56
Sacramento (Municipal)*	AP	23	N38	31	W121	30	48-57
Salinas	FAA	74	N36	40	W121	37	49-54
San Bernardino (Norton)	AFB	1125					
Sandberg	WSCO	4523	N34	45	W118	44	48-54
San Diego*	WSAP	37	N32	44	W117	10	35-39,48-57
San Fernando		977					
San Francisco	WSAP	18	N37	37	W122	23	48-57
San Francisco	WSCO	52					
San Jose	FAA	70ᵣ					
San Luis Obispo		315ᵣ					
San Rafael (Hamilton)	AFB	2	N38	4	W122	31	49-56
Santa Ana	FAA	115ᵣ					
Santa Barbara	FAA	13ᵣ	N34	26	W119	50	49-54
Santa Barbara	WSCO	100					
Santa Cruz		125					
Santa Maria	WSAP	238	N34	56	W120	25	48-54
Santa Monica	WSCO	57					
Santa Paula		263					
Santa Rosa		167					
Stockton	FAA	28	N37	54	W121	15	49-54
Sunnyvale (Moffett)	NAS	39	N37	25	W122	4	48-56
Thermal	FAA	117	N33	38	W116	10	50-54
Ukiah	CAA	620	N39	8	W123	12	50-54
Visalia		354					
Williams	FAA	128	N39	6	W122	9	35-39
Yreka		2625					
Yuba City		70					

TABLE 1—Continued

DIRECTORY OF WEATHER STATIONS
Type, Elevation, Latitude, Longitude, Period of Recording

Station	Type	Elev. (ft.)	Latitude Degrees	Minutes	Longitude Degrees	Minutes	Period of Recording (Inclusive)	Station	Type	Elev. (ft.)	Latitude Degrees	Minutes	Longitude Degrees	Minutes	Period of Recording (Inclusive)
COLORADO								Savannah (Travis)*	WSAP	52	N32	8	W 81	12	36-39,51-56
Akron*	FAA	4621	N40	7	W103	10	48-54	Valdosta	WSAP	223	N30	47	W 83	17	49-54
Alamosa	WSAP	7536						Washington		630					
Boulder		5385						Waycross		140					
Burlington		4165													
Canon City		5343						**HAWAII**							
Colorado Springs	WSAP	6173	N38	49	W104	42	1949-56	Hilo		31					
Craig		6280						Honolulu	WSAP	39	N21	20	W157	25	50-57
Denver*	WSAP	5332	N39	46	W104	53	35-39,48-57	Kaneohe		198					
Durango		6550						Lihue	WSAP	115					
Eagle -	FAA	6598	N39	39	W106	55	48-57	Wahiawa		215					
Fort Collins		5001						Wailuku		200					
Fort Morgan		4321													
Glenwood Springs		5823						**IDAHO**							
Grand Junction*	WSAP	4839	N39	6	W108	32	48-53,56	Boise*	WSAP	2858	N43	34	W116	13	35-39,48-57
Greeley		4648						Burley	FAA	4180	N42	33	W113	46	35-39,48-54
Gunnison		7664						Coeur d'Alene	FAA	2973	N47	46	W116	49	48-53
La Junta	FAA	4188	N38	3	W103	31	48-54	Dubois -	FAA	5129	N44	10	W112	18	48-54
Lamar		3635						Gooding -	FAA	3668	N42	55	W114	46	48-54
Leadville		10177						Grangeville		3355					
Limon		5360						Hailey	AP	5328					
Montrose		5830						Idaho Falls	FAA	4730	N43	31	W112	4	35-39,48-54
Pueblo	WSAP	4639	N38	14	W104	38	35-39,48-53	Lewiston	WSAP	1413					
Sterling		3939						Malad City -	FAA	4480	N42	10	W112	19	48-54
Trinidad	FAA	5746	N37	16	W104	20	48-54	McCall		5025					
								Montpelier		6950					
CONNECTICUT								Moscow		2660					
Bridgeport	WSAP	7						Mountain Home	AFB	2992	N43	3	W115	51	49,51-56
Falls Village		580						Mullan Pass -	FAA	6037	N47	27	W115	41	48-54
Hartford (Brainard)	WSAP	15	N41	44	W 72	39	35-39,49-53	Pocatello	WSAP	4444	N42	55	W112	32	35-39,48-57
New Haven	WSAP	6	N41	16	W 72	53	35-39	Rexburg		4810					
New London		60						Salmon		3961					
Norwald		37						Sandpoint		2100					
Norwich		20						Twin Falls	AP	4148					
Waterbury		605						Weiser		2120					
Windsor Locks (Bradley)*	WSAP	179	N41	56	W 72	41	49-56							
								ILLINOIS							
DELAWARE								Aurora		744					
Dover*	AFB	38						Belleville (Scott)	AFB	447	N38	33	W 89	59	49-56
Wilmington	WSAP	78	N39	40	W 75	36	48-57	Bloomington		775					
								Cairo	WSCO	314					
DISTRICT OF COLUMBIA								Carbondale		380					
Andrews	AFB	279						Champaign/Urbana		743					
Washington, D.C.*	WSAP	65	N38	50	W 77	2	35-39,48-57	Charleston		686					
								Chicago-Midway*	WSAP	623	N41	47	W 87	44	35-39,48-57
FLORIDA								Chicago-O'Hare	WSAP	658					
Avon Park		145						Chicago	WSCO	594					
Belle Glade		16						Danville		558					
Cape Kennedy	AP	16						Decatur		670					
Crestview -	FAA	272	N30	48	W 86	34	48-54	Dixon		696					
Cross City	FAA	46	N29	38	W 83	6	49-54	Effingham		595					
Daytona Beach	WSAP	31	N29	11	W 81	3	48-57	Elgin		820					
Fort Lauderdale		13						Freeport		780					
Fort Myers	WSAP	13	N26	34	W 81	52	48-54	Galesburg		771					
Fort Pierce		10						Greenville		563					
Gainesville	FAA	155						Harrisburg		366					
Homestead	AFB	10						Joliet	WSAP	588	N41	30	W 88	10	48-52
Jacksonville*	WSAP	39	N30	25	W 81	39	35-39,48-57	Kankakee		625					
Key West	AP	6						La Salle/Peru		520					
Lakeland	WSCO	214						Macomb		702					
Miami*	WSAP	24	N25	49	W 80	17	35-39,48-57	Moline	WSAP	582	N41	27	W 90	31	35-39,48-57
Miami Beach	WSCO	9						Mt. Vernon		500					
Ocala		86						Olney		450					
Orlando	WSAP	106	N28	33	W 81	20	48-57	Peoria	WSAP	652	N40	40	W 89	41	35-39,48-51,57
Panama City (Tyndall)	.AFB	22	N30	4	W 85	35	49-56	Quincy	FAA	762	N39	56	W 91	11	49-54
Pensacola -	NAS	33	N30	21	W 87	19	48-54	Rantoul (Chanute)	AFB	740	N40	18	W 88	9	49-56
Pensacola	WSCO	13						Rockford*		724					
St. Augustine		15						Springfield	WSAP	587	N39	45	W 89	41	35-39,48-57
St. Petersburg		35						Waukegan		680					
Sanford		14													
Sarasota		30						**INDIANA**							
Tallahassee	WSCO	58	N30	26	W 84	20	48-57	Anderson		847					
Tampa*	WSAP	36	N27	58	W 82	32	48-57	Bedford		670					
Titusville -	WSAP	14	N28	34	W 80	51	35-39	Bloomington		820					
Valparaiso (Elgin)	AFB	66						Columbus (Bakalar)	AFB	661	N39	15	W 85	53	50-56
Vero Beach -	FAA	54	N27	39	W 80	24	49-54	Crawfordsville		752					
West Palm Beach	WSAP	15	N26	41	W 80	6	48-57	Evansville*	WSAP	388	N38	2	W 87	32	48-57
								Fort Wayne	WSAP	791	N41	0	W 85	12	48-57
GEORGIA								Goshen	AP	823					
Albany (Turner)	AFB	224	N31	32	W 84	11	49-54	Helmer -	WSAP	976	N41	33	W 85	12	35-39
Alma -	FAA	203	N31	32	W 82	31	49-54	Hobart		600					
Americus		476						Huntington		802					
Athens		700						Indianapolis*	WSAP	793	N39	44	W 86	16	35-39,48-57
Atlanta*	WSAP	993	N33	39	W 84	25	35-39,48-57	Jefferson		455					
Augusta	WSAP	143	N33	22	W 81	58	51-56	Kokomo		790					
Baxley		205						Lafayette		600					
Brunswick		14						La Porte		810					
Columbus (Lawson)	AFB	242						Madison		455					
Covington		770						Marion		791					
Dalton		720						Muncie		955					
Dublin		215						Peru (Bunker Hill)	AFB	804					
Fitzgerald		371						Richmond	FAA	1138					
Gainesville		1254						Rochester		770					
Griffin		980						Shelbyville		765					
La Grange		715						South Bend	WSAP	773	N41	42	W 86	19	48-57
Louisville		337						Terre Haute	WSAP	601	N39	28	W 87	18	48-54
Macon	WSAP	356	N32	42	W 83	39	49-56	Valparaiso		801					
Marietta (Dobbins)	AFB	1016						Vincennes		420					
Milledgeville		320													
Moultrie		340													
Newnan		990													
Rome	WSAP	637													

Station	Type	Elev. (ft.)	Latitude Degrees	Minutes	Longitude Degrees	Minutes	Period of Recording (Inclusive)
IOWA							
Ames		1004					
Atlantic		1195					
Burlington	WSAP	694	N40	47	W 91	8	48-57
Carroll		1250					
Cedar Rapids	FAA	863					
Chariton		940					
Clarinda		1048					
Clinton		595					
Council Bluffs		1210					
Des Moines*	WSAP	963	N41	32	W 93	39	35-39,48-57
Dubuque		1065					
Estherville		1298					
Fort Dodge		1111					
Grinnell		1009					
Iowa City	FAA	645	N41	38	W 91	33	48-52
Keokuk		526					
Marshalltown		898					
Lamoni -	FAA	1173	N40	39	W 94	0	50-54
Mason City	FAA	1194	N43	9	W 93	20	48-57
Newton		946					
Oskaloosa		770					
Ottumwa	FAA	842	N40	6	W 92	27	48-54
Sioux City	WSAP	1095	N42	23	W 96	22	48-57
Storm Lake		1425					
Washington	•	762					
Waterloo		868					
KANSAS							
Atchison		945					
Chanute	FAA	977	N37	40	W 95	29	48-54
Concordia	WSAP	1470					
Dodge City*	WSAP	2592	N37	46	W 99	58	48-57
El Dorado		1282					
Emporia		1209					
Garden City	FAA	2882	N37	58	W100	49	48-54
Goodland	WSAP	3645	N39	21	W101	42	48-57
Great Bend		1940					
Hill City -	FAA	2221	N39	22	W 99	50	49-54
Hutchison	FAA	1524	N38	4	W 97	52	48-54
Liberal		2838					
McPherson		1495					
Manhattan		1076					
Norton		2298					
Ottawa		915					
Parsons		908					
Pratt		1868					
Russell	FAA	1864	N38	52	W 98	49	50-56
Salina		1271					
Scott City		2971					
Topeka	WSAP	877	N39	4	W 95	37	48-57
Wichita*	WSAP	1392	N37	38	W 97	16	35-39,48-57
Winfield		1205					
KENTUCKY							
Ashland		551					
Bowling Green	FAA	535	N36	58	W 86	26	48-54
Corbin	FAA	1175	N36	58	W 84	8	50-54
Covington Gr. Cin.*	AP	888	N39	4	W 84	40	48-57
Danville		955					
Ft. Knox (Godman)	AFB	735					
Hopkinsville (Campbell)	AFB	540					
Lexington	WSAP	979	N38	2	W 84	36	48-57
Louisville*	WSAP	488	N38	11	W 85	44	35-39,48-57
Madisonville		439					
Maysville		515					
Owensboro		420					
Paducah	FAA	398	N37	3	W 88	14	50-54
Pikeville		686					
LOUISIANA							
Alexandria (England)	AFB	92	N31	19	W 92	33	52-56
Baton Rouge*	WSAP	76	N30	31	W 91	9	49-57
Bogalusa		103					
DeRidder		180					
Hammond		45					
Houma		13					
Lafayette	FAA	38	N30	21	W 91	59	48-54
Lake Charles*	WSAP	32	N30	13	W 93	9	49-57
Minden		250					
Monroe	FAA	78	N32	31	W 92	3	48-54
Natchitoches		120					
New Orleans	WSAP	3	N29	59	W 90	15	35-39,45-57
Shreveport*	WSAP	251	N32	28	W 93	49	35-39,49-57
Barksdale	AFB	168					
Tallulah		85					
Winnsboro		80					
MAINE							
Augusta	FAA	350	N44	19	W 69	48	49-54
Bangor (Dow)	AFB	162					
Caribou	WSAP	624	N46	53	W 67	58	48-57
Eastport		40					
Ellsworth		24					
Farmington		420					
Houlton		496					
Lewiston		182					
Loring	AFB	752					
Millinocket	FAA	405					
Old Town -	FAA	124	N44	57	W 68	40	49-56
Portland	WSAP	61	N43	39	W 70	19	48-57
Rockland		40					
Rumford		674					
Waterville		89					
MARYLAND							
Baltimore	WSAP	146	N39	11	W 76	40	35-39,54-56
Baltimore	WSCO	14					
Cumberland		945					
Frederick	AP	294					
Hagerstown		660					
Lexington Park (Patuxent River)	NAS	45					
Salisbury		52					
MASSACHUSETTS							
Amherst		160					
Bedford (Hanscom)	AFB	143					
Boston*	WSAP	29	N42	22	W 71	2	35-39,48-57
Blue Hills Obs.		629					
Clinton		398					
Fall River		190					
Framingham		170					
Gloucester		10					
Greenfield		205					
Lawrence		57					
Lowell		90					
Nantucket	WSAP	43	N41	15	W 70	4	48-57
New Bedford		70					
Otis	AFB	137					
Pittsfield	WSAP	1170					
Springfield (Westover)	AFB	247					
Taunton		20					
Worcester	FAA	986	N42	16	W 71	52	49-54
MICHIGAN							
Adrain		754					
Alpena	WSAP	689					
Bad Axe		715					
Battle Creek	FAA	939	N42	18	W 85	14	49-54
Benton Harbor	FAA	649					
Big Rapids		930					
Cadillac		1390					
Cheboygan		600					
Detroit-Met. CAP*		626	N42	24	W 83	0	35-39,48-57
Escanaba		594					
Flint	FAA	766	N42	58	W 83	44	49-54
Grand Rapids*	WSAP	689	N42	54	W 85	40	48-57
Grayling		1175					
Holland		612					
Houghton		1079					
Jackson	FAA	1003					
Kalamazoo		930					
Lansing	WSAP	852	N42	47	W 84	36	49-54
Ludington		650					
Marquette	WSCO	677					
Sawyer	AFB	1214					
Mt. Clemens (Selfridge)	AFB	602					
Mt. Pleasant		796					
Muskegon	WSAP	627	N43	10	W 86	14	48-52
Pellston -	FAA	715	N45	34	W 84	48	49-54
Pontiac		974					
Port Huron		586					
Saginaw	FAA	662	N43	26	W 83	52	49-54
Sault Ste. Marie*	WSAP	724	N46	28	W 84	22	48-57
Traverse City	FAA	618	N44	44	W 85	35	49-56
Ypsilanti	WSAP	777	N42	14	W 83	32	48-57
MINNESOTA							
Albert Lea		1235					
Alexandria	FAA	1421	N45	52	W 95	23	49-54
Bemidji	AP	1392					
Brainerd		1214					
Detroit Lakes		1375					
Duluth	WSAP	1426	N46	50	W 92	11	48-57
Fairmont		1187					
Faribault		1190					
Fergus Falls		1210					
Grand Rapids		1310					
International Falls	WSAP	1179					
Mankato		785					
Marshall		1165					
Minneapolis/St. Paul*	WSAP	838	N44	53	W 93	15	48-57
Redwood Falls -	FAA	1030	N44	33	W 95	5	50-54
Rochester		1297	N44	0	W 92	29	48-57
Roseau		1047					
St. Cloud	WSAP	1034	N45	35	W 94	11	48-57
Thief River Falls		1120					
Virginia		1435					
Willmar		1133					
Winona		652					
Worthington		1593					

TABLE 1—Continued

DIRECTORY OF WEATHER STATIONS
Type, Elevation, Latitude, Longitude, Period of Recording

Station	Type	Elev. (ft.)	Latitude Degrees	Minutes	Longitude Degrees	Minutes	Period of Recording (Inclusive)
MISSISSIPPI							
ABBoxi (Keesler)		25					
Clarksdale		178					
Columbus	AFB	224					
Corinth		438					
Greenville	AFB	139					
Greenwood	FAA	128	N33	30	W 90	12	48-54
Hattiesburg		200					
Jackson*	WSAP	332	N32	20	W 90	13	49-57
Kosciusko		468					
Laurel		264					
McComb	FAA	458	N31	15	W 90	28	49-54
Meridian	WSAP	294	N32	20	W 88	45	49-57
Natchez		168					
Oxford		270					
Tupelo		289					
Vicksburg	WSCO	234					
Yazoo City		107					
MISSOURI							
Bethany		900					
Butler -	FAA	878	N38	18	W 94	20	50-54
Chillicothe		700					
Clinton		740					
Columbia	WSAP	778	N38	58	W 92	22	48-57
Farmington	FAA	928	N37	46	W 90	24	50-54
Grand View (Richards Gebaur)	AFB	1101					
Hannibal		489					
Jefferson City		640					
Joplin	FAA	982	N37	10	W 94	30	48-54
Kansas City*	WSAP	750	N39	7	W 94	35	35-39,48-57
Kirksville	FAA	966	N40	6	W 92	33	48-54
Lebanon		1240					
Marshall		775					
Maryville		1169					
Mexico		775					
Moberly		850					
Nevada		780					
Poplar Bluff		322					
Rolla		1202					
St. Joseph	WSAP	809	N39	46	W 94	55	48-54
St. Louis*	WSAP	564	N38	45	W 90	23	35-39,48-57
St. Louis	WSCO	465					
Sedalia (Whiteman)	AFB	838					
Sikeston		318					
Springfield*	WSAP	1270	N37	14	W 93	23	35-39,48-57
Vichy -	FAA	1137	N38	8	W 91	46	48-54
Washington		660					
West Plains		1006					
MONTANA							
Billings	WSAP	3567	N45	48	W108	32	35-39,48-57
Boseman		4856					
Butte	FAA	5526	N45	58	W112	30	35-39,48-54
Cut Bank	FAA	3838	N48	37	W112	22	48-57
Deer Lodge		4530					
Dillon		5228					
Glasgow	WSAP	2277	N48	11	W106	38	55-57
Glendive		2076					
Great Falls*	WSAP	3687	N47	30	W111	21	48-57
Hardin		2855					
Havre		2488					
Helena	WSAP	3893	N46	36	W112	0	48-57
Kalispell	WSAP	2965	N48	18	W114	16	49-52
Lewistown	FAA	4132	N47	4	W109	27	48-57
Libby		2080					
Livingston	FAA	4653	N45	40	W110	32	48-54
Malta		2255					
Miles City*	FAA	2634	N44	26	W105	52	48-57
Missoula	WSAP	3200	N46	55	W114	5	48-57
Polson	AP	2927					
Roundup		3227					
Sidney		1920					
Wolf Point		1975					
NEBRASKA							
Alliance		3971					
Beatrice		1235					
Bellevue (Offutt)	AFB	1030					
Burwell		2180					
Chadron	FAA	3300	N42	50	W103	5	48-54
Columbus		1442					
Fremont		1203					
Grand Island	WSAP	1841	N40	58	W 98	19	48-57
Hastings		1932					
Kearney		2146					
Lexington -	FAA	2408	N40	48	W 99	46	50-54
Lincoln	WSAP	1189	N40	53	W 96	46	35-39,48-53
Lincoln WSCO		1150					
McCook		2565					
Norfolk		1532					
North Platte*	WSAP	2787	N41	8	W100	42	35-39,48-57
Ogallala		3250					
Omaha*	WSAP	982	N41	18	W 95	54	35-39,48-57
O'Neill		1975					
Scottsbluff	WSAP	3950	N41	52	W103	36	48-57
Sidney	FAA	4292	N41	8	W103	2	48-54
Valentine		2587					
York		1636					
NEVADA							
Austin		6600					
Caliente		4402					
Carson City		4675					
Elko	WSAP	5075	N40	50	W115	47	35-39,48-57
Ely	WSAP	6257	N39	17	W114	51	48,53-56
Fallon	NAS	3934					
Hawthorne		4330					
Las Vegas	WSAP	2180	N36	4	W115	10	35-39,49-56
Nellis	AFB	1881					
Lovelock	WSAP	3900	N40	4	W118	33	49-56
Reno	WSAP	4404	N39	30	W119	47	35-39,48-57
Stead	AFB	5046					
Reno	WSCO	4490					
Tonopah	FAA	5426	N38	5	W117	8	51-56
Winnemucca*	FAA	4299					
NEW HAMPSHIRE							
Berlin		1110					
Claremont		420					
Concord	WSAP	339	N43	12	W 71	30	49-57
Keene		490					
Laconia		505					
Manchester (Grenier)	AFB	253					
Portsmouth (Pease)	AFB	127					
West Lebanon -	FAA	550	N43	38	W 72	19	49-54
NEW JERSEY							
Atlantic City*	WSAP	11	N39	22	W 74	27	49-54
Long Branch		20					
Camden -	WSAP	219	N39	56	W 74	5	35-39
McGuire	AFB	117					
Millville -	FAA	68	N39	22	W 75	4	49-54
Newark	WSAP	11	N40	43	W 74	10	35-39,48-57
New Brunswick		86					
Patterson		100					
Phillipsburg		180					
Trenton	WSCO	144					
Vineland		95					
NEW MEXICO							
Alamogordo (Holloman)	AFB	4070	N37	51	W106	5	49-56
Albuquerque*	WSAP	5314	N35	3	W106	37	35-39,49-57
Artesia		3375					
Carlsbad	FAA	3234	N32	21	W104	15	49-54
Clayton	AP	4969					
Clovis	AP	4279					
Deming		4331					
El Morro -	FAA	7121	N35	1	W108	24	35-39
Farmington*	FAA	5509	N36	45	W108	15	53-57
Gallup		6465					
Grants		6520					
Hobbs	FAA	3664	N32	41	W103	8	49-54
Las Cruces		3900					
Las Vegas	FAA	6857	N35	37	W105	11	35-39,49-56
Los Alamos		7410					
Raton	AP	6379					
Rodeo -		4120	N31	56	W108	59	35-39,40-53
Roswell (Walker)	AFB	3643	N33	18	W104	32	49-56
Santa Fe -	FAA	6308	N35	36	W106	5	48-54
Santa Fe	WSCO	7045					
Silver City	WSAP	5373					
Socorro	AP	4617					
Truth or Consequences	FAA	4820	N33	14	W107	16	50-56
Tucumcari	FAA	4053	N35	11	W103	36	35-39,49-57
Zuni -	FAA	6440	N35	6	W108	47	49-56
NEW YORK							
Albany*	WSAP	292	N42	45	W 73	48	35-39,48-57
Albany	WSCO	19					
Auburn		715					
Batavia		900					
Binghamton -	WSAP	1630	N42	13	W 75	59	52-56
Binghamton	WSCO	858					
Buffalo*	WSAP	705	N42	56	W 78	43	35-39,48-57
Canton	WSCO	458					
Cortland		1129					
Dunkirk		590					
Elmira	FAA	860	N42	10	W 76	54	35-39,49-56
Geneva		590					
Glen Falls		321					
Gloversville		770					
Hempstead (Mitchell)	AFB	125					
Hornell		1325					
Ithaca		950					
Jamestown		1390					
Kingston		279					
Lockport		520					
Massena	FAA	202	N44	56	W 74	50	49-56
Newburgh (Stewart)	AFB	460	N41	30	W 74	6	49-56
NYC-Central Park		132					
New York-Kennedy	WSAP	16	N40	39	W 73	47	49-56
New York-LaGuardia	WSAP	19	N40	46	W 73	52	49-57
Niagara Falls	AP	596					
Olean		1420					
Oneonta		1150					
Oswego	WSCO	300					
Plattsburg	AFB	165					
Poughkeepsie		103					
Rochester	WSAP	543	N43	4	W 76	16	35-39,48-57
Rome (Griffiss)	AFB	515					

TABLE 1—Continued   **DIRECTORY OF WEATHER STATIONS**
Type, Elevation, Latitude, Longitude, Period of Recording

Station	Type	Elev. (ft.)	Latitude Degrees	Minutes	Longitude Degrees	Minutes	Period of Recording (Inclusive)
Schenectady		217					
Suffolk County	AFB	57					
Syracuse	WSAP	424	N43	4	W76	16	35-39,48-57
Tupper Lake		680					
Utica		479					
Watertown	.	497					
NORTH CAROLINA							
Asheville	WSAP	2170r	N35	26	W82	29	49-54
Charlotte*	WSAP	769	N35	14	W80	56	35-39,48-57
Durham		406					
Elizabeth City	FAA	10	N36	15	W76	11	49-54
Fayetteville (Pope)	AFB	95					
Goldsboro							
(Seymour-Johnson)	AFB	88					
Greensboro	WSAP	897	N36	5	W79	57	35-39,49-56
Greenville		25					
Hatteras	WSCO	5	N35	15	W75	40	48-56
Havelock (Cherry Pt.)	MCAS	35					
Henderson		510					
Hickory		1165					
Jacksonville		24					
Lumberton	FAA	132	N34	38	W79	4	49-54
New Bern	FAA	17	N35	5	W77	2	49-54
Raleigh/Durham*	WSAP	444	N35	52	W78	47	35-39,49-56
Rocky Mount		81					
Wilmington	WSAP	30	N34	14	W77	57	48-57
Winston-Salem	WSAP	967	N36	7	W80	12	48-57
NORTH DAKOTA							
Bismarck*	WSAP	1660	N46	46	W100	45	35-39,48-57
Bottineau		1640					
Carrington		1586					
Crosby		1952					
Devils Lake		1471					
Dickinson	FAA	2595	N46	48	W102	48	35-39,49-54
Ellendale		1460					
Fargo*	WSAP	899	N46	54	W96	48	35-39,48-57
Grafton		827					
Grand Forks	FAA	832	N47	55	W97	5	49-54
Jamestown	FAA	1492	N46	55	W98	41	49-54
Kermare		1300					
Langdon		1615					
McClusky		1943					
Minot	FAA	1713	N48	15	W101	17	49-56
Mott		2420					
Pembina -	FAA	803	N48	57	W97	15	35-39
Valley City		1230					
Wahpeton		960					
Williston		1877					
OHIO							
Akron/Canton	WSAP	1210	N40	55	W81	26	35-39
Ashtabula		690					
Athens		700					
Bellefontaine		1185					
Bowling Green		675					
Cambridge		800					
Chillicothe		638					
Cincinnati (Muncipal) -	WSAP	483	N39	6	W84	25	35-39
Greater Cincinnati	WSAP	888	N39	4	W84	40	48-59
Cincinnati	WSCO	761					
Cleveland*	WSAP	805	N41	24	W81	51	35-39,48-57
Columbus*	WSAP	833	N40	0	W82	53	35-39,48-57
Columbus (Lockbourne)	AFB	744					
Dayton	WSAP	997	N39	46	W84	10	48-57
Wright-Patterson	AFB	822					
Defiance		700					
Findlay	FAA	797	N41	1	W83	40	49-54
Fremont		600					
Greenville		1035					
Hamilton		650					
Lancaster		920					
Lima		860					
Mansfield	FAA	1297	N40	49	W83	31	49-54
Marion		920					
Middletown		635					
Newark		825					
Norwalk		720					
Oberlin		817					
Portsmouth		530					
Sandusky	WSCO	606					
Springfield		1020					
Steubenville		992					
Toledo	WSAP	676r	N41	34	W83	28	35-39,48-57
Van Wert		795					
Warren		900					
Wilmington (Clinton Co.)	AFB	1065					
Wooster		1030					
Youngstown	WSAP	1178	N41	16	W80	40	48-57
Zanesville	FAA	881	N39	57	W81	54	49-54
OKLAHOMA							
Ada		1015					
Altus	AFB	1390					
Alva		1374					
Ardmore	FAA	880	N34	18	W97	9	35-39,49-54
Bartlesville		715					
Chickasha		1085					
Clinton							
(Clinton-Sherman)	AFB	1928					
Enid (Vance)	AFB	1287					
Gage -	FAA	2202	N36	18	W99	46	49-54
Guyman		3124					
Hobart	FAA	1562	N35	0	W99	3	49-54
Hugo		540					
Lawton	FAA	1108					
McAlester		760					
Muskogee	FAA	610					
Norman		1109					
Oklahoma City*	WSAP	1304	N35	24	W97	36	35-39,49-57
Oklahoma City (Tinker)	AFB	1262					
Ponca City	FAA	996	N36	43	W97	6	49-54
Seminole		865					
Stillwater		884					
Tulsa*	WSAP	674	N36	11	W95	54	35-39,49-57
Vinita		740					
Waynoka -	WSAP	1529	N36	35	W98	51	35-39
Woodward		1900					
OREGON							
Albany		224					
Arlington -	WSAP	350	N45	43	W120	11	35-39
Astoria	WSAP	8					
Baker	FAA	3368	N44	50	W117	49	35-39,48-54
Bend		3599					
Burns	WSCO	4151					
Corvallis		221					
Eugene	WSAP	364	N44	7	W123	13	35-39,48-54
Forest Grove		180					
Grants Pass		925					
Klamath Falls	AP	4091					
LaGrande		2805					
Lakeview		4774					
Medford	WSAP	1298	N42	23	W122	52	35-39,48-54
Newport	AP	136					
North Bend	AP	11					
Pendleton	WSAP	1492	N45	41	W118	51	48-57
Portland*	WSAP	26	N45	36	W122	36	35-39,48-54
Portland	WSCO	57					
Prineville		2840					
Redmond -	FAA	3084	N44	16	W121	8	48-57
Roseburg	AP	505					
Salem	WSAP	195	N44	55	W123	0	48-57
The Dalles		102					
PENNSYLVANIA							
Allentown	WSAP	376	N40	39	W75	26	48-57
Altoona	FAA	1468	N40	18	W78	19	49-54
Butler		1100					
Chambersburg		650					
Clarion		1114					
Curwensville -	FAA	2222	N41	3	W78	35	35-39
DuBois		1670					
Erie	FAA	732	N42	5	W80	12	35-39,48-54
Franklin		987					
Harrisburg*	WSAP	351	N40	13	W76	51	35-39,48-57
Johnstown		1214					
Lancaster		255					
Meadville		1065					
Middletown (Olmstead)	AFB	306					
New Castle		825					
Philadelphia*	WSAP	114	N39	53	W75	14	48-57
Philipsburg -	FAA	1914	N40	53	W78	5	49-54
Pittsburgh*	WSAP	1273	N40	21	W79	56	35-39,48-57
Pittsburgh	WSCO	749r					
Reading	WSCO	226					
Scranton/Wilkes Barre	FAA	940	N41	21	W75	43	49-54
State College		1175					
Sunbury	FAA	480	N40	54	W76	47	35-39
Uniontown		1040					
Warren		1280					
West Chester		440					
Williamsport	WSAP	527	N41	14	W76	55	49-54
York		390					
RHODE ISLAND							
Newport		20					
Providence	WSAP	55	N41	44	W71	25	48-57
SOUTH CAROLINA							
Anderson		764					
Charleston	WSAP	41	N32	54	W80	2	35-39,48-57
Charleston	WSCO	9					
Columbia*	WSAP	220	N33	56	W81	7	48-57
Florence	WSAP	146	N34	11	W79	43	48-57
Georgetown		14					
Greenville	WSAP	957	N34	51	W82	21	48-57
Greenwood		671					
Myrtle Beach	FAA	25	N33	41	W78	56	49-54
Orangeburg		244					
Rock Hill		470					
Spartanburg	WSAP	816	N34	58	W81	57	48-54
Sumter-Shaw AFB	AFB	291					
SOUTH DAKOTA							
Aberdeen	FAA	1296	N45	27	W98	26	48-54
Brookings		1642					
Hot Springs		3535					
Huron	WSAP	1282	N44	23	W98	13	48-57
Lead		5245					

TABLE 1—Continued

DIRECTORY OF WEATHER STATIONS
Type, Elevation, Latitude, Longitude, Period of Recording

Station	Type	Elev. (ft.)	Latitude Degrees	Minutes	Longitude Degrees	Minutes	Period of Recording (Inclusive)
Lemmon		2596					
Mitchell		1346					
Mobridge		1664					
Philip -	FAA	2212	N44	3	W101	36	48-54
Pierre	FAA	1718	N44	23	W100	17	48-57
Rapid City*	WSAP	3168	N44	2	W103	3	51-56
Sioux Falls*	WSAP	1427	N43	34	W 96	44	48-57
Watertown	FAA	1746	N44	45	W 97	10	48-54
Winner		1965					
Yankton		1280					
TENNESSEE							
Athens		940					
Bristol-Tri City	WSAP	1519	N36	30	W 82	21	48-53
Chattanooga	WSAP	670	N35	2	W 85	12	35-39,48-57
Clarksville		470					
Columbia		690					
Cookeville		1162					
Dyersburg	FAA	334	N36	1	W 89	24	49-54
Greenville		1320					
Jackson		413	N35	36	W 88	55	49-54
Knoxville*	WSAP	974	N35	49	W 83	59	48-57
Memphis*	WSAP	282	N35	3	W 89	59	35-39,48-57
Murfreesboro		608					
Nashville*	WSAP	601	N36	7	W 86	41	35-39,48-57
Smithville -	FAA	1078	N35	58	W 85	47	49-53
Smyrna (Sewart)	AFB	522					
Tulahoma		1075					
Union City		340					
TEXAS							
Abilene	WSAP	1759	N32	27	W 99	41	35-39,49-57
Dyess	AFB	1777					
Alice	FAA	180	N27	44	W 98	1	49-54
Alpine		4433					
Amarillo*	WSAP	3604	N35	14	W101	42	35-39,49-57
Austin	WSAP	597	N30	18	W 97	42	49-57
Bergstrom	AFB	507					
Bay City		52					
Beaumont		18					
Beeville		225					
Big Spring	FAA	2537	N32	14	W101	30	49-53
Brownsville	WSAP	16	N25	55	W 97	28	49-57
Brownwood		1435					
Bryan	FAA	275	N30	38	W 96	28	52-56
Childress	FAA	1880	N34	26	W100	17	49-54
Corpus Christi*	WSAP	44	N27	46	W 97	26	49-57
Coriscana		425					
Cotulla	AFB	425	N28	27	W 99	13	50-54
Dalhart	FAA	3989	N36	1	W102	33	49-54
Dallas (Love)*	WSAP	488	N32	51	W 96	51	35-39,49-57
Del Rio (Laughlin)	AFB	1072	N29	22	W100	47	54-57
Denton		655					
Eagle Pass		743					
El Paso*	WSAP	3916	N31	48	W106	24	35-39,49-57
Biggs	AFB	3923					
Fort Worth (Meacham)	WSAP	706	N32	49	W 97	21	49-52
Carswell	AFB	617					
Galveston	WSAP	5	N29	16	W 94	52	49-57
Greenville		575					
Harlingen		37					
Houston*	WSAP	62	N29	39	W 94	17	35-39,49-57
Houston	WSCO	158					
Ellington	AFB	39					
Huntsville		494					
Junction	FAA	1705	N30	29	W 99	46	49-57
Kerrville		1650					
Killeen (Gray)	AFB	1021					
Lamesa		2965					
Laredo	AFB	503	N27	32	W 99	29	49-57
Longview		345					
Lubbock	WSAP	3243	N33	29	W101	50	49-57
Reese	AFB	3340					
Lufkin	FAA	286	N31	14	W 94	45	49-56
McAllen		122					
Marfa -	FAA	4885	N30	15	W103	53	49-54
Midland	WSAP	2815	N31	56	W102	12	49-57
Mineral Wells	FAA	934	N32	47	W 98	4	49-54
Palacias -	FAA	13	N28	43	W 96	15	49-54
Palestine	WSCO	580					
Pampa		3230					
Pecos		2580					
Plainview		3400					
Port Arthur	WBAS	16	N29	58	W 94	1	49-57
Salt Flat -	FAA	3715	N31	45	W105	5	49-54
San Angelo*	WSAP	1919	N31	22	W100	30	48-52,55-56
San Antonio	WSAP	792	N29	32	W 98	28	35-39,49-57
Kelly	AFB	682					
Randolph	AFB	743					
Sherman (Perrin)	AFB	763					
Snyder		2325					
Temple		675					
Tyler	FAA	527	N32	21	W 95	24	48-54
Uvalde		905					
Vernon		1225					
Victoria	WSAP	104	N28	47	W 97	5	50-56
Waco	WSAP	500	N31	37	W 97	13	36-39,49-57
Connally	AFB	475					
Wichita Falls	WSAP	994	N33	59	W 98	31	49-57
Wink	FAA	2820	N31	47	W103	12	35-39,49-54

Station	Type	Elev. (ft.)	Latitude Degrees	Minutes	Longitude Degrees	Minutes	Period of Recording (Inclusive)
UTAH							
Bryce Canyon* -	FAA	7589	N37	42	W112	9	49-56
Cedar City*	FAA	5660	N37	43	W113	6	49-56
Delta	FAA	4759	N39	23	W112	30	49-54
Dugway Proving Gd.		4359					
Hanksville -	FAA	4462	N38	25	W110	41	49-54
Logan		4775					
Milford	WSAP	5028	N38	26	W113	1	35-39,49-51
Moab		3965					
Ogden	WSAP	4400	N41	12	W112	1	48-54
Hill	AFB	4787					
Price		5580					
Provo		4470					
Richfield		5300					
St. George	FAA	2899	N37	2	W113	31	49-54
Salt Lake City*	WSAP	4240	N40	46	W111	58	35-39,48-57
Vernal	FAA	5280					
Wendover	FAA	4239	N40	44	W114	2	50-54
VERMONT							
Barre		1120					
Bennington		670					
Burlington	WSAP	331	N44	28	W 73	9	48-57
Newport		766					
Rutland		620					
VIRGINIA							
Blackstone	FAA	435	N37	4	W 77	57	49-54
Charlottesville		870					
Covington		1245					
Danville	FAA	590	N36	34	W 79	20	49-54
Fredericksburg		50					
Front Royal -	FAA	680	N39	0	W 78	14	49-54
Gordonsville -	FAA	440	N38	4	W 78	10	49-54
Harrisonburg		1340					
Langley	AFB	13					
Lynchburg	WSAP	947	N37	20	W 79	12	48-53
Norfolk*	WSAP	30	N36	53	W 76	12	48-57
Petersburg		194					
Pulaski		1850					
Richmond	WSAP	162	N37	30	W 77	20	35-39,48-57
Roanoke*	WSAP	1176	N37	19	W 79	58	36-39,48-57
Staunton		1480					
Winchester		750					
WASHINGTON							
Aberdeen		12					
Bellingham	FAA	150	N48	48	W122	33	49-54
Bremerton		162					
Buckley		685					
Centralia		185					
Dallesport (The Dalles) -	FAA	236	N45	37	W121	9	48-54
Ellensburg	FAA	1729	N47	2	W120	31	35-39,48-54
Euphrata -	FAA	1271	N47	18	W119	31	48-54
Everett (Paine)	AFB	598					
Forks		350					
Kennewick		392					
Longview		12					
Moses Lake (Larson)	AFB	1183					
Olympia	WSAP	190	N46	58	W122	53	48-57
Omak		1228					
Port Angeles		99					
Seattle (Boeing)	WSAP	14	N47	32	W122	18	48-57
Seattle/Tacoma*	WSAP	383	N47	26	W122	20	35-39,48-57
Seattle	WSCO	14					
Spokane*	WSAP	2365	N47	37	W117	31	35-39,48-57
Fairchild	AFB	2437					
Tacoma (McChord)	AFB	350					
Tatoosh Island -	WSCO	119	N48	23	W124	44	48-57
Walla Walla	FAA	1185	N46	6	W118	17	48-54
Wenatchee		634					
Yakima	WSAP	1061	N46	34	W120	32	48-57
WEST VIRGINIA							
Beckely		2330					
Bluefield	FAA	2850					
Charleston*	WSAP	989	N38	22	W 81	36	49-56
Clarksburg		977					
Elkins	WSAP	1970	N38	53	W 79	51	48-53
Huntington	WSCO	565					
Martinsburg	FAA	537	N39	24	W 77	59	49-54
Morgantown	FAA	1245	N39	38	W 79	55	49-54
Parkersburg	FAA	637	N39	21	W 81	26	49-54
Wheeling		659					
White Sulfur Springs		1914					
WISCONSIN							
Appleton		742					
Ashland		650					
Beloit		780					
Eau Claire	FAA	888	N44	52	W 91	29	50-56
Fond du Lac		760					
Green Bay	WSAP	683	N44	29	W 88	8	50-56
La Crosse*	WSAP	672	N43	56	W 91	17	35-39,48-57
Lone Rock -	FAA	721	N43	12	W 90	11	49-54
Madison*	WSAP	866	N43	8	W 89	20	35-39,48-57
Manitowoc		660					
Marinette		605					
Milwaukee*	WSAP	693	N42	57	W 87	54	35-39,48-57

Station	Type	Elev. (ft.)	Latitude Degrees	Minutes	Longitude Degrees	Minutes	Period of Recording (Inclusive)
Montello		822					
Prairie du Chien		658					
Racine		640					
Rhinelander		1560					
Rice Lake		1115					
Sheboygan		648					
Stevens Point		1079					
Waukesha		860					
Wausau	FAA	1196	N44	55	W 69	37	50-54
WYOMING							
Casper*	WSAP	5321	N42	55	W106	28	50-56
Cheyenne	WSAP	6126	N41	9	W104	49	35-39,48-57
Cody	AP	5090					
Douglas -	FAA	4853	N42	45	W105	21	48-54
Evanston		6860					
Fort Bridger -	FAA	7024	N41	24	W110	25	48-54
Gillette		4556					
Jackson		6244					
Lander	WSAP	5563					
Laramie	FAA	7266	N41	19	W105	41	48-54
New Castle		4480					
Rawlins		6736					
Rock Springs*	FAA	6745	N41	36	W109	4	35-39,48-56
Sheridan	WSAP	3942	N44	46	W106	58	48-57
Thermopolis		4336					
Torrington		4098					

FOREIGN WEATHER STATIONS

Station	Type	Elev. (ft.)	Latitude Degrees	Minutes	Longitude Degrees	Minutes	Period of Recording (Inclusive)
BERMUDA							
St. George (Kindley)	AFB	17	N32	22	W 64	40	49-57
CANADA							
Calgary	DOT	3540	N51	6	W114	1	49-57
Edmonton	DOT	2219	N53	34	W113	31	50-57
Halifax (Dartmouth)	DOT	136	N44	38	W 63	30	50-57
Montreal (Dorval)	DOT	98	N45	28	W 73	45	48-57
Ottawa (Uplands)	DOT	339	N45	19	W 75	40	48-57
Regina	DOT	1884	N50	26	W104	40	48-57
Toronto (Malton)	DOT	578	N43	41	W 79	38	48-57
Vancouver	DOT	16	N49	11	W123	10	49-57
Winnipeg	DOT	786	N49	54	W 97	14	48-57
CANAL ZONE							
Balboa (Albrook)	AFB	20	N 8	59	W 79	34	48-56
CUBA							
Guantanamo Bay	NAS	54	N19	54	W 75	9	48-56
ENGLAND							
Wethersfield (RAF St.)	—	310	N51	59	E 0	30	52-56
FRENCH MOROCCO							
Fort Lyautey	FWC	39	N34	18	W 6	36	49-57
GERMANY							
Furstenfeldbruck	AB	1740	N48	12	W 11	16	49-56
Wiesbaden	AB	468	N50	3	E 8	20	48-56
JAPAN							
Osaka Honshu (Itami)	AB	54	N34	48	W135	26	49-56
Tokyo Honshu (Int'l AP)	—	10	N35	34	E139	46	49-54
KOREA							
Seoul (Kimpo)	AB	71	N37	34	E126	42	51-56
LIBYA							
Tripoli (Wheelus Field)	—	14	N32	54	E 13	17	49-56
MARIANA ISLANDS							
Guam (Agana Field)	FWC	245	N13	36	E144	48	48-56
MEXICO							
Aguascalientes	MGO	6132	N21	53	W102	18	48-57
Chihuahua	MGO	4692	N28	38	W106	4	53-57
Guadalajara	MGO	5053	N20	36	W103	19	48-57
Hermosillo	MGO	778	N29	6	W110	55	48-57
Merida	MGO	30	N20	56	W 89	41	48-57
Mexico City	MGO	7349	N19	26	W 99	8	48-57
Monterrey	MGO	1765	N25	40	W100	18	48-57
Tampico	MGO	70	N22	18	W 97	51	48-57
Torreon	MGO	3696	N25	32	W103	28	48-57
Zacatecas	MGO	8012	N22	47	W102	34	49-57
NEWFOUNDLAND							
Stephenville (Marmon)	AFB	44	N48	33	W 58	34	49-57
PHILIPPINE ISLANDS							
Cavite (Sangley Point)	FWC	11	N14	30	E120	55	48-56
PUERTO RICO							
San Juan	NAS	43	N18	29	W 66	7	49-57
RYUKU ISLANDS							
Okinawa (Kadena)	AB	163	N26	21	W127	45	49-57
SAUDI ARABIA							
Dhahran Airfield	—	78	N26	17	E 50	9	48-56

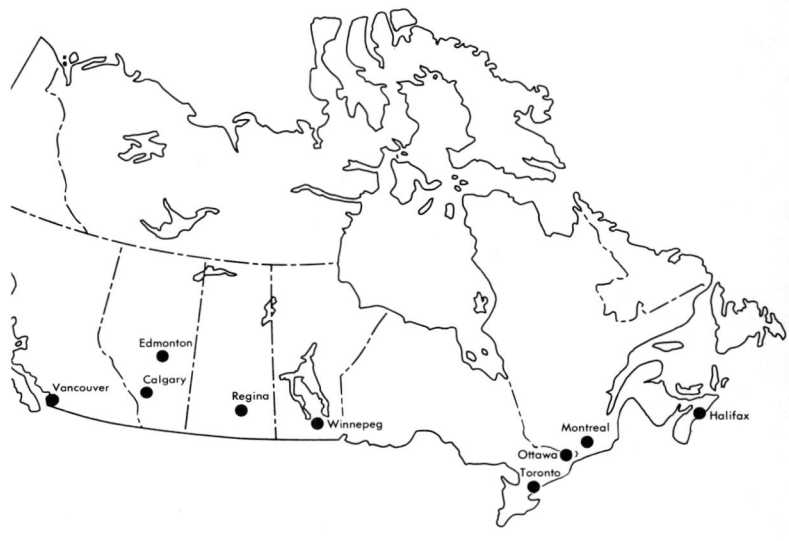

FIGURE 2
SELECTED CANADIAN OFFICIAL WEATHER STATIONS

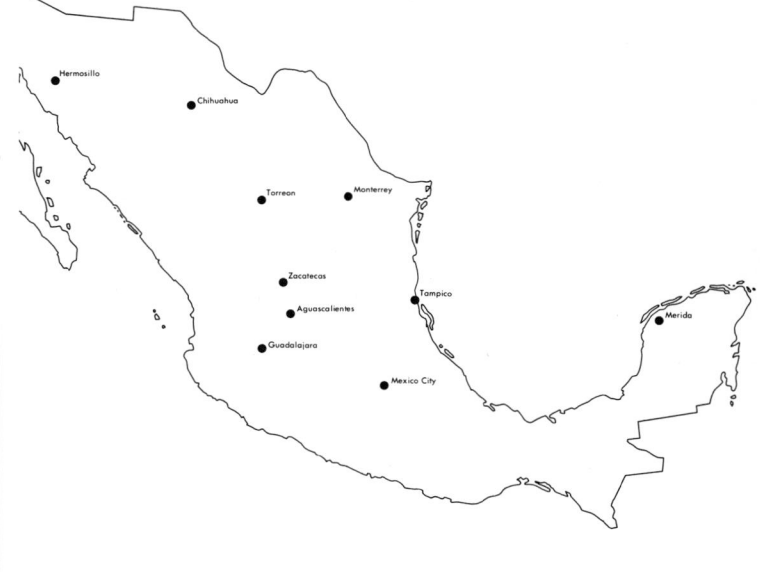

FIGURE 3
SELECTED MEXICAN OFFICIAL WEATHER STATIONS

Section 1: TYPICAL DAILY CURVES

The daily fluctuations in temperatures at any location are the result of the balance of radiation from the sun to the earth or from the earth to the outer atmosphere. Fig. 4 shows the fundamental temperature profile near the ground and the contrast between day and night.

As a part of RP-23, the daily sequences of both cold and warm extremes were examined for the extreme days in 14 past seasons. For these same dates, vertical soundings obtained by radiosonde balloons furnished detailed information regarding the variation in temperature with height.

When extremely cold temperatures occur and winds are light or very light, the stable air near the ground can record temperatures that are more than 10°F colder than temperatures at 400 feet above the ground.

When high winds accompany cold temperatures, the air is mechanically well mixed and temperatures are often one to two degrees warmer at the ground than at 400 feet above the ground during either nighttime or daytime periods.

Fig. 5 presents a typical early morning profile in the lowest 400 feet with four different wind conditions. (See page 6-3 regarding coincident winds.) The temperature at 400 feet remains nearly constant for each situation. The spread of temperature near the ground as shown in

Fig. 5 is up to 10°F.

From the temperature observations made at various towers equipped with multi-level sensors, it is possible to prepare vertical profiles of conditions during the time of the maximum temperatures on extremely hot days. Very close collaboration was obtained between tower data from the states of Texas, Washington and New York. The composite result is shown in Fig. 6. It can be concluded that the top of a building 400 feet high will be immersed in air approximately 5.5° cooler than the portion of the building only five feet above the earth's surface. Most weather observations are made in a sheltered screen with the thermometer located approximately five feet above the ground.

At any particular location the maximum wet bulb temperature is reached at a time when there is high moisture content. The dry bulb temperature generally would not be at its record maximum for that location at the same time. Conversely, the conditions which exist when the dry bulb temperature maximum is reached will ordinarily occur at periods when there is less total moisture content and thus lower wet bulb temperatures.

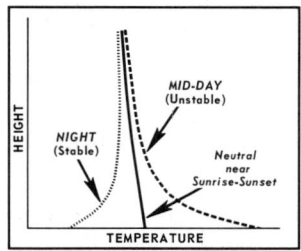

Fig. 4. The shape of the temperature profile near the ground under different stability conditions.

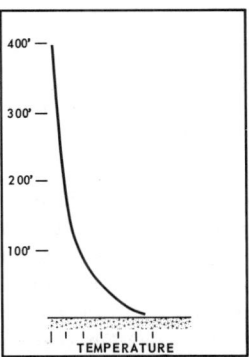

Fig. 6. Typical vertical profile of temperature between 5' and 400' at time of maximum summer dry bulb temperature.

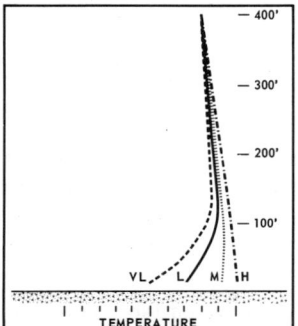

Fig. 5. Schematic vertical temperature profile for Very Light, Light, Moderate, and High coincident winds.

To illustrate this point, Fig. 7 shows a comparison between the actual daily wet bulb and dry bulb sequence at Dallas, Texas, on the peak wet bulb and dry bulb days in 1957. The plot of the hourly data on a psychrometric chart, Fig. 8, illustrates the marked contrast in the two days. Somewhat by coincidence, these two days occurred only two days apart in the 1957 season.

The air mass which prevailed through the evening hours of July 30 was a dry, hot air mass with air moving from the southwest or west over Dallas. At midnight the dry bulb temperature was 90°F and the wet bulb temperature was 74°F. The hourly sequence of wet bulb and dry bulb temperatures shows a decrease in both of these

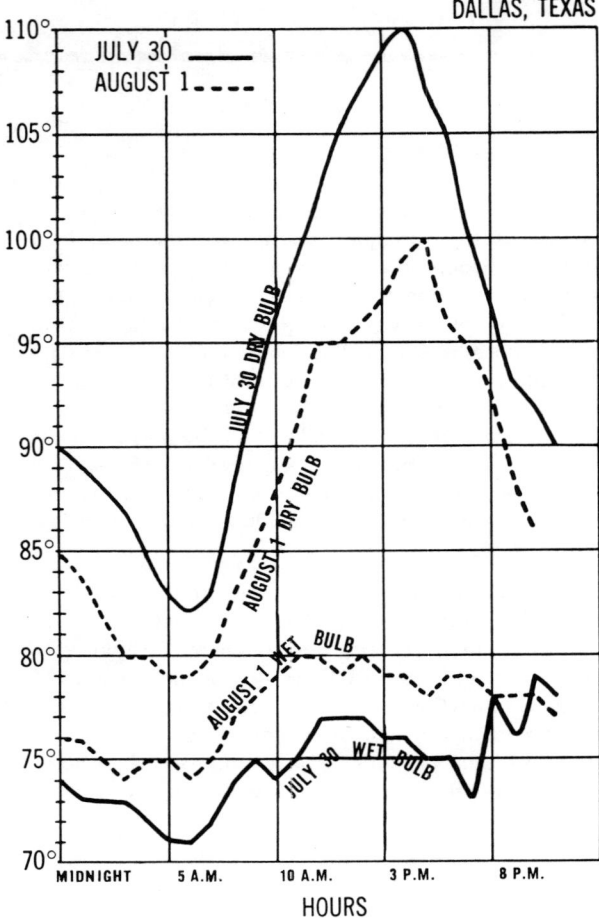

DALLAS, TEXAS

Fig. 7. Hourly sequence of dry bulb and wet bulb temperatures on hottest dry bulb day and hottest wet bulb day at Dallas, Texas during 1957 summer season.

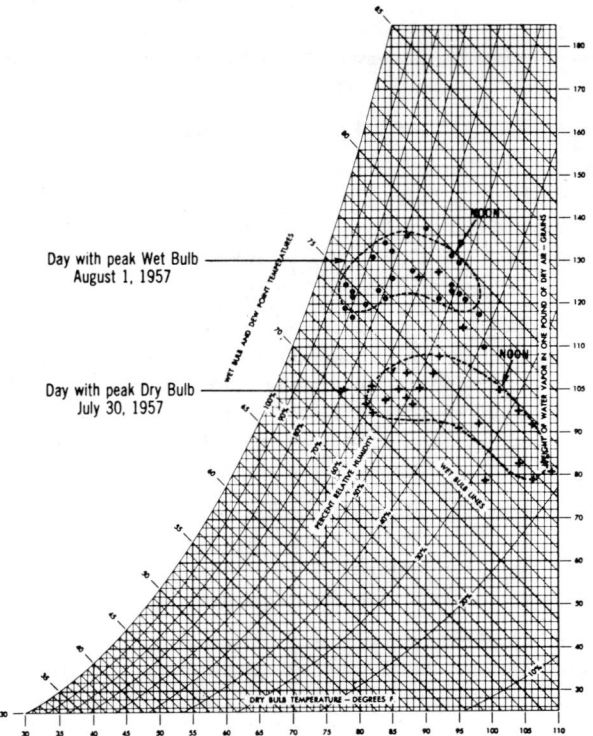

Fig. 8. Dallas, Texas — Psychrometric chart areas for peak wet bulb temperature day and peak dry bulb temperature day during 1957.

The maximum dry bulb temperature of 100°F occurred at 5:00 p.m., six hours after the maximum wet bulb temperature had been recorded. The temperature fell rapidly from this peak, being only 95°F at 7:00 p.m. Both temperatures dropped from 7:00 p.m. to midnight.

A comparison of the two extreme days shows that:

The maximum wet bulb temperature at Dallas was reached when the dry bulb temperature was between 90°F and 95°F.

The actual maximum dry bulb temperature on the hottest dry bulb day was some 15°F higher than 95°F (110°F).

The peak dry bulb temperature on the hottest dry bulb day was reached when the wet bulb temperature was 3°F less than it was on the peak wet bulb day.

Section 2: ANNUAL CLIMATIC RANGES OF WET BULB TEMPERATURES

In some problems of calculating the total power load required for a cooling tower installation, it is useful to know the annual range of wet bulb temperature frequencies. There are also problems incident to the occurrence of freezing temperatures during the winter months.

In Table 2, the average patterns of wet bulb temperatures are shown for the months of July and January at 30 representative locations throughout the United States.

elements between midnight and 6:00 a.m. A rapid increase in both wet bulb and dry bulb temperatures took place from 6:00 a.m. until noon, except for a hesitation in the wet bulb climb at 9:00 a.m., probably caused by convective currents carrying moisture aloft and bringing in dry air from above. The maximum wet bulb temperature was reached by noon. This held steady for two hours as the dry bulb temperature continued its movement upward. The peak dry bulb temperature of 110°F was reached at 4:00 p.m., at which time the wet bulb temperature had decreased by 1°F from its maximum, which prevailed from noon to 2:00 p.m.

On that particular day, between 7:00 and 8:00 p.m., the wind shifted and a different air mass which had originated in the Gulf of Mexico moved over Dallas. This brought a sharp rise in the moisture content. July 31 was a relatively hot, moist day, and the peak day for wet bulb temperatures was reached on August 1. The hourly sequence shows a pattern similar to that for July 30, but the wet bulb temperatures are higher while the dry bulbs are lower. The maximum wet bulb temperature was reached on August 1 at 11:00 a.m. and continued high through 7:00 p.m.

TABLE 2 ANNUAL RANGE OF WET BULB TEMPERATURES

AS DEFINED BY EXTREME MONTHS OF JANUARY (COLDEST) AND JULY (HOTTEST)

(Figures shown are average number of hours for each degree wet bulb—taken from a five-year sample.)

Wet Bulb Temp. °F	Amarillo, Tex. Ja.	Jy.	Atlanta, Ga. Ja.	Jy.	Bismarck, N.D. Ja.	Jy.	Boise, Ida. Ja.	Jy.	Boston, Mass. Ja.	Jy.	Chicago, Ill. Ja.	Jy.	Dallas, Tex. Ja.	Jy.	Denver, Colo. Ja.	Jy.	Detroit, Mich. Ja.	Jy.	El Paso, Tex. Ja.	Jy.	Fresno, Calif. Ja.	Jy.	Houston, Tex. Ja.	Jy.	Jacksonville, Fla. Ja.	Jy.	Kansas City, Mo. Ja.	Jy.	Louisville, Ky. Ja.	Jy.
84°																														
83																														
82																														
81						1								1											2		1		1
80						2						2		2											6		8		3
79				1		3						1		7				1							21		11		8
78				2		6				4		3		20				4							49		16		14
77				9		8				7		8		39				6							78		29		27
76				24		11				11		19		70				10						1	101		40		39
75				49		11		1		12		23		103		1		16				1		11	106		53		52
74		1		81		21		2		19		39		125				24				3		18	101		65		54
73		1		101		21				22		34		118				34				6	2	45	1	96		60		57
72		2		101		27		4		32		43		107		1		31				12	8	58		68		68		60
71		14		111		23		6		45		45		64		2		37		2		16		74	5	54		74		62
70		24		95		30		12		45		48		34		4		47		4		23	13	70	12	29		69		73
69	50			72		39		30		44		49		16		4		50		19		36	21	76	13	15		62		55
68	79			35		47		23		52		48		12		8		38		46		40	29	47	16	5		52		41
67	80			18		53		28		47		46		12		8		43		76		44	21	51	13	5		37		34
66	80		1	10		47		40		42		39	1	6		14		49		98		57	14	39	22	2		27		31
65	97		3	6		56		39		53		45	2	3		24		54		99		51	13	34	23	2		23		27
64	68		5	4		44		44		52		47	6	1		39		41		98		56	11	33	23	1		18		22
63	61		7	2		45		46		47		40	5	1		48		34		73		56	15	27	25			9		15
62	58		9	5		42		44		44		29	3	1		67		35		73		46	14	21	29	1		8		15
61	45		12			42		50		49		35	5	1		73		36		53		55	22	18	26			4	2	15
60	25		9	3		35		41		37		21	11			60		24		28		42	19	15	26			3	2	8
59		24	9	5		29		51		29		16	6	1		71		25		23	1	46	11	13	29			3	4	7
58		12	12	3		23		46	1	29		16	9			72		25		18	2	54	16	9	30	1		2	2	4
57		10	16	1		20		37		18		13	12			58		20		9	2	34	14	9	29	1		1	3	4
56		5	18	1		14		34	1	13		12	10			42		10		8	3	20	17	7	26				5	2
55		2	11	1		13		32	1	13	1	7	9	1		46		16	2	8	3	20	20	5	25		1		5	2
54	1	2	11	1		8		27	3	7	1	5	13	1		33		11		5	8	15	15	2	19		2		5	1
53	1		14			7		23	3	4	1	5	18			20	1	8	1		15	9	20	3	21		3		3	1
52	2		15			7		20	3	1	2	1	23			17	1	8	1		15	6	20		24		2		6	1
51	2		13			5		16	3	1	2	2	18			18		2	3	1	21	3	23		24		2		4	1
50	3		13			1		12		1	1	2	22			7	1	3	4	1	28	1	25		21		2		4	1
49	4		15			2			8		5		1			4	1	2	5		36	2	29		15		3		5	
48	10		22			1			6		6		2		1	1	1	1	8		40	1	24		17		3		9	
47	6		22			1			3		5		1		1		2		16		38	1	21		15		3		9	
46	10		24						5		6		2		1		3		14		44		29		15		5		9	
45	11		28				2		6		7		3		3		4		23		44		26		15		9		9	
44	14		17				3		7		10		5		3		4		24		42		27		16		9		11	
43	17		25				5		8		8		5		5		5		34		35		21		13		8		16	
42	21		29				5		8		8		4		5		5		33		40		19		13		15		11	
41	20		28				8		10		10		5		8		6		38		42		21		14		15		11	
40	19		28				16		10		10		8		8		6		42		39		18		17		14		18	
39	20		27				17		11		13		24		12		9		35		41		18		14		18		21	
38	25		25				22		12		12		28		15		8		40		36		16		13		19		22	
37	25		22				24		16		10		19		14		7		45		29		15		8		19		14	
36	24		25		1		29		21		20		24		18		20		41		28		12		11		23		25	
35	34		26		2		38		32		21		24		23		18		45		19		10		9		31		32	
34	25		17		4		35		24		32		21		18		26		34		16		7		9		28		28	
33	32		23		6		34		21		26		18		28		21		29		11		9		6		34		32	
32	45		19		4		43		31		18		32		32		32		35		15		7		6		32		38	
31	26		18		4		39		24		24		26		26		20		26		9		10				27		23	
30	32		16		2		42		24		32		20		39		23		25		6		8		8		22		25	
29	26		10		7		33		19		25		15		25		17		22		5		3		6		20		15	
28	29		12		8		40		24		27		14		28		30		18		8		1		3		29		15	
27	23		14		11		31		26		32		10		30		37		19		5		2		2		27		19	
26	23		8		12		29		18		27		11		30		29		13		3		4		3		18		8	
25	22		9		15		28		29		31		7		33		32		17		3				3		15		11	
24	15		9		12		26		19		25		6		30		26		13		2		1		1		17		10	
23	22		6		13		19		17		21		7		22		32		9		2		1		1		16		9	
22	17		8		11		17		19		19		6		19		26		10		3		1		1		11		6	
21	22		5		12		13		16		16		8		23		25		6				1				15		5	
20	18		6		11		10		16		16		6		20		29		6								12		6	
19	11		4		13		7		20		17		2		18		27		5				1				11		5	
18	15		2		10		9		21		14		2		16		16		3				1				12		4	
17	9		2		14		10		20		20		2		12		18		1								12		3	
16	11		2		11		7		18		13				15		22						1				13		5	
15	7		3		9		6		15		15		3		13		17		1								10		5	
14	7		2		9		7		16		17				13		18										8		3	
13	6		2		8		6		13		18				13		16										11		2	
12	3		2		11		7		12		10		1		13		13		1				1				10		3	
11	4				10		7		11		11				8		15		1				1				11		6	
10	2								10						8		12										10		4	
9	3				10		6		10		10				7		11										10		5	
8	4				10		3		11		10				6		7										10		4	
7	3				9		2		6		6				6		7										9		2	
6	2				10		3		8		7				5		5										7		3	
5	3				13		5		5		7				6		6										10		2	
4	1				11		2		6		5				4		5										9		2	
3	1				11		4		5		5				4		3										9		1	
2	1				13		5		1		5				3		5										4		2	
1	1				14		4				4				5		4										5		2	
0					18		2				4				2		2										4		1	
−5	3				69		10		7		20		12		2												9		5	
−10					73		5				15		10		2												7		5	
−15					65		4				4		10																2	
−20					35		1				3		1																	
−25					21																									
−30					8																									
−35					1																									

TABLE 2—Continued   ANNUAL RANGE OF WET BULB TEMPERATURES

AS DEFINED BY EXTREME MONTHS OF JANUARY (COLDEST) AND JULY (HOTTEST)

(Figures shown are average number of hours for each degree wet bulb—taken from a five-year sample.)

Wet Bulb Temperatures Degrees Fahrenheit	Medford, Ore.		Memphis, Tenn.		Miami, Fla.		Mobile, Ala.		Newark, N.J.		New Orleans, La.		Oklahoma City, Okla.		Phoenix, Ariz.		Pittsburgh, Pa.		San Antonio, Tex.		San Diego, Calif.		Seattle, Wash.		St. Paul, Minn.		St. Louis, Mo.		Washington, D.C.	
	Ja.	Jy.	Ja.	Jy.	Ja.	Jy.	Ja.	Jy.	Ja.	Jy.	Ja.	Jy.	Ja.	Jy.	Ja.	Jy.	Ja.	Jy.	Ja.	Jy.	Ja.	Jy.	Ja.	Jy.	Ja.	Jy.	Ja.	Jy.	Ja.	Jy.
84°				1								1								1										
83				2								1								1										
82				8				4				6								2										
81				11				10				10								4								1		2
80				16		3		27				24								6						1		7		3
79				34		18		55		1		67		1						13						4		11		11
78				48		62		81		4		95		1		2				33						7		13		14
77				67		124		118		6		116		4		9				71						12		23		29
76				78		147		110		17		122		10		18		1		117						11		36		40
75				71		115		91		24		122		19		42		6		171						22		45		55
74				78	2	92		71		45	1	87		45		64		15		137						31		65		69
73				71	7	65	2	56		49	2	57		73		81		21		52						37		66		67
72		3		66	23	50	5	51		53	6	21		81		85		27		45		2				42		57		69
71		3		56	40	36		34		61	18	8		100		79		31	2	24		3				42		58		65
70		10		38	54	21	9	18		63	17	4		95		71		40	4	13		12		1		47		68		54
69		10		24	50	9	13	9		43	22	2		87		50		47	6	6		24		3		49		58		49
68		14		15	48	3	16	4		33	26	1		65		48		43	16	5		37		13		51		55		43
67		21	1	14	68	1	22	1		39	24			60		28		55	17	5		61		9		48		43		26
66		30	2	9	49	1	28	1		34	22			39		28		45	12	2		84		8		42		29		24
65		36	2	8	45		25	1		35	17			23		29		40	9	1		83		12		50		23		24
64		36	3	5	34		22	1		34	20			12		17		37	9			87		17		39		21	2	26
63		41	5	4	32		25			29	19			8		17		23	15			86		27		36		12	2	16
62		41	4	5	27		28		1	36	18			6		16		28	15			95		29		34		10	1	17
61		46	3	3	27		22		1	34	15			7		14		28	17			76		48		32		13	1	14
60		43	9	3	25		16		1	30	20			3		7		31	17		2	34		46		27		8		9
59		51	8	3			23		19		23		20	3	2	7	1	28	18		6	34	1	58		27	1	5	2	7
58		53	12	2			21		17		17		18	3	1	7	2	21	20		12	15	1	67		15	2	4	3	6
57		51	11	1			22		17		11		19	2	5	3	3	20	15		16	5	1	72		12	1	2	3	2
56		47	8	1			15		16		8		17	4	9	5	3	13	26		22	2	2	65		9	1	2	3	
55		45	10				19		17		6		26	5	1	9	3	10	26		33		2	78		5	3	1	3	
54		41	10				11		14		2		24	4	11	3	4	9	20		40		2	56		3	4	1	3	
53		29	15				12		23				25	5	16	2	4	21	21		57		4	57		4	5	1	4	
52		26	13				12		19				21	5	19	1	4	7	25		61		3	33		3	5	1	4	
51	1	21	12	9			21		21				20	5	20	1	4	3	22		55		2	22		2	4	1	4	
50	1	13	14	9			22		22				23	10	23		6	1	29		58		2	16			1	3	6	
49	1	9	14				8		21		5		22	9	28	1	6	1	21		56		6	11			5		8	
48	3	10	13				8		24		7		27	17	30		6		27		48		14	5			7		9	
47	4	4	15				8		24		5		22	17	37		10		28		40		25	1			9		10	
46	11	3	18				8		16		5		21	18	35		8		25		40		30				6		8	
45	14	3	18				6		19		7		21	15	42		6		24		42		38				9		12	
44	18	1	16				6		18		11		22	18	33		10		24		28		43				7		11	
43	26	2	24				5		18		8		19	21	7		7		30		22		46		1		7		12	
42	24	1	22				4		19		10		13	23	31		8		26		25		41				9		14	
41	29		25				4		19		14		23	29	6		6		26		15		42		1		10		18	
40	33		27				4		16		14		9	33	13		13		23		16		37		1		15		15	
39	33		26		1		14		13		9		24		26		17		17		14		34		1		17		24	
38	40		31		1		14		16		8		23		35		23		14		9		27		2		19		32	
37	44		30		1		13		17		11		26		26		17		12		6		28		1		24		29	
36	45		37		1		10		27		8		28		28		23		16		4		30		1		26		34	
35	52		22		1		13		26		9		25		31		25		15		5		28		2		38		32	
34	51		21		1		8		29		8		27		24		27		14		5		25		6		38		40	
33	52		22				9		27		8		21		21		32		9		5		28		8		33		36	
32	56		30				8		38		4		20		23		27		9		2		24		13		46		40	
31	40		22				9		38		5		23		21		20		8		1		17		9		31		32	
30	32		16				6		28		7		29		27		27		11		2		17		16		31		39	
29	18		13				3		27		4		23		14		30		4				11		12		23		21	
28	19		18				5		26		2		23		10		33		4				13		19		30		26	
27	13		20				5		30		2		25		11		28		4		1		14		18		23		21	
26	9		12				2		20		3		19		5		22		2				11		16		19		17	
25	7		11				3		26		1		18		6		25		2				11		18		16		12	
24	8		9				3		22				16		3		24		1				5		18		19		14	
23	8		8				4		17		1		11		3		23		1				6		18		16		14	
22	5		8				2		14				11		4		20		2				7		14		11		10	
21	6		8				1		16				9		1		18		1				6		15		14		12	
20	5		6				1		19				8		1		17		2				4		17		12		16	
19	5		5						17		10		13		1		4								20		12		10	
18	4		4						19		11		14				4								20		13		11	
17	5		4						13		6		9				3								20		12		9	
16	3		3						13		10		8				4								17		12		9	
15	2		3						12		9		12				5								17		11		9	
14	3		3						10		7		10				6								14		8		5	
13	1		3						10		7		9				1								15		8		6	
12	1		3						7		6		9												14		7		6	
11	2		4						5		4		8												16		5		4	
10	2		2						6		5		6												17		9		4	
9	1		1						7		2						7								20		8		2	
8	2								5		3						7								21		7		4	
7	1								5								4								16		3		2	
6	1								3		1						4								13		4		2	
5									2								4								14		3			
4									4								4								16		4		1	
3									2								5								16		3			
2									2								5								13		5			
1									1								2								14		5		1	
0									1								3								14		3		1	
−5									3								7								72		10		2	
−10																	6								57		9			
−15																	1								30		2			
−20																									17					
−25																									8					
−30																									5					
−35																									1					

Section 3: CLOUD COVER

While there is a relative abundance of stations with sky cover records, there are only a few locations where solar radiation has been measured (204 vs. 26). The original sky cover observations included both thick and thin cloud cover and both low and high clouds. Opaque cloudiness, which permits a large fraction of penetration of diffuse solar radiation, has been included in the sky cover amounts.

In a general sense, amounts of sky cover can be used to represent the availability or non-availability of solar radiation. 30% or less sky cover can essentially be treated as clear for estimating solar radiation. Even when the sky is covered with 40 to 60% of sky cover, a very high fraction of possible solar radiation is recorded. Most of the diffuse solar radiation reaches the ground until dense and thick cloud cover prevails (100%).
Small amounts of diffuse solar radiation are measured even when continuous precipitation is added to thick, dense cloud cover.

The three-month maps of sky cover in the 48 contiguous states show ranges of sky cover from sunrise to sunset. Each original hourly observation was recorded in 10% intervals of sky coverage.

FIGURE 9. SKY COVER BY THREE-MONTH PERIODS

The three-month sky cover maps for the 48 contiguous states have been arranged to indicate ranges of sky cover with band widths of ten percentiles of sky cover. The lowest sky cover measurements are made in central and eastern California, western Nevada and western Arizona during the three months of June, July and August. Less than 30% of the sky is covered in this area with the exception of some high mountain ridges. A large part of the Great Lakes region records more than 60% sky cover throughout most of the year. Coastal areas often have more sky cover than inland stations.

DEC - JAN - FEB

U.S. DEPARTMENT OF COMMERCE
WEATHER BUREAU

TRUE SCALE 1:22,500,000 AT LAT 60 N.
POLAR STEREOGRAPHIC PROJECTION

MEAN SKY COVER IN TENTHS
SUNRISE TO SUNSET

A 7.5 - 8.5
B 6.5 - 7.5
C 5.5 - 6.5
D 4.5 - 5.5
E 3.5 - 4.5

MAR - APR - MAY

U.S. DEPARTMENT OF COMMERCE
WEATHER BUREAU

TRUE SCALE 1:22,500,000 AT LAT 60 N
POLAR STEREOGRAPHIC PROJECTION

MEAN SKY COVER IN TENTHS
SUNRISE TO SUNSET

A 7.5 - 8.5
B 6.5 - 7.5
C 5.5 - 6.5
D 4.5 - 5.5
E 3.5 - 4.5
F 2.5 - 3.5

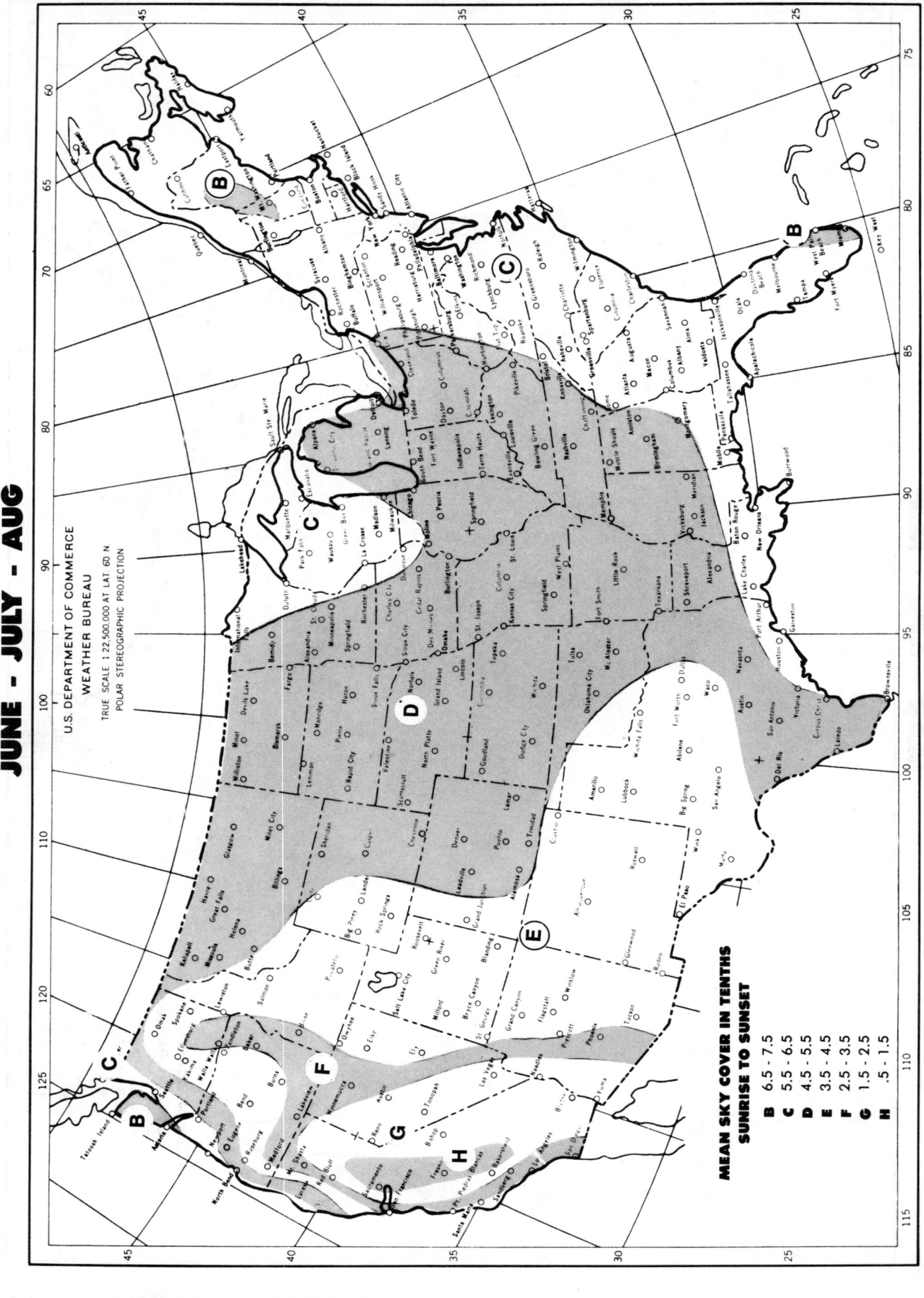

JUNE - JULY - AUG

U.S. DEPARTMENT OF COMMERCE
WEATHER BUREAU

TRUE SCALE 1 22,500,000 AT LAT 60 N
POLAR STEREOGRAPHIC PROJECTION

MEAN SKY COVER IN TENTHS
SUNRISE TO SUNSET

B 6.5 - 7.5
C 5.5 - 6.5
D 4.5 - 5.5
E 3.5 - 4.5
F 2.5 - 3.5
G 1.5 - 2.5
H .5 - 1.5

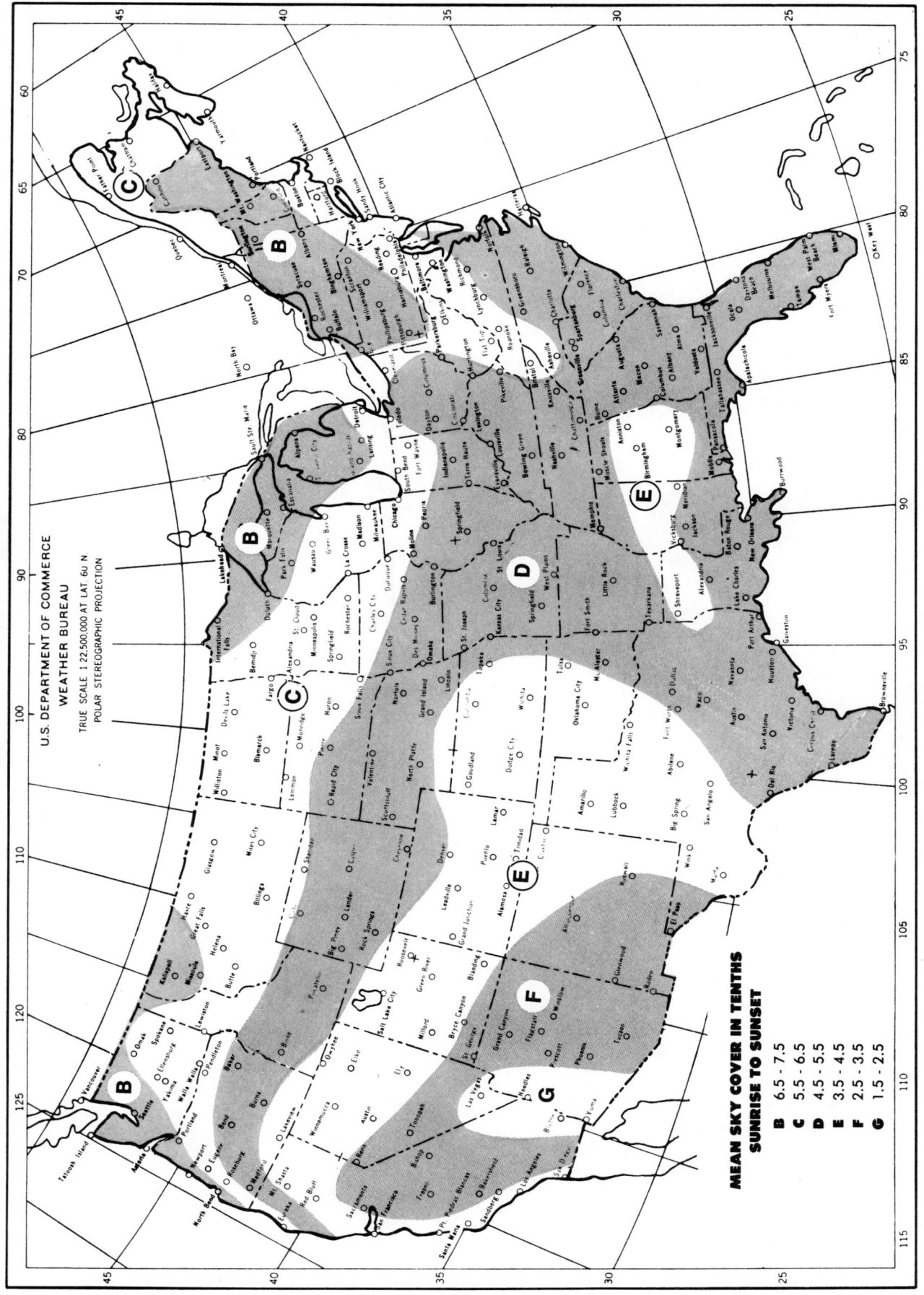

SEPT - OCT - NOV

U.S. DEPARTMENT OF COMMERCE
WEATHER BUREAU

TRUE SCALE 1:22,500,000 AT LAT 60°N
POLAR STEREOGRAPHIC PROJECTION

MEAN SKY COVER IN TENTHS
SUNRISE TO SUNSET

B 6.5 - 7.5
C 5.5 - 6.5
D 4.5 - 5.5
E 3.5 - 4.5
F 2.5 - 3.5
G 1.5 - 2.5

Part 3 — SUMMER WET BULB TEMPERATURE

Section 1: PERTINENT CONSIDERATIONS

As previously noted, the data upon which the reported information is based were obtained from the most reliable sources available. Hourly observations in the majority of cases were made continuously for a ten-year period. The portion representing the four-month period, June, July, August and September, has been analyzed and the results presented in such a way that the designer can choose the particular wet bulb temperature for a given locality that will be above the wet bulb temperatures of any given percentage of the total hours of the period. This wet bulb temperature is more usefully designated as the value equaled or exceeded a given number of hours or a given percent of the total hours.

There are 2928 hours in the four-month summer period. A 1% design criterion would entail approximately 30 hours. Therefore, a statement that a particular wet bulb temperature had to do with the 1% level would mean that for any year during the months of June, July, August and September the normal expectancy would be for 30 hours to be at or above the noted wet bulb temperature. Similarly, the 5% and 15% levels would have to do with the wet bulbs that would be equaled or exceeded for approximately 150 hours and 450 hours, respectively.

It should be noted that 15% of the four-month period would be only 5% of the entire year, and therefore this adjustment should be made when pertinent.

The frequency array shown in Table 3 is a cumulative total of the number of hours at which the noted wet bulb temperatures were equaled or exceeded, starting from the highest temperature and working downward through the entire sample of wet bulb temperatures for each station. The figures are the averages to the closest degree and the closest hour for the 5- to 10-year period represented by the data. All major industrial areas were based on the 10-year period of 1948 through 1957.

The 1% level of wet bulb frequency — down from the top — of the four-month summer period can be considered as an adequate design value for almost any given location. In effect, the 1% temperature might be equaled or exceeded only 29 hours during the "average" summer season.

It is the responsibility of each engineer to determine the level of risk permissible in a particular design.

Obviously, any design temperature below the 15th percentile of the average cumulative total would certainly expose the subject equipment to weather for appreciable periods of time during which it would be operating under conditions more severe than those for which it was designed. The 15% level — down from the top — would "on the average" have approximately 450 hours in which the design wet bulb would be equaled or exceeded and should be considered as being a low design point.

Section 2: WET BULB TABULATION AND 1% ISO-LINE MAP

To facilitate the sorting and tabulation of the great mass of primary data available on punched cards, two main groups were established. Warmer stations are indicated in black, while cooler stations are indicated in grey. These groups were processed to yield the wet bulb frequencies for one-degree increments for the higher wet bulbs at each station and for larger increments for the lower temperatures. The tabulated information is presented in Table 3.

Figure 10, the 1% iso-line map which follows Table 3, contains lines of equal wet bulb temperatures representing respectively three frequencies in the average summer season wet bulb array. This figure shows the various values of wet bulb temperatures that might be considered adequate design values throughout the United States and which can be expected "on the average" to be equaled or exceeded about 1% of the time (approximately 30 hours) during the summer season.

It is not unusual for the design engineer to round off the design wet bulb temperature to the nearest whole degree. This practice can in certain geographical locations involve several percentile points. The engineer must use discretion in designs for Gulf Coast and similar areas, especially when close approaches to the wet bulb temperatures are to be used.

TABLE 3
HOURLY FREQUENCY
OF
SUMMER WET BULB TEMPERATURES

This table indicates the average expected number of hours during which each wet bulb temperature would be equalled or exceeded during the four summer months, June to September, inclusive.

The 1%, 5%, 15%, and 50% wet bulb specific frequencies were obtained by linear interpolation between the integral wet bulb temperatures of the table.

The hours reported under each wet bulb temperature actually include those that can be said to have higher wet bulb temperatures in addition to the hours at the subject temperature.

It should be noted for the record that although the temperatures reported in this table would be the ones normally used in design work, the precise temperatures that might be considered the dividing lines between the temperature cells of the table in all cases would be ½ degree lower in value.

TABLE 3

Number of hours during average summer season (June through September) that wet bulb temperatures equal or exceed any particular degree Fahrenheit value and wet bulb temperatures at four specific frequency levels—1%, 5%, 15% and 50%.

LOCATION	ALT.	SPECIFIC FREQ. LEVELS 1%	5%	15%	50%	83† 73†	82 72	81 71	80 70	79 69	78 68	77 67	76 66	75 65	74 64	73 63
ALABAMA																
ANNISTON	599	79.9	78.1	76.0	71.5	....	1	6	25	68	151	273	442	659	895	1118
BIRMINGHAM	630	78.5	76.6	74.9	71.1	....	....	1	6	14	42	103	208	420	668	930
DOTHAN	321	81.5	79.7	77.9	74.1	3	14	46	111	230	417	641	878	1173	1496	1774
EVERGREEN	257	81.0	79.5	77.8	73.6	2	12	29	94	204	398	618	842	1122	1365	1633
MOBILE	217	80.1	78.7	77.3	74.3	1	3	8	33	100	255	517	824	1210	1564	1880
MONTGOMERY	195	79.6	77.9	76.4	73.1		1	3	15	51	136	295	524	857	1176	1481
MUSCLE SHOALS	562	79.4	77.6	75.8	71.5	2	4	7	16	40	102	215	388	601	827	1078
TUSCALOOSA	170	80.7	78.9	77.1	72.9	1	3	16	65	138	276	460	661	951	1191	1441
ALASKA																
ANCHORAGE (Elmendorf)	258	63.8	59.4	56.1	51.4	....	....	1	2	3	4	7	12	19	27	37
FAIRBANKS, Ladd AFB	484	65.1	61.9	58.5	52.0	....	....	1	3	4	7	10	17	30	54	88
ARIZONA																
DOUGLAS	4075	69.4	67.8	66.0	62.8	....	....	....	....	....	....	....	....	....	....	....
FLAGSTAFF	6973	61.8	59.5	56.6	51.0	....	....	....	....	....	....	....	1	1	3	10
GILA BEND	853	76.2	74.7	73.0	67.5	....	....	....	....	1	3	8	34	107	244	438
KINGMAN	3446	70.0	68.5	66.4	60.8	....	....	....	....	....	....	....	....	....	....	1
PHOENIX	1112	76.8	75.3	73.4	68.1	....	....	1	1	2	4	18	69	176	330	514
PRESCOTT	5014	66.6	65.2	63.2	58.2											
TUCSON	2558	72.9	71.4	69.8	65.3	....	....	....	....	....	....	....	....	1	6	24
WINSLOW	4880	66.0	64.3	62.3	56.7	....	....	....	•	....	1	9	28	84	178	312
YUMA	199	78.9	77.4	75.4	69.4	....	....	1	5	25	82	183	321	512	697	885
ARKANSAS																
EL DORADO	252	81.7	79.7	77.8	74.0	5	20	54	114	220	399	639	906	1205	1460	1710
FAYETTEVILLE	1253	78.0	76.3	74.4	69.5	....	1	1	2	9	28	81	178	339	518	716
FORT SMITH	449	79.6	77.8	75.9	71.7	1	2	4	18	49	127	247	409	688	924	1156
LITTLE ROCK	265	80.1	78.4	76.5	72.3	....	4	11	32	78	184	347	551	825	1074	1303
PINE BLUFF	204	81.8	80.0	78.0	73.3	6	21	60	150	274	446	652	852	1079	1297	1536
TEXARKANA	361	80.0	78.5	77.0	73.7	....	3	9	28	80	217	428	698	1046	1362	1655
WALNUT RIDGE	275	80.2	78.1	75.9	71.1	....	2	13	33	75	156	276	425	626	841	1066
CALIFORNIA																
ARCATA	217	60.3	58.2	56.1	53.0	....	....	....	....	....	....	....	....	....	1	3
BAKERSFIELD	494	72.4	69.8	67.3	61.9	*19	36	69	132	224	348	486	644	847	1038	1229
BLYTHE	395	77.9	75.9	73.9	67.3	2	2	3	5	8	24	64	129	265	422	596
BURBANK	699	71.5	69.1	66.4	62.0	....	....	....	....	....	....	....	....	1	2	6
CRESCENT CITY	50	60.8	58.7	56.6	53.4	....	....	....	....	....	....	....	....	....	1	3
DAGGETT	1929	73.2	70.7	67.3	61.0	....	....	....	....	....	....	1	2	6	15	33
EL CENTRO	-30	81.4	79.0	76.4	68.9	6	16	38	85	146	247	366	490	639	778	908
EL TORO	380	71.9	69.0	66.3	62.4	....	....	....	....	....	....	....	1	2	6	13
FRESNO	326	73.2	70.5	67.5	62.4	....	....	....	....	....	....	....	1	5	15	34
LONG BEACH	34	71.7	68.8	66.0	62.6	....	....	....	....	....	1	1	2	5	7	14
LOS ANGELES (Int'l. AP)	122	69.4	66.9	64.7	61.5	1	2	7	17	37	73	133	235	383	603	894
MERCED, Castle AFB	178	73.9	70.7	67.9	62.2	....	....	....	....	1	2	3	6	13	27	46
MONTAGUE	2635	67.6	64.8	61.6	54.5	....	1	2	3	9	22	40	70	135	206	296
NEEDLES	913	75.8	74.3	72.3	66.0	....	....	....	....	1	1	4	18	76	175	308
OAKLAND	3	65.6	62.8	60.3	56.5	....	....	....	1	1	3	9	21	41	77	131
PALMDALE	2517	70.0	66.7	63.7	57.2	3	7	15	30	48	79	126	202	293	403	527
RED BLUFF	344	71.3	68.5	65.8	60.3	6	17	35	62	113	183	279	404	548	717	903
REDDING	435	70.1	67.1	64.5	59.7	....	3	13	32	57	99	153	241	368	525	720
RIVERSIDE, March AFB	1511	72.3	69.1	66.1	61.4	....	....	....	....	....	....	....	2	5	10	19
SACRAMENTO	23	71.9	69.1	66.0	60.3	....	....	....	....	....	....	....	1	2	6	12
SALINAS	74	66.7	63.6	60.9	56.0	....	1	2	4	8	13	25	39	75	118	188
SANDBERG	4523	62.5	60.0	57.4	52.5	....	....	....	....	....	....	....	1	2	7	19
SAN DIEGO	37	70.7	68.4	66.2	63.2	....	....	....	....	....	....	....	....	....	1	2
SAN FRANCISCO	18	64.7	61.7	59.3	55.4	....	....	....	1	2	3	6	13	23	41	74
SAN RAFAEL (Hamilton)	2	70.8	67.0	63.6	56.5	9	17	26	43	65	99	145	200	291	391	504
SANTA BARBARA	13	67.4	64.8	62.7	59.1	....	....	....	1	6	19	37	69	124	219	376
SANTA MARIA	250	65.4	62.7	60.3	55.7	....	....	....	....	1	4	7	17	36	65	118
STOCKTON	28	71.4	68.8	65.9	60.3	....	....	....	....	....	....	....	....	1	3	8
SUNNYVALE	39	68.5	65.5	62.8	58.1	....	1	4	10	20	38	67	104	182	274	413
THERMAL	117	79.8	77.4	74.7	66.8	....	1	5	22	52	103	173	275	402	530	642
UKIAH	620	71.0	68.4	65.0	57.4	4	13	29	72	108	167	242	315	445	557	677
WILLIAMS	128	76.5	72.0	68.6	62.0	2	3	5	8	13	17	24	35	49	73	102

*Wet bulb temperature range extends above 73°F, but the number of hours with 74°, 75°, etc., can be estimated.

WET BULB TEMPERATURES

Wet bulb frequency arrays are shown in gray at stations having cooler temperatures. This allows greater detailed analysis of these stations in their higher range of wet bulb values.

72 62	71 61	70 60	69 59	68 58	67 57	66 56	64 55	62 54	60 53	55 52	50 50	45 45	40 40	39‡ 39‡	LOCATION
															ALABAMA
1362	1580	1820	2003	2152	2270	2372	2550	2664	2751	2875	2918	2927	2928	2928	ANNISTON
1231	1480	1765	1948	2111	2236	2341	2527	2661	2755	2880	2920	2927	2928	2928	BIRMINGHAM
2043	2249	2414	2517	2606	2673	2720	2799	2851	2885	2924	2927	2928	2928	2928	DOTHAN
1886	2093	2294	2423	2527	2607	2666	2754	2821	2868	2919	2927	2928	2928	2928	EVERGREEN
2135	2311	2462	2558	2636	2697	2742	2809	2855	2886	2924	2927	2928	2928	2928	MOBILE
1771	1988	2199	2321	2433	2517	2587	2719	2793	2848	2914	2927	2928	2928	2928	MONTGOMERY
1353	1565	1793	1960	2108	2217	2320	2496	2628	2729	2867	2913	2926	2928	2928	MUSCLE SHOALS
1690	1902	2101	2235	2350	2435	2502	2641	2736	2805	2892	2922	2927	2928	2928	TUSCALOOSA
															ALASKA
54	74	116	164	236	331	452	627	822	1035	1275	1735	2493	2808	2928	ANCHORAGE (Elmendorf)
138	195	282	378	499	630	779	962	1122	1285	1454	1780	2348	2631	2928	FAIRBANKS, Ladd AFB
															ARIZONA
1	2	14	42	121	246	430	1017	1503	1851	2393	2686	2841	2912	2928	DOUGLAS
25	53	112	181	276	385	518	695	872	1071	1254	1550	2172	2543	2928	FLAGSTAFF
650	857	1076	1246	1398	1538	1664	1921	2157	2360	2719	2871	2919	2928	2928	GILA BEND
3	8	30	89	199	343	517	873	1249	1594	2227	2645	2853	2916	2928	KINGMAN
735	950	1146	1314	1485	1638	1792	2079	2318	2514	2809	2909	2927	2928	2928	PHOENIX
....	....	....	1	3	17	48	223	555	894	1700	2320	2682	2864	2928	PRESCOTT
85	194	386	605	842	1064	1280	1647	1943	2194	2625	2838	2913	2927	2928	TUCSON
485	655	878	1060	1240	1415	1575	1738	1877	2002	2136	2340	2688	2867	2928	WINSLOW
1076	1235	1391	1516	1649	1771	1887	2132	2339	2523	2836	2920	2928	2928	2928	YUMA
															ARKANSAS
1923	2088	2233	2340	2429	2496	2550	2662	2747	2807	2886	2921	2928	2928	2928	EL DORADO
924	1121	1360	1564	1741	1912	2055	2284	2432	2562	2757	2871	2915	2927	2928	FAYETTEVILLE
1417	1594	1808	1948	2090	2211	2308	2487	2613	2712	2858	2911	2925	2928	2928	FORT SMITH
1531	1724	1923	2060	2186	2299	2385	2538	2646	2743	2876	2920	2928	2928	2928	LITTLE ROCK
1749	1917	2079	2194	2300	2387	2456	2588	2692	2775	2873	2914	2927	2928	2928	PINE BLUFF
1913	2088	2243	2346	2442	2517	2577	2693	2766	2822	2896	2920	2927	2928	2928	TEXARKANA
1294	1494	1680	1838	1980	2099	2208	2398	2537	2644	2816	2897	2919	2927	2928	WALNUT RIDGE
															CALIFORNIA
5	12	37	81	164	281	454	732	1065	1476	1909	2512	2883	2925	2928	ARCATA
1440	1627	1844	2025	2207	2360	2485	2608	2694	2772	2825	2888	2922	2928	2928	BAKERSFIELD
767	923	1099	1236	1376	1511	1635	1934	2190	2418	2796	2908	2927	2928	2928	BLYTHE
16	41	87	150	234	343	492	854	1308	1820	2685	2887	2922	2928	2928	BURBANK
9	20	57	113	215	363	576	853	1197	1629	2026	2559	2881	2926	2928	CRESCENT CITY
67	127	193	269	366	475	593	876	1190	1525	2318	2799	2913	2927	2928	DAGGETT
1046	1164	1317	1447	1583	1707	1827	2083	2318	2532	2847	2922	2928	2928	2928	EL CENTRO
27	46	87	148	236	351	481	897	1382	1941	2734	2893	2926	2928	2928	EL TORO
66	108	181	272	380	509	646	1017	1411	1804	2563	2874	2923	2927	2928	FRESNO
26	40	79	127	207	319	445	879	1439	2119	2838	2923	2928	2928	2928	LONG BEACH
1264	1651	2034	2338	2569	2726	2815	2866	2895	2910	2918	2925	2928	2928	2928	LOS ANGELES (Int'l. AP)
77	120	211	302	421	565	701	1029	1377	1741	2528	2881	2925	2928	2928	MERCED, Castle AFB
397	504	641	770	913	1068	1209	1387	1555	1723	1876	2180	2661	2862	2928	MONTAGUE
490	650	840	995	1156	1309	1452	1757	2038	2286	2720	2898	2926	2928	2928	NEEDLES
211	325	493	706	975	1285	1634	2000	2312	2557	2729	2878	2926	2928	2928	OAKLAND
667	806	981	1142	1313	1492	1665	1824	1973	2117	2260	2495	2812	2904	2928	PALMDALE
1118	1322	1537	1737	1933	2115	2291	2439	2561	2662	2740	2836	2917	2927	2928	RED BLUFF
935	1174	1396	1621	1847	2048	2243	2416	2557	2662	2748	2846	2923	2928	2928	REDDING
35	56	100	153	234	328	447	783	1193	1631	2512	2862	2924	2928	2928	RIVERSIDE, March AFB
28	52	96	153	230	319	428	712	1015	1342	2288	2856	2923	2928	2928	SACRAMENTO
297	426	622	795	991	1211	1449	1800	2107	2381	2594	2826	2921	2927	2928	SALINAS
40	80	149	227	346	499	677	876	1106	1343	1599	2035	2711	2891	2928	SANDBERG
8	19	51	95	181	304	464	1013	1702	2288	2901	2928	2928	2928	2928	SAN DIEGO
123	201	316	488	702	966	1256	1578	1909	2227	2499	2803	2926	2928	2928	SAN FRANCISCO
644	765	930	1063	1228	1385	1535	1747	1951	2163	2381	2714	2923	2928	2928	SAN RAFAEL (Hamilton)
603	859	1171	1504	1834	2106	2334	2511	2623	2699	2763	2850	2924	2928	2928	SANTA BARBARA
207	323	497	688	899	1115	1361	1691	2021	2308	2509	2718	2891	2925	2928	SANTA MARIA
17	39	78	127	206	299	414	692	1009	1365	2329	2853	2925	2928	2928	STOCKTON
571	734	981	1221	1493	1765	1998	2255	2430	2566	2673	2814	2921	2928	2928	SUNNYVALE
764	879	1009	1133	1275	1431	1592	1945	2270	2515	2860	2925	2928	2928	2928	THERMAL
813	922	1094	1220	1363	1532	1667	1872	2028	2176	2326	2580	2876	2924	2928	UKIAH
146	194	276	381	514	641	816	1142	1461	1748	2421	2818	2917	2928	2928	WILLIAMS

†Includes all wet bulb hours which were 83° or 73° or higher.   ‡Includes all wet bulb hours which were 39° or lower.

TABLE 3—Continued   **HOURLY FREQUENCY OF SUMMER**

Number of hours during average summer season (June through September) that wet bulb temperatures equal or exceed any particular degree Fahrenheit value and wet bulb temperatures at four specific frequency levels—1%, 5%, 15% and 50%.

LOCATION	ALT.	1%	5%	15%	50%	83†/73†	82/72	81/71	80/70	79/69	78/68	77/67	76/66	75/65	74/64	73/63
COLORADO																
AKRON	4621	70.6	67.6	65.2	59.6	....	....	....	....	1	2	2	3	5	7	9
COLORADO SPRINGS	6173	63.0	60.8	58.8	54.1							1	3	10	28	
DENVER	5332	64.6	62.5	60.2	55.4						1	3	6	17	46	100
EAGLE	6598	63.5	60.9	58.2	51.3							1	2	6	17	41
GRAND JUNCTION	4839	65.1	62.9	60.4	55.1						1	2	8	32	80	137
LA JUNTA	4188	73.2	70.3	67.4	62.0	⁻34	57	92	167	245	351	489	655	869	1070	1259
PUEBLO	4639	67.6	65.5	63.3	58.5			1	2	6	19	47	100	198	329	498
TRINIDAD	5746	66.1	63.9	61.7	56.9	1	1	2	3	3	6	11	31	67	133	230
CONNECTICUT																
HARTFORD, Brainard Field	15	77.2	74.4	71.5	64.7	....	....	....	2	6	14	32	61	110	168	258
NEW HAVEN	6	77.0	74.7	71.9	64.7	....	....	....	1	9	29	67	125	209	301	
WINDSOR LOCKS	179	76.4	73.7	70.6	63.6	....	....	1	2	3	8	18	38	73	124	192
DELWARE																
DOVER	38	78.9	77.3	73.9	67.6	—	2	7	20	48	92	152	248	368	519	675
WILMINGTON	79	78.6	76.2	73.5	66.7	....	....	1	9	19	45	95	160	263	375	509
DIST. OF COLUMBIA																
WASHINGTON	65	78.3	76.1	73.8	67.9	....	....	....	3	13	36	75	152	267	406	567
FLORIDA																
CRESTVIEW	272	80.6	78.8	77.3	74.0	1	4	17	45	117	278	512	820	1144	1475	1765
CROSS CITY	46	82.0	80.5	78.8	75.1	6	27	84	207	399	653	918	1184	1506	1829	2143
DAYTONA BEACH	31	80.7	79.0	77.7	74.8	1	4	17	56	149	344	628	971	1387	1771	2126
FORT MYERS	13	80.3	79.1	78.1	75.9	....	....	6	39	159	460	897	1406	1894	2306	2572
JACKSONVILLE	39	80.0	78.6	77.2	74.6	1	2	8	29	92	242	504	877	1282	1721	2080
MIAMI	24	79.8	78.8	77.8	76.0	....	....	2	19	87	354	869	1473	2010	2387	2630
ORLANDO	106	79.4	78.2	77.1	74.9	....	....	1	10	40	175	471	842	1404	1869	2258
PANAMA CITY (Tyndall)	22	82.0	80.5	78.9	76.0	8	28	79	218	409	732	1097	1462	1854	2131	2345
PENSACOLA	33	81.6	79.9	78.6	76.1	6	15	48	128	294	671	1097	1524	1890	2139	2325
TALLAHASSEE	58	80.2	78.5	76.9	73.8	....	2	9	34	85	209	416	699	1034	1401	1766
TAMPA	36	79.9	78.6	77.4	75.0	....	1	5	24	83	250	556	989	1455	1937	2328
TITUSVILLE	14	80.7	79.4	78.1	75.1	1	2	10	63	197	455	789	1143	1533	1836	2152
VERO BEACH	54	80.7	79.5	78.4	75.9	....	3	12	72	223	600	1024	1423	1882	2233	2529
WEST PALM BEACH	15	80.7	79.5	78.5	76.3	1	2	11	65	239	616	1107	1603	2076	2406	2626
GEORGIA																
ALBANY	224	80.0	78.4	76.7	73.5	....	1	6	29	77	185	355	596	949	1296	1612
ALMA	203	80.9	79.1	77.3	73.4	3	8	25	77	153	303	509	734	1036	1302	1587
ATLANTA	993	77.6	75.8	74.1	70.4				4	16	51	121	255	458	698	
AUGUSTA	143	80.1	78.5	76.5	72.6	....	....	7	33	91	202	349	548	809	1070	1347
MACON	356	79.5	77.7	75.8	72.4	....	1	3	13	44	110	224	396	661	954	1279
SAVANNAH, Travis Field	52	80.5	78.8	77.0	73.5	1	3	12	48	118	247	429	664	1003	1320	1629
VALDOSTA	223	79.5	77.9	76.5	73.3	1	1	4	14	45	134	310	558	866	1217	1562
IDAHO																
BOISE	2858	67.9	64.7	61.4	54.6		1	2	7	13	28	49	80	127	185	264
BURLEY	4180	67.9	64.3	60.9	53.7	1	1	2	8	15	27	45	66	110	162	231
COEUR D'ALENE	2973	66.4	63.3	60.3	54.1				1	3	8	19	35	66	107	167
DUBOIS	5129	62.6	59.5	56.3	50.7							1	5	10	22	
GOODING	3668	67.6	64.1	60.5	53.7	2	2	3	7	14	22	40	66	103	149	204
IDAHO FALLS	4730	65.4	61.8	58.5	51.9					1	3	7	19	37	57	88
MALAD CITY	4180	68.5	65.4	62.0	53.7		1	3	10	18	40	68	110	170	235	321
MOUNTAIN HOME	2992	68.4	64.9	61.6	54.4		1	4	11	20	36	58	91	142	206	285
MULLAN PASS	6037	58.3	54.9	51.9	47.5											1
POCATELLO	4444	64.6	61.6	58.7	52.2	....						1	3	8	21	40	71
ILLINOIS																
BELLEVILLE, Scott AFB	447	79.9	77.6	75.0	68.6	2	4	10	25	57	112	189	290	442	588	735
CHICAGO-Midway	623	77.7	74.8	71.5	64.6	....	1	2	4	10	21	46	79	131	207	286
JOLIET	588	78.5	75.3	71.8	64.6	....	1	3	8	19	38	69	108	162	233	315
MOLINE	582	78.9	75.9	72.5	65.4	....	1	3	9	25	55	93	141	210	297	388
PEORIA	652	78.3	75.6	72.4	65.1	....	....	2	6	16	34	64	117	193	279	367
QUINCY	762	80.1	77.4	74.2	67.1	2	5	13	31	57	107	172	252	362	464	587
RANTOUL, Chanute AFB	740	79.1	76.3	73.1	65.7	1	2	5	14	32	60	106	161	254	345	451
ROCKFORD	724	76.9	74.0	70.5	63.3	—	—	1	3	9	20	39	67	105	161	236
SPRINGFIELD	587	79.1	76.8	73.8	66.7	....	....	4	13	32	70	130	211	300	411	534

*Wet bulb temperature range extends above 73°F, but the number of hours with 74°, 75°, etc., can be estimated.

WET BULB TEMPERATURES

Wet bulb frequency arrays are shown in gray at stations having cooler temperatures. This allows greater detailed analysis of these stations in their higher range of wet bulb values.

72 / 62	71 / 61	70 / 60	69 / 59	68 / 58	67 / 57	66 / 56	64 / 55	62 / 54	60 / 53	55 / 52	50 / 50	45 / 45	40 / 40	39‡ / 39†	LOCATION
															COLORADO
14	21	41	69	120	195	282	551	870	1233	2066	2559	2780	2877	2928	AKRON
63	126	254	396	576	783	991	1253	1488	1697	1890	2206	2672	2863	2928	COLORADO SPRINGS
188	309	478	668	894	1108	1336	1560	1770	1955	2111	2363	2733	2882	2928	DENVER
85	133	237	333	461	606	751	921	1071	1205	1345	1594	2124	2505	2928	EAGLE
230	334	508	667	861	1056	1258	1493	1683	1857	2022	2318	2754	2900	2928	GRAND JUNCTION
1474	1658	1872	2031	2179	2300	2403	2505	2585	2643	2694	2780	2885	2919	2928	LA JUNTA
705	903	1163	1368	1582	1756	1910	2077	2206	2332	2441	2606	2822	2905	2928	PUEBLO
381	555	770	987	1224	1453	1661	1861	2036	2174	2298	2499	2793	2892	2928	TRINIDAD
															CONNECTICUT
382	509	659	780	926	1066	1197	1480	1749	2023	2502	2783	2886	2916	2928	HARTFORD, Brainard Field
418	550	713	859	1005	1146	1271	1570	1859	2147	2631	2828	2908	2927	2928	NEW HAVEN
287	387	519	639	774	904	1039	1322	1617	1885	2425	2751	2873	2912	2928	WINDSOR LOCKS
															DELAWARE
840	1012	1180	1320	1475	1615	1749	2104	2240	2429	2743	2877	2913	2976	2928	DOVER
661	811	983	1130	1278	1419	1549	1845	2097	2332	2697	2860	2912	2925	2928	WILMINGTON
															DIST. OF COLUMBIA
763	954	1145	1301	1454	1587	1737	2029	2287	2484	2767	2889	2920	2928	2928	WASHINGTON
															FLORIDA
2051	2258	2424	2536	2621	2684	2735	2811	2864	2901	2925	2927	2928	2928	2928	CRESTVIEW
2401	2575	2708	2785	2836	2873	2891	2910	2916	2922	2928	2928	2928	2928	2928	CROSS CITY
2411	2599	2737	2811	2851	2874	2888	2911	2920	2925	2927	2928	2928	2928	2928	DAYTONA BEACH
2743	2829	2877	2898	2910	2917	2921	2926	2928	2928	2928	2928	2928	2928	2928	FORT MYERS
2375	2560	2689	2763	2815	2846	2871	2901	2915	2921	2927	2928	2928	2928	2928	JACKSONVILLE
2779	2850	2887	2904	2914	2920	2925	2928	2928	2928	2928	2928	2928	2928	2928	MIAMI
2556	2707	2800	2843	2876	2896	2907	2921	2925	2927	2928	2928	2928	2928	2928	ORLANDO
2511	2610	2699	2749	2790	2820	2847	2888	2910	2919	2927	2928	2928	2928	2928	PANAMA CITY (Tyndall)
2472	2570	2665	2730	2782	2815	2843	2879	2903	2920	2927	2928	2928	2928	2928	PENSACOLA
2092	2331	2496	2609	2685	2740	2786	2849	2889	2908	2926	2928	2928	2928	2928	TALLAHASSEE
2576	2725	2803	2845	2877	2894	2906	2918	2924	2927	2928	2928	2928	2928	2928	TAMPA
2412	2628	2772	2841	2882	2902	2916	2925	2926	2927	2928	2928	2928	2928	2928	TITUSVILLE
2718	2813	2877	2900	2915	2920	2923	2927	2928	2928	2928	2928	2928	2928	2928	VERO BEACH
2766	2842	2886	2902	2914	2921	2924	2928	2928	2928	2928	2928	2928	2928	2928	WEST PALM BEACH
															GEORGIA
1897	2109	2306	2434	2542	2622	2682	2785	2845	2888	2924	2927	2928	2928	2928	ALBANY
1879	2102	2345	2473	2567	2649	2701	2801	2861	2898	2924	2927	2928	2928	2928	ALMA
983	1283	1583	1821	2006	2147	2270	2481	2637	2739	2878	2920	2927	2928	2928	ATLANTA
1621	1843	2042	2176	2289	2398	2492	2636	2735	2802	2899	2924	2928	2928	2928	AUGUSTA
1583	1829	2062	2208	2338	2435	2514	2657	2752	2821	2904	2924	2928	2928	2928	MACON
1928	2157	2346	2464	2562	2643	2703	2799	2863	2893	2924	2928	2928	2928	2928	SAVANNAH, Travis Field
1903	2160	2373	2518	2633	2706	2755	2839	2892	2918	2926	2927	2928	2928	2928	VALDOSTA
															IDAHO
367	479	629	755	905	1052	1210	1390	1556	1710	1870	2173	2684	2873	2928	BOISE
324	418	565	689	838	991	1133	1286	1423	1560	1695	1964	2503	2791	2928	BURLEY
248	345	475	616	762	922	1098	1296	1476	1658	1842	2159	2677	2868	2928	COEUR D'ALENE
42	68	116	174	252	350	479	633	792	962	1138	1493	2222	2648	2928	DUBOIS
286	376	499	628	778	940	1035	1253	1419	1572	1736	2045	2603	2844	2928	GOODING
136	194	283	378	501	633	788	946	1106	1258	1419	1745	2404	2752	2928	IDAHO FALLS
437	547	696	806	932	1056	1168	1309	1429	1539	1659	1899	2383	2714	2928	MALAD CITY
393	499	643	775	923	1057	1194	1365	1524	1666	1813	2113	2620	2835	2928	MOUNTAIN HOME
3	5	9	19	34	55	91	139	208	289	401	686	1583	2365	2928	MULLEN PASS
118	182	285	393	532	683	831	1021	1180	1339	1499	1808	2433	2766	2928	POCATELLO
															ILLINOIS
893	1046	1240	1392	1555	1694	1821	2092	2282	2454	2732	2865	2911	2926	2928	BELLEVILLE, Scott AFB
387	504	632	751	889	1038	1182	1475	1762	2041	2520	2779	2885	2921	2928	CHICAGO
420	525	660	782	926	1065	1193	1458	1736	2017	2473	2734	2857	2906	2928	JOLIET
497	614	768	914	1069	1203	1339	1628	1893	2132	2559	2779	2879	2915	2928	MOLINE
492	627	775	917	1052	1184	1332	1634	1902	2156	2582	2797	2881	2919	2928	PEORIA
729	871	1045	1179	1327	1473	1607	1889	2119	2326	2650	2815	2893	2919	2928	QUINCY
579	697	872	1002	1145	1279	1405	1717	1959	2205	2597	2807	2892	2921	2928	RANTOUL, Chanute AFB
331	441	573	707	845	987	1143	1435	1696	1950	2430	2731	2861	2914	2928	ROCKFORD
682	820	976	1116	1276	1423	1564	1841	2086	2306	2644	2822	2896	2921	2928	SPRINGFIELD

†Includes all wet bulb hours which were 83° or 73° or higher.   ‡Includes all wet bulb hours which were 39° or lower.

TABLE 3—Continued　　　　　　　　　　　　　　　　　　　**HOURLY FREQUENCY OF SUMMER**

Number of hours during average summer season (June through September) that wet bulb temperatures equal or exceed any particular degree Fahrenheit value and wet bulb temperatures at four specific frequency levels—1%, 5%, 15% and 50%.

LOCATION	ALT.	SPECIFIC FREQ. LEVELS				83+ 73†	82 72	81 71	80 70	79 69	78 68	77 67	76 66	75 65	74 64	73 63
		1%	5%	15%	50%											
MICHIGAN—Continued																
SAGINAW	662	76.6	73.2	69.3	61.8	....	....	....	1	4	10	22	41	70	106	159
SAULT STE. MARIE	724	73.2	68.9	64.9	58.2	....	....	....	....	....	....	1	4	9	20	31
TRAVERSE CITY	618	75.3	71.6	68.1	60.8	....	....	....	2	4	10	18	33	54	83
YPSILANTI	777	75.8	73.1	69.9	62.8	....	....	....	1	4	12	25	51	93	152
MINNESOTA																
ALEXANDRIA	1421	75.9	72.0	67.9	60.6	....	....	....	1	3	8	14	27	46	74	103
DULUTH	1426	73.0	68.8	64.9	58.2	....	....	....	....	....	1	2	6	12	19	30
MINNEAPOLIS	838	77.5	73.7	69.7	62.6	....	1	2	6	11	21	37	57	92	133	181
REDWOOD FALLS	1030	77.3	73.4	69.5	62.2	....	....	....	3	9	19	33	54	81	116	166
ROCHESTER	1297	77.4	73.7	69.8	62.4	....	....	1	4	9	20	37	59	91	130	185
ST. CLOUD	1034	76.5	72.7	68.5	61.2	....	....	....	2	7	14	23	35	60	92	129
MISSISSIPPI																
GREENWOOD	128	81.1	79.6	77.7	73.7	1	7	31	102	212	379	599	835	1106	1382	1629
JACKSON	332	79.6	78.0	76.5	73.0	....	1	3	15	53	150	332	562	878	1172	1460
McCOMB	458	79.9	78.5	77.0	73.6	....	....	3	26	90	215	436	698	1011	1344	1659
MERIDIAN	294	79.6	78.0	76.5	72.9	....	....	2	9	58	149	324	564	848	1152	1449
MISSOURI																
BUTLER	878	80.0	77.3	74.7	68.6	1	6	12	29	52	95	173	263	399	524	682
COLUMBIA	778	79.0	76.7	74.0	67.6	....	1	3	12	28	68	120	203	318	440	574
FARMINGTON	928	79.2	77.1	74.4	68.3	....	1	3	11	33	82	153	230	363	492	645
JOPLIN	982	78.9	76.7	74.3	69.4	....	1	2	12	28	62	118	203	335	490	680
KANSAS CITY	750	78.7	76.4	74.1	68.1	....	1	2	7	19	50	101	178	311	452	618
KIRKSVILLE	966	79.2	76.4	73.1	66.0	1	2	5	15	33	64	111	169	255	340	446
ST. JOSEPH	809	79.7	77.1	74.2	67.3	....	1	6	21	48	94	153	240	354	464	574
ST. LOUIS, Lambert	564	79.0	76.8	74.3	68.1	....	....	2	8	29	69	130	216	347	488	647
SPRINGFIELD	1270	78.0	75.8	73.5	68.3	....	....	....	3	10	28	65	126	232	357	520
VICHY	1137	79.6	77.5	75.2	69.3	....	3	7	20	44	101	192	312	481	648	819
MONTANA																
BILLINGS	3567	67.7	64.7	61.5	55.1	1	2	3	7	12	23	42	74	126	186	270
BUTTE	5526	60.0	57.2	54.3	48.9										1	2
CUT BANK	3838	64.8	61.1	57.5	51.2			1	1	2	4	8	15	27	42	68
GLASGOW	2277	68.8	65.4	62.2	55.7	1	2	3	10	24	48	78	104	175	250	353
GREAT FALLS	3687	64.3	60.9	57.9	52.1				1	2	4	6	10	19	34	57
HELENA	3893	64.7	61.4	58.2	51.9				1	1	3	6	11	22	44	72
KALISPELL	2965	64.9	61.7	58.5	51.9		1	1	2	4	8	13	28	51	82
LEWISTOWN	4132	65.0	61.7	58.5	51.9					1	3	7	14	29	49	78
LIVINGSTON	4653	63.3	60.7	57.7	51.7							1	2	7	15	34
MILES CITY	2634	70.8	67.5	64.1	57.4	8	14	24	48	72	116	173	243	348	454	576
MISSOULA	3200	64.6	61.4	58.2	52.0				1	1	2	4	11	23	41	68
NEBRASKA																
CHADRON	3300	72.2	68.8	65.8	59.6	*17	32	52	89	135	204	293	412	564	730	897
GRAND ISLAND	1841	76.2	73.7	70.8	64.6	....	....	....	....	2	6	16	32	68	122	200
LEXINGTON	2408	76.1	73.3	70.3	64.0	....	....	....	1	7	16	30	66	107	163
LINCOLN	1189	78.3	75.6	72.4	65.4	....	1	1	5	15	36	72	120	190	268	361
NORTH PLATTE	2787	74.4	71.8	69.1	63.0	....	....	....	....	1	2	6	18	38	76
OMAHA	982	78.9	76.4	73.3	66.1	....	1	4	12	28	59	108	171	261	364	469
SCOTTSBLUFF	3950	70.1	67.4	64.8	58.7	2	4	14	30	58	105	176	277	408	559	729
SIDNEY	4292	70.3	67.5	65.2	59.6	....	....	....	....	....	....	....	....	1	1	3
NEVADA																
ELKO	5075	64.1	61.0	57.8	50.9					1	1	3	7	15	32	57
ELY	6257	61.5	59.3	56.0	48.4										3	9
LAS VEGAS	2180	71.7	69.5	66.3	59.9	....	....	....	....	....	....	....	....	....	2	6
LOVELOCK	3900	64.7	61.6	58.7	52.5						1	5	9	22	45	75
RENO	4404	63.7	60.7	57.6	51.6							1	3	10	23	42
TONOPAH	5426	64.0	61.6	58.3	51.3						1	1	3	10	28	67
WINNEMUCCA	4299	62.7	59.9	58.0	50.6	—	—	—	—	—	—	—	2	12	33	68
NEW HAMPSHIRE																
CONCORD	339	75.0	71.9	68.4	61.2	....	....	....	1	2	5	14	30	56	92
WEST LEBANON	550	75.2	71.7	68.0	60.0	*90	134	182	257	339	438	546	647	788	911	1042

*Wet bulb temperature range extends above 73°F, but the number of hours with 74°, 75°, etc., can be estimated

WET BULB TEMPERATURES

Wet bulb frequency arrays are shown in gray at stations having cooler temperatures. This allows greater detailed analysis of these stations in their higher range of wet bulb values.

72 / 62	71 / 61	70 / 60	69 / 59	68 / 58	67 / 57	66 / 56	64 / 55	62 / 54	60 / 53	55 / 52	50 / 50	45 / 45	40 / 40	39‡ / 39‡	LOCATION
															MICHIGAN—Cont.
220	276	370	464	573	685	800	1072	1351	1624	2242	2631	2824	2905	2928	SAGINAW
49	71	105	142	195	251	311	480	692	953	1659	2300	2683	2855	2928	SAULT STE. MARIE
125	178	277	347	452	557	666	927	1195	1481	2122	2578	2806	2895	2928	TRAVERSE CITY
229	307	432	544	672	797	924	1201	1492	1784	2395	2737	2871	2916	2928	YPSILANTI
															MINNESOTA
145	194	262	337	428	525	632	889	1183	1456	2094	2546	2775	2884	2928	ALEXANDRIA
51	73	106	137	186	237	299	482	695	945	1659	2288	2676	2854	2928	DULUTH
242	312	411	506	618	743	872	1165	1454	1749	2322	2681	2847	2913	2928	MINNEAPOLIS
233	299	397	482	598	710	825	1124	1403	1702	2274	2631	2826	2896	2928	REDWOOD FALLS
251	321	419	508	621	745	869	1154	1435	1707	2254	2616	2803	2888	2928	ROCHESTER
183	232	313	390	484	594	703	983	1261	1562	2164	2573	2792	2887	2928	ST. CLOUD
															MISSISSIPPI
1832	1999	2147	2267	2362	2444	2526	2641	2729	2791	2881	2917	2927	2928	2928	GREENWOOD
1732	1949	2160	2287	2397	2490	2563	2681	2755	2817	2896	2923	2928	2928	2928	JACKSON
1931	2142	2345	2471	2559	2638	2689	2761	2814	2850	2907	2926	2928	2928	2928	McCOMB
1717	1983	2185	2341	2463	2551	2630	2745	2805	2850	2905	2923	2927	2928	2928	MERIDIAN
															MISSOURI
859	1021	1221	1391	1557	1718	1845	2127	2336	2497	2743	2858	2915	2926	2928	BUTLER
726	882	1071	1241	1404	1567	1716	1978	2208	2395	2697	2850	2907	2925	2928	COLUMBIA
818	969	1174	1328	1515	1672	1797	2074	2277	2443	2717	2841	2899	2919	2928	FARMINGTON
919	1134	1355	1529	1704	1859	2005	2242	2427	2562	2764	2881	2921	2927	2928	JOPLIN
802	964	1151	1319	1478	1632	1780	2067	2284	2456	2736	2875	2919	2927	2928	KANSAS CITY
570	696	881	1021	1186	1331	1462	1771	2020	2242	2617	2799	2883	2918	2928	KIRKSVILLE
735	855	1047	1193	1364	1506	1634	1956	2213	2411	2689	2843	2906	2923	2928	ST. JOSEPH
823	977	1162	1316	1485	1630	1765	2048	2266	2438	2738	2873	2916	2927	2928	ST. LOUIS, Lambert
722	902	1134	1329	1512	1686	1827	2114	2318	2480	2733	2867	2914	2926	2928	SPRINGFIELD
1002	1178	1351	1508	1664	1802	1929	2171	2360	2509	2744	2864	2912	2925	2928	VICHY
															MONTANA
376	499	650	796	964	1133	1312	1491	1660	1820	1970	2244	2663	2842	2928	BILLINGS
6	12	29	57	104	157	241	346	470	611	771	1094	1860	2426	2928	BUTTE
104	149	218	289	387	501	623	775	922	1084	1254	1605	2319	2689	2928	CUT BANK
467	599	761	908	1080	1255	1407	1590	1736	1874	1988	2253	2636	2826	2928	GLASGOW
94	141	220	305	423	568	718	907	1092	1286	1480	1858	2513	2792	2928	GREAT FALLS
112	169	251	348	463	595	730	908	1073	1243	1415	1748	2394	2731	2928	HELENA
130	187	280	376	495	625	758	939	1104	1255	1436	1775	2402	2737	2928	KALISPELL
125	190	274	379	498	632	784	940	1110	1277	1440	1736	2368	2716	2928	LEWISTON
72	123	198	284	404	543	686	856	1021	1198	1391	1734	2408	2744	2928	LIVINGSTON
717	856	1038	1198	1371	1529	1678	1834	1967	2090	2212	2415	2712	2853	2928	MILES CITY
109	167	252	342	457	592	739	916	1095	1271	1450	1776	2447	2793	2928	MISSOULA
															NEBRASKA
1077	1231	1408	1541	1707	1845	1970	2102	2198	2287	2381	2525	2751	2857	2928	CHADRON
304	407	557	688	839	996	1159	1479	1762	2031	2478	2732	2863	2911	2928	GRAND ISLAND
251	341	485	612	760	898	1047	1364	1674	1944	2413	2674	2814	2891	2928	LEXINGTON
492	618	767	903	1073	1218	1348	1654	1951	2207	2574	2786	2878	2914	2928	LINCOLN
133	209	331	453	593	730	880	1222	1534	1836	2364	2663	2814	2894	2928	NORTH PLATTE
598	719	880	1015	1184	1343	1485	1796	2057	2269	2619	2816	2900	2923	2928	OMAHA
896	1057	1246	1407	1575	1731	1875	2013	2130	2238	2333	2480	2739	2870	2928	SCOTTSBLUFF
8	16	35	65	114	178	268	554	896	1244	2030	2510	2747	2862	2928	SIDNEY
															NEVADA
97	147	230	319	419	542	678	824	970	1113	1253	1519	2075	2494	2928	ELKO
18	42	93	165	243	327	438	543	684	819	963	1260	1902	2352	2928	ELY
20	47	113	183	282	377	470	711	971	1278	2095	2671	2885	2926	2928	LAS VEGAS
124	181	287	397	534	695	854	1042	1212	1374	1538	1861	2464	2779	2928	LOVELOCK
76	121	197	278	391	523	671	852	1024	1202	1368	1698	2347	2736	2928	RENO
123	186	276	370	470	573	691	824	986	1149	1314	1608	2232	2659	2928	TONOPAH
113	171	261	33	377	502	656	821	994	1154	1305	1635	2207	2604	2928	WINNEMUCCA
															NEW HAMPSHIRE
143	203	289	376	483	610	735	985	1255	1534	2135	2546	2771	2870	2928	CONCORD
1172	1304	1464	1589	1720	1856	1952	2070	2174	2267	2357	2505	2749	2861	2928	WEST LEBANON

†Includes all wet bulb hours which were 83° or 73° or higher.   ‡Includes all wet bulb hours which were 39° or lower.

TABLE 3—Continued

Number of hours during average summer season (June through September) that wet bulb temperatures equal or exceed any particular degree Fahrenheit value and wet bulb temperatures at four specific frequency levels—1%, 5%, 15% and 50%.

LOCATION	ALT.	SPECIFIC FREQ. LEVELS 1%	5%	15%	50%	83† 73†	82 72	81 71	80 70	79 69	78 68	77 67	76 66	75 65	74 64	73 63
INDIANA																
COLUMBUS, Bakalar AFB	661	80.0	77.0	73.8	67.2	1	4	11	30	58	98	147	209	306	416	549
EVANSVILLE	388	79.3	77.2	74.8	68.9	....	....	2	13	36	86	161	263	408	574	749
FORT WAYNE	791	77.4	74.6	71.4	64.7	....	....	1	3	7	17	39	69	122	183	272
HELMER	976	77.4	74.7	71.3	63.9	....	....	....	3	5	13	38	72	123	185	265
INDIANAPOLIS	793	78.4	75.7	72.7	66.0	....	1	3	8	17	36	70	123	199	292	401
SOUTH BEND	773	77.6	74.8	71.4	64.4	....	....	1	3	9	20	41	78	131	198	275
TERRE HAUTE	601	79.3	76.5	73.4	66.8	....	2	7	17	34	68	112	179	264	363	485
IOWA																
BURLINGTON	694	79.5	76.6	73.3	65.9		1	5	19	38	75	126	184	269	363	471
DES MOINES	963	79.0	75.9	72.7	65.3		1	3	12	28	53	90	142	222	306	405
IOWA CITY	645	80.1	76.3	72.6	65.2	....	6	13	31	54	85	117	159	231	305	393
LAMONI	1173	79.5	76.7	72.9	65.6	1	2	8	20	39	81	130	185	266	338	431
MASON CITY	1194	77.6	74.3	70.5	63.2		....	1	3	7	22	41	70	110	161	225
OTTUMWA	842	78.9	76.3	72.8	65.9		....	3	11	27	62	112	162	244	326	421
SIOUX CITY	1095	78.7	75.7	72.1	65.0		1	3	11	23	43	75	121	195	265	352
KANSAS																
CHANUTE	977	79.2	76.8	74.6	69.3			4	14	32	67	125	221	373	533	724
DODGE CITY	2592	74.3	72.2	70.0	65.3	....	....	....	1	1	3	6	13	36	83
GARDEN CITY	2882	75.9	73.4	70.7	65.4	....	....	1	1	3	9	28	59	106	175
GOODLAND	3645	71.6	69.1	66.6	61.6	....	....	....	....	....	1	2	4	9
HILL CITY	2221	76.2	74.1	71.6	65.7				3	12	35	84	157	248
HUTCHINSON	1524	77.2	75.0	72.7	67.9	....		1	4	15	34	73	150	253	390
RUSSELL	1864	77.9	75.1	72.5	66.7	2	4	6	10	15	26	49	87	151	234	352
TOPEKA	877	79.6	77.1	74.5	68.2		1	5	19	45	89	150	235	369	502	657
WICHITA	1392	77.0	75.0	72.9	68.2	....	....	2	4	11	28	66	142	264	425
KENTUCKY																
BOWLING GREEN	535	79.2	77.0	74.7	69.2		1	3	14	34	71	143	250	393	560	737
CORBIN	1175	78.5	76.0	73.5	67.7	....	....	6	17	41	87	146	259	371	500
COVINGTON	888	77.2	74.9	72.2	66.0	....	....	1	5	15	33	69	136	224	331
LEXINGTON	979	77.6	75.5	73.0	67.3	....	....	1	6	18	49	106	190	297	432
LOUISVILLE	488	79.0	76.8	74.3	68.4		1	2	13	30	70	131	213	347	484	642
PADUCAH	398	80 1	78.0	75.8	70.2		2	10	31	67	148	269	403	582	767	955
LOUISIANA																
ALEXANDRIA, England AFB	92	80.3	78.9	77.5	74.3		1	8	39	117	312	594	864	1251	1542	1829
BATON ROUGE	76	80.5	78.9	77.5	74.5	....	2	12	50	125	304	575	887	1292	1615	1904
LAFAYETTE	38	81.1	80.0	78.6	75.3	2	9	31	138	321	602	920	1206	1586	1910	2167
LAKE CHARLES	32	80.5	79.2	78.0	75.4	....	2	12	50	174	445	826	1255	1633	1949	2201
MONROE	78	81.5	80.0	78.4	74.6	3	13	45	147	305	543	795	1052	1362	1615	1859
NEW ORLEANS	3	80.6	79.2	77.9	75.4	1	3	15	51	165	411	770	1217	1644	2000	2263
SHREVEPORT	251	80.5	78.9	77.5	74.3	1	2	10	45	128	314	569	875	1230	1544	1810
MAINE																
AUGUSTA	350	74.4	70.9	66.9	59.7	*62	98	139	202	264	348	433	530	667	803	938
CARIBOU	624	72.0	67.9	63.9	55.9	15	29	45	71	100	143	194	257	335	425	524
OLD TOWN	124	73.7	70.3	66.2	58.8	*45	76	108	165	220	289	371	461	581	696	819
PORTLAND	61	75.0	71.3	67.3	60.8	....	....	....	....	1	2	7	14	30	49	76
MARYLAND																
BALTIMORE	146	78.8	76.6	73.9	67.1	....	....	3	9	23	52	114	203	298	421	558
MASSACHUSETTS																
BOSTON	29	75.9	72.8	69.6	63.2	....	....	....	1	1	5	13	26	51	85	132
NANTUCKET	43	73.8	71.2	68.9	63.6	....	....	....	....	....	1	2	6	12	24	48
WORCESTER	986	74.6	71.3	68.3	61.4	....	....	....	1	2	3	5	10	22	41	66
MICHIGAN																
BATTLE CREEK	939	76 2	73.3	69.8	62.6	....	....	....	....	1	3	14	34	65	107	165
DETROIT	626	76.4	73.6	70.4	63.4					2	6	18	36	66	118	182
FLINT	766	76.8	73.8	69.9	62.4	....	....	....	1	5	13	25	49	87	134	191
GRAND RAPIDS	689	75.9	73.2	69.9	62.6					1	4	10	25	56	99	160
LANSING	852	76.7	73.3	69.7	62.0					2	7	22	44	73	111	163
MUSKEGON	627	75.5	72.7	69.3	62.0	....	....	....	....	1	4	16	41	70	122
PELLSTON	715	74.4	70.5	66.5	59.2	....	....	....	....	1	2	5	9	21	35	49

*Wet bulb temperature range extends above 73°F, but the number of hours with 74°, 75°, etc., can be estimated.

WET BULB TEMPERATURES

Wet bulb frequency arrays are shown in gray at stations having cooler temperatures. This allows greater detailed analysis of these stations in their higher range of wet bulb values.

72 62	71 61	70 60	69 59	68 58	67 57	66 56	64 55	62 54	60 53	55 52	50 50	45 45	40 40	39‡ 39‡	LOCATION
															INDIANA
701	844	1034	1177	1342	1486	1622	1898	2138	2349	2675	2834	2899	2924	2928	COLUMBUS, Bakalar AFB
930	1101	1281	1443	1594	1732	1862	2102	2304	2473	2738	2860	2909	2926	2928	EVANSVILLE
378	480	628	758	910	1058	1187	1485	1754	2014	2505	2767	2871	2916	2928	FORT WAYNE
364	470	605	759	910	1064	1193	1455	1696	1908	2402	2690	2849	2906	2928	HELMER
539	683	844	995	1161	1309	1456	1741	1986	2220	2606	2811	2892	2920	2928	INDIANAPOLIS
368	480	609	737	875	1011	1149	1433	1712	1983	2473	2752	2876	2915	2928	SOUTH BEND
638	780	948	1118	1289	1443	1580	1849	2076	2291	2638	2814	2893	2917	2928	TERRE HAUTE
															IOWA
589	704	867	1010	1161	1301	1434	1724	1974	2203	2593	2799	2886	2920	2928	BURLINGTON
519	618	760	885	1032	1183	1321	1628	1905	2145	2550	2778	2882	2918	2928	DES MOINES
509	611	769	883	1033	1167	1284	1582	1837	2105	2536	2764	2860	2905	2928	IOWA CITY
543	654	811	949	1100	1236	1363	1662	1947	2183	2573	2795	2881	2921	2928	LAMONI
303	391	494	596	714	841	982	1278	1545	1807	2341	2662	2828	2898	2928	MASON CITY
533	653	820	968	1129	1281	1424	1742	2000	2218	2617	2813	2892	2920	2928	OTTUMWA
452	556	692	815	956	1096	1248	1548	1815	2066	2500	2738	2863	2911	2928	SIOUX CITY
															KANSAS
927	1114	1342	1509	1687	1840	1973	2237	2420	2546	2760	2869	2917	2927	2928	CHANUTE
162	266	436	631	847	1051	1266	1667	2002	2245	2598	2807	2899	2924	2928	DODGE CITY
277	387	554	723	929	1129	1323	1713	2026	2279	2627	2808	2889	2919	2928	GARDEN CITY
22	42	91	153	254	383	534	916	1296	1663	2320	2639	2817	2901	2928	GOODLAND
383	527	693	866	1041	1212	1389	1713	1981	2215	2569	2756	2862	2912	2928	HILL CITY
571	769	1015	1222	1445	1627	1788	2085	2295	2460	2723	2850	2911	2926	2928	HUTCHINSON
513	681	867	1047	1243	1414	1579	1886	2126	2312	2620	2808	2900	2924	2928	RUSSELL
820	975	1186	1337	1501	1650	1786	2070	2272	2441	2707	2846	2909	2925	2928	TOPEKA
633	849	1105	1304	1506	1674	1818	2093	2299	2460	2729	2867	2919	2928	2928	WICHITA
															KENTUCKY
932	1114	1335	1503	1680	1826	1951	2188	2379	2532	2764	2875	2914	2926	2928	BOWLING GREEN
661	804	1030	1217	1411	1591	1740	2030	2241	2418	2686	2836	2897	2920	2928	CORBIN
466	624	812	974	1142	1304	1461	1754	2010	2232	2632	2827	2902	2922	2928	COVINGTON
598	773	983	1161	1348	1517	1659	1932	2170	2372	2702	2853	2910	2925	2928	LEXINGTON
831	1002	1211	1367	1533	1681	1802	2074	2288	2480	2751	2874	2914	2926	2928	LOUISVILLE
1143	1314	1504	1652	1806	1944	2057	2280	2459	2601	2807	2891	2920	2927	2928	PADUCAH
															LOUISIANA
2067	2225	2380	2462	2535	2598	2650	2733	2798	2843	2908	2926	2928	2928	2928	ALEXANDRIA, England AFB
2173	2327	2487	2579	2651	2707	2744	2808	2849	2880	2918	2927	2928	2928	2928	BATON ROUGE
2377	2502	2616	2673	2723	2760	2788	2839	2869	2889	2921	2927	2928	2928	2928	LAFAYETTE
2388	2502	2581	2646	2699	2742	2782	2837	2871	2894	2922	2928	2928	2928	2928	LAKE CHARLES
2058	2210	2347	2441	2514	2576	2624	2720	2791	2836	2898	2923	2927	2928	2928	MONROE
2450	2580	2667	2727	2770	2804	2833	2876	2901	2917	2927	2928	2928	2928	2928	NEW ORLEANS
2041	2191	2324	2424	2507	2573	2626	2718	2791	2842	2907	2926	2928	2928	2928	SHREVEPORT
															MAINE
1101	1241	1414	1575	1723	1870	2007	2156	2280	2395	2492	2634	2832	2902	2928	AUGUSTA
632	745	891	1020	1160	1304	1444	1600	1735	1855	1992	2223	2617	2817	2928	CARIBOU
971	1110	1284	1440	1584	1715	1850	1985	2098	2201	2300	2474	2741	2855	2928	OLD TOWN
116	159	221	287	374	470	581	861	1168	1495	2170	2600	2803	2888	2928	PORTLAND
															MARYLAND
682	811	980	1147	1307	1474	1618	1921	2208	2406	2724	2875	2922	2926	2928	BALTIMORE
															MASSACHUSETTS
197	276	397	513	641	777	923	1250	1567	1895	2481	2794	2892	2921	2928	BOSTON
93	157	283	417	585	760	933	1296	1645	1951	2535	2826	2906	2926	2928	NANTUCKET
112	160	259	363	475	609	739	1014	1290	1584	2241	2666	2854	2909	2928	WORCESTER
															MICHIGAN
234	317	417	523	650	786	915	1171	1453	1736	2335	2689	2855	2913	2928	BATTLE CREEK
272	356	489	607	734	864	992	1296	1583	1867	2436	2762	2877	2917	2928	DETROIT
255	326	431	535	656	784	921	1185	1449	1720	2319	2656	2835	2907	2928	FLINT
237	315	431	535	652	774	899	1174	1453	1731	2331	2686	2848	2907	2928	GRAND RAPIDS
232	308	408	513	631	747	870	1136	1393	1671	2291	2657	2844	2911	2928	LANSING
196	255	379	469	588	693	808	1094	1384	1671	2320	2701	2862	2913	2928	MUSKEGON
82	118	173	226	305	390	480	708	959	1219	1861	2414	2695	2841	2928	PELLSTON

†Includes all wet bulb hours which were 83° or 73° or higher. ‡Includes all wet bulb hours which were 39° or lower.

TABLE 3—Continued

Number of hours during average summer season (June through September) that wet bulb temperatures equal or exceed any particular degree Fahrenheit value and wet bulb temperatures at four specific frequency levels—1%, 5%, 15% and 50%.

LOCATION	ALT.	1%	5%	15%	50%	83†/73†	82/72	81/71	80/70	79/69	78/68	77/67	76/66	75/65	74/64	73/63
NEW JERSEY																
ATLANTIC CITY	11	79.4	76.4	74.2	67.1	2	5	13	28	53	96	151	238	338	474	614
CAMDEN	219	78.9	76.5	73.7	66.7	....	2	4	10	26	61	110	177	279	405	539
MILLVILLE	68	78.9	76.6	74.0	67.0	....	1	2	10	25	62	115	196	307	435	565
NEWARK	11	77.4	75.0	72.2	65.4	....	....	1	4	8	17	38	79	143	232	334
NEW MEXICO																
ALAMOGORDO (Holloman)	4070	70.9	68.8	66.9	63.4	....	....	....	....	....	....	....	....	1	2	4
ALBUQUERQUE	5314	66.3	64.8	62.9	58.6				1	1	2	11	38	117	243	418
CARLSBAD	3234	72.1	70.6	68.9	65.4									....	1	7
EL MORRO	7121	66.7	63.5	60.9	55.5			1	3	7	12	24	40	71	117	181
FARMINGTON	5509	67.7	64.8	62.4	57.0			2	7	13	24	38	72	132	224	347
HOBBS	3664	73.0	70.9	69.1	65.4				....	....	....	1	3	6	13	30
LAS VEGAS	6857	64.6	62.4	60.2	55.3					1	2	4	7	18	46	89
RODEO	4120	71.7	68.9	67.0	63.4									1	6	12
ROSWELL, Walker AFB	3643	71.7	69.8	67.9	64.6					1	1	1	1	3	5	9
SANTA FE	6308	64.9	63.0	60.8	56.0							2	7	27	69	145
TRUTH OR CONSEQUENCES	4820	68.1	66.3	64.6	60.3			1	2	10	32	81	175	347	553	800
TUCUMCARI	4053	70.9	69.1	67.0	63.2				....	....	....	....	....	....	1	2
ZUNI	6440	64.4	62.3	60.0	54.7				1	2	6	15	39	85		
NEW YORK																
ALBANY	292	76.0	72.9	69.6	62.4					2	6	16	30	56	92	140
BINGHAMTON	1630	73.7	70.7	67.4	60.6						1	4	13	23	41	
BUFFALO	705	74.7	72.1	69.0	62.4						1	3	10	21	49	88
ELMIRA	860	74.8	71.8	68.7	61.6					1	2	5	12	25	51	82
MASSENA	202	75.7	72.3	68.3	60.8			1	3	4	7	13	22	45	73	108
NEWBURGH, Stewart AFB	460	78.5	74.6	71.2	64.2	3	6	8	15	23	34	51	76	125	180	255
NEW YORK, Idlewild	16	76.8	74.8	72.0	65.6					1	7	24	57	126	209	313
NEW YORK, La Guardia	19	77.0	74.9	72.2	65.7				1	4	13	29	66	138	221	321
ROCHESTER	543	75.3	72.4	69.0	62.2					1	3	8	18	35	64	110
SYRACUSE	424	75.5	72.5	69.5	62.4					1	4	9	21	39	71	118
NORTH CAROLINA																
ASHEVILLE	2170	75.7	73.7	71.4	65.9	....	....	....	....	....	2	7	19	56	121	217
CHARLOTTE	769	77.7	76.0	74.2	70.1	....	....	....	1	4	16	62	147	302	482	697
ELIZABETH CITY	10	80.7	78.6	76.5	71.7	1	6	19	57	111	212	350	523	752	971	1197
GREENSBORO	897	77.3	75.5	73.4	68.8				1	3	12	38	94	200	344	515
HATTERAS	5	81.1	79.6	77.9	74.2	4	11	32	98	210	412	681	962	1266	1503	1710
LUMBERTON	132	81.1	78.9	76.7	72.3	6	13	32	79	139	246	386	560	800	1030	1296
NEW BERN	17	81.5	79.5	77.3	72.9	6	17	40	108	182	320	491	693	938	1207	1439
RALEIGH	444	78.8	76.9	74.9	70.1	....	....	1	5	23	66	136	252	414	591	787
WILMINGTON	30	81.9	79.7	77.7	73.5	8	27	55	118	208	373	587	822	1091	1342	1573
WINSTON SALEM	967	76.6	74.9	72.9	68.5	....	....	....	....	1	3	15	51	135	252	412
NORTH DAKOTA																
BISMARCK	1660	74.7	70.6	66.5	59.9	....	....	....	....	1	3	5	12	23	41	62
DICKINSON	2595	72.0	68.2	64.1	56.0	*16	30	48	73	113	153	212	271	352	444	537
FARGO	899	75.8	72.0	67.8	60.6	....	....	1	2	3	8	14	26	43	66	99
GRAND FORKS	832	74.0	70.6	66.4	58.4	*53	83	123	176	235	306	384	472	589	711	835
JAMESTOWN	1491	74.6	71.0	66.7	58.2	*70	101	145	203	265	339	411	495	587	699	818
MINOT	1713	72.7	68.7	64.6	56.8	*25	40	59	95	132	180	245	309	400	499	615
PEMBINA	803	74.1	71.5	67.5	60.0	*79	123	169	233	303	392	491	596	710	831	962
OHIO																
AKRON/CANTON	1210	76.1	73.7	70.7	64.1					1	4	12	31	68	125	194
CINCINNATI	483	79.1	76.9	74.4	68.2		1	3	13	31	69	133	235	356	492	626
CLEVELAND	805	76.3	73.8	70.6	64.4				1	4	15	35	76	133	199	
COLUMBUS	833	77.5	75.0	72.1	65.6				2	6	17	40	74	145	220	319
DAYTON, Vandalia	997	76.6	74.1	71.5	65.2				1	2	6	19	44	95	156	249
FINDLAY	797	77.6	74.9	71.7	64.9				1	6	21	44	87	137	208	301
MANSFIELD	1297	76.1	73.5	70.4	64.0				1	1	4	13	30	64	118	180
TOLEDO	676	76.9	74.3	71.0	64.2				1	5	13	28	57	105	166	241
YOUNGSTOWN	1178	75.1	72.5	69.3	62.8				....	....	2	5	13	31	64	113
ZANESVILLE	801	78.2	75.5	72.4	65.7	....	1	1	5	14	33	62	109	183	268	364
OKLAHOMA																
ARDMORE	880	78.9	77.4	75.7	71.8	....		1	6	23	80	189	372	601	854	1129
GAGE	2202	76.8	74.7	72.6	67.8		1	1	2	5	12	24	55	118	224	365

*Wet bulb temperature range extends above 73°F, but the number of hours with 74°, 75°, etc., can be estimated.

WET BULB TEMPERATURES

Wet bulb frequency arrays are shown in gray at stations having cooler temperatures. This allows greater detailed analysis of these stations in their higher range of wet bulb values.

72 62	71 61	70 60	69 59	68 58	67 57	66 56	64 55	62 54	60 53	55 52	50 50	45 45	40 40	39‡ 39‡	LOCATION
															NEW JERSEY
770	932	1096	1253	1404	1551	1681	1952	2187	2380	2710	2860	2909	2983	2928	ATLANTIC CITY
687	827	982	1118	1264	1424	1541	1847	2151	2384	2743	2874	2919	2927	2928	CAMDEN
717	876	1048	1200	1338	1469	1604	1879	2122	2351	2685	2851	2908	2926	2928	MILLVILLE
465	597	755	907	1061	1206	1353	1650	1939	2212	2653	2853	2912	2925	2928	NEWARK
															NEW MEXICO
9	25	59	125	250	428	635	1182	1649	2029	2564	2801	2904	2927	2928	ALAMOGORDO (Holloman)
636	860	1141	1363	1588	1787	1950	2124	2250	2356	2451	2611	2848	2920	2928	ALBUQUERQUE
33	82	235	420	678	965	1243	1823	2196	2441	2760	2883	2922	2928	2928	CARLSBAD
273	420	569	764	950	1179	1372	1572	1738	1895	2030	2242	2563	2756	2928	EL MORRO
504	695	902	1094	1286	1467	1617	1764	1893	2014	2126	2315	2656	2847	2928	FARMINGTON
66	130	261	449	686	946	1229	1767	2165	2429	2755	2882	2918	2928	2928	HOBBS
178	294	471	659	880	1091	1300	1523	1728	1904	2073	2337	2709	2876	2928	LAS VEGAS
22	43	78	138	263	432	666	1210	1668	2011	2481	2727	2855	2912	2928	RODEO
22	50	129	240	422	645	889	1452	1898	2230	2666	2849	2913	2927	2928	ROSWELL, Walker AFB
268	403	597	791	1031	1256	1469	1684	1861	2010	2153	2372	2709	2870	2928	SANTA FE
1073	1296	1547	1732	1913	2067	2190	2316	2404	2494	2570	2694	2861	2921	2928	TRUTH OR CONSEQUENCES
7	23	75	156	276	432	622	1147	1631	2038	2575	2816	2909	2926	2928	TUCUMCARI
170	273	435	600	796	992	1196	1405	1584	1742	1892	2139	2519	2750	2928	ZUNI
															NEW YORK
215	291	397	500	622	756	885	1163	1433	1735	2322	2683	2846	2900	2928	ALBANY
77	125	192	282	382	482	600	898	1147	1441	2126	2593	2825	2904	2928	BINGHAMTON
154	220	320	438	560	690	828	1117	1421	1722	2335	2703	2860	2915	2928	BUFFALO
134	204	307	401	520	647	769	1047	1333	1614	2205	2587	2804	2895	2928	ELMIRA
165	221	302	379	470	570	665	919	1193	1482	2123	2561	2783	2877	2928	MASSENA
359	455	590	706	856	988	1118	1415	1680	1957	2473	2770	2881	2918	2928	NEWBURGH, Stewart AFB
442	581	763	926	1084	1228	1375	1714	1992	2253	2694	2869	2917	2926	2928	NEW YORK, Idlewild
465	601	784	935	1091	1237	1391	1727	2014	2271	2702	2872	2916	2927	2928	NEW YORK, La Guardia
172	239	336	438	565	683	807	1105	1397	1690	2315	2687	2854	2911	2928	ROCHESTER
180	268	382	493	617	743	879	1163	1449	1735	2340	2699	2858	2911	2928	SYRACUSE
															NORTH CAROLINA
357	487	682	857	1052	1258	1440	1826	2113	2341	2653	2812	2889	2921	2928	ASHEVILLE
953	1204	1484	1691	1882	2038	2162	2381	2537	2664	2845	2909	2926	2928	2928	CHARLOTTE
1411	1580	1786	1933	2071	2196	2312	2506	2658	2761	2884	2916	2927	2928	2928	ELIZABETH CITY
734	951	1218	1430	1636	1801	1940	2201	2390	2543	2785	2884	2918	2927	2928	GREENSBORO
1911	2065	2229	2342	2450	2541	2620	2757	2836	2885	2925	2928	2928	2928	2928	HATTERAS
1534	1727	1931	2079	2211	2316	2405	2565	2682	2777	2883	2917	2925	2928	2928	LUMBERTON
1680	1860	2055	2184	2304	2413	2493	2652	2746	2825	2899	2922	2928	2928	2928	NEW BERN
1011	1237	1491	1671	1840	1979	2104	2317	2481	2618	2818	2899	2921	2927	2928	RALEIGH
1786	1953	2122	2246	2362	2458	2541	2681	2779	2839	2906	2923	2928	2928	2928	WILMINGTON
640	845	1130	1358	1575	1747	1902	2190	2388	2553	2796	2889	2920	2928	2928	WINSTON SALEM
															NORTH DAKOTA
91	122	186	243	312	398	487	735	1003	1303	1971	2444	2703	2850	2928	BISMARCK
648	765	892	1021	1165	1313	1467	1610	1741	1871	1995	2213	2600	2800	2928	DICKINSON
147	196	268	329	416	511	625	872	1139	1436	2090	2517	2753	2874	2928	FARGO
970	1098	1251	1388	1518	1645	1782	1911	2022	2129	2232	2409	2708	2856	2928	GRAND FORKS
953	1081	1236	1362	1497	1629	1753	1892	2012	2112	2210	2381	2682	2838	2928	JAMESTOWN
745	876	1034	1162	1302	1441	1574	1728	1856	1974	2078	2293	2648	2821	2928	MINOT
1126	1289	1445	1606	1727	1838	1955	2076	2186	2266	2349	2472	2710	2837	2928	PEMBINA
															OHIO
287	401	541	692	868	1040	1184	1477	1721	1953	2460	2757	2887	2921	2928	AKRON/CANTON
796	968	1160	1331	1496	1641	1761	1996	2204	2377	2703	2860	2907	2923	2928	CINCINNATI
290	389	531	675	826	972	1116	1432	1718	1984	2494	2773	2889	2923	2928	CLEVELAND
447	560	753	904	1076	1228	1368	1671	1920	2155	2573	2796	2890	2919	2928	COLUMBUS
371	495	670	818	983	1149	1294	1602	1873	2114	2575	2809	2892	2920	2928	DAYTON, Vandalia
406	518	662	798	945	1096	1247	1536	1796	2033	2508	2780	2876	2916	2928	FINDLAY
268	351	499	631	774	933	1067	1396	1658	1912	2438	2734	2871	2914	2928	MANSFIELD
340	444	584	705	843	979	1112	1419	1704	1968	2497	2776	2877	2915	2928	TOLEDO
177	255	358	478	612	753	899	1193	1494	1771	2333	2695	2854	2913	2928	YOUNGSTOWN
484	608	775	933	1098	1260	1406	1689	1926	2139	2516	2746	2862	2907	2928	ZANESVILLE
															OKLAHOMA
1409	1658	1891	2057	2180	2281	2370	2503	2611	2700	2857	2915	2927	2928	2928	ARDMORE
545	746	982	1207	1431	1642	1826	2135	2336	2483	2711	2852	2914	2926	2928	GAGE

†Includes all wet bulb hours which were 83° or 73° or higher.   ‡Includes all wet bulb hours which were 39° or lower.

Number of hours during average summer season (June through September) that wet bulb temperatures equal or exceed any particular degree Fahrenheit value and wet bulb temperatures at four specific frequency levels—1%, 5%, 15% and 50%.

LOCATION	ALT.	1%	5%	15%	50%	83†/73†	82/72	81/71	80/70	79/69	78/68	77/67	76/66	75/65	74/64	73/63
OKLAHOMA—Cont.																
HOBART	1562	78.5	76.6	74.7	70.3	1	3	4	9	16	41	104	205	380	567	781
OKLAHOMA CITY	1304	77.9	75.9	74.2	70.1	....	....	1	2	9	24	59	139	287	478	727
PONCA CITY	996	80.7	78.6	76.3	71.3	4	10	20	52	108	207	337	479	682	882	1097
TULSA	674	79.0	77.2	75.4	70.9	....	2	4	11	29	74	165	306	532	753	993
WAYNOKA	1529	76.1	74.5	72.7	68.7	....	....	....	....	1	3	9	31	91	201	359
OREGON																
ARLINGTON	350	69.8	66.6	63.6	58.0	2	4	10	26	46	78	121	188	283	390	520
BAKER	3368	66.4	63.2	59.4	51.9			1	2	4	10	20	37	69	109	154
EUGENE	364	68.9	65.3	62.2	56.3	2	4	7	16	27	47	70	110	165	242	334
MEDFORD	1298	69.9	66.4	63.0	56.3	2	5	11	27	45	74	117	167	249	338	440
PENDLETON	1492	66.3	63.4	60.5	54.8	....	....	1	2	4	10	19	34	67	108	171
PORTLAND	26	69.4	65.7	62.4	57.2	2	6	10	22	35	58	84	127	183	265	361
REDMOND	3084	64.0	61.0	57.8	51.3	....	....	....	....	....	....	2	6	15	30	56
SALEM	195	69.2	65.5	62.2	56.3	2	4	9	18	32	52	83	117	180	253	344
PENNSYLVANIA																
ALLENTOWN	376	76.9	74.2	71.2	64.9	....	....	....	2	5	13	26	51	99	162	250
ALTOONA	1468	74.8	72.5	69.5	63.2	....	....	....	....	....	....	1	4	22	54	103
CURWENSVILLE	2222	74.9	71.3	68.0	61.1	....	....	....	....	....	2	5	12	26	47	71
ERIE	732	75.7	72.9	69.7	63.0	....	....	....	....	....	3	8	23	48	84	139
HARRISBURG	351	76.2	73.8	71.3	65.0	....	....	....	....	....	3	15	32	68	131	229
PHILADELPHIA	114	73.4	76.0	73.3	66.6	....	1	2	6	15	40	87	148	240	351	483
PHILIPSBURG	1914	74.1	71.1	68.0	61.0	....	....	....	....	....	....	1	5	13	31	56
PITTSBURGH	1273	74.9	72.7	70.0	64.2	....	....	....	....	....	....	2	11	27	61	121
SUNBURY	480	77.6	74.7	71.6	64.9	....	....	....	1	5	20	43	73	128	203	286
WILKES BARRE	940	75.4	72.6	69.7	63.2	....	1	1	1	3	6	9	20	35	65	115
WILLIAMSPORT	527	76.3	73.7	70.6	63.8	....	....	....	1	2	5	16	34	77	128	198
RHODE ISLAND																
PROVIDENCE	55	76.2	73.5	70.4	63.6	....	....	....	1	3	8	16	33	64	110	180
SOUTH CAROLINA																
CHARLESTON	41	81.2	79.2	77.2	73.5	4	12	33	79	160	294	485	738	1028	1318	1594
COLUMBIA	220	79.4	77.6	75.8	72.2	....	....	3	12	41	104	213	383	640	916	1223
FLORENCE	146	80.1	78.3	76.5	72.7	1	3	10	32	76	177	330	542	801	1094	1378
GREENVILLE	957	77.1	75.3	73.4	69.2	....	....	....	....	1	11	32	79	177	325	503
MYRTLE BEACH	25	82.4	80.2	78.2	74.3	15	37	80	165	285	479	732	991	1283	1531	1744
SPARTANBURG	816	77.6	75.8	74.0	70.1	....	....	....	1	3	16	52	119	260	436	668
SOUTH DAKOTA																
ABERDEEN	1296	77.3	73.5	68.6	61.2	....	....	1	4	10	20	34	57	86	126	164
HURON	1282	77.2	73.9	70.0	62.8	....	1	1	3	7	17	32	57	94	143	201
PHILIP	2212	74.4	70.9	67.2	60.0	*63	97	137	202	269	360	462	569	710	849	987
PIERRE	1718	75.7	72.8	69.0	62.0	....	....	....	1	2	6	13	22	49	88	132
RAPID CITY	3168	72.3	69.0	65.5	58.2	*17	36	54	100	146	203	281	367	503	617	742
SIOUX FALLS	1427	76.7	73.6	69.8	62.4	....	....	....	1	3	11	24	45	78	123	179
WATERTOWN	1746	76.4	72.8	68.6	61.0	....	....	1	2	6	12	21	36	58	94	135
TENNESSEE																
BRISTOL	1519	76.5	74.5	72.0	67.1	....	....	....	....	....	3	13	44	106	190	289
CHATTANOOGA	670	78.3	76.6	74.7	70.3	....	....	....	1	9	38	107	207	375	572	799
DYERSBURG	334	81.8	79.7	77.2	71.9	7	23	54	119	211	332	475	632	837	1051	1249
JACKSON	413	80.4	78.6	76.4	71.6	....	2	8	41	101	205	331	500	717	943	1168
KNOXVILLE	974	77.4	75.6	73.6	69.4	....	....	....	2	13	39	93	218	366	549	
MEMPHIS	282	80.4	78.6	76.5	72.1	....	2	10	42	103	208	353	533	776	1013	1250
NASHVILLE	601	78.8	77.0	75.1	70.4	....	....	1	5	22	64	146	266	457	659	877
SMITHVILLE	1078	78.8	76.6	74.2	69.1	....	....	1	8	23	55	108	198	318	468	630
TEXAS																
ABILENE	1759	75.9	73.9	72.4	69.2	....	....	....	1	4	11	24	68	139	280	
ALICE	180	82.2	80.3	78.8	76.4	12	34	73	185	384	746	1223	1659	2119	2358	2520
AMARILLO	3604	72.2	70.2	68.3	64.6	....	....	....	....	....	....	....	1	4	12	
AUSTIN	597	78.5	77.0	75.9	73.6	....	....	....	3	11	46	143	375	828	1304	1710
BIG SPRING	2537	73.9	72.4	70.8	67.5	....	....	....	....	....	....	....	5	24	72	
BROWNSVILLE	16	80.4	79.3	78.4	76.7	1	2	9	43	193	622	1262	1879	2269	2507	2661
BRYAN	275	79.6	78.2	77.0	74.6	....	1	3	15	51	168	441	811	1308	1665	1988

*Wet bulb temperature range extends above 73°F, but the number of hours with 74°, 75°, etc., can be estimated.

WET BULB TEMPERATURES

Wet bulb frequency arrays are shown in gray at stations having cooler temperatures. This allows greater detailed analysis of these stations in their higher range of wet bulb values.

72 62	71 61	70 60	69 59	68 58	67 57	66 56	64 55	62 54	60 53	55 52	50 50	45 45	40 40	39‡ 39‡	LOCATION
															OKLAHOMA—Cont.
1027	1258	1547	1751	1943	2101	2214	2420	2548	2640	2816	2902	2925	2928	2928	HOBART
982	1235	1492	1700	1888	2033	2167	2370	2512	2626	2823	2906	2925	2928	2928	OKLAHOMA CITY
1331	1523	1738	1890	2032	2141	2241	2419	2541	2646	2813	2898	2924	2927	2928	PONCA CITY
1241	1452	1674	1835	1981	2102	2209	2402	2542	2653	2831	2909	2926	2928	2928	TULSA
588	845	1150	1389	1627	1816	1970	2233	2433	2565	2761	2857	2908	2924	2928	WAYNOKA
															OREGON
678	845	1050	1265	1470	1672	1853	2069	2232	2365	2492	2674	2872	2923	2928	ARLINGTON
215	287	386	482	600	728	855	989	1131	1269	1432	1728	2321	2690	2928	BAKER
464	590	758	931	1130	1329	1525	1744	1936	2109	2271	2526	2840	2915	2928	EUGENE
568	696	855	1002	1178	1350	1522	1714	1880	2040	2207	2463	2821	2913	2928	MEDFORD
259	357	507	649	822	998	1187	1416	1613	1802	1985	2311	2785	2909	2928	PENDLETON
486	639	833	1033	1276	1517	1760	1995	2210	2392	2548	2746	2908	2926	2928	PORTLAND
93	146	220	305	408	533	672	821	980	1138	1306	1623	2297	2701	2928	REDMOND
459	576	770	930	1134	1339	1514	1758	1940	2109	2266	2520	2845	2917	2928	SALEM
															PENNSYLVANIA
358	465	623	763	918	1068	1210	1529	1811	2076	2558	2795	2889	2919	2928	ALLENTOWN
187	264	379	493	633	785	937	1266	1564	1865	2399	2723	2865	2914	2928	ALTOONA
109	159	233	317	435	585	710	1017	1323	1630	2203	2600	2816	2908	2928	CURWENSVILLE
209	290	403	512	643	782	922	1226	1510	1804	2406	2736	2878	2922	2928	ERIE
350	487	657	803	962	1121	1271	1567	1859	2116	2583	2819	2900	2923	2928	HARRISBURG
640	787	950	1107	1256	1404	1546	1830	2098	2331	2698	2865	2915	2925	2928	PHILADELPHIA
102	152	252	335	436	556	691	975	1239	1528	2087	2480	2709	2836	2928	PHILIPSBURG
204	306	442	592	758	927	1087	1408	1710	1981	2475	2765	2883	2917	2928	PITTSBURGH
393	515	666	810	976	1135	1286	1602	1882	2119	2588	2814	2902	2923	2928	SUNBURY
198	289	409	527	668	810	963	1249	1537	1817	2380	2713	2871	2914	2928	WILKES BARRE
290	382	523	652	794	931	1053	1350	1640	1925	2453	2746	2883	2920	2928	WILLIAMSPORT
															RHODE ISLAND
266	367	498	620	756	897	1027	1319	1623	1915	2456	2762	2874	2915	2928	PROVIDENCE
															SOUTH CAROLINA
1857	2071	2247	2378	2484	2570	2641	2755	2824	2867	2916	2927	2928	2928	2928	CHARLESTON
1531	1762	1975	2132	2258	2364	2457	2602	2713	2792	2886	2921	2928	2928	2928	COLUMBIA
1652	1856	2047	2184	2300	2398	2484	2632	2739	2815	2898	2922	2926	2928	2928	FLORENCE
735	964	1284	1518	1741	1927	2068	2341	2512	2650	2843	2910	2927	2928	2928	GREENVILLE
1956	2093	2236	2341	2441	2523	2589	2712	2797	2849	2906	2924	2928	2928	2928	MYRTLE BEACH
953	1205	1504	1719	1917	2076	2195	2438	2576	2682	2849	2908	2925	2928	2928	SPARTANBURG
															SOUTH DAKOTA
211	256	326	400	497	607	713	974	1250	1538	2158	2533	2752	2871	2928	ABERDEEN
272	350	441	548	667	791	925	1199	1479	1746	2296	2627	2803	2883	2928	HURON
1147	1294	1460	1605	1745	1874	1994	2114	2212	2305	2390	2535	2753	2863	2928	PHILIP
190	248	346	443	555	668	792	1082	1374	1661	2251	2612	2801	2895	2928	PIERRE
894	1027	1205	1343	1501	1658	1797	1949	2065	2172	2263	2430	2712	2847	2928	RAPID CITY
253	326	421	522	641	756	877	1155	1435	1713	2285	2622	2806	2885	2928	SIOUX FALLS
191	248	320	402	494	594	706	978	1254	1527	2155	2573	2782	2881	2928	WATERTOWN
															TENNESSEE
443	606	833	1032	1266	1481	1669	2010	2252	2456	2747	2873	2915	2927	2928	BRISTOL
1049	1275	1547	1750	1933	2087	2216	2429	2571	2681	2850	2909	2926	2928	2928	CHATTANOOGA
1444	1623	1816	1951	2089	2195	2288	2457	2580	2684	2846	2904	2922	2928	2928	DYERSBURG
1386	1585	1783	1933	2072	2172	2272	2449	2578	2682	2836	2902	2922	2927	2928	JACKSON
782	1014	1324	1557	1768	1944	2089	2346	2525	2656	2841	2910	2926	2928	2928	KNOXVILLE
1488	1669	1865	2001	2125	2231	2323	2485	2610	2715	2857	2912	2926	2927	2928	MEMPHIS
1117	1322	1558	1733	1899	2032	2142	2364	2519	2640	2830	2902	2924	2928	2928	NASHVILLE
834	1047	1261	1479	1673	1842	1994	2237	2442	2590	2806	2890	2920	2928	2928	SMITHVILLE
															TEXAS
546	818	1220	1515	1779	2001	2155	2433	2581	2699	2864	2918	2928	2928	2928	ABILENE
2639	2705	2761	2799	2829	2851	2867	2894	2912	2922	2927	2928	2928	2928	2928	ALICE
32	77	168	299	488	715	948	1448	1887	2205	2631	2829	2914	2928	2928	AMARILLO
2010	2211	2379	2482	2565	2627	2677	2772	2833	2867	2916	2927	2928	2928	2928	AUSTIN
199	368	702	1000	1328	1631	1875	2286	2495	2661	2849	2919	2928	2928	2928	BIG SPRING
2750	2801	2839	2866	2885	2898	2909	2923	2927	2928	2928	2928	2928	2928	2928	BROWNSVILLE
2214	2365	2485	2560	2626	2681	2722	2791	2831	2865	2915	2928	2928	2928	2928	BRYAN

†Includes all wet bulb hours which were 83° or 73° or higher.   ‡Includes all wet bulb hours which were 39° or lower.

TABLE 3—Continued   **HOURLY FREQUENCY OF SUMMER**

Number of hours during average summer season (June through September) that wet bulb temperatures equal or exceed any particular degree Fahrenheit value and wet bulb temperatures at four specific frequency levels—1%, 5%, 15% and 50%.

LOCATION	ALT.	1%	5%	15%	50%	83†/73†	82/72	81/71	80/70	79/69	78/68	77/67	76/66	75/65	74/64	73/63
TEXAS—Cont.																
CHILDRESS	1880	76.8	74.8	72.8	68.8	......	1	2	2	4	8	22	54	121	237	398
CORPUS CHRISTI	44	80.9	79.9	78.9	77.1	......	3	19	121	388	925	1521	1957	2290	2473	2597
COTULLA	425	80.5	78.8	77.5	75.2	1	5	14	44	115	269	581	1027	1592	1991	2267
DALHART	3989	74.1	70.7	68.2	63.4	*54	84	126	205	312	469	650	847	1113	1333	1556
DALLAS	488	79.3	77.6	76.0	73.1	......	2	6	14	35	93	218	428	777	1140	1500
DEL RIO, Laughlin AFB	1072	80.3	77.4	75.2	72.2	5	9	19	34	61	108	174	278	485	784	1159
EL PASO	3916	69.7	68.0	66.5	63.6	......	......	......	......	......	......	......	......	......	......	......
FORT WORTH (Meacham)	706	77.7	76.1	74.8	72.0	......	......	......	1	3	17	53	160	362	697	1090
GALVESTON	5	81.9	80.7	79.6	77.4	5	24	78	301	658	1157	1646	2004	2328	2473	2573
HOUSTON	62	80.4	78.9	77.8	75.5	......	3	10	41	126	364	762	1198	1725	2039	2266
JUNCTION	1705	76.8	75.0	73.5	70.4	......	......	......	2	4	9	24	55	144	301	554
LAREDO	503	79.7	78.0	76.7	74.7	1	3	6	20	55	149	344	683	1293	1797	2164
LUBBOCK	3243	73.1	71.5	69.8	65.9	......	......	......	......	......	......	......	1	4	12	32
LUFKIN	286	80.5	78.9	77.6	74.3	1	3	12	45	127	313	616	930	1261	1564	1841
MARFA	4805	67.8	66.4	65.4	62.6	......	......	......	......	......	......	......	......	......	......	......
MIDLAND	2815	73.8	72.0	70.3	66.7	......	......	......	......	......	......	......	1	7	22	57
MINERAL WELLS	934	78.7	77.0	75.6	72.2	......	......	1	5	18	60	147	323	605	896	1203
PALACIAS	13	82.8	81.5	80.4	78.2	18	80	213	605	1039	1575	1974	2210	2432	2536	2610
PORT ARTHUR	16	81.1	79.9	78.7	76.1	3	10	31	122	342	705	1123	1501	1877	2135	2328
SALT FLAT	3715	70.9	69.2	67.5	64.6	......	......	......	......	......	......	......	......	1	1	5
SAN ANGELO	1919	74.0	72.6	71.1	68.4	......	......	......	......	......	......	......	2	10	27	86
SAN ANTONIO	792	77.3	75.9	74.8	72.7	......	......	......	1	4	12	38	130	370	801	1324
TYLER	527	80.6	78.6	76.9	74.0	4	8	18	44	95	219	407	689	1079	1467	1782
VICTORIA	104	80.0	78.9	77.9	76.0	......	1	3	29	124	409	926	1458	2006	2304	2476
WACO	500	78.8	77.5	76.0	73.4	......	......	......	4	21	75	208	438	850	1256	1627
WICHITA FALLS	994	77.4	75.7	74.1	70.7	......	......	......	1	4	14	41	106	248	467	754
WINK	2820	74.8	72.6	70.7	67.2	......	......	1	2	3	4	7	12	23	48	103
UTAH																
BRYCE CANYON	7589	64.9	59.9	55.7	49.2	......	......	1	1	2	5	9	16	28	39	56
CEDAR CITY	5660	64.9	62.5	59.8	53.3	......	......	......	......	......	1	4	11	26	53	108
DELTA	4759	67.4	65.0	62.0	55.3	......	......	......	3	6	14	40	80	147	225	322
HANKSVILLE	4462	69.7	66.5	63.7	57.4	*11	14	19	26	38	66	112	186	280	397	523
MILFORD	5028	66.9	64.4	61.6	55.2	......	......	1	3	5	14	27	55	105	175	277
OGDEN	4400	66.5	64.0	61.1	55.2	......	......	......	......	1	5	18	43	88	145	221
ST. GEORGE	2899	70.8	68.9	66.4	60.0	1	3	19	71	139	237	364	482	652	800	958
SALT LAKE CITY	4240	66.9	64.4	61.7	55.8	......	......	......	2	6	14	27	53	105	178	275
WENDOVER	4239	65.7	63.4	60.3	54.1	......	......	......	......	......	1	5	19	58	109	170
VERMONT																
BURLINGTON (Ethan Allen)	331	75.0	71.9	68.3	60.5	*94	142	202	291	372	474	585	701	835	969	1108
VIRGINIA																
BLACKSTONE	432	79.6	77.4	75.0	69.7	......	1	4	18	47	98	179	287	443	604	800
DANVILLE	590	79.0	76.9	74.6	69.4	......	1	3	12	29	73	135	228	373	524	698
FRONT ROYAL	680	78.0	75.5	72.5	65.9	......	......	......	4	11	29	60	109	179	267	375
GORDONSVILLE	440	79.3	76.7	73.9	67.5	1	4	7	16	36	72	125	206	312	433	558
LYNCHBURG	947	77.4	75.3	72.8	67.4	......	......	......	......	4	15	40	80	174	278	399
NORFOLK	30	79.4	77.5	75.5	70.6	......	2	4	15	39	99	202	334	532	729	952
RICHMOND	162	79.3	77.1	74.8	69.4	......	1	3	15	35	78	151	251	398	575	770
ROANOKE	1176	76.1	74.1	71.8	66.6	......	......	......	......	1	4	11	32	75	155	267
WASHINGTON																
BELLINGHAM	150	67.3	63.2	60.0	55.1	1	1	2	5	10	20	33	48	73	112	156
DALLESPORT, The Dalles	236	70.3	66.9	63.7	58.1	4	10	17	35	60	94	142	203	284	399	527
ELLENSBURG	1729	66.5	63.5	60.2	54.0	......	......	1	1	4	11	19	39	71	114	174
EPHRATA	1271	67.9	65.0	62.0	56.2	1	1	2	5	13	27	51	86	144	214	307
OLYMPIA	190	66.7	63.3	60.0	54.9	......	......	1	3	6	12	23	43	72	109	162
SEATTLE, Boeing Field	14	66.5	63.5	60.6	56.2	......	......	1	2	4	10	20	39	73	116	180
SEATTLE/TACOMA	383	66.0	62.8	59.8	55.2	......	......	1	2	3	7	14	30	50	83	131
SPOKANE	2365	65.6	62.6	59.5	53.3	......	......	......	1	1	4	11	22	42	72	120
TATOOSH ISLAND	119	59.8	58.0	56.3	53.4	......	......	......	......	......	......	......	......	......	......	1
WALLA WALLA	1185	69.3	65.9	62.7	56.7	2	5	9	18	34	57	94	142	204	293	399
YAKIMA	1061	68.8	65.3	61.8	55.4	2	3	7	14	26	42	67	108	161	225	315

*Wet bulb temperature range extends above 73°F, but the number of hours with 74°, 75°, etc., can be estimated.

WET BULB TEMPERATURES

Wet bulb frequency arrays are shown in gray at stations having cooler temperatures. This allows greater detailed analysis of these stations in their higher range of wet bulb values.

72 62	71 61	70 60	69 59	68 58	67 57	66 56	64 55	62 54	60 53	55 52	50 50	45 45	40 40	39‡ 39‡	LOCATION
															TEXAS—Cont.
620	861	1158	1403	1665	1867	2057	2338	2509	2631	2819	2907	2928	2928	2928	CHILDRESS
2687	2740	2793	2824	2853	2874	2892	2912	2922	2926	2928	2928	2928	2928	2928	CORPUS CHRISTI
2449	2558	2640	2697	2745	2791	2826	2869	2893	2908	2926	2928	2928	2928	2928	COTULLA
1792	1955	2139	2251	2359	2439	2507	2575	2624	2668	2709	2779	2889	2923	2928	DALHART
1812	2019	2202	2315	2416	2498	2560	2671	2753	2818	2903	2926	2928	2928	2928	DALLAS
1560	1875	2179	2355	2490	2601	2677	2789	2847	2883	2924	2928	2928	2928	2928	DEL RIO, Laughlin AFB
1	3	17	54	149	322	537	1189	1710	2105	2641	2863	2923	2928	2928	EL PASO
1483	1812	2047	2215	2326	2407	2488	2606	2700	2796	2895	2924	2928	2928	2928	FORT WORTH (Meacham)
2660	2715	2780	2816	2845	2864	2881	2908	2918	2925	2928	2928	2928	2928	2928	GALVESTON
2431	2522	2624	2683	2731	2769	2798	2848	2884	2904	2925	2928	2928	2928	2928	HOUSTON
894	1213	1609	1889	2112	2279	2398	2596	2715	2787	2876	2912	2924	2928	2928	JUNCTION
2428	2566	2683	2737	2784	2821	2852	2890	2912	2922	2928	2928	2928	2928	2928	LAREDO
91	200	386	611	876	1149	1415	1894	2233	2467	2754	2881	2924	2928	2928	LUBBOCK
2079	2251	2407	2505	2574	2634	2679	2750	2802	2842	2903	2922	2928	2928	2928	LUFKIN
....	....	....	3	20	75	196	787	1494	2074	2716	2880	2922	2927	2928	MARFA
146	268	521	787	1093	1397	1661	2153	2436	2623	2836	2913	2927	2928	2928	MIDLAND
1542	1801	2026	2184	2305	2405	2483	2617	2718	2796	2897	2924	2928	2928	2928	MINERAL WELLS
2670	2713	2763	2794	2826	2855	2871	2898	2913	2921	2927	2928	2928	2928	2928	PALACIAS
2471	2558	2640	2693	2738	2773	2798	2848	2881	2901	2923	2928	2928	2928	2928	PORT ARTHUR
11	25	74	165	332	566	843	1452	1894	2219	2641	2814	2893	2925	2928	SALT FLAT
234	460	896	1272	1617	1927	2138	2466	2645	2756	2877	2922	2928	2928	2928	SAN ANGELO
1767	2068	2275	2413	2526	2613	2670	2763	2826	2867	2913	2928	2928	2928	2928	SAN ANTONIO
2025	2177	2327	2426	2506	2568	2626	2720	2781	2834	2902	2923	2928	2928	2928	TYLER
2600	2672	2739	2779	2821	2853	2887	2916	2922	2928	2928	2928	2928	2928	2928	VICTORIA
1923	2114	2285	2400	2486	2558	2625	2728	2798	2851	2906	2925	2928	2928	2928	WACO
1089	1375	1690	1901	2075	2212	2316	2489	2608	2707	2868	2920	2928	2928	2928	WICHITA FALLS
210	364	647	908	1224	1520	1791	2225	2480	2643	2841	2904	2924	2927	2928	WINK
															UTAH
75	96	142	186	242	314	393	535	664	795	939	1243	1855	2286	2928	BRYCE CANYON
186	275	412	544	683	839	998	1190	1350	1507	1661	1950	2490	2795	2928	CEDAR CITY
438	556	704	848	1001	1166	1343	1513	1663	1808	1948	2201	2653	2853	2928	DELTA
676	829	1034	1194	1375	1530	1684	1841	1971	2091	2219	2412	2717	2866	2928	HANKSVILLE
380	530	660	845	1020	1200	1350	1490	1620	1750	1900	2120	2600	2800	2928	MILFORD
330	453	611	766	949	1129	1308	1492	1665	1826	1984	2276	2734	2884	2928	OGDEN
1122	1273	1469	1618	1765	1902	2025	2172	2287	2384	2480	2648	2873	2924	2928	ST. GEORGE
396	531	710	870	1063	1245	1425	1623	1787	1942	2088	2365	2756	2892	2928	SALT LAKE CITY
256	343	474	589	736	902	1077	1299	1476	1679	1870	2227	2739	2895	2928	WENDOVER
															VERMONT
1254	1386	1550	1687	1821	1948	2070	2199	2298	2391	2478	2628	2816	2888	2928	BURLINGTON (Ethan Allen)
															VIRGINIA
1021	1198	1407	1581	1739	1877	2008	2252	2438	2589	2816	2893	2919	2928	2928	BLACKSTONE
918	1116	1357	1534	1724	1886	2015	2270	2456	2604	2811	2891	2920	2927	2928	DANVILLE
500	637	795	957	1134	1290	1443	1737	1997	2225	2602	2803	2886	2918	2928	FRONT ROYAL
720	865	1066	1220	1390	1540	1679	1948	2186	2371	2668	2815	2887	2915	2928	GORDONSVILLE
567	737	968	1163	1359	1531	1677	1984	2219	2419	2738	2876	2915	2927	2928	LYNCHBURG
1170	1368	1584	1738	1881	2023	2151	2402	2577	2719	2881	2918	2928	2928	2928	NORFOLK
974	1164	1372	1535	1690	1817	1947	2194	2398	2553	2804	2893	2919	2927	2928	RICHMOND
401	569	782	975	1194	1399	1575	1906	2178	2391	2711	2856	2909	2925	2928	ROANOKE
															WASHINGTON
223	312	434	575	770	988	1241	1500	1768	1987	2197	2494	2841	2914	2928	BELLINGHAM
698	861	1072	1269	1494	1694	1898	2084	2246	2376	2506	2673	2878	2920	2928	DALLESPORT, The Dalles
251	339	464	587	737	893	1061	1264	1463	1651	1835	2163	2685	2876	2928	ELLENSBURG
443	566	748	922	1138	1330	1508	1703	1888	2062	2233	2483	2814	2915	2928	EPHRATA
242	324	444	584	772	972	1192	1435	1649	1853	2043	2377	2794	2904	2928	OLYMPIA
267	375	547	749	992	1248	1522	1784	2023	2232	2425	2687	2904	2927	2928	SEATTLE, Boeing Field
203	288	411	567	763	999	1255	1518	1776	2010	2216	2568	2885	2926	2928	SEATTLE/TACOMA
182	258	378	497	645	804	970	1154	1339	1530	1723	2065	2658	2874	2928	SPOKANE
3	6	23	61	144	284	498	820	1202	1615	1993	2540	2920	2928	2928	TATOOSH ISLAND
534	674	845	1016	1213	1403	1604	1789	1971	2136	2291	2544	2846	2916	2928	WALLA WALLA
420	545	689	844	1007	1179	1359	1533	1704	1867	2017	2276	2706	2878	2928	YAKIMA

†Includes all wet bulb hours which were 83° or 73° or higher.   ‡Includes all wet bulb hours which were 39° or lower.

TABLE 3—Continued   **HOURLY FREQUENCY OF SUMMER**

Number of hours during average summer season (June through September) that wet bulb temperatures equal or exceed any particular degree Fahrenheit value and wet bulb temperatures at four specific frequency levels—1%, 5%, 15% and 50%.

LOCATION	ALT.	1%	5%	15%	50%	83†/73†	82/72	81/71	80/70	79/69	78/68	77/67	76/66	75/65	74/64	73/63
WEST VIRGINIA																
CHARLESTON	989	77.2	75.0	72.6	67.1	....	....	....	1	4	11	34	72	149	256	381
ELKINS	1970	74.9	72.4	69.5	63.8	....	....	....	....	....	1	2	5	26	53	95
MARTINSBURG	537	78.6	75.9	72.8	66.2	1	1	2	6	17	46	89	139	223	307	419
MORGANTOWN	1245	76.7	74.3	71.5	65.4	....	....	....	....	1	7	20	47	96	170	257
PARKERSBURG	637	77.9	75.4	72.7	66.6	....	....	1	2	7	25	57	96	177	271	392
WISCONSIN																
EAU CLAIRE	888	76.1	72.3	68.5	61.4	....	....	....	1	3	9	17	31	55	81	116
GREEN BAY	683	74.9	71.0	67.6	60.3	....	....	....	....	1	3	7	13	28	42	67
LA CROSSE	672	78.2	74.6	70.8	63.8	....	....	....	5	15	34	58	84	128	177	236
LONE ROCK	721	78.7	75.1	71.2	63.8	....	2	4	13	24	45	70	102	151	210	279
MADISON	866	77.1	73.7	70.2	62.8	....	....	1	2	7	16	30	53	88	127	183
MILWAUKEE	693	76.6	73.2	70.0	62.8	....	....	....	1	2	8	20	41	66	105	155
WAUSAU	1196	74.0	70.5	67.0	59.9	....	....	....	....	1	2	5	10	17	29	46
WYOMING																
CASPER	5321	63.8	61.0	58.4	52.6	....	....	....	....	....	....	1	3	10	23	48
CHEYENNE	6126	63.1	60.7	58.5	53.3	....	....	....	....	....	....	....	1	5	14	31
DOUGLAS	4853	68.4	65.0	61.7	55.4	1	4	6	12	22	34	58	87	145	214	303
FORT BRIDGER	7024	61.2	58.0	54.9	49.6	....	....	....	....	....	....	....	1	2	5	9
LARAMIE	7266	60.9	58.2	55.7	50.7	....	....	....	....	....	....	....	....	1	2	4
ROCK SPRINGS	6745	58.9	56.4	53.8	49.6	....	....	....	....	....	....	....	....	....	....	....
SHERIDAN	3942	67.0	64.3	61.4	55.0	....	....	1	3	7	15	29	55	103	166	250

FOREIGN WEATHER STATIONS

LOCATION	ALT.	1%	5%	15%	50%	83†/73†	82/72	81/71	80/70	79/69	78/68	77/67	76/66	75/65	74/64	73/63
BERMUDA																
ST. GEORGE, Kindley AFB	17	79.4	78.2	77.0	74.8	....	....	1	10	44	166	425	847	1389	1804	2114
CANADA																
CALGARY	3540	64.7	60.9	57.2	51.0	....	....	1	2	2	4	9	15	25	40	60
EDMONTON	2219	67.1	62.7	58.9	52.5	1	2	4	7	14	22	31	46	65	92	129
HALIFAX, Dartmouth	136	69.9	66.7	63.7	57.6	2	6	13	27	46	81	124	200	283	401	513
MONTREAL, Dorval	98	75.7	72.0	68.2	61.0	....	....	....	....	1	5	11	24	40	66	94
OTTAWA, Uplands	339	74.9	71.4	67.4	60.3	....	....	....	1	2	4	7	13	26	50	76
REGINA	1884	70.8	66.4	62.4	54.9	*11	17	26	42	60	85	119	166	227	296	376
TORONTO, Malton	578	76.1	72.5	68.5	61.2	....	....	1	3	6	11	17	31	53	81	120
VANCOUVER	16	67.1	64.3	61.5	56.7	....	....	....	1	5	15	30	63	105	169	243
WINNEPEG	786	73.7	69.8	65.4	57.4	*46	70	93	137	177	235	301	387	472	582	695
CANAL ZONE																
BALBOA, Albrook AFB	20	81.6	80.3	78.9	76.5	4	14	53	181	390	724	1182	1721	2274	2642	2834
CUBA																
GUANTANAMO BAY	54	81.6	80.1	78.7	76.0	4	15	48	152	332	685	1086	1481	1985	2397	2686
ENGLAND																
WETHERSFIELD, RAF Sta.	310	67.7	64.0	60.7	55.4	....	2	3	6	12	25	41	67	101	144	208
FRENCH MOROCCO																
PORT LYAUTEY	39	74.8	72.7	70.8	67.1	....	....	....	....	....	1	3	8	23	60	108
GERMANY																
FURSTENFELDBRUCK	1740	70.2	66.2	62.9	56.5	7	13	19	33	49	74	109	157	236	324	421
WIESBADEN	468	71.0	67.5	63.9	58.0	*12	19	29	52	78	120	170	232	326	430	555
HAWAII																
HONOLULU (John Rodgers)	39	75.2	73.3	71.9	69.9	....	....	....	....	....	....	3	10	33	78	174
JAPAN																
OSAKA HONSHU, Itami AB	54	82.6	80.2	77.8	72.6	20	46	86	163	261	407	567	758	986	1193	1390
TOKYO HONSHU, Int'l AP	10	82.4	80.2	77.9	72.5	17	37	73	160	262	412	614	824	1070	1230	1386

*Wet bulb temperature range extends above 73°F, but the number of hours with 74°, 75°, etc., can be estimated.

WET BULB TEMPERATURES

Wet bulb frequency arrays are shown in gray at stations having cooler temperatures. This allows greater detailed analysis of these stations in their higher range of wet bulb values.

72 62	71 61	70 60	69 59	68 58	67 57	66 56	64 55	62 54	60 53	55 52	50 50	45 45	40 40	39‡ 39‡	LOCATION
															WEST VIRGINIA
537	712	929	1124	1318	1485	1640	1939	2166	2356	2687	2837	2907	2924	2928	CHARLESTON
177	250	381	508	656	821	978	1325	1636	1898	2383	2658	2816	2890	2928	ELKINS
548	683	854	1009	1177	1333	1491	1774	2023	2253	2616	2808	2890	2919	2928	MARTINSBURG
377	493	662	824	997	1174	1345	1658	1934	2157	2573	2797	2885	2917	2928	MORGANTOWN
550	678	901	1065	1246	1418	1549	1858	2095	2292	2654	2829	2898	2921	2928	PARKERSBURG
															WISCONSIN
162	219	306	385	496	605	728	1028	1294	1594	2200	2603	2801	2895	2928	EAU CLAIRE
100	148	226	311	397	493	592	844	1103	1389	2101	2553	2790	2885	2928	GREEN BAY
329	408	544	643	769	914	1049	1346	1618	1892	2415	2722	2863	2912	2928	LA CROSSE
369	462	583	697	819	953	1068	1348	1607	1857	2372	2668	2825	2890	2928	LONE ROCK
260	343	462	568	688	820	951	1215	1482	1781	2344	2675	2843	2902	2928	MADISON
235	324	437	544	662	786	920	1194	1487	1783	2377	2693	2857	2912	2928	MILWAUKEE
74	113	181	258	346	442	547	789	1064	1334	2017	2529	2792	2892	2928	WAUSAU
															WYOMING
92	145	253	355	488	643	799	1023	1203	1394	1572	1900	2463	2755	2928	CASPER
64	117	222	348	517	708	896	1123	1325	1518	1706	2020	2548	2786	2928	CHEYENNE
404	515	699	848	1024	1202	1353	1550	1705	1849	1982	2226	2596	2794	2928	DOUGLAS
19	32	58	91	146	217	309	425	559	708	886	1227	1985	2574	2928	FORT BRIDGER
10	25	53	94	163	261	391	556	736	922	1123	1502	2224	2652	2928	LARAMIE
1	3	10	27	58	104	175	274	406	562	743	1161	2051	2614	2928	ROCK SPRINGS
369	491	658	806	972	1127	1282	1471	1637	1787	1930	2196	2610	2819	2928	SHERIDAN

FOREIGN WEATHER STATIONS

															BERMUDA
2365	2534	2678	2740	2789	2826	2855	2905	2924	2927	2928	2928	2928	2928	2928	ST. GEORGE, Kindley AFB
															CANADA
96	138	201	272	355	458	580	715	888	1042	1225	1582	2323	2744	2928	CALGARY
182	242	337	429	559	685	856	1032	1222	1381	1565	1885	2416	2676	2928	EDMONTON
668	818	1012	1190	1391	1563	1748	1902	2070	2188	2320	2525	2824	2918	2928	HALIFAX, Dartmouth
147	201	284	358	462	560	683	952	1231	1542	2195	2622	2812	2895	2928	MONTREAL, Dorval
116	165	236	302	390	479	590	828	1104	1397	2058	2537	2785	2881	2928	OTTAWA. Uplands
484	586	720	852	1009	1154	1304	1455	1603	1732	1866	2107	2533	2763	2928	REGINA
175	232	314	392	496	598	719	998	1270	1565	2209	2628	2823	2901	2928	TORONTO, Malton
368	502	696	893	1154	1387	1682	1934	2179	2359	2528	2749	2912	2926	2928	VANCOUVER
838	953	1103	1232	1385	1521	1667	1785	1912	2017	2133	2332	2674	2839	2928	WINNEPEG
															CANAL ZONE
2901	2921	2927	2928	2928	2928	2928	2928	2928	2928	2928	2928	2928	2928	2928	BALBOA, Albrook AFB
															CUBA
2857	2908	2925	2927	2928	2928	2928	2928	2928	2928	2928	2928	2928	2928	2928	GUANTANAMO BAY
															ENGLAND
291	390	538	694	891	1098	1301	1555	1775	1990	2176	2460	2840	2920	2928	WETHERSFIELD, RAF Sta.
															FRENCH MOROCCO
228	368	657	898	1225	1497	1789	2326	2630	2799	2915	2928	2928	2928	2928	PORT LYAUTEY
															GERMANY
546	670	853	1007	1194	1377	1563	1774	1964	2128	2283	2525	2828	2909	2928	FURSTENFELDBRUCK
711	862	1077	1268	1474	1667	1856	2065	2229	2369	2508	2705	2897	2926	2928	WIESBADEN
															HAWAII
387	765	1427	2049	2524	2802	2898	2928	2928	2928	2928	2928	2928	2928	2928	HONOLULU (John Rodgers)
															JAPAN
1566	1713	1886	2020	2166	2292	2398	2589	2734	2827	2916	2928	2928	2928	2928	OSAKA HONSHU, Itami AB
1528	1669	1842	1982	2125	2247	2361	2606	2749	2848	2918	2928	2928	2928	2928	TOKYO HONSHU (Int'l AP)

†Includes all wet bulb hours which were 83° or 73° or higher.   ‡Includes all wet bulb hours which were 39° or lower.

TABLE 3—Continued　　　　　　　　　　　　　　　　　**HOURLY FREQUENCY OF SUMMER**

Number of hours during average summer season (June through September) that wet bulb temperatures equal or exceed any particular degree Fahrenheit value and wet bulb temperatures at four specific frequency levels—1%, 5%, 15% and 50%.

LOCATION	ALT.	SPECIFIC FREQ. LEVELS 1%	5%	15%	50%	83† 73†	82 72	81 71	80 70	79 69	78 68	77 67	76 66	75 65	74 64	73 63
KOREA																
SEOUL, Kimpo AB	71	81.4	78.9	76.3	69.0	12	20	36	76	134	228	347	470	637	772	900
LIBYA																
TRIPOLI, Wheelus Field	14	79.8	77.6	75.5	71.0	1	3	8	23	50	104	200	329	534	746	986
MARIANA ISLANDS																
GUAM, Agana Field	245	80.0	78.9	78.1	76.7	....	1	4	28	117	492	1212	2061	2646	2840	2901
MEXICO																
AGUASCALIENTES	6132	71.6	67.1	64.6	60.7	14	24	36	51	71	101	151	231	371	571	811
CHIHUAHUA	4692	74.6	69.2	65.7	62.3	....	....	....	....	....	....	5	13	23	38	56
GUADALAJARA	5053	68.3	65.9	63.6	60.3		2	4	9	19	34	74	134	234	364	534
HERMOSILLO	778	82.1	78.4	75.7	72.0	15	30	50	80	120	165	225	365	605	880	1180
MERIDA	30	79.7	78.3	77.1	75.0	....	....	2	17	67	187	457	917	1477	2017	2467
MEXICO CITY	7349	60.5	58.7	57.3	54.4											
MONTERREY	1765	81.0	78.6	75.9	71.6	2	10	30	60	115	190	300	430	580	770	1010
TAMPICO	70	83.7	81.3	79.3	77.2	50	95	165	285	515	975	1555	2055	2395	2625	2755
TORREON	3696	78.2	73.5	70.5	66.5	....	....	....	8	18	32	47	67	92	122	172
ZACATECAS	8012	55.4	56.3	53.8	50.4											2
NEWFOUNDLAND																
STEPHENVILLE (Harmon)	44	67.9	64.4	61.2	54.7	3	4	5	9	14	28	44	67	109	172	249
PHILIPPINE ISLANDS																
CAVITE, Sangley Point	11	81.6	80.5	79.5	77.8	3	13	53	245	661	1358	2015	2535	2823	2905	2921
PUERTO RICO																
SAN JUAN	43	80.7	79.5	78.4	76.5	1	4	13	74	226	592	1136	1735	2261	2633	2816
RYUKYU ISLANDS																
OKINAWA, Kadena AB	163	83.5	82.0	80.6	78.2	52	145	303	640	1058	1573	2023	2325	2540	2665	2735
SAUDI ARABIA																
DHAHRAN AIRFIELD	78	86.9	84.9	82.2	74.6	339	458	561	704	825	948	1076	1219	1391	1562	1739

WET BULB TEMPERATURES

Wet bulb frequency arrays are shown in gray at stations having cooler temperatures. This allows greater detailed analysis of these stations in their higher range of wet bulb values.

72 62	71 61	70 60	69 59	68 58	67 57	66 56	64 55	62 54	60 53	55 52	50 50	45 45	40 40	39‡ 39‡	LOCATION
															KOREA
1026	1155	1310	1462	1631	1787	1917	2216	2449	2638	2856	2911	2926	2928	2928	SEOUL, Kimpo AB
															LIBYA
1241	1473	1746	1952	2155	2314	2453	2679	2808	2880	2925	2928	2928	2928	2928	TRIPOLI, Wheelus Field
															MARIANA ISLANDS
2923	2927	2928	2928	2928	2928	2928	2928	2928	2928	2928	2928	2928	2928	2928	GUAM, Agana Field
															MEXICO
1071	1391	1611	1851	2081	2281	2461	2601	2701	2776	2831	2886	2924	2928	2928	AGUASCALIENTES
76	96	121	151	191	266	376	836	1596	2111	2681	2861	2923	2928	2928	CHiHUAHUA
764	1144	1614	2054	2414	2609	2729	2809	2854	2882	2900	2918	2928	2928	2928	GUADALAJARA
1470	1720	1920	2070	2200	2305	2395	2550	2670	2760	2870	2928	2928	2928	2928	HERMOSILLO
2747	2862	2897	2912	2922	2928	2928	2928	2928	2928	2928	2928	2928	2928	2928	MERIDA
3	13	43	103	253	503	853	1233	1593	1923	2198	2588	2906	2928	2928	MEXICO CITY
1320	1680	2020	2320	2575	2715	2795	2863	2898	2928	2928	2928	2928	2928	2928	MONTERREY
2825	2865	2895	2915	2925	2928	2928	2928	2928	2928	2928	2928	2928	2928	2928	TAMPICO
242	352	512	752	1022	1312	1582	2002	2322	2577	2892	2925	2928	2928	2928	TORREON
6	12	22	34	54	94	164	264	404	594	864	1604	2674	2909	2928	ZACATECAS
															NEWFOUNDLAND
352	461	625	771	931	1081	1230	1414	1570	1716	1875	2166	2641	2862	2928	STEPHENVILLE (Harmon)
															PHILIPPINE ISLANDS
2926	2927	2928	2928	2928	2928	2928	2928	2928	2928	2928	2928	2928	2928	2928	CAVITE, Sangley Point
															PUERTO RICO
2900	2920	2927	2928	2928	2928	2928	2928	2928	2928	2928	2928	2928	2928	2928	SAN JUAN
															RYUKYU ISLANDS
2791	2822	2850	2871	2889	2904	2913	2926	2928	2928	2928	2928	2928	2928	2928	OKINAWA, Kadena AB
															SAUDI ARABIA
1928	2088	2273	2412	2537	2631	2706	2830	2893	2919	2928	2928	2928	2928	2928	DHAHRAN AIRFIELD

†Includes all wet bulb hours which were 83° or 73° or higher.   ‡Includes all wet bulb hours which were 39° or lower.

WET BULB TEMPERATURE

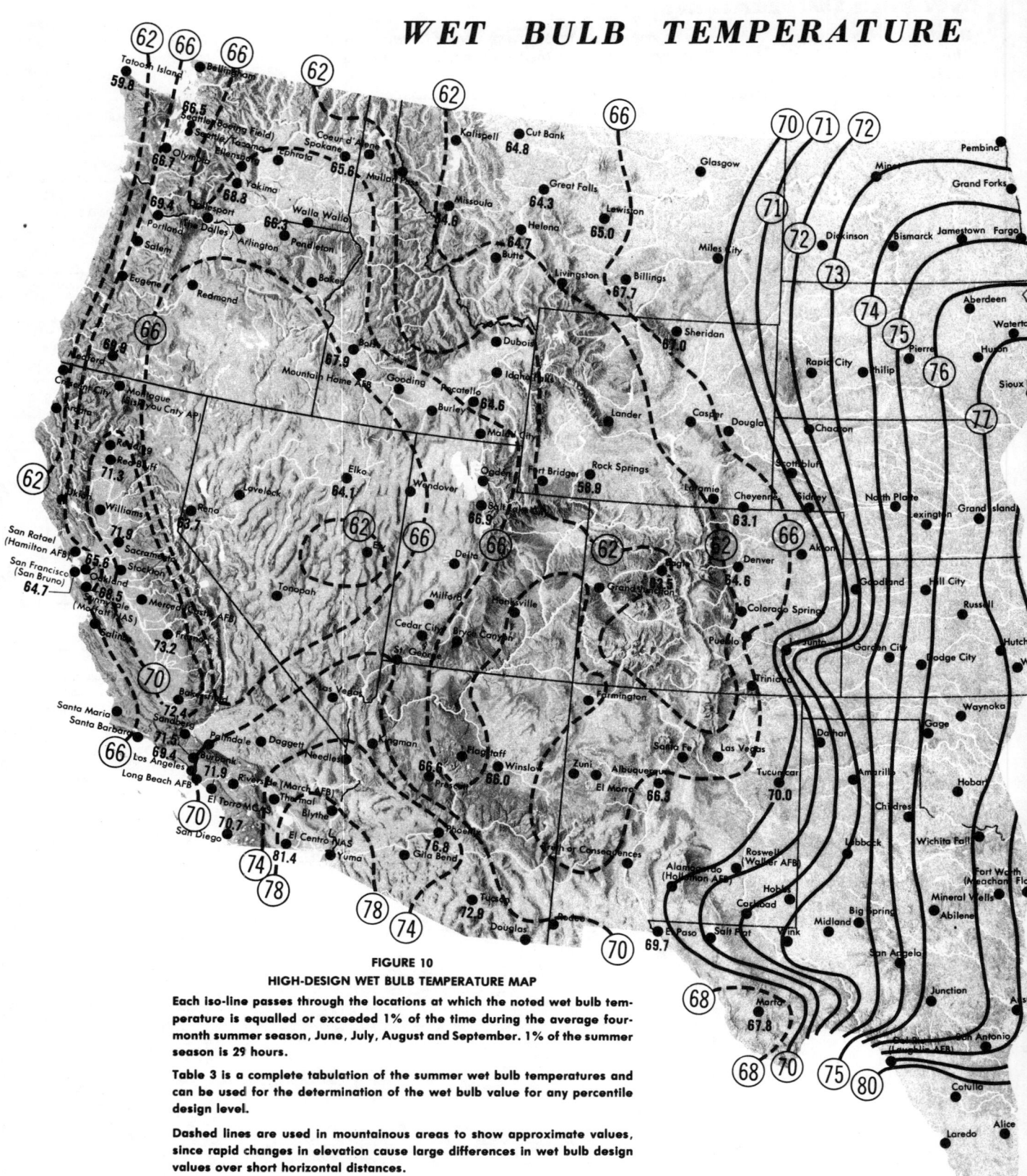

FIGURE 10

HIGH-DESIGN WET BULB TEMPERATURE MAP

Each iso-line passes through the locations at which the noted wet bulb temperature is equalled or exceeded 1% of the time during the average four-month summer season, June, July, August and September. 1% of the summer season is 29 hours.

Table 3 is a complete tabulation of the summer wet bulb temperatures and can be used for the determination of the wet bulb value for any percentile design level.

Dashed lines are used in mountainous areas to show approximate values, since rapid changes in elevation cause large differences in wet bulb design values over short horizontal distances.

ISO-LINES AT THE 1% LEVEL

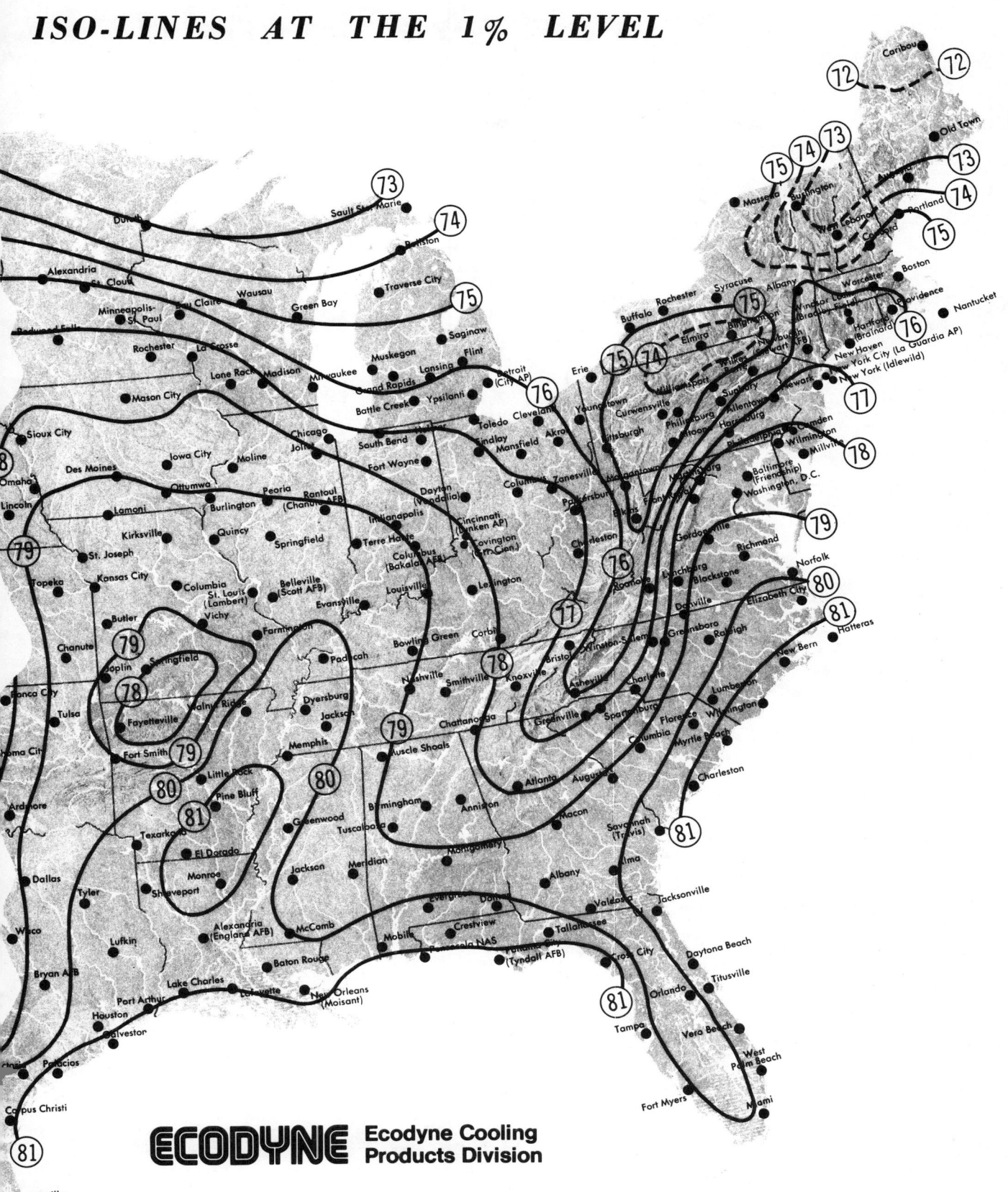

ECODYNE Ecodyne Cooling Products Division

Section 1: VELOCITY CHANGES WITH HEIGHT ABOVE GROUND

Wind velocities tend to increase with elevation, the greatest rate of change occurring in the lower few feet of the atmosphere. Even with strong winds at the 30-foot level, the layers of air lying immediately above the earth's surface move with low velocities.

Figure 11 illustrates the general pattern of wind velocities. Since the wind measurements are generally made at approximately the 30-foot level at Weather Bureau stations throughout the United States, it should be assumed that cooling towers would have lower wind velocities at their air intakes.

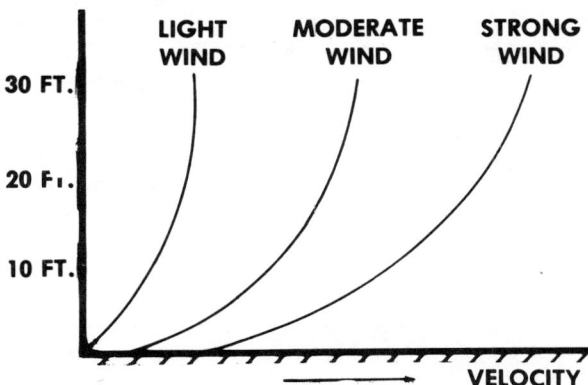

Fig. 11. Wind velocities in lower 30 feet of the atmosphere.

Section 2: DAILY CHANGES IN WIND

During the summer months, the wind is generally strongest in the afternoon hours. This is caused by atmospheric turbulence and the mixing of a deep layer of the atmosphere due to vertical motion. Nighttime velocities during the summer months are almost always very low unless there is a large-scale disturbance or air mass frontal boundary moving through the immediate area.

Section 3: UPSLOPE AND DOWNSLOPE WINDS

Because the atmosphere is a fluid, it tends to react in a characteristic manner with varying densities. At night the lower layer of the atmosphere is cooled by contact with the ground surface, which in turn is cooled by radiation. As this air becomes denser, downslope drainage takes place, filling the lower pockets and basins. A reverse process takes place in the daytime, when the air nearest the earth's surface is heated first and this heated air expands and becomes lighter than adjacent higher layers. It initially moves upslope in reverse of the nighttime direction and eventually, if sufficiently warmed, will rise vertically into the upper atmosphere.

Section 4: SEA AND LAKE BREEZES

Due to the comparatively unequal heating of the earth's surface over land and water, circulation is established during the summer months along sizable water bodies.

During the warmer parts of the day the air rises rapidly as it is heated over the land surface, allowing the cooler, denser air immediately adjacent over the water to move inland and replace this warmer, lighter air as it moves aloft.

Generally, the air moving in from the water surface has a nearly constant wet bulb temperature and fluctuates only as the temperature of the water surface fluctuates gradually throughout the season.

If the water is considerably cooler than the land surface, lower rather than higher wet bulb temperatures may be recorded during the sea breeze. The high wet bulb readings at Chicago are coincident with southwest winds and hot, dry bulb temperatures, even though the moisture source for that air mass is the Gulf of Mexico rather than nearby Lake Michigan.

Section 5: COOLING TOWER ORIENTATION

Some of the reasons for the orientation of a cooling tower in a particular manner relative to the prevailing winds coincident with the higher wet bulbs are quite obvious, others are not.

Any evaporative cooling equipment that depends on natural air movement should be oriented to take the fullest advantage of this natural movement during the high wet bulb periods when the cooling task is the most difficult.

An important phenomenon caused by natural winds blowing over and around a cooling tower is recirculation. It is defined as the contamination of the air entering the tower by a portion of the exhaust air leaving the tower. This degradation of the inlet air raises the entering air wet bulb temperature above ambient, thus reducing the overall tower performance that might otherwise be expected.

Also, the locating of towers close to other structures may lead to eddy currents that carry the exhaust air back to the inlet.

Cooling tower manufacturers generally agree that, in multiple cell mechanical draft installations, the long axis should be parallel to the prevailing wind.

Ground space or other considerations might dictate the division of a large installation into several towers. The optimum arrangement in this case consists of units not over 300 to 400 feet long with their long axes parallel to the prevailing wind coincident with high wet bulb temperatures. Wherever possible, these units should be placed side by side, separated by a distance not less than the length of the longest unit. Also, because of ground space limitations, it might be necessary to overlap the ends of the towers. This should be done with due consideration for the predominant wind shift direction. See Figure 12.

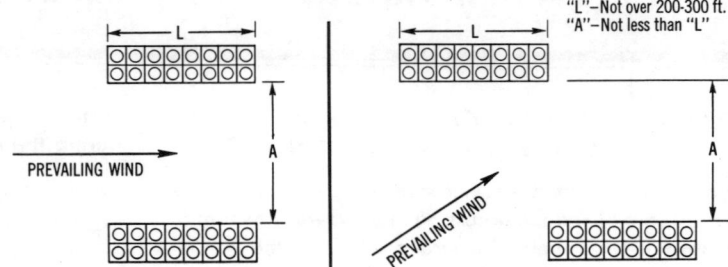

"L"–Not over 200-300 ft.
"A"–Not less than "L"

Figure 12 — Preferred multiple tower orientations.

PREVAILING WIND

PREVAILING WIND

Section 6: WINDS COINCIDENT WITH HIGH WET BULB TEMPERATURES

The performance of a natural draft or an atmospheric cooling tower is influenced greatly by the wind or movement of air. The orientation of such cooling towers is important because of the gain experience from taking the greatest advantage of the wind flow pattern in the area.

Even with mechanical air moving equipment, favorable ventilation afforded by the natural air movement tends to decrease the load on fan motors and, especially with industrial cooling towers, is a factor in the control of recirculation.

Prior to the research and tabulations for this manual, wind data were furnished on the basis of including *all* winds for a given period of time. However, since the ultimate test of any cooling tower occurs during periods of high wet bulb temperatures, it is fundamentally important that the wind direction and velocity be known for these periods. Therefore those winds which were coincident with approximately the top 20% of the summer wet bulb temperatures have been tabulated and reported in Table 4 and shown on the map (Figure 13). These values have real meaning to the designer. The predominant directions shown in the table and on the accompanying map, Figure 13, are the predominant directions which prevail when high wet bulb temperatures are experienced at each of the locations indicated.

Generally speaking, air that moves from mid-continent toward the oceanic areas will have low wet bulb temperatures. Air moving from the moisture sources toward the drier mid-continent will carry moisture and generally have higher wet bulb temperatures. The predominant wind directions, as shown in Table 4, are the directions from which warm, moist air is moving toward the station during periods of high wet bulb temperatures.

Section 7: DETERMINATION OF PREDOMINANT DIRECTION

Coastal stations located in tropical areas having a single prevailing wind direction can be expected to have almost one single predominant direction coincident with high wet bulbs. This direction would be from the water surface toward the land, with little variation throughout the entire summer period.

In contrast to this, the mountainous stations near the middle of a large continent have no nearby moisture source and the local directions coincident with high wet bulb may often be influenced by local thunderstorms. These thunderstorms are most frequent when high wet bulb temperatures occur.

On the map (Figure 13) are 28 locations which failed to have any single 45° range of direction with 20% or more of all the wind readings coincident with high wet bulb temperatures. Note that the symbol used shows no predominant direction.

The three directional classifications used in the map (Figure 13) were chosen after examining the results of tabulations at all stations. Three broad ranges of concentration of direction are presented. At stations having the higher concentration of predominant direction (above 60% in a 135° azimuth range), distinct advantages can be gained by proper orientation of a cooling tower relative to that wind direction.

In contrast to this, other reasons for specific tower orientation would probably be used at Butte or Livingston, Montana, where winds coincident with high wet bulbs blow from almost all directions.

Section 8: RANGES OF VELOCITY

From the mass of wind data recorded at the many stations, tabulations were made for the four ranges: calm, 1 to 10 mph, 11 to 19 mph, and 20 or more mph.

There is a very high predominance of velocities in the range between 1 and 10 mph at the time that high wet bulbs are experienced. This is compatible with the horizontal stratification of air that lends itself to high wet bulb temperatures in the lower layers of atmosphere. When high velocities are experienced, air is mixed to high levels and the drier, cooler air from aloft is brought nearer the surface.

Treating the 376 stations in the continental area of the United States as one group, the following are the percentage values in each of the four velocity ranges:

Calm	1-10 mph	11-19 mph	20 or more mph
4.29%	60.57%	29.67%	5.47%

The key to Figure 13 describes the classification which has been used to divide the velocities into three (not four) main ranges, with supplementary indications of extremes of calm or exceptionally high winds. The choice was made after examining the results of the tabulations, and is primarily intended to show relative ranges of velocities at different locations.

The light winds which are coincident with high wet bulbs in Alabama and Georgia are in sharp contrast with the strong velocities coincident with high wet bulbs in Oklahoma and Kansas. More than half of the entire sample fell in the middle range of the three velocity ranges. (See key on map, Figure 13.)

Annual frequencies of winds when relative humidities are about 85% are presented in Part 9 of this book.

TABLE 4

DIRECTION OF WIND
COINCIDENT WITH HIGH WET BULB TEMPERATURES

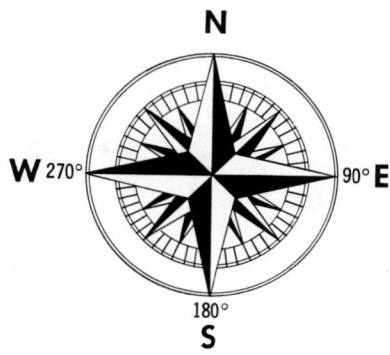

N
W 270°   90° E
180°
S

Direction from which predominant winds blow during periods of high wet bulb temperatures are given in degrees clockwise from north.

The wind speed and concentration of direction are most readily obtained from the map of "Prevailing Winds Coincident with High Wet Bulb Temperatures" (Figure 13).

Parentheses ( ) are used around the direction when this direction has only slight predominance over other directions.

STATION	DIRECTION	STATION	DIRECTION	STATION	DIRECTION	STATION	DIRECTION
ALABAMA		DENVER	(190)	FORT WAYNE	230	DULUTH	210
ANNISTON	240	EAGLE	250	INDIANAPOLIS	230	MINNEAPOLIS	180
BIRMINGHAM	230	GRAND JUNCTION	270	SOUTH BEND	210	REDWOOD FALLS	180
DOTHAN	230	LA JUNTA	110	TERRE HAUTE	200	ROCHESTER	190
EVERGREEN	260	PUEBLO	100			ST. CLOUD	180
MOBILE	200	TRINIDAD	(110)	**IOWA**			
MONTGOMERY	230			BURLINGTON	200	**MISSISSIPPI**	
MUSCLE SHOALS	250	**CONNECTICUT**		DES MOINES	190	GREENWOOD	200
TUSCALOOSA	200	HARTFORD		IOWA CITY	190	JACKSON	260
		(Brainard Field)	200	LAMONI	180	McCOMB	220
ALASKA		WINDSOR LOCKS		MASON CITY	180	MERIDIAN	260
ANCHORAGE		(Bradley Field)	200	OTTUMWA	190		
(Elmendorf AFB)	270			SIOUX CITY	180	**MISSOURI**	
FAIRBANKS		**DELAWARE**				BUTLER	190
(Ladd AFB)	240	WILMINGTON	230	**KANSAS**		COLUMBIA	190
				CHANUTE	190	FARMINGTON	190
ARIZONA		**DISTRICT OF COLUMBIA**		DODGE CITY	180	JOPLIN	190
DOUGLAS	160	WASHINGTON	200	GARDEN CITY	160	KANSAS CITY	190
FLAGSTAFF	230			GOODLAND	160	KIRKSVILLE	220
GILA BEND	240	**FLORIDA**		HILL CITY	180	ST. JOSEPH	200
PHOENIX	(290)	CRESTVIEW	210	HUTCHINSON	180	ST. LOUIS	
PRESCOTT	240	CROSS CITY	240	RUSSELL	180	(Lambert)	180
TUCSON	290	DAYTONA BEACH	100	TOPEKA	180	SPRINGFIELD	200
WINSLOW	240	FORT MYERS	110	WICHITA	180	VICHY	190
YUMA	160	JACKSONVILLE	230				
		MIAMI	120	**KENTUCKY**		**MONTANA**	
ARKANSAS		ORLANDO	210	BOWLING GREEN	230	BILLINGS	(220)
EL DORADO	200	PANAMA CITY		CORBIN	220	BUTTE	(330)
FAYETTEVILLE	200	(Tyndall AFB)	230	COVINGTON	230	CUT BANK	(150)
FORT SMITH	210	PENSACOLA	230	LEXINGTON	210	GLASGOW	120
LITTLE ROCK	200	TALLAHASSEE	190	LOUISVILLE	220	GREAT FALLS	(220)
PINE BLUFF	220	TAMPA	260	PADUCAH	210	HELENA	(30)
TEXARKANA	190	VERO BEACH	80			KALISPELL	180
WALNUT RIDGE	190	WEST PALM BEACH	120	**LOUISIANA**		LEWISTOWN	100
				ALEXANDRIA		LIVINGSTON	(230)
CALIFORNIA		**GEORGIA**		(England AFB)	160	MILES CITY	140
ARCATA	310	ALBANY	220	BATON ROUGE	240	MISSOULA	(310)
BAKERSFIELD	290	ALMA	240	LAFAYETTE	230		
BLYTHE	170	ATLANTA	290	LAKE CHARLES	210	**NEBRASKA**	
BURBANK	180	AUGUSTA	210	MONROE	200	CHADRON	(160)
CRESCENT CITY	310	MACON	240	NEW ORLEANS	200	GRAND ISLAND	180
DAGGETT	310	SAVANNAH		SHREVEPORT	190	LEXINGTON	180
EL CENTRO	140	(Travis Field)	190			LINCOLN	180
EL TORO	290	VALDOSTA	230	**MAINE**		NORTH PLATTE	160
FRESNO	290			AUGUSTA	200	OMAHA	160
LONG BEACH	200	**IDAHO**		CARIBOU	200	SCOTTSBLUFF	120
LOS ANGELES	250	BOISE	320	OLD TOWN	200	SIDNEY	150
MERCED		BURLEY	280	PORTLAND	200		
(Castle AFB)	320	COEUR D'ALENE	150			**NEVADA**	
MONTAGUE	10	DUBOIS	180	**MARYLAND**		ELKO	240
NEEDLES	200	GOODING	290	BALTIMORE	230	LAS VEGAS	(220)
OAKLAND	280	IDAHO FALLS	190			LOVELOCK	200
PALMDALE	240	MALAD CITY	180	**MASSACHUSETTS**		RENO	290
RED BLUFF	150	MOUNTAIN HOME	320	BOSTON	230	TONOPAH	180
RIVERSIDE		MULLAN PASS	(320)	NANTUCKET	230		
(March AFB)	310	POCATELLO	(210)	WORCESTER	260	**NEW HAMPSHIRE**	
SACRAMENTO	230					CONCORD	200
SALINAS	320	**ILLINOIS**		**MICHIGAN**		WEST LEBANON	190
SANDBERG	160	BELLEVILLE		BATTLE CREEK	220		
SAN DIEGO	300	(Scott AFB)	220	DETROIT	220	**NEW JERSEY**	
SAN FRANCISCO	320	CHICAGO	210	FLINT	220	MILLVILLE	210
SAN RAFAEL		JOLIET	210	GRAND RAPIDS	230	NEWARK .	230
(Hamilton AFB)	140	MOLINE	210	LANSING	220		
SANTA BARBARA	220	PEORIA	200	MUSKEGON	230	**NEW MEXICO**	
SANTA MARIA	280	QUINCY	200	PELLSTON	260	ALAMOGORDO	
SUNNYVALE	330	RANTOUL		SAGINAW	230	(Holloman AFB)	190
STOCKTON	300	(Chanute AFB)	210	SAULT STE. MARIE	240	ALBUQUERQUE	240
THERMAL	160	SPRINGFIELD	220	TRAVERSE CITY	220	CARLSBAD	140
UKIAH	(140)			YPSILANTI	230	FARMINGTON	(100)
		INDIANA				HOBBS	150
COLORADO		COLUMBUS		**MINNESOTA**		LAS VEGAS	200
AKRON	150	(Bakalar AFB)	220	ALEXANDRIA	170	RODEO	200
COLORADO SPRINGS	150	EVANSVILLE	220				

PREVAILING WINDS COINCIDENT

Shown are winds which are coincident with

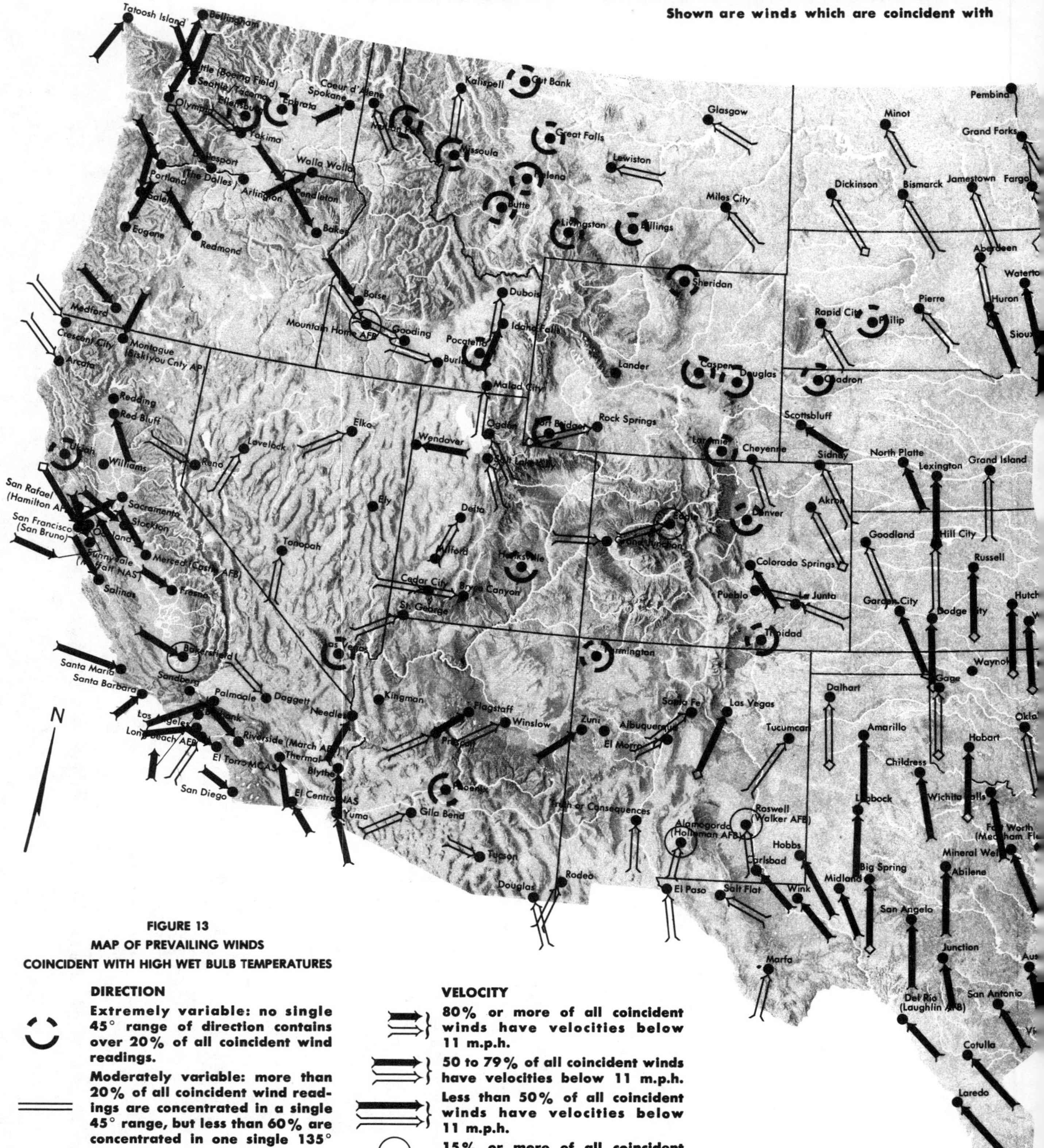

FIGURE 13

MAP OF PREVAILING WINDS

COINCIDENT WITH HIGH WET BULB TEMPERATURES

DIRECTION

Extremely variable: no single 45° range of direction contains over 20% of all coincident wind readings.

Moderately variable: more than 20% of all coincident wind readings are concentrated in a single 45° range, but less than 60% are concentrated in one single 135° range.

Moderately directional: more than 60% of all coincident wind readings are concentrated in one 135° range.

VELOCITY

80% or more of all coincident winds have velocities below 11 m.p.h.

50 to 79% of all coincident winds have velocities below 11 m.p.h.

Less than 50% of all coincident winds have velocities below 11 m.p.h.

15% or more of all coincident winds reported as calm.

15% or more of all coincident winds reported as 20 m.p.h. or more.

WITH HIGH WET BULB TEMPERATURES
approximately top 20% of Summer wet bulb temperatures.

ECODYNE Ecodyne Cooling Products Division

NOTE: Table 4 shows predominant wind directions at all locations.

STATION	DIRECTION	STATION	DIRECTION	STATION	DIRECTION	STATION	DIRECTION
ROSWELL		**OKLAHOMA**		JACKSON	210	**VERMONT**	
(Walker AFB)	170	ARDMORE	160	KNOXVILLE	250	BURLINGTON	
SANTA FE	230	GAGE	180	MEMPHIS	210	(Ethan Allen AFB)	200
TRUTH OR CONSEQUENCES	180	HOBART	180	NASHVILLE	220		
TUCUMCARI	210	OKLAHOMA CITY	170	SMITHVILLE	210	**VIRGINIA**	
ZUNI	230	PONCA CITY	180			BLACKSTONE	220
		TULSA	180	**TEXAS**		DANVILLE	230
NEW YORK				ABILENE	180	FRONT ROYAL	230
ALBANY	180	**OREGON**		ALICE	130	GORDONSVILLE	230
BINGHAMTON	230	BAKER	320	AMARILLO	180	LYNCHBURG	220
BUFFALO	220	EUGENE	10	AUSTIN	170	NORFOLK	220
ELMIRA	240	MEDFORD	310	BIG SPRING	180	RICHMOND	210
MASSENA	240	PENDLETON	310	BROWNSVILLE	140	ROANOKE	(230)
NEWBURGH		PORTLAND	320	BRYAN	160		
(Stewart AFB)	230	REDMOND	320	CHILDRESS	170	**WASHINGTON**	
NEW YORK		SALEM	360	CORPUS CHRISTI	140	BELLINGHAM	190
(Idlewild)	200			COTULLA	140	DALLESPORT	
NEW YORK		**PENNSYLVANIA**		DALHART	180	(The Dalles)	320
(La Guardia)	210	ALLENTOWN	230	DALLAS	160	ELLENSBURG	(120)
ROCHESTER	230	ALTOONA	230	DEL RIO		EPHRATA	(220)
SYRACUSE	230	ERIE	240	(Laughlin AFB)	140	OLYMPIA	20
		HARRISBURG	230	EL PASO	170	SEATTLE (Boeing)	330
NORTH CAROLINA		PHILADELPHIA	230	FORT WORTH		SEATTLE/TACOMA	10
ASHEVILLE	170	PHILIPSBURG	260	(Meacham Field)	170	SPOKANE	230
CHARLOTTE	220	PITTSBURGH	230	GALVESTON	180	TATOOSH ISLAND	200
ELIZABETH CITY	220	WILKES BARRE	230	HOUSTON	170	WALLA WALLA	230
GREENSBORO	230	WILLIAMSPORT	(240)	JUNCTION	170	YAKIMA	300
HATTERAS	200			LAREDO	140		
LUMBERTON	230	**RHODE ISLAND**		LUBBOCK	180	**WEST VIRGINIA**	
NEW BERN	210	PROVIDENCE	210	LUFKIN	180	CHARLESTON	220
RALEIGH	220			MARFA	190	ELKINS	260
WILMINGTON	210	**SOUTH CAROLINA**		MIDLAND	160	MARTINSBURG	(190)
WINSTON SALEM	230	CHARLESTON	200	MINERAL WELLS	160	MORGANTOWN	210
		COLUMBIA	220	PALACIAS	170	PARKERSBURG	210
NORTH DAKOTA		FLORENCE	220	PORT ARTHUR	180		
BISMARCK	150	GREENVILLE	220	SALT FLAT	120	**WISCONSIN**	
DICKINSON	150	MYRTLE BEACH	210	SAN ANGELO	180	EAU CLAIRE	170
FARGO	150	SPARTANBURG	230	SAN ANTONIO	150	GREEN BAY	230
GRAND FORKS	150			TYLER	180	LA CROSSE	180
JAMESTOWN	160	**SOUTH DAKOTA**		VICTORIA	140	LONE ROCK	190
MINOT	150	ABERDEEN	170	WACO	180	MADISON	210
		HURON	160	WICHITA FALLS	170	MILWAUKEE	220
OHIO		PHILIP	(150)	WINK	140	WAUSAU	220
CLEVELAND	210	PIERRE	140				
COLUMBUS	200	RAPID CITY	150	**UTAH**		**WYOMING**	
DAYTON		SIOUX FALLS	180	BRYCE CANYON	270	CASPER	(230)
(Vandalia)	230	WATERTOWN	170	CEDAR CITY	270	CHEYENNE	160
FINDLEY	230			DELTA	200	DOUGLAS	(130)
MANSFIELD	230	**TENNESSEE**		HANKSVILLE	(180)	FORT BRIDGER	(280)
TOLEDO	230	BRISTOL	260	OGDEN	150	LARAMIE	(240)
YOUNGSTOWN	220	CHATTANOOGA	220	ST. GEORGE	240	ROCK SPRINGS	250
ZANESVILLE	200	DYERSBURG	210	SALT LAKE CITY	160	SHERIDAN	(350)
				WENDOVER	90		

FOREIGN STATIONS

STATION	DIRECTION	STATION	DIRECTION	STATION	DIRECTION	STATION	DIRECTION
BERMUDA		**CANAL ZONE**		**HAWAII**		**MARIANA ISLANDS**	
ST. GEORGE		BALBOA		HONOLULU		GUAM	
(Kindley AFB)	200	(Albrook AFB)	320	(John Rodgers Fld., WBAS)	60	(Agana Fld. FWC)	110
CANADA		**CUBA**		**JAPAN**		**NEWFOUNDLAND**	
CALGARY	140	GUANTANAMO BAY NAS	120	OSAKA HONSHU		STEPHENVILLE	
EDMONTON	(150)			(Itami AB)	230	(Harmon AFB)	230
HALIFAX		**ENGLAND**		TOKYO HONSHU			
(Dartmouth DOT)	200	WETHERSFIELD		(Int'l. Airport)	170	**PHILIPPINE ISLANDS**	
MONTREAL		(RAF Station)	240			CAVITE	
(Dorval DOT)	230			**KOREA**		(Sangley Point FWC)	250
OTTAWA		**FRENCH MOROCCO**		SEOUL		**PUERTO RICO**	
(Uplands DOT)	230	PORT LYAUTEY FWC	310	(Kimpo AB)	230	SAN JUAN, NAS	70
REGINA, DOT	140					**RYUKYU ISLANDS**	
TORONTO		**GERMANY**		**LIBYA**		OKINAWA	
(Malton DOT)	230	FURSTENFELDBRUCK AB	(80)	TRIPOLI		(Kadena AB)	150
VANCOUVER, DOT	260	WIESBADEN AB	(190)	(Wheelus Fld.)	80	**SAUDI ARABIA**	
WINNIPEG, DOT	180					DHAHRAN AIRFIELD	50

In terms of enthalpy (heat content), an interval of 3°F dry bulb is approximately equal to a single degree wet bulb in the temperature ranges which prevail in the United States during the summer. The combination of Figs. 14 and 15, summer dry bulb design values can be determined at both the 1% and 5% levels — down from the top — for the four months June-September.

The need for 1% design level is much less important for dry bulb temperatures than for wet bulb temperatures. Therefore, the iso-line map presented in Fig. 15 shows the pattern throughout the country of the 5% level of summer dry bulb temperatures.

The small set of lines shown in Fig. 14 furnishes a way to derive the 1% level of summer dry bulb temperatures in conjunction with the iso-lines shown in Fig. 15. For instance, at Birmingham, Alabama, the 5% level is approximately 92°F. The 1% level would be 96°F, which is 4° warmer than the 5% level.

The effect of continentality is quite noticeable in the Texas and Oklahoma areas. Dry bulb temperatures increase as one moves inland from the Gulf of Mexico toward Dallas. Farther north the decrease in temperatures due to latitude becomes more apparent.

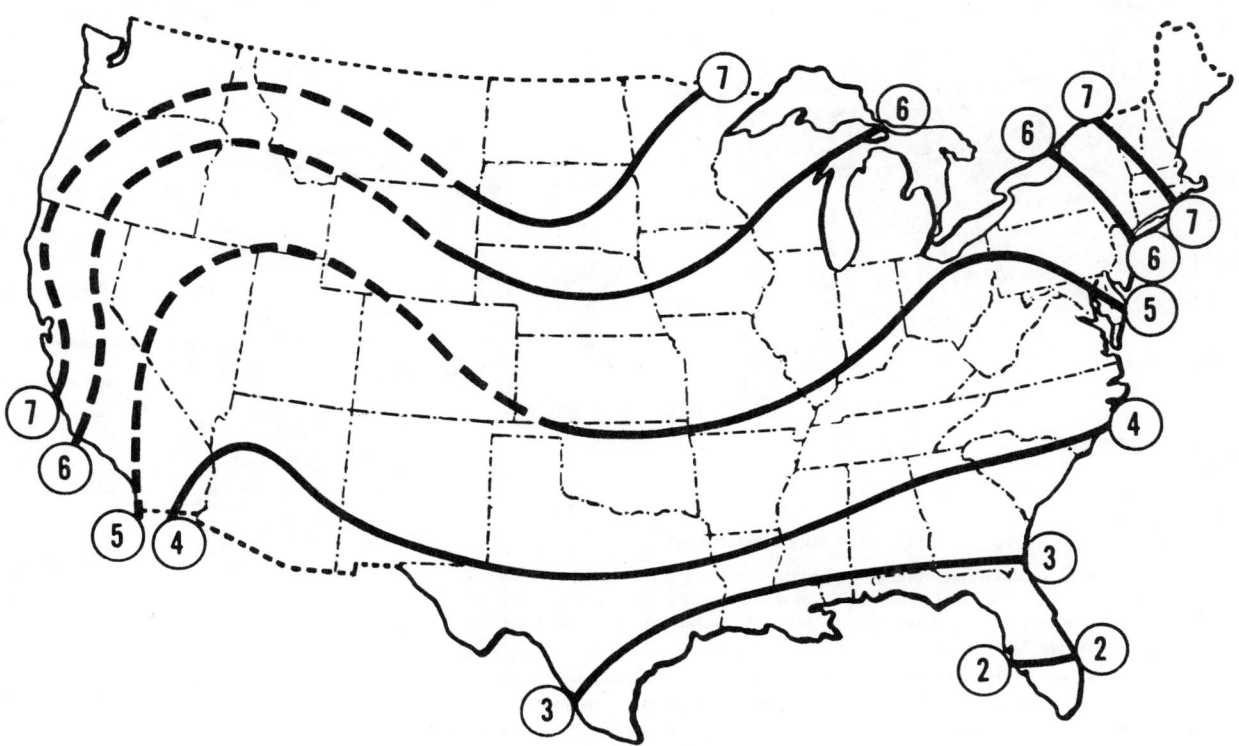

FIGURE 14 — Number of degrees Fahrenheit difference between the highest 1% and 5% hours of dry bulb temperatures during the summer months of June through September.

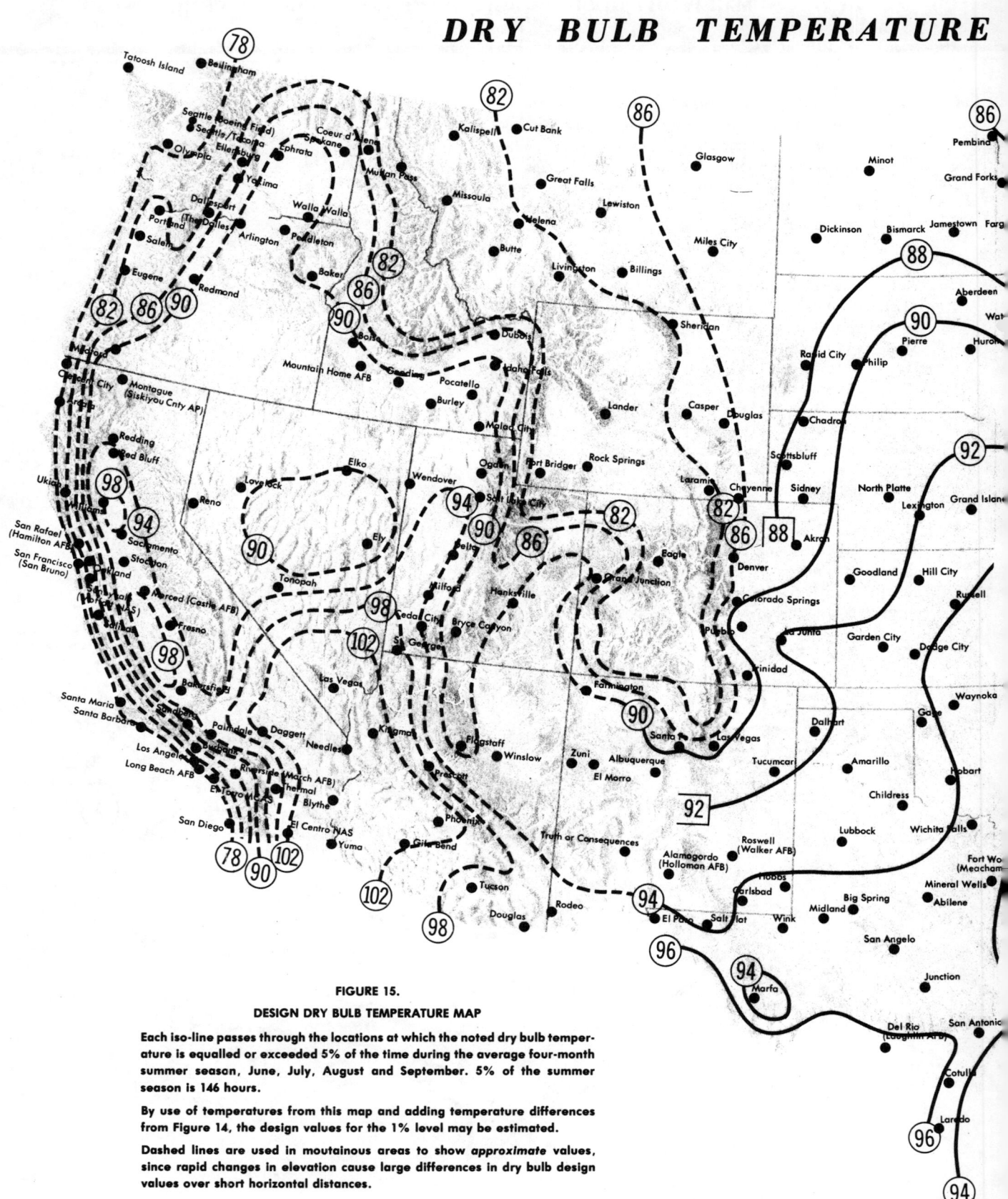

FIGURE 15.

DESIGN DRY BULB TEMPERATURE MAP

Each iso-line passes through the locations at which the noted dry bulb temperature is equalled or exceeded 5% of the time during the average four-month summer season, June, July, August and September. 5% of the summer season is 146 hours.

By use of temperatures from this map and adding temperature differences from Figure 14, the design values for the 1% level may be estimated.

Dashed lines are used in moutainous areas to show *approximate* values, since rapid changes in elevation cause large differences in dry bulb design values over short horizontal distances.

ISO-LINES AT THE 5% LEVEL

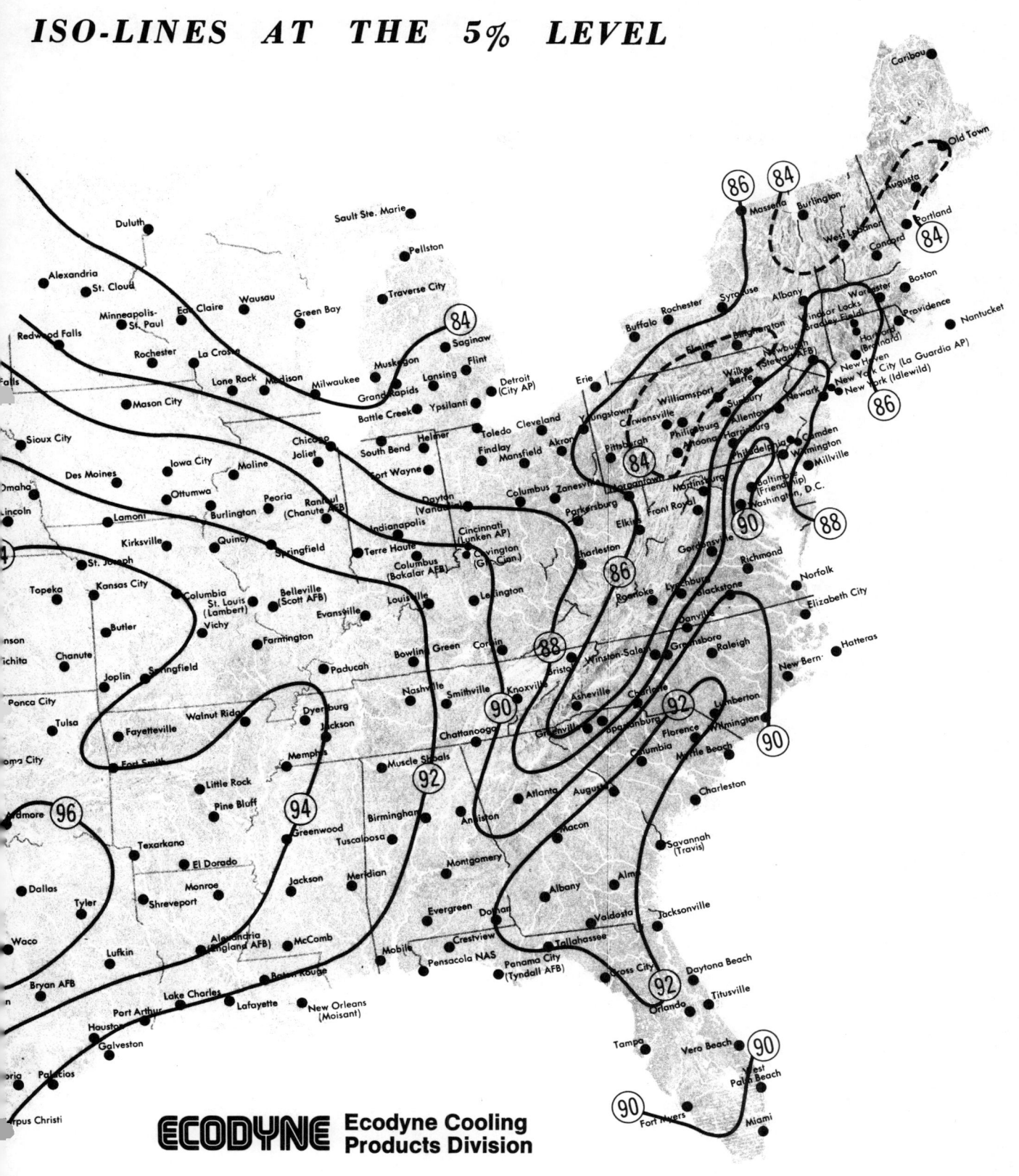

ECODYNE Ecodyne Cooling
Products Division

Section 1: SOURCE REGIONS FOR EXTREME TEMPERATURE CONDITIONS

Design temperatures, both cold and hot, at any particular location are determined by the ease and frequency with which abnormally cold or abnormally hot air can be imported. The speed of movement from a major source region to each respective location also affects the extreme temperatures. Figs. 16 and 17 are presented to show the major source regions for most of the temperature extremes throughout the United States.

The major source region for cold air lies across northern Canada. With strong winds this extreme cold air can be moved easily from northern Canada to the northern portion of the United States within one day. In the bottom part of fig. 16 we see the range of two-day travel distances from the extreme cold source region.

The air reaching the shaded zone has been modified by traveling through two days of solar heating. During the first day's travel southward across Canada brief and low-angle sunshine would have a negligible influence in heating the air. On the second day, as the air moves down across the United States, sunshine would have a more important warming effect. Furthermore, the ground surfaces over which this cold air passes would be considerably warmer than the air itself.

Mountainous terrain presents a physical barrier to the spread of dense cold air. This is quite noticeable in the case of the Continental Divide. The lower mountains in the eastern part of the United States have a similar but less important effect.

Fig. 17 presents the typical source regions and paths of movement from these source regions for hot summer extremes. The speed of movement of the abnormally warm air masses is relatively slow.

On most summer days air flows inward toward the center of the "heat low" in the desert regions of the southwestern United States. Air flow patterns sometimes arrange themselves to spread this abnormally hot air away from the source regions, as shown in the lower left portion of fig.18. In the northwest portion of the United States and along the extreme Pacific Coastline, instances of warm, dry air have a fairly reliable frequency of occurrence once each year, but are not repeated several times per year.

The major source region for extra high dry bulb temperatures having a high moisture content lies inland from the Gulf of Mexico and the Atlantic Ocean. When air which has originated from the warm ocean is permitted to stagnate over land some 100 to 200 miles inland, it can build up to higher and higher temperatures. The further

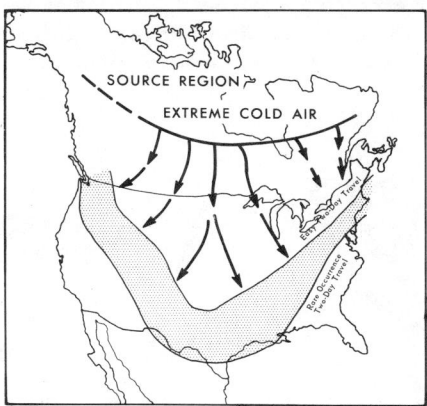

Fig. 16. Extreme cold temperatures throughout the United States are caused by rapid movement of much colder air within the one- or two-day travel time from Polar source regions.

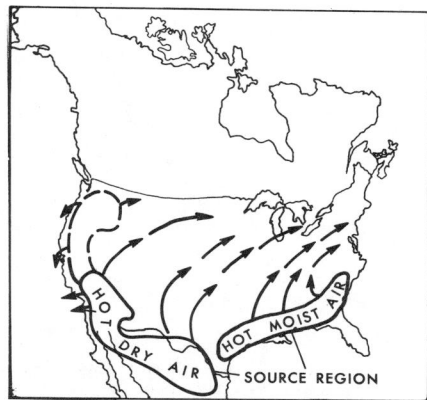

Fig. 17. Source regions and typical flow patterns which produce the high temperature extremes throughout the United States.

northward flow of this air produces the season's highest temperatures in most of the eastern third of the United States.

Although it is not shown in fig. 17, there is a zone in the Middle West which can alternate from year to year in whether its maximum seasonal temperatures come from hot, dry air moving up from the southwest, or from the hot, moist air moving up from the southeast.

Section 2: COINCIDENT WINDS WITH COLD DESIGN TEMPERATURES

Heat loss from the perimeter area of a building is directly proportional to coincident wind speeds.

As a part of a study of temperature and wind frequencies for North America and Greenland, the Arctic Meteorological Research Group at McGill University prepared tables which gave a double array of temperature and wind frequencies. By examining the winds related to the coldest 3 percent of winter temperatures, it is possible to summarize the pattern produced by 61 stations throughout the United States.

Fig. 18 presents the geographic arrangement of four classifications of winds coincident with cold temperatures. Most of the area west of the Rocky Mountains sustains either calm or very light winds coincident with cold temperatures. East of the Rocky Mountains two areas are notable for their high coincident velocities. One area is located in Texas, Oklahoma, and Kansas. The second area is along the East Coast to the north of Cape Hatteras. The hills of Kentucky and Tennessee and the Appalachian Mountain chain furnish a barrier and permit coincident light winds for a large area east and south of the Ohio River.

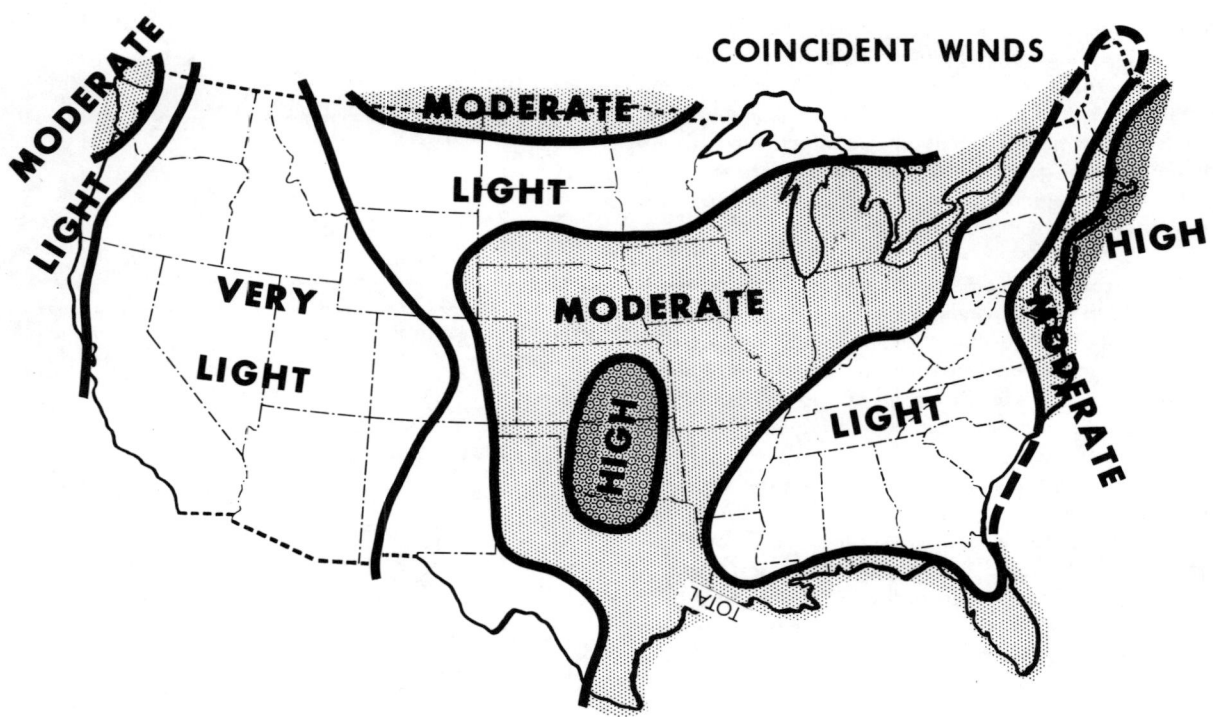

Fig. 18. General coincident wind velocity pattern for coldest 3% of December-February hours.
VL - Very Light, 70% or more of cold extreme hours ≤ 7 mph.
L - Light,   50% to 69% cold extreme hours ≤ 7 mph.
M - Moderate,   50% to 74% cold extreme hours > 7 mph.
H - High,   75% or more cold extreme hours > 7 mph., and 50% are > 12 mph.

Section 3: WINTER AND SUMMER DESIGN DATA BY STATES

WINTER

The annual minimum outdoor temperature, shown in the Median of Annual Extremes Column of Table 5, will be equaled or exceeded in five out of ten years. The columns headed 99% and 97½% show the temperatures which are equaled or exceeded in that percentage of the 2160 hours in an "average" three-month winter season, December through February.

Data in the column headed "Coincident Winds" relates to typical velocities in the coldest 3% of all winter hours.

SUMMER

Dry Bulb

Data appearing in the three columns for Summer Design Dry Bulb show the temperatures which are equaled or exceeded that percentage of the 2928 hours of June through September in an "average" year.

The column headed "Outdoor Daily Range" shows the average difference between the minimum and maximum dry bulb temperatures during the warmest month of the year at each respective location.

Wet Bulb

The three design levels shown in the table are 1%, 2½%, and 5% of the 2928 summer hours, June through September, rounded off to the nearest whole degree.

TABLE 5

WINTER AND SUMMER DESIGN DATA BY STATES

Station[a]	Elev.[b] Ft.	WINTER Dec. – Feb.				SUMMER June – Sept.						
		Median of annual Extremes	99%	97½%	Coincident Wind	Design 1%	Dry Bulb 2½%	Bulb 5%	Outdoor Daily Range[c]	Design 1%	Wet 2½%	Bulb 5%

ALABAMA

Station												
Alexander City	660	12	16	20	L	96	94	93	21	79	78	77
Andalusia	260	18	22	26	L	97	95	94	19	80	79	78
Anniston AP	599	12	17	19	L	96	94	93	21	79	78	77
Auburn	730	17	21	25	L	98	96	95	21	80	79	78
Birmingham AP	630	14	19	22	L	97	94	93	21	79	78	77
Brewton	85	17	21	25	L	97	95	94	19	80	79	78
Citronelle	331	19	23	27	L	95	93	92	19	80	79	78
Decatur	580	10	15	19	L	97	95	94	22	79	78	77
Demopolis	100	15	19	23	L	97	95	94	22	80	79	78
Dothan AP	321	19	23	27	L	97	95	94	20	81	80	79
Eufaula	207	18	22	26	L	98	96	95	20	80	79	78
Florence AP	562	8	13	17	L	97	95	94	22	79	78	77
Gadsden	570	11	16	20	L	96	94	93	22	78	77	76
Greenville	444	18	22	26	L	97	95	94	20	80	79	78
Haleyville	947	10	15	19	L	95	93	92	22	78	77	76
Huntsville AP	619	8	13	17	L	97	95	94	23	78	77	76
Jasper	525	12	17	21	L	96	94	93	22	79	78	77
Mobile AP	217	21	26	29	M	95	93	91	18	80	79	79
Mobile CO	119	24	28	32	M	96	94	93	16	80	79	79
Montgomery AP	195	18	22	26	L	98	95	93	21	80	79	78
Ozark	380	18	22	26	L	97	95	94	20	80	79	78
Selma (Craig) AFB	207	18	23	27	L	98	96	94	21	81	80	79
Talladega	565	11	15	19	L	97	95	94	21	79	78	77
Thomasville	405	16	20	24	L	97	95	94	20	80	79	78
Troy	580	17	21	25	L	97	95	94	20	80	79	78
Tuscaloosa AP	170r	14	19	23	L	98	96	95	22	81	80	79

a When airport temperature observations were used to develop design data, "AP" follows station name. Military airports -- AFB - Air Force Base, NAS - Naval Air Station, MCAS - Marine Corps Air Station. Data for stations followed by "CO" came from city office locations and generally reflect an influence of surrounding metropolitan area. Stations without designation can be considered semi-rural and may be directly compared with most airport data.

b Elevations are ground elevations for each station as of 1964. Temperature readings are generally made at an elevation of 5 feet above the ground, except for locations marked "r", indicating roof exposure of thermometer.

c The difference between the average maximum and average minimum temperatures during the warmest month.

All temperatures shown in these tables are in degrees Fahrenheit.

Station[a]	Elev.[b] Ft.	WINTER Dec. – Feb. Median of annual Extremes	99%	97½%	Coincident Wind	SUMMER June – Sept. Design 1%	Dry Bulb 2½%	5%	Outdoor Daily Range[c]	Design 1%	Wet Bulb 2½%	5%
ALASKA												
Anchorage AP	90	−29	−25	−20	VL	73	70	67	15	63	61	59
Barrow	22	−49	−45	−42	M	58	54	50	12	54	51	48
Bethel AP	125	−36	−32	−28	VL	74	69	66	14	65	63	61
Cordova AP	41	−17	−13	− 8	L	70	66	63	14	62	60	58
Fairbanks AP	436	−59	−53	−50	VL	82	78	75	24	64	63	61
Juneau AP	17	−11	− 7	− 4	L	75	71	68	15	66	64	62
Kodiak	21	4	8	12	M	71	66	63	10	62	60	58
Kotzebue AP	10	−44	−39	−36	VL	68	64	61	12	60	58	56
Nome AP	13	−37	−32	−28	L	66	62	59	10	58	56	54
ARIZONA												
Ajo	1763	30	35	39	VL	107	105	102	26	75	74	73
Casa Grande	1405	22	28	32	VL	110	108	105	32	77	76	75
Douglas AP	4076	13	18	22	VL	100	98	96	31	70	69	68
Flagstaff AP	6973	−10	0	5	VL	84	82	80	31	61	60	59
Fort Huachuca AP	4664	18	25	28	VL	95	93	91	27	69	68	67
Gila Bend AP	853	24	30	34	VL	111	109	106	29	77	76	75
Globe	3540	16	23	27	VL	103	101	98	28	72	71	70
Kingman AP	3446	18	25	29	VL	103	100	97	30	70	69	69
Luke AFB	1087	27	33	35	VL	110	107	105	27	77	76	75
Nogales	3800	15	20	24	VL	100	98	96	31	72	71	70
Page	4270	11	20	24	VL	101	99	96	30	70	69	68
Phoenix AP	1112	25	31	34	VL	108	106	104	27	77	76	75
Prescott AP	5014	7	15	19	VL	96	94	91	30	67	66	65
Safford	2900	18	25	29	VL	105	103	100	31	74	73	72
Tucson AP	2558	23	29	32	VL	105	102	100	26	74	73	72
Williams AFB	1351	24	30	32	VL	108	106	104	27	77	76	75
Winslow AP	4880	2	9	13	VL	97	95	92	32	66	65	64
Yuma AP	199	32	37	40	VL	111	109	107	27	79	78	77

TABLE 5—Continued

WINTER AND SUMMER DESIGN DATA BY STATES

Station[a]	Elev.[b] Ft.	WINTER Dec. – Feb.				SUMMER June – Sept.						
		Median of annual Extremes	99%	97½%	Coincident Wind	Design 1%	Dry Bulb 2½%	5%	Outdoor Daily Range[c]	Design 1%	Wet Bulb 2½%	5%

ARKANSAS

Arkadelphia	200	11	17	21	M	99	97	96	22	80	79	78
Batesville	277	7	13	17	M	98	96	95	22	80	79	78
Blytheville AFB	264	6	12	17	L	98	96	93	21	80	79	78
Brinkley	205	11	17	22	L	99	97	96	21	81	80	79
Camden	116	13	19	23	L	99	97	96	21	81	80	79
El Dorado AP	252	13	19	23	L	98	96	95	21	81	80	79
Fayetteville AP	1253	3	9	13	M	97	95	93	23	77	76	75
Fort Smith AP	449	9	15	19	M	101	99	96	24	79	78	77
Harrison	1150	3	9	13	M	98	96	93	23	77	76	75
Hot Springs Nat. Pk.	710	12	18	22	M	99	97	96	22	79	78	77
Jacksonville-Little Rock AFB	337	12	18	23	M	99	96	94	22	80	79	78
Jonesboro	345	8	14	18	M	98	96	95	21	80	79	78
Little Rock AP	257	13	19	23	M	99	96	94	22	80	79	78
Pine Bluff AP	204	14	20	24	L	99	96	95	22	81	80	79
Russelville	360	9	15	19	M	99	97	96	22	79	78	77
Texarkana AP	361	16	22	26	M	99	97	96	21	80	79	78

NORTHERN

SOUTHERN

*Indicates rare penetration to Coast.

Auburn	1297	25	31	35	VL	98	96	93	36	70	68	67
Bakersfield AP	494	26	31	33	VL	103	101	99	32	72	71	70
Banning	2349	20	26	30	VL	101	98	95	34	73	72	71
Barstow AP	2142	18	24	28	VL	104	102	99	37	73	72	71
Bishop AP	4108	9	16	20	VL	100	98	96	42	64	63	62
Blythe AP	395	26	31	35	VL	111	109	106	28	78	77	76
Burbank AP	699	30	36	38	VL	97	94	91	25	72	70	69
Chico	205	23	29	33	VL	102	100	97	34	71	70	69
Coalinga	676	26	30	34	VL	101	99	97	34	72	71	70
Concord	195	27	32	36	VL	96	92	88	20	69	67	66

TABLE 5—Continued   WINTER AND SUMMER DESIGN DATA BY STATES

Station[a]	Elev.[b] Ft.	Median of annual Extremes	99%	97½%	Coincident Wind	Design 1%	Dry 2½%	Bulb 5%	Outdoor Daily Range[c]	Design 1%	Wet 2½%	Bulb 5%
Covina	575	32	38	41	VL	100	97	94	31	73	72	71
Crescent City AP	50	28	33	36	L	72	69	65	12	61	60	59
Downey	116	30	35	38	VL	93	90	87	22	72	71	70
El Cajon	525	26	31	34	VL	98	95	92	30	74	73	72
El Centro AP	− 30	26	31	35	VL	111	109	106	34	81	80	79
Escondido	660	28	33	36	VL	95	92	89	30	73	72	71
Eureka/Arcata AP	203	30	35	38	L	67	65	63	11	60	59	58
Fairfield (Travis) AFB	72	26	32	34	VL	98	94	90	28	71	69	67
Fresno AP	326	25	28	31	VL	101	99	97	36	73	72	71
Indio	11	25	31	34	VL	111	109	106	30	80	79	78
Laguna Beach	35	32	37	39	VL	83	80	77	18	69	68	67
Livermore	545	23	28	30	VL	99	97	94	24	70	69	68
Lompoc (Vandenburg) AFB	552	32	36	38	VL	82	79	76	20	65	63	61
Long Beach AP	34	31	36	38	VL	87	84	81	22	72	70	69
Los Angeles AP	122	36	41	43	VL	86	83	80	15	69	68	67
Los Angeles CO	312	38	42	44	VL	94	90	87	20	72	70	69
Mather AFB	92	25	31	33	VL	101	98	95	36	72	70	69
McClellan AFB	86	26	32	34	VL	102	99	96	36	71	70	69
Merced (Castle) AFB	178	24	30	32	VL	102	99	96	36	73	72	70
Modesto	91	26	32	36	VL	101	98	96	34	73	71	70
Monterey	38	29	34	37	VL	81	78	75	18	64	63	61
Napa	16	26	31	34	VL	94	92	89	24	70	69	68
Needles AP	913	27	33	37	VL	112	110	107	27	76	75	74
Oakland AP	3	30	35	37	VL	85	81	77	19	65	63	62
Oceanside	30	33	38	40	VL	84	81	78	13	69	68	67
Ontario	995	26	32	34	VL	100	97	94	36	72	71	70
Oxnard AFB	43	32	35	37	VL	84	80	78	19	70	69	67
Palmdale AP	2517	18	24	27	VL	103	101	98	35	70	68	67
Palm Springs	411	27	32	36	VL	110	108	105	35	79	78	77
Pasadena	864	31	36	39	VL	96	93	90	29	72	70	69
Petaluma	27	24	29	32	VL	94	90	87	20	70	68	67
Redding AP	495	25	31	35	VL	103	101	98	32	70	69	67
Redlands	1318	28	34	37	VL	99	96	93	33	72	71	70
Richmond	55	28	35	38	VL	85	81	77	19	66	64	63
Riverside (March) AFB	1511	26	32	34	VL	99	96	94	37	72	71	69
Sacramento (Municipal) AP	23	24	30	32	VL	100	97	94	36	72	70	69
Salinas AP	74	27	32	35	VL	87	85	82	20	64	62	61
San Bernardino (Norton) AFB	1125	26	31	33	VL	101	98	96	38	75	73	71
San Diego AP	37	38	42	44	VL	86	83	80	12	71	70	68
San Fernando	977	29	34	37	VL	100	97	94	38	73	72	71
San Francisco AP	18	32	35	37	L	83	79	75	20	65	63	62
San Francisco CO	52	38	42	44	VL	80	77	73	14	64	62	61
San Jose AP	70r	30	34	36	VL	90	88	85	20	70	69	67
San Luis Obispo	315	30	35	37	VL	89	85	82	26	65	64	63
San Rafael (Hamilton) AFB	2	28	33	35	VL	87	85	81	20	71	68	66
Santa Ana AP	115r	28	33	36	VL	92	89	86	28	72	71	70
Santa Barbara AP	13	28	32	34	VL	85	82	79	24	66	65	64
Santa Barbara CO	100	30	34	36	VL	87	84	81	24	67	66	65
Santa Cruz	125	28	32	34	VL	87	84	80	18	66	65	63
Santa Maria AP	238	28	32	34	VL	85	82	79	23	65	64	63

TABLE 5—Continued   WINTER AND SUMMER DESIGN DATA BY STATES

Station[a]	Elev.[b] Ft.	Median of annual Extremes	WINTER Dec. – Feb. 99%	97½%	Coincident Wind	SUMMER June – Sept. Design 1%	Dry Bulb 2½%	Bulb 5%	Outdoor Daily Range[c]	Design 1%	Wet 2½%	Bulb 5%
Santa Monica CO	57	38	43	45	VL	80	77	74	16	69	68	67
Santa Paula	263	28	33	36	VL	91	89	86	36	72	71	70
Santa Rosa	167	24	29	32	VL	95	93	90	24	70	68	67
Stockton AP	28	25	30	34	VL	101	98	96	34	72	70	69
Sunnyvale (Moffett) NAS	39	29	34	36	VL	85	80	76	18	68	67	65
Ukiah	620	22	27	30	VL	98	96	93	26	71	70	68
Visalia	354	26	32	36	VL	102	100	97	36	72	71	70
Yreka	2625	7	13	17	VL	96	94	91	36	68	66	65
Yuba City	70	24	30	34	VL	102	100	97	34	71	70	69

COLORADO

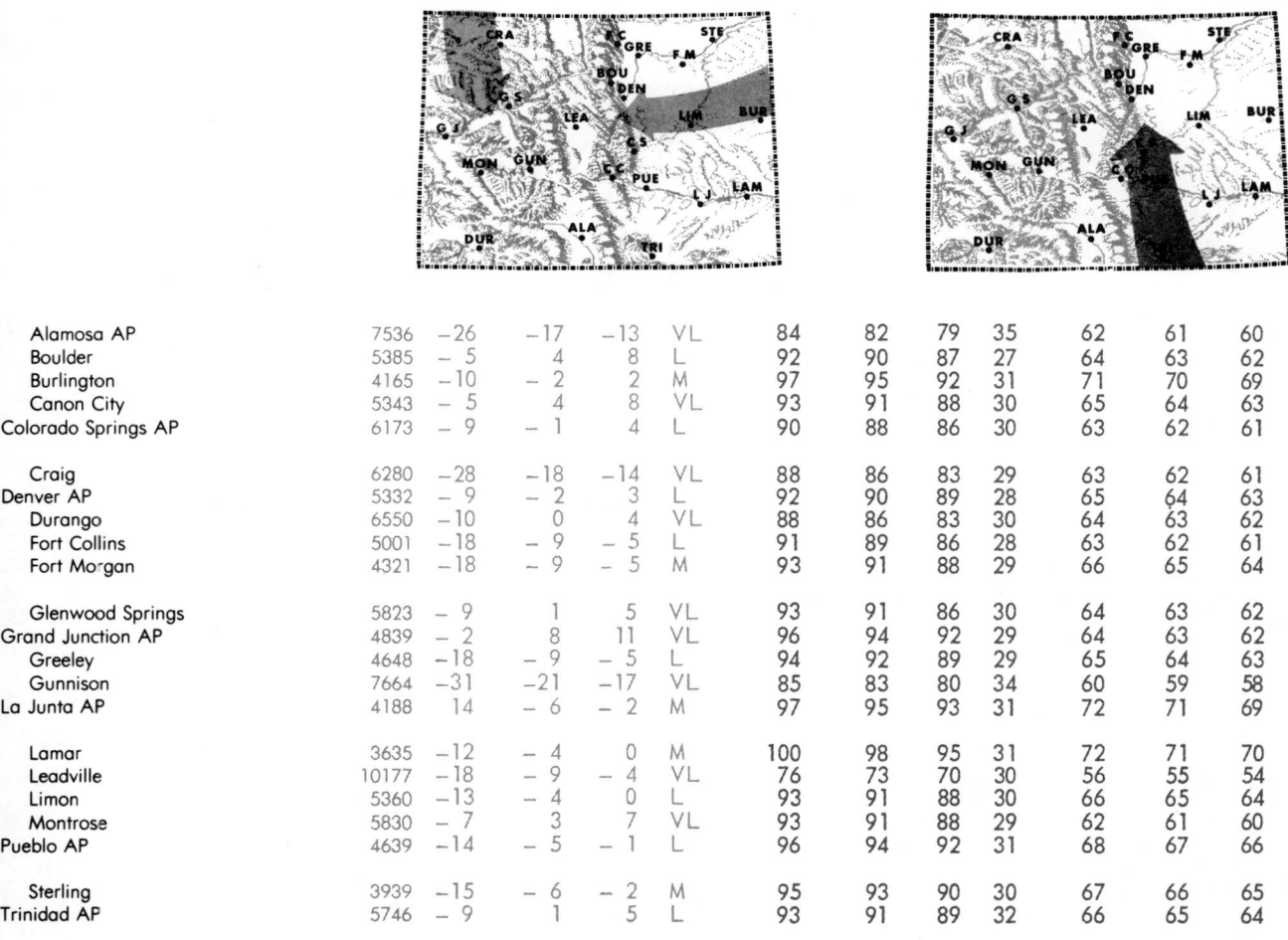

Station[a]	Elev.[b] Ft.	Median of annual Extremes	WINTER 99%	97½%	Coincident Wind	SUMMER Design 1%	Dry Bulb 2½%	Bulb 5%	Outdoor Daily Range[c]	Design 1%	Wet 2½%	Bulb 5%
Alamosa AP	7536	−26	−17	−13	VL	84	82	79	35	62	61	60
Boulder	5385	− 5	4	8	L	92	90	87	27	64	63	62
Burlington	4165	−10	− 2	2	M	97	95	92	31	71	70	69
Canon City	5343	− 5	4	8	VL	93	91	88	30	65	64	63
Colorado Springs AP	6173	− 9	− 1	4	L	90	88	86	30	63	62	61
Craig	6280	−28	−18	−14	VL	88	86	83	29	63	62	61
Denver AP	5332	− 9	− 2	3	L	92	90	89	28	65	64	63
Durango	6550	−10	0	4	VL	88	86	83	30	64	63	62
Fort Collins	5001	−18	− 9	− 5	L	91	89	86	28	63	62	61
Fort Morgan	4321	−18	− 9	− 5	M	93	91	88	29	66	65	64
Glenwood Springs	5823	− 9	1	5	VL	93	91	86	30	64	63	62
Grand Junction AP	4839	− 2	8	11	VL	96	94	92	29	64	63	62
Greeley	4648	−18	− 9	− 5	L	94	92	89	29	65	64	63
Gunnison	7664	−31	−21	−17	VL	85	83	80	34	60	59	58
La Junta AP	4188	14	− 6	− 2	M	97	95	93	31	72	71	69
Lamar	3635	−12	− 4	0	M	100	98	95	31	72	71	70
Leadville	10177	−18	− 9	− 4	VL	76	73	70	30	56	55	54
Limon	5360	−13	− 4	0	L	93	91	88	30	66	65	64
Montrose	5830	− 7	3	7	VL	93	91	88	29	62	61	60
Pueblo AP	4639	−14	− 5	− 1	L	96	94	92	31	68	67	66
Sterling	3939	−15	− 6	− 2	M	95	93	90	30	67	66	65
Trinidad AP	5746	− 9	1	5	L	93	91	89	32	66	65	64

TABLE 5—Continued   **WINTER AND SUMMER DESIGN DATA BY STATES**

		WINTER		Dec. – Feb.		SUMMER			June – Sept.			
Station[a]	Elev.[b] Ft.	Median of annual Extremes	99%	97½%	Coincident Wind	Design 1%	Dry Bulb 2½%	5%	Outdoor Daily Range[c]	Design 1%	Wet Bulb 2½%	5%

CONNECTICUT

Bridgeport AP	7	– 1	4	8	M	90	88	85	18	77	76	75
Falls Village	580	–13	– 8	– 4	L	90	88	85	22	76	75	73
Hartford (Brainard)	15	– 4	1	5	M	90	88	85	22	77	76	74
New Haven AP	6	0	5	9	H	88	86	83	17	77	76	75
New London	60	0	4	8	H	89	86	83	16	77	75	74
Norwalk	37	– 5	0	4	M	91	89	86	19	77	76	75
Norwich	20	– 7	– 2	2	M	88	86	83	18	77	76	75
Waterbury	605	– 5	0	4	M	90	88	85	21	77	76	75
Windsor Locks (Bradley)	179	– 7	– 2	2	M	90	88	85	22	76	75	73

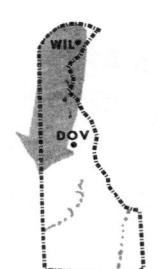 

DELAWARE

Dover AFB	38	8	13	15	M	93	90	88	18	79	78	77
Wilmington AP	78	6	12	15	M	93	90	87	20	79	77	76

DISTRICT OF COLUMBIA

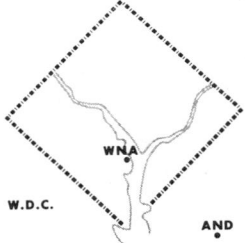 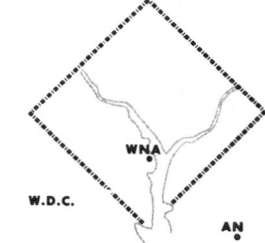

Andrews AFB	279	9	13	16	M	94	91	88	18	79	77	76
Washington National AP	65	12	16	19	M	94	92	90	18	78	77	76

TABLE 5—Continued　　　　**WINTER AND SUMMER DESIGN DATA BY STATES**

Station[a]	Elev.[b] Ft.	WINTER Dec. – Feb. Median of annual Extremes	99%	97½%	Coincident Wind	SUMMER June – Sept. Design 1%	Dry Bulb 2½%	5%	Outdoor Daily Range[c]	Design 1%	Wet Bulb 2½%	5%
Avon Park	145	32	36	40	M	96	94	93	17	80	79	78
Belle Glade	16	31	35	39	M	93	91	90	16	80	79	79
Cape Kennedy AP	16	33	37	40	L	90	89	88	15	81	80	79
Cross City AP	46	20	25	29	L	96	94	93	18	81	80	79
Daytona Beach AP	31	28	32	36	L	94	92	91	15	81	80	79
Fort Lauderdale	13	37	41	45	M	91	90	89	15	81	80	79
Fort Myers AP	13	34	38	42	M	94	92	91	18	80	80	79
Fort Pierce	10	33	37	41	M	93	91	90	15	81	80	79
Gainesville AP	155	24	28	32	L	96	94	93	18	80	79	79
Homestead AFB	10	39	43	46	M	91	90	89	15	80	79	79
Jacksonville AP	39	26	29	32	L	96	94	92	19	80	79	79
Key West AP	6	50	55	58	M	90	89	88	9	80	79	79
Lakeland CO	214	31	35	39	M	95	93	91	17	80	79	78
Miami AP	24	39	44	47	M	92	90	89	15	80	79	79
Miami Beach CO	9	40	45	48	M	91	89	88	10	80	79	79
Ocala	86	25	29	33	L	96	94	93	18	80	79	79
Orlando AP	106r	29	33	37	L	96	94	93	17	80	79	78
Panama City (Tyndall) AFB	22	28	32	35	M	92	91	90	14	81	80	80
Pensacola CO	13	25	29	32	M	92	90	89	14	82	81	80
St. Augustine	15	27	31	35	L	94	92	90	16	81	80	79
St. Petersburg	35	35	39	42	M	93	91	90	16	81	80	79
Sanford	14	29	33	37	L	95	93	92	17	80	79	79
Sarasota	30	31	35	39	M	93	91	90	17	80	80	79
Tallahassee AP	58	21	25	29	L	96	94	93	19	80	79	79
Tampa AP	36	32	36	39	M	92	91	90	17	81	80	79
Valparaiso (Elgin) AFB	66	23	27	31	M	96	94	92	14	82	81	80
West Palm Beach AP	15	36	40	44	M	92	91	89	16	81	80	80

TABLE 5—Continued   **WINTER AND SUMMER DESIGN DATA BY STATES**

Station[a]	Elev.[b] Ft.	WINTER Dec. — Feb. Median of annual Extremes	99%	97½%	Coincident Wind	SUMMER June — Sept. Design 1%	Dry Bulb 2½%	5%	Outdoor Daily Range[c]	Design 1%	Wet Bulb 2½%	5%
GEORGIA												
Albany (Turner) AFB	224	21	26	30	L	98	96	94	20	80	79	78
Americus	476	18	22	25	L	98	96	93	20	80	79	78
Athens	700	12	17	21	L	96	94	91	21	78	77	76
Atlanta AP	993	14	18	23	H	95	92	90	19	78	77	76
Augusta AP	143	17	20	23	L	98	95	93	19	80	79	78
Baxley	205	19	23	27	L	97	95	93	20	80	79	78
Brunswick	14	24	27	31	L	97	95	92	18	81	80	79
Columbus (Lawson) AFB	242	19	23	26	L	98	96	94	21	80	79	78
Covington	770	13	17	21	L	97	95	92	21	79	78	77
Dalton	720	10	15	19	L	97	95	92	22	78	77	76
Dublin	215	17	21	25	L	98	96	93	20	80	79	78
Fitzgerald	371	19	23	27	L	97	95	93	20	80	79	78
Gainesville	1254	11	16	20	L	94	92	89	21	78	77	76
Griffin	980	13	17	22	L	95	93	90	21	79	78	77
La Grange	715	12	16	20	L	96	94	92	21	79	78	77
Louisville	337	16	20	24	L	98	96	94	20	80	79	78
Macon AP	356	18	23	27	L	98	96	94	22	80	79	78
Marietta (Dobbins) AFB	1016	12	17	21	L	95	93	91	21	78	77	76
Milledgeville	320	15	19	23	L	98	96	93	21	79	78	77
Moultrie	340	22	26	30	L	97	95	93	20	80	79	78
Newnan	990	12	17	21	L	95	93	90	21	79	78	77
Rome AP	637	11	16	20	L	97	95	93	23	78	77	76
Savannah (Travis) AP	52	21	24	27	L	96	94	92	20	81	80	79
Valdosta AFB	223	24	28	31	L	96	94	92	20	80	79	78
Washington	630	13	18	22	L	97	95	92	20	79	78	77
Waycross	140	20	24	28	L	97	95	93	20	80	79	78
HAWAII												
Hilo AP	31	56	59	61	L	85	83	82	15	74	73	72
Honolulu AP	39	58	60	62	L	87	85	84	12	75	74	73
Kaneohe	198	58	60	61	L	85	83	82	12	74	73	73
Lihue AP	115	56	58	60	L	84	82	81	11	74	73	72
Wahiawa	215	57	59	61	L	86	84	83	14	75	74	73
Wailuku	200	57	59	61	L	85	83	82	12	74	73	72

TABLE 5—Continued   **WINTER AND SUMMER DESIGN DATA BY STATES**

Station[a]	Elev.[b] Ft.	WINTER Dec. – Feb.				SUMMER June – Sept.						
		Median of annual Extremes	99%	97½%	Coincident Wind	Design Dry Bulb 1%	2½%	5%	Outdoor Daily Range[c]	Design Wet Bulb 1%	2½%	5%

IDAHO

Boise AP	2858	0	4	10	L	96	93	91	31	68	66	65
Burley	4180	− 5	4	8	VL	95	93	89	35	68	66	64
Couer d'Alene AP	2973	− 4	2	7	VL	94	91	88	31	66	65	63
Grangeville	3355	− 9	− 1	3	VL	91	89	86	34	64	63	61
Hailey AP	5328	−16	− 7	− 3	VL	90	87	84	34	63	61	60
Idaho Falls AP	4730r	−17	−12	− 6	VL	91	88	85	38	65	64	62
Lewiston AP	1413	1	6	12	VL	98	96	93	32	67	66	65
McCall	5025	−21	−13	− 9	VL	85	82	79	32	61	60	58
Montpelier	5960	−19	− 9	− 5	VL	68	86	82	33	62	61	59
Moscow	2660	−11	− 3	1	VL	91	89	86	32	64	63	61
Mountain Home AFB	2992	− 3	2	9	L	99	96	93	36	68	66	64
Pocatello AP	4466	−12	− 8	− 2	VL	94	91	88	35	65	63	62
Rexburg	4810	−21	−11	− 7	VL	88	85	82	36	64	63	61
Salmon	3961	−19	−10	− 6	VL	93	90	87	36	63	62	60
Sandpoint	2100	− 8	0	4	VL	87	83	80	30	64	63	61
Twin Falls AP	4148	− 5	4	8	L	96	94	91	34	66	64	63
Weiser	2120	− 4	4	8	VL	97	95	92	31	68	66	64

TABLE 5—Continued   **WINTER AND SUMMER DESIGN DATA BY STATES**

Station[a]	Elev.[b] Ft.	WINTER Dec. – Feb. Median of annual Extremes	99%	97½%	Coincident Wind	SUMMER June – Sept. Design 1%	Dry Bulb 2½%	5%	Outdoor Daily Range[c]	Design 1%	Wet Bulb 2½%	5%

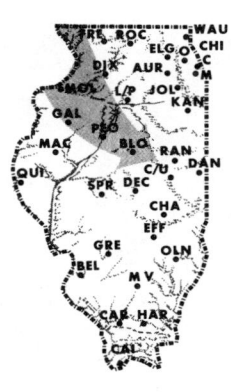

ILLINOIS

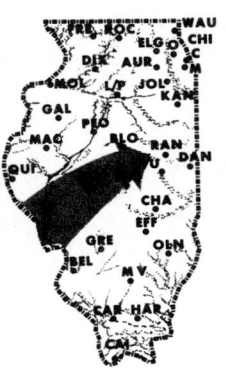

Station[a]	Elev.[b] Ft.	Median of annual Extremes	99%	97½%	Coincident Wind	Design 1%	Dry Bulb 2½%	5%	Outdoor Daily Range[c]	Design 1%	Wet Bulb 2½%	5%
Aurora	744	−13	− 7	− 3	M	93	91	88	20	78	77	75
Belleville (Scott) AFB	447	0	6	10	M	97	95	92	21	79	78	77
Bloomington	775	− 7	− 1	3	M	94	92	89	21	79	78	77
Cairo CO	314	5	11	15	L	97	95	93	20	80	79	78
Carbondale	380	1	7	11	M	98	96	94	21	80	79	78
Champaign/Urbana	743	− 6	0	4	M	96	94	91	21	79	78	77
Charleston	686	− 6	0	4	M	96	94	92	21	79	78	77
Chicago - Midway AP	623	− 7	− 4	1	M	95	92	89	20	78	76	75
Chicago - O'Hare AP	658	− 9	− 4	0	M	93	90	87	20	77	75	74
Chicago CO	594	− 5	− 3	1	M	94	91	88	15	78	76	75
Danville	558	− 6	− 1	4	M	96	94	91	21	79	78	76
Decatur	670	− 6	0	4	M	96	93	91	21	79	78	77
Dixon	696	−13	− 7	− 3	M	93	91	89	23	78	77	76
Effingham	595	− 5	1	5	M	96	94	92	21	79	78	77
Elgin	820	−14	− 8	− 4	M	92	90	87	21	78	76	75
Freeport	780	−16	−10	− 6	M	92	90	87	24	78	77	75
Galesburg	771	−10	− 4	0	M	95	92	89	22	79	78	76
Greenville	563	− 3	3	7	M	96	94	92	21	79	78	77
Harrisburg	366	1	7	11	M	98	96	94	21	80	79	78
Joliet AP	588	−11	− 5	− 1	M	94	92	89	20	78	77	75
Kankakee	625	−10	− 4	1	M	94	92	89	21	78	77	76
La Salle/Peru	520	− 9	− 3	1	M	94	93	90	22	78	77	76
Macomb	702	− 5	− 3	1	M	95	93	90	22	79	78	77
Moline AP	582	−12	− 7	− 3	M	94	91	88	23	79	77	76
Mt. Vernon	500	0	6	10	M	97	95	92	21	79	78	77
Olney	450	− 4	2	6	M	97	95	93	21	79	78	77
Peoria AP	652	− 8	− 2	2	M	94	92	89	22	78	77	76
Quincy AP	762	− 8	− 2	2	M	97	95	92	22	80	79	77
Rantoul (Chanute) AFB	740	− 7	− 1	3	M	94	92	89	21	78	77	76
Rockford	724	−13	− 7	− 3	M	92	90	87	24	77	76	75
Springfield AP	587	− 7	− 1	4	M	95	92	90	21	79	78	77
Waukegan	680	−11	− 5	− 1	M	92	90	87	21	77	76	75

TABLE 5—Continued   **WINTER AND SUMMER DESIGN DATA BY STATES**

Station[a]	Elev.[b] Ft.	WINTER Dec. – Feb. Median of annual Extremes	99%	97½%	Coincident Wind	SUMMER June – Sept. Design 1%	Dry Bulb 2½%	5%	Outdoor Daily Range[c]	Design 1%	Wet Bulb 2½%	5%

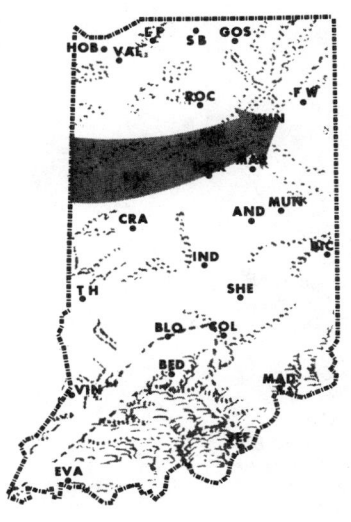

INDIANA

Anderson	847	− 5	0	5	M	93	91	88	22	78	77	76
Bedford	670	− 3	3	7	M	95	93	90	22	79	78	77
Bloomington	820	− 3	3	7	M	95	92	90	22	79	78	76
Columbus (Bakalar) AFB	661	− 3	3	7	M	95	92	90	22	79	78	76
Crawfordsville	752	− 8	− 2	2	M	95	93	90	22	79	77	76
Evansville AP	388	1	6	10	M	96	94	91	22	79	78	77
Fort Wayne AP	791	− 5	0	5	M	93	91	88	24	77	76	75
Goshen AP	823	−10	− 4	0	M	92	90	87	23	77	76	74
Hobart	600	−10	− 4	0	M	93	91	88	21	78	76	75
Huntington	802	− 8	− 2	2	M	94	92	89	23	78	76	75
Indiananpolis AP	793	− 5	0	4	M	93	91	88	22	78	77	76
Jeffersonville	455	3	9	13	M	96	94	91	23	79	78	77
Kokomo	790	− 6	0	4	M	94	92	89	22	78	76	75
Lafayette	600	− 7	− 1	3	M	94	92	89	22	78	77	76
La Porte	810	−10	− 4	0	M	93	91	88	22	77	76	74
Madison	455	3	9	13	M	96	94	91	22	79	78	76
Marion	791	− 8	− 2	2	M	93	91	88	23	78	76	75
Muncie	955	− 8	− 2	2	M	93	91	88	22	78	77	75
Peru (Bunker Hill) AFB	804	− 9	− 3	1	M	91	89	86	22	77	76	74
Richmond AP	1138	− 7	− 1	3	M	93	91	88	22	78	77	75
Rochester	770	− 7	− 1	3	M	94	92	89	22	77	76	75
Shelbyville	765	− 4	2	6	M	94	92	89	22	78	77	76
South Bend AP	773	− 6	− 2	3	M	92	89	87	22	77	76	74
Terre Haute AP	601	− 3	3	7	M	95	93	91	22	79	78	77
Valparaiso	801	−12	− 6	− 2	M	92	90	87	22	78	76	75
Vincennes	420	− 1	5	9	M	96	94	91	22	79	78	77

TABLE 5—Continued   **WINTER AND SUMMER DESIGN DATA BY STATES**

		WINTER		Dec. – Feb.		SUMMER			June – Sept.			
Station[a]	Elev.[b] Ft.	Median of annual Extremes	99%	97½%	Coincident Wind	Design 1%	Dry Bulb 2½%	5%	Outdoor Daily Range[c]	Design 1%	Wet Bulb 2½%	5%

IOWA

Ames	1004	−17	−11	− 7	M	94	92	89	23	79	78	76
Atlantic	1195	−18	−11	− 7	M	94	92	89	23	79	78	76
Burlington AP	694	−10	− 4	0	M	95	92	89	22	80	78	77
Carroll	1250	−18	−13	− 7	M	94	92	89	23	78	77	76
Cedar Rapids AP	863	−14	− 8	− 4	M	92	90	87	23	78	76	75
Chariton	940	−16	−10	− 6	M	96	94	91	23	79	78	77
Clarinda	1048	−15	− 8	− 4	M	96	94	91	23	79	78	76
Clinton	595	−13	− 7	− 3	M	92	90	87	23	78	77	76
Council Bluffs	1210	−14	− 7	− 3	M	97	94	91	22	79	78	76
Des Moines AP	963	−13	− 7	− 3	M	95	92	89	23	79	77	76
Dubuque	1065	−17	−11	− 7	M	92	90	87	22	78	76	75
Estherville	1298	−19	−12	− 8	M	92	90	87	24	77	76	75
Fort Dodge	1111	−18	−12	− 8	M	94	92	89	23	78	77	75
Grinnell	1009	−16	−10	− 6	M	95	93	90	23	79	77	76
Iowa City	645	−14	− 8	− 4	M	94	91	88	22	79	77	76
Keokuk	526	− 9	− 3	1	M	95	93	90	22	79	78	77
Marshalltown	898	−16	−10	− 6	M	93	91	88	23	79	77	76
Mason City AP	1194	−20	−13	− 9	M	91	88	85	24	77	75	74
Newton	946	−15	− 9	− 5	M	95	93	90	23	79	77	76
Oskaloosa	770	−14	− 8	− 4	M	95	93	90	22	79	77	76
Ottumwa AP	842	−12	− 6	− 2	M	95	93	90	22	79	78	76
Sioux City AP	1095	−17	−10	− 6	M	96	93	90	24	79	77	76
Storm Lake	1425	−19	−12	− 8	M	92	90	87	23	78	76	75
Washington	762	−13	− 7	− 3	M	94	92	89	22	79	78	76
Waterloo	868	−18	−12	− 8	M	91	89	86	23	78	76	75

KANSAS

Atchison	945	− 9	− 2	2	M	97	95	92	23	79	78	77
Chanute AP	977	− 3	3	7	H	99	97	95	23	79	78	77
Concordia AP	1470	− 7	0	4	M	100	98	95	22	77	76	74
Dodge City AP	2592	− 5	3	7	M	99	97	95	25	74	73	72
El Dorado	1282	− 3	4	8	H	101	99	96	24	78	77	76

TABLE 5—Continued   **WINTER AND SUMMER DESIGN DATA BY STATES**

Station[a]	Elev.[b] Ft.	WINTER Dec. – Feb.				SUMMER June – Sept.						
		Median of annual Extremes	99%	97½%	Coincident Wind	Design 1%	Dry Bulb 2½%	5%	Outdoor Daily Range[c]	Design 1%	Wet Bulb 2½%	5%
Emporia	1209	– 4	3	7	H	99	97	94	25	78	77	76
Garden City AP	2882	–10	– 1	3	M	100	98	96	28	74	73	72
Goodland AP	3645	–10	– 2	4	M	99	96	93	31	71	70	69
Great Bend	1940	– 5	2	6	M	101	99	96	28	77	76	75
Hutchinson AP	1524	– 5	2	6	H	101	99	96	28	77	76	75
Liberal	2838	– 4	4	8	M	102	100	99	28	74	73	71
McPherson	1495	– 5	2	6	H	101	99	96	25	77	76	75
Manhattan	1076	– 7	– 1	4	H	101	98	95	24	79	78	77
Norton	2298	–10	– 2	2	M	100	98	95	29	75	74	72
Ottawa	915	– 3	4	8	M	99	97	94	23	79	78	77
Parsons	908	– 2	5	9	H	99	97	94	23	79	78	77
Pratt	1868	– 2	5	9	H	101	99	96	27	76	75	74
Russell AP	1864	– 7	0	4	M	102	100	97	29	78	76	75
Salina	1271	– 4	3	7	H	101	99	96	26	78	76	75
Scott City	2971	–10	– 2	2	M	100	98	95	29	74	72	71
Topeka AP	877	– 4	3	6	M	99	96	94	24	79	78	77
Wichita AP	1392	– 1	5	9	H	102	99	96	23	77	76	75
Winfield	1205	– 1	6	10	H	101	99	96	23	78	77	76

KENTUCKY

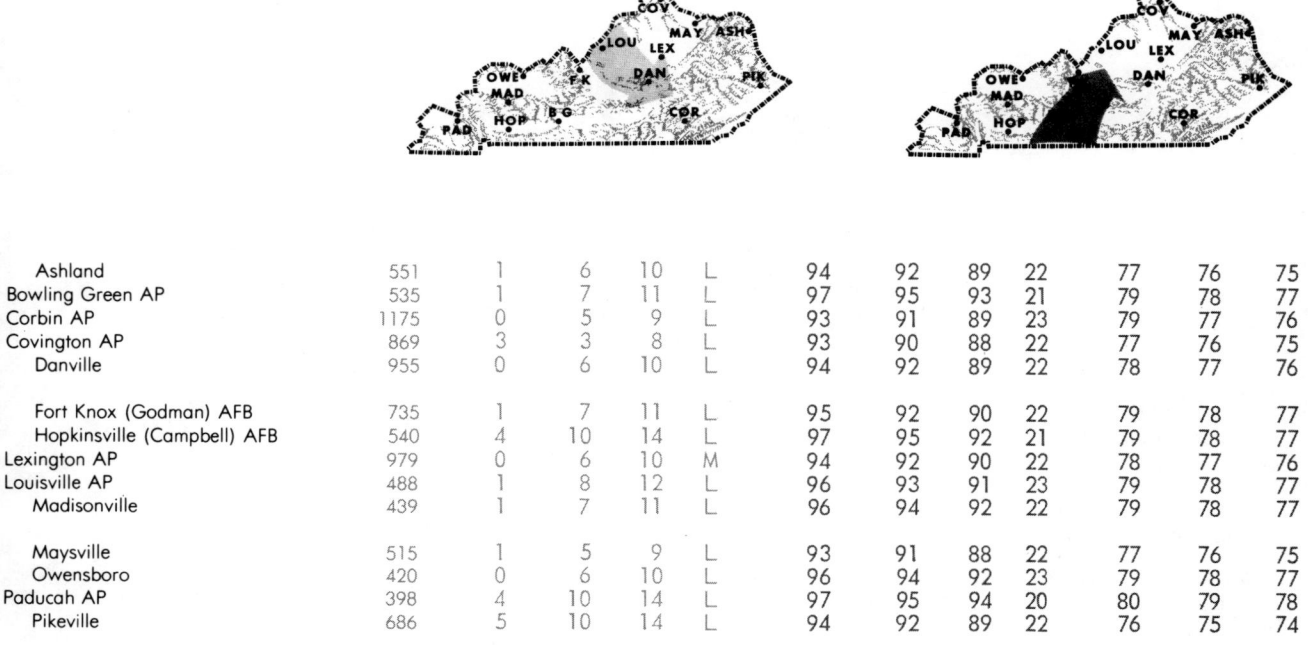

Ashland	551	1	6	10	L	94	92	89	22	77	76	75
Bowling Green AP	535	1	7	11	L	97	95	93	21	79	78	77
Corbin AP	1175	0	5	9	L	93	91	89	23	79	77	76
Covington AP	869	3	3	8	L	93	90	88	22	77	76	75
Danville	955	0	6	10	L	94	92	89	22	78	77	76
Fort Knox (Godman) AFB	735	1	7	11	L	95	92	90	22	79	78	77
Hopkinsville (Campbell) AFB	540	4	10	14	L	97	95	92	21	79	78	77
Lexington AP	979	0	6	10	M	94	92	90	22	78	77	76
Louisville AP	488	1	8	12	L	96	93	91	23	79	78	77
Madisonville	439	1	7	11	L	96	94	92	22	79	78	77
Maysville	515	1	5	9	L	93	91	88	22	77	76	75
Owensboro	420	0	6	10	L	96	94	92	23	79	78	77
Paducah AP	398	4	10	14	L	97	95	94	20	80	79	78
Pikeville	686	5	10	14	L	94	92	89	22	76	75	74

TABLE 5—Continued   **WINTER AND SUMMER DESIGN DATA BY STATES**

Station[a]	Elev.[b] Ft.	WINTER Dec. – Feb.				SUMMER June – Sept.						
		Median of annual Extremes	99%	97½%	Coincident Wind	Design 1%	Dry Bulb 2½%	5%	Outdoor Daily Range[c]	Design 1%	Wet Bulb 2½%	5%

LOUISIANA

Station	Elev.	Median	99%	97½%	Wind	Design 1%	2½%	5%	Daily Range	Design 1%	2½%	5%
Alexandria (England) AFB	92	20	25	29	L	97	95	94	20	80	80	79
Baton Rouge AP	76	22	25	30	L	96	94	92	19	81	80	79
Bogalusa	103	20	24	28	L	96	94	93	19	80	79	78
DeRidder	180	18	22	26	L	96	94	93	20	81	80	79
Hammond	45	21	25	29	L	95	93	92	18	81	80	79
Houma	13	25	29	33	L	94	92	91	15	81	80	79
Lafayette AP	38	23	28	32	L	95	93	92	18	81	81	80
Lake Charles AP	32	25	29	33	M	95	93	91	17	80	79	79
Minden	250	17	22	26	L	98	96	95	20	81	80	79
Monroe AP	78	18	23	27	L	98	96	95	20	81	81	80
Natchitoches	120	17	22	26	L	99	97	96	20	81	80	79
New Orleans AP	3	29	32	35	M	93	91	90	16	81	80	79
Shreveport AP	251	18	22	26	M	99	96	94	20	81	80	79
Barksdale AFB	168	17	21	27	M	99	97	95	20	80	79	78
Tallulah	85	17	22	26	L	96	94	93	20	81	80	79
Winnsboro	80	18	23	27	L	98	96	95	20	81	80	79

MAINE

Station	Elev.	Median	99%	97½%	Wind	Design 1%	2½%	5%	Daily Range	Design 1%	2½%	5%
Augusta AP	350	−13	−7	−3	M	88	86	83	22	74	73	71
Bangor (Dow) AFB	162	−14	−8	−4	M	88	85	81	22	75	73	71
Caribou AP	624	−24	−18	−14	L	85	81	78	21	72	70	68
Eastport	40	−9	−3	1	H	82	80	77	22	71	70	68
Ellsworth	24	−10	−4	1	H	85	83	80	22	73	72	70
Farmington	420	−20	−14	−10	L	88	86	83	22	74	72	70
Houlton	496	−23	−17	−13	L	86	84	81	22	73	72	70
Lewiston	182	−14	−8	−4	M	88	86	83	22	74	73	71
Loring AFB	752	−22	−16	−11	L	84	81	77	21	71	69	67
Millinocket AP	405	−22	−16	−12	L	87	85	82	22	74	72	70

TABLE 5—Continued   **WINTER AND SUMMER DESIGN DATA BY STATES**

Station[a]	Elev.[b] Ft.	Median of annual Extremes	99%	97½%	Coincident Wind	Design 1%	Dry Bulb 2½%	5%	Outdoor Daily Range[c]	Design 1%	Wet Bulb 2½%	5%
Portland AP	61	−14	− 5	0	L	88	85	81	22	75	73	71
Rockland	40	−11	− 5	− 1	H	87	85	82	22	73	71	69
Rumford	674	−16	−10	− 6	L	88	86	83	22	74	73	71
Waterville	89	−15	− 9	− 5	M	88	86	82	22	74	73	71

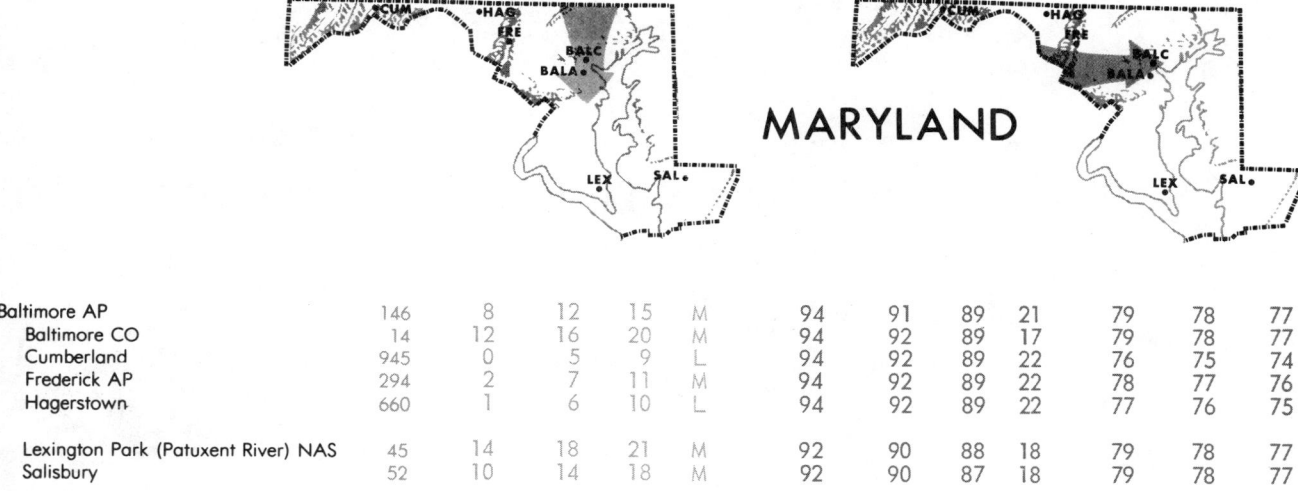

MARYLAND

Station[a]	Elev.[b] Ft.	Median of annual Extremes	99%	97½%	Coincident Wind	Design 1%	Dry Bulb 2½%	5%	Outdoor Daily Range[c]	Design 1%	Wet Bulb 2½%	5%
Baltimore AP	146	8	12	15	M	94	91	89	21	79	78	77
Baltimore CO	14	12	16	20	M	94	92	89	17	79	78	77
Cumberland	945	0	5	9	L	94	92	89	22	76	75	74
Frederick AP	294	2	7	11	M	94	92	89	22	78	77	76
Hagerstown	660	1	6	10	L	94	92	89	22	77	76	75
Lexington Park (Patuxent River) NAS	45	14	18	21	M	92	90	88	18	79	78	77
Salisbury	52	10	14	18	M	92	90	87	18	79	78	77

MASSACHUSETTS

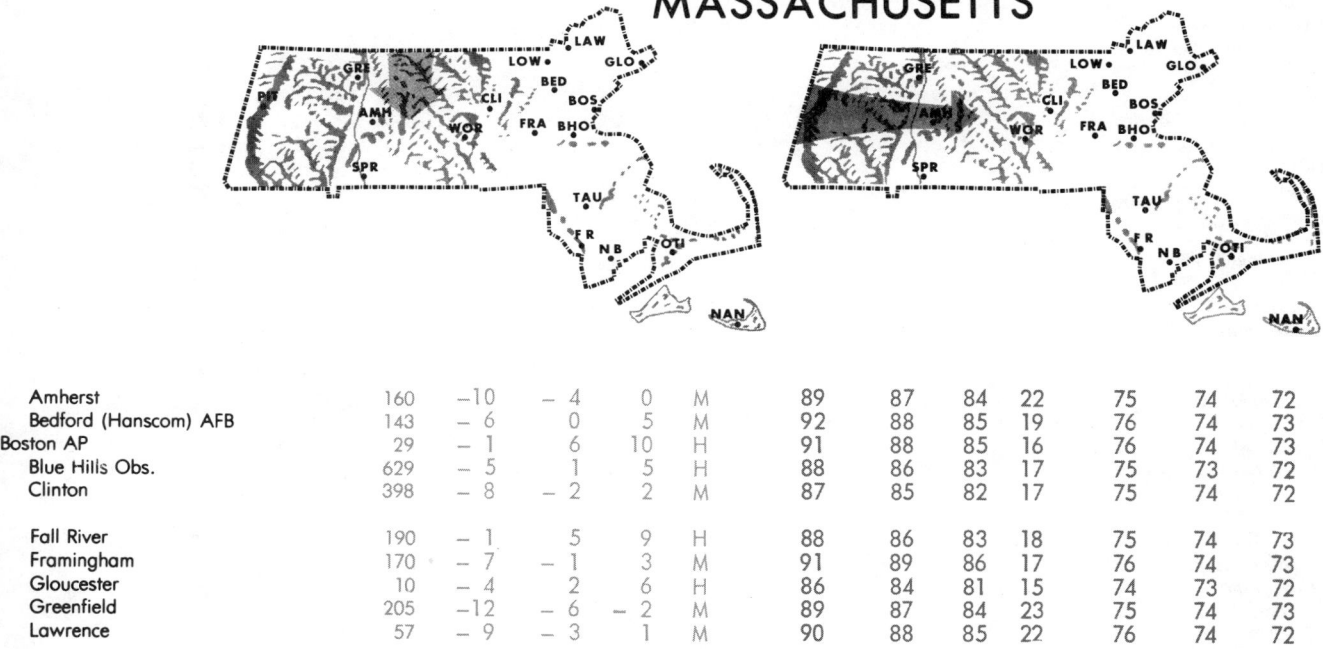

Station[a]	Elev.[b] Ft.	Median of annual Extremes	99%	97½%	Coincident Wind	Design 1%	Dry Bulb 2½%	5%	Outdoor Daily Range[c]	Design 1%	Wet Bulb 2½%	5%
Amherst	160	−10	− 4	0	M	89	87	84	22	75	74	72
Bedford (Hanscom) AFB	143	− 6	0	5	M	92	88	85	19	76	74	73
Boston AP	29	− 1	6	10	H	91	88	85	16	76	74	73
Blue Hills Obs.	629	− 5	1	5	H	88	86	83	17	75	73	72
Clinton	398	− 8	− 2	2	M	87	85	82	17	75	74	72
Fall River	190	− 1	5	9	H	88	86	83	18	75	74	73
Framingham	170	− 7	− 1	3	M	91	89	86	17	76	74	73
Gloucester	10	− 4	2	6	H	86	84	81	15	74	73	72
Greenfield	205	−12	− 6	− 2	M	89	87	84	23	75	74	73
Lawrence	57	− 9	− 3	1	M	90	88	85	22	76	74	72

TABLE 5—Continued   **WINTER AND SUMMER DESIGN DATA BY STATES**

		WINTER		Dec. – Feb.		SUMMER			June – Sept.			
Station[a]	Elev.[b] Ft.	Median of annual Extremes	99%	97½%	Coincident Wind	Design 1%	Dry Bulb 2½%	5%	Outdoor Daily Range[c]	Design 1%	Wet Bulb 2½%	5%
Lowell	90	– 7	– 1	3	M	91	89	86	21	76	74	72
Nantucket AP	43	7	13	17	M	80	78	76	14	74	73	71
New Bedford	70	3	9	13	H	86	84	81	19	75	73	72
Otis AFB	137	1	7	11	H	85	82	80	17	75	73	72
Pittsfield AP	1170	–11	– 5	– 1	M	86	84	81	23	74	72	71
Springfield (Westover) AFB	247	– 8	– 3	2	M	91	88	85	19	76	74	73
Taunton	20	– 9	– 4	0	H	88	86	83	18	76	75	74
Worcester AP	986	– 8	– 3	1	M	89	87	84	18	75	73	71

MICHIGAN

Station[a]	Elev.[b] Ft.	Median of annual Extremes	99%	97½%	Coincident Wind	Design 1%	Dry Bulb 2½%	5%	Outdoor Daily Range[c]	Design 1%	Wet Bulb 2½%	5%
Adrian	754	– 6	0	4	M	93	91	88	23	76	75	74
Alpena AP	689	–11	– 5	– 1	M	87	85	82	27	74	73	71
Bad Axe	715	– 8	– 2	2	M	89	87	84	23	75	74	72
Battle Creek AP	939	– 6	1	5	M	92	89	86	23	76	74	73
Benton Harbor AP	649	– 7	– 1	3	M	90	88	85	20	76	74	73
Big Rapids	930	–11	– 5	– 1	M	88	86	83	22	75	74	73
Cadillac	1390	–15	– 9	– 5	M	87	85	82	22	74	73	71
Cheboygan	600	–13	– 7	– 3	M	85	83	80	23	74	72	70
Detroit Met. CAP	626	0	4	8	M	92	88	85	20	76	75	74
Escanaba	594	–13	– 7	– 3	M	82	80	77	17	73	71	69
Flint AP	766	– 7	– 1	3	M	89	87	84	25	76	75	74
Grand Rapids AP	689	– 3	2	6	M	91	89	86	24	76	74	73
Grayling	1175	–18	–12	– 8	M	86	84	81	24	74	73	71
Holland	612	– 4	2	6	M	90	88	85	22	76	74	73
Houghton	1079	–14	– 8	– 4	L	84	80	77	18	72	70	68
Jackson AP	1003	– 6	0	4	M	92	89	86	23	76	75	74
Kalamazoo	930	– 5	1	5	M	92	89	86	23	76	75	74
Lansing AP	852	– 4	2	6	M	89	87	84	24	76	75	73
Ludington	650	– 4	2	6	M	84	82	79	22	75	74	72
Marquette CO	677	–14	– 8	– 4	L	88	86	83	18	73	71	69
Sawyer AFB	1214	–17	–11	– 7	L	86	83	80	18	72	70	68
Mt. Clemens (Selfridge) AFB	602	– 3	3	7	M	91	88	85	20	77	75	74
Mt. Pleasant	796	– 9	– 3	1	M	89	87	84	24	75	74	73
Muskegon AP	627	– 2	4	8	M	87	85	82	21	75	74	73
Pontiac	974	– 6	0	4	M	90	88	85	21	76	75	73
Port Huron	586	– 6	– 1	3	M	90	88	85	21	76	74	73

		WINTER		Dec. — Feb.			SUMMER			June — Sept.		
Station[a]	Elev.[b] Ft.	Median of annual Extremes	99%	97½%	Coincident Wind	Design 1%	Dry Bulb 2½%	Bulb 5%	Outdoor Daily Range[c]	Design 1%	Wet 2½%	Bulb 5%
Saginaw AP	662	− 7	− 1	3	M	88	86	83	23	76	75	73
Sault Ste. Marie AP	724	−18	−12	− 8	L	83	81	78	23	73	71	69
Traverse City AP	618	− 6	0	4	M	89	86	83	22	75	73	72
Ypsilanti	777	− 3	− 1	5	M	92	89	86	22	76	74	73

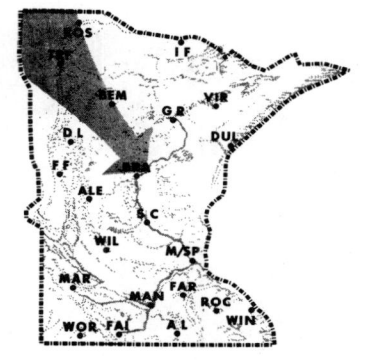 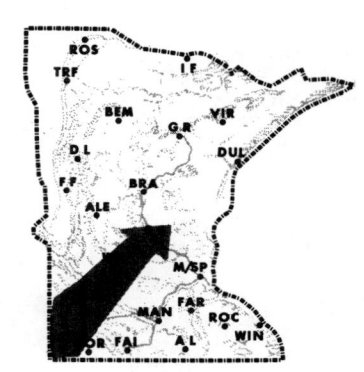

Albert Lea	1235	−20	−14	−10	M	91	89	86	24	77	76	74
Alexandria AP	1421	−26	−19	−15	L	90	88	85	24	76	74	72
Bemidji AP	1392	−38	−32	−28	L	87	84	81	24	73	72	71
Brainerd	1214	−31	−24	−20	L	88	85	82	24	74	73	72
Detroit Lakes	1375	−35	−28	−24	L	88	86	83	24	74	73	72
Duluth AP	1426	−25	−19	−15	M	85	82	79	22	73	71	69
Fairmont	1187	−19	−12	− 8	M	91	89	86	24	77	76	74
Faribault	1190	−23	−16	−12	L	90	88	85	24	77	75	74
Fergus Falls	1210	−28	−21	−17	L	92	89	86	24	75	74	72
Grand Rapids	1310	−37	−30	−26	L	86	83	80	24	73	72	71
International Falls AP	1179	−35	−29	−24	L	86	82	79	26	72	69	68
Mankato	785	−23	−16	−12	L	91	89	86	24	77	75	74
Marshall	1165	−23	−16	−12	L	91	89	86	24	77	76	74
Minneapolis/St. Paul AP	838	−19	−14	−10	L	92	89	86	24	77	75	74
Rochester AP	1297	−23	−17	−13	M	90	88	85	24	77	75	74
Roseau	1047	−38	−31	−27	M	86	83	80	25	72	70	69
St. Cloud AP	1034	−26	−20	−16	L	90	88	85	24	77	75	73
Thief River Falls	1120	−33	−26	−22	M	86	83	80	24	73	72	70
Virginia	1435	−32	−25	−21	L	86	83	80	23	73	71	69
Willmar	1133	−25	−18	−14	L	91	88	85	24	77	75	73
Winona	652	−19	−12	− 8	M	91	89	86	24	77	76	74
Worthington	1593	−20	−13	− 9	M	92	89	86	24	78	76	74

TABLE 5—Continued   **WINTER AND SUMMER DESIGN DATA BY STATES**

Station[a]	Elev.[b] Ft.	Median of annual Extremes	99%	97½%	Coincident Wind	Design 1%	Dry Bulb 2½%	5%	Outdoor Daily Range[c]	Design 1%	Wet Bulb 2½%	5%

MISSISSIPPI

Biloxi (Keesler) AFB	25	26	30	32	M	93	92	90	16	82	81	80
Clarksdale	178	14	20	24	L	98	96	95	21	81	80	79
Columbus AFB	224	13	18	22	L	97	95	93	22	79	79	78
Corinth	438	10	15	19	L	98	96	95	22	80	79	78
Greenville AFB	139	16	21	24	L	98	96	94	21	81	80	79
Greenwood	128	14	19	23	L	98	96	94	21	81	80	79
Hattiesburg	200	18	22	26	L	97	95	94	21	80	79	78
Jackson AP	332	17	21	24	L	98	96	94	21	79	78	78
Kosciusko	468	14	19	23	L	97	95	94	22	80	79	78
Laurel	264	18	22	26	L	97	95	94	21	80	79	78
McComb AP	458	18	22	26	L	96	94	93	18	80	79	79
Meridian AP	294	15	20	24	L	97	95	94	22	80	79	78
Natchez	168	18	22	26	L	96	94	93	21	80	80	79
Oxford	270	9	14	18	L	98	96	95	21	80	79	78
Tupelo	289	13	18	22	L	98	96	95	22	80	79	78
Vicksburg CO	234	18	23	26	L	97	95	94	21	80	80	79
Yazoo City	107	16	21	25	L	97	95	94	21	80	79	78

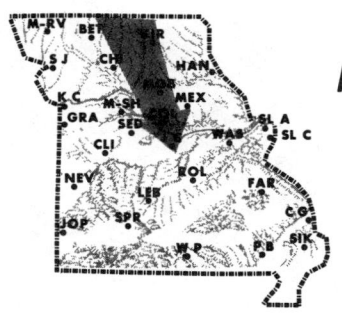

MISSOURI

Bethany	900	−15	−8	−4	M	96	94	91	23	79	78	77
Cape Girardeau	330	2	8	12	M	98	96	94	21	80	79	78
Chillicothe	700	−10	−4	0	M	97	95	92	23	79	78	77
Clinton	740	−5	1	5	M	98	96	94	22	79	78	77
Columbia AP	778	−4	2	6	M	97	95	92	22	79	78	77

Station[a]	Elev.[b] Ft.	WINTER Dec. – Feb.				SUMMER June – Sept.						
		Median of annual Extremes	99%	97½%	Coincident Wind	Design 1%	Dry 2½%	Bulb 5%	Outdoor Daily Range[c]	Design 1%	Wet 2½%	Bulb 5%
Farmington AP	928	− 2	4	8	M	97	95	93	22	79	78	77
Grandview (Richards Gebaur) AFB	1101	− 3	3	7	M	97	94	92	21	78	77	76
Hannibal	489	− 7	− 1	4	M	96	94	91	22	79	78	77
Jefferson City	640	− 4	2	6	M	97	95	93	23	79	78	77
Joplin AP	982	1	7	11	M	97	95	93	24	79	78	77
Kansas City AP	750	− 2	4	8	M	100	97	94	20	79	77	76
Kirksville AP	966	−13	− 7	− 3	M	96	94	91	24	79	78	77
Lebanon	1240	− 4	2	6	M	97	95	93	22	78	77	76
Marshall	775	− 7	− 1	3	M	96	94	91	21	79	78	77
Maryville	1169	−15	− 8	− 4	M	96	94	91	22	79	78	77
Mexico	775	− 7	− 1	3	M	96	94	91	22	79	78	77
Moberly	850	− 8	− 2	2	M	96	94	91	23	79	78	77
Nevada	780	− 3	3	7	M	98	96	94	22	79	78	77
Poplar Bluff	322	3	9	13	M	98	96	94	22	80	79	78
Rolla	1202	− 3	3	7	M	97	95	93	22	79	78	77
St. Joseph AP	809	− 8	− 1	3	M	97	95	92	23	79	78	77
St. Louis AP	564	− 2	4	8	M	98	95	92	21	79	78	77
St. Louis CO	465	1	7	11	M	96	94	92	18	79	78	77
Sedalia (Whiteman) AFB	838	− 2	4	9	M	97	94	92	22	79	77	76
Sikeston	318	4	10	14	L	98	96	94	21	80	79	78
Springfield AP	1270	0	5	10	M	97	94	91	23	78	77	76
Washington	660	− 7	− 1	3	M	97	95	93	21	79	78	77
West Plains	1006	0	6	10	M	97	95	93	22	78	77	76

MONTANA

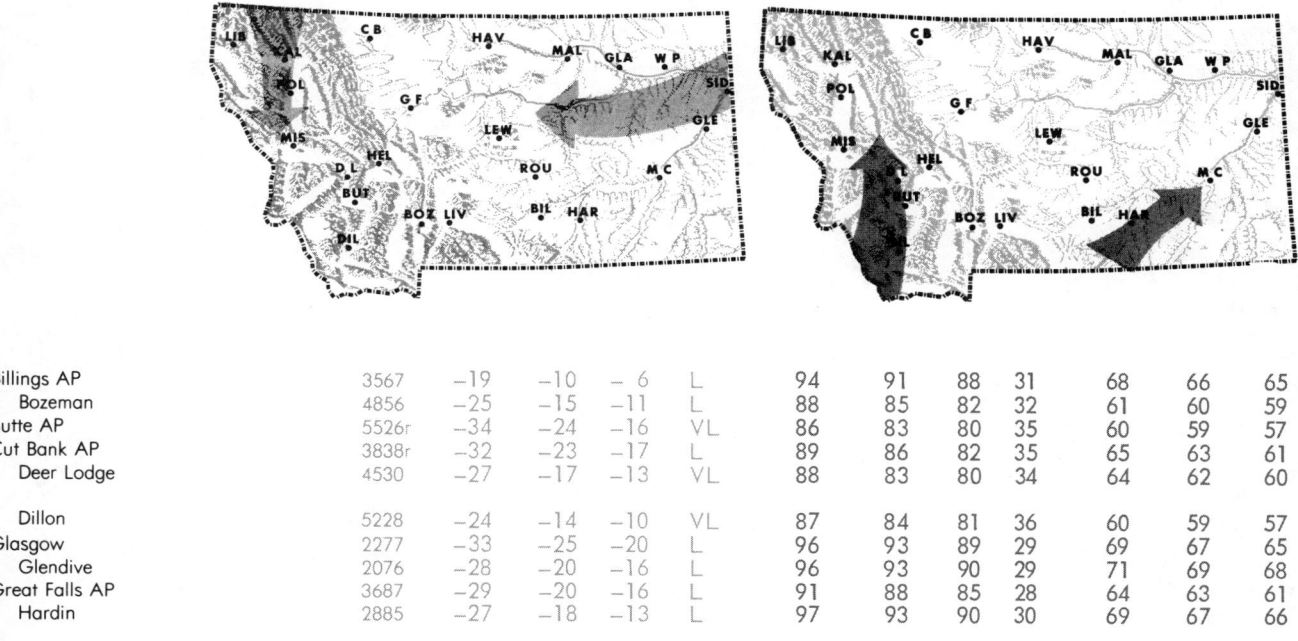

Billings AP	3567	−19	−10	− 6	L	94	91	88	31	68	66	65
Bozeman	4856	−25	−15	−11	L	88	85	82	32	61	60	59
Butte AP	5526r	−34	−24	−16	VL	86	83	80	35	60	59	57
Cut Bank AP	3838r	−32	−23	−17	L	89	86	82	35	65	63	61
Deer Lodge	4530	−27	−17	−13	VL	88	83	80	34	64	62	60
Dillon	5228	−24	−14	−10	VL	87	84	81	36	60	59	57
Glasgow	2277	−33	−25	−20	L	96	93	89	29	69	67	65
Glendive	2076	−28	−20	−16	L	96	93	90	29	71	69	68
Great Falls AP	3687	−29	−20	−16	L	91	88	85	28	64	63	61
Hardin	2885	−27	−18	−13	L	97	93	90	30	69	67	66

Station[a]	Elev.[b] Ft.	WINTER Dec. – Feb. Median of annual Extremes	99%	97½%	Coincident Wind	SUMMER June – Sept. Design 1%	Dry Bulb 2½%	5%	Outdoor Daily Range[c]	Design 1%	Wet Bulb 2½%	5%
Havre	2488	−32	−22	−15	M	91	87	84	33	66	64	63
Helena AP	3893	−27	−17	−13	L	90	87	84	32	65	63	61
Kalispell AP	2965	−17	− 7	− 3	VL	88	84	81	34	65	63	62
Lewiston AP	4132	−27	−18	−14	L	89	86	83	30	65	63	62
Libby	2080	−22	−13	− 9	VL	93	89	86	35	66	64	63
Livingston AP	4653	−26	−17	−13	L	91	88	85	32	63	62	61
Malta	2255	−32	−24	−20	M	92	88	85	29	68	66	64
Miles City AP	2634	−27	−19	−15	L	97	94	91	30	71	69	68
Missoula AP	3200	−16	− 7	− 3	VL	92	89	86	36	65	63	61
Polson AP	2927	−11	− 1	3	VL	86	83	81	34	64	62	61
Roundup	3227	−28	−19	−15	L	94	91	88	31	67	65	64
Sidney	1920	−31	−23	−19	L	94	91	88	26	71	69	68
Wolf Point	1975	−34	−26	−22	L	96	92	89	28	70	68	67

NEBRASKA

Station[a]	Elev.[b] Ft.	Median of annual Extremes	99%	97½%	Coincident Wind	Design 1%	Dry Bulb 2½%	5%	Outdoor Daily Range[c]	Design 1%	Wet Bulb 2½%	5%
Alliance	3971	−16	− 8	− 4	M	95	92	89	30	72	70	68
Beatrice	1235	−10	− 3	1	M	99	97	94	24	78	77	76
Bellevue (Offutt) AFB	1030	−11	− 4	− 1	M	97	94	91	24	79	78	76
Burwell	2180	−17	− 9	− 5	M	97	94	92	28	76	75	73
Chadron AP	3300	−21	−13	− 9	M	97	95	92	30	72	70	69
Columbus	1442	−14	− 7	− 3	M	98	96	93	25	78	76	75
Fremont	1203	−14	− 7	− 3	M	99	97	94	22	78	77	76
Grand Island AP	1841	−14	− 6	− 2	M	98	95	92	28	76	75	74
Hastings	1932	−11	− 3	1	M	98	96	94	27	77	75	74
Kearney	2146	−14	− 6	− 2	M	97	95	92	28	76	75	74
Lincoln AFB	1189	−10	− 4	0	M	100	96	93	25	78	77	76
Lincoln CO	1150	−10	− 4	0	M	100	96	93	24	78	77	76
McCook	2565	−12	− 4	0	M	99	97	94	28	74	72	71
Norfolk	1532	−18	−11	− 7	M	97	95	92	30	78	76	75
North Platte AP	2787	−13	− 6	− 2	M	97	94	90	28	74	73	72
Ogallala	3250	−15	− 7	− 3	M	97	95	92	30	73	72	70
Omaha AP	982	−12	− 5	− 1	M	97	94	91	22	79	78	76
O'Neill	1975	−19	−11	− 7	M	97	95	92	28	77	76	74
Scottsbluff AP	3950	−16	− 8	− 4	M	96	94	91	31	70	69	67
Sidney AP	4292	−15	− 7	− 2	M	95	92	89	31	70	69	67
Valentine	2587	−19	−11	− 7	M	97	94	91	30	73	72	71
York	1636	−15	− 8	− 4	M	99	97	94	25	78	76	75

TABLE 5—Continued   **WINTER AND SUMMER DESIGN DATA BY STATES**

Station[a]	Elev.[b] Ft.	WINTER Dec. — Feb.				SUMMER June — Sept.						
		Median of annual Extremes	99%	97½%	Coincident Wind	Design 1%	Dry Bulb 2½%	5%	Outdoor Daily Range[c]	Design 1%	Wet Bulb 2½%	5%

NEVADA

Station	Elev	Med	99%	97½%	Wind	1%	2½%	5%	Range	1%	2½%	5%
Austin	6600	− 3	5	9	VL	91	89	86	30	59	58	57
Caliente	4402	− 4	4	8	VL	100	98	95	41	67	66	65
Carson City	4675	− 4	3	7	VL	93	91	88	42	62	61	60
Elko AP	5075	−21	−13	− 7	VL	94	92	90	42	64	62	61
Ely AP	6257	−15	− 6	− 2	VL	90	88	86	39	60	59	58
Fallon NAS	3934	− 2	5	9	VL	98	96	94	42	64	62	61
Hawthorne	4330	8	15	19	VL	96	94	91	36	66	65	64
Las Vegas AP	2180	18	23	26	VL	108	106	104	30	72	71	70
Nellis AFB	1881	17	24	27	VL	110	108	106	32	73	72	71
Lovelock AP	3900	0	7	11	VL	98	96	93	42	65	64	62
Reno AP	4404	− 2	2	7	VL	95	92	90	45	64	62	61
Stead AFB	5046	− 2	5	9	VL	91	89	87	44	62	60	59
Reno CO	4490	8	12	17	VL	94	92	89	45	64	62	61
Tonopah AP	5426	2	9	13	VL	95	92	90	40	64	63	62
Winnemucca	4299	− 8	1	5	VL	97	95	93	42	64	62	61

NEW HAMPSHIRE

Station	Elev	Med	99%	97½%	Wind	1%	2½%	5%	Range	1%	2½%	5%
Berlin	1110	−25	−19	−15	L	87	85	82	22	73	71	70
Claremont	420	−19	−13	− 9	L	89	87	84	24	74	73	72
Concord AP	339	−17	−11	− 7	M	91	88	85	26	75	73	72
Keene	490	−17	−12	− 8	M	90	88	85	24	75	73	72
Laconia	505	−22	−16	−12	M	89	87	84	25	74	73	72

TABLE 5—Continued   **WINTER AND SUMMER DESIGN DATA BY STATES**

		WINTER	Dec. — Feb.			SUMMER	June — Sept.				
Station[a]	Elev.[b] Ft.	Median of annual Extremes	99%	97½%	Coin- cident Wind	Design 1%	Dry Bulb 2½%	5%	Outdoor Daily Range[c]	Design 1%	Wet 2½%	Bulb 5%
Manchester (Grenier) AFB	253	−11	− 5	1	M	92	89	86	24	76	74	73
Portsmouth (Pease) AFB	127	− 8	− 2	3	M	88	86	83	22	75	73	72

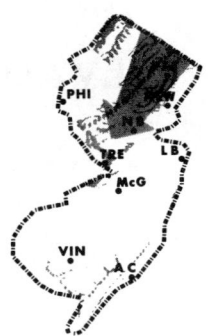
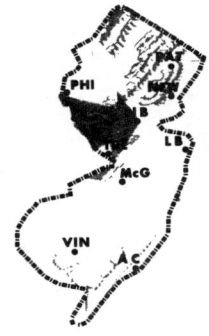

NEW JERSEY

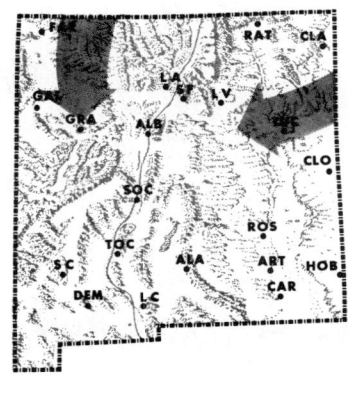
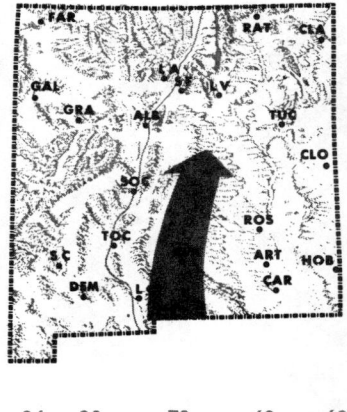

NEW MEXICO

Station	Elev.	Median	99%	97½%	Wind	1%	2½%	5%	Range	1%	2½%	5%
Alamogordo (Holloman) AFB	4070	12	18	22	L	100	98	96	30	70	69	68
Albuquerque AP	5314	6	14	17	L	96	94	92	27	66	65	64
Artesia	3375	9	16	19	L	101	99	97	30	71	70	69
Carlsbad AP	3234	11	17	21	L	101	99	97	28	72	71	70
Clayton AP	4969	− 6	2	6	M	95	93	90	28	70	69	68
Clovis AP	4279	2	14	17	L	99	97	95	28	70	69	68
Deming	4331	9	15	19	L	102	100	97	29	70	69	68
Farmington AP	5509	− 3	6	9	VL	95	93	91	30	66	65	64
Gallup	6465	−13	− 5	− 1	VL	92	90	87	32	64	63	62
Grants	6520	−15	− 7	− 3	VL	91	89	86	32	64	63	62

TABLE 5—Continued   WINTER AND SUMMER DESIGN DATA BY STATES

		WINTER		Dec. – Feb.		SUMMER				June – Sept.		
Station^a	Elev.^b Ft.	Median of annual Extremes	99%	97½%	Coincident Wind	Design 1%	Dry Bulb 2½%	5%	Outdoor Daily Range^c	Design 1%	Wet 2½%	Bulb 5%
Hobbs AP	3664	9	15	19	L	101	99	96	29	72	71	70
Las Cruces	3900	13	19	23	L	102	100	97	30	70	69	68
Las Vegas	6857	−11	− 3	1	L	91	89	86	29	64	63	62
Los Alamos	7410	− 4	5	9	L	88	86	83	32	64	63	62
Raton AP	6379	−11	− 2	2	L	92	90	88	34	66	65	64
Roswell (Walker) AFB	3643	5	16	19	L	101	99	97	33	71	70	69
Santa Fe CO	7045	− 2	7	11	L	90	88	85	28	65	63	62
Silver City AP	5373	8	14	18	VL	95	93	91	30	68	67	66
Socorro AP	4617	6	13	17	L	99	97	94	30	67	66	65
Truth or Consequences	4820	8	14	18	L	100	98	96	31	68	67	66
Tucumari AP	4053	1	9	13	L	99	97	95	28	71	70	69

NEW YORK

Station^a	Elev.^b Ft.	Median of annual Extremes	99%	97½%	Coincident Wind	Design 1%	Dry Bulb 2½%	5%	Outdoor Daily Range^c	Design 1%	Wet 2½%	Bulb 5%
Albany AP	292	−14	− 5	0	L	91	88	85	23	76	74	73
Albany CO	19	− 5	1	5	L	91	89	86	20	76	74	73
Auburn	715	−10	− 2	2	M	89	87	84	22	75	73	72
Batavia	900	− 7	− 1	3	M	89	87	84	22	75	74	72
Binghamton CO	858	− 8	− 2	2	L	91	89	86	20	74	72	71
Buffalo AP	705r	− 3	3	6	M	88	86	83	21	75	73	72
Canton CO	458	−25	−19	−15	M	86	84	81	20	74	73	71
Cortland	1129	−11	− 5	− 1	L	90	88	85	23	75	73	72
Dunkirk	590	− 2	4	8	M	88	86	83	18	75	74	72
Elmira AP	860	− 5	1	5	L	92	90	87	24	75	73	72
Geneva	590	− 8	− 2	2	M	91	89	86	22	75	73	72
Glens Falls	321	−17	−11	− 7	L	88	86	83	23	74	72	71
Gloversville	770	−12	− 6	− 2	L	89	87	84	23	75	73	71
Hempstead (Mitchel) AFB	125	5	10	14	H	91	88	85	17	77	76	75
Hornell	1325	−15	− 9	− 5	L	87	85	82	24	74	72	71
Ithaca	950	−10	− 4	0	L	91	88	85	24	75	73	72
Jamestown	1390	− 5	1	5	M	88	86	83	20	75	73	72
Kingston	279	− 8	− 2	2	L	92	90	87	22	76	74	73
Lockport	520	− 4	2	6	M	87	85	82	21	75	74	72
Massena AP	202r	−22	−16	−12	M	86	84	81	20	75	74	72
Newburgh (Stewart) AFB	460	− 4	2	6	M	92	89	86	21	78	76	74
NYC - Central Park	132	6	11	15	H	94	91	88	17	77	76	75
NYC - Kennedy AP	16	12	17	21	H	91	87	84	16	77	76	75
NYC - LaGuardia AP	19	7	12	16	H	93	90	87	16	77	76	75
Niagara Falls AP	596	− 2	4	7	M	88	86	83	20	75	74	73

TABLE 5—Continued   **WINTER AND SUMMER DESIGN DATA BY STATES**

Station[a]	Elev.[b] Ft.	Median of annual Extremes	99%	97½%	Coincident Wind	Design 1%	Dry Bulb 2½%	5%	Outdoor Daily Range[c]	Design 1%	Wet Bulb 2½%	5%
		WINTER Dec. – Feb.				**SUMMER June – Sept.**						
Olean	1420	−13	− 8	− 3	L	87	85	82	23	74	72	71
Oneonta	1150	−13	− 7	− 3	L	89	87	84	24	74	72	71
Oswego CO	300	− 4	2	6	M	86	84	81	20	75	74	72
Plattsburg AFB	165	−16	−10	− 6	L	86	84	81	22	74	73	71
Poughkeepsie	103	− 6	− 1	3	L	93	90	87	21	77	75	74
Rochester AP	543	− 5	2	5	M	91	88	85	22	75	74	72
Rome (Griffiss) AFB	515	−13	− 7	− 3	L	90	87	84	22	76	74	73
Schenectady	217	−11	− 5	− 1	L	90	88	85	22	75	73	72
Suffolk County AFB	57	4	9	13	H	87	84	81	16	76	75	74
Syracuse AP	424	−10	− 2	2	M	90	87	85	20	76	74	73
Tupper Lake	680	−26	−20	−16	L	85	83	80	23	73	72	70
Utica	714	−12	− 6	− 2	L	89	87	84	22	75	73	72
Watertown	497	−20	−14	−10	M	86	84	81	20	75	74	72

NORTH CAROLINA

Station[a]	Elev.[b] Ft.	Median of annual Extremes	99%	97½%	Coincident Wind	Design 1%	Dry Bulb 2½%	5%	Outdoor Daily Range[c]	Design 1%	Wet Bulb 2½%	5%
Asheville AP	2170r	8	13	17	L	91	88	86	21	75	74	73
Charlotte AP	769	13	18	22	L	96	94	92	20	78	77	76
Durham	406	11	15	19	L	94	92	89	20	78	77	76
Elizabeth City AP	10	14	18	22	M	93	91	89	18	80	79	78
Fayetteville (Pope) AFB	95	13	17	20	L	97	94	92	20	80	79	78
Goldsboro (Seymour-Johnson) AFB	88	14	18	21	M	95	92	90	18	80	79	78
Greensboro AP	897	9	14	17	L	94	91	89	21	77	76	75
Greenville	25	14	18	22	M	95	93	90	19	81	80	79
Hatteras	5	24	28	32	M	86	84	82	12	81	80	79
Havelock (Cherry Point) MCAS	35	19	23	27	M	94	92	90	18	81	80	79
Henderson	510	8	12	16	L	94	92	89	20	79	78	77
Hickory	1165	9	14	18	L	93	91	88	21	77	76	75
Jacksonville	24	17	21	25	M	94	92	89	18	81	80	79
Lumberton	132	14	18	22	L	95	93	90	20	81	80	79
New Bern AP	17	14	18	22	L	94	92	89	18	81	80	79
Raleigh/Durham AP	444	13	16	20	L	95	92	90	20	79	78	77
Rocky Mount	81	12	16	20	L	95	93	90	19	80	79	78
Wilmington AP	30	19	23	27	L	93	91	89	18	82	81	80
Winston-Salem AP	967	9	14	17	L	94	91	89	20	77	76	75

TABLE 5—Continued   **WINTER AND SUMMER DESIGN DATA BY STATES**

Station[a]	Elev.[b] Ft.	Median of annual Extremes	99%	97½%	Coincident Wind	Design 1%	Dry Bulb 2½%	5%	Outdoor Daily Range[c]	Design 1%	Wet Bulb 2½%	5%
WINTER Dec. – Feb.						**SUMMER** June – Sept.						

NORTH DAKOTA

Station	Elev. Ft.	Median of annual Extremes	99%	97½%	Coincident Wind	Design 1%	Dry Bulb 2½%	5%	Outdoor Daily Range	Design 1%	Wet Bulb 2½%	5%
Bismarck AP	1660	−31	−24	−19	VL	95	91	88	27	74	72	70
Bottineau	1640	−35	−28	−24	M	92	88	85	25	73	71	69
Carrington	1586	−30	−23	−19	L	94	90	87	26	74	73	71
Crosby	1952	−31	−24	−20	M	94	90	87	25	71	69	67
Devils Lake	1471	−30	−23	−19	M	93	89	86	25	73	71	69
Dickinson AP	2595	−31	−23	−19	L	96	93	90	25	72	70	68
Ellendale	1460	−26	−19	−15	L	95	91	88	26	76	74	72
Fargo AP	899	−28	−22	−17	L	92	88	85	25	76	74	72
Grafton	827	−31	−24	−20	M	93	89	86	25	73	71	69
Grand Forks AP	832	−30	−26	−23	L	91	87	84	25	74	72	70
Jamestown AP	1492	−29	−22	−18	L	95	91	88	26	75	73	71
Kenmare	1300	−30	−23	−19	M	93	89	86	25	72	70	68
Langdon	1615	−35	−28	−24	M	92	88	85	25	73	71	69
McClusky	1943	−31	−24	−20	L	94	90	87	25	74	72	70
Minot AP	1713	−31	−24	−20	M	91	88	84	25	72	70	68
Mott	2420	−30	−22	−18	L	96	92	89	26	73	71	69
Valley City	1230	−29	−22	−18	L	93	89	86	26	75	73	71
Wahpeton	960	−28	−21	−17	L	94	90	87	26	76	74	72
Williston	1877	−28	−21	−17	M	94	90	87	25	71	69	67

OHIO

Station	Elev. Ft.	Median of annual Extremes	99%	97½%	Coincident Wind	Design 1%	Dry Bulb 2½%	5%	Outdoor Daily Range	Design 1%	Wet Bulb 2½%	5%
Akron/Canton AP	1210	− 5	1	6	M	89	87	84	21	75	73	72
Ashtabula	690	− 3	3	7	M	89	87	84	18	76	75	74
Athens	700	− 3	3	7	M	93	91	88	22	77	76	75
Bellefontaine	1185	− 6	0	4	M	92	90	87	24	77	76	75
Bowling Green	675	− 7	− 1	3	M	93	91	88	23	77	75	74

TABLE 5—Continued　　　　WINTER AND SUMMER DESIGN DATA BY STATES

Station[a]	Elev.[b] Ft.	WINTER Dec. – Feb. Median of annual Extremes	99%	97½%	Coincident Wind	SUMMER June – Sept. Design 1%	Dry Bulb 2½%	5%	Outdoor Daily Range[c]	Design 1%	Wet Bulb 2½%	5%
Cambridge	800	− 6	0	4	M	91	89	86	23	77	76	75
Chillicothe	638	− 1	5	9	M	93	91	88	22	77	76	75
Cincinnati (Covington) AP	888	3	3	8	L	93	90	88	22	77	76	75
Cincinnati CO	761	2	8	12	L	94	92	90	21	78	77	76
Cleveland AP	805	− 2	2	7	M	91	89	86	22	76	75	74
Columbus AP	833	− 1	2	7	M	92	88	86	24	77	76	75
Columbus (Lockbourne) AFB	744	− 5	1	7	M	93	91	88	24	77	76	75
Dayton AP	997	− 2	0	6	M	92	90	87	20	77	75	74
Wright-Patterson AFB	822	− 3	3	8	M	93	90	88	22	77	76	75
Defiance	700	− 7	− 1	1	M	93	91	88	24	77	76	74
Findlay AP	797	− 6	0	4	M	92	90	88	24	77	76	75
Fremont	600	− 7	− 1	3	M	92	90	87	24	76	75	74
Greenville	1035	− 8	− 2	2	M	92	90	87	23	77	76	75
Hamilton	650	− 2	4	8	M	94	92	90	22	78	77	76
Lancaster	920	− 5	1	5	M	93	91	88	23	77	76	75
Lima	860	− 6	0	4	M	93	91	88	24	77	76	75
Mansfield AP	1297	− 7	1	3	M	91	89	86	22	76	75	74
Marion	920	− 5	1	6	M	93	91	88	23	77	76	75
Middletown	635	− 3	3	7	M	93	91	88	22	77	76	75
Newark	825	− 7	− 1	3	M	92	90	87	23	77	76	75
Norwalk	720	− 7	− 1	3	M	92	90	87	22	76	75	74
Oberlin	817	− 4	2	6	M	90	88	85	22	76	75	74
Portsmouth	530	0	5	9	L	94	92	89	22	77	76	75
Sandusky CO	606	− 2	4	8	M	92	90	87	21	76	75	74
Springfield	1020	− 3	3	7	M	93	90	88	21	77	76	75
Steubenville	992	− 2	4	9	M	91	89	86	22	76	75	74
Toledo AP	676r	− 5	1	5	M	92	90	87	25	77	75	74
Van Wert	795	− 8	− 2	2	M	93	91	88	24	77	76	75
Warren	900	− 6	0	4	M	90	88	85	23	75	74	73
Wilmington (Clinton County) AFB	1065	− 5	1	5	M	92	90	87	22	77	76	75
Wooster	1030	− 7	− 1	3	M	90	88	85	22	76	75	74
Youngstown AP	1178	− 5	1	6	M	89	86	84	23	75	74	73
Zanesville AP	881	− 7	− 1	3	M	92	89	87	23	77	76	75
Ada	1015	6	12	16	H	102	100	98	23	79	78	77
Altus AFB	1390	7	14	18	H	103	101	99	25	77	76	75
Alva	1374	− 1	6	10	H	103	101	99	25	76	75	74
Ardmore	880	9	15	19	H	103	101	99	23	79	78	77
Bartlesville	715	− 1	5	9	H	101	99	97	23	79	78	77

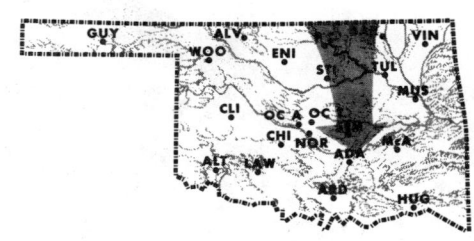

OKLAHOMA

Station[a]	Elev.[b] Ft.	WINTER Dec. – Feb. Median of annual xtremes	99%	97½%	Coincident Wind	SUMMER June – Sept. Design 1%	Dry Bulb 2½%	5%	Outdoor Daily Range[c]	Design 1%	Wet Bulb 2½%	5%
Chickasha	1085	5	12	16	H	103	101	99	24	77	76	75
Clinton (Clinton-Sherman) AFB	1928	3	10	15	H	103	100	97	26	78	77	76
Enid (Vance) AFB	1287	3	10	14	H	103	100	98	24	78	77	76
Guymon	3124	− 5	3	7	M	101	99	96	28	74	72	70
Hugo	540	9	15	19	M	102	100	98	22	79	78	77
Lawton AP	1108	6	13	16	H	103	101	98	24	78	77	76
McAlester	760	7	13	17	H	102	100	98	23	79	78	77
Muskogee AP	610	6	12	16	M	102	99	96	23	79	78	77
Norman	1109	5	11	15	H	101	99	97	24	78	77	76
Oklahoma City AP	1304	4	11	15	H	100	97	95	23	78	77	76
Oklahoma City (Tinker) AFB	1262	4	11	15	H	101	98	96	23	78	77	76
Ponca City	996	1	8	12	H	102	100	97	24	78	77	76
Seminole	865	6	12	16	H	102	100	98	23	78	77	76
Stillwater	884	2	9	13	H	101	99	97	24	78	77	76
Tulsa AP	674	4	12	16	H	102	99	96	22	79	78	77
Vinita	740	1	7	11	M	101	99	96	23	79	78	77
Woodward	1900	− 3	4	8	H	103	101	98	26	76	74	73

OREGON

Albany	224	17	23	27	VL	91	88	84	31	69	67	65
Astoria AP	8	22	27	30	M	79	76	72	16	61	60	59
Baker AP	3368	−10	− 3	1	VL	94	92	89	30	66	65	63
Bend	3599	− 7	0	4	VL	89	87	84	33	64	62	61
Burns CO	4151	− 9	− 2	2	VL	92	90	87	35	65	64	62
Corvallis	221	17	23	27	VL	91	88	84	31	69	67	65
Eugene AP	364	16	22	26	VL	91	88	84	31	69	67	65
Forest Grove	180	14	20	24	L	90	88	85	28	67	66	65
Grants Pass	925	16	22	26	VL	94	92	89	33	68	66	65
Klamath Falls AP	4091	− 5	1	5	VL	89	87	84	36	63	62	61
LaGrande	2805	− 6	1	5	VL	94	92	89	28	66	65	63
Lakeview	4774	− 7	0	3	VL	89	87	84	36	63	62	61
Medford AP	1298	15	21	23	VL	98	94	91	35	70	68	66
Newport AP	136	25	30	33	L	77	74	70	14	60	59	58
North Bend AP	11	25	30	33	L	76	73	69	16	61	60	59
Pendleton AP	1492	− 2	3	10	VL	97	94	91	29	66	65	63
Portland AP	26	17	21	24	L	89	85	81	23	69	67	66
Portland CO	57	21	26	29	L	91	88	84	21	69	68	67
Prineville	2840	− 6	1	5	VL	91	89	86	34	65	63	62
Roseburg AP	505	19	25	29	VL	93	91	88	30	69	67	65
Salem AP	195	15	21	25	VL	92	88	84	31	69	67	66
The Dalles	102	7	13	17	VL	93	91	88	28	70	68	67

TABLE 5—Continued   **WINTER AND SUMMER DESIGN DATA BY STATES**

Station[a]	Elev.[b] Ft.	WINTER Dec. – Feb. Median of annual Extremes	99%	97½%	Coincident Wind	SUMMER June – Sept. Design 1%	Dry Bulb 2½%	5%	Outdoor Daily Range[c]	Design 1%	Wet Bulb 2½%	5%

PENNSYLVANIA

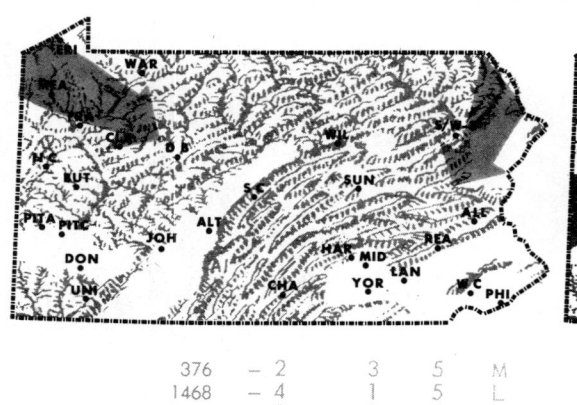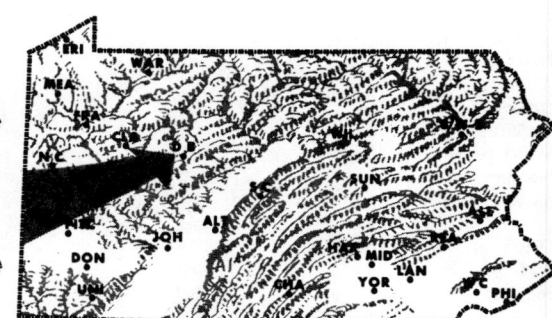

Station	Elev.	Extremes	99%	97½%	Wind	1%	2½%	5%	Range	1%	2½%	5%
Allentown AP	376	− 2	3	5	M	92	90	87	22	77	75	74
Altoona	1468	− 4	1	5	L	89	87	84	23	74	73	72
Butler	1100	− 8	− 2	2	L	91	89	86	22	75	74	73
Chambersburg	640	0	5	9	L	94	92	89	23	76	75	74
Clarion	1114	−11	− 7	− 1	L	89	87	84	24	74	73	72
Donora	814	0	5	9	L	92	90	87	22	75	74	73
DuBois	1670	−11	− 5	0	L	89	87	84	24	74	73	71
Erie AP	732	1	7	11	M	88	85	82	18	76	74	73
Franklin	987	− 7	− 1	3	L	88	86	83	24	75	73	72
Harrisburg AP	351	4	9	13	L	92	89	86	21	76	75	74
Johnstown	1214	− 4	1	5	L	91	87	85	23	74	73	72
Lancaster	255	− 3	2	6	L	92	90	87	22	77	76	75
Meadville	1065	− 6	0	4	M	88	86	83	21	75	73	72
Middletown (Olmstead) AFB	306	5	10	14	L	95	92	88	21	77	76	75
New Castle	825	− 7	− 1	4	M	91	89	86	23	75	74	73
Philadelphia AP	114	7	11	15	M	93	90	87	21	78	77	76
Pittsburgh AP	1273	− 1	5	9	M	90	87	85	22	75	74	73
Pittsburgh CO	749r	1	7	11	M	90	88	85	19	75	74	73
Reading CO	226	1	6	9	M	92	90	87	19	77	76	75
Scranton/Wilkes Barre	940	− 3	2	6	L	89	87	84	19	75	74	73
State College	1175	− 3	2	6	L	89	87	84	23	74	73	72
Sunbury	480	− 2	3	7	L	91	89	86	22	76	75	74
Uniontown	1040	− 1	4	8	L	90	88	85	22	75	74	73
Warren	1280	− 8	− 3	1	L	89	87	84	24	75	73	72
West Chester	440	4	9	13	M	92	90	87	20	77	76	75
Williamsport AP	527	− 5	1	5	L	91	89	86	23	76	75	74
York	390	− 1	4	8	L	93	91	88	22	77	76	75

RHODE ISLAND

Station	Elev.	Extremes	99%	97½%	Wind	1%	2½%	5%	Range	1%	2½%	5%
Newport	20	1	5	11	H	86	84	81	16	75	74	73
Providence AP	55	0	6	10	M	89	86	83	19	76	75	74

		WINTER	Dec. – Feb.			SUMMER	June – Sept.				
Station[a]	Elev.[b] Ft.	Median of annual Extremes	99%	97½%	Coincident Wind	Design 1%	Dry Bulb 2½%	5%	Outdoor Daily Range[c]	Design 1%	Wet Bulb 2½%	5%

SOUTH CAROLINA

Anderson	764	13	18	22	L	96	94	91	21	77	76	75
Charleston	41	19	23	27	L	94	92	90	18	81	80	79
Charleston CO	9	23	26	30	L	95	93	90	13	81	80	79
Columbia AP	220	16	20	23	L	98	96	94	22	79	79	78
Florence AP	146	16	21	25	L	96	94	92	21	80	79	78
Georgetown	14	19	23	26	L	93	91	88	18	81	80	79
Greenville AP	957	14	19	23	L	95	93	91	21	77	76	75
Greenwood	671	15	19	23	L	97	95	92	21	78	77	76
Myrtle Beach	25	18	22	25	L	92	89	88	18	81	80	79
Orangeburg	244	17	21	25	L	97	95	92	20	80	79	78
Rock Hill	470	13	17	21	L	97	95	92	20	78	77	76
Spartanburg AP	816	13	18	22	L	95	93	90	20	77	76	75
Sumter - Shaw AFB	291	18	23	26	L	96	94	92	21	80	79	78

SOUTH DAKOTA

Aberdeen AP	1296	−29	−22	−18	L	95	92	89	27	77	75	74
Brookings	1642	−26	−19	−15	M	93	90	87	25	77	75	74
Hot Springs	3535	−20	−12	− 8	M	97	95	91	30	72	70	68
Huron AP	1282	−24	−16	−12	L	97	93	90	28	77	75	74
Lead	5245	−19	−11	− 7	L	89	86	82	28	68	66	64
Lemmon	2596	−27	−19	−15	L	96	92	89	28	73	71	69
Mitchell	1346	−22	−15	−11	M	96	94	91	28	77	76	74
Mobridge	1664	−26	−18	−14	L	97	94	91	28	75	74	72
Pierre AP	1718r	−21	−13	− 9	M	98	96	93	29	76	74	73
Rapid City AP	3168	−17	− 9	− 6	M	96	94	91	28	72	71	69

TABLE 5—Continued   **WINTER AND SUMMER DESIGN DATA BY STATES**

Station[a]	Elev.[b] Ft.	WINTER Dec. – Feb. Median of annual Extremes	99%	97½%	Coincident Wind	SUMMER June – Sept. Design 1%	Dry Bulb 2½%	5%	Outdoor Daily Range[c]	Design 1%	Wet Bulb 2½%	5%
Sioux Falls AP	1427	−21	−14	−10	M	95	92	89	24	77	75	74
Watertown AP	1746	−27	−20	−16	L	93	90	87	26	76	74	73
Winner	1965	−19	−11	− 7	M	98	95	93	28	76	74	73
Yankton	1280	−18	−11	− 7	M	96	94	91	25	78	76	75

TENNESSEE

Station	Elev. Ft.	Median of annual Extremes	99%	97½%	Coincident Wind	Design 1%	Dry Bulb 2½%	5%	Outdoor Daily Range	Design 1%	Wet Bulb 2½%	5%
Athens	940	10	14	18	L	96	94	91	22	77	76	75
Bristol (Tri City) AP	1519	6	11	16	L	92	90	88	22	76	75	74
Chattanooga AP	670	11	15	19	L	97	94	92	22	78	78	77
Clarksville	470	6	12	16	L	98	96	94	21	79	78	77
Columbia	690	8	13	17	L	97	95	93	21	79	78	77
Cookeville	1162	5	11	15	L	96	94	91	22	78	77	76
Dyersburg	334	7	13	17	L	98	96	94	21	80	79	78
Greenville	1320	5	10	14	L	93	91	88	22	76	75	74
Jackson AP	413	8	14	17	L	97	95	94	21	80	79	78
Knoxville AP	974	9	13	17	L	95	92	90	21	77	76	75
Memphis AP	282	11	17	21	L	98	96	94	21	80	79	78
Murfreesboro	608	7	13	17	L	97	94	92	22	79	78	77
Nashville AP	601	6	12	16	L	97	95	92	21	79	78	77
Smyrna (Sewart) AFB	522	6	12	17	L	98	95	93	22	78	77	77
Tullahoma	1075	7	13	17	L	96	94	92	22	79	78	77
Union City	340	6	12	16	L	98	96	94	21	80	79	78

TEXAS

Station	Elev. Ft.	Median of annual Extremes	99%	97½%	Coincident Wind	Design 1%	Dry Bulb 2½%	5%	Outdoor Daily Range	Design 1%	Wet Bulb 2½%	5%
Abilene AP	1759	12	17	21	M	101	99	97	22	76	75	74
Dyess AFB	1777	11	17	21	M	101	99	97	22	75	74	74
Alice AP	180	26	30	34	M	101	99	97	20	81	80	79
Alpine	4433	10	15	19	L	97	94	91	25	68	67	66
Amarillo AP	3604	2	8	12	M	98	96	93	26	72	71	70

TABLE 5—Continued   WINTER AND SUMMER DESIGN DATA BY STATES

Station[a]	Elev.[b] Ft.	WINTER Dec. — Feb. Median of annual Extremes	99%	97½%	Coincident Wind	SUMMER June — Sept. Design 1%	Dry Bulb 2½%	5%	Outdoor Daily Range[c]	Design 1%	Wet Bulb 2½%	5%
Austin AP	597	19	25	29	M	101	98	96	22	79	78	77
Bergstrom AFB	507	20	25	29	M	101	100	98	22	79	78	78
Bay City	52	25	29	33	M	95	93	91	16	81	80	79
Beaumont	18	25	29	33	M	96	94	93	19	81	80	79
Beeville	225	24	28	32	M	99	97	96	18	81	80	79
Big Spring AP	2537	12	18	22	M	100	98	96	26	75	73	72
Brownsville AP	16	32	36	40	M	94	92	91	18	80	80	79
Brownwood	1435	15	20	25	M	102	100	98	22	76	75	74
Bryan AP	275	22	27	31	M	100	98	96	20	79	78	78
Childress	1880	6	13	17	M	103	101	99	26	76	75	74
Corpus Christi AP	44	28	32	36	M	95	93	91	19	81	80	80
Corsicana	425	16	21	25	M	102	100	98	21	79	78	77
Cotulla FAA	425	24	28	32	L	104	102	100	22	80	79	78
Dalhart AP	3989	3	5	9	M	99	97	94	28	71	70	69
Dallas (Love) AP	488	14	19	24	H	101	99	97	20	79	78	78
Del Rio (Laughlin) AFB	1072	24	28	31	M	101	99	98	24	79	77	76
Denton	655	12	18	22	H	102	100	98	22	79	78	77
Eagle Pass	743	23	27	31	L	106	104	102	24	80	79	78
El Paso AP	3916	16	21	25	L	100	98	96	27	70	69	68
Biggs AFB	3923	15	20	24	L	100	98	96	27	70	69	68
Fort Worth AP	706	14	20	24	H	102	100	98	22	79	78	77
Carswell AFB	617	14	20	24	H	103	101	99	22	79	78	77
Galveston AP	5	28	32	36	M	91	89	88	10	82	81	81
Greenville	575	13	19	24	H	101	99	97	21	79	78	78
Harlingen	37	30	34	38	M	96	95	94	19	80	80	79
Houston AP	62	23	28	32	M	96	94	92	18	80	80	79
Houston CO	158r	24	29	33	M	96	94	92	18	80	80	79
Ellington AFB	39	25	30	33	M	96	94	93	18	81	80	80
Huntsville	494	22	27	31	M	99	97	96	20	80	79	78
Junction AP	1705	15	20	24	L	103	101	99	22	76	75	74
Kerrville	1650	15	20	24	L	101	99	97	22	77	76	75
Killeen (Gray) AFB	1021	17	22	26	M	100	99	97	22	78	77	76
Lamesa	2965	7	14	18	M	100	98	96	26	74	73	72
Laredo AFB	503	29	32	36	L	103	101	100	23	79	78	78
Longview	345	16	21	25	M	100	98	96	20	81	80	79
Lubbock AP	3243	4	11	15	M	99	97	94	26	73	72	71
Reese AFB	3340	5	12	17	M	98	96	94	26	73	72	70
Lufkin AP	286	19	24	28	M	98	96	95	20	81	80	79
McAllen	122	30	34	38	M	102	100	98	21	80	79	78
Midland AP	2815r	13	19	23	M	100	98	96	26	74	73	72
Mineral Wells AP	934	12	18	22	H	102	100	98	22	78	77	76
Palestine CO	580	16	21	25	M	99	97	96	20	80	79	78
Pampa	3230	0	7	11	M	100	98	95	26	73	72	71
Pecos	2580	10	15	19	L	102	100	97	27	72	71	70
Plainview	3400	3	10	14	M	100	98	95	26	73	72	71
Port Arthur AP	16	25	29	33	M	94	92	91	19	81	80	80
San Angelo	1919	15	20	25	M	101	99	97	24	76	75	74
San Antonio AP	792	22	25	30	L	99	97	96	19	77	77	76
Kelly AFB	682	24	28	32	L	100	99	97	19	78	78	77
Randolph AFB	743	23	27	32	L	99	98	96	19	78	77	76

Station[a]	Elev.[b] Ft.	WINTER Dec. — Feb. Median of annual Extremes	99%	97½%	Coincident Wind	SUMMER June — Sept. Design 1%	Dry Bulb 2½%	5%	Outdoor Daily Range[c]	Design 1%	Wet Bulb 2½%	5%
Sherman (Perrin) AFB	763	12	18	23	H	101	99	97	22	79	78	77
Snyder	2325	9	15	19	M	102	100	97	26	75	74	73
Temple	675	18	23	27	M	101	99	97	22	79	78	77
Tyler AP	527	15	20	24	M	99	97	96	21	80	79	78
Uvalde	905	20	24	28	L	104	102	99	23	78	77	76
Vernon	1225	7	14	18	H	103	101	99	24	77	76	75
Victoria AP	104	24	28	32	M	98	96	95	18	80	79	79
Waco AP	500	16	21	26	M	101	99	98	22	79	78	78
Connally AFB	475	16	21	26	M	101	100	98	22	79	78	78
Wichita Falls AP	994	9	15	19	H	103	100	98	24	77	76	75

UTAH

Cedar City AP	5660	−10	− 1	6	VL	94	91	89	32	65	64	62
Delta AP	4759	− 9	0	4	VL	97	94	92	34	67	66	65
Dugway Proving Ground	4359	− 9	0	6	VL	99	97	94	34	67	65	64
Logan	4775	− 7	3	7	VL	93	91	89	33	66	65	63
Milford AP	5028	−14	− 5	− 1	VL	97	94	91	37	67	66	64
Moab	3965	2	12	16	VL	100	98	95	30	66	65	64
Ogden	4400	− 3	7	11	VL	94	92	89	33	66	65	64
Hill AFB	4787	− 4	6	10	VL	93	91	89	33	66	65	63
Price	5580	− 7	3	7	L	93	91	88	33	65	64	63
Provo	4470	− 6	2	6	L	96	93	91	32	67	66	65
Richfield	5300	−10	− 1	3	L	94	92	89	34	66	65	64
St. George	2899	13	22	26	VL	104	102	99	33	71	70	69
Salt Lake City AP	4240	− 2	5	9	L	97	94	92	32	67	66	65
Vernal AP	5280	−20	−10	− 6	VL	90	88	84	32	64	63	62
Wendover AP	4239	− 6	3	9	VL	97	95	92	35	67	66	64

TABLE 5—Continued   **WINTER AND SUMMER DESIGN DATA BY STATES**

Station[a]	Elev.[b] Ft.	WINTER Dec. — Feb. Median of annual Extremes	99%	97½%	Coincident Wind	SUMMER June — Sept. Design 1%	Dry 2½%	Bulb 5%	Outdoor Daily Range[c]	Design 1%	Wet 2½%	Bulb 5%

VERMONT

Station	Elev	Med	99%	97½%	Wind	1%	2½%	5%	Range	1%	2½%	5%
Barre	1120	23	−17	−13	L	86	84	81	23	73	72	70
Bennington	670	16	−10	− 6	L	89	87	84	23	75	74	72
Burlington AP	331	18	−12	− 7	M	88	85	83	23	74	73	71
Newport	766	27	−19	−17	L	85	83	80	24	73	72	70
Rutland	620	18	−12	− 8	L	87	85	82	23	74	73	71

VIRGINIA

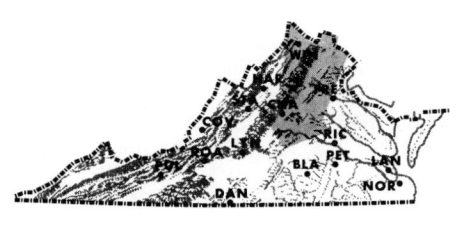

Station	Elev	Med	99%	97½%	Wind	1%	2½%	5%	Range	1%	2½%	5%
Blackstone AP	435	11	15	19	L	95	92	90	20	79	78	77
Charlottsville	870	7	11	15	L	93	90	88	23	79	77	76
Covington	1245	4	9	13	L	92	90	89	23	75	74	73
Danville AP	590	9	13	17	L	95	92	90	21	78	77	76
Fredericksburg	50	6	10	14	M	94	92	89	21	79	78	76
Harrisonburg	1340	0	5	9	L	92	90	87	23	78	77	76
Langley AFB	13	15	19	22	M	94	92	89	18	80	79	78
Lynchburg AP	947	10	15	19	L	94	92	89	21	77	76	75
Norfolk AP	30	18	20	23	M	94	91	89	18	79	78	78
Petersburg	194	10	15	18	L	96	94	91	20	80	79	78
Pulaski	1850	3	8	12	L	92	90	87	23	75	74	73
Richmond AP	162	10	14	18	L	96	93	91	21	79	78	77
Roanoke AP	1176	9	15	18	L	94	91	89	23	76	75	74
Staunton	1480	3	8	12	L	92	90	87	23	78	77	75
Winchester	750	1	6	10	L	94	92	89	21	78	76	75

TABLE 5—Continued   **WINTER AND SUMMER DESIGN DATA BY STATES**

Station[a]	Elev.[b] Ft.	WINTER Dec. – Feb.				SUMMER June – Sept.						
		Median of annual Extremes	99%	97½%	Coincident Wind	Design 1%	Dry Bulb 2½%	5%	Outdoor Daily Range[c]	Design 1%	Wet Bulb 2½%	5%

WASHINGTON

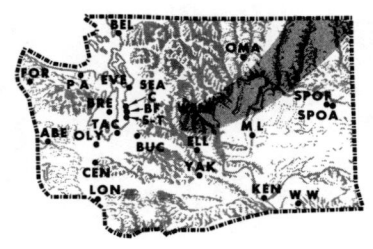
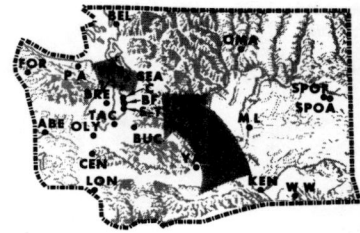

Station	Elev.	Median	99%	97½%	Wind	1%	2½%	5%	Range	1%	2½%	5%
Aberdeen	12	19	24	27	M	83	80	77	16	62	61	60
Bellingham AP	150	8	14	18	L	76	74	71	19	67	65	63
Bremerton	162	17	24	29	L	85	81	77	20	68	66	65
Buckley	685	14	20	24	L	83	81	78	22	67	65	64
Centralia	185	13	19	23	L	88	86	83	30	67	65	64
Ellensburg AP	1729	− 5	2	6	VL	91	89	86	34	67	65	63
Everett (Paine) AFB	598	13	19	24	L	82	78	74	20	67	65	63
Forks	350	17	22	25	M	81	78	74	16	60	59	58
Kennewick	392	4	11	15	VL	98	96	93	30	69	68	66
Longview	12	14	20	24	L	88	86	83	30	68	66	65
Moses Lake (Larson) AFB	1183	−14	− 7	− 1	VL	96	93	90	32	68	66	65
Olympia AP	190	15	21	25	L	85	83	80	32	67	65	63
Omak	1228	−15	− 8	− 4	VL	93	91	87	30	67	65	63
Port Angeles	99	20	26	29	M	75	73	70	18	60	58	57
Seattle (Boeing)	14	17	23	27	L	82	80	77	24	67	65	64
Seattle CO	14	22	28	32	L	81	79	76	19	67	65	64
Seattle/Tacoma AP	383	14	20	24	L	85	81	77	22	66	64	63
Spokane AP	2365	− 5	− 2	4	VL	93	90	87	28	66	64	63
Fairchild AFB	2437	−12	− 5	1	VL	91	88	85	30	65	63	62
Tacoma (McChord) AFB	350	14	20	24	L	85	81	78	22	68	66	64
Walla Walla AP	1185	5	12	16	VL	98	96	93	27	69	68	66
Wenatchee	634	− 2	5	9	VL	95	92	89	32	68	66	64
Yakima AP	1061	− 1	6	10	VL	94	92	89	36	69	67	65

TABLE 5—Continued   **WINTER AND SUMMER DESIGN DATA BY STATES**

Station[a]	Elev.[b] Ft.	WINTER Dec. – Feb.				SUMMER June – Sept.						
		Median of annual Extremes	99%	97½%	Coincident Wind	Design 1%	Dry Bulb 2½%	5%	Outdoor Daily Range[c]	Design 1%	Wet Bulb 2½%	5%

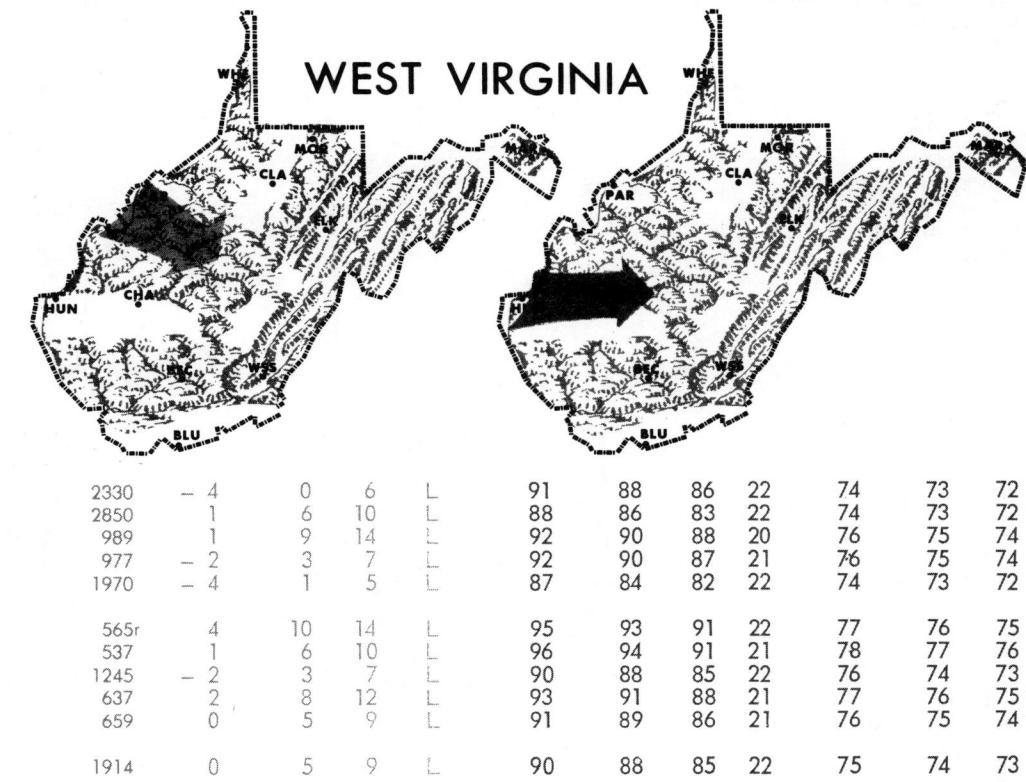

WEST VIRGINIA

Beckley	2330	− 4	0	6	L	91	88	86	22	74	73	72
Bluefield AP	2850	1	6	10	L	88	86	83	22	74	73	72
Charleston AP	989	1	9	14	L	92	90	88	20	76	75	74
Clarksburg	977	− 2	3	7	L	92	90	87	21	76	75	74
Elkins AP	1970	− 4	1	5	L	87	84	82	22	74	73	72
Huntington	565r	4	10	14	L	95	93	91	22	77	76	75
Martinsburg AP	537	1	6	10	L	96	94	91	21	78	77	76
Morgantown AP	1245	− 2	3	7	L	90	88	85	22	76	74	73
Parkersburg	637	2	8	12	L	93	91	88	21	77	76	75
Wheeling	659	0	5	9	L	91	89	86	21	76	75	74
White Sulfur Springs	1914	0	5	9	L	90	88	85	22	75	74	73

WISCONSIN

Appleton	742	−16	−10	− 6	M	89	87	84	23	75	74	72
Ashland	650	−27	−21	−17	L	85	83	80	23	73	71	69
Beloit	780	−13	− 7	− 3	M	92	90	87	24	77	76	75
Eau Claire AP	888	−21	−15	−11	L	90	88	85	23	76	74	72
Fond du Lac	760	−17	−11	− 7	M	89	87	84	23	76	74	73
Green Bay AP	683	−16	−12	− 7	M	88	85	82	23	75	73	72
La Crosse AP	672	−18	−12	− 8	M	90	88	85	22	78	76	75
Madison AP	866	−13	− 9	− 5	M	92	88	85	22	77	75	73
Manitowoc	660	−11	− 5	− 1	M	88	86	83	21	75	74	72
Marinette	605	−14	− 8	− 4	M	88	86	83	20	74	72	70

TABLE 5—Continued   **WINTER AND SUMMER DESIGN DATA BY STATES**

Station[a]	Elev.[b] Ft.	WINTER Dec. – Feb. Median of annual Extremes	99%	97½%	Coincident Wind	SUMMER June – Sept. Design 1%	Dry Bulb 2½%	5%	Outdoor Daily Range[c]	Design 1%	Wet Bulb 2½%	5%
Milwaukee AP	693	−11	− 6	− 2	M	90	87	84	21	77	75	73
Montello	822	−19	−13	− 9	M	89	87	84	23	76	75	73
Prairie du Chien	658	−18	−12	− 8	M	92	90	87	22	78	76	75
Racine	640	−10	− 4	0	M	90	88	85	21	77	75	73
Rhinelander	1560	−27	−21	−17	L	86	84	81	23	74	72	70
Rice Lake	1115	−25	−19	−15	M	88	86	83	23	74	72	70
Sheboygan	648	−10	− 4	0	M	89	87	84	20	76	74	72
Stevens Point	1079	−22	−16	−12	M	89	87	84	23	75	73	71
Waukesha	860	−12	− 6	− 2	M	91	89	86	22	77	75	74
Wausau AP	1196	−24	−18	−14	M	89	86	83	23	74	72	70

WYOMING

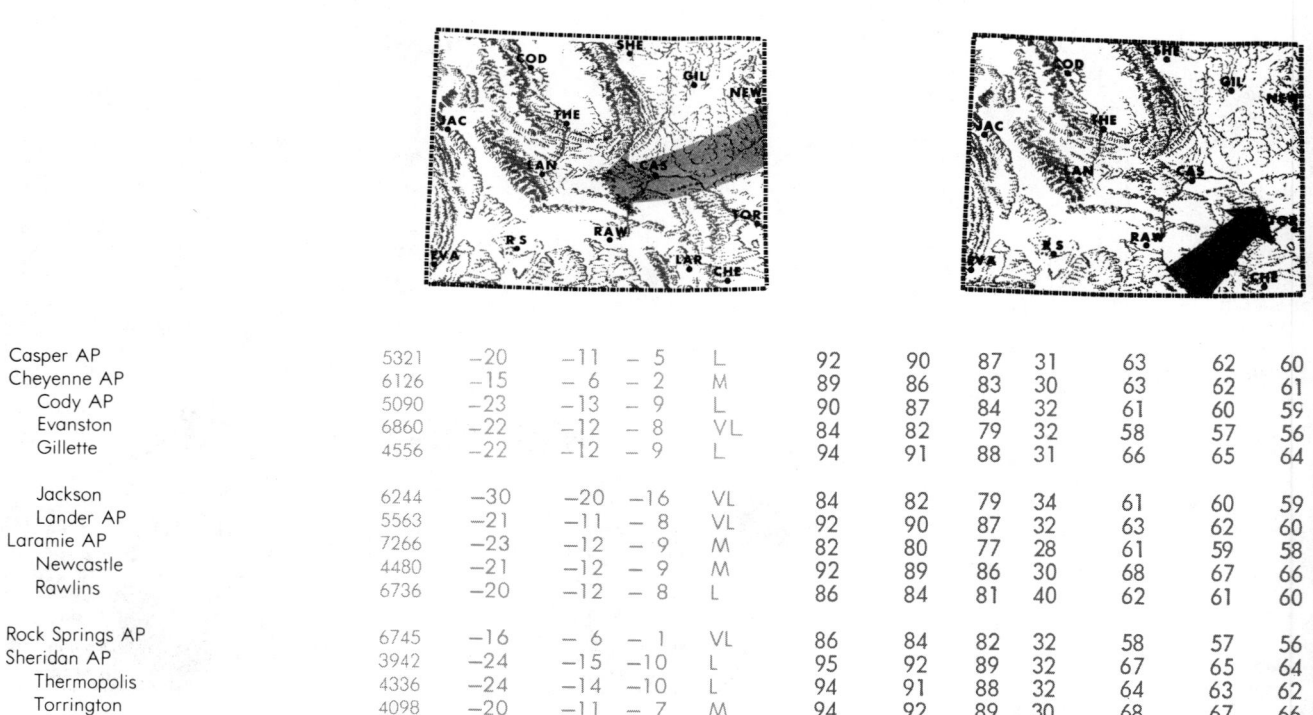

Station[a]	Elev.[b] Ft.	Median of annual Extremes	99%	97½%	Coincident Wind	Design 1%	Dry Bulb 2½%	5%	Outdoor Daily Range[c]	Design 1%	Wet Bulb 2½%	5%
Casper AP	5321	−20	−11	− 5	L	92	90	87	31	63	62	60
Cheyenne AP	6126	−15	− 6	− 2	M	89	86	83	30	63	62	61
Cody AP	5090	−23	−13	− 9	L	90	87	84	32	61	60	59
Evanston	6860	−22	−12	− 8	VL	84	82	79	32	58	57	56
Gillette	4556	−22	−12	− 9	L	94	91	88	31	66	65	64
Jackson	6244	−30	−20	−16	VL	84	82	79	34	61	60	59
Lander AP	5563	−21	−11	− 8	VL	92	90	87	32	63	62	60
Laramie AP	7266	−23	−12	− 9	M	82	80	77	28	61	59	58
Newcastle	4480	−21	−12	− 9	M	92	89	86	30	68	67	66
Rawlins	6736	−20	−12	− 8	L	86	84	81	40	62	61	60
Rock Springs AP	6745	−16	− 6	− 1	VL	86	84	82	32	58	57	56
Sheridan AP	3942	−24	−15	−10	L	95	92	89	32	67	65	64
Thermopolis	4336	−24	−14	−10	L	94	91	88	32	64	63	62
Torrington	4098	−20	−11	− 7	M	94	92	89	30	68	67	66

Part 7 — TWELVE-MONTH DRY BULB TEMPERATURES AND TWELVE-MONTH WET BULB TEMPERATURES VS. RELATIVE HUMIDITY

Section 1: INTRODUCTION

At 91 stations throughout the United States, computer runs have been made to tabulate the relationship of wet bulb temperatures with other weather parameters. These include relative humidity, wind direction, wind speed, and various combinations of visibility and cloud cover.

In the analysis of feasibility for use of various combinations of WET-DRY cooling towers, there is a need for detailed data throughout each month of the year. In special problems in which cooling tower fogging may need to be studied, some frequency of occurrence data are needed. Natural low clouds and/or low visibility often may obscure any view of a cooling tower plume. The frequency of obscuring conditions needs to be studied along with the frequency of high relative humidity which also relates to plumes that are visible in the absence of clouds. Sample data are presented for dry bulb temperatures by months and wet bulb temperatures within eight separate relative humidity ranges.

In this part and other parts which follow, examples will be given of the type of detailed data that have been computed. Some monthly and annual data are presented in this manual for Nashville, Tennessee, and Rock Springs, Wyoming. The data sets for all stations are available through Ecodyne Corporation.

Section 2: MONTHLY DRY BULB TEMPERATURES

The average monthly dry bulb temperatures in degrees Fahrenheit for each month of the year plus the annual average temperature for 91 stations located throughout the United States are presented in Table 6.

At three month intervals, the daily maximum-minimum range in outdoor temperatures is presented in Table 6. For instance, the average monthly dry bulb temperature in July at Birmingham is 80°F. The range between the minimum and maximum is 21°F. An average minimum of 69°F and a maximum of 90°F fits such an average daily range. In October at Birmingham a daily minimum of 50°F and a maximum of 75°F would produce an average monthly temperature of 63°F and an average daily range of 25°F.

The potential for dry surface heat exchange equipment will be directly related to the comparative temperature of the heated surface and the ambient air moving past the cooling device.

Section 3: WET BULB TEMPERATURE VS. RELATIVE HUMIDITY

The efficiency of an evaporative natural draft cooling tower at any time during the year is primarily related to the ambient wet bulb temperature and its coincident relative humidity. The amount of water evaporated to produce a given quantity of cooling with a wet-dry tower is directly related to the ambient wet bulb temperature and the relative humidity. First approximation estimates of cooling tower efficiency and water usage can be developed from sets of data similar to those presented in Tables 7 and 8 for Nashville and Rock Springs. The frequency distribution for January, July, and Annual in 2° intervals of wet bulb vs. 10% ranges of relative humidity above 30% are presented in the three segments of Tables 7 and 8. The relative humidity equal to or less than 30% and all wet bulb temperatures less than 30°F have been consolidated to conserve tabular space.

All data presented in Tables 7 and 8 are still in 10-year total hours. The appropriate average value for an individual month or a single year can be derived by inserting a decimal point immediately before the final digit.

Section 4: SUMMARY DATA ON WET BULB VS. RELATIVE HUMIDITY

For each of 91 stations throughout the United States, detailed tables were developed for monthly and annual data relating wet bulb temperatures to 10% ranges of relative humidity. Two summary-type lines of data from each of the 91 stations are presented in Table 9. The first line at each station contains the distribution for the combinations of wet bulb temperatures within the 10% ranges above 30% relative humidity. All hours when relative humidities were 30% or less are consolidated into the first number of each upper line.

During periods of cold weather operations, cooling tower icing conditions can result in structural failures. All cold weather problems in which cooling tower process water can reach a frozen state are essentially included in all the hours per year when wet bulb temperatures are below 30°F. The typical number of hours when wet bulb temperatures are below 30°F are presented in the second line for each of the 91 stations.

All data appearing in Table 9 have been reduced to annual frequencies.

TABLE 6

AVERAGE MONTHLY DRY BULB TEMPERATURES AND OUTDOOR DAILY RANGE FROM MINIMUM TO MAXIMUM EACH THIRD MONTH IN DEGREES FAHRENHEIT.

Station	Jan	Feb	Mar	Apr	May	Jun	Jul	Aug	Sep	Oct	Nov	Dec	Ann
Birmingham	44	47	53	63	71	77	80	79	74	63	52	45	62
Max-min range	20			24			21			25			22
Mobile	51	54	59	68	75	80	82	82	78	69	59	53	67
	20			20			18			22			20
Phoenix	51	55	60	68	76	85	91	89	84	72	60	53	70
	27			32			27			31			30
Tucson	51	54	58	66	74	82	86	84	80	70	59	52	68
	26			32			24			28			28
Little Rock	40	43	50	62	70	78	81	81	73	62	50	42	61
	21			24			23			27			24
Bakersfield	48	52	57	63	70	77	84	82	77	67	56	48	65
	20			26			30			28			26
Blythe	53	58	63	70	78	85	92	91	85	74	61	53	72
	33			31			25			35			32
Los Angeles	57	58	59	62	65	68	73	74	73	68	63	58	65
	20			18			19			19			19
Sacramento	45	50	53	58	64	71	75	74	72	63	53	46	60
	16			26			35			27			26
San Diego	55	57	58	61	63	66	70	71	66	61	58	63	55
	19			14			11			16			15
Akron	26	30	35	47	56	66	73	72	62	51	37	29	49
	27			26			29			29			28
Denver	30	33	37	48	57	66	73	72	63	52	39	33	50
	28			27			28			30			28
Grand Junction	27	34	41	52	62	71	79	75	67	55	40	30	53
	20			26			29			26			25
Windsor Locks	25	27	36	48	56	68	73	70	63	53	41	28	49
	17			22			22			23			20
Dover	35	37	44	55	64	73	77	75	70	59	48	37	56
	20			21			19			20			19
Washington, D.C.	36	37	45	56	66	75	79	77	71	60	48	37	57
	16			21			19			20			19
Jacksonville	55	56	61	68	74	79	81	81	78	71	61	55	68
	20			22			18			17			19
Miami	67	68	71	75	78	81	82	83	82	78	72	68	76
	17			16			13			14			15
Tampa	60	62	66	72	77	81	82	82	81	75	67	62	72
	21			20			16			18			19
Atlanta	42	45	51	61	69	76	78	78	72	62	51	44	61
	18			20			18			19			19
Savannah	50	52	58	66	73	79	81	81	76	67	57	50	66
	22			24			20			22			22
Boise	29	36	41	49	57	65	75	72	63	52	40	32	50
	15			25			32			25			24
Chicago	24	27	37	50	60	71	75	74	66	55	40	29	51
	15			19			19			19			17
Rockford	20	24	34	48	59	69	73	72	63	53	38	25	48
	17			22			22			23			22
Evansville	33	36	44	57	66	75	78	76	69	58	45	35	56
	18			22			22			26			45
Des Moines	19	24	34	50	61	71	75	73	64	54	38	25	49
	16			21			20			21			19
Dodge City	31	35	41	54	64	74	79	78	69	58	43	33	55
	24			25			24			26			25
Wichita	31	36	44	57	66	76	81	80	71	60	45	35	57
	20			23			22			23			22
Louisville	33	36	44	56	65	73	77	76	69	58	45	36	56
	17			22			22			24			21
Baton Rouge	51	54	60	68	75	80	82	82	78	69	59	53	67
	21			21			18			24			20
Lake Charles	52	55	60	69	75	81	82	82	78	70	60	54	68
	19			18			18			23			19
Shreveport	47	51	57	66	73	80	83	83	77	68	56	49	66
	19			21			21			24			21
Boston	29	30	38	49	59	68	73	71	65	55	45	33	51
	13			15			16			16			15
Detroit	25	27	35	48	58	68	72	71	64	53	40	29	49
	15			21			22			22			19
Grand Rapids	23	25	33	47	57	67	72	70	62	52	39	27	49
	14			22			22			22			19
Sault St. Marie	14	15	24	38	49	59	64	63	55	46	33	20	40
	16			18			23			17			18
Minneapolis	12	17	28	45	57	67	72	70	60	50	32	19	44
	18			21			21			21			19
Jackson	47	50	56	66	73	79	82	81	76	66	55	49	65
	22			25			22			28			24
Kansas City	28	33	41	55	65	74	79	77	69	59	44	32	55
	17			20			18			21			19
St. Louis	31	35	43	57	66	75	79	77	70	59	45	35	56
	17			21			21			24			21
Springfield	33	37	44	57	65	74	78	77	69	59	46	36	56
	20			23			23			24			22
Great Falls	21	27	31	43	53	61	69	67	57	48	35	27	45
	18			22			29			22			22
Miles City	15	22	30	45	56	65	74	73	60	49	32	22	45
	21			25			29			27			25
North Platte	23	28	34	48	58	68	74	73	62	51	36	27	49
	27			27			27			32			27
Omaha	23	28	37	52	63	72	77	76	66	56	40	28	52
	20			24			23			26			23
Las Vegas	44	49	55	64	73	82	90	87	80	67	53	45	66
	23			28			29			28			27
Winnemucca	28	34	38	45	54	62	71	68	59	48	37	30	48
	25			28			40			30			31
Atlantic City	33	34	41	52	62	70	75	73	67	57	46	35	54
	17			21			19			22			20
Albuquerque	35	40	46	56	65	75	79	77	70	58	45	36	57
	23			29			27			27			27
Farmington	29	35	41	50	60	68	75	73	65	53	39	30	51
	29			28			36			44			35
Albany	22	24	33	47	58	68	72	70	62	51	40	26	48
	18			22			24			23			21
Buffalo	24	24	32	45	55	66	70	68	62	52	40	28	47
	12			17			19			18			16
Charlotte	42	44	51	61	69	76	79	78	72	62	51	43	61
	20			24			20			23			21
Raleigh	41	42	49	60	67	74	78	77	71	60	50	41	59
	21			26			24			24			23
Bismarck	8	14	25	43	54	64	71	69	58	47	29	16	41
	22			24			27			27			24
Fargo	6	11	24	42	55	65	71	69	58	47	29	13	41
	19			21			24			23			21
Cincinnati (Covington)	31	33	42	54	63	72	76	74	68	57	44	34	54
	17			22			22			24			21
Cleveland	27	28	36	48	58	68	71	70	64	54	42	30	50
	13			20			20			20			18
Columbus	28	30	39	51	61	70	74	72	65	54	42	31	52
	16			23			23			24			21
Oklahoma City	37	41	48	60	68	77	82	81	73	62	49	40	60
	22			23			22			24			22
Tulsa	37	41	48	61	69	77	83	81	73	63	49	40	60
	21			22			21			24			22
Portland	38	43	46	51	57	62	67	67	62	54	45	41	53
	11			20			24			18			18
Harrisburg	30	32	41	53	63	72	76	74	67	56	44	33	53
	15			23			21			21			20
Philadelphia	32	34	42	53	63	72	77	75	68	57	46	35	55
	16			21			20			21			19
Pittsburgh	31	32	40	53	62	71	75	73	67	56	44	33	53
	14			20			22			21			18
Columbia	45	48	54	64	72	79	81	80	75	64	54	46	64
	23			26			22			26			24
Rapid City	22	26	31	45	55	64	73	72	61	50	35	27	47
	25			25			28			27			25
Sioux Falls	14	19	30	46	58	68	73	72	61	50	33	20	45
	21			23			24			25			22
Knoxville	41	43	50	60	68	76	78	77	72	61	49	42	60
	17			23			20			22			20
Memphis	41	44	51	63	71	79	82	80	74	63	51	43	62
	18			20			20			24			20
Nashville	38	41	49	60	69	77	80	79	72	61	48	40	59
	19			23			21			25			21
Amarillo	36	40	46	57	66	75	79	78	70	60	46	39	57
	27			29			26			27			27
Corpus Christi	56	60	65	73	78	82	85	85	81	74	65	59	72
	20			19			19			20			20
Dallas	45	49	55	65	73	81	85	85	78	68	56	48	66
	22			22			22			22			22
El Paso	44	48	55	64	72	80	82	81	74	64	52	44	63
	27			29			25			29			27
Houston	52	55	61	69	76	81	83	83	79	71	61	55	69
	21			20			20			25			22
San Angelo	46	50	57	67	75	82	85	85	77	67	56	48	66
	26			26			25			25			25
Bryce Canyon	24	23	29	38	46	54	62	60	53	43	31	22	40
	31			26			34			36			32
Cedar City	29	33	38	47	56	65	73	71	63	52	39	31	50
	26			22			32			33			28
Salt Lake City	28	33	40	49	58	66	77	75	65	52	39	30	51
	19			25			32			28			26
Norfolk	41	41	48	58	67	75	78	77	72	62	52	42	59
	17			20			17			17			17
Roanoke	36	38	45	56	64	72	75	74	68	58	47	37	56
	18			24			22			24			22
Seattle	40	44	46	50	56	61	66	65	61	54	46	42	53
	10			17			20			15			15
Spokane	25	32	38	46	55	62	70	68	60	48	36	29	47
	12			22			29			21			20
Charleston	35	37	45	56	65	72	75	74	68	57	45	36	55
	18			24			24			24			22
LaCrosse	16	20	31	48	59	69	73	71	62	52	35	22	46
	18			20			21			20			19
Madison	17	20	30	45	56	66	70	69	60	50	35	22	45
	17			21			23			22			20
Milwaukee	19	23	31	45	54	65	70	69	61	51	37	24	46
	16			20			21			21			19
Casper	23	27	31	43	53	62	71	70	59	48	34	26	45
	21			28			32			28			28
Rock Springs	19	23	29	40	50	59	68	66	56	45	31	23	43
	21			25			31			33			27

TABLE 7 EXAMPLES OF JANUARY AND JULY FREQUENCY ARRAYS OF WET BULB TEMPERATURES VS. RELATIVE HUMIDITY. PLUS THE ANNUAL SUMMARY FOR ALL 12 MONTHS, FOR NASHVILLE, TENNESSEE.

WET BULB TEMPERATURE VS. RELATIVE HUMIDITY

STATION #13897 — NASHVILLE, TN — JAN — PERIOD OF RECORD 48-57

WET BULB TEMPS C	F	R.H.% ≤30	31-40	41-50	51-60	61-70	71-80	81-90	91-100	TOTAL
20.0/20.6	68/69	0	0	0	0	1	0	0	0	1
18.9/19.5	66/67	0	0	0	3	5	3	1	0	12
17.8/18.4	64/65	0	0	0	1	8	20	21	5	55
16.7/17.3	62/63	0	0	3	2	21	52	37	19	134
15.6/16.2	60/61	0	0	0	1	13	47	84	46	191
14.5/15.0	58/59	0	0	0	11	18	24	51	72	176
13.4/13.9	56/57	0	1	3	9	20	48	60	87	228
12.3/12.8	54/55	0	1	4	2	34	50	46	102	239
11.2/11.7	52/53	0	1	6	12	16	43	75	99	252
10.0/10.6	50/51	0	0	11	13	27	40	39	104	234
8.9/9.5	48/49	0	10	13	18	13	27	37	89	207
7.8/8.4	46/47	0	9	30	13	14	27	33	91	217
6.7/7.3	44/45	1	10	39	33	27	32	33	114	289
5.6/6.2	42/43	1	18	44	52	41	28	30	94	308
4.5/5.0	40/41	3	11	42	59	51	42	61	124	393
3.4/3.9	38/39	6	29	49	72	61	51	58	167	493
2.3/2.8	36/37	3	27	56	66	76	75	74	162	539
1.2/1.7	34/35	0	14	60	76	80	94	78	147	549
0.1/0.6	32/33	0	9	26	70	62	121	135	138	561
-1.1/-0.5	30/31	0	3	19	29	65	112	126	100	454
<-1.1	<30	0	5	79	207	372	552	500	193	1908
TOTAL		14	148	484	749	1025	1488	1579	1953	7440

STATION #13897 — NASHVILLE, TN — JUL — PERIOD OF RECORD 48-57

WET BULB TEMPS C	F	R.H.% ≤30	31-40	41-50	51-60	61-70	71-80	81-90	91-100	TOTAL
27.8/28.4	82/83	0	0	0	1	0	0	0	0	1
26.7/27.3	80/81	0	2	4	8	2	2	1	0	19
25.6/26.2	78/79	0	15	46	102	54	26	11	0	254
24.5/25.0	76/77	0	33	189	276	204	134	77	14	927
23.4/23.9	74/75	16	88	189	277	284	325	307	173	1659
22.3/22.8	72/73	6	84	134	142	187	258	407	386	1604
21.2/21.7	70/71	19	43	72	81	105	168	279	398	1165
20.0/20.6	68/69	22	50	82	66	71	92	145	185	713
18.9/19.5	66/67	23	36	62	37	51	64	65	59	397
17.8/18.4	64/65	10	44	29	50	46	61	57	29	326
16.7/17.3	62/63	2	24	30	16	39	26	47	14	198
15.6/16.2	60/61	0	3	6	8	17	33	30	20	117
14.5/15.0	58/59	0	0	0	2	6	11	26	4	49
13.4/13.9	56/57	0	90	0	0	0	3	4	2	9
12.3/12.8	54/55	0	0	0	0	0	2	0	0	2
TOTAL		98	422	843	1066	1066	1205	1456	1284	7440

STATION #13897 — NASHVILLE, TN — ANNUAL — PERIOD OF RECORD 48-57

WET BULB TEMPS C	F	R.H.% ≤30	31-40	41-50	51-60	61-70	71-80	81-90	91-100	TOTAL
27.8/28.4	82/83	0	0	0	1	0	0	0	0	1
26.7/27.3	80/81	0	2	13	22	9	5	1	0	52
25.6/26.2	78/79	0	27	122	229	126	72	21	0	597
24.5/25.0	76/77	3	91	402	585	476	303	164	41	2065
23.4/23.9	74/75	29	231	548	774	766	757	631	342	4078
22.3/22.8	72/73	34	287	509	594	710	855	1073	842	4904
21.2/21.7	70/71	67	271	524	598	668	774	1048	1193	5143
20.0/20.6	68/69	95	384	552	616	582	702	823	982	4736
18.9/19.5	66/67	94	318	467	499	554	652	763	745	4092
17.8/18.4	64/65	87	351	484	498	598	780	892	929	4619
16.7/17.3	62/63	105	286	367	427	528	716	819	754	4002
15.6/16.2	60/61	93	295	361	377	544	668	875	832	4045
14.5/15.0	58/59	66	218	271	372	467	529	711	841	3475
13.4/13.9	56/57	89	202	286	330	465	496	689	836	3393
12.3/12.8	54/55	76	256	322	313	431	524	569	738	3229
11.2/11.7	52/53	73	298	310	269	358	413	567	603	2891
10.0/10.6	50/51	70	250	342	314	333	434	537	659	2939
8.9/9.5	48/49	103	276	347	356	350	361	400	633	2826
7.8/8.4	46/47	97	268	383	360	334	375	390	566	2773
6.7/7.3	44/45	94	258	383	398	405	399	392	647	2976
5.6/6.2	42/43	67	284	363	416	399	361	423	686	2999
4.5/5.0	40/41	45	200	374	428	438	423	450	639	2997
3.4/3.9	38/39	17	172	281	460	467	426	479	599	2901
2.3/2.8	36/37	16	133	260	393	462	446	491	564	2765
1.2/1.7	34/35	12	94	247	335	429	486	498	564	2665
0.1/0.6	32/33	11	40	183	337	364	557	566	455	2513
-1.1/-0.5	30/31	1	15	75	216	361	458	508	349	1983
<-1.1	<30	0	25	207	640	1273	1725	1573	563	6006
		1444	5532	8983	1157	12897	14697	16353	16602	87665

WET BULB TEMPERATURE VS. RELATIVE HUMIDITY

STATION #24027 — ROCK SPRINGS, WY — JAN — PERIOD OF RECORD 49-58

WET BULB TEMPS C	F	≤30	31-40	41-50	51-60	61-70	71-80	81-90	91-100	TOTAL
3.4/ 3.9	38/39	0	0	3	17	2	2	0	0	24
2.3/ 2.8	36/37	0	2	1	14	17	17	7	0	58
1.2/ 1.7	34/35	3	6	14	27	44	33	31	15	173
0.1/ 0.6	32/33	4	10	24	34	64	77	53	42	308
−1.1/−0.5	30/31	4	8	38	41	66	73	51	37	318
<−1.1	<30	20	48	253	796	1571	2256	1310	304	6558
TOTAL		31	74	333	929	1764	2458	1452	398	7439

STATION #24027 — ROCK SPRINGS, WY — JUL — PERIOD OF RECORD 49-58

WET BULB TEMPS C	F	≤30	31-40	41-50	51-60	61-70	71-80	81-90	91-100	TOTAL
17.8/18.4	64/65	0	0	0	0	0	0	0	1	1
16.7/17.3	62/63	0	0	1	0	1	0	0	0	2
15.6/16.2	60/61	27	18	11	6	5	4	3	0	74
14.5/15.0	58/59	133	102	49	49	34	11	11	1	390
13.4/13.9	56/57	303	150	99	89	70	42	23	4	780
12.3/12.8	54/55	589	178	122	113	87	74	60	11	1234
11.2/11.7	52/53	657	148	124	114	75	61	33	6	1218
10.0/10.6	50/51	588	173	153	106	92	43	24	3	1182
8.9/ 9.5	48/49	399	116	100	72	55	58	20	3	823
7.8/ 8.4	46/47	288	131	51	62	45	34	26	2	639
6.7/ 7.3	44/45	214	138	59	26	18	20	12	2	489
5.6/ 6.2	42/43	117	84	38	11	7	27	11	4	299
4.5/ 5.0	40/41	89	38	29	10	4	5	7	5	187
3.4/ 3.9	38/39	35	15	3	6	5	1	3	2	70
2.3/ 2.8	36/37	16	5	2	2	2	2	0	0	29
1.2/ 1.7	34/35	7	5	1	0	0	0	0	0	13
TOTAL		3462	1301	842	666	500	382	233	44	7430

STATION #24027 — ROCK SPRINGS, WY — ANNUAL — PERIOD OF RECORD 49-58

WET BULB TEMPS C	F	≤30	31-40	41-50	51-60	61-70	71-80	81-90	91-100	TOTAL
18.9/19.5	66/67	0	0	1	0	0	0	0	0	1
17.8/18.4	64/65	0	1	0	0	0	0	0	1	2
16.7/17.3	62/63	0	1	3	3	3	0	0	0	10
15.6/16.2	60/61	38	29	25	10	6	6	7	0	121
14.5/15.0	58/59	254	155	88	82	59	19	20	10	687
13.4/13.9	56/57	609	282	187	161	117	64	46	13	1479
12.3/12.8	54/55	1220	406	295	240	169	124	99	20	2573
11.2/11.7	52/53	1805	479	369	299	212	175	92	21	3452
10.0/10.6	50/51	2340	571	481	349	288	182	91	12	4314
8.9/ 9.5	48/49	2271	627	499	367	281	258	124	37	4464
7.8/ 8.4	46/47	2012	745	496	397	300	229	186	79	4444
6.7/ 7.3	44/45	1924	781	539	358	261	286	206	89	4444
5.6/ 6.2	42/43	1659	767	501	321	273	319	258	95	4193
4.5/ 5.0	40/41	1460	750	568	365	272	262	252	142	4071
3.4/ 3.9	38/39	1076	748	501	449	410	280	287	168	3919
2.3/ 2.8	36/37	927	705	589	507	436	340	302	173	3979
1.2/ 1.7	34/35	675	647	699	603	552	451	364	240	4231
0.1/ 0.6	32/33	520	530	744	675	752	631	573	468	4893
−1.1/−0.5	30/31	301	447	642	756	890	689	614	416	4755
<−1.1	<30	413	1024	2161	4406	6771	8842	6285	1690	31592
		19504	9695	9388	10348	12052	13157	9806	3674	87624

TABLE 9 WET BULB VS. RELATIVE HUMIDITY
Within 10% ranges above 30% relative humidity and total hours when wet bulb temperatures are below 30°F.

Station		Below 30% RH	31-40	41-50	51-60	61-70	71-80	81-90	91-100	Total HRS/YR.
Birmingham, AL	Total hrs/yr.	342	665	940	1050	1155	1368	1834	1406	8760
	Hrs. < 30°F. WB	4	18	35	51	62	65	80	28	343
Mobile, AL	Total hrs/yr.	194	393	615	880	1143	1307	1720	2508	8760
	Hrs. < 30°F. WB	2	6	17	27	21	16	8	1	98
Phoenix, AZ	Total hrs/yr.	3144	1665	1367	923	619	445	370	227	8760
	Hrs. < 30°F. WB	2	8	17	12	11	8	9	2	69
Tucson, AZ	Total hrs/yr.	4434	1340	932	712	514	390	324	114	8760
	Hrs. < 30°F. WB	23	24	25	23	13	12	12	0	132
Little Rock, AR	Total hrs/yr.	259	613	992	1239	1407	1470	1543	1237	8760
	Hrs. < 30°F. WB	4	22	52	79	89	66	54	13	379.
Bakersfield, CA	Total hrs/yr.	1655	1375	1352	1182	919	774	800	703	8760
	Hrs. < 30°F. WB	0	1	2	5	7	10	13	5	43
Blythe, CA	Total hrs/yr.	5196	1449	905	527	296	187	123	74	8760
	Hrs. < 30°F. WB	40	18	10	7	3	0	0	0	68
Los Angeles AP, CA	Total hrs/yr.	408	299	429	841	1532	1813	2491	947	8760
	Hrs. < 30°F. WB	1	2	1	0	0	0	0	0	4
Sacramento, CA	Total hrs/yr.	724	795	952	1028	1105	1279	1597	1280	8760
	Hrs. < 30°F. WB	2	2	7	4	8	12	22	10	67
San Diego, CA	Total hrs/yr.	308	279	429	1014	1848	2114	2209	559	8760
	Hrs. < 30°F. WB	–	1	1	0	0	0	0	0	2
Akron, OH	Total hrs/yr.	921	917	1034	1131	1261	1271	1282	943	8760
	Hrs. < 30°F. WB	19	61	147	280	448	592	541	234	2322
Denver, CO	Total hrs/yr.	2475	1247	1190	1070	916	848	709	305	8760
	Hrs. < 30°F. WB	142	198	306	342	343	365	316	74	2086
Grand Junction, CO	Total hrs/yr.	2852	1224	1015	946	914	822	612	375	8760
	Hrs. < 30°F. WB	56	98	199	332	419	387	245	122	1858
Windsor Locks, CT	Total hrs/yr.	212	554	929	1218	1292	1257	1457	1841	8760
	Hrs. < 30°F. WB	31	90	222	363	351	272	212	107	1648
Dover, DE	Total hrs/yr.	38	255	722	1157	1433	1570	1747	1838	8760
	Hrs. < 30°F. WB	3	23	94	217	238	186	101	42	904
Washington, D.C.	Total hrs/yr.	287	775	1264	1445	1336	1231	1336	1086	8760
	Hrs. < 30°F. WB	17	107	214	224	138	82	53	17	852
Jacksonville, FL	Total hrs/yr.	218	375	715	1032	1144	1392	2087	1797	8760
	Hrs. < 30°F. WB	1	5	8	9	9	7	4	0	43
Miami, FL	Total hrs/yr.	33	96	412	1211	1734	1976	2094	1204	8760
	Hrs. < 30°F. WB	0	0	0	0	0	0	1	0	1
Tampa, FL	Total hrs/yr.	118	240	608	1056	1223	1440	2101	1974	8760
	Hrs. < 30°F. WB	0	1	1	1	1	0	1	0	5
Atlanta, GA	Total hrs/yr.	322	660	988	1199	1254	1301	1334	1702	8760
	Hrs. < 30°F. WB	6	28	56	73	78	51	15	2	309
Savannah, GA	Total hrs/yr.	179	397	667	985	1173	1295	1866	2198	8760
	Hrs. < 30°F. WB	2	8	14	29	41	31	33	7	165
Boise, ID	Total hrs/yr.	1240	1200	1174	1141	1125	1106	1076	698	8760
	Hrs. < 30°F. WB	2	11	50	130	253	380	382	178	1386
Chicago-Midway, IL	Total hrs/yr.	193	534	932	1353	1713	1780	1513	742	8760
	Hrs. < 30°F. WB	7	32	119	302	483	500	259	40	1742
Rockford, IL	Total hrs/yr.	133	399	700	1007	1427	1717	2081	1296	8760
	Hrs. < 30°F. WB	0	8	66	225	491	627	637	208	2262
Evansville, IN	Total hrs/yr.	156	506	848	1103	1323	1505	1761	1558	8760
	Hrs. < 30°F. WB	0	10	45	124	210	258	231	71	949
Des Moines, IA	Total hrs/yr.	213	441	742	1095	1410	1689	1770	1400	8760
	Hrs. < 30°F. WB	0	11	64	208	406	568	577	327	2161
Dodge City, KS	Total hrs/yr.	1042	1017	1130	1176	1167	1158	1091	979	8760
	Hrs. < 30°F. WB	14	47	123	216	287	352	319	190	1548
Wichita, KS	Total hrs/yr.	525	745	1034	1194	1323	1416	1486	1037	8760
	Hrs. < 30°F. WB	11	47	107	167	238	315	297	152	1334
Louisville, KY	Total hrs/yr.	197	574	913	1181	1391	1567	1669	1268	8760
	Hrs. < 30°F. WB	1	14	64	151	242	254	160	31	917
Baton Rouge, LA	Total hrs/yr.	203	427	710	1043	1130	1275	1860	2112	8760
	Hrs. < 30°F. WB	0	3	8	16	17	19	15	3	81

Station		Below 30% RH	31-40	41-50	51-60	61-70	71-80	81-90	91-100	Total HRS/YR.
Lake Charles, LA	Total hrs/yr.	151	327	622	941	1099	1211	1900	2509	8760
	Hrs. < 30°F. WB	0	1	5	8	12	9	7	5	47
Shreveport, LA	Total hrs/yr.	206	537	938	1138	1269	1357	1754	1561	8760
	Hrs. < 30°F. WB	1	8	20	28	31	31	32	10	161
Boston, MD	Total hrs/yr.	251	701	1160	1442	1410	1231	1288	1277	8760
	Hrs. < 30°F. WB	51	208	364	393	256	139	97	52	1560
Detroit, MI	Total hrs/yr.	128	448	859	1237	1735	1891	1564	898	8760
	Hrs. < 30°F. WB	1	14	89	274	542	567	294	58	1839
Grand Rapids, MI	Total hrs/yr.	152	387	691	933	1291	1721	2022	1563	8760
	Hrs. < 30°F. WB	0	2	24	128	361	622	682	251	2070
Sault Ste. Marie, MI	Total hrs/yr.	48	152	373	685	1149	1707	2361	2285	8760
	Hrs. < 30°F. WB	1	8	43	149	406	781	1116	380	2884
Minneapolis, MN	Total hrs/yr.	189	452	844	1244	1609	1745	1690	987	8760
	Hrs. < 30°F. WB	2	31	167	409	645	709	579	211	2753
Jackson, MS	Total hrs/yr.	303	594	871	1073	1195	1339	1681	1704	8760
	Hrs. < 30°F. WB	2	8	24	38	52	44	35	15	218
Kansas City, MO	Total hrs/yr.	452	801	1184	1477	1556	1413	1170	707	8760
	Hrs. < 30°F. WB	1	22	110	254	348	324	204	54	1317
St. Louis, MO	Total hrs/yr.	220	625	1042	1423	1615	1602	1400	833	8760
	Hrs. < 30°F. WB	3	36	118	259	338	336	209	68	136
Springfield, MO	Total hrs/yr.	210	563	889	1190	1330	1378	1492	1708	8760
	Hrs. < 30°F. WB	1	9	45	130	216	267	276	189	1133
Great Falls, MT	Total hrs/yr.	1281	1120	1335	1422	1205	996	808	593	8760
	Hrs. < 30°F. WB	16	66	194	416	499	552	461	232	2436
Miles City, MT	Total hrs/yr.	905	878	978	1135	1292	1396	1371	805	8760
	Hrs. < 30°F. WB	6	19	90	242	479	732	736	307	2611
North Platte, NB	Total hrs/yr.	548	710	910	1093	1260	1465	1670	1104	8760
	Hrs. < 30°F. WB	3	20	84	222	413	622	714	250	2328
Omaha, NB	Total hrs/yr.	307	603	937	1264	1546	1648	1569	886	8760
	Hrs. < 30°F. WB	2	23	98	246	438	543	437	143	1930
Las Vegas, NV	Total hrs/yr.	5723	1076	735	471	309	227	156	63	8760
	Hrs. < 30°F. WB	128	97	88	64	39	30	15	1	462
Winnemucca, NV	Total hrs/yr.	2581	1098	993	890	873	893	864	568	8760
	Hrs. < 30°F. WB	51	114	157	200	292	416	448	200	1878
Atlantic City, NJ	Total hrs/yr.	84	311	633	993	1306	1488	1771	2174	8760
	Hrs. < 30°F. WB	6	34	92	178	213	195	133	41	892
Albuquerque, NM	Total hrs/yr.	3324	1508	1267	1034	756	462	267	142	8760
	Hrs. < 30°F. WB	106	179	263	283	199	110	43	15	1198
Farmington, NM	Total hrs/yr.	2391	1280	1171	1059	934	818	693	414	8760
	Hrs. < 30°F. WB	35	78	152	268	333	398	304	110	1678
Albany, NY	Total hrs/yr.	133	431	799	1189	1451	1574	1681	1502	8760
	Hrs. < 30°F. WB	3	34	156	336	463	445	385	130	195.
Buffalo, NY	Total hrs/yr.	64	326	632	1092	1639	1934	1842	1231	8760
	Hrs. < 30°F. WB	1	6	48	187	473	601	431	104	1851
Charlotte, NC	Total hrs/yr.	312	722	1079	1203	1227	1187	1327	1703	8760
	Hrs. < 30°F. WB	5	30	81	106	100	65	43	11	441
Raleigh, NC	Total hrs/yr.	277	626	962	1113	1168	1185	1388	2041	8760
	Hrs. < 30°F. WB	8	36	92	120	128	99	74	29	586
Bismarck, ND	Total hrs/yr.	334	550	723	922	1328	2000	1977	926	8760
	Hrs. < 30°F. WB	1	7	39	146	509	1167	994	266	3129
Fargo, ND	Total hrs/yr.	281	472	687	986	1584	2033	1811	906	8760
	Hrs. < 30°F. WB	2	10	56	256	773	1111	797	153	3158
Cincinnati, OH (Covington)	Total hrs/yr.	236	558	915	1224	1460	1548	1561	1258	8760
	Hrs. < 30°F. WB	1	11	62	184	333	356	250	51	1248
Cleveland, OH	Total hrs/yr.	105	382	754	1140	1514	1770	1845	1250	8760
	Hrs. < 30°F. WB	1	4	29	143	361	491	432	127	1588
Columbus, OH	Total hrs/yr.	107	412	784	1094	1439	1701	1889	1334	8760
	Hrs. < 30°F. WB	0	2	30	144	351	440	339	67	1373
Oklahoma City, OK	Total hrs/yr.	440	680	989	1172	1267	1384	1506	1322	8760
	Hrs. < 30°F. WB	13	39	67	107	155	182	200	118	881

Station		Below 30% RH	31-40	41-50	51-60	61-70	71-80	81-90	91-100	Total HRS/YR.
Tulsa, OK	Total hrs/yr.	469	794	1102	1286	1388	1396	1289	1036	8760
	Hrs. < 30°F. WB	3	21	64	117	161	160	154	68	748
Portland, OR	Total hrs/yr.	127	262	575	829	1152	1614	2398	1803	8760
	Hrs. < 30°F. WB	2	8	26	46	50	57	75	39	303
Harrisburg, PA	Total hrs/yr.	285	750	1271	1461	1316	1223	1402	1052	8760
	Hrs. < 30°F. WB	40	154	335	317	196	126	96	21	1285
Philadelphia, PA	Total hrs/yr.	199	668	1159	1361	1350	1300	1406	1317	8760
	Hrs. < 30°F. WB	19	107	235	275	189	98	55	17	995
Pittsburgh, PA	Total hrs/yr.	163	508	964	1247	1506	1684	1732	956	8760
	Hrs. < 30°F. WB	2	29	117	253	413	452	229	28	1523
Columbia, SC	Total hrs/yr.	361	696	953	982	1042	1153	1560	2013	8760
	Hrs. < 30°F. WB	4	16	29	37	40	44	83	43	296
Rapid City, SD	Total hrs/yr.	951	973	1163	1314	1365	1342	1193	459	8760
	Hrs. < 30°F. WB	10	44	147	326	507	640	635	166	2475
Sioux Falls, SD	Total hrs/yr.	400	637	924	1220	1553	1780	1579	667	8760
	Hrs. < 30°F. WB	11	56	174	383	649	835	584	86	2778
Knoxville, TN	Total hrs/yr.	183	563	959	1237	1355	1525	1564	1374	8760
	Hrs. < 30°F. WB	3	14	49	93	139	148	97	18	561
Memphis, TN	Total hrs/yr.	218	606	996	1212	1383	1529	1633	1183	8760
	Hrs. < 30°F. WB	2	18	51	90	89	101	83	15	449
Nashville, TN	Total hrs/yr.	144	553	898	1114	1288	1468	1635	1660	8760
	Hrs. < 30°F. WB	0	2	21	64	127	173	157	56	600
Amarillo, TX	Total hrs/yr.	1713	1227	1221	1104	997	898	854	746	8760
	Hrs. < 30°F. WB	43	100	150	167	199	211	188	94	1152
Corpus Christi, TX	Total hrs/yr.	147	245	480	962	1240	1398	2068	2220	8760
	Hrs. < 30°F. WB	1	3	3	5	6	4	4	2	28
Dallas, TX	Total hrs/yr.	506	906	1245	1370	1395	1279	1177	882	8760
	Hrs. < 30°F. WB	2	10	29	51	54	52	42	17	257
El Paso, TX	Total hrs/yr.	3792	1660	1211	834	544	377	252	90	8760
	Hrs. < 30°F. WB	49	84	92	81	47	32	28	8	421
Houston, TX	Total hrs/yr.	193	367	655	996	1165	1261	1957	2166	8760
	Hrs. < 30°F. WB	2	3	10	10	8	8	8	4	53
San Angelo, TX	Total hrs/yr.	1534	1274	1250	1179	1080	1002	848	593	8760
	Hrs. < 30°F. WB	11	33	53	60	53	57	31	25	323
Bryce Canyon, UT	Total hrs/yr.	1319	898	941	1110	1176	1321	1319	676	8760
	Hrs. < 30°F. WB	35	101	230	428	580	867	879	305	3425
Cedar City, UT	Total hrs/yr.	2633	1185	1065	984	883	841	749	420	8760
	Hrs. < 30°F. WB	45	86	155	269	356	458	409	155	1933
Salt Lake City, UT	Total hrs/yr.	1579	1092	1162	1176	1102	1058	1061	530	8760
	Hrs. < 30°F. WB	5	20	58	151	272	390	468	186	1550
Norfolk, VA	Total hrs/yr.	88	360	812	1223	1346	1478	1827	1626	8760
	Hrs. < 30°F. WB	4	22	69	101	79	62	50	12	399
Roanoke, VA	Total hrs/yr.	428	737	1143	1386	1274	1154	1275	1363	8760
	Hrs. < 30°F. WB	18	60	169	234	166	105	68	27	847
Seattle, WA	Total hrs/yr.	76	241	520	780	1017	1377	2168	2581	8760
	Hrs. < 30°F. WB	1	8	21	40	57	60	74	60	321
Spokane, WA	Total hrs/yr.	880	857	947	991	1083	1241	1620	1141	8760
	Hrs. < 30°F. WB	3	15	46	105	218	386	558	233	1564
Charleston, WV	Total hrs/yr.	334	644	962	1118	1235	1285	1530	1652	8760
	Hrs. < 30°F. WB	12	39	97	162	226	244	166	47	993
La Crosse, WI	Total hrs/yr.	139	432	859	1220	1609	1788	1591	1122	8760
	Hrs. < 30°F. WB	11	18	128	336	595	743	539	163	2533
Madison, WI	Total hrs/yr.	136	445	821	1113	1524	1812	1758	1151	8760
	Hrs. < 30°F. WB	4	44	162	352	588	673	448	110	2381
Milwaukee, WI	Total hrs/yr.	99	280	677	1171	1692	1936	1715	1190	8760
	Hrs. < 30°F. WB	2	26	124	352	599	608	343	69	2123
Casper, WY	Total hrs/yr.	1798	1054	1164	1250	1160	933	880	521	8760
	Hrs. < 30°F. WB	30	109	271	477	556	486	507	216	2652
Rock Springs, WY	Total hrs/yr.	1950	969	939	1035	1205	1315	980	367	8760
	Hrs. < 30°F. WB	41	102	216	441	677	884	629	169	3159

Section 1:   STATION EXAMPLES

The annual distribution — which has been derived from tabulations of monthly data — of wet bulb temperatures by 2° intervals vs. four separate ranges of relative humidity and five wind speed ranges at Nashville and Rock Springs is presented in Tables 10 and 11. The data have been reduced to annual frequency from the original ten-year sample of data. (The annual totals which exceed slightly the annual total of 8760 hours are partly the result of some additional hours from February 29 in leap years.)

In Table 10 for Nashville, the distribution of wet bulb frequency by 2° intervals extends from 6° and 7°F through 82° and 83°F. All hours when the wet bulb temperatures were equal to or colder than 5°F have been consolidated. However, in Nashville the annual frequency is only seven hours per year in that category. At Rock Springs there are 263 hours in the average year when wet bulb temperatures are 5°F or colder. (See Table 11.)

Section 2:   WET BULB FREQUENCIES BELOW 32°F

In the tables developed to show the array of wet bulb temperatures vs. wind speeds and relative humidity, hourly frequencies were developed for temperature ranges below 32°F down through 6°F in 2° intervals with a consolidation of all hours equal to or below 5°F. In the operation of cooling tower equipment in cold climates, maintenance engineers can apply operational procedures which prevent cooling tower "freeze up." In Table 12 the pattern of hourly frequencies per year of wet bulb temperatures occurring below 32°F is presented for 91 stations. It is easy to see that stations in most southern states have very few hours of freezing conditions. Many northern stations have several hundred hours per year when wet bulb temperatures are colder than 32°F.

For extremely cold temperatures — those colder than 5°F — there is essentially no spread betwen wet bulb and dry bulb temperatures. Therefore, for a distribution of temperature frequencies below 5°F, any available data sets of dry bulb temperatures can be effectively used as if they were also the true array of wet bulb frequencies.

STATION: 13897
NASHVILLE, TN.

WET BULB TEMPERATURE, WIND SPEED AND RELATIVE HUMIDITY
PERIOD OF RECORD 1948-1957

WIND SPEED		0-4 M.P.H.					5-10 M.P.H.				
R.H. (%)		≤70	71 80	81 90	91 100	TOT	≤70	71 80	81 90	91 100	TOT
WET BULB TEMPERATURE											
C	F										
.>28.3	>83										
27.8/28.3	82/83						+				+
26.7/27.2	80/81	+	+	+		1	3	+			3
25.6/26.1	78/79	10	2	1		14	30	5	1		36
24.4/25.0	76/77	32	13	10	2	57	85	15	5	2	107
23.3/23.9	74/75	58	26	33	23	139	127	41	27	11	207
22.2/22.8	72/73	59	33	51	56	198	116	41	51	27	234
21.1/21.7	70/71	61	29	46	70	205	107	38	53	46	243
20.0/20.6	68/69	60	28	35	53	177	115	31	38	41	225
18.9/19.4	66/67	56	26	35	41	157	91	28	33	28	180
17.8/18.3	64/65	60	28	41	49	178	99	34	35	35	202
16.7/17.2	62/63	44	25	34	38	141	82	27	29	27	166
15.6/16.1	60/61	41	21	33	35	129	76	26	34	37	172
14.4/15.0	58/59	36	17	29	36	119	63	20	24	36	144
13.3/13.9	56/57	36	15	23	32	106	59	20	27	35	141
12.2/12.8	54/55	34	18	20	26	98	56	19	24	33	132
11.1/11.7	52/53	28	12	23	24	87	58	17	21	27	123
10.0/10.6	50/51	27	14	22	26	89	60	19	20	30	129
8.9/9.4	48/49	31	11	13	22	77	66	15	18	29	128
7.8/8.3	46/47	30	11	14	21	76	65	16	16	25	121
6.7/7.2	44/45	29	15	17	24	84	75	18	14	26	133
5.6/6.1	42/43	29	12	19	27	88	75	15	15	28	133
4.4/5.0	40/41	32	13	18	23	86	75	18	16	28	137
3.3/3.9	38/39	26	12	19	20	77	70	18	17	26	130
2.2/2.8	36/37	24	13	19	15	71	64	20	19	24	126
1.1/1.7	34/35	21	15	16	22	73	56	21	20	19	117
0.0/0.6	32/33	20	16	20	15	72	49	28	24	16	117
−1.1/−0.6	30/31	13	13	20	20	66	36	21	20	8	84
−2.2/−1.7	28/29	9	17	20	12	58	25	21	18	4	69
−3.3/−2.8	26/27	9	7	14	11	40	22	16	14	4	55
−4.4/−3.9	24/25	9	8	13	5	34	17	13	12	3	45
−5.6/−5.0	22/23	5	8	8	5	25	8	8	6	2	25
−6.7/−6.1	20/21	2	3	7	2	13	7	4	4	1	15
−7.8/−7.2	18/19	2	2	6	1	11	4	2	3	+	9
−8.9/−8.3	16/17	2	2	2	+	6	6	2	2		10
−10.0/−9.4	14/15	1	2	2		6	4	2	1	+	7
−11.1/−10.6	12/13	1	1	1	+	3	3	1	+		4
−12.2/−11.7	10/11	1	1	1		3	1	2	+		3
−13.3/−12.8	8/9	1	1	1		3	2	2			3
−14.4/−13.9	6/7	1	1			1	1				1
<−15.0	<5	2	2	1		5	1	+			1
TOTAL		939	490	687	755	2871	1956	643	660	657	3917

NOTE: OCCURRENCES ARE FOR THE AVERAGE YEAR (TOTALS DIVIDED BY NUMBER OF YEARS). VALUES ARE ROUNDED TO THE NEAREST WHOLE, BUT NOT ADJUSTED TO MAKE THEIR SUMS EXACTLY EQUAL TO COLUMN OR ROW TOTALS.   + INDICATES MORE THAN 0 BUT LESS THAN 0.5

RANGES OF WIND SPEED AND RELATIVE HUMIDITY AT NASHVILLE, TENNESSEE

WET BULB TEMPERATURE, WIND SPEED AND RELATIVE HUMIDITY
PERIOD OF RECORD 1948-1957

STATION: 13897
NASHVILLE, TN.

11-16 M.P.H.					17-22 M.P.H.					≥ 23 M.P.H.					ANNUAL
≤70	71 80	81 90	91 100	TOT	≤70	71 80	81 90	91 100	TOT	≤70	71 80	81 90	91 100	TOT	TOTAL
															+
2				2	+				+						5
10	+			10	1				1						60
34	2	+	+	37	4	1	+		5	+				+	207
43	8	2	1	53	7	1	+		8	1	+			1	408
33	10	5	2	49	5	2	1		8	1		+	+	1	490
38	10	6	3	57	7	1	+	1	8	1	+	+	+	1	514
40	9	7	4	60	6	2	1	1	10	2	+	+		2	474
35	9	7	5	55	10	3	1	1	15	1	+		+	2	409
35	12	11	7	65	7	3	3	2	16	1	1	+	+	2	462
35	15	14	8	72	8	5	4	2	19	2	1	+	+	4	400
37	14	17	9	77	11	5	4	3	22	1	1	1	+	4	405
30	10	12	9	61	9	5	6	3	22	2	1	+	1	3	348
30	12	15	13	69	11	3	4	3	20	1	1	+	1	3	339
37	11	9	12	68	11	3	3	3	20	2	1	1	+	5	323
34	9	10	7	60	10	3	3	2	16	1	+	1	1	2	289
35	9	9	7	60	9	2	2	2	14	1	+	1	+	2	294
35	8	8	9	60	10	2	1	2	15	2	1	+	+	3	283
39	8	7	9	62	10	2	2	2	16	2	+	+	+	3	277
37	6	7	11	61	12	2	2	3	18	1	+	+	1	2	298
37	7	6	10	59	10	3	2	2	17	2	+	+	1	3	300
31	9	8	10	58	9	2	2	3	15	3	+	1	1	4	300
33	8	10	12	63	10	3	2	2	17	2	1	+	+	3	290
29	9	8	14	60	9	3	3	3	17	1	+	+	1	2	277
26	10	9	11	56	8	2	4	4	18	1	+	1	1	3	267
18	8	8	11	45	6	3	4	4	17	+	+	+	+	1	251
14	9	8	5	36	3	3	3	2	11	+	+	+	+	1	198
14	12	6	3	34	3	3	2	+	8	+	1	+		1	170
9	6	3	2	20	3	3	1	+	7	+		+		1	123
7	5	3	1	17	2	1	1	+	4	+	+	+		1	100
5	4	1	+	10	1	1	+	+	2	+	1			1	62
3	3	1	+	7	2	1	+		3	1	+			1	38
4	2	1		6	2	+			3	+	+			1	30
3	1	1	+	4	2	1	+		3						23
3	1	+		5	1	+	+		1	+				+	19
1	1	+		2	+	+	+		1		1			+	10
1	+			1	+	+	+		+						8
+	+	+		1	+	+	+		1						8
+				+											2
1				1	+				+						7
856	255	219	192	1521	217	70	61	48	396	34	11	9	8	61	8767

NOTE: OCCURRENCES ARE FOR THE AVERAGE YEAR (TOTALS DIVIDED BY NUMBER OF YEARS). VALUES ARE ROUNDED TO THE NEAREST WHOLE, BUT NOT ADJUSTED TO MAKE THEIR SUMS EXACTLY EQUAL TO COLUMN OR ROW TOTALS. + INDICATES MORE THAN 0 BUT LESS THAN 0.5

TABLE 11

EXAMPLES OF ANNUAL ARRAYS OF WET BULB TEMPERATURES WITH VARIOUS

STATION: 24027
ROCK SPRINGS, WY.

WET BULB TEMPERATURE, WIND SPEED AND RELATIVE HUMIDITY
PERIOD OF RECORD 1949-1958

WIND SPEED		0-4 M.P.H.					5-10 M.P.H.				
R.H. (%)		≤70	71 80	81 90	91 100	TOT	≤70	71 80	81 90	91 100	TOT
WET BULB TEMPERATURE											
C	F										
>28.3	>83										
27.8/28.3	82/83										
26.7/27.2	80/81										
25.6/26.1	78/79										
24.4/25.0	76/77										
23.3/23.9	74/75										
22.2/22.8	72/73										
21.1/21.7	70/71										
20.0/20.6	68/69										
18.9/19.4	66/67	+				+					
17.8/18.3	64/65									+	+
16.7/17.2	62/63						+				+
15.6/16.1	60/61	+				+	4	+	+		5
14.4/15.0	58/59	8	+	+	+	8	27	1	1	1	30
13.3/13.9	56/57	16	1	1	+	17	53	3	2	1	59
12.2/12.8	54/55	26	2	2	+	30	86	6	4	1	98
11.1/11.7	52/53	32	3	1	1	37	114	10	4	1	129
10.0/10.6	50/51	42	5	1	+	49	139	9	5	1	153
8.9/9.4	48/49	47	5	2	1	56	137	12	5	1	155
7.8/8.3	46/47	51	3	3	2	59	151	10	9	4	174
6.7/7.2	44/45	51	4	3	1	60	148	13	9	4	175
5.6/6.1	42/43	50	3	3	3	58	132	14	11	4	161
4.4/5.0	40/41	47	2	3	2	54	125	12	12	7	155
3.3/3.9	38/39	44	3	4	3	54	109	13	12	6	140
2.2/2.8	36/37	43	3	6	3	55	105	11	11	5	132
1.1/1.7	34/35	43	5	4	4	56	99	11	10	9	129
0.0/0.6	32/33	43	6	7	6	61	92	15	15	13	135
−1.1/−0.6	30/31	39	7	8	5	59	86	17	15	16	133
−2.2/−1.7	28/29	35	8	7	4	54	73	20	19	11	123
−3.3/−2.8	26/27	31	10	7	5	52	66	19	18	13	115
−4.4/−3.9	24/25	25	12	9	3	49	55	22	20	10	107
−5.6/−5.0	22/23	22	11	9	4	46	42	20	22	7	90
−6.7/−6.1	20/21	18	10	11	3	43	37	19	18	8	81
−7.8/−7.2	18/19	15	10	10	3	38	26	18	21	5	70
−8.9/−8.3	16/17	14	9	9	2	33	28	16	12	5	60
−10.0/−9.4	14/15	11	10	7	2	31	20	16	11	2	48
−11.1/−10.6	12/13	12	8	6	1	27	16	15	10	1	42
−12.2/−11.7	10/11	7	7	6	1	21	15	13	8	1	37
−13.3/−12.8	8/9	8	7	6	1	22	12	11	8	+	31
−14.4/−13.9	6/7	5	5	3	1	14	10	9	5	+	25
≤−15.0	≤5	18	33	14	3	67	28	43	15	2	88
	TOTAL	802	194	152	61	1210	2033	397	312	137	2878

NOTE: OCCURRENCES ARE FOR THE AVERAGE YEAR (TOTALS DIVIDED BY NUMBER OF YEARS). VALUES ARE ROUNDED TO THE NEAREST WHOLE, BUT NOT ADJUSTED TO MAKE THEIR SUMS EXACTLY EQUAL TO COLUMN OR ROW TOTALS.   + INDICATES MORE THAN 0 BUT LESS THAN 0.5

RANGES OF WIND SPEED AND RELATIVE HUMIDITY AT ROCK SPRINGS, WYOMING

WET BULB TEMPERATURE, WIND SPEED AND RELATIVE HUMIDITY

PERIOD OF RECORD 1949-1958

STATION: 24027
ROCK SPRINGS, WY.

11-16 M.P.H.					17-22 M.P.H.					≥ 23 M.P.H.					ANNUAL
≤70	71 80	81 90	91 100	TOT	≤70	71 80	81 90	91 100	TOT	≤70	71 80	81 90	91 100	TOT	TOTAL
															+
+				+											+
1				1	+				+						1
4	+	+		4	2	+			2	1				1	12
15	+	+		16	9	+	+		9	6	+	+		6	69
39	1	1	+	42	19	1	1		21	9	+			9	148
64	3	3	+	70	38	1	1	+	39	20	+			20	257
84	3	3	1	90	51	2	1	+	54	35	1			36	345
104	3	2	+	109	65	1	1	+	67	54	+	+	+	55	431
103	7	4	1	115	66	2	1	+	69	51	1	+	+	53	446
99	7	5	2	114	55	1	1	+	58	39	1	+	+	40	444
89	7	6	3	105	56	3	2	1	61	42	1	+	+	44	444
77	9	9	3	97	49	4	2	+	56	44	2	1	+	48	419
79	7	7	4	97	45	3	2	1	51	45	3	1	1	49	407
71	7	8	5	89	46	3	4	2	55	49	3	2	1	54	392
71	9	6	6	92	48	5	4	2	59	50	6	3	2	60	398
66	12	9	6	93	52	9	7	3	70	57	9	7	3	75	423
72	14	14	14	114	55	12	11	8	86	60	17	11	6	94	489
72	15	16	11	114	49	12	11	6	77	57	18	12	4	92	476
57	18	16	7	97	45	14	13	5	76	46	17	15	4	81	430
56	22	14	7	98	39	17	12	2	70	39	19	12	5	75	410
48	15	17	6	86	32	17	14	3	66	32	16	11	3	62	370
36	17	17	5	75	27	14	14	4	59	29	15	10	2	55	325
27	17	15	5	63	22	16	13	2	52	25	15	13	3	56	295
22	14	18	3	56	17	11	14	1	42	19	14	10	2	45	252
19	16	12	2	49	18	14	8	1	40	15	8	5	+	28	211
15	13	9	1	38	13	12	4	+	30	11	11	5	+	26	173
12	11	7	1	30	9	11	4	+	24	8	9	4	+	22	145
10	10	6	1	26	6	9	3		18	6	8	3		17	117
7	9	4	+	21	4	5	2	+	11	4	6	2	1	13	98
5	6	4		15	4	4	1	+	9	4	4	2	1	10	72
22	23	5	+	50	12	12	2		26	14	17	2		33	263
1443	294	236	91	2064	950	214	149	41	1354	871	218	131	36	1256	8762

NOTE: OCCURRENCES ARE FOR THE AVERAGE YEAR (TOTALS DIVIDED BY NUMBER OF YEARS). VALUES ARE ROUNDED TO THE NEAREST WHOLE, BUT NOT ADJUSTED TO MAKE THEIR SUMS EXACTLY EQUAL TO COLUMN OR ROW TOTALS.   + INDICATES MORE THAN 0 BUT LESS THAN 0.5

TABLE 12 ANNUAL NUMBER OF HOURS WITH WET BULB TEMPERATURES BELOW 32°

WET BULB TEMPERATURES IN 2°F INTERVALS

Station	≤5°F	6/7	8/9	10/11	12/13	14/15	16/17	18/19	20/21	22/23	24/25	26/27	28/29	30/31
Birmingham, AL	1	2	2	2	2	4	9	16	27	38	55	73	112	152
Mobile, AL				+	1	1	1	2	5	9	19	26	34	50
Phoenix, AZ							+	1	2	3	11	19	32	52
Tucson, AZ						+	1	2	5	12	22	35	56	95
Little Rock, AR	1	+	1	2	4	10	12	16	23	37	69	85	119	170
Bakersfield, CA										2	6	12	24	48
Blythe, CA									2	4	11	21	40	65
Los Angeles, CA											+	1	3	8
Sacramento, CA								+	1	3	6	17	40	69
San Diego, CA												+	1	3
Akron, CO	196	50	58	78	97	120	119	148	203	241	318	334	359	381
Denver, CO	98	35	40	51	70	86	112	145	178	224	291	357	401	438
Grand Junction, CO	46	21	28	40	58	89	99	122	172	219	280	305	346	392
Windsor Locks, CT	61	24	34	52	57	79	97	117	151	192	228	253	305	322
Dover, DE	2	2	6	10	19	38	44	64	84	104	151	194	221	289
Washington, D.C.	1	2	7	12	13	25	36	61	82	98	140	161	214	304
Jacksonville, FL								1	2	3	6	11	20	29
Miami, FL														+
Tampa, FL											1	2	3	7
Atlanta, GA	1	1	2	2	5	7	8	12	17	32	53	69	100	142
Savannah, GA					1	1	2	4	11	20	33	41	54	78
Boise, ID	56	16	20	29	33	50	71	78	115	149	208	255	308	420
Chicago-Midway, IL	124	38	43	47	58	80	97	122	145	182	236	261	310	364
Rockford, IL	348	71	72	80	90	114	126	130	159	220	263	276	312	318
Evansville, IN	15	9	14	19	20	24	40	50	67	101	153	194	245	281
Des Moines, IA	337	63	76	98	104	119	119	140	174	183	217	243	289	321
Dodge City, KS	56	24	42	44	54	73	90	108	135	170	219	243	292	343
Wichita, KS	54	27	30	47	58	63	84	98	113	141	173	213	235	288
Louisville, KY	14	9	14	18	20	31	45	48	70	93	142	175	238	270
Baton Rouge, LA					+	1	1	2	3	5	14	19	35	54
Lake Charles, LA					+	1	2	1	2	2	7	12	21	34
Shreveport, LA	1	+	+	2	1	3	3	5	12	17	25	35	59	93
Boston, MA	40	26	36	48	62	86	99	122	143	181	216	256	246	291
Detroit, MI	33	24	34	48	68	91	112	138	163	202	274	314	339	357
Grand Rapids, MI	51	28	41	58	80	101	123	157	193	243	289	328	378	380
Sault Ste. Marie, MI	393	105	126	145	168	179	179	205	220	249	301	297	319	370
Minneapolis, MN	586	107	119	132	142	155	158	163	186	207	247	261	292	298
Jackson, MS	1	1	1	1	1	1	3	8	17	25	39	54	68	104
Kansas City, MO	41	22	31	46	59	72	71	91	127	134	166	201	259	289
St. Louis, MO	75	27	35	50	62	62	74	81	104	138	187	216	258	314
Springfield, MO	27	11	16	25	28	39	52	79	102	121	180	201	252	305
Great Falls, MT	526	57	61	71	73	97	98	127	167	217	271	314	359	418
Miles City, MT	583	73	93	103	108	140	138	151	177	197	249	276	325	358
North Platte, NB	231	64	77	85	92	119	140	171	204	242	291	291	323	360
Omaha, NB	204	60	68	77	102	107	114	138	157	177	208	242	277	313

+ Indicates more than 0 but less than 0.5

TABLE 12—Continued

WET BULB TEMPERATURES IN 2°F INTERVALS

Station	≤5°F	6/7	8/9	10/11	12/13	14/15	16/17	18/19	20/21	22/23	24/25	26/27	28/29	30/31
Las Vegas, NV				+	1	2	6	13	26	43	76	125	170	249
Winnemucca, NV	82	44	50	58	76	95	111	124	153	177	221	288	347	425
Atlantic City, NJ	4	7	9	14	22	32	41	56	85	113	136	157	202	260
Albuquerque, NM	5	3	5	12	19	35	47	66	101	142	211	241	313	386
Farmington, NM	27	13	22	30	42	61	69	102	127	169	228	252	283	314
Albany, NY	136	42	54	69	92	109	120	142	173	200	250	274	293	329
Buffalo, NY	42	27	43	61	68	85	123	157	192	211	240	279	323	333
Charlotte, NC	+	1	1	2	4	7	12	15	27	45	71	112	144	181
Raleigh, NC		1	1	3	8	10	16	29	44	61	115	140	158	194
Bismarck, ND	974	118	134	153	142	157	146	158	190	205	235	241	277	315
Fargo, ND	1015	113	129	137	144	162	159	179	191	197	239	250	246	272
Cincinnati, OH (Covington)	29	17	22	24	33	42	52	72	105	142	201	232	277	313
Cleveland, OH	36	14	24	37	49	72	88	105	144	194	236	271	319	350
Columbus, OH	37	14	23	32	42	62	66	90	120	147	218	236	287	351
Oklahoma City, OK	18	8	17	21	25	33	47	63	76	100	129	162	185	232
Tulsa, OK	6	6	7	14	16	23	35	53	70	88	109	138	182	220
Portland, OR	2	1	4	6	6	11	16	22	31	34	44	51	75	116
Harrisburg, PA	7	8	14	20	32	49	69	81	114	148	201	243	299	345
Philadelphia, PA	2	5	7	10	23	37	48	67	81	117	159	192	250	302
Pittsburgh, PA	30	16	27	38	54	75	79	109	139	179	226	262	290	339
Columbia, SC	+	+	+	1	1	4	8	13	20	27	47	71	103	144
Rapid City, SD	304	77	92	109	113	131	130	160	205	217	283	312	344	372
Sioux Falls, SD	527	100	106	118	127	149	177	201	212	223	265	270	305	326
Knoxville, TN	4	2	4	7	7	12	16	24	45	56	83	125	176	230
Memphis, TN	1	3	3	5	5	10	13	20	38	46	73	100	132	184
Nashville, TN	7	2	8	8	10	19	23	30	38	62	100	123	170	198
Amarillo, TX	14	9	15	26	33	43	60	75	99	128	175	220	255	341
Corpus Christi, TX							+	1	2	4	9	6	7	15
Dallas, TX	1	1	1	1	3	9	10	11	16	23	43	61	79	122
El Paso, TX		+	+	2	3	6	9	15	28	45	80	98	135	198
Houston, TX					1	1	1	2	2	4	10	14	18	28
San Angelo, TX	1	1	2	2	5	9	7	13	25	36	49	70	92	144
Bryce Canyon, UT	381	79	114	128	149	196	202	250	310	357	411	406	443	483
Cedar City, UT	106	31	36	56	63	88	95	123	168	208	278	322	360	423
Salt Lake City, UT	51	21	28	38	50	60	73	96	126	178	231	277	324	377
Norfolk, VA					+	1	8	17	32	44	64	99	134	188
Roanoke, VA	1	3	5	10	13	24	29	49	68	99	134	186	227	313
Seattle, WA	1	1	3	6	8	13	16	23	26	34	46	52	93	166
Spokane, WA	134	29	34	36	44	50	62	72	95	153	216	280	358	463
Charleston, WV	11	10	12	18	26	34	48	62	84	114	158	189	220	265
La Crosse, WI	359	69	92	102	110	129	121	139	192	204	241	224	256	290
Madison, WI	274	73	79	93	105	130	138	171	206	224	278	295	316	370
Milwaukee, WI	184	52	62	72	85	105	128	161	168	202	241	320	344	400
Casper, WY	204	48	65	85	101	130	160	195	238	295	355	381	396	449
Rock Springs, WY	263	72	98	117	145	173	211	252	295	325	370	410	430	476

+ Indicates more than 0 but less than 0.5

Section 1: **EXAMPLES OF WIND DIRECTION VS. HIGH RELATIVE HUMIDITIES**

Wind speeds and wind direction often play an important part in the development of appropriate tower orientation as they relate to either recirculation or cooling tower plume problems. The peak frequency of wind direction coincident with relative humidity in the range between 85% and 100% at Nashville fits the two directions of south and south-southeast. With the exception of calm conditions, which account for 12.2% of all hours, only those two directions show a frequency of more than 9%.

The data presented in Table 13 remain in ten-year total numbers rather than in annual averages. At Nashville there is an average of 2656 hours per year when the relative humidity is 85% or higher. By contrast, at Rock Springs there are only 862 hours per year, slightly less than 10% of all hours, when relative humidities are 85% or higher.

The three most frequent wind directions with high relative humidities at Rock Springs are west, west-southwest, and southwest.

Section 2: **SUMMARY DATA ON WIND DIRECTION VS. HIGH RELATIVE HUMIDITY**

Detailed tabulations of monthly data for wind directions in three ranges, 70-84%, 85-100% and equal to or above 93%, have been tabulated for 91 stations throughout the United States. Only the frequencies by 16 points of the compass and for calm conditions when relative humidities were 85% to 100% are presented in Table 14. The directions which have frequency of occurrence levels of 99% or more have been emphasized in Table 14. The selection of 9% as a threshold level of importance is based on a total distribution for 16 direction ranges plus the fact that for some few hours the wind direction is measured as calm. If 96% of all hours are scattered within 16 points of the compass, totally random frequency would produce 6% within each direction range. Any direction range which has a 9% or greater frequency would therefore represent a frequency level which is 50% greater than random chance.

The lower line in each of the three sections of data in Table 14 indicates the percentage fraction of all hours in the year which experienced relative humidity measurements of 85% or greater. It is easy to note a sharp contrast between Tucson and Little Rock. Only 3% of all hours per year have relative humidities equal to or greater than 85% at Tucson, whereas 25% of all hours have relative humidity measurements in that same high range at Little Rock.

Although the emphasized wind directions in Table 14 can be used in planning for recirculation problems, they have limited use as related to fogging problems. Most fogging problems are unique to a particular geographic location and very few of the worst fogging problems are found in the immediate vicinity of the airports from which data were taken to prepare Table 14. Detailed meteorological measurements from very near the site are required when fogging problems are to be evaluated appropriately.

See Part 4 for winds related to highest summer wet bulb temperatures.

TABLE 13
EXAMPLES OF WIND DIRECTION AND
WIND SPEED RANGES FOR ALL HOURS WITH RELATIVE HUMIDITY
BETWEEN 85% AND 100% AT NASHVILLE AND ROCK SPRINGS

NASHVILLE, TN.
STATION 13897

85-100% RH

ANNUAL
PERIOD OF RECORD 1948-1957

MO	CODE	DIR	0-4	5-7	8-10	11-13	14-16	17-19	20-22	23-25	26&GR	TOTAL	PERCENT	AVG SPEED
AN	2	N	515	531	395	177	106	31	7	1	1	1764	6.6	7.0
		NNE	278	282	178	54	23	2				817	3.1	8.0
		NE	411	249	111	32	15	3	1	1		823	3.1	4.9
		ENE	317	153	57	9	3		1			540	2.0	4.2
		E	737	214	56	12		1	1			1021	3.8	3.4
		ESE	764	281	91	18	14	4	2	1		1175	4.4	3.9
		SE	1037	569	254	90	57	21	8	3	1	2040	7.7	5.1
		SSE	818	671	543	279	219	94	35	11	6	2676	10.1	7.0
		S	1241	1045	505	207	148	59	23	8		3236	12.2	6.1
		SSW	363	362	229	113	74	27	9	1		1178	4.4	6.9
		SW	446	301	171	59	40	5	9			1031	3.9	5.7
		WSW	340	245	136	59	62	14	9	3	2	870	3.3	6.4
		W	388	340	242	78	56	39	9	2	6	1160	4.4	6.8
		WNW	214	257	232	149	127	77	49	29	15	1149	4.3	9.8
		NW	459	534	465	304	251	131	81	25	10	2260	8.5	9.2
		NNW	328	449	349	203	170	59	14	6	1	1579	5.9	8.3
		CALM	3240									3240	12.2	
		TOTAL	11896	6483	4014	1843	1365	567	258	91	42	26559	100.0	5.8
		PERCENT	44.8	24.4	15.1	6.9	5.1	2.1	1.0	.3	.2		100.0	

TABLE 13—Continued

MO	CODE	DIR	0-4	5-7	8-10	11-13	14-16	17-19	20-22	23-25	26&GR	TOTAL	PERCENT	AVG SPEED
AN	2	N	41	54	27	18	11	4	3		3	161	1.9	7.8
		NNE	25	45	23	11	12	10	11	4	10	151	1.8	11.1
		NE	56	75	72	59	70	28	38	27	93	518	6.0	15.9
		ENE	24	73	114	92	102	55	50	40	91	641	7.4	15.8
		E	36	99	152	119	67	16	8	3	7	507	5.9	10.5
		ESE	17	47	36	17	11	4	1			133	1.5	8.3
		SE	12	60	41	26	10	2	1	1		153	1.8	8.5
		SSE	17	53	54	32	18	4	7	5		190	2.2	9.7
		S	35	111	95	48	25	5	9	3	1	332	3.9	8.9
		SSW	29	103	91	46	36	5	9	6	5	330	3.8	9.7
		SW	62	205	313	227	170	79	55	30	15	1156	13.4	11.4
		WSW	41	192	303	255	308	181	229	152	182	1843	21.4	15.7
		W	42	133	153	100	122	96	138	93	171	1048	12.2	16.7
		WNW	30	66	57	42	32	26	25	13	19	310	3.6	12.4
		NW	29	53	33	21	18	4	7	2	4	171	2.0	9.2
		NNW	20	40	27	10	7	4	5	1	4	118	1.4	9.1
		CALM	853									853	9.9	
		TOTAL	1369	1409	1591	1123	1019	523	596	380	605	8615	100.0	12.0
		PERCENT	15.9	16.4	18.5	13.0	11.8	6.1	6.9	4.4	7.0		100.0	

ROCK SPRINGS, WY.
STATION 24027

85-100% RH

ANNUAL
PERIOD OF RECORD 1949-1958

SPEED GROUPS IN MILES

TABLE 14   FREQUENCY OF WINDS WHEN RELATIVE HUMIDITY IS 85-100%

	N	NNE	NE	ENE	E	ESE	SE	SSE	S	SSW	W	WSW	W	WNW	NW	NNW	CALM	% Hrs. HIGH Rel. Hum.
Baton Rouge	5	4	6	6	9	7	11	7	6	2	4	3	4	2	3	3	20	38
Louisville	9	3	5	2	4	3	13	9	11	5	6	4	3	4	7	5	8	26
Wichita	11	8	5	4	3	5	8	13	13	4	2	2	2	3	4	9	4	22
Dodge City																		
Des Moines																		
Evansville	6	4	5	4	4	3	6	6	6	7	5	3	3	5	8	10	16	27
Rockford																		
Chicago	5	6	6	6	6	3	5	6	10	9	7	6	7	5	7	5	1	18
Boise	3	1	2	2	2	9	21	7	5	2	3	3	6	12	11	3	10	15
Savannah	5	9	11	6	4	4	5	5	7	7	10	6	4	3	4	3	8	39
Atlanta																		
Tampa	7	8	11	11	14	8	6	6	7	4	3	2	2	2	2	2	7	38
Miami	16	10	7	4	4	4	6	4	5	4	6	4	3	2	4	8	10	28
Jacksonville	7	7	7	4	3	3	5	4	6	6	19	7	5	4	9	7	4	36
Washington, D.C.	6	7	8	8	3	3	3	4	12	13	7	4	2	3	5	6	8	22
Dover	6	5	5	4	5	4	6	4	9	6	8	4	6	3	5	3	19	31
Windsor Locks																		
Grand Junction	5	3	3	5	11	13	8	3	3	1	2	2	6	8	10	8	10	8
Denver	15	9	9	5	5	3	4	3	7	6	3	3	3	4	9	11	2	8
Akron	6	6	6	5	4	7	7	8	6	5	5	5	6	5	5	9	5	19
San Diego	13	12	14	5	4	2	3	3	6	6	4	3	3	3	5	6	8	20
Sacramento	5	2	3	1	5	5	19	15	12	6	7	2	3	2	6	5	5	26
Los Angeles	3	3	5	6	10	7	7	3	3	3	4	7	10	5	3	2	21	27
Blythe																		
Bakersfield	3	3	2	6	8	6	3	2	1	1	1	1	3	5	6	4	51	14
Little Rock	6	6	7	6	6	4	7	6	9	7	9	5	4	4	6	5	7	25
Tucson	3	2	2	2	4	11	21	13	13	4	3	4	6	4	3	2	3	3
Phoenix	3	1	5	4	20	11	11	2	2	1	3	2	4	2	3	1	26	5
Mobile	7	4	7	4	7	4	10	8	12	6	7	3	5	3	5	3	7	41
Birmingham																		

9-4   WEATHER DATA HANDBOOK

	N	NNE	NE	ENE	E	ESE	SE	SSE	S	SSW	SW	WSW	W	WNW	NW	NNW	CALM	% Hrs. HIGH Rel. Hum.
Oklahoma City	12	8	5	3	2	4	8	23	12	5	2	1	1	1	3	9	1	25
Columbus	4	3	3	3	4	4	11	9	10	7	5	3	2	4	9	8	12	28
Cleveland	5	4	3	2	2	3	5	8	16	9	10	8	6	6	5	4	3	27
Cincinnati	9	6	5	5	3	2	3	5	10	15	12	6	5	5	4	4	4	25
Fargo	12	6	4	3	5	4	6	9	9	4	4	3	6	6	7	12	1	22
Bismarck	4	4	5	10	13	9	4	5	2	2	3	4	6	9	9	7	5	23
Raleigh/Durham	8	8	8	4	5	3	4	3	7	8	11	4	3	2	3	3	17	33
Charlotte	8	8	10	9	4	3	3	5	6	9	9	8	4	3	2	4	10	29
Buffalo	4	4	7	4	3	2	6	6	13	10	15	8	5	4	4	3	0	26
Albany	10	4	2	1	1	1	2	12	20	5	4	2	5	5	4	6	17	29
Farmington	4	3	13	16	14	4	2	1	1	1	4	6	9	4	2	1	17	8
Albuquerque	17	8	4	2	3	5	12	7	8	2	3	2	2	3	6	10	6	3
Atlantic City	6	6	6	7	4	5	4	7	9	11	5	7	5	5	4	5	6	37
Winnemucca	3	3	8	2	5	3	11	5	15	3	5	3	6	3	4	1	19	12
Las Vegas	3	2	3	1	3		1	1	3	2	7	6	9	6	4	2	42	2
Omaha	12	4	3	3	4	6	10	17	6	2	2	1	2	3	6	12	7	20
North Platte																		
Miles City	4	10	9	6	2	2	6	8	4	2	4	3	6	12	10	8	4	18
Great Falls	10	6	13	5	4	4	3	2	1	2	10	9	6	6	8	9	2	12
Springfield	7	5	5	4	4	3	8	21	14	3	3	2	4	5	6	6	1	30
St. Louis	4	4	5	4	4	7	8	8	9	4	4	5	7	8	8	5	7	19
Kansas City	8	6	13	11	5	3	3	3	6	6	6	3	3	5	7	6	8	16
Jackson	5	4	4	3	3	5	9	15	12	6	5	3	3	3	6	6	10	32
Minneapolis	6	4	3	4	5	9	13	8	7	6	7	5	4	4	5	4	7	22
Sault Ste. Marie	3	1	5	7	18	9	8	2	3	2	7	3	8	11	9	1	3	43
Grand Rapids																		
Detroit	11	5	5	4	9	4	6	3	11	5	8	5	8	4	7	3	2	20
Boston	8	7	9	9	9	6	4	4	7	8	9	4	3	3	4	6	1	23
Shreveport	5	6	4	4	5	6	10	13	12	7	4	3	3	4	4	5	5	31
Lake Charles																		

	N	NNE	NE	ENE	E	ESE	SE	SSE	S	SSW	SW	WSW	W	WNW	NW	NNW	CALM	% Hrs. HIGH Rel. Hum.
Rock Springs	2	2	6	7	6	2	2	2	4	4	13	21	12	4	2	1	10	10
Casper	8	13	10	8	8	4	2	1	1	2	6	9	5	5	5	4	10	12
Milwaukee	7	13	6	3	3	4	7	6	9	7	8	5	5	6	5	4	2	25
Madison	5	5	8	7	6	5	6	7	8	5	4	4	5	5	6	5	9	23
La Crosse	7	4	4	4	8	8	12	8	10	3	2	1	2	3	9	7	9	20
Charleston	4	3	8	4	5	2	5	3	8	4	8	5	4	4	3	3	27	30
Spokane	1	3	15	9	3	4	8	8	8	16	12	3	1	1	1	1	8	25
Seattle-Tacoma	4	6	5	2	3	6	9	7	11	14	13	3	1	1	1	1	14	46
Roanoke																		
Norfolk	6	6	9	6	5	4	6	5	11	9	11	4	4	3	5	3	4	32
Salt Lake City	5	2	2	1	2	5	18	15	9	3	4	2	5	5	6	6	10	13
Cedar City	7	5	5	2	2	2	8	5	6	7	12	4	3	2	3	2	27	10
Bryce Canyon	2	2	2	1	2	8	9	2	2	1	8	13	23	5	4	2	15	16
San Angelo	4	5	10	9	9	5	4	3	5	6	7	6	5	2	2	2	19	12
Houston	4	5	6	6	7	9	14	15	10	6	4	3	2	2	3	3	2	40
El Paso	21	11	9	4	4	3	6	7	11	3	3	2	1	2	4	7	2	3
Dallas	8	6	8	4	4	5	12	15	12	3	3	1	2	2	6	7	3	18
Corpus Christi	4	5	5	3	5	7	17	24	10	3	1	1	1	1	2	4	7	41
Amarillo	9	8	6	4	4	4	10	12	13	8	6	2	2	3	4	4	2	14
Nashville	7	3	3	2	4	4	8	10	12	4	4	3	4	4	9	6	12	30
Memphis	6	5	7	3	5	3	9	8	13	9	7	2	3	2	4	4	11	25
Knoxville																		
Sioux Falls	6	8	9	5	6	6	8	7	6	3	6	3	3	5	6	5	8	18
Rapid City	11	7	5	4	6	8	10	6	4	2	2	1	2	2	6	17	8	13
Columbia	5	6	8	5	4	2	3	3	5	8	9	6	5	3	3	3	25	34
Pittsburgh	3	3	2	4	5	6	5	5	7	7	8	14	7	7	7	4	6	23
Philadelphia	5	4	5	12	8	4	4	4	5	6	9	9	4	3	3	3	13	25
Harrisburg	2	2	3	9	12	13	6	3	2	3	4	7	9	7	4	3	13	22
Portland	2	1	1	1	3	15	10	5	8	9	5	2	4	6	8	3	18	38
Tulsa	13	8	5	3	2	3	8	15	15	4	2	1	1	3	5	7	5	20

Section 1: VISIBLE PLUMES

Nearly all persistent cooling tower plumes which form in the immediate vicinity of the cooling tower and travel for long distances before being evaporated occur when relative humidities are 93% or more near ground level.

Typically there is a nearly total absence of atmospheric observations *at plume height*. Instead, assumptions are made based on atmospheric observations made near the ground. One of the most critical atmospheric measurements related to persistent visible plumes is the wind direction. In many cases there is a favorite wind direction related to persistent visible plumes at any particular location.

For the 91 stations for which detailed tabulations have been made relating to WET-DRY cooling tower combinations, a set of data has developed from the ten-year series which included the complete hourly observations for all hours when relative humidities were equal to or greater than 93%. When and if a particular cooling tower is located very near the observing station listed, a detailed analysis of all these hours can be made to determine what weather conditions prevailed when a persistent cooling tower plume might be expected.

All persistent cooling tower plumes which are visible at considerable distance would need coincident absence of clouds in the path of the plume. Wind speeds would need to be sufficiently strong to "bend" the plume into a horizontal pattern a short distance above the cooling tower outlet. Light wind speeds would permit a rapid rise of the cooling tower plumes in the absence of any inversion layer and the horizontal path could be similar to that of a low natural cloud.

Section 2: NATURAL PLUME OBSCURATION

The occurrence of natural low cloud and/or low visibility can prevent the observation of cooling tower plumes.

The set of detailed hourly observations for all hours when relative humidity is equal to or greater than 93% contains many sequences when low ceilings or low visibilities would render a cooling tower plume indistinguishable from surrounding, naturally occurring cloud cover. These sets of data for each of 91 locations can be examined to determine the critical conditions for a particular cooling tower complex at a location near the stations for which data are being presented. Some examples of the hourly observations are given for both Nashville and Rock Springs. They are identified in Tables 15 and 16.

In Table 15 a series of hourly observations which occurred in January, 1951 and 1952 is shown. The first column of numbers identifies the year, the second column identifies the month. On this one page of data there were two periods lasting three hours or more when visibility was less than one mile and the ceiling height was less than 500 feet. The first three-hour period occurred on January 31, 1951 from 1400 – 1600 hours. The ceiling heights were reported as 100 and 300 feet above the ground. Visibilities were reported as three-fourths mile and one-half mile. Coincident wind and the coincident dry bulb temperature, wet bulb temperature, and relative humidity have been underlined. Under these limiting ceiling heights and visibility ranges a cooling tower plume would have joined with the cloud cover very soon after leaving the tower and would not be visible as a separate entity.

At the bottom of the table there is a period of seven hours with low ceilings and low visibility. During four of these hours the sky was totally obscured and therefore the ceiling was listed as zero.

The unique characteristics of any particular cooling tower and its respective plume dispersal pattern would help establish the criteria required for identifying repeatable episodes when natural low cloud and low visibility conditions would obscure the plume. Some relevant sets of frequency-of-occurrence data can be derived by detailed analysis of the ten-year period of hourly data.

In Table 16 an episode of low visibility and low ceilings occurred on March 7, 1949 at Rock Springs. Note that there can be a rapid change in ceiling height even while horizontal visibility remained less than one mile. At 0300 hours the ceiling height was only 200 feet and the visibility was one-fourth mile. One hour later the ceiling height was 14,000 feet, but the visibility was only one-half mile. At 0500 hours the ceiling height was again at 200 feet, and the visibility was one-fourth mile.

Small circles have been used to identify ceiling heights equal to or greater than 500 feet coincident with visibility measurements less than one mile. It is important to note that the wind speeds were light in all instances as shown on this particular page of reference data at Rock Springs when ceiling heights and visibility measurements were low. The direction of air flow was near random.

YEAR	MO.	DAY	HOUR	CEILING HT HNDS OF FEET	SKY CONDITIONS 1 2 3 4	VISIBILITY (MILES)	WEATHER AND OR OBSTRUCTION TO VISION	SEA LEVEL PRESSURE (MBS)	DEW POINT (°F)	WIND DIR (16 PTS)	WIND SPEED (MPH OR KNOTS)	STATION PRESSURE (INCHES)	DRY BULB (°F)	WET BULB (°F)	REL HUM (°+)	TOTAL SKY COVER	LOWEST AMT	LOWEST TYPE	LOWEST HT (HNDS OF FEET)	2nd LAYER AMT	2nd LAYER TYPE	2nd LAYER HT (HNDS OF FEET)	SUMM AMT
51	01	28	16	008	8052	1 1/2	01000011	10217	39	NW	08	29.52	39	39	*100	10							
51	01	28	17	003	8--5	1 1/2	01000011	10230	38	NW	08	29.55	38	38	*100	10							
51	01	28	18	008	0--6	3 0	01000010	10234	37	NW	10	29.56	37	37	* 99	10	10	3	008				
51	01	28	19	008	8032	3 0	01000010	10237	36	NW	10	29.57	36	36	* 98	10							
51	01	28	20	011	0--8	3 0	01000010	10247	34	NW	09	29.60	34	34	* 98	10							
51	01	28	21	005	0--8	3 0	01000010	10251	33	NW	10	29.61	33	33	* 99	10	10	2	005				
51	01	28	22	006	0--8	5 0	01000010	10254	32	N	08	29.62	32	32	* 99	10							
51	01	28	23	006	0--8	3 0	01000010	10257	32	NNW	09	29.63	32	32	* 99	10							
51	01	29	00	013	8072	5 0	07000010	10257	31	NNW	11	29.63	31	31	*100	10	2	2	007	10	2	013	10
51	01	29	01	011	8--5	4 0	08000010	10257	30	N	07	29.62	31	31	95	10							
51	01	29	02	014	8072	4 0	07000210	10264	30	N	09	29.64	31	30	96	10							
51	01	29	03	009	0--8	4 0	00000210	10261	30	N	10	29.63	31	30	96	10	10	2	009				
51	01	29	04	018	8062	4 0	07000110	10271	29	NNW	10	29.66	30	30	95	10							
51	01	29	05	006	0--8	1 1/2	07000210	10271	30	N	06	29.66	30	30	*100	10							
51	01	29	06	010	0--8	4 0	00000110	10281	26	N	10	29.68	28	28	94	10	10	2	010				
51	01	29	07	009	8072	4 0	07000010	10288	26	NNW	10	29.70	27	27	93	10							
51	01	29	08	008	0--8	4 0	00000011	10298	25	NNW	10	29.73	26	26	95	10							
51	01	29	09	009	0--8	4 0	00000011	10301	24	NNW	10	29.74	25	25	94	10	10	3	009				
51	01	29	12	007	0--8	3 0	00700001	10301	21	N	09	29.74	23	23	93	10	10	3	007				
51	01	29	13	007	8--5	2 0	00700001	10298	21	NNW	10	29.73	23	23	93	10							
51	01	31	02	004	0---	3 0	00000211	10234	20	N	11	29.54	22	22	93	10							
51	01	31	03	007	0--8	3 0	00000211	10237	21	NW	08	29.55	22	22	95	10	10	2	007				
51	01	31	04	005	0--8	4 0	07000111	10217	25	NE	07	29.49	26	26	95	10							
51	01	31	05	006	0--8	3 0	08000111	10220	26	N	03	29.50	27	27	96	10							
51	01	31	06	007	0--8	3 0	07000011	10224	27	N	03	29.51	27	27	* 97	10	10	2	007				
51	01	31	07	005	8032	4 0	07000011	10220	28	NNE	02	29.50	29	29	96	10							
51	01	31	08	003	0--8	2 0	07000011	10213	29	W	03	29.48	29	29	* 97	10							
51	01	31	09	003	0--8	2 1/2	07000011	10207	29	ENE	01	29.46	30	30	* 97	10	10	2	003				
51	01	31	10	003	8--5	3 0	07000011	10190	30	ENE	03	29.42	31	31	95	10							
51	01	31	11	003	8--5	3 0	02000011	10169	31	NE	02	29.36	32	31	* 97	10							
51	01	31	12	003	0--8	1 1/4	02000011	10135	32	NNE	02	29.26	32	32	* 99	10	10	O	003				
51	01	31	13	002	0--8	1 1/4	02000011	10132	32	NNW	01	29.25	32	32	* 99	10							
51	01	31	14	001	0--8	3/4	08000011	10122	32	NW	12	29.22	32	32	*100	10							
51	01	31	15	003	0--8	3/4	08000011	10125	32	S E	07	29.23	32	32	*100	10	10	O	003				
51	01	31	16	003	0--8	1/2	08000011	10115	32	NW	04	29.21	32	32	*100	10							
51	01	31	17	004	0--8	1 0	08000011	10122	32	NW	10	29.23	32	32	*100	10							
51	01	31	18	006	0--8	2 0	08000011	10125	32	NW	09	29.24	32	32	*100	10	10	O	006				
51	01	31	19	006	0--8	2 0	08000011	10129	31	N	04	29.25	31	31	*100	10							
51	01	31	20	005	0--8	1 0	00000211	10149	26	NW	06	29.30	27	27	* 97	10							
51	01	31	21	005	0--8	1 0	00000211	10139	26	NW	04	29.27	27	27	* 97	10	10	O	005				
51	01	31	22	005	0--8	1 0	00000211	10142	26	NNW	04	29.28	28	27	95	10							
51	01	31	23	005	0--8	1 0	07000200	10142	26	NW	10	29.28	27	27	* 97	10							
52	01	01	23	002	-000	1 0	00000011	10227	46	N	07	29.55	48	47	93	10	10	1	002				
52	01	02	00	002	-000	3/4	00000011	10227	47	NNW	09	29.55	47	47	*100	10	10	1	002				
52	01	02	01	001	-000	* 0 1/4	00000011	10227	45	N	06	29.55	45	45	*100	10	10	1	001				
52	01	02	02	000	-000	* 0 1/16	00000011	10234	44	NNW	05	29.57	44	44	*100	10	10	1	000				
52	01	02	03	000	-000	* 0 1/16	00000011	10230	44	N	03	29.56	44	44	*100	10	10	1	000				
52	01	02	04	000	-000	* 0 1/16	00000011	10234	43	NW	03	29.57	43	43	*100	10	10	1	000				
52	01	02	05	000	-000	* 0 1/16	00000011	10234	43	NW	04	29.57	43	43	*100	10	10	1	000				
52	01	02	06	002	-000	3/4	00400011	10240	42	NW	06	29.59	42	42	*100	10	10	1	002				

YEAR	MO.	DAY	HOUR	CEILING HT HNDS OF FEET	SKY CONDITIONS 1 2 3 4	VISIBILITY (MILES)	WEATHER AND OR OBSTRUCTION TO VISION (THNDR/LIQUID/FROZEN/PRECIP/OBSTRUC)	SEA LEVEL PRESSURE (MBS)	DEW POINT (°F)	WIND DIR (16 PTS)	WIND SPEED (MPH OR KNOTS)	STATION PRESSURE (INCHES)	DRY BULB (°F)	WET BULB (°F)	REL HUM (%)	TOTAL SKY COVER	LOWEST AMT TYPE	LOWEST HT (HNDS OF FEET)	2nd LAYER AMT TYPE	2nd LAYER HT (HNDS OF FEET)	SUMM AMT
49	03	05	15	010	0---	2 0	00001000	10200	27	WSW	10	23.38	28	28	94	10					
49	03	05	16	040	8072	10 0	00001000	10200	29	NW	03	23.39	30	30	95	10					
49	03	05	17	018	8--5	10 0	00001000	10200	30	NW	01	23.39	30	30	* 99	10	3 K	004	6 3	018	9
49	03	05	18	014	8--5	15 0	00001000	10207	28	WSW	07	23.40	30	29	93	10					
49	03	05	20	025	8--5	15 0	00000000	10200	28	SW	10	23.42	30	29	93	10	6 3	025	4 6	047	10
49	03	06	01	014	0--8	20 0	00000000	10227	28	W	05	23.50	29	29	94	10					
49	03	06	02	015	0--8	15 0	00000000	10244	26	W	04	23.51	29	28	94	10	10 3	015			
49	03	06	03	012	0--8	15 0	00000000	10251	28	WSW	07	23.52	30	29	93	10					
49	03	07	03	002	0---	* 0 1/4	00000010	10186	22	WSW	05	23.40	23	23	95	10					
49	03	07	04	140	4--	1/2	00000010	10180	21	WNW	01	23.38	22	22	95	9					
49	03	07	05	002	0---	* 0 1/4	00000010	10180	21	W	03	23.38	22	22	95	10	10 1	002			
49	03	07	06	003	0---	* 0 1/4	00000010	10186	22	SSW	06	23.37	23	23	95	10					
49	03	07	07	200	5--	* 0 1/8	00000010	10186	22	SW	02	23.36	23	23	95	9					
49	03	07	08	001	0---	* 0 1/8	00000010	10190	21	CLM	00	23.36	22	22	95	10	10 1	001			
49	03	07	09	001	0---	* 0 1/8	00000010	10186	22	WNW	01	23.35	24	24	96	10					
49	03	07	10	001	0---	1/2	00000010	10176	24	CLM	00	23.33	25	25	96	10					
49	03	07	11	010	7--5	8 0	00000000	10166	26	W	02	23.31	27	27	* 97	10	7 2	010	3 8	200	10
49	03	07	12	200	7992	15 0	00000000	10146	27	NNW	02	23.27	29	28	94	10					
49	03	07	19	050	7212	2 0	00001000	10132	26	W	08	23.23	28	28	93	10					
49	03	07	20	110	7202	15 0	00000000	10132	26	WSW	03	23.22	28	27	93	10	3 M	020	7 6	110	10
49	03	07	21	110	0--7	10 0	00000000	10132	25	S	06	23.22	26	26	95	10					
49	03	07	22	090	0--7	10 0	00000000	10129	25	W	07	23.22	27	26	94	10					
49	03	07	23	060	0--7	15 0	00000000	10125	25	WSW	05	23.22	27	27	93	10	10 6	060			
49	03	08	01	003	8--5	7 0	00000000	10105	26	WSW	10	23.21	27	27	93	10					
49	03	08	02	023	8051	5 0	00001000	10098	26	W	11	23.21	27	27	93	10	4 K	005	6 3	023	10
49	03	08	03	040	-252	2 0	00001000	10098	26	W	09	23.21	27	27	96	10					
49	03	08	05	025	0---	2 0	00001000	10115	24	NW	05	23.22	26	25	93	10	10 -	025			
49	03	08	06	010	8--5	10 0	00001000	10125	23	W	01	23.23	25	25	93	10					
49	03	12	02	060	8202	20 0	00000000	10081	27	W	15	23.20	29	28	93	10	4 3	020	6 6	060	10
49	03	23	03	017	0---	3 0	00001000	09966	30	W	07	22.94	32	31	93	10					
49	03	23	04	016	0--8	15 0	00001000	09980	29	WSW	03	22.95	30	30	94	10					
49	03	23	05	037	0--8	10 0	00001000	09976	29	SSW	03	22.95	30	30	94	10	10 3	037			
49	03	23	06	012	0---	1/2	00002000	09983	29	S	09	22.96	30	30	96	10					
49	03	23	07	030	0--8	15 0	00001000	09993	29	SSW	03	22.97	29	29	* 97	10					
49	03	23	16	012	0---	5/8	00001000	10010	28	W	10	22.97	29	29	95	10					
49	03	23	17	040	8152	15 0	00000000	10010	28	CLM	00	22.98	29	29	93	10	0 K	005	1 4	015	1
49	03	23	19	045	8152	15 0	00001000	10024	29	SE	10	23.00	30	29	* 98	10					
49	03	23	23	008	0---	3/8	00002000	10034	26	E	09	23.05	27	27	93	10	10 -	008			
49	03	24	00	009	0---	3/4	00001000	10044	24	ENE	03	23.05	26	26	94	10					
49	03	24	02	012	0--8	3 0	00001000	10047	23	NE	07	23.06	25	25	94	10	10 3	012			
49	03	24	23	UNI	0302	25 0	00000000	10132	25	SW	07	23.25	27	26	93	2	2 3	030	0 0	---	2
49	03	29	07	006	0---	* 0 1/16	00002005	10156	17	NE	35	23.25	19	19	93	10					
50	03	06	01	009	0---	1/2	00020000	10027	26	W	21	23.10	27	27	* 97	10					
50	03	06	02	008	0---	3/4	00010005	10020	24	WSW	20	23.08	25	25	* 97	10	10 -	008			
50	03	07	00	014	0---	3/4	00010000	10169	19	NW	17	23.30	20	20	94	10					
50	03	10	02	011	0---	2 0	00010000	10102	26	CLM	00	23.21	27	27	96	10	10 -	011			
50	03	10	03	030	0--8	5 0	00010000	10098	26	CLM	00	23.20	27	27	95	10					
50	03	10	04	040	0--8	8 0	00010000	10102	25	WNW	03	23.20	26	26	96	10					
50	03	10	05	010	0---	3 0	00010000	10102	25	CLM	00	23.20	26	26	* 97	10	10 -	010			
50	03	10	06	030	0--8	5 0	00010000	10108	24	W	08	23.20	25	25	96	10					

Section 1: THE GENERAL RELATIONSHIP

Highest wet bulb temperatures do not occur coincidentally with the highest dry bulb values. All extreme conditions at any location are the result of imported air from some other area. The highest wet bulb temperatures will occur when the extremely hot air moves to the location from some moist source. The hottest dry bulb temperatures will occur when air moves to the location from some hot dry air source.

During the warmer part of the day when moist air prevails, clouds develop and the shaded ground surface thereby helps to reduce the high dry bulb temperatures.

Some general conclusions may be drawn regarding coincident wet bulb and dry bulb temperatures in the typical design ranges. Design dry bulb temperatures at any station generally have wet bulb temperatures which are from 2°F to 6°F colder than the peak wet bulb temperatures at that same station. A difference of 4°F is probably the most common.

In some instances the highest wet bulb temperatures occur when the dry bulb temperatures may be 10°F to 15°F below the peak dry bulb temperature for a particular station. Table 17 lists the approximate 5°F dry bulb temperature range which is coincident with the high wet bulb temperature readings at 49 locations. It will be noted that most of the stations have their peak wet bulb temperatures when the dry bulb temperature is 95°F or less.

TABLE 17

The approximate 5° dry bulb temperature range with which the highest wet bulb temperature is most likely to be coincident.

ABILENE	90-94	DALLAS	95-99	*LAS VEGAS (NEV.)	80-100	OKLAHOMA CITY	91-95
ALBUQUERQUE	87-91	DENVER	76-80	LITTLE ROCK	93-97	OMAHA	91-95
AMARILLO	87-91	DETROIT	88-92	LOS ANGELES	80-84		
ATLANTA	89-93			LOUISVILLE	90-94	PHOENIX	95-99
		EL PASO	88-92			PITTSBURGH	86-90
BIRMINGHAM	90-94						
BISMARCK	91-95	FRESNO	98-102	MEDFORD	93-97	ST. LOUIS	90-94
BOISE	90-94			MEMPHIS	90-94	SALT LAKE CITY	87-91
BOSTON	90-94	GREAT FALLS	86-90	MIAMI	86-90	SAN ANTONIO	88-92
BROWNSVILLE	88-92			MINNEAPOLIS	91-95	SAN DIEGO	80-84
BURBANK	91-95	HOUSTON	91-95	MOBILE	88-92	SAN FRANCISCO	80-84
		HURON	91-95			SEATTLE	82-86
CHARLESTON	90-94			NEW ORLEANS	90-94	SYRACUSE	88-92
CHARLOTTE	89-93	JACKSONVILLE	90-94	NEW YORK CITY,			
CHICAGO	92-96			La Guardia	89-93	WASHINGTON, D.C.	89-93
CLEVELAND	88-92	KANSAS CITY	92-96	NORTH PLATTE	87-91	WICHITA	90-94

*Entire 20° range has nearly equal frequency of coincident high wet bulb temperatures at Las Vegas, Nevada.

Table 17 lists the approximate 5°F dry bulb temperature range which is coincident with the highest wet bulb temperature readings at 49 locations. It will be noted that most of the stations have their peak wet bulb temperatures when the dry bulb temperature is 95°F or less.

If a constant moisture content in outdoor air could be maintained during hot summer weather, the wet bulb temperature should increase about one degree for each three-degree increase in dry bulb. However, with the vertical mixing of air which takes place during the hottest part of summer days, drier air from a few hundred feet above the surface is brought down and mixed with the more moist air near the surface. Thus there is no fixed relationship between wet bulb and dry bulb temperatures. Both geographic locations and time of day are contributing factors to a very complex inter-relationship.

From the detailed hourly data for a large sample of hottest days at five widely separated stations it was noted that the wet bulb temperatures tend to remain nearly flat during the mid part of the hot extreme days while the dry bulb temperatures moved through their daytime peak arch. These coincident data are summarized in Fig. 19.

Section 3: POSSIBLE HIGHEST EXTREMES

At the 91 stations for which detailed data have been tabulated to assist in studying WET-DRY cooling tower combinations, the ten-year extremes of both high dry bulb and wet bulb temperatures were tabulated. From those data, the nine highest wet bulb temperatures and the nine highest dry bulb temperatures within a ten-year span have been identified and are reproduced in Fig. 20. The nine instances represent the highest *one hundredth of 1%*. In a sample of 87,600 hourly values, 1% would equal 876 hours. One hundredth of 1% would equal 8.76 hours. The center of the population of coincident dry bulb for coincident wet bulb values is represented by a small horizontal bar at each station.

At Birmingham the nine highest wet bulb temperatures in a ten-year span were all 81°F. The central value for coincident dry bulb temperatures was 95°F. For this same station the nine highest dry bulb values in the ten-year period consisted of three at 105°F, five at 104°F, and two at 103°F. However, the central value for coincident wet bulb within those same hours was only 74°F which is 7°F cooler than the nine highest wet bulb temperatures.

The pattern of coincident temperature values in a very dry climate can be represented by the data for Tucson. At this station the dry bulb temperature coincident with the high wet bulb values in only 88°F. By contrast eight of the nine highest dry bulb temperatures are 21° warmer at 109°. However, the mean coincident wet bulb with the 109°F dry bulb values is only 67°F.

The occurrence of the highest one, two, or three hours in a sample of 87,600 hourly values should not be considered as a reliable all-time extreme. It is entirely possible that minor mechanical failures of measuring equipment could produce erroneous data for a few very rare high readings. Furthermore, if the highest wet bulb or dry bulb temperature should occur for only a brief period, the "fly wheel effect" of the system would decrease the importance of that very rare short period measurement. The ninth highest value, which is at a level of one hundredth of 1% in the entire sample, should be high enough to be considered the extreme condition for almost all cooling tower applications.

All wet bulb and dry bulb values shown in Table 17 are generally much higher than would be required for typical design values at the 1%, 2½%, or 5% frequency levels.

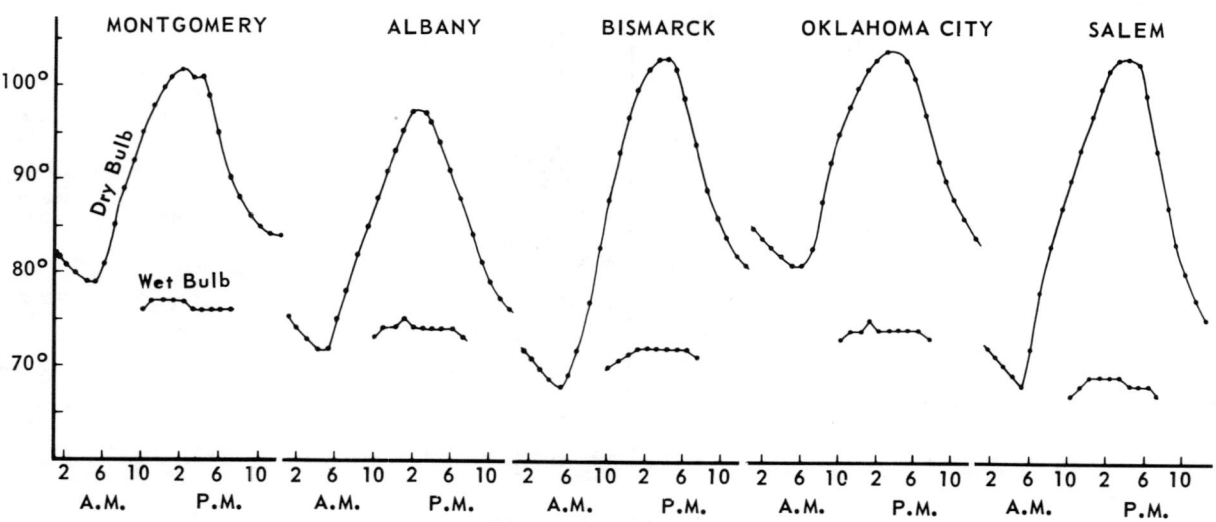

Fig. 19. Coincident wet bulb temperatures on extreme dry bulb hot days.

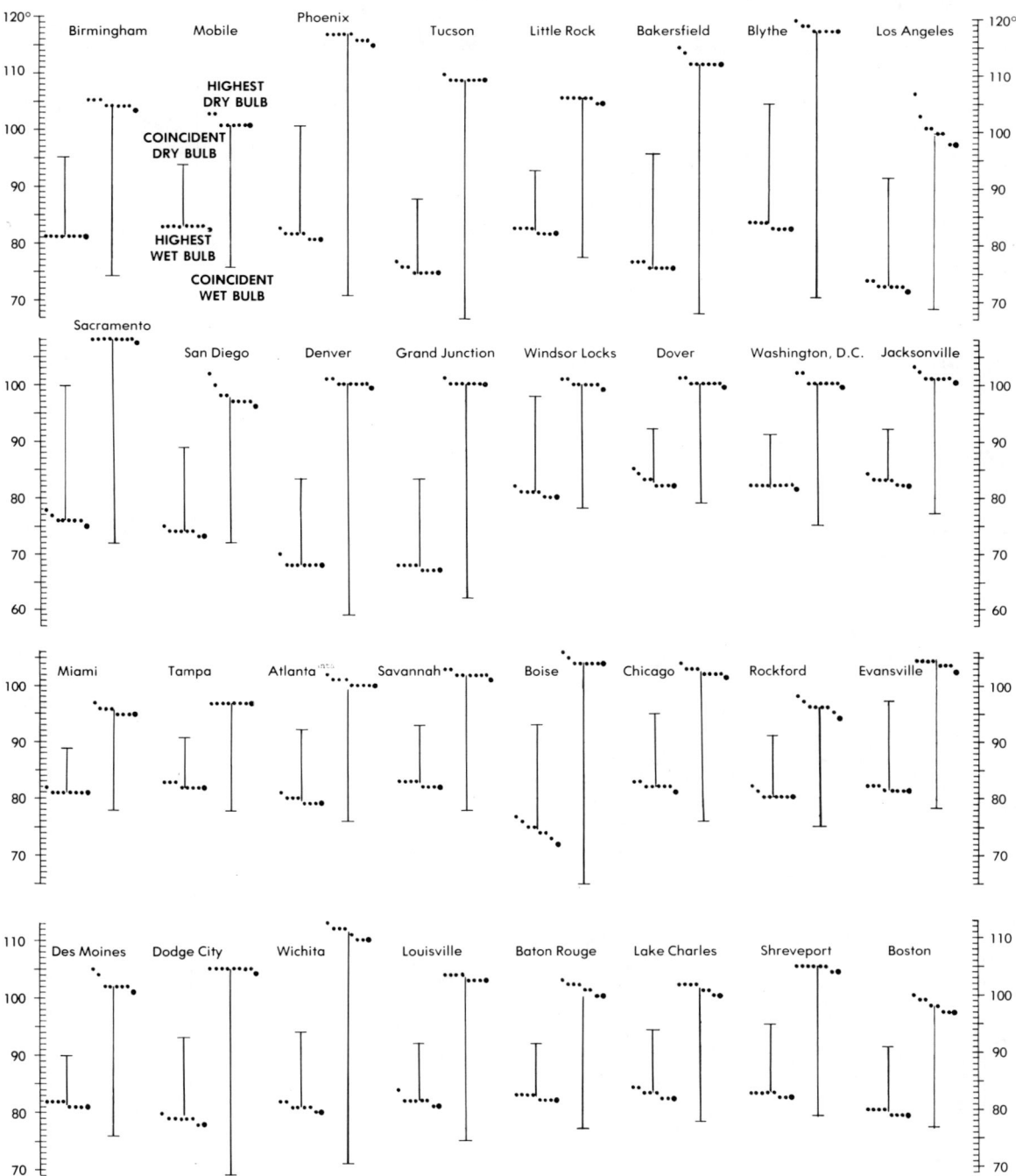

Figure 20. Combinations of:
- Nine highest wet bulb temperatures with mean coincident dry bulb readings.
- Nine highest dry bulb temperatures with mean coincident wet bulb readings.

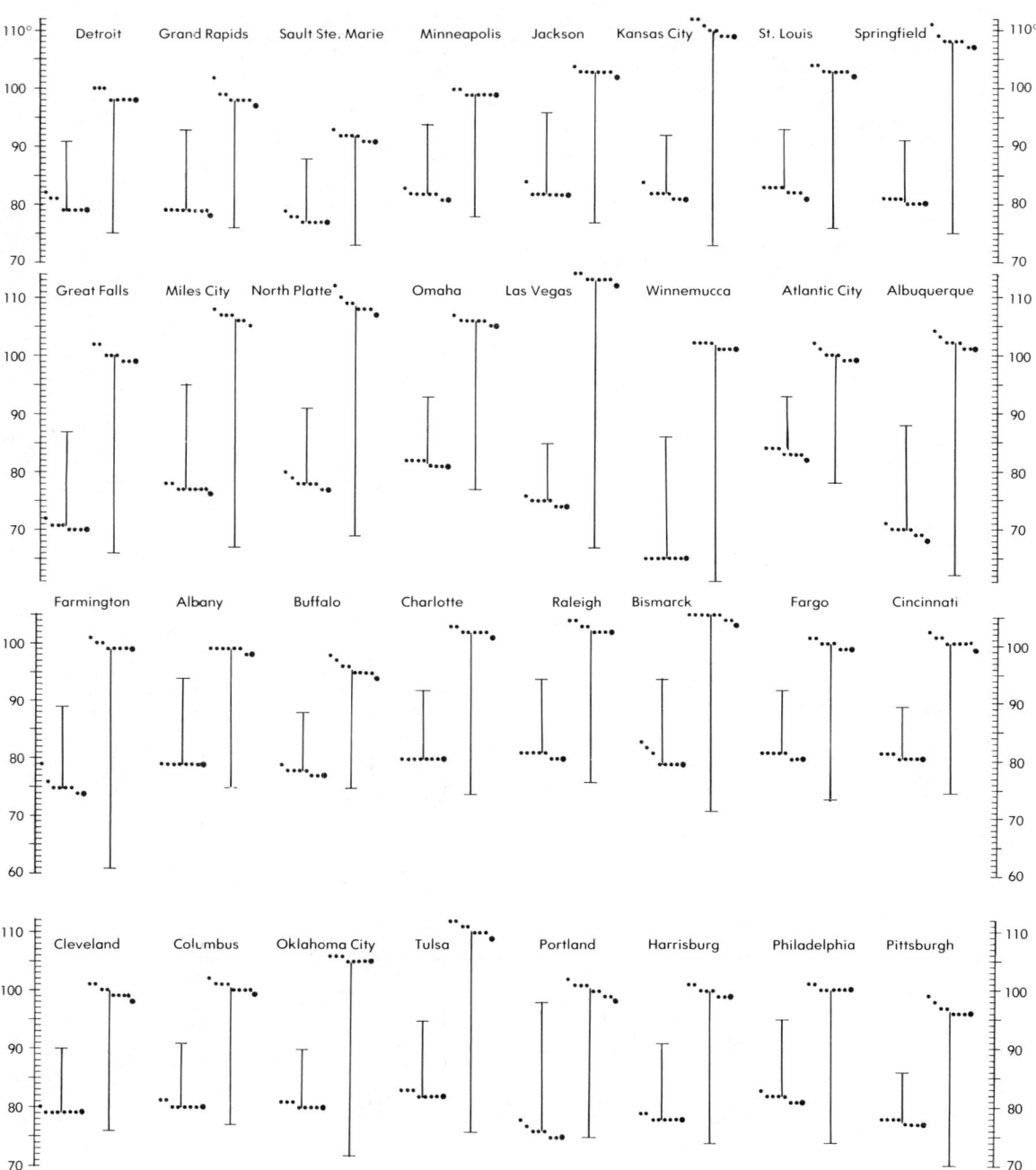

Figure 20—Continued. Combinations of:
- Nine highest wet bulb temperatures with mean coincident dry bulb readings.
- Nine highest dry bulb temperatures with mean coincident wet bulb readings.

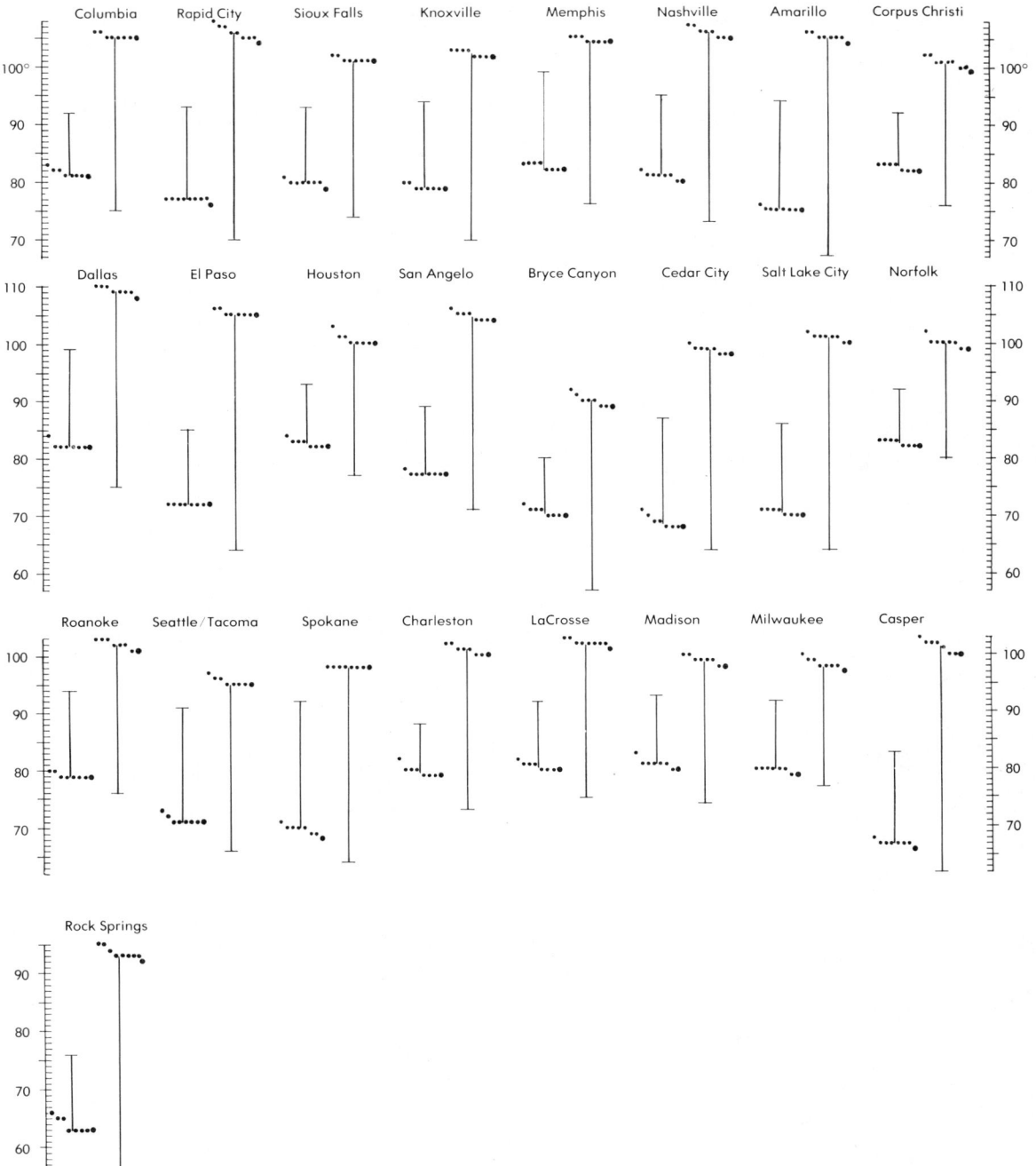

Figure 20—Continued.   Combinations of:
 – Nine highest wet bulb temperatures with mean coincident dry bulb readings.
 – Nine highest dry bulb temperatures with mean coincident wet bulb readings.

The data presented in Table 18 are intended for use in figuring estimates of energy consumption for the locations included. They are reprinted from AFM 88-29 and were compiled by the Engineering Meteorology Section (ENE) of the U.S. Air Force Environmental Technical Applications Center (USAAFETAC). Similar and other data for over 100 additional stations can be found in AFM 88-29.

The locations shown in Table 18 have recorded 24 hourly observations a day for at least five years. (Because of rounding, the counts in columns may not correspond to a count of hours in an eight-hour period for the month.)

Distributions of dry bulb temperatures (temperature range) are listed in five degree intervals on a monthly and annual basis. They are further broken down into three daily periods to roughly coincide with the three main categories of facility use, i.e. sleep, one a.m. to eight a.m. (01 to 08); work, nine a.m. to four p.m. (09 to 16); and recreation, five p.m. to midnight (17 to 24).

Mean coincident wet bulb temperature (MCWB) values are the average (arithmetic mean) values of all wet bulb temperatures occurring simultaneously with each noted five degree dry bulb temperature interval. At the upper end of the MCWB distribution, values sometimes reverse their trend as the highest wet bulb temperatures are not necessarily coincident with highest dry bulb temperatures.

Where possible, the stations listed in Table 18 coincide with the 91 stations covered in depth elsewhere in this book. (See Part 1, Section 4 and Table 1.) This is true for 52 stations:

Albany, New York	Little Rock, Arkansas
Albuquerque, New Mexico	Los Angeles, California
Amarillo, Texas	Madison, Wisconsin
Atlanta, Georgia	Memphis Tennessee
Birmingham, Alabama	North Platte, Nebraska
Bismark, North Dakota	Oklahoma City, Oklahoma
Casper, Wyoming	Pittsburgh, Pennsylvania
Charleston, West Virginia	Portland, Oregon
Chicago, Illinois	Rapid City, South Dakota
Cincinnati, Ohio	Roanoke, Virginia
Corpus Christi, Texas	Rock Springs, Wyoming
Denver, Colorado	Sacramento, California
Des Moines, Iowa	St. Louis, Missouri
Dodge City, Kansas	St. Paul (Minneapolis), Minnesota
Dover, Delaware	San Diego, California
Evansville, Indiana	Savannah, Georgia
Farmington, New Mexico	Seattle, Washington
Grand Junction, Colorado	Shreveport, Louisiana
Harrisburg, Pennsylvania	Sioux Falls, South Dakota
Houston, Texas	Spokane, Washington
Jackson, Mississippi	Springfield, Missouri
Jacksonville, Florida	Tampa, Florida
Knoxville, Tennessee	Tucson, Arizona
La Crosse, Wisconsin	Tulsa, Oklahoma
Lake Charles, Louisiana	Wichita, Kansas
Las Vegas, Nevada	Winnemucca, Nevada

For eight stations, readings were taken at sites in close approximation to those covered in this book. In such cases, stations are listed by the site names which correspond to those used elsewhere in this book and then by the sites at which the readings were actually taken:

Site Name	Readings taken at
Boise, Idaho	Mountain Home AFB, Idaho
Boston, Massachusetts	Hanscom AFB/Bedford, Massachussetts
Detroit, Michigan	Selfridge ANGB/Mt. Clemens, Michigan
El Paso, Texas	Fort Bliss/Biggs AFB, Texas
Great Falls, Montana	Malmstrom AFB, Montana
Kansas City, Missouri	Richards-Gebaur AFB/Grandview, Missouri
Norfolk, Virginia	Langley AFB/Hampton, Virginia
Omaha, Nebraska	Offutt AFB, Nebraska

Twenty-six stations fall into a category wherein readings were taken nearby but far enough away to require comparative information. This information consists of comparative elevations and design temperatures. Please note that the comparative design temperature information *cannot* be used in determining estimates of energy consumption as it is a measurement of extremes rather than central tendencies. The stations containing notes on comparative data are:

Site Name	Readings taken at
Atlantic City, New Jersey	McGuire AFB, New Jersey
Bakersfield, California	Castle AFB/Merced, California
Baton Rouge, Louisiana	England AFB/Alexandria, Louisiana
Blythe, California	Yuma MCAS/IAP, Arizona
Buffalo, New York	Niagara Falls IAP, New York
Charlotte, North Carolina	Fort Bragg/Simmons AAF, North Carolina
Cleveland, Ohio	Akron/Akron-Canton APRT, Ohio
Columbia, South Carolina	Shaw AFB/Sumter, South Carolina
Columbus, Ohio	Wright-Patterson AFB/Dayton, Ohio
Dallas, Texas	Carswell AFB/Forth Worth, Texas
Grand Rapids, Michigan	Lansing/Capital City ARPT, Michigan
Indianapolis, Indiana	Terre Haute/Hulman FLD, Indiana
Louisville, Kentucky	Fort Knox/Godman AAF, Kentucky
Miami, Florida	Homestead AFB, Florida
Milwaukee, Wisconsin	Madison/Traux Field, Wisconsin
Mobile, Alabama	Pensacola NAS/F Sherman FLD, Florida
Nashville, Tennessee	Sewart AFB/Smyrna APRT, Tennessee
Philadelphia, Pennsylvania	McGuire AFB, New Jersey
Phoenix, Arizona	Luke AFB/Glendale, Arizona
Raleigh, North Carolina	Seymour Johnson AFB, North Carolina
Rockford, Illinois	Moline/Quad City ARPT, Illinois
Salt Lake City, Utah	Hill AFB/Ogden, Utah
San Angelo, Texas	Dyers AFB/Abilene, Texas
Sault Ste. Marie, Michigan	Kincheloe AFB, Michigan
Washington, D.C.	Andrews AFB, Maryland
Windsor Locks, Connecticut	Westover AFB, Massachussetts

Billings, Montana and Grand Forks, North Dakota have been substituted for Miles City, Montana and Fargo, North Dakota respectively.

There are no entries in Table 18 for Akron, Colorado, Bryce Canyon or Cedar City, Utah.

Locations included in Table 18 are listed alphabetically within the states.

BIRMINGHAM MAP ALABAMA
LAT 33 34N   LONG 86 45W   ELEV 620 FT

MEAN FREQUENCY OF OCCURRENCE OF DRY BULB TEMPERATURE (DEGREES F) WITH MEAN COINCIDENT WET BULB TEMPERATURE (DEGREES F) FOR EACH DRY BULB TEMPERATURE RANGE

Temperature Range	MAY 01–08	MAY 09–16	MAY 17–24	MAY Total Obsn	MAY MCWB	JUNE 01–08	JUNE 09–16	JUNE 17–24	JUNE Total Obsn	JUNE MCWB	JULY 01–08	JULY 09–16	JULY 17–24	JULY Total Obsn	JULY MCWB	AUG 01–08	AUG 09–16	AUG 17–24	AUG Total Obsn	AUG MCWB	SEP 01–08	SEP 09–16	SEP 17–24	SEP Total Obsn	SEP MCWB	OCT 01–08	OCT 09–16	OCT 17–24	OCT Total Obsn	OCT MCWB
105/109												0		0	74															
100/104							1	0	1	75		3	0	3	74		0		0	76										
95/99		2	0	2	71		10	1	11	74		12	2	14	75		15	1	16	75				0						
90/94		16	3	19	70	0	45	9	54	74		56	13	69	75		64	11	75	75		6	0	6	71		2		2	73
85/89	0	49	12	61	69	3	68	24	95	72	3	86	29	118	74	3	86	29	118	74		28	3	31	72		13	1	14	68
80/84	4	62	26	92	68	15	62	43	120	71	22	56	52	130	73	19	54	55	128	73	1	53	13	67	71		37	4	41	66
75/79	15	50	41	106	67	51	36	66	153	70	75	28	86	189	72	65	23	88	176	72	4	64	28	96	70	2	52	13	67	65
70/74	47	34	58	139	65	93	14	66	173	68	121	8	59	188	70	118	5	52	175	69	29	46	52	127	69	19	49	33	101	64
65/69	75	22	58	155	63	51	5	22	78	64	22	1	6	29	66	32	1	10	43	65	74	27	70	171	67	35	38	46	119	61
60/64	49	9	27	85	58	18	1	6	25	59	5		1	6	60	9	0	2	11	61	64	12	44	120	63	41	30	48	119	57
55/59	30	3	14	47	54	6	0	2	8	56	1			1	57	2	0	0	2	57	38	3	21	62	59	44	17	40	101	53
50/54	14	1	6	21	49	2	0		2	50									0	53	22	1	8	31	54	45	8	33	86	49
45/49	9	0	4	13	45	0			0	45											8	0	2	10	50	26	3	18	47	44
40/44	5	0		5	41																1			1	46	22	1	9	32	40
35/39	0			0	38																					9	0	3	12	35
30/34																										3		1	4	31
25/29																										1			1	27

BIRMINGHAM MAP ALABAMA

Temperature Range	Nov 01–08	Nov 09–16	Nov 17–24	Nov Total Obsn	Nov MCWB	Dec 01–08	Dec 09–16	Dec 17–24	Dec Total Obsn	Dec MCWB	Jan 01–08	Jan 09–16	Jan 17–24	Jan Total Obsn	Jan MCWB	Feb 01–08	Feb 09–16	Feb 17–24	Feb Total Obsn	Feb MCWB	Mar 01–08	Mar 09–16	Mar 17–24	Mar Total Obsn	Mar MCWB	Apr 01–08	Apr 09–16	Apr 17–24	Apr Total Obsn	Apr MCWB	Annual 01–08	Annual 09–16	Annual 17–24	Annual Total Obsn	Annual MCWB
105/109																																		0	74
100/104																																4		4	74
95/99																																45	4	49	74
90/94																													0	65		211	39	250	74
85/89																											6		6	67	10	361	108	479	72
80/84		1		1	67														0	66				0			37	7	44	65	64	379	216	659	71
75/79		11	1	12	64		1		1	67		2		2	65		4	1	5	65		6	1	7	65	1	43	21	65	63	238	309	374	921	69
70/74	4	32	9	45	62		8	2	10	62		8	2	10	64		15	5	20	61		13	5	18	63	13	46	38	97	62	491	274	407	1172	67
65/69	11	38	19	68	59	6	17	8	31	60	7	19	13	39	61	6	24	14	44	59	2	28	13	43	61	37	41	51	129	59	362	255	319	936	61
60/64	20	41	31	92	55	14	29	17	60	57	17	24	18	59	57	14	35	26	75	55	16	37	28	81	58	54	30	39	123	56	300	243	272	815	57
55/59	26	34	30	90	51	20	35	25	80	52	17	30	25	72	52	26	36	31	93	51	21	41	36	98	54	36	20	32	88	51	264	214	249	727	52
50/54	32	33	36	101	47	25	40	31	96	47	22	37	28	87	47	26	29	29	84	46	34	38	42	114	51	33	12	24	69	47	243	194	225	662	47
45/49	36	24	37	97	43	25	42	36	103	43	27	42	36	105	43	30	30	35	95	42	36	34	36	106	46	27	5	18	50	43	211	170	215	596	43
40/44	32	16	32	80	38	32	35	39	106	38	32	33	36	101	38	32	21	33	86	38	30	24	31	85	42	21	1	8	30	39	215	123	187	525	38
35/39	34	8	25	67	34	35	23	41	99	34	38	28	39	105	34	32	15	23	70	34	39	16	30	85	38	14		2	16	35	197	80	150	427	34
30/34	27	3	13	43	30	42	13	29	84	30	34	13	26	73	30	26	8	14	48	30	35	6	17	58	34	4			4	31	162	40	90	292	30
25/29	12	1	4	17	26	29	4	15	48	25	26	6	15	47	25	15	4	8	27	25	26	3	7	36	30				0	28	90	15	44	149	25
20/24	6	1	1	8	21	14	1	5	20	21	18	3	6	27	21	9	1	3	13	20	7		2	9	26						48	6	16	70	21
15/19	0	0	0	0	16	5	0	1	6	16	4	1	3	8	16	3	1	1	5	16	1		1	2	20						13	2	5	20	16
10/14	0	0	0	0	10	1	0	0	1	11	3	1	1	5	12	1		1	2	11			1	1	16						5		2	8	11
5/9	0			0	5	1	0	0	1	5			1	1	5	2			2	7				0	13						3		1	4	6
0/4						0			0	2	1			1	1																1	1		1	1
-5/-1											0	0		0	-2																			0	-2

MOBILE, ALABAMA*
READINGS TAKEN AT PENSACOLA NAS/F SHERMAN FIELD, FL

LAT 30 21N   LONG 87 19W   ELEV   30 FT

MEAN FREQUENCY OF OCCURRENCE OF DRY BULB TEMPERATURE (DEGREES F) WITH MEAN COINCIDENT WET BULB TEMPERATURE (DEGREES F) FOR EACH DRY BULB TEMPERATURE RANGE

Hour Gp columns: 01 to 08, 09 to 16, 17 to 24. "Total Obsn" = total observations. "MC WB" = Mean Coincident Wet Bulb.

Temperature Range	MAY 01–08	MAY 09–16	MAY 17–24	MAY Total	MAY WB	JUNE 01–08	JUNE 09–16	JUNE 17–24	JUNE Total	JUNE WB	JULY 01–08	JULY 09–16	JULY 17–24	JULY Total	JULY WB	AUG 01–08	AUG 09–16	AUG 17–24	AUG Total	AUG WB	SEP 01–08	SEP 09–16	SEP 17–24	SEP Total	SEP WB	OCT 01–08	OCT 09–16	OCT 17–24	OCT Total	OCT WB
100/104																			0	79										
95/99												1		1	78		1		1	80				0	77					
90/94		2		2	71	0	1	0	1	77	0	40	2	42	79		44	2	46	79	0	22	1	23	77				0	77
85/89		35	1	36	73		20	1	21	77	12	130	31	173	78	8	123	32	163	78	3	78	15	96	76	0	19	0	19	74
80/84	13	110	30	153	73	8	106	18	132	76	74	55	125	254	76	68	54	120	242	76	35	85	76	196	75	5	59	15	79	72
75/79	54	61	90	205	71	59	82	99	240	75	125	18	78	221	74	123	21	79	223	74	83	36	88	207	73	22	67	41	130	69
70/74	90	29	82	201	68	92	22	91	205	73	34	4	12	50	71	43	5	14	62	71	77	13	42	132	69	42	52	68	162	66
65/69	53	8	30	91	63	60	8	26	94	70	2	0	1	3	66	4	0	0	4	66	27	4	13	44	64	57	31	58	146	62
60/64	21	2	9	32	58	17	0	5	22	65	1			1	60	1			1	62	13	1	3	17	59	54	15	34	103	58
55/59	10	1	4	15	53	3	0	0	3	58											2	0	1	3	54	32	5	20	57	53
50/54	6	0	1	7	49	0		0	0	53											1	0	0	1	49	20	1	10	31	48
45/49	0	0	0	0	45																0	0	0	0	45	11	0	3	14	44
40/44	0	0	0	0	43																					4	0	0	4	40
35/39																										1			1	37

*Comparative design data note:

	Elevation	WINTER 97 1/2%	SUMMER DB 2 1/2%	SUMMER WB 2 1/2%
Mobile AP, AL.	211 ft.	29° F	93° F	79° F
Pensacola NAS/F, FL.	30 ft.	30° F	91° F	80° F

COINCIDENT WET BULB TEMPERATURE FOR EACH DRY BULB TEMPERATURE RANGE

MOBILE, ALABAMA*
READINGS TAKEN AT PENSACOLA NAS/F SHERMAN FIELD, FL

Temperature Range	NOV 01 to 08	NOV 09 to 16	NOV 17 to 24	NOV Total Obsn	NOV MCWB	DEC 01 to 08	DEC 09 to 16	DEC 17 to 24	DEC Total Obsn	DEC MCWB	JAN 01 to 08	JAN 09 to 16	JAN 17 to 24	JAN Total Obsn	JAN MCWB	FEB 01 to 08	FEB 09 to 16	FEB 17 to 24	FEB Total Obsn	FEB MCWB	MAR 01 to 08	MAR 09 to 16	MAR 17 to 24	MAR Total Obsn	MAR MCWB	APR 01 to 08	APR 09 to 16	APR 17 to 24	APR Total Obsn	APR MCWB	ANNUAL 01 to 08	ANNUAL 09 to 16	ANNUAL 17 to 24	ANNUAL Total Obsn	ANNUAL MCWB
100/104																																0		0	79
95/99																																3	0	3	78
90/94																															0	128	6	134	78
85/89																											1		1	69	31	492	97	620	77
80/84		3		3	70																0	0	0	0	73		21	1	22	72	254	469	466	1189	75
75/79	1	29	2	32	68		5		5	68		0		0	62		0		0	68		8	0	8	65	10	64	17	91	70	510	331	486	1327	72
70/74	20	60	31	111	66	4	26	4	34	67		11		11	67		18	3	21	67	3	39	6	48	65	50	87	73	210	67	423	352	361	1136	68
65/69	34	48	45	127	62	29	41	33	103	63	11	32	16	59	64	19	38	24	81	64	31	70	47	148	63	72	47	78	197	63	356	319	350	1025	63
60/64	33	44	45	122	57	29	53	42	124	58	33	42	39	114	59	32	47	42	121	58	53	58	74	185	58	48	15	46	109	58	321	277	334	932	58
55/59	39	27	41	107	52	29	46	45	120	52	28	49	40	117	53	29	43	40	112	52	40	38	50	128	52	28	5	17	50	53	237	214	258	709	52
50/54	41	16	33	90	48	35	35	42	112	47	31	40	42	113	48	32	35	44	111	47	45	22	34	101	48	23	1	7	31	48	234	150	213	597	48
45/49	30	11	22	63	43	34	21	32	87	43	32	30	40	102	43	34	23	31	88	43	32	10	22	64	43	8		2	10	44	181	95	152	428	43
40/44	21	2	14	37	39	36	11	27	74	39	39	24	35	98	38	30	12	23	65	38	26	3	12	41	38	2		0	2	39	158	52	111	321	38
35/39	14	1	5	20	34	25	5	14	44	34	29	12	20	61	34	23	6	14	43	34	12	1	2	15	34	0			0	36	104	25	55	184	34
30/34	6	0	1	7	30	17	2	7	26	30	28	5	9	42	29	17	2	3	22	29	4	0	1	5	30						72	9	21	102	29
25/29	1	1	0	1	27	8	1	1	10	25	10	2	5	17	25	6	0	1	7	25	1			1	25						26	3	7	36	25
20/24	0	0		0	24	1	0	0	1	21	4	1	2	7	20	1			1	20											6	1	2	9	20
15/19						0	0	0	0	15	1	0	0	2	16																1	1	0	2	16
10/14						0	0	0	0	11	2	0	0	2	8																2	0	0	2	11
5/9						0	0	0	0	8				0																	0			0	8

PHOENIX, ARIZONA*
READINGS TAKEN AT GLENDALE/LUKE AFB
LAT 33 33N LONG 112 22W ELEV 1101 FT

MEAN FREQUENCY OF OCCURRENCE OF DRY BULB TEMPERATURE (DEGREES F) WITH MEAN COINCIDENT WET BULB TEMPERATURE (DEGREES F) FOR EACH DRY BULB TEMPERATURE RANGE

Temperature Range	MAY 01–08	MAY 09–16	MAY 17–24	MAY Total	MAY MCWB	JUNE 01–08	JUNE 09–16	JUNE 17–24	JUNE Total	JUNE MCWB	JULY 01–08	JULY 09–16	JULY 17–24	JULY Total	JULY MCWB	AUG 01–08	AUG 09–16	AUG 17–24	AUG Total	AUG MCWB	SEP 01–08	SEP 09–16	SEP 17–24	SEP Total	SEP MCWB	OCT 01–08	OCT 09–16	OCT 17–24	OCT Total	OCT MCWB
115/119							1	0	1	70		1	1	2	73															
110/114		0	0	0	66		7	5	12	70		9	7	16	72		0		0	75										
105/109		2	2	4	66		24	17	41	69		39	30	69	72		2	1	3	74		3		3	71				0	
100/104		11	7	18	65		38	27	65	67		67	50	117	71		19	12	31	73		6	3	9	70		0		0	
95/99		32	21	53	63	0	50	40	90	65	2	61	56	119	71	1	52	37	89	73		26	14	40	69		8	2	10	66
90/94	0	45	29	74	61	7	46	44	97	63	27	47	61	135	70	12	65	49	115	72		45	25	70	67		27	9	36	64
85/89	2	47	37	86	59	24	36	43	103	62	92	18	29	139	68	61	58	28	128	71	1	55	42	98	66		46	20	66	62
80/84	9	44	44	97	57	48	23	32	103	59	81	6	9	96	67	92	36	13	146	71	11	49	45	105	65		50	28	78	60
75/79	30	33	45	108	55	57	11	20	88	57	38	1	3	42	66	64	11	3	78	70	39	34	48	121	64	4	44	41	89	59
70/74	51	19	31	101	53	53	3	8	64	54	7	0	0	7	60	16	3	1	20	69	62	17	35	114	60	23	35	49	107	57
65/69	61	9	20	90	51	34	0	3	37	52	1			1	54	3	0		3	64	63	6	20	89	57	51	22	49	122	55
60/64	53	4	9	66	49	14	0	0	14	49						1			1	54	40	1	6	47	56	70	10	31	111	52
55/59	31	1	3	35	46	2			2	46										50	19	0	1	20	53	62	4	14	80	48
50/54	10	0	1	11	44	0			0	46										41	4	0	1	5	49	27	1	4	32	44
45/49	2		0	2	38																1			1	49	8	1	1	10	41
40/44	0			0	35																					2		0	2	36
35/39																										1			1	30
30/34																										0			0	27

*Comparative design data note:

	Elevation	WINTER 97 1/2%	SUMMER DB 2 1/2%	SUMMER WB 2 1/2%
Phoenix AP, AZ.	1117 ft.	34° F	106° F	76° F
Luke AFB	1101 ft.	35° F	107° F	76° F

PHOENIX, ARIZONA*
READINGS TAKEN AT GLENDALE/LUKE AFB

Temperature Range	NOVEMBER					DECEMBER					JANUARY					FEBRUARY					MARCH					APRIL					ANNUAL TOTAL				
	Obsn Hour Gp			Total Obsn	MCWB	Obsn Hour Gp			Total Obsn	MCWB	Obsn Hour Gp			Total Obsn	MCWB	Obsn Hour Gp			Total Obsn	MCWB	Obsn Hour Gp			Total Obsn	MCWB	Obsn Hour Gp			Total Obsn	MCWB	Obsn Hour Gp			Total Obsn	MCWB
	01 to 08	09 to 16	17 to 24			01 to 08	09 to 16	17 to 24			01 to 08	09 to 16	17 to 24			01 to 08	09 to 16	17 to 24			01 to 08	09 to 16	17 to 24			01 to 08	09 to 16	17 to 24			01 to 08	09 to 16	17 to 24		
115/119																																2	1	3	72
110/114																																18	13	31	71
105/109																																90	64	154	71
100/104																																194	135	329	70
95/99																											0			0	64	3	265	195	463	68
90/94		0		0	64									0	60				0	64		1	1	2	59		4	2	6	62	47	293	252	592	67
85/89		4	1	5	59				0	54				0	57		1	0	1	60		6	3	9	58		14	8	22	60	190	274	245	709	65
80/84		15	3	18	57		1		1	54		3	1	4	54		5	2	7	58		20	11	31	56	0	31	18	49	58	269	252	232	753	62
75/79		34	10	44	56		8	1	9	54		18	6	24	52		13	7	20	55	0	31	19	50	55	0	41	27	68	56	256	244	230	730	59
70/74	0	46	19	65	54		21	5	26	52		39	17	56	51		30	16	46	53		41	31	72	53	1	46	37	84	54	222	257	231	710	55
65/69	4	48	33	85	53	0	35	13	48	51	1	48	31	80	49	0	42	29	71	51	4	45	42	91	51	9	38	44	91	52	229	274	256	759	52
60/64	14	45	54	113	51	2	48	27	77	49	13	48	49	110	47	5	46	44	95	47	18	45	49	112	48	31	33	44	108	50	256	267	278	801	49
55/59	47	27	60	134	48	9	47	45	101	47	34	41	57	132	44	28	39	50	117	44	46	33	45	124	47	59	21	32	112	48	308	208	285	801	47
50/54	71	15	38	124	44	24	39	65	128	44	55	26	47	128	40	50	28	42	120	41	75	17	30	122	44	66	9	18	93	46	337	144	244	725	44
45/49	59	5	16	80	41	64	29	56	149	41	67	17	25	109	36	60	14	24	98	36	61	7	12	80	41	45	3	7	55	43	332	83	158	573	41
40/44	32	2	5	39	37	82	15	29	126	37	46	5	11	62	32	48	5	9	62	33	30	1	4	35	37	23	1	2	26	40	266	40	72	378	37
35/39	11	0	2	13	34	53	3	6	62	33	26	2	4	32	28	26	1	2	29	28	11	0	1	12	33	5		0	5	37	148	9	22	179	33
30/34	3		0	3	31	12	1	1	14	29	6	0	0	6	23	6			6	25	2			2	28	0			0	37	49	3	5	57	28
25/29						1			1	25	1			1	20	0			0		0			0	23						7	0	0	7	24
20/24																					0			0	23						1	0		1	20

MEAN FREQUENCY OF OCCURRENCE OF DRY BULB TEMPERATURE (DEGREES F) WITH MEAN COINCIDENT WET BULB TEMPERATURE (DEGREES F) FOR EACH DRY BULB TEMPERATURE RANGE

TUCSON, ARIZONA/DAVIS-MONTHAN AFB
LAT 32 11N   LONG 110 54W   ELEV 2654 FT

Temperature Range	MAY					JUNE					JULY					AUGUST					SEPTEMBER					OCTOBER				
	Obsn 01 to 08	Hour 09 to 16	Gp 17 to 24	Total Obsn	MWB	01 to 08	09 to 16	17 to 24	Total Obsn	MWB	01 to 08	09 to 16	17 to 24	Total Obsn	MWB	01 to 08	09 to 16	17 to 24	Total Obsn	MWB	01 to 08	09 to 16	17 to 24	Total Obsn	MWB	01 to 08	09 to 16	17 to 24	Total Obsn	MWB
110/114							0		0	68							0		0	68										
105/109							5	1	6	67		3	1	4	68		9	3	12	69										
100/104		3	1	4	64		28	13	41	66		28	14	42	68		37	20	57	69		3	0	3	69					
95/99		15	7	22	62	0	50	32	82	64		61	34	95	68	0	75	39	114	69		34	10	44	66		2	0	2	61
90/94		43	21	64	59	1	63	47	111	62	2	71	50	123	68	5	67	51	123	69		54	26	80	65		18	4	22	61
85/89	1	56	34	91	57	12	47	49	108	60	20	51	55	126	67	39	42	62	143	68	1	64	44	109	65		41	14	55	59
80/84	5	53	42	100	55	39	30	42	111	59	72	23	49	144	67	110	14	49	173	67	20	47	54	121	64	0	56	23	79	58
75/79	15	38	46	99	54	50	12	30	92	57	100	8	31	139	66	84	3	20	107	66	57	23	52	132	63	3	52	40	95	57
70/74	36	22	43	101	51	57	3	18	78	54	51	3	13	67	66	10	0	3	13	63	80	11	37	128	61	21	37	50	108	55
65/69	57	11	30	98	49	48	0	6	54	50	3	0	1	4	63		0	0	0	61	55	0	13	71	57	53	21	49	123	53
60/64	67	4	15	86	46	26		1	27	47											21	0	3	24	52	70	11	37	118	50
55/59	41	2	6	49	44	7			7	44											5	0	1	6	48	54	6	19	79	47
50/54	19	1	2	22	41	0			0	41											1			1	43	29	2	8	39	44
45/49	6	0	1	7	38																					12	1	3	16	40
40/44	2	0		2	34																					4	1	1	6	38
35/39	0			0	28																					0		0	0	30
30/34																										0			0	26

COINCIDENT WET BULB TEMPERATURE FOR EACH DRY BULB TEMPERATURE RANGE

TUCSON, ARIZONA/DAVIS-MONTHAN AFB

(MCWB = Mean Coincident Wet Bulb temperature. Obsn Hour Gp = Observation Hour Group.)

NOVEMBER

Temperature Range	Obsn Hour Gp 01 to 08	Obsn Hour Gp 09 to 16	Obsn Hour Gp 17 to 24	Total Obsn	MCWB
85/89		1		1	55
80/84		16	2	18	55
75/79	0	34	8	42	53
70/74	3	45	17	62	52
65/69	18	47	31	81	50
60/64	51	42	49	109	48
55/59	65	27	54	132	46
50/54	58	18	42	125	43
45/49	28	7	23	88	40
40/44	13	3	10	41	37
35/39	4	1	3	17	34
30/34	0	0	1	5	31
25/29		0		0	26

DECEMBER

Temperature Range	Obsn Hour Gp 01 to 08	Obsn Hour Gp 09 to 16	Obsn Hour Gp 17 to 24	Total Obsn	MCWB
90/94		0		0	63
85/89		1	1	1	53
80/84	0	8	4	9	52
75/79	3	24	12	28	50
70/74	16	41	26	53	49
65/69	42	41	46	70	47
60/64	60	46	59	108	46
55/59	68	39	50	140	43
50/54	38	28	32	138	40
45/49	16	12	14	112	37
40/44	4	6	3	58	33
35/39	1	1	1	20	29
30/34		0		5	25
25/29		0		1	21

JANUARY

Temperature Range	Obsn Hour Gp 01 to 08	Obsn Hour Gp 09 to 16	Obsn Hour Gp 17 to 24	Total Obsn	MCWB
80/84		1	0	1	55
75/79		5	1	6	52
70/74	0	19	5	24	50
65/69	1	34	12	46	48
60/64	12	51	28	80	47
55/59	37	49	48	109	45
50/54	53	41	55	133	43
45/49	70	26	47	126	39
40/44	37	14	30	114	36
35/39	20	7	15	65	32
30/34	9	2	6	28	28
25/29	3	1	2	12	23
20/24	1	0	0	3	18
15/19				1	16

FEBRUARY

Temperature Range	Obsn Hour Gp 01 to 08	Obsn Hour Gp 09 to 16	Obsn Hour Gp 17 to 24	Total Obsn	MCWB
85/89		1	0	1	59
80/84		3	1	4	56
75/79	0	12	3	15	53
70/74	1	24	11	35	51
65/69	4	38	21	60	49
60/64	21	43	37	84	47
55/59	40	43	44	108	45
50/54	54	32	46	118	42
45/49	48	17	32	103	39
40/44	36	8	18	74	36
35/39	17	3	8	47	32
30/34	3	1	2	20	28
25/29	0	3	0	3	24
20/24		0		0	22

MARCH

Temperature Range	Obsn Hour Gp 01 to 08	Obsn Hour Gp 09 to 16	Obsn Hour Gp 17 to 24	Total Obsn	MCWB
90/94		0	0	0	58
85/89		3	1	4	56
80/84		16	5	21	54
75/79	0	28	15	43	52
70/74	1	43	25	69	50
65/69	2	42	35	79	48
60/64	11	43	45	99	46
55/59	32	33	46	111	44
50/54	66	22	38	126	42
45/49	63	12	24	99	39
40/44	45	4	10	59	36
35/39	20	1	1	25	32
30/34	7	0	1	8	28
25/29	1	0		1	22
20/24	0			0	17

APRIL

Temperature Range	Obsn Hour Gp 01 to 08	Obsn Hour Gp 09 to 16	Obsn Hour Gp 17 to 24	Total Obsn	MCWB
100/104		0	0	0	62
95/99		1	0	1	61
90/94		9	3	12	58
85/89		19	8	27	56
80/84	0	42	21	63	54
75/79	6	50	33	83	52
70/74	20	46	42	94	50
65/69	44	33	46	99	48
60/64	61	21	40	105	46
55/59	58	11	28	100	44
50/54	35	6	12	76	41
45/49	14	1	5	41	39
40/44	3	0	1	15	36
35/39	0		0	3	34
30/34				0	33

ANNUAL TOTAL

Temperature Range	Obsn Hour Gp 01 to 08	Obsn Hour Gp 09 to 16	Obsn Hour Gp 17 to 24	Total Obsn	MCWB
110/114				0	68
105/109	8		2	10	68
100/104	0	71	31	102	67
95/99	0	200	103	303	66
90/94	3	333	190	526	65
85/89	39	350	256	645	63
80/84	175	330	301	806	62
75/79	335	284	309	928	60
70/74	336	280	285	901	56
65/69	252	270	259	781	51
60/64	265	256	281	802	48
55/59	300	217	292	809	45
50/54	357	161	262	780	42
45/49	341	92	185	618	40
40/44	279	42	102	423	36
35/39	153	18	44	215	32
30/34	64	4	13	81	29
25/29	17	1	3	21	24
20/24	4	0	0	4	19
15/19	1			1	16

LITTLE ROCK AFB ARKANSAS
LAT 34 55N   LONG 92 09W   ELEV 311 FT

MEAN FREQUENCY OF OCCURRENCE OF DRY BULB TEMPERATURE (DEGREES F) WITH MEAN COINCIDENT WET BULB TEMPERATURE (DEGREES F) FOR EACH DRY BULB TEMPERATURE RANGE

Temperature Range	MAY 01–08	MAY 09–16	MAY 17–24	MAY Total	MAY MCWB	JUNE 01–08	JUNE 09–16	JUNE 17–24	JUNE Total	JUNE MCWB	JULY 01–08	JULY 09–16	JULY 17–24	JULY Total	JULY MCWB	AUG 01–08	AUG 09–16	AUG 17–24	AUG Total	AUG MCWB	SEP 01–08	SEP 09–16	SEP 17–24	SEP Total	SEP MCWB	OCT 01–08	OCT 09–16	OCT 17–24	OCT Total	OCT MCWB
105/109																			0	79										
100/104																			0	77										
95/99		0		0	75			0	0	77		3	0	3	78		2	0	2	77										
90/94		9	1	10	71		7	1	8	76		25	6	31	78		13	3	16	76		3	0	3	75		2		2	66
85/89		31	12	43	70		42	13	55	75	0	62	24	86	77		55	17	72	74		22	4	26	76		12	2	14	70
80/84	1	59	33	93	69	1	68	36	105	74	3	74	46	123	75	1	74	38	113	74		45	15	60	73		31	8	39	67
75/79	12	53	50	115	67	12	59	58	129	72	30	48	64	142	74	37	36	63	136	73	2	53	34	89	71	1	39	22	62	65
70/74	45	39	55	139	65	57	39	60	156	70	99	26	69	194	72	103	10	71	184	72	28	52	56	136	70	11	44	35	90	63
65/69	71	32	47	150	62	89	20	50	159	68	84	9	31	124	69	98	3	41	142	69	72	36	59	167	68	32	44	47	123	60
60/64	51	16	28	95	58	53	5	16	74	64	22	1	6	29	64	47	0	13	60	64	60	19	39	118	63	42	37	44	123	56
55/59	34	7	14	55	53	19	1	4	24	59	7		1	8	59	15		2	17	60	37	6	20	63	58	44	25	40	109	52
50/54	20	2	7	29	49	7		1	8	55	2			2	56	3			3	56	27	2	9	38	54	48	11	31	90	48
45/49	12	0	1	13	45	1		0	1	50											10	0	2	12	50	39	3	13	55	43
40/44	2			2	41	0			0	47											2		1	3	45	21		5	26	39
35/39																					1		0	1	40	7		1	8	36
30/34																										2			2	31
25/29																													0	28

LITTLE ROCK AFB ARKANSAS

Temperature Range	NOV 01–08	NOV 09–16	NOV 17–24	NOV Total Obsn	NOV MCWB	DEC 01–08	DEC 09–16	DEC 17–24	DEC Total Obsn	DEC MCWB	JAN 01–08	JAN 09–16	JAN 17–24	JAN Total Obsn	JAN MCWB	FEB 01–08	FEB 09–16	FEB 17–24	FEB Total Obsn	FEB MCWB	MAR 01–08	MAR 09–16	MAR 17–24	MAR Total Obsn	MAR MCWB	APR 01–08	APR 09–16	APR 17–24	APR Total Obsn	APR MCWB	ANN 01–08	ANN 09–16	ANN 17–24	ANN Total Obsn	ANN MCWB
105/109																																	0	0	79
100/104																																		0	77
95/99																																5		5	77
90/94																											1	0	1	68		48	10	58	76
85/89																						2	1	3	67	0	6	2	8	67		193	59	252	74
80/84		2	0	2	68		0	0	0	66		0		0	63		0		0	63		5	2	7	64	0	25	11	36	66	63	312	152	469	71
75/79	0	8	1	9	64	1	0	1	6	63		1	0	1	64	0	1	1	2	62	0	9	6	15	63	2	36	25	63	65	276	337	273	673	70
70/74	2	22	8	32	62	2	4	5	18	60	2	4	1	5	62	0	5	2	7	59	2	16	12	30	59	18	44	39	101	62	415	300	361	937	66
65/69	8	32	21	61	59	8	11	15	44	56	9	9	6	17	60	0	9	6	15	56	8	24	18	50	57	35	46	45	126	59	337	253	334	1002	61
60/64	16	38	32	86	55	14	21	22	62	52	10	14	13	36	57	5	16	11	32	54	15	32	30	77	54	39	46	42	127	56	271	235	269	841	56
55/59	27	36	39	102	51	15	26	26	77	46	8	20	14	44	51	8	22	19	49	50	23	35	34	92	50	29	38	38	105	51	241	219	242	732	51
50/54	39	40	43	122	47	26	36	40	107	42	15	27	19	54	46	17	31	23	71	46	27	39	37	103	45	33	25	25	83	47	229	198	230	669	47
45/49	39	30	37	106	42	39	41	49	129	38	31	33	33	81	42	22	36	38	96	42	37	35	43	115	42	20	14	9	43	43	221	200	215	642	42
40/44	40	16	30	86	38	47	41	42	121	34	35	36	36	103	38	36	38	43	117	38	54	25	33	112	38	13	5	3	21	38	241	183	199	619	38
35/39	35	9	17	61	34	41	32	25	85	29	48	34	39	108	33	38	29	35	102	33	41	15	19	75	33	4	1	0	5	34	208	157	153	597	33
30/34	21	5	7	33	29	30	19	16	57	25	42	32	42	122	29	42	20	29	91	29	25	8	11	44	29	1	0	1	2	31	180	119	115	480	29
25/29	9	1	3	13	25	15	11	5	24	20	25	20	22	84	25	35	12	13	60	25	12	2	3	17	25						128	84	57	231	25
20/24	3	0	1	4	20	8	4	3	13	16	12	10	13	48	20	14	3	4	21	20	3	1	1	5	20						60	46	24	102	20
15/19	1	0	0	1	16	2	2	1	3	11	6	5	6	23	15	5	1	1	7	16	1	0		1	16						27	18	10	45	15
10/14						0	0	0	0	6	3	3	2	11	11	1			1	12											9	8	3	15	11
5/9											1	1	1	5	7																3	3	1	5	7
0/4						0			0	4	2	0	0	2	2																2	0		2	2
-5/-1											0			0	-2																0			0	-2

BAKERSFIELD, CALIFORNIA*
READINGS TAKEN AT CASTLE AFB/MERCED
LAT 37 23N   LONG 120 34W   ELEV   188 FT

MEAN FREQUENCY OF OCCURRENCE OF DRY BULB TEMPERATURE (DEGREES F) WITH MEAN COINCIDENT WET BULB TEMPERATURE (DEGREES F) FOR EACH DRY BULB TEMPERATURE RANGE

Temperature Range	MAY 01–08	MAY 09–16	MAY 17–24	MAY Total Obsn	MAY MCWB	JUNE 01–08	JUNE 09–16	JUNE 17–24	JUNE Total Obsn	JUNE MCWB	JULY 01–08	JULY 09–16	JULY 17–24	JULY Total Obsn	JULY MCWB	AUG 01–08	AUG 09–16	AUG 17–24	AUG Total Obsn	AUG MCWB	SEP 01–08	SEP 09–16	SEP 17–24	SEP Total Obsn	SEP MCWB	OCT 01–08	OCT 09–16	OCT 17–24	OCT Total Obsn	OCT MCWB
110/114							1	0	1	74		0	0	0	73															
105/109							3	1	4	72		3	1	4	71		0	0	0	70		0	0	0	71					
100/104		0	0	0	66		9	5	14	70		17	6	23	70		11	3	14	70		2	0	2	71					
95/99		3	1	4	67		16	9	25	69		44	22	66	69		36	14	50	69		11	3	14	69		0	0	0	66
90/94		11	5	16	65	0	30	16	46	67	0	57	33	90	67		57	28	85	67		30	9	39	66		7	1	8	66
85/89		22	10	32	63	1	38	26	65	65	3	52	37	92	65	0	51	35	86	66		43	20	63	65		14	3	17	64
80/84	0	34	17	51	62	5	44	33	82	63	10	38	45	93	64	5	42	45	92	64	0	49	29	78	63		26	9	35	62
75/79	1	44	27	72	60	15	42	37	94	61	30	25	47	102	61	25	28	50	103	62	6	46	43	95	62	0	41	16	57	60
70/74	6	51	36	93	58	28	32	38	98	59	60	10	32	102	59	55	16	42	113	59	20	34	51	105	59	1	53	31	85	58
65/69	17	40	45	102	56	44	17	34	95	57	73	2	18	93	57	71	5	21	97	58	47	19	49	115	57	8	50	47	105	56
60/64	45	27	48	120	54	65	5	27	97	54	52	0	5	57	55	63	0	9	72	55	86	6	28	120	55	35	35	61	131	54
55/59	80	12	38	130	51	57	2	12	71	52	19	0	1	20	53	26	1	2	29	53	58	0	8	66	52	72	17	52	141	52
50/54	72	18	2	92	48	23	0	2	25	49	2	0	0	2	49	2	0	0	2	50	20	0	1	21	48	79	4	23	106	48
45/49	21	3	0	24	44	1	0	0	1	45											2	0	0	2	44	42	0	4	46	44
40/44	6	0	0	6	40	0	0	0	0	42											0	0	0	0	39	9	0	1	10	39
35/39	0	0	0	0	36																					2	0	0	2	33
30/34																										0	0	0	0	28

*Comparative design data note:

	Elevation	WINTER 97 1/2%	SUMMER DB 2 1/2%	SUMMER WB 2 1/2%
Castle AFB-Merced, CA.	188 ft.	32° F	99° F	72° F
Bakersfield AP	475 ft.	33° F	101° F	71° F

BAKERSFIELD, CALIFORNIA*
READINGS TAKEN AT CASTLE AFB/MERCED

Obsn Hour Gp columns: 01 to 08, 09 to 16, 17 to 24. Then Total Obsn and MCWB.

Temp. Range	Nov 01-08	Nov 09-16	Nov 17-24	Nov Total	Nov MCWB	Dec 01-08	Dec 09-16	Dec 17-24	Dec Total	Dec MCWB	Jan 01-08	Jan 09-16	Jan 17-24	Jan Total	Jan MCWB	Feb 01-08	Feb 09-16	Feb 17-24	Feb Total	Feb MCWB	Mar 01-08	Mar 09-16	Mar 17-24	Mar Total	Mar MCWB	Apr 01-08	Apr 09-16	Apr 17-24	Apr Total	Apr MCWB	Ann 01-08	Ann 09-16	Ann 17-24	Ann Total	Ann MCWB
110/114																																1	0	1	74
105/109																																6	2	8	71
100/104																																39	14	53	70
95/99																															0	110	49	159	69
90/94																											0	0	0	66	0	194	93	287	67
85/89																						0	0	0	64		2	1	3	65	4	227	133	364	65
80/84		0		0	60																	1	0	1	62		7	2	9	63	20	252	185	457	63
75/79		6	0	6	60																	8	2	10	60		18	7	25	61	77	268	236	581	61
70/74	0	18	3	21	57																	21	7	28	58		28	14	42	59	170	275	262	707	59
65/69		32	9	41	55		4	0	4	55		2	0	2	58		2	0	2	59		36	17	53	55	0	38	22	60	57	263	265	276	804	56
60/64	2	50	27	79	54	1	17	4	22	53	0	13	5	18	55		14	4	18	57	1	61	35	97	53	3	44	32	79	55	367	292	306	965	54
55/59	21	59	58	138	52	6	33	16	55	51	8	38	21	67	52	1	38	16	55	54	12	64	59	135	50	16	40	41	97	53	416	325	359	1100	51
50/54	54	46	69	169	48	20	47	39	106	48	20	57	44	121	48	14	63	48	125	51	57	42	69	168	47	43	36	44	123	50	454	273	371	1098	48
45/49	64	21	46	131	44	33	60	58	151	44	40	53	56	149	44	38	54	61	153	48	86	13	42	141	44	67	21	45	133	47	420	188	294	902	44
40/44	59	8	21	88	40	68	54	76	198	40	52	47	64	163	40	57	35	59	151	44	63	3	13	79	40	74	6	26	106	44	345	126	210	681	40
35/39	31	1	6	38	36	69	26	42	137	36	65	25	42	132	36	59	14	29	102	40	23	0	3	26	35	29	0	6	35	40	242	55	100	397	36
30/34	9		0	9	31	40	6	12	58	31	46	11	16	73	31	45	3	7	55	35	5	0	0	5	30	7	0	0	7	36	113	17	29	159	31
25/29	0	0		0	28	11	0	1	12	27	17	1	1	19	27	12	0	1	13	31	1			1	25	1			1	32	29	1	2	32	27
20/24						0	0	0	0	21			1	1	22	0		0	0	26													1	1	22
15/19						0			0	17																							0	0	17

BLYTHE, CALIFORNIA*
READINGS TAKEN AT YUMA, AZ

LAT 32 39N   LONG 114 37W   ELEV 213 FT

MEAN FREQUENCY OF OCCURRENCE OF DRY BULB TEMPERATURE (DEGREES F) WITH MEAN COINCIDENT WET BULB TEMPERATURE (DEGREES F) FOR EACH DRY BULB TEMPERATURE RANGE

MAY

Temperature Range	Obsn Hour Gp 01 to 08	09 to 16	17 to 24	Total Obsn	MCWB
120/124					
115/119					
110/114		1	0	1	66
105/109		3	2	5	65
100/104	0	14	7	21	64
95/99	0	37	20	57	62
90/94	0	50	31	81	61
85/89	2	48	36	86	59
80/84	10	42	44	96	58
75/79	33	29	45	107	56
70/74	61	16	31	108	55
65/69	69	7	17	93	53
60/64	41	1	12	54	50
55/59	24	0	3	27	47
50/54	6		0	6	45
45/49	1			1	42

JUNE

Temperature Range	Obsn Hour Gp 01 to 08	09 to 16	17 to 24	Total Obsn	MCWB
115/119		1	0	1	70
110/114		9	6	15	69
105/109		27	16	43	68
100/104	0	42	25	67	67
95/99		55	35	90	65
90/94	3	46	44	93	64
85/89	28	34	44	106	63
80/84	55	17	37	109	61
75/79	69	6	22	97	58
70/74	53	2	7	62	57
65/69	24	1	2	27	54
60/64	7		1	8	51
55/59	2		0	2	49

JULY

Temperature Range	Obsn Hour Gp 01 to 08	09 to 16	17 to 24	Total Obsn	MCWB
115/119		1	1	2	73
110/114		14	7	21	73
105/109		50	30	80	72
100/104	0	70	42	112	72
95/99	1	57	51	109	72
90/94	23	39	64	126	71
85/89	112	13	39	164	70
80/84	83	3	10	96	69
75/79	22	1	3	26	64
70/74	5		0	5	58
65/69	0			0	54

AUGUST

Temperature Range	Obsn Hour Gp 01 to 08	09 to 16	17 to 24	Total Obsn	MCWB
115/119				0	74
110/114		7	2	9	72
105/109		45	19	64	73
100/104	0	70	38	108	73
95/99		59	49	108	73
90/94	16	44	72	132	72
85/89	104	17	47	168	72
80/84	89	5	17	111	70
75/79	28	2	3	33	66
70/74	9	0	1	10	62
65/69	1			1	55

SEPTEMBER

Temperature Range	Obsn Hour Gp 01 to 08	09 to 16	17 to 24	Total Obsn	MCWB
115/119				0	72
110/114				0	72
105/109		4	0	4	72
100/104	0	28	9	37	71
95/99	0	49	21	70	70
90/94	0	55	33	88	70
85/89	3	48	48	99	69
80/84	33	33	59	125	69
75/79	71	16	42	129	67
70/74	61	5	21	87	64
65/69	46	1	6	53	59
60/64	21		1	22	56
55/59	3			3	53
50/54				0	46

OCTOBER

Temperature Range	Obsn Hour Gp 01 to 08	09 to 16	17 to 24	Total Obsn	MCWB
105/109		0		0	68
100/104		13	3	16	67
95/99		33	10	43	65
90/94		45	18	63	64
85/89		48	31	79	63
80/84	8	39	48	95	62
75/79	31	32	53	116	60
70/74	53	22	43	118	58
65/69	72	10	26	108	55
60/64	54	3	11	68	52
55/59	21	1	4	26	47
50/54	8	0	1	9	44
45/49	1			1	41

*Comparative design data note:

	WINTER 97 1/2%	SUMMER DB 2 1/2%	SUMMER WB 2 1/2%	Elevation
Blythe, CA.	35° F	109° F	77° F	390 ft.
Yuma, AZ.	40° F	109° F	78° F	213 ft.

COINCIDENT WET BULB TEMPERATURE FOR EACH DRY BULB TEMPERATURE RANGE

BLYTHE, CALIFORNIA*
READINGS TAKEN AT YUMA, AZ

Temperature Range	NOV 01-08	NOV 09-16	NOV 17-24	NOV Total Obsn	NOV MCWB	DEC 01-08	DEC 09-16	DEC 17-24	DEC Total Obsn	DEC MCWB	JAN 01-08	JAN 09-16	JAN 17-24	JAN Total Obsn	JAN MCWB	FEB 01-08	FEB 09-16	FEB 17-24	FEB Total Obsn	FEB MCWB	MAR 01-08	MAR 09-16	MAR 17-24	MAR Total Obsn	MAR MCWB	APR 01-08	APR 09-16	APR 17-24	APR Total Obsn	APR MCWB	ANN 01-08	ANN 09-16	ANN 17-24	ANN Total Obsn	ANN MCWB
120/124																																0	0	0	72
115/119																																2	1	3	72
110/114																																35	15	50	72
105/109																											0	0	0	64		153	76	229	71
100/104																										0	3	1	4	63	0	261	137	398	71
95/99		0	0	0	61																					0	12	5	17	61	1	308	203	512	69
90/94		2	0	2	60												0	0	0	60		4	1	5	58	0	27	13	40	59	45	305	291	641	67
85/89		15	3	18	59		0	0	0	55		0	0	0	58		5	1	6	58		19	8	27	57	0	42	24	66	58	279	274	292	845	66
80/84		32	6	38	58		4	0	4	56		3	0	3	56	0	14	5	19	56		35	17	52	55	0	46	31	77	57	316	256	257	829	63
75/79	0	44	18	62	56		20	3	23	54		13	3	16	54	0	26	12	38	54		42	25	67	53	3	44	42	89	55	247	264	250	761	58
70/74	2	47	34	83	54		42	11	53	51		32	11	43	52	0	39	22	61	52	1	45	38	84	52	23	35	46	104	53	253	281	250	784	55
65/69	11	42	52	105	52	0	53	26	79	50		49	24	73	50	3	48	40	91	50	9	43	49	101	50	57	20	38	115	52	267	273	275	815	52
60/64	43	30	57	130	49	6	51	51	108	48	3	50	45	98	48	18	40	49	107	48	39	35	50	124	48	70	9	23	102	50	284	219	299	802	49
55/59	66	17	41	124	46	35	39	70	144	46	28	46	63	137	46	45	28	48	121	46	77	16	36	129	46	53	2	12	67	47	351	149	277	777	46
50/54	65	8	21	94	43	71	24	55	150	42	62	29	54	145	43	63	15	30	108	42	72	6	19	97	43	25	0	4	29	44	372	82	184	638	43
45/49	36	2	7	45	40	81	12	27	120	39	73	16	32	121	39	57	6	12	75	39	36	2	4	42	40	7		0	7	41	292	38	82	412	40
40/44	13	1	2	16	36	43	3	4	52	36	52	7	12	72	36	26	1	4	31	36	12	0	0	12	36	1			1	38	147	12	23	182	36
35/39	3	0		3	33	11	0	1	12	31	24	2	3	29	32	9	0	0	9	30	2	0		2	31						49	2	4	55	31
30/34	0			0	31	1		0	1	29	7	0	0	7	27	2			2	27				0	29						10	0	0	10	27
25/29														0	22																			0	22

LOS ANGELES IAP CALIFORNIA
LAT 33 56N   LONG 118 24W   ELEV   97 FT

MEAN FREQUENCY OF OCCURRENCE OF DRY BULB TEMPERATURE (DEGREES F) WITH MEAN COINCIDENT WET BULB TEMPERATURE (DEGREES F) FOR EACH DRY BULB TEMPERATURE RANGE

Temperature Range	MAY 01–08	MAY 09–16	MAY 17–24	MAY Total Obsn	MAY MC WB	JUNE 01–08	JUNE 09–16	JUNE 17–24	JUNE Total Obsn	JUNE MC WB	JULY 01–08	JULY 09–16	JULY 17–24	JULY Total Obsn	JULY MC WB	AUG 01–08	AUG 09–16	AUG 17–24	AUG Total Obsn	AUG MC WB	SEP 01–08	SEP 09–16	SEP 17–24	SEP Total Obsn	SEP MC WB	OCT 01–08	OCT 09–16	OCT 17–24	OCT Total Obsn	OCT MC WB
105/109																							0	0	73					
100/104		0		0	63		0		0	63		0		0	68		0		0	71		1		1	72		1		1	67
95/99		0		0	60		0		0	61		0		0	70		0		0	70	0	2	0	2	69		1		1	65
90/94		1	0	1	58		1	0	1	64		3	0	3	68		1		1	70		1		1	69		3		3	63
85/89		2	0	2	57		1	0	1	66		15	1	16	69	0	16	0	16	69		5	1	6	68		4	0	4	62
80/84																					2	17	2	21	68	1	10	2	13	62
75/79	0	6	1	7	60	0	22	1	23	65	3	62	6	71	67	2	70	6	78	67	5	49	9	63	66	1	22	3	26	63
70/74	1	34	3	38	61	3	66	12	81	63	21	117	41	179	65	21	121	45	187	65	16	93	35	144	64	6	65	13	84	62
65/69	6	103	19	128	58	25	113	53	191	61	104	47	117	268	63	119	37	132	288	63	69	63	98	230	62	34	100	64	198	61
60/64	72	91	100	263	56	139	37	141	317	58	104	3	77	184	59	100	2	63	165	60	122	8	91	221	60	97	40	127	264	58
55/59	126	11	114	251	54	68	1	33	102	55	16	0	6	22	56	6	0	1	7	57	26	0	4	30	56	88	2	37	127	55
50/54	39	0	11	50	50	5	0	0	5	51	0			0	53						0			0	53	21		1	22	50
45/49	2	2	0	2	45	0			0	47																0			0	43

COINCIDENT WET BULB TEMPERATURE FOR EACH DRY BULB TEMPERATURE RANGE

LOS ANGELES IAP CALIFORNIA

Temperature Range	NOV 01-08	NOV 09-16	NOV 17-24	NOV Total	NOV MCWB	DEC 01-08	DEC 09-16	DEC 17-24	DEC Total	DEC MCWB	JAN 01-08	JAN 09-16	JAN 17-24	JAN Total	JAN MCWB	FEB 01-08	FEB 09-16	FEB 17-24	FEB Total	FEB MCWB	MAR 01-08	MAR 09-16	MAR 17-24	MAR Total	MAR MCWB	APR 01-08	APR 09-16	APR 17-24	APR Total	APR MCWB	ANN 01-08	ANN 09-16	ANN 17-24	ANN Total	ANN MCWB
105/109																																0	0	0	73
100/104		0		0																												2		2	70
95/99		1		1	60																										0	3	0	3	67
90/94		4		4	60		0		0	59							0		0	63							0		0	59	0	5	0	5	65
85/89		10		10	59		0		0	55		0		0	60		1		1	59		1		1	56		1		1	62		22	1	23	64
80/84	0	19	1	20	56		5	0	5	56		3		3	57		2	0	2	57		3	0	3	56		4	0	4	62	3	88	5	96	64
75/79		30	5	35	56		10	0	10	54		7	0	7	55		6	0	6	56		6	0	6	55		6	2	8	61	11	285	29	325	64
70/74	5	61	22	88	57		19	2	21	53		16	1	17	54		15	1	16	54	0	15	2	17	56	1	20	4	25	59	69	611	164	844	63
65/69	34	78	80	192	56	0	40	8	48	53		29	5	34	53	2	32	6	40	53	2	41	7	50	55	3	51	12	66	58	369	717	543	1629	60
60/64	86	32	97	215	55	10	82	36	128	53	3	60	26	89	52	5	72	30	107	53	5	95	31	131	54	24	114	45	183	55	715	682	847	2244	57
55/59	80	4	31	115	52	51	69	106	226	52	33	85	86	204	51	48	71	95	214	52	61	71	116	248	52	113	41	141	295	53	722	383	836	1941	53
50/54	31	1	5	37	48	92	20	78	190	48	83	38	89	210	48	83	23	75	181	48	108	16	82	206	49	81	3	35	119	50	592	104	402	1098	48
45/49	4			4	43	73	2	16	91	43	81	10	33	124	43	66	2	16	84	43	61	0	9	70	44	17	0	1	18	45	331	15	80	426	43
40/44	0			0	38	19	0	2	21	38	39	1	8	48	39	19		1	20	38	10		1	11	40	0			0	41	91	1	12	104	39
35/39					33	2			2	32	9		0	9	33	1			1	34	1			1	37						13		0	13	33
30/34						0			0	29	0			0	28																0			0	28

SACRAMENTO, CALIFORNIA/MC CLELLAN AFB

LAT 38 40N   LONG 121 24W   ELEV 76 FT

MEAN FREQUENCY OF OCCURRENCE OF DRY BULB TEMPERATURE (DEGREES F) WITH MEAN COINCIDENT WET BULB TEMPERATURE (DEGREES F) FOR EACH DRY BULB TEMPERATURE RANGE

Within each month the "Obsn Hour Gp" columns are 01 to 08, 09 to 16, 17 to 24; "Tot" = Total Obsn; "WB" = Mean Coincident Wet Bulb.

Temperature Range	May 01-08	May 09-16	May 17-24	May Tot	May WB	Jun 01-08	Jun 09-16	Jun 17-24	Jun Tot	Jun WB	Jul 01-08	Jul 09-16	Jul 17-24	Jul Tot	Jul WB	Aug 01-08	Aug 09-16	Aug 17-24	Aug Tot	Aug WB	Sep 01-08	Sep 09-16	Sep 17-24	Sep Tot	Sep WB	Oct 01-08	Oct 09-16	Oct 17-24	Oct Tot	Oct WB
110/114							0	0	0	71																				
105/109							2	1	3	70		2	1	3	70		1	0	1	72										
100/104		0		0	70		8	4	12	70		16	8	24	69		13	6	19	70										
95/99		2	1	3	68		16	8	24	68		36	17	53	68		32	15	47	68		3	1	4	69		0		0	67
90/94		8	4	12	65		25	11	36	66		49	25	74	67		48	23	71	67		12	4	16	67		1	0	1	65
85/89	0	18	7	25	64	1	34	19	54	65		46	27	73	66		44	24	68	66		32	11	43	65		5	1	6	65
80/84	0	34	15	49	62	3	44	26	73	63	2	38	32	72	64	2	42	32	76	64		40	17	57	64		16	3	19	63
75/79	1	39	20	60	60	8	42	32	82	61	12	30	38	80	62	10	31	44	85	62		44	25	69	63		25	8	33	61
70/74	3	46	27	76	58	18	34	35	87	60	34	21	44	99	60	37	23	46	106	60	14	33	33	80	61		42	15	57	59
65/69	10	48	39	97	56	35	21	39	95	57	65	9	36	110	58	69	12	36	117	58	26	22	45	93	59	1	50	28	79	58
60/64	34	34	54	122	54	65	9	39	113	55	88	1	17	106	55	89	2	19	110	56	59	9	51	119	58	9	49	46	104	56
55/59	82	14	53	149	52	79	3	21	103	52	42	0	3	45	53	40	0	3	43	54	89	1	36	126	55	35	36	65	136	55
50/54	89	3	24	116	48	30	0	4	34	49	2	0	0	2	50	1	0	0	1	51	72	0	15	87	52	89	19	56	164	52
45/49	23	0	4	27	44	2	0	0	2	45	0			0	46	0			0	48	20	0	2	22	48	68	3	19	90	48
40/44	6	0	0	6	40																4	0	0	4	43	32	1	6	39	43
35/39	0			0	35																			0		11	0	1	12	39
30/34																										3		0	3	34

SACRAMENTO, CALIFORNIA/MC CLELLAN AFB

Temperature Range	NOV 01–08	NOV 09–16	NOV 17–24	NOV Total Obsn	NOV MCWB	DEC 01–08	DEC 09–16	DEC 17–24	DEC Total Obsn	DEC MCWB	JAN 01–08	JAN 09–16	JAN 17–24	JAN Total Obsn	JAN MCWB	FEB 01–08	FEB 09–16	FEB 17–24	FEB Total Obsn	FEB MCWB	MAR 01–08	MAR 09–16	MAR 17–24	MAR Total Obsn	MAR MCWB	APR 01–08	APR 09–16	APR 17–24	APR Total Obsn	APR MCWB	ANN 01–08	ANN 09–16	ANN 17–24	ANN Total Obsn	ANN MCWB
110/114																																	0	0	71
105/109																																5	2	7	70
100/104																															0	40	19	59	70
95/99																															0	99	45	144	68
90/94																															0	167	75	242	66
85/89		0	0	0	63																						0		0	63	1	202	98	301	65
80/84		0	2	2	60		0	0	0	56				0	57							1	0	1	63		4	1	5	63	8	245	144	397	63
75/79		7	0	7	59		0	0	0	53				0	55		0		0	59		1	0	1	63		16	6	22	61	34	267	196	497	61
70/74		15	3	18	57		5	0	5	54		1		1	57		3	0	3	59		7	2	9	60		25	12	37	59	108	279	254	641	59
65/69		33	9	42	55	2	13	5	20	53	1	15	5	21	55		13	3	16	57		17	7	24	57		37	19	56	57	235	286	300	821	57
60/64	3	55	31	89	54	10	43	21	74	51	10	39	20	69	52	1	42	15	58	53		29	13	42	55	1	44	28	73	55	412	319	355	1086	54
55/59	33	60	64	157	52	28	58	46	132	48	26	61	44	131	48	18	66	50	134	52	1	59	30	90	52	12	44	39	95	53	522	353	415	1290	52
50/54	64	43	71	178	48	42	58	63	163	44	39	61	68	168	44	43	56	66	165	48	14	70	57	141	50	34	38	52	124	51	506	293	400	1199	48
45/49	60	18	40	118	44	73	49	72	194	40	56	43	64	163	40	55	30	56	141	44	59	45	75	179	48	76	24	49	149	48	418	193	313	924	44
40/44	47	7	17	71	40	57	18	31	106	36	62	20	32	114	36	58	13	27	98	40	86	18	48	152	44	75	7	28	110	44	343	116	201	660	40
35/39	26	1	4	31	35	26	3	8	37	31	37	8	12	57	31	40	2	5	47	35	60	3	14	77	40	32	1	6	39	40	218	41	74	333	36
30/34	6	0	0	6	31	8			8	27	16	1	1	18	26	10	0	1	11	31	21	0	2	23	35	9		0	9	36	84	11	21	116	31
25/29	0			0	25				0	23	1		1	2	22	1			1	26	5		0	5	30				0	32	26	1	1	28	26
20/24																					1			1	27						2			2	22

TABLE 18—Continued   MEAN FREQUENCY OF OCCURRENCE OF DRY BULB TEMPERATURE WITH MEAN

SAN DIEGO FWF CALIFORNIA
LAT 32 43N   LONG 117 09W   ELEV   48 FT

MEAN FREQUENCY OF OCCURRENCE OF DRY BULB TEMPERATURE (DEGREES F) WITH MEAN COINCIDENT WET BULB TEMPERATURE (DEGREES F) FOR EACH DRY BULB TEMPERATURE RANGE

Temperature Range	MAY 01–08	MAY 09–16	MAY 17–24	MAY Total Obsn	MAY MCWB	JUNE 01–08	JUNE 09–16	JUNE 17–24	JUNE Total Obsn	JUNE MCWB	JULY 01–08	JULY 09–16	JULY 17–24	JULY Total Obsn	JULY MCWB	AUGUST 01–08	AUGUST 09–16	AUGUST 17–24	AUGUST Total Obsn	AUGUST MCWB	SEPTEMBER 01–08	SEPTEMBER 09–16	SEPTEMBER 17–24	SEPTEMBER Total Obsn	SEPTEMBER MCWB	OCTOBER 01–08	OCTOBER 09–16	OCTOBER 17–24	OCTOBER Total Obsn	OCTOBER MCWB
100/104																														
95/99									0	64												0		0	64					
90/94				0	63				0	64		0		0	69		0		0	76		1	0	1	64		0		0	68
85/89		1		1	61				0	65		2	0	2	69		1		1	73		1	0	1	66		1	1	1	64
80/84	0	2	0	2	59		1		1	66	0	6	1	7	70	0	11	2	13	71	0	4	0	4	67		4	2	5	63
75/79	0	2	1	3	60	0	4	1	5	66	2	35	9	46	69	7	58	17	82	70	0	8	3	11	68		7	5	9	61
70/74	0	15	4	19	62	0	36	8	45	64	33	84	55	172	66	68	87	85	240	67	4	29	10	43	68	1	12	5	18	61
65/69	7	78	23	108	60	36	86	65	187	62	99	37	88	224	63	88	8	60	156	64	27	86	48	161	66	5	52	15	72	63
60/64	111	112	122	345	57	110	52	82	244	59	32	13	15	60	60	3	14	2	19	56	95	34	88	217	63	41	97	78	216	61
55/59	74	28	64	166	54	30	38	28	96	54	11	39	17	67	53	8	41	20	69	52	32	34	15	81	58	88	57	82	227	58
50/54	25	21	8	53	51	23	17	31	71	50	28	22	35	85	50	30	21	34	85	49	19	33	30	82	54	59	16	37	112	54
45/49	15	8	1	24	46	20	4	15	39	46	19	6	16	41	45	17	5	16	38	46	25	8	28	61	50	32	2	21	55	50
40/44	9	1	3	13	42	10	1	6	17	41	12	2	10	24	41	13	1	8	22	41	19	1	13	33	46	16	0	7	23	46
35/39	5	0	1	6	37	7	1	3	11	37	7	1	3	11	37	11	0	4	15	37	14		4	18	42	6		1	7	42
30/34	1			1	33	3	0	0	3	33	6	0	1	7	32	4	0		4	32	5		0	5	38	1			1	38
25/29	0			0	29	0			0	29	1			1	28	0			0	29	0			0	34					

COINCIDENT WET BULB TEMPERATURE FOR EACH DRY BULB TEMPERATURE RANGE

SAN DIEGO FWF CALIFORNIA

Temperature Range	Nov 01–08	Nov 09–16	Nov 17–24	Nov Total Obsn	Nov MCWB	Dec 01–08	Dec 09–16	Dec 17–24	Dec Total Obsn	Dec MCWB	Jan 01–08	Jan 09–16	Jan 17–24	Jan Total Obsn	Jan MCWB	Feb 01–08	Feb 09–16	Feb 17–24	Feb Total Obsn	Feb MCWB	Mar 01–08	Mar 09–16	Mar 17–24	Mar Total Obsn	Mar MCWB	Apr 01–08	Apr 09–16	Apr 17–24	Apr Total Obsn	Apr MCWB	Ann 01–08	Ann 09–16	Ann 17–24	Ann Total Obsn	Ann MCWB
100/104																																0		0	64
95/99		0	0	0	65																											1	0	1	65
90/94		0	0	0	63																										0	2	0	2	65
85/89		0	0	0	61												2	0	2	66		1		1	58		1	0	1	59	0	13	1	14	65
80/84		1	0	1	59	0	0	0	0	60	0	4	0	4	67												2	0	2	59	0	45	8	53	67
75/79	0	8	0	8	57	0	12	1	13	63	0	23	5	28	66	0	20	4	24	66	0	11	1	12	64		6	1	7	60	14	220	55	289	67
70/74	0	29	5	34	59	0	42	10	52	61	2	44	16	62	63	3	41	17	61	64	2	43	10	55	63	0	22	5	27	62	141	581	278	1000	65
65/69	3	85	26	114	59	11	51	28	90	59	23	31	35	89	61	19	33	32	84	61	14	51	32	97	60	7	71	27	105	60	443	662	582	1687	62
60/64	59	88	103	250	57	39	74	65	178	57	33	63	49	145	57	30	60	50	140	57	33	90	77	200	57	56	100	98	254	57	626	757	760	2143	57
55/59	97	25	82	204	54	63	49	84	196	52	59	52	82	193	53	69	51	81	201	54	112	47	102	261	54	108	34	89	231	53	709	453	716	1878	53
50/54	62	3	21	86	49	81	16	52	149	48	72	26	48	146	48	66	16	35	117	49	67	6	24	97	49	49	3	14	66	50	560	147	364	1071	49
45/49	16	0	3	19	45	46	2	8	56	44	46	4	12	62	43	32	1	5	38	45	19	0	2	21	45	15	0	5	20	47	280	24	110	414	45
40/44	3	0		3	41	7	0	1	8	38	12	0	1	13	38	4			4	40	2			2	42	4		1	5	42	96	5	35	136	41
35/39						1			1	35	1			1	33	0			0	36						1			1	39	39	2	11	52	37
30/34																															14	0	1	15	32
25/29																															1			1	29

DENVER, COLORADO/BUCKLEY ANGB

LAT 39 42N LONG 104 45W ELEV 5663 FT

MEAN FREQUENCY OF OCCURRENCE OF DRY BULB TEMPERATURE (DEGREES F) WITH MEAN COINCIDENT WET BULB TEMPERATURE (DEGREES F) FOR EACH DRY BULB TEMPERATURE RANGE

Temperature Range	MAY 01-08	MAY 09-16	MAY 17-24	MAY Total Obsn	MAY MC WB	JUNE 01-08	JUNE 09-16	JUNE 17-24	JUNE Total Obsn	JUNE MC WB	JULY 01-08	JULY 09-16	JULY 17-24	JULY Total Obsn	JULY MC WB	AUGUST 01-08	AUGUST 09-16	AUGUST 17-24	AUGUST Total Obsn	AUGUST MC WB	SEPTEMBER 01-08	SEPTEMBER 09-16	SEPTEMBER 17-24	SEPTEMBER Total Obsn	SEPTEMBER MC WB	OCTOBER 01-08	OCTOBER 09-16	OCTOBER 17-24	OCTOBER Total Obsn	OCTOBER MC WB
100/104																														
95/99												2	0	2	61		0	0	0	64										
90/94							2	0	2	60	0	31	5	36	60	0	3	0	3	63		0		0	60					
85/89		4	0	4	55	0	12	3	15	58	0	62	14	76	60	0	18	2	20	60	0	13	2	15	56		0		0	54
80/84		20	4	24	53	0	23	6	29	58	3	60	25	88	61	0	41	9	50	60	0	38	6	44	56	0	7	0	7	52
75/79	0	32	9	41	52	1	32	12	45	57	10	44	37	91	60	2	62	19	83	59	0	48	13	61	55	0	23	2	25	51
70/74	2	41	18	61	51	3	44	21	68	56	26	29	56	111	59	6	51	30	87	59	3	43	23	69	54	0	32	4	36	49
65/69	5	38	25	68	50	9	42	30	81	55	62	12	60	134	57	18	37	48	103	58	10	32	36	78	52	1	35	10	46	48
60/64	17	39	39	95	48	19	38	37	94	54	90	5	37	132	56	48	20	59	127	56	33	22	51	106	51	6	39	20	65	46
55/59	34	23	43	100	46	45	23	48	116	52	45	3	13	61	53	82	11	54	147	55	62	16	45	123	49	17	30	35	82	44
50/54	50	22	39	111	44	63	11	41	115	51	11	0	2	13	50	63	5	20	88	52	54	10	27	91	46	33	27	42	102	41
45/49	56	14	34	104	42	58	9	29	96	48	1	1	1	3	45	25	1	5	31	48	38	7	17	62	42	48	18	47	113	39
40/44	46	11	23	80	38	33	5	10	48	44	1			1	43	5	0	1	6	43	21	4	8	33	39	55	12	39	106	36
35/39	24	3	9	36	35	9	1	2	12	41						0			0	43	11	4	6	21	35	41	10	20	71	33
30/34	10	1	5	16	30	1	0	1	2	37											5	4	4	13	31	27	10	17	54	30
25/29	3	0	0	3	26																2	0	1	3	27	12	3	7	22	25
20/24																					0	0		0	23	6	2	4	12	21
15/19																										1	1	1	3	17
10/14																										1	0	1	2	12
5/9																										1	0	0	1	6

DENVER, COLORADO/BUCKLEY ANGB

Temperature Range	NOV 01–08	NOV 09–16	NOV 17–24	NOV Total Obsn	NOV MCWB	DEC 01–08	DEC 09–16	DEC 17–24	DEC Total Obsn	DEC MCWB	JAN 01–08	JAN 09–16	JAN 17–24	JAN Total Obsn	JAN MCWB	FEB 01–08	FEB 09–16	FEB 17–24	FEB Total Obsn	FEB MCWB	MAR 01–08	MAR 09–16	MAR 17–24	MAR Total Obsn	MAR MCWB	APR 01–08	APR 09–16	APR 17–24	APR Total Obsn	APR MCWB	ANN 01–08	ANN 09–16	ANN 17–24	ANN Total Obsn	ANN MCWB
100/104																																		0	64
95/99																																7	0	7	61
90/94																																61	10	71	60
85/89																																143	31	174	59
80/84																					0	0	0	0	53	0	0	0	0	50	6	219	66	291	58
75/79	0	0	0	0	48	0	0	0	0	51						0	1	0	1	48	0	1	0	1	51	0	8	2	10	49	19	251	114	384	56
70/74	0	3	0	3	47	0	2	1	3	45						0	4	0	4	46	0	5	1	6	47	0	18	5	23	47	58	251	185	494	55
65/69	0	12	0	12	46	0	10	1	11	43	0	1	0	1	46	0	7	1	8	43	0	13	3	16	44	0	27	8	35	46	146	234	238	618	53
60/64	0	28	1	29	44	1	20	2	23	40	0	7	1	8	43	0	12	3	15	41	1	22	6	29	42	2	32	14	48	44	276	245	273	794	51
55/59	1	37	6	44	42	2	27	5	34	38	1	16	1	18	41	1	26	8	35	38	1	25	9	35	41	7	39	26	72	42	295	237	244	776	47
50/54	6	32	19	57	39	6	28	11	45	35	2	27	5	34	38	5	34	16	55	36	4	26	14	44	38	18	37	36	91	40	264	244	231	739	43
45/49	16	33	31	80	37	16	34	25	75	32	5	31	13	49	36	12	30	24	66	33	8	26	24	58	36	32	31	43	106	38	253	228	248	729	39
40/44	42	26	49	117	34	29	31	35	95	29	16	30	26	72	33	29	30	35	94	30	25	28	32	85	33	48	17	40	105	35	291	193	268	752	35
35/39	48	21	45	114	31	43	33	46	122	27	32	30	40	102	30	36	23	42	101	27	37	22	32	91	31	52	15	31	98	33	304	166	254	724	31
30/34	47	22	33	102	28	42	25	41	108	23	38	30	35	103	27	43	20	34	97	24	44	25	42	111	28	49	10	23	82	30	299	158	247	704	28
25/29	41	19	30	90	25	42	15	32	89	20	41	24	35	100	24	41	18	26	85	20	42	25	33	100	24	19	4	9	32	25	245	120	190	555	24
20/24	21	6	18	45	20	30	10	25	65	15	33	16	27	76	19	24	7	16	47	15	36	14	25	75	20	8	2	2	12	21	187	73	134	394	20
15/19	13	1	8	22	16	19	7	11	37	11	27	11	22	60	15	15	6	8	29	11	21	9	11	41	16	3	1	1	5	17	119	40	84	243	15
10/14	4	0	1	5	11	10	4	7	21	7	19	6	13	38	10	8	3	4	15	6	13	5	7	25	11	1	0	0	1	13	72	24	41	137	11
5/9	1	0	0	1	8	5	1	4	10	2	13	7	9	29	6	7	2	5	14	1	8	3	6	17	7						41	17	26	84	6
0/4						2	0	1	3	-3	8	6	8	22	2	2	0	1	3	-4	5	1	2	8	1						25	10	19	54	2
-5/-1						1	0	1	2	-8	6	4	4	14	-3	1	0	0	1	-9	2	0	0	2	-3						11	5	6	22	-3
-10/-6						0	0	0	0	-14	5	1	4	10	-8	1	0	0	1	-13	0	0	0	0	-6						7	1	5	13	-8
-15/-11											2	1	0	3	-13																3	1	1	5	-13
-20/-16											1	0	0	1	-18																1	0	2	3	-18
-25/-21											1	0	0	1	-24																1	0	0	1	-24
-30/-26											0	0	0	0	-28																0	0	0	0	-28

GRAND JUNCTION/WALKER FIELD COLORADO
LAT 39 07N   LONG 108 32W   ELEV 4843 FT

MEAN FREQUENCY OF OCCURRENCE OF DRY BULB TEMPERATURE (DEGREES F) WITH MEAN COINCIDENT WET BULB TEMPERATURE (DEGREES F) FOR EACH DRY BULB TEMPERATURE RANGE

Column key per month: Obsn Hour Gp (01–08, 09–16, 17–24), Total Obsn, MC WB = Mean Coincident Wet Bulb.

Temp. Range	MAY 01–08	MAY 09–16	MAY 17–24	MAY Tot	MAY WB	JUN 01–08	JUN 09–16	JUN 17–24	JUN Tot	JUN WB	JUL 01–08	JUL 09–16	JUL 17–24	JUL Tot	JUL WB	AUG 01–08	AUG 09–16	AUG 17–24	AUG Tot	AUG WB	SEP 01–08	SEP 09–16	SEP 17–24	SEP Tot	SEP WB	OCT 01–08	OCT 09–16	OCT 17–24	OCT Tot	OCT WB
100/104																														
95/99													1	1	61															
90/94		2	0	2	55		0	0	0	61		1	1	2	60		7	3	10	60		0	0	0	59					
85/89		10	4	14	54		6	3	9	58		21	10	31	59		32	14	46	59		6	2	8	58		0	0	0	54
80/84		29	11	40	52		35	15	50	57		63	28	91	59		57	29	86	59		27	9	36	57		6	1	7	54
75/79	0	46	22	68	51		51	27	78	55	0	63	37	100	58	2	56	39	97	58		44	19	63	55		26	5	31	52
70/74	4	46	34	84	49	1	49	35	85	54	4	52	53	109	57	15	49	57	121	57	1	49	30	80	54		39	12	51	50
65/69	21	37	46	104	48	15	42	45	102	53	39	32	62	133	55	52	31	53	136	56	11	42	43	96	53	2	47	27	76	48
60/64	42	31	45	118	46	42	29	46	117	51	84	12	39	135	54	89	12	35	136	55	38	35	50	123	51	15	37	40	96	46
55/59	60	23	34	117	44	59	14	35	108	49	84	3	14	101	52	70	4	15	89	54	59	9	43	122	49	33	25	51	121	44
50/54	54	14	25	93	43	59	8	18	85	48	33	1	4	38	50	18	0	2	20	50	63	4	29	101	47	51	17	49	125	41
45/49	40	7	17	64	40	38	4	10	52	46	4	0	0	4	47	2	0	0	2	44	45	1	8	57	44	63	7	34	114	39
40/44	18	2	6	26	37	17	1	4	22	43	0			0		0			0	40	15	0	4	21	41	52	2	21	80	36
35/39	8	1	2	11	34	5	0	2	7	40											6		2	9	39	22	0	7	31	33
30/34	1		0	1	30	2	0	0	2	37											1			1	33	9		2	11	29
25/29						0			0																	2			2	24

COINCIDENT WET BULB TEMPERATURE FOR EACH DRY BULB TEMPERATURE RANGE

GRAND JUNCTION/WALKER FIELD COLORADO

Column key for each month: **Obsn Hour Gp** = (01 to 08 / 09 to 16 / 17 to 24); **Tot** = Total Obsn; **MCWB** = M C W B

Temperature Range	NOV 01–08	NOV 09–16	NOV 17–24	NOV Tot	NOV MCWB	DEC 01–08	DEC 09–16	DEC 17–24	DEC Tot	DEC MCWB	JAN 01–08	JAN 09–16	JAN 17–24	JAN Tot	JAN MCWB	FEB 01–08	FEB 09–16	FEB 17–24	FEB Tot	FEB MCWB	MAR 01–08	MAR 09–16	MAR 17–24	MAR Tot	MAR MCWB	APR 01–08	APR 09–16	APR 17–24	APR Tot	APR MCWB	ANN 01–08	ANN 09–16	ANN 17–24	ANN Tot	ANN MCWB
100/104																															0	1	1	2	61
95/99																															0	34	16	50	59
90/94																															0	138	59	197	58
85/89																															0	208	106	314	57
80/84																										0	3	1	4	51	7	239	159	405	56
75/79		0	0	0	48																0	3	1	4	47	0	9	3	12	49	70	253	224	547	54
70/74		3	0	3	47																0	9	3	12	45	0	24	9	33	48	193	226	237	656	53
65/69		12	2	14	45		0	0	0	47							0		0	45	0	17	7	24	43	1	38	19	58	46	294	198	229	721	51
60/64	1	29	7	37	43	0	2	1	3	45						0	3	1	4	43	2	28	16	46	41	7	39	31	77	44	285	176	206	667	48
55/59	6	37	18	61	41	1	8	1	10	40	0	1	0	1	42	0	8	2	10	42	7	36	25	68	39	23	37	41	101	42	242	178	193	613	44
50/54	14	46	33	93	38	2	21	5	28	37	0	4	1	5	40	1	17	6	24	40	19	42	39	100	37	41	35	43	119	40	225	181	180	586	41
45/49	29	38	46	113	35	5	36	14	55	35	1	12	4	17	37	3	28	16	47	38	37	43	47	127	34	46	30	38	114	38	208	205	192	605	38
40/44	45	33	51	129	32	14	50	33	97	32	2	30	11	43	34	10	43	31	84	35	53	38	47	138	31	50	18	33	101	35	211	218	211	640	35
35/39	67	24	47	138	29	37	57	64	158	28	9	46	29	84	32	31	48	50	129	32	58	23	38	119	28	43	6	16	65	32	226	224	235	685	32
30/34	48	13	23	84	24	62	39	58	159	24	35	56	60	151	29	58	36	53	147	28	45	10	20	75	24	25	1	5	31	29	290	197	269	756	29
25/29	22	3	8	33	20	57	22	37	116	20	56	40	56	152	24	50	21	33	104	24	21	1	5	27	19	4	0	0	4	25	267	123	190	580	24
20/24	6	1	3	10	15	39	8	20	67	15	54	30	37	121	20	33	9	15	57	20	6	0	1	7	15	1			1	20	188	65	102	355	20
15/19	3	0	1	4	10	19	4	7	30	11	38	16	25	79	15	18	6	8	32	15	1			1	12						107	31	57	195	15
10/14	1			1	6	6	2	5	13	6	26	7	15	48	11	10	2	6	18	11											59	13	29	101	11
5/9						3	0	2	5	2	14	4	7	25	6	5	1	2	8	6											26	7	14	47	6
0/4						1	0	1	2	-3	8	1	3	12	1	2	1	1	4	2											13	2	6	21	1
-5/-1						1	0	0	1	-8	2	1	1	4	-3	1	0	0	1	-4											4	1	2	7	-3
-10/-6						0			0	-12	0	0	0	0	-9	0			0	-9											2	0	0	2	-9
-15/-11											0	0	0	0	-14																0	0	0	0	-14
-20/-16											1	0	0	1	-18																1	0	0	1	-18

WINDSOR LOCKS (BRADLEY FIELD) CONNECTICUT*
READINGS TAKEN AT WESTOVER AFB, MA
LAT 42 12N   LONG 72 32W   ELEV 245 FT

MEAN FREQUENCY OF OCCURRENCE OF DRY BULB TEMPERATURE (DEGREES F) WITH MEAN COINCIDENT WET BULB TEMPERATURE (DEGREES F) FOR EACH DRY BULB TEMPERATURE RANGE

MAY

Temperature Range	Obsn Hour Gp 01 to 08	Obsn Hour Gp 09 to 16	Obsn Hour Gp 17 to 24	Total Obsn	MCWB
100/104					
95/99				0	71
90/94		1	0	1	72
85/89	0	1	0	1	70
80/84	0	6	2	8	68
75/79	1	12	4	16	64
70/74	2	24	9	34	61
65/69	9	34	20	56	58
60/64	21	46	32	87	56
55/59	42	48	42	111	53
50/54	53	36	49	127	51
45/49	47	22	41	116	47
40/44	43	12	29	88	43
35/39	21	6	16	65	39
30/34	9	1	4	26	35
25/29	2		0	9	30
20/24		2		2	26
15/19					

JUNE

Temperature Range	Obsn Hour Gp 01 to 08	Obsn Hour Gp 09 to 16	Obsn Hour Gp 17 to 24	Total Obsn	MCWB
100/104					
95/99					
90/94		1	0	1	73
85/89		7	2	9	72
80/84		20	6	26	70
75/79	0	39	16	55	67
70/74	3	46	28	77	65
65/69	15	51	46	112	63
60/64	46	37	50	133	61
55/59	54	23	41	118	57
50/54	55	15	33	103	54
45/49	39	2	14	55	49
40/44	18	0	2	20	45
35/39	7	1	1	8	41
30/34	2		0	2	36
25/29	1			1	32

JULY

Temperature Range	Obsn Hour Gp 01 to 08	Obsn Hour Gp 09 to 16	Obsn Hour Gp 17 to 24	Total Obsn	MCWB
95/99				0	72
90/94		1	0	1	72
85/89		10	2	12	73
80/84	0	31	8	39	71
75/79	1	58	25	84	68
70/74	8	66	47	121	66
65/69	42	52	65	159	65
60/64	78	25	63	165	61
55/59	59	4	27	90	59
50/54	34	0	8	42	54
45/49	20		3	23	50
40/44	5		2	7	46
35/39	1			1	42

AUGUST

Temperature Range	Obsn Hour Gp 01 to 08	Obsn Hour Gp 09 to 16	Obsn Hour Gp 17 to 24	Total Obsn	MCWB
95/99				0	76
90/94		6	1	7	74
85/89		24	5	29	71
80/84		54	18	72	69
75/79	5	64	39	108	66
70/74	34	53	64	151	65
65/69	60	31	56	147	62
60/64	63	13	38	114	59
55/59	44	2	17	63	55
50/54	22	0	6	28	50
45/49	15		3	18	45
40/44	5		0	5	41
35/39	1			1	37
30/34	0			0	31

SEPTEMBER

Temperature Range	Obsn Hour Gp 01 to 08	Obsn Hour Gp 09 to 16	Obsn Hour Gp 17 to 24	Total Obsn	MCWB
90/94		2	0	2	74
85/89		8	2	10	73
80/84		22	5	27	70
75/79	1	34	15	50	66
70/74	15	51	34	100	64
65/69	30	43	43	116	61
60/64	35	38	41	114	57
55/59	44	27	43	114	53
50/54	41	12	34	87	49
45/49	34	2	15	51	45
40/44	21	0	7	28	41
35/39	13		2	15	36
30/34	4		1	5	31
25/29		1		1	27

OCTOBER

Temperature Range	Obsn Hour Gp 01 to 08	Obsn Hour Gp 09 to 16	Obsn Hour Gp 17 to 24	Total Obsn	MCWB
85/89				0	64
80/84		2	0	2	66
75/79		11	1	12	63
70/74		17	5	22	61
65/69	11	31	15	49	59
60/64	17	42	29	86	55
55/59	31	51	41	116	51
50/54	48	48	52	139	47
45/49	44	27	42	113	43
40/44	41	12	31	84	39
35/39	37	5	21	63	34
30/34	29	1	9	39	30
25/29	13	3	3	16	26
20/24	3	0	0	3	22
15/19	0			0	18

*Comparative design data note:

	WINTER 97 1/2%	SUMMER DB 2 1/2%	SUMMER WB 2 1/2%	Elevation
Westover AFB, MA.	2° F	88° F	74° F	245 ft.
Windsor Locks, CT.	2° F	88° F	75° F	169 ft.

COINCIDENT WET BULB TEMPERATURE FOR EACH DRY BULB TEMPERATURE RANGE

WINDSOR LOCKS (BRADLEY FIELD) CONNECTICUT*
READINGS TAKEN AT WESTOVER AFB, MA

Each month group column headings: Obsn Hour Gp (01 to 08 | 09 to 16 | 17 to 24) | Total Obsn | MCWB

Temperature Range	NOV 01-08	NOV 09-16	NOV 17-24	NOV Total	NOV MCWB	DEC 01-08	DEC 09-16	DEC 17-24	DEC Total	DEC MCWB	JAN 01-08	JAN 09-16	JAN 17-24	JAN Total	JAN MCWB	FEB 01-08	FEB 09-16	FEB 17-24	FEB Total	FEB MCWB	MAR 01-08	MAR 09-16	MAR 17-24	MAR Total	MAR MCWB	APR 01-08	APR 09-16	APR 17-24	APR Total	APR MCWB	ANN 01-08	ANN 09-16	ANN 17-24	ANN Total	ANN MCWB
100/104																																		0	71
95/99																															0	3		3	72
90/94																																26	5	31	73
85/89																											0		0	62		89	23	112	71
80/84																											0		0	64	1	189	68	258	68
75/79		1		1	62																	0		0	59		2	0	2	62	18	251	140	409	65
70/74	1	4	2	7	61																	1		1	56	0	6	1	7	58	108	271	238	617	64
65/69	3	9	5	17	56												0		0	57		3	1	4	53	0	11	4	15	56	227	236	269	732	61
60/64	9	23	14	46	52	0	1	1	2	56	0			0	51		0		0	56		3	2	5	51		16	8	24	53	253	210	243	706	56
55/59	17	40	25	82	47	1	3	2	6	52		1	0	1	50		1	0	1	52	0	8	5	13	48	3	29	17	49	51	264	205	241	710	52
50/54	25	41	34	100	42	2	7	2	11	47	1	1	2	4	49	1	2	2	5	47	1	19	10	30	43	11	38	29	78	48	255	195	228	678	47
45/49	36	52	40	128	38	6	12	7	25	42	1	3	1	5	42	1	8	4	13	41	6	32	19	57	40	19	42	37	98	44	239	178	199	616	42
40/44	41	40	51	132	33	11	25	16	52	37	5	17	7	29	37	4	19	12	35	37	16	49	37	102	36	35	41	43	119	41	242	217	217	676	38
35/39	45	24	45	114	29	22	40	33	95	33	17	38	29	84	33	19	40	27	86	33	43	57	63	163	33	52	37	50	139	37	269	236	266	771	33
30/34	33	6	16	55	25	44	53	54	151	29	37	49	43	129	29	38	51	55	144	29	74	46	59	179	29	53	15	36	104	34	319	227	279	825	29
25/29	19	1	7	27	21	47	46	46	139	24	29	41	41	111	24	35	39	43	117	24	51	19	32	102	24	38	3	13	54	29	231	151	183	565	24
20/24	8	0	1	9	17	36	30	36	102	20	33	33	38	104	20	37	27	34	98	20	31	7	11	49	20	20	0	2	22	25	164	98	126	388	20
15/19	1			1	13	26	18	26	70	15	33	31	35	99	15	28	18	21	67	15	15	2	5	22	15	5	0	0	5	21	112	69	88	269	15
10/14						22	8	14	44	11	33	19	27	79	10	20	9	13	42	10	6	2	3	11	10	2	0	0	2	16	83	38	57	178	10
5/9						13	4	6	23	6	24	8	14	46	6	17	7	10	34	6	3	0	0	3	3	1	0	0	1	11	57	19	30	106	6
0/4						10	2	2	14	2	14	4	6	24	1	11	2	3	16	1	0	0		0	0	0			0	8	35	8	11	54	1
-5/-1						6	0	1	7	-3	8	2	3	13	-3	7	0	1	8	-3	0	0		0	-4						21	2	5	28	-3
-10/-6						1	0	0	1	-8	6	0	1	7	-8	4	0	0	4	-8	0	0		0	-8						11	0	1	12	-8
-15/-11						0	0		0	-13	5	0	0	5	-13	1			1	-13	0			0	-13						6	0	0	6	-13
-20/-16						0	0		0	-16	1		0	1	-18	0			0	-17											1	0	0	1	-18
-25/-21											0			0	-22																0			0	-22

DOVER AFB DELAWARE
LAT 39 08N   LONG 75 28W   ELEV 28 FT

MEAN FREQUENCY OF OCCURRENCE OF DRY BULB TEMPERATURE (DEGREES F) WITH MEAN COINCIDENT WET BULB TEMPERATURE (DEGREES F) FOR EACH DRY BULB TEMPERATURE RANGE

Temperature Range	MAY 01–08	MAY 09–16	MAY 17–24	MAY Total	MAY MWB	JUNE 01–08	JUNE 09–16	JUNE 17–24	JUNE Total	JUNE MWB	JULY 01–08	JULY 09–16	JULY 17–24	JULY Total	JULY MWB	AUG 01–08	AUG 09–16	AUG 17–24	AUG Total	AUG MWB	SEP 01–08	SEP 09–16	SEP 17–24	SEP Total	SEP MWB	OCT 01–08	OCT 09–16	OCT 17–24	OCT Total	OCT MWB
100/104							0		0	78		1		1	79															
95/99		0		0	76	0	3	0	3	76	0	2	0	2	76	0	1	0	1	78		0		0	76					
90/94		2	0	2	73	0	14	3	17	75	0	19	3	22	75	0	11	1	12	76	0	6	0	6	75		0		0	74
85/89		9	2	11	70	1	32	11	44	73	0	49	17	66	74	0	42	9	51	74	0	20	4	24	74		1	0	1	71
80/84	0	18	7	25	68	4	52	26	82	71	7	76	38	121	72	2	71	30	103	72	0	34	11	45	72		6	1	7	69
75/79	2	30	16	48	65	21	51	41	113	69	49	67	69	185	70	32	77	68	177	70	13	51	31	95	69	0	13	3	16	66
70/74	13	40	28	81	63	54	47	60	161	66	90	29	75	194	68	97	36	84	217	68	42	55	54	151	67	5	33	10	48	64
65/69	29	48	36	113	60	66	28	53	147	63	66	6	37	109	64	70	9	40	119	64	56	40	57	153	63	13	50	26	89	61
60/64	44	47	54	145	56	54	10	35	99	59	31	0	6	37	60	32	1	14	47	59	50	22	43	115	58	39	59	52	150	57
55/59	60	35	53	148	52	31	2	10	43	54	4		0	4	55	13	0	2	15	54	42	10	28	80	54	46	42	52	140	52
50/54	54	15	37	106	48	8	0	2	10	50	0			0	50	2			2	50	23	1	10	34	49	49	29	47	125	48
45/49	33	3	13	49	44	1		0	1	45											12		2	14	45	45	11	34	90	44
40/44	12	0	0	14	39	0		0	0	42											2		0	2	40	30	4	16	50	39
35/39	2			2	34																0			0	38	17	0	5	22	35
30/34	0			0	29																					5		1	6	30
25/29																										1		0	1	25

DOVER AFB DELAWARE

Temperature Range	NOV 01–08	NOV 09–16	NOV 17–24	NOV Total Obsn	NOV MCWB	DEC 01–08	DEC 09–16	DEC 17–24	DEC Total Obsn	DEC MCWB	JAN 01–08	JAN 09–16	JAN 17–24	JAN Total Obsn	JAN MCWB	FEB 01–08	FEB 09–16	FEB 17–24	FEB Total Obsn	FEB MCWB	MAR 01–08	MAR 09–16	MAR 17–24	MAR Total Obsn	MAR MCWB	APR 01–08	APR 09–16	APR 17–24	APR Total Obsn	APR MCWB	ANN 01–08	ANN 09–16	ANN 17–24	ANN Total Obsn	ANN MCWB
100/104																																1	0	1	79
95/99																																6	0	6	76
90/94																																52	7	59	75
85/89		0		0	68																						2	0	2	68	1	155	43	199	74
80/84																						0		0	60		7	2	9	65	13	264	115	392	71
75/79	0	2	0	2	68	0	1	0	1	63		0		0	60		0		0	61		2	0	2	60	0	10	4	14	63	117	303	232	652	69
70/74	0	4	1	5	64	0	2	1	3	60		1	0	1	59		2	0	2	58	0	6	1	7	59	2	17	10	29	61	303	268	323	894	66
65/69	4	10	4	18	60	3	6	3	12	57	1	2	1	4	58	0	3	2	5	57	1	8	3	12	56	8	22	17	47	58	313	226	274	813	62
60/64	9	27	13	49	56	6	10	6	22	52	3	5	4	12	52	4	6	3	13	52	3	10	8	21	53	17	35	23	75	54	283	222	254	759	57
55/59	18	48	26	92	52	7	21	10	38	47	5	8	4	17	47	3	13	6	22	46	4	15	10	29	50	25	45	32	102	50	256	218	226	700	52
50/54	31	49	39	119	47	14	35	26	75	43	7	23	10	40	42	6	20	11	37	42	9	33	17	59	45	36	48	52	136	46	227	217	224	668	47
45/49	39	43	49	131	43	30	42	37	109	38	16	43	28	87	38	19	41	28	88	38	20	45	37	102	41	51	36	55	142	42	228	216	237	681	43
40/44	46	33	48	127	38	43	52	47	142	34	37	51	50	138	34	41	53	57	151	33	46	57	64	167	38	54	17	33	104	38	255	237	256	748	38
35/39	47	17	38	102	34	54	41	53	148	29	50	42	55	147	29	49	39	52	140	29	68	44	63	175	34	33	2	10	45	34	288	219	270	777	34
30/34	32	4	15	51	29	39	25	39	103	24	44	33	41	118	24	48	22	35	105	24	58	18	29	105	29	11	0	1	12	29	259	144	206	609	29
25/29	11	1	5	17	25	30	11	18	59	20	34	22	28	84	20	25	15	17	57	19	25	7	11	43	24	1			1	26	169	88	131	388	24
20/24	4	0	1	5	19	17	2	7	26	15	26	11	16	53	15	16	7	9	32	15	9	3	5	17	20						102	51	69	222	20
15/19	0	0		0	16	5	1	1	7	11	16	5	8	29	10	9	2	3	14	11	5	0	1	6	15						64	20	33	117	15
10/14						1	0		1	6	7	1	2	10	6	3	1	0	4	6	1	0	0	1	12						31	8	12	51	11
5/9																1	0		1	1				0	8						11	2	2	15	6
0/4											1			1	2	1			1	1											2	0	0	2	2

MEAN FREQUENCY OF OCCURRENCE OF DRY BULB TEMPERATURE (DEGREES F) WITH MEAN COINCIDENT WET BULB TEMPERATURE (DEGREES F) FOR EACH DRY BULB TEMPERATURE RANGE

WASHINGTON, D.C.*
READINGS TAKEN AT ANDREWS AFB, MD
LAT 38 49N   LONG 76 52W   ELEV 279 FT

Hour groups: 01 to 08, 09 to 16, 17 to 24. Total Obsn. MCWB = Mean Coincident Wet Bulb.

Temperature Range	MAY 01-08	MAY 09-16	MAY 17-24	MAY Total	MAY MCWB	JUN 01-08	JUN 09-16	JUN 17-24	JUN Total	JUN MCWB	JUL 01-08	JUL 09-16	JUL 17-24	JUL Total	JUL MCWB	AUG 01-08	AUG 09-16	AUG 17-24	AUG Total	AUG MCWB	SEP 01-08	SEP 09-16	SEP 17-24	SEP Total	SEP MCWB	OCT 01-08	OCT 09-16	OCT 17-24	OCT Total	OCT MCWB
100/104																														
95/99									0	80				0	76															
90/94				0	72		2	0	2	78		2	1	3	76		1		1	74									0	75
85/89		3		3	70		14	2	16	74		22	4	26	75		16	2	18	75		0		0	77		0	0	1	72
80/84	0	13	3	16	69	0	40	13	53	72	0	58	18	76	75		50	14	64	73		8	0	8	74		1	1	9	67
75/79	2	25	11	36	66	3	52	29	84	70	5	75	41	121	70	2	71	35	108	71		22	5	27	73		8	3	21	65
70/74	13	37	21	60	64	15	54	48	117	67	35	55	67	157	69	26	63	65	154	69	0	38	15	53	71	4	18	15	56	63
65/69	35	45	37	95	62	56	42	62	160	66	102	28	78	208	68	97	34	78	209	67	9	50	34	93	68	14	37	32	91	60
60/64	53	44	51	130	60	73	22	49	144	63	73	8	33	114	63	71	12	37	120	63	43	49	49	141	66	34	45	48	132	56
55/59	54	40	48	141	56	51	11	24	86	58	28	1	5	34	59	37	1	13	51	59	55	39	53	147	62	46	50	48	136	52
50/54	49	24	41	119	52	29	3	10	42	54	5	0	0	5	54	11	0	3	14	54	52	20	42	114	57	50	42	47	129	47
45/49	29	13	24	86	48	11	0	2	13	50						3	0	0	3	50	44	10	26	80	53	44	32	31	86	43
40/44	9	3	10	42	44	1		0	1	45						0			0	47	24	2	11	37	49	32	11	16	51	38
35/39	1	1	2	12	39																12	0	3	15	45	18	3	5	24	35
30/34	0	0	0	1	34																2		1	3	40	7	1	1	8	30
25/29				0	31																0		0	0	36	0	0	0	0	26

*Comparative design data note:

	Elevation	WINTER 97 1/2%	SUMMER DB 2 1/2%	SUMMER WB 2 1/2%
Andrews AFB, MD.	279 ft.	16° F	91° F	77° F
Washington National AP	14 ft.	19° F	92° F	77° F

WASHINGTON, D.C.*
READINGS TAKEN AT ANDREWS AFB, MD

Temperature Range	NOVEMBER					DECEMBER					JANUARY					FEBRUARY					MARCH					APRIL					ANNUAL TOTAL				
	01 to 08	09 to 16	17 to 24	Total Obsn	MCWB	01 to 08	09 to 16	17 to 24	Total Obsn	MCWB	01 to 08	09 to 16	17 to 24	Total Obsn	MCWB	01 to 08	09 to 16	17 to 24	Total Obsn	MCWB	01 to 08	09 to 16	17 to 24	Total Obsn	MCWB	01 to 08	09 to 16	17 to 24	Total Obsn	MCWB	01 to 08	09 to 16	17 to 24	Total Obsn	MCWB
100/104																																		0	77
95/99																																5	1	6	76
90/94																																64	8	72	74
85/89		1		1	69																						1		1	71		189	54	243	72
80/84																						1		1	61		5	1	6	66	10	282	136	428	70
75/79		2		2	67		1		1	59		1		1	59				0	58		4	1	5	60		11	4	15	63	88	296	247	631	68
70/74	1	6	2	9	61		4	1	5	58		1	1	2	58				0	57		8	3	11	57	1	13	8	22	61	318	270	337	925	66
65/69	4	14	5	23	58	3	7	5	15	55	1	3	1	5	55		2	1	3	55	1	9	5	15	55	2	19	13	34	58	337	229	292	858	61
60/64	8	31	17	56	55	6	13	7	26	50	3	5	4	12	51	1	3	2	6	50	4	15	10	29	52	11	29	24	64	56	292	218	245	755	56
55/59	19	42	28	89	51	7	20	13	40	46	4	13	6	23	45	2	10	6	18	46	7	19	17	43	48	20	36	30	86	53	255	207	226	688	51
50/54	31	47	41	119	46	16	30	27	73	42	7	24	15	46	41	5	14	9	28	41	12	30	24	66	44	29	39	36	104	49	233	213	225	671	46
45/49	41	41	45	127	42	30	44	36	110	37	22	41	32	95	37	10	21	17	48	37	24	43	38	105	41	37	42	48	127	45	236	201	228	665	42
40/44	47	34	46	127	37	45	50	50	145	33	36	46	46	128	33	18	40	34	92	33	46	51	55	152	37	52	28	42	122	42	257	229	248	734	37
35/39	43	16	34	93	33	55	41	51	147	28	55	46	55	156	29	39	46	49	134	29	60	39	50	149	33	51	15	26	92	38	268	200	240	708	33
30/34	33	6	15	54	29	37	23	32	92	24	39	32	39	110	24	50	43	49	142	24	56	19	30	105	29	26	2	6	34	34	264	155	202	621	29
25/29	10	1	4	15	25	29	11	19	59	19	34	21	23	78	19	48	23	32	103	19	25	7	9	41	24	8		1	9	30	160	86	116	362	24
20/24	4		2	6	20	13	3	6	22	15	25	10	14	49	15	24	13	15	52	14	10	3	4	17	20	1			1	25	101	48	63	212	19
15/19	0			0	15	6	1	1	8	10	15	5	8	28	10	13	6	7	26	10	4			4	16						55	19	27	101	15
10/14						1			1	7	6	1	2	9	6	10	2	3	15	7	0			0	13						31	8	12	51	10
5/9											1			1	2	3			3												10	1	2	13	6
0/4											0			0	-2				0	2												1		1	2
-5/-1																																		0	-2

JACKSONVILLE/CECIL FLD NAS FLORIDA
LAT 30 13N   LONG 81 53W   ELEV   80 FT

MEAN FREQUENCY OF OCCURRENCE OF DRY BULB TEMPERATURE (DEGREES F) WITH MEAN COINCIDENT WET BULB TEMPERATURE (DEGREES F) FOR EACH DRY BULB TEMPERATURE RANGE

Temperature Range	MAY 01–08	MAY 09–16	MAY 17–24	MAY Total Obsn	MAY MCWB	JUNE 01–08	JUNE 09–16	JUNE 17–24	JUNE Total Obsn	JUNE MCWB	JULY 01–08	JULY 09–16	JULY 17–24	JULY Total Obsn	JULY MCWB	AUGUST 01–08	AUGUST 09–16	AUGUST 17–24	AUGUST Total Obsn	AUGUST MCWB	SEPTEMBER 01–08	SEPTEMBER 09–16	SEPTEMBER 17–24	SEPTEMBER Total Obsn	SEPTEMBER MCWB	OCTOBER 01–08	OCTOBER 09–16	OCTOBER 17–24	OCTOBER Total Obsn	OCTOBER MCWB
100/104		0	0	0	74				0	80				0	78															
95/99		5	1	6	74		6	1	7	77		13	2	15	78		0		0	81										
90/94		24	6	30	72		43	9	52	76		68	14	82	77		8	1	9	78		1		1	77		3	0	3	75
85/89		63	17	80	71		81	23	104	75		85	25	110	77	0	63	9	72	77		28	3	31	76		29	3	32	73
80/84	0	75	35	110	70	6	68	48	122	74	12	56	54	122	76		86	25	111	76		76	15	91	75		65	14	79	71
75/79	12	47	55	114	69	50	28	83	161	73	92	19	98	209	74	7	58	51	116	75	37	40	42	119	74	7	64	40	111	70
70/74	68	24	78	170	68	133	12	65	210	70	132	8	53	193	71	79	25	98	202	74	70	15	95	180	73	50	44	76	170	68
65/69	90	7	41	138	64	42	1	10	53	66	12	0	2	14	67	145	6	59	210	71	151	4	68	223	70	74	26	61	161	64
60/64	55	2	13	70	60	9		1	10	61	0			0	63	17	2	4	23	68	45	0	14	59	66	51	12	33	96	59
55/59	17		2	19	55	1			1	57						0	0	0	0	64	10		2	12	60	35	4	14	53	54
50/54	5			5	50																2			2	55	16	1	6	23	49
45/49	0			0	47																			0	48	11	0	2	13	45
40/44																								0	46	3		0	3	40
35/39																										0			0	38

JACKSONVILLE/CECIL FLD NAS FLORIDA

Temperature Range	NOVEMBER Obsn Hour Gp 01 to 08	09 to 16	17 to 24	Total Obsn	MCWB	DECEMBER Obsn Hour Gp 01 to 08	09 to 16	17 to 24	Total Obsn	MCWB	JANUARY Obsn Hour Gp 01 to 08	09 to 16	17 to 24	Total Obsn	MCWB
100/104															
95/99															
90/94															
85/89		2		2	70		0		0	70					
80/84		20	2	22	69		7	0	7	68		3	0	3	67
75/79		42	9	51	66		19	3	22	65		12	3	15	65
70/74	3	50	25	78	64	1	28	12	41	64	1	22	8	31	63
65/69	25	44	50	119	62	11	35	25	71	61	4	30	18	52	61
60/64	53	34	56	143	59	22	41	38	101	57	18	38	36	92	58
55/59	44	23	40	107	54	29	38	41	108	53	31	37	41	109	53
50/54	45	14	30	89	49	46	38	52	136	49	39	41	43	123	49
45/49	33	6	16	55	44	40	22	35	97	44	42	28	40	110	44
40/44	19	3	8	30	39	37	12	23	72	39	40	22	33	95	39
35/39	11	1	3	15	35	33	5	13	51	35	34	9	17	60	35
30/34	6	0	1	7	31	20	2	4	26	30	26	5	7	38	30
25/29	1	0	0	1	25	7	1	1	9	26	9	1	2	12	25
20/24	1		0	1	21	1	0	0	1	21	3	1		4	21
15/19						0	0		0	15					
10/14						0			0	13					

Temperature Range	FEBRUARY Obsn Hour Gp 01 to 08	09 to 16	17 to 24	Total Obsn	MCWB	MARCH Obsn Hour Gp 01 to 08	09 to 16	17 to 24	Total Obsn	MCWB	APRIL Obsn Hour Gp 01 to 08	09 to 16	17 to 24	Total Obsn	MCWB
100/104															
95/99															
90/94							0		0	66		5	1	6	72
85/89		1	0	1	70		8	2	10	70		30	8	38	70
80/84		8	2	10	69		22	7	29	68		52	19	71	68
75/79		16	5	21	66		35	14	49	64	1	61	32	94	66
70/74	2	23	14	39	63	5	43	29	77	63	17	48	56	121	64
65/69	12	25	22	59	60	25	38	42	105	61	52	24	57	133	63
60/64	21	33	31	85	56	41	38	49	128	57	72	15	43	130	59
55/59	23	41	36	100	52	49	32	46	127	53	54	4	18	76	54
50/54	38	35	46	119	48	50	19	31	100	48	30	1	7	38	49
45/49	37	22	33	92	44	35	8	18	61	44	11		1	12	45
40/44	39	13	25	77	39	25	4	9	38	39	3		0	3	40
35/39	32	5	7	44	34	15	1	1	17	35	0			0	38
30/34	15	2	2	19	30	4	0	0	4	30					
25/29	5	1	0	6	25	0			0	29					
20/24	0			0	20										
15/19															
10/14															

Temperature Range	ANNUAL TOTAL Obsn Hour Gp 01 to 08	09 to 16	17 to 24	Total Obsn	MCWB
100/104		0	0	0	76
95/99		33	5	38	77
90/94		234	42	276	76
85/89	0	461	118	579	74
80/84	26	510	274	810	72
75/79	286	408	535	1229	71
70/74	697	323	543	1563	68
65/69	405	236	346	987	63
60/64	352	213	302	867	58
55/59	285	179	238	702	53
50/54	269	149	215	633	49
45/49	209	86	145	440	44
40/44	166	54	98	318	39
35/39	125	21	41	187	35
30/34	71	9	14	94	30
25/29	22	3	3	28	25
20/24	5	1	0	6	21
15/19	0	0		0	15
10/14	0			0	13

MIAMI, FLORIDA*
READINGS TAKEN AT HOMESTEAD AFB

LAT 25 29N LONG 80 24W ELEV 7 FT

MEAN FREQUENCY OF OCCURRENCE OF DRY BULB TEMPERATURE (DEGREES F) WITH MEAN COINCIDENT WET BULB TEMPERATURE (DEGREES F) FOR EACH DRY BULB TEMPERATURE RANGE

Temperature Range	MAY 01 to 08	09 to 16	17 to 24	Total Obsn	MCWB	JUNE 01 to 08	09 to 16	17 to 24	Total Obsn	MCWB	JULY 01 to 08	09 to 16	17 to 24	Total Obsn	MCWB	AUGUST 01 to 08	09 to 16	17 to 24	Total Obsn	MCWB	SEPTEMBER 01 to 08	09 to 16	17 to 24	Total Obsn	MCWB	OCTOBER 01 to 08	09 to 16	17 to 24	Total Obsn	MCWB
95/99																	0		0	80										
90/94		1		1	74		7	0	7	78		9	0	9	78		18	1	19	78		10	1	11	78		0		0	77
85/89		37	3	40	75	2	91	14	107	77	5	174	35	214	77	4	168	35	207	78	2	132	18	152	77		56	3	59	76
80/84	13	138	48	199	73	49	107	93	249	75	89	50	136	275	76	89	46	132	267	76	67	71	123	261	76	23	124	70	217	74
75/79	104	60	134	298	71	136	27	108	271	73	143	13	71	227	74	141	14	74	229	74	143	24	88	255	74	102	52	115	269	72
70/74	97	10	55	162	69	52	8	25	85	71	11	2	5	18	71	14	2	6	22	72	28	3	10	41	71	80	13	48	141	69
65/69	27	1	7	35	64	1		0	1	66																30	3	11	44	63
60/64	7		1	8	59																					9		2	11	59
55/59	1			1	55																					2		0	2	55
50/54																													0	47

* Comparative design data note:

	WINTER 97 1/2%	SUMMER DB 2 1/2%	WB 2 1/2%	Elevation
Miami AP, FL.	47° F	90° F	79° F	7 ft.
Homestead AFB	46° F	90° F	79° F	7 ft.

MIAMI, FLORIDA*
READINGS TAKEN AT HOMESTEAD AFB

Temperature Range	NOVEMBER 01 to 08	09 to 16	17 to 24	Total Obsn	MCWB	DECEMBER 01 to 08	09 to 16	17 to 24	Total Obsn	MCWB	JANUARY 01 to 08	09 to 16	17 to 24	Total Obsn	MCWB	FEBRUARY 01 to 08	09 to 16	17 to 24	Total Obsn	MCWB	MARCH 01 to 08	09 to 16	17 to 24	Total Obsn	MCWB	APRIL 01 to 08	09 to 16	17 to 24	Total Obsn	MCWB	ANNUAL TOTAL 01 to 08	09 to 16	17 to 24	Total Obsn	MCWB
95/99																																0		0	80
90/94																											1		1	76		46	2	48	78
85/89		4		4	75		0		0	71							2		2	74		5	0	5	73		18	3	21	74	13	687	111	811	77
80/84	0	69	5	74	72		24	0	24	72		21	1	22	71		36	3	39	72		53	7	60	72	1	84	16	101	72	331	823	634	1788	75
75/79	29	109	69	207	70	5	89	24	118	69	1	76	16	93	69	9	65	30	104	69	12	87	45	144	69	42	109	90	241	70	867	725	864	2456	72
70/74	86	35	106	227	67	60	64	85	209	66	42	67	75	184	66	48	49	65	162	67	78	60	94	232	66	108	24	101	233	67	704	337	675	1716	67
65/69	69	12	38	119	63	58	37	68	163	62	71	39	78	188	63	46	35	54	135	62	68	23	60	151	62	57	4	24	85	63	427	154	340	921	63
60/64	34	6	13	53	58	44	19	37	100	58	50	20	40	110	58	42	18	41	101	58	41	13	24	78	57	23	0	5	28	58	250	76	163	489	58
55/59	12	3	7	22	52	35	9	21	65	53	36	15	21	72	53	37	13	18	68	53	22	6	14	42	52	8		1	9	54	153	46	82	281	53
50/54	7	2	2	11	47	26	4	10	40	48	25	7	11	43	48	23	5	9	37	48	19	1	4	24	47	1	0	0	1	49	101	19	36	156	48
45/49	2	0	1	3	43	12	1	3	16	43	12	3	5	20	43	13	1	4	18	43	8	0	0	8	44	0			0	44	47	5	13	65	43
40/44	1		0	1	37	5	0	1	6	39	8	1	3	12	38	5	0	0	5	39	1		0	1	39						20	1	4	25	38
35/39						2	0	0	2	35	3	0	0	3	34	1			1	34	0			0	37						6	0	0	6	35
30/34											0			0	32																0			0	32

TAMPA, FLORIDA/MAC DILL AFB

LAT 27 51N   LONG 82 30W   ELEV   13 FT

MEAN FREQUENCY OF OCCURRENCE OF DRY BULB TEMPERATURE (DEGREES F) WITH MEAN COINCIDENT WET BULB TEMPERATURE (DEGREES F) FOR EACH DRY BULB TEMPERATURE RANGE

Temperature Range	MAY 01 to 08	MAY 09 to 16	MAY 17 to 24	MAY Total Obsn	MAY MCWB	JUNE 01 to 08	JUNE 09 to 16	JUNE 17 to 24	JUNE Total Obsn	JUNE MCWB	JULY 01 to 08	JULY 09 to 16	JULY 17 to 24	JULY Total Obsn	JULY MCWB	AUG 01 to 08	AUG 09 to 16	AUG 17 to 24	AUG Total Obsn	AUG MCWB	SEP 01 to 08	SEP 09 to 16	SEP 17 to 24	SEP Total Obsn	SEP MCWB	OCT 01 to 08	OCT 09 to 16	OCT 17 to 24	OCT Total Obsn	OCT MCWB
95/99		0	0	0	75		1	0	1	77		1	0	1	78		1	0	1	79		1	0	1	78					
90/94		9	1	10	73		31	5	36	76		48	6	54	77		50	6	56	78		32	4	36	77		5	0	5	76
85/89		74	14	88	72	1	107	36	144	76	2	120	48	170	77	1	109	41	151	77		104	27	131	76	0	59	9	68	74
80/84	2	102	54	158	71	31	75	80	186	75	65	60	97	222	76	56	65	94	215	76	20	73	78	171	75	2	84	39	125	72
75/79	49	46	95	190	70	128	23	90	241	73	147	17	80	244	74	163	21	97	281	74	154	25	110	289	73	58	58	86	202	71
70/74	131	14	72	217	68	76	4	28	108	69	33	4	18	55	71	27	2	11	40	71	62	5	20	87	70	95	31	71	197	67
65/69	52	2	11	65	63	4			4	65	0		0	0	67	0			0	67	3	0	1	4	62	55	8	29	92	62
60/64	11	0	1	12	58																0		0	0	58	22	3	10	35	57
55/59	1		0	1	53																					11	1	3	15	52
50/54																										4	0	1	5	47
45/49																										1		0	1	43
40/44																										0			0	40

COINCIDENT WET BULB TEMPERATURE FOR EACH DRY BULB TEMPERATURE RANGE

TAMPA, FLORIDA/MAC DILL AFB

Temperature Range	NOVEMBER					DECEMBER					JANUARY					FEBRUARY					MARCH					APRIL					ANNUAL TOTAL				
	01 to 08	09 to 16	17 to 24	Total Obsn	MCWB	01 to 08	09 to 16	17 to 24	Total Obsn	MCWB	01 to 08	09 to 16	17 to 24	Total Obsn	MCWB	01 to 08	09 to 16	17 to 24	Total Obsn	MCWB	01 to 08	09 to 16	17 to 24	Total Obsn	MCWB	01 to 08	09 to 16	17 to 24	Total Obsn	MCWB	01 to 08	09 to 16	17 to 24	Total Obsn	MCWB
95/99																															4		0	4	78
90/94		0		0	72																						1	0	1	73		176	22	198	77
85/89		6	1	7	72														0	68		1		1	70		18	2	20	71	4	598	178	780	75
80/84		35	5	40	70		10	0	10	69		3	0	3	69		11	1	12	70		23	3	26	69		80	18	98	70	176	621	469	1266	74
75/79	3	69	25	97	68	0	38	7	45	67		26	4	30	67		27	8	35	68		57	18	75	67	5	75	55	135	68	707	482	675	1864	71
70/74	27	54	60	141	66	6	49	31	86	65	1	44	19	64	65	10	40	30	80	65	19	58	52	129	65	69	44	85	198	66	556	349	497	1402	67
65/69	69	39	68	176	63	35	46	61	142	62	25	47	51	123	62	35	46	43	124	62	57	45	68	170	62	90	18	54	162	63	425	251	386	1062	62
60/64	68	21	44	133	58	58	44	51	153	58	57	46	59	162	58	43	41	48	132	57	71	34	52	157	57	52	4	20	76	57	382	193	285	860	58
55/59	34	9	22	65	53	50	31	42	123	53	55	36	44	135	53	43	27	41	111	52	47	19	30	96	52	19	1	5	25	52	260	124	187	571	53
50/54	23	4	8	35	48	40	17	30	87	47	39	24	36	99	48	44	18	31	93	48	32	10	21	63	47	4	0	1	5	48	186	73	128	387	47
45/49	8	2	4	14	42	28	8	16	52	42	34	14	21	69	43	30	11	16	57	43	15	2	4	21	42	1		0	1	44	117	37	61	215	43
40/44	6	1	2	9	38	20	4	7	31	38	22	5	10	37	38	15	3	5	23	38	6	0	1	7	38	0			0	41	69	13	25	107	38
35/39	2	0	1	3	32	7	1	2	10	33	10	3	3	16	33	5	1	1	7	33	0	0	0	0	34						24	5	7	36	33
30/34	0	0	0	0	27	2	0	1	3	28	3	1	1	5	28	1	0	0	1	28											6	1	2	9	28
25/29	0			0	25	1	0	0	1	24	1	0	0	1	25																2	0	0	2	24
20/24						0	0	0	0	19																					0	0	0	0	19

ATLANTA/HARTSFIELD IAP GEORGIA
LAT 33 39N   LONG 84 26W   ELEV 1010 FT

MEAN FREQUENCY OF OCCURRENCE OF DRY BULB TEMPERATURE (DEGREES F) WITH MEAN COINCIDENT WET BULB TEMPERATURE (DEGREES F) FOR EACH DRY BULB TEMPERATURE RANGE

Temperature Range	MAY 01-08	MAY 09-16	MAY 17-24	MAY Total Obsn	MAY MCWB	JUNE 01-08	JUNE 09-16	JUNE 17-24	JUNE Total Obsn	JUNE MCWB	JULY 01-08	JULY 09-16	JULY 17-24	JULY Total Obsn	JULY MCWB	AUGUST 01-08	AUGUST 09-16	AUGUST 17-24	AUGUST Total Obsn	AUGUST MCWB	SEPTEMBER 01-08	SEPTEMBER 09-16	SEPTEMBER 17-24	SEPTEMBER Total Obsn	SEPTEMBER MCWB	OCTOBER 01-08	OCTOBER 09-16	OCTOBER 17-24	OCTOBER Total Obsn	OCTOBER MCWB
100/104																														
95/99							0		0	77		1	0	1	72		0	0	0	76		2		2	72		0		0	74
90/94		4	1	5	70		4	1	5	74		5	1	6	74		6	1	7	74		9	2	11	71		1	0	1	73
85/89		33	13	46	69		29	10	39	74		30	10	40	74		30	9	39	74		31	11	42	71		3	1	4	70
80/84	0	53	28	81	67	0	52	25	77	72	0	61	30	91	74		72	33	105	73		60	31	91	70		16	4	20	68
75/79	3	57	46	106	66	5	65	44	114	71	5	81	57	143	73	3	76	58	137	72	8	57	53	118	68	1	42	14	57	64
70/74	32	47	62	141	64	31	50	62	143	69	46	51	74	171	72	47	42	76	165	71	72	43	71	186	67	8	52	34	94	63
65/69	94	30	52	176	62	93	28	64	185	68	147	18	69	234	70	133	19	59	211	69	82	21	40	143	63	28	53	54	135	60
60/64	59	15	26	100	58	82	11	28	121	64	46	2	7	55	66	54	3	11	68	65	49	14	23	86	59	51	39	59	149	57
55/59	30	7	15	52	53	23	1	4	28	59	5	0	1	6	60	10	0	1	11	60	22	2	6	30	54	60	23	40	123	52
50/54	19	1	5	25	48	5	1	1	7	55						0	0		0	56	6	1	1	8	49	51	12	24	87	48
45/49	8	0	1	9	44	1		0	1	49											1	0	0	1	45	28	4	11	43	43
40/44	3	0	0	3	40	0			0	44											0			0	42	14	2	4	20	39
35/39																										7	0	1	8	33
30/34																										2		0	2	29

COINCIDENT WET BULB TEMPERATURE FOR EACH DRY BULB TEMPERATURE RANGE

ATLANTA/HARTSFIELD IAP GEORGIA

Temperature Range	Nov 01-08	Nov 09-16	Nov 17-24	Nov Total Obsn	Nov MCWB	Dec 01-08	Dec 09-16	Dec 17-24	Dec Total Obsn	Dec MCWB	Jan 01-08	Jan 09-16	Jan 17-24	Jan Total Obsn	Jan MCWB	Feb 01-08	Feb 09-16	Feb 17-24	Feb Total Obsn	Feb MCWB	Mar 01-08	Mar 09-16	Mar 17-24	Mar Total Obsn	Mar MCWB	Apr 01-08	Apr 09-16	Apr 17-24	Apr Total Obsn	Apr MCWB	Annual 01-08	Annual 09-16	Annual 17-24	Annual Total Obsn	Annual MCWB
100/104																																1	0	1	73
95/99																																17	3	20	74
90/94																															0	103	32	135	74
85/89		1		1	67																						2	0	2	66	0	254	113	367	72
80/84																						1	0	1	64		17	7	24	64	13	370	229	612	70
75/79		5	1	6	64		3	0	3	60		0	0	0	64	0	2	0	2	63	0	9	4	13	62	0	38	20	58	62	136	353	350	839	69
70/74	0	20	5	25	60	1	13	5	19	60	0	4	1	5	63	0	8	3	11	60	0	18	9	27	59	2	41	36	79	61	487	301	413	1201	67
65/69	5	32	17	54	59	9	22	16	47	57	2	11	5	18	60	2	16	10	28	57	5	27	24	56	57	22	43	48	113	59	423	262	301	986	62
60/64	18	39	35	92	56	13	26	22	61	52	9	19	19	47	57	7	25	20	52	55	16	34	34	84	54	55	40	48	143	56	311	248	286	845	57
55/59	28	40	43	111	51	17	36	33	86	47	17	29	23	69	53	17	32	33	82	51	30	45	42	117	50	54	29	38	121	52	276	234	263	773	52
50/54	34	38	41	113	47	29	44	41	114	42	21	34	34	89	47	26	34	37	97	47	38	40	44	122	47	42	17	22	81	46	255	213	241	709	47
45/49	45	30	42	117	42	39	44	53	136	38	25	42	39	106	43	32	37	37	106	42	44	34	37	115	42	31	9	14	54	42	243	200	222	665	42
40/44	44	20	30	94	38	55	29	37	121	34	36	38	43	117	38	43	30	35	108	38	48	21	30	99	38	22	3	6	31	38	249	158	201	608	38
35/39	35	9	16	60	33	43	19	25	87	29	46	37	40	123	34	41	21	25	87	34	34	12	15	61	33	10	0	1	11	34	228	108	135	471	34
30/34	20	4	7	31	29	23	7	11	41	24	45	18	28	91	29	29	10	14	53	29	25	6	6	37	29	2	0	0	2	29	166	57	80	303	29
25/29	8	1	3	12	25	13	2	3	18	20	28	9	9	46	24	15	5	6	26	24	5	1	3	9	25						79	23	32	134	24
20/24	3	0	0	3	21	13	1	3	18	20	9	4	4	17	20	7	2	2	11	19	1	0	1	2	20						33	8	10	51	20
15/19	1	0	1	2	14	2	1	0	3	15	5	1	3	9	15	3	1	2	6	15	1	0	0	1	16						13	3	7	23	15
10/14	0	0	0	0	10	0	0	0	0	5	3	1	0	4	11	2	0	0	2	11	0	0	0	0	11						7	2	0	9	11
5/9	0	0	0	0	6	1	0	0	1	1	0	0	0	0	6	1	0	0	1	6											1	0	0	1	6
0/4	0	0	0	0	3						0	0	0	0	0																1	0		1	1
-5/-1											0	0	0	0	-3																0			0	-3

SAVANNAH, GEORGIA/HUNTER AAF

LAT 32 01N LONG 81 08W ELEV 42 FT

MEAN FREQUENCY OF OCCURRENCE OF DRY BULB TEMPERATURE (DEGREES F) WITH MEAN COINCIDENT WET BULB TEMPERATURE (DEGREES F) FOR EACH DRY BULB TEMPERATURE RANGE

Temperature Range	MAY 01 to 08	MAY 09 to 16	MAY 17 to 24	MAY Total Obsn	MAY MC WB	JUNE 01 to 08	JUNE 09 to 16	JUNE 17 to 24	JUNE Total Obsn	JUNE MC WB	JULY 01 to 08	JULY 09 to 16	JULY 17 to 24	JULY Total Obsn	JULY MC WB	AUG 01 to 08	AUG 09 to 16	AUG 17 to 24	AUG Total Obsn	AUG MC WB	SEP 01 to 08	SEP 09 to 16	SEP 17 to 24	SEP Total Obsn	SEP MC WB	OCT 01 to 08	OCT 09 to 16	OCT 17 to 24	OCT Total Obsn	OCT MC WB
105/109																	0		0	79										
100/104												0	0	0	80		1	0	1	77										
95/99		0	0	0	76		2	0	2	79		8	1	9	79		10	1	11	78							0	0	0	78
90/94		3		3	74		8	1	9	78		49	8	57	78		50	6	56	78		1		1	76			1	1	76
85/89		15	3	18	73		29	5	34	77	1	103	28	132	77	1	91	28	120	76		12	1	13	76		10	1	11	73
80/84	0	40	7	47	72	1	74	17	92	75	21	61	75	157	75	16	63	74	153	75		62	7	69	75		46	6	52	71
75/79	2	76	21	99	71	14	76	53	143	73	117	21	101	239	74	109	27	104	240	74	3	77	36	116	74	6	54	26	86	68
70/74	19	61	58	138	69	70	38	94	202	72	103	5	36	144	71	108	6	32	146	71	52	57	99	208	72	29	57	52	138	66
65/69	76	33	87	196	68	104	10	57	171	69	7	0	0	7	65	14	0	2	16	66	108	22	68	198	70	45	38	64	147	62
60/64	81	13	50	144	64	38	2	10	50	65						1			1	63	55	7	22	84	64	64	27	48	139	58
55/59	39	5	16	60	59	10	1	3	14	60											17	2	6	25	59	42	10	26	78	54
50/54	23	2	4	29	54	3	0	0	3	56											4	0	1	5	54	29	3	16	48	49
45/49	6	1	2	9	50																1			1	51	20	1	7	28	44
40/44	2	0	0	2	46																					10	0	3	13	40
35/39	0	0	0	0	42																					3		0	3	35
30/34																										0			0	31

COINCIDENT WET BULB TEMPERATURE FOR EACH DRY BULB TEMPERATURE RANGE

SAVANNAH, GEORGIA/HUNTER AAF

The data below are arranged by month. Each month group contains the observation hour groups (01 to 08, 09 to 16, 17 to 24), the Total Obsn, and the MCWB (Mean Coincident Wet Bulb).

Temperature Range	Nov 01–08	Nov 09–16	Nov 17–24	Nov Total	Nov MCWB	Dec 01–08	Dec 09–16	Dec 17–24	Dec Total	Dec MCWB	Jan 01–08	Jan 09–16	Jan 17–24	Jan Total	Jan MCWB	Feb 01–08	Feb 09–16	Feb 17–24	Feb Total	Feb MCWB	Mar 01–08	Mar 09–16	Mar 17–24	Mar Total	Mar MCWB	Apr 01–08	Apr 09–16	Apr 17–24	Apr Total	Apr MCWB	Ann 01–08	Ann 09–16	Ann 17–24	Ann Total	Ann MCWB
105/109																															0	0	0	0	79
100/104																															0	3	0	3	78
95/99																															0	30	3	33	78
90/94																					0	0	0	0	69	0	1	0	1	73	0	157	23	180	77
85/89		0	0	0	70						0	0	0	0	69						0	2	1	3	68	0	8	1	9	69	3	390	90	483	75
80/84	0	7	0	7	69	0	1	0	1	68	0	1	0	1	68	0	3	0	3	66	0	10	2	12	67	0	33	5	38	68	56	454	272	782	73
75/79	0	26	2	28	66	0	6	0	6	66	0	7	1	8	66	0	10	2	12	64	0	25	5	30	64	1	59	18	78	66	374	391	510	1275	71
70/74	21	45	11	77	63	0	19	1	20	62	0	17	3	20	63	0	23	5	28	62	1	38	15	54	61	15	56	46	117	64	545	331	413	1289	68
65/69	21	49	45	115	61	8	31	17	56	61	4	27	11	42	60	6	36	19	61	60	21	44	38	103	60	51	42	71	164	61	351	289	349	989	62
60/64	38	44	48	130	57	18	40	29	87	56	19	37	32	88	57	30	35	38	103	57	40	45	50	135	56	65	27	52	144	58	341	263	322	926	57
55/59	38	34	46	118	53	24	40	36	100	52	28	39	38	105	52	28	36	37	101	52	39	34	45	118	52	45	11	26	82	53	274	206	259	739	52
50/54	44	20	37	101	48	29	40	46	115	47	30	37	39	106	47	32	32	42	106	47	45	23	42	110	47	28	4	15	47	48	244	160	239	643	48
45/49	39	10	28	77	43	36	33	43	112	43	32	35	42	109	43	38	25	39	102	43	35	15	27	77	43	25	1	6	32	44	227	120	192	539	43
40/44	31	4	15	50	39	42	22	37	101	38	45	25	41	111	38	35	13	22	70	39	35	7	15	57	38	9	0	1	10	40	207	71	134	412	38
35/39	19	1	7	27	34	39	10	22	71	34	37	15	24	76	34	25	7	12	44	34	20	4	5	29	34	2	0	0	2	36	145	37	70	252	34
30/34	7	0	2	9	30	30	5	11	46	29	28	5	12	45	29	19	3	5	27	30	9	0	2	11	30	0			0	33	93	13	32	138	29
25/29	0	2	0	2	25	16	1	4	21	25	17	3	5	25	25	8	1	1	10	25	2	0	0	2	26						45	5	10	60	25
20/24	0	1	0	1	22	6	0	1	7	21	7	1	1	9	20	2	0	0	2	21	0	0	0	0	20						16	1	2	19	21
15/19						1	0	0	1	16	2	0	0	2	17	1	0	0	1	15											4	0	0	4	16
10/14						0	0	0	0	12	0	0	0	0	10																0	0	0	0	11

BOISE, IDAHO
READINGS TAKEN AT MOUNTAIN HOME AFB

LAT 43 02N   LONG 115 54W   ELEV 2996 FT

MEAN FREQUENCY OF OCCURRENCE OF DRY BULB TEMPERATURE (DEGREES F) WITH MEAN COINCIDENT WET BULB TEMPERATURE (DEGREES F) FOR EACH DRY BULB TEMPERATURE RANGE

Temperature Range	MAY					JUNE					JULY					AUGUST					SEPTEMBER					OCTOBER				
	01 to 08	09 to 16	17 to 24	Total Obsn	MCWB	01 to 08	09 to 16	17 to 24	Total Obsn	MCWB	01 to 08	09 to 16	17 to 24	Total Obsn	MCWB	01 to 08	09 to 16	17 to 24	Total Obsn	MCWB	01 to 08	09 to 16	17 to 24	Total Obsn	MCWB	01 to 08	09 to 16	17 to 24	Total Obsn	MCWB
105/109								0	0	66		1	1	2	65		1	1	2	67										
100/104							2	1	3	64		7	5	12	64		5	3	8	64										
95/99		0	0	0	59		6	5	11	63		25	22	47	63		20	15	35	63		2	1	3	61					
90/94		3	2	5	60		15	11	26	62		47	37	84	61		39	29	68	61		10	5	15	60		0	0	0	59
85/89		8	6	14	58	0	25	18	43	60	0	51	39	90	60	0	45	32	77	60		20	12	32	59		2	1	3	57
80/84		19	11	30	57	1	35	25	61	58	4	49	37	90	58	3	42	32	77	58		29	17	46	57		6	2	8	55
75/79	0	27	18	45	55	3	36	29	68	57	15	37	41	93	57	10	37	38	85	57	1	31	23	55	55	0	13	6	19	54
70/74	2	32	25	59	53	11	37	34	82	55	40	20	34	94	55	32	28	40	100	55	5	41	30	76	53	0	20	10	30	52
65/69	8	37	32	77	51	30	33	37	100	54	67	9	22	98	53	57	15	27	99	52	13	36	36	85	51	1	30	17	48	50
60/64	19	41	36	96	49	50	25	32	107	52	67	2	9	78	50	65	8	16	89	50	38	31	31	100	50	4	38	24	66	48
55/59	32	35	40	107	47	56	17	27	100	49	38	0	3	41	47	45	5	10	60	47	52	22	32	106	46	10	42	36	88	46
50/54	54	26	38	118	45	51	7	16	74	47	13	0	0	13	43	23	2	4	29	45	57	12	25	94	43	28	43	45	116	43
45/49	62	13	24	99	41	29	2	4	35	43	3	0	0	3	39	10	0	1	11	41	40	6	13	59	40	51	28	45	124	41
40/44	41	5	10	56	38	6	0	0	6	38				0	35	2			2	37	28	2	5	35	37	53	17	34	104	37
35/39	19	1	4	24	33	1			1	34				0	34	1			1	34	9	1	2	12	33	53	7	19	79	33
30/34	8	0	1	9	29																4		0	4	29	34	2	7	43	29
25/29	2			2	26																1			1	25	10	1	1	12	25
20/24	0			0	23																0			0	20	2	0	0	2	21
15/19																										1			1	16

COINCIDENT WET BULB TEMPERATURE FOR EACH DRY BULB TEMPERATURE RANGE

BOISE, IDAHO
READINGS TAKEN AT MOUNTAIN HOME AFB

Temperature Range	NOV 01–08	NOV 09–16	NOV 17–24	NOV Total Obsn	NOV MCWB	DEC 01–08	DEC 09–16	DEC 17–24	DEC Total Obsn	DEC MCWB	JAN 01–08	JAN 09–16	JAN 17–24	JAN Total Obsn	JAN MCWB	FEB 01–08	FEB 09–16	FEB 17–24	FEB Total Obsn	FEB MCWB	MAR 01–08	MAR 09–16	MAR 17–24	MAR Total Obsn	MAR MCWB	APR 01–08	APR 09–16	APR 17–24	APR Total Obsn	APR MCWB	ANNUAL 01–08	ANNUAL 09–16	ANNUAL 17–24	ANNUAL Total Obsn	ANNUAL MCWB
105/109																																2	2	4	66
100/104																																14	9	23	64
95/99																															0	53	43	96	63
90/94																															0	114	84	198	61
85/89																													0	57	0	151	108	259	60
80/84																											2	1	3	55	8	182	125	315	58
75/79		1		1	50																	1		1	53		6	3	9	53	29	188	158	375	56
70/74		2	0	2	48																	3	1	4	51		13	8	21	51	90	195	182	467	54
65/69	0	8	2	10	47												0		0	49		7	4	11	48		19	13	32	49	176	188	188	552	52
60/64	1	23	9	33	45			0	0	52	0		0	0	45	0	3	2	5	47		12	7	19	46	1	31	21	53	47	236	199	188	623	49
55/59						2		1	3	46		1	0	1	46	0	9	4	13	45	0	24	15	39	44	6	41	32	79	44	240	221	209	670	46
50/54	6	33	19	58	43	1	8	3	12	42	1	6	2	9	44	2	20	13	35	43	5	39	29	73	41	18	47	42	107	42	259	243	236	738	43
45/49	15	45	37	97	41	3	22	9	34	40	3	21	10	34	40	7	36	26	69	40	12	51	42	105	39	36	44	47	127	40	271	268	258	797	40
40/44	39	55	56	150	37	19	38	29	86	37	15	34	29	78	38	13	46	41	100	37	33	52	52	137	36	55	28	41	124	37	304	277	297	878	37
35/39	53	39	49	141	33	34	54	47	135	33	30	47	43	120	33	48	50	57	155	33	54	36	48	138	33	66	9	23	98	33	368	244	292	904	33
30/34	54	22	39	115	29	53	57	65	175	29	52	54	57	163	29	67	36	48	151	30	68	18	35	121	29	40	1	8	49	29	380	190	260	830	29
25/29	39	9	20	68	25	55	34	48	137	25	39	39	45	123	25	47	15	22	84	25	47	5	12	64	25	14	0	1	15	25	254	103	149	506	25
20/24	23	3	7	33	21	46	19	29	94	21	45	24	32	101	20	26	7	9	42	21	21	1	2	24	21	3		0	3	20	166	54	79	299	21
15/19	8	1	1	10	16	21	8	11	40	16	33	11	18	62	16	9	2	3	14	16	5	0	1	6	15				0	16	77	22	34	133	16
10/14	1	0	0	1	11	11	4	4	19	12	16	6	6	28	11	4	1	0	5	11	2		0	2	11						34	11	10	55	11
5/9	0			0	8	3	1	2	6	7	5	3	3	11	6	1	0	0	1	7											9	4	5	18	7
0/4						3	0	1	4	2	3	1	3	7	1	0			0	4											6	1	4	11	1
-5/-1						1	0		1	-3	3	1	1	5	-3																4	1	1	6	-3
-10/-6											1	0	0	1	-9																1	0	0	1	-9
-15/-11											1	0	0	1	-13																1	0	0	1	-13
-20/-16											0			0	-17																0			0	-17
-25/-21											0			0	-22																0			0	-22

CHICAGO/O HARE IAP ILLINOIS
LAT 41 59N   LONG 87 54W   ELEV 658 FT

MEAN FREQUENCY OF OCCURRENCE OF DRY BULB TEMPERATURE (DEGREES F) WITH MEAN COINCIDENT WET BULB TEMPERATURE (DEGREES F) FOR EACH DRY BULB TEMPERATURE RANGE

Temperature Range	MAY Obsn Hour Gp 01–08	09–16	17–24	MAY Total Obsn	MAY MCWB	JUNE 01–08	09–16	17–24	JUNE Total	JUNE MCWB	JULY 01–08	09–16	17–24	JULY Total	JULY MCWB	AUG 01–08	09–16	17–24	AUG Total	AUG MCWB	SEPT 01–08	09–16	17–24	SEPT Total	SEPT MCWB	OCT 01–08	09–16	17–24	OCT Total	OCT MCWB
100/104																														
95/99																														
90/94		2	0	2	71		0	0	0	77		0	0	0	78		2	0	2	75		2	0	2	73					
85/89		9	2	11	70		1	0	1	78		1	0	1	78		17	2	19	75		8	1	9	73		0		0	66
80/84	0	21	7	28	68	0	13	2	15	74		12	1	13	76	0	31	7	38	73	0	15	3	18	72		2		2	70
75/79	3	32	15	50	64		31	10	41	72	1	43	10	54	73	3	55	21	79	71	0	24	8	32	69		11	1	12	66
70/74	12	33	23	68	61	4	43	21	68	69	4	67	29	100	70	18	66	42	126	68	7	35	16	58	66	0	16	3	19	63
65/69	25	34	29	88	59	17	43	32	92	67	23	58	48	129	68	50	48	64	162	66	19	47	30	96	63	2	26	9	37	61
60/64	31	31	32	94	55	36	42	44	122	64	56	43	64	163	66	68	23	60	151	63	33	50	45	128	60	9	37	20	66	59
55/59	38	33	39	110	51	50	29	44	123	61	78	17	57	152	63	56	6	34	96	59	48	35	53	136	57	23	38	30	91	55
50/54	46	29	39	114	47	50	20	38	108	57	54	4	28	86	59	33	0	13	46	55	43	19	40	102	53	32	37	41	110	51
45/49	44	17	35	96	43	37	11	27	75	53	23	0	7	30	55	15		4	19	50	42	5	25	72	49	38	36	43	117	47
40/44	30	5	20	55	39	30	5	17	52	49	8	0	2	10	50	4		1	5	46	26	1	13	40	45	49	24	42	115	44
35/39	16	2	6	24	35	13	0	6	19	45	1	0	0	1	45	1			1	42	14	0	6	20	41	37	13	28	78	39
30/34	3		0	3	31	3	0	1	4	40											5		2	7	36	29	7	18	54	35
25/29						0			0	36											1			1	32	20	1	8	29	30
20/24																										6	0	3	9	26
15/19																										2	0	0	2	18

COINCIDENT WET BULB TEMPERATURE FOR EACH DRY BULB TEMPERATURE RANGE

CHICAGO/O HARE IAP ILLINOIS

Column key for each month block: Obsn Hour Gp (01 to 08 / 09 to 16 / 17 to 24), Total Obsn, MCWB.

Temp. Range	NOV 01-08	NOV 09-16	NOV 17-24	NOV Total	NOV MCWB	DEC 01-08	DEC 09-16	DEC 17-24	DEC Total	DEC MCWB	JAN 01-08	JAN 09-16	JAN 17-24	JAN Total	JAN MCWB	FEB 01-08	FEB 09-16	FEB 17-24	FEB Total	FEB MCWB	MAR 01-08	MAR 09-16	MAR 17-24	MAR Total	MAR MCWB	APR 01-08	APR 09-16	APR 17-24	APR Total	APR MCWB	ANN 01-08	ANN 09-16	ANN 17-24	ANN Total	ANN MCWB
100/104																																0	0	0	77
95/99																																6	0	6	76
90/94																																52	6	58	74
85/89																											1	0	1	65	1	132	32	165	72
80/84																								0	62		4	1	5	64	11	225	88	324	70
75/79		1		1	66																			0	61		9	3	12	63	68	260	159	487	67
70/74		3	1	4	61																	1	1	2	57	1	18	8	27	60	176	262	243	681	64
65/69	1	8	2	11	58									0	63				0	60		2	2	4	55	6	19	11	36	57	270	220	269	759	61
60/64	5	11	8	24	56		1	0	1	54		0	0	0	58		1	0	1	55		3	5	8	53	13	24	18	55	54	280	176	244	700	57
55/59	9	20	13	42	51		3	2	5	53		1	1	2	55	1	2	1	4	52	3	9	5	17	50	14	25	22	61	50	233	160	211	604	52
50/54	10	27	19	56	47	2	7	4	13	48	1	2	1	4	50	1	4	2	7	47	4	14	9	27	46	25	33	32	90	46	222	163	196	581	47
45/49	22	38	29	89	43	4	10	6	20	43	2	5	3	10	44	2	8	4	14	43	10	22	14	46	42	35	39	36	110	42	212	164	189	565	43
40/44	33	35	38	106	38	9	21	13	43	39	4	13	5	22	39	4	18	10	32	38	15	39	27	81	37	44	37	49	130	38	194	181	197	572	38
35/39	39	36	43	118	34	28	36	34	98	34	17	34	26	77	34	18	42	30	90	34	41	57	51	149	34	50	23	35	108	34	243	237	245	725	34
30/34	46	28	35	109	30	46	52	52	150	30	45	56	54	155	30	53	57	61	171	30	72	50	69	191	30	33	7	20	60	30	319	251	299	869	30
25/29	38	17	27	82	25	42	41	44	127	25	41	40	41	122	25	45	37	46	128	25	41	24	36	101	25	12	3	5	20	25	227	160	202	589	25
20/24	18	9	14	41	20	35	27	27	89	21	34	29	30	93	20	30	21	28	79	21	31	14	17	62	21	3	1	1	5	20	154	100	117	371	21
15/19	10	3	7	20	16	22	17	18	57	16	26	22	23	71	16	23	13	16	52	16	16	5	9	30	16	1	0	0	1	16	98	60	73	231	16
10/14	5	2	4	11	11	19	14	17	50	11	20	17	19	56	11	16	9	8	33	11	9	2	3	14	11						69	43	52	164	11
5/9	2	1	2	5	6	12	9	12	33	6	18	15	18	51	6	9	5	8	22	6	3	1	0	4	6						44	30	41	115	6
0/4	2		1	3	1	11	5	9	25	1	16	8	15	39	1	8	5	6	19	1	3	0	0	3	2						40	18	31	89	1
-5/-1	1		0	1	-3	8	3	6	17	-3	11	4	7	22	-3	7	2	4	13	-4				0	-3						27	9	17	53	-3
-10/-6						5	1	3	9	-8	7	2	3	12	-8	5	0	1	6	-8				0	-7						17	3	7	27	-8
-15/-11						3	0	1	4	-13	4	1	1	6	-13	1	0	0	1	-13											8	1	2	11	-13
-20/-16						1		0	1	-17	1	0	0	1	-17				0	-16											2	0	0	2	-17
-25/-21											0			0	-21																		0	0	-21

ROCKFORD, ILLINOIS*
READINGS TAKEN AT MOLINE/QUAD CITY AP

LAT 41 27N   LONG 90 31W   ELEV 582 FT

MEAN FREQUENCY OF OCCURRENCE OF DRY BULB TEMPERATURE (DEGREES F) WITH MEAN COINCIDENT WET BULB TEMPERATURE (DEGREES F) FOR EACH DRY BULB TEMPERATURE RANGE

Temperature Range	MAY 01–08	MAY 09–16	MAY 17–24	MAY Total Obsn	MAY MC WB	JUNE 01–08	JUNE 09–16	JUNE 17–24	JUNE Total Obsn	JUNE MC WB	JULY 01–08	JULY 09–16	JULY 17–24	JULY Total Obsn	JULY MC WB	AUG 01–08	AUG 09–16	AUG 17–24	AUG Total Obsn	AUG MC WB	SEP 01–08	SEP 09–16	SEP 17–24	SEP Total Obsn	SEP MC WB	OCT 01–08	OCT 09–16	OCT 17–24	OCT Total Obsn	OCT MC WB
100/104																														
95/99														0	74															
90/94		3	1	4	71		4	0	4	76		4	1	5	78		3	0	3	75									0	67
85/89		9	3	12	69		20	6	26	74		21	6	27	76		18	4	22	75		3		3	73		4		4	69
80/84	0	24	9	33	67	1	36	13	50	72	1	48	20	69	73	0	42	14	56	73		9	1	10	73		14	1	15	66
75/79	4	39	21	64	64	7	49	30	86	70	9	71	42	122	71	5	64	34	103	71		16	4	20	71		22	6	28	63
70/74	16	41	33	90	61	22	47	42	111	67	32	58	58	148	69	23	59	51	133	69	1	27	9	37	69	2	32	16	50	61
65/69	29	39	42	110	59	43	39	54	136	65	68	31	60	159	67	58	42	64	164	67	8	39	22	69	66	13	31	24	68	58
60/64	41	38	46	125	56	53	24	45	122	62	66	11	42	119	64	66	15	44	125	63	23	46	34	103	63	24	36	32	92	55
55/59	46	28	41	115	52	54	14	30	98	58	50	3	15	68	60	54	5	27	86	59	35	46	48	129	61	32	38	38	108	51
50/54	45	17	29	91	48	37	6	14	57	54	17	0	3	20	56	28	0	9	37	55	42	33	43	118	57	36	30	40	106	47
45/49	34	6	15	55	44	18	2	4	24	50	5	0	0	5	51	11		2	13	51	42	15	38	95	53	40	22	40	102	43
40/44	22	2	7	31	39	5		0	5	45				0	48	3		0	3	46	41	5	25	71	49	42	12	25	79	39
35/39	9	0	2	11	35	1			1	42							0		0	43	29	1	10	40	45	31	5	18	54	35
30/34	2		0	2	32																12		4	16	41	19	1	7	27	31
25/29																					6		1	7	37	6		1	7	26
20/24																					1			1	33	2			2	21
15/19																												0	0	17

* Comparative design data note:

	Elevation	WINTER 97 1/2%	SUMMER DB 2 1/2%	SUMMER WB 2 1/2%
Rockford, IL.	724 ft.	-3° F	90° F	76° F
Moline/Quad City AP	582 ft.	-3° F	91° F	77° F

ROCKFORD, ILLINOIS*
READINGS TAKEN AT MOLINE/QUAD CITY AP

Temperature Range	NOV 01-08	NOV 09-16	NOV 17-24	NOV Total	NOV MCWB	DEC 01-08	DEC 09-16	DEC 17-24	DEC Total	DEC MCWB	JAN 01-08	JAN 09-16	JAN 17-24	JAN Total	JAN MCWB	FEB 01-08	FEB 09-16	FEB 17-24	FEB Total	FEB MCWB	MAR 01-08	MAR 09-16	MAR 17-24	MAR Total	MAR MCWB	APR 01-08	APR 09-16	APR 17-24	APR Total	APR MCWB	ANN 01-08	ANN 09-16	ANN 17-24	ANN Total	ANN MCWB
100/104																																0		0	74
95/99																																14	1	15	76
90/94																																71	18	89	75
85/89																											0		0	65	2	157	54	213	72
80/84																											2	0	2	64	22	256	127	405	70
75/79		1		1	65																	1		1	59		7	2	9	63	89	277	205	571	67
70/74		4	1	5	60																	3	1	4	56		11	5	16	62	211	257	271	739	65
65/69	1	10	3	14	58		0		0	59		0		0	61		0		0	59		3	2	5	54	1	19	8	28	59	270	203	267	740	61
60/64	6	16	10	32	55	1	2	1	4	55		0		0	57		1	0	1	55	1	6	4	11	52	7	24	17	48	56	289	181	233	703	57
55/59	7	19	13	39	50	1	4	1	6	50	0	2	1	3	53	1	2	1	4	51	2	12	7	21	48	16	27	25	68	54	232	154	196	582	52
50/54	12	27	19	58	46	3	7	4	14	46	1	2	1	4	47	1	7	3	11	46	6	20	13	39	44	19	28	30	77	50	207	151	175	533	47
45/49	21	34	30	85	42	4	12	6	22	42	2	6	3	11	42	2	12	6	20	42	8	26	20	54	41	28	34	35	97	46	184	154	167	505	43
40/44	29	35	33	97	38	9	19	13	41	38	4	16	9	29	38	5	22	14	41	38	21	38	30	89	37	36	35	37	108	42	182	173	169	524	38
35/39	40	34	40	114	34	23	36	36	95	34	18	30	25	73	34	19	37	32	88	34	40	49	48	137	34	37	29	34	100	38	233	208	233	674	34
30/34	45	25	35	105	30	45	50	46	141	30	31	41	41	113	30	53	48	54	155	30	67	44	58	169	30	47	17	31	95	34	297	215	252	764	30
25/29	35	17	27	79	25	43	39	45	127	25	37	40	40	117	25	40	36	40	116	25	43	22	32	97	25	34	6	11	51	30	216	155	189	560	25
20/24	22	9	16	47	21	37	27	33	97	21	36	31	32	99	21	28	21	26	75	21	25	14	17	56	20	12	1	4	17	25	153	102	124	379	21
15/19	12	5	7	24	16	24	19	17	60	16	32	23	27	82	16	21	15	16	52	16	16	7	9	32	16	3	0	0	3	21	105	69	76	250	16
10/14	5	3	3	11	11	19	13	17	49	11	23	21	22	66	11	17	9	12	38	11	9	2	1	12	11						73	48	59	180	11
5/9	2	1	2	5	6	12	9	10	31	6	21	16	21	58	6	12	7	10	29	6	4	1	2	7	6						51	34	45	130	6
0/4	2		1	3	2	9	7	10	26	1	19	12	15	46	1	10	4	6	20	1	3	0	1	4	2						43	23	33	99	1
-5/-1	0			0	-2	7	3	5	15	-3	12	4	6	22	-3	7	2	3	12	-3	1	0	0	1	-3						27	9	14	50	-3
-10/-6						7	1	2	10	-8	8	2	4	14	-8	4	1	1	6	-8	1			1	-8						20	4	7	31	-8
-15/-11						2	0	1	3	-12	4	1	1	6	-13	2	0		2	-13	1			1	-13						9	1	2	12	-13
-20/-16						1	0	0	1	-18	1	0	0	1	-17	0			0	-17	0			0	-17						2	0	0	2	-17
-25/-21						0	0		0	-21	0			0	-23																0	0		0	-22

EVANSVILLE/DRESS RGNL APRT INDIANA
LAT 38 03N LONG 87 32W ELEV 381 FT

MEAN FREQUENCY OF OCCURRENCE OF DRY BULB TEMPERATURE (DEGREES F) WITH MEAN COINCIDENT WET BULB TEMPERATURE (DEGREES F) FOR EACH DRY BULB TEMPERATURE RANGE

Column key for each month: Obsn Hour Gp (01 to 08 | 09 to 16 | 17 to 24), Total Obsn, MCWB (Mean Coincident Wet Bulb)

MAY

Temperature Range	01–08	09–16	17–24	Total Obsn	MCWB
90/94		6	0	6	73
85/89		23	6	29	70
80/84	2	42	16	60	68
75/79	9	52	31	92	66
70/74	25	43	42	110	64
65/69	52	35	50	137	61
60/64	48	22	43	113	57
55/59	42	14	28	84	53
50/54	37	8	18	63	49
45/49	19	3	9	31	45
40/44	10	1	5	16	40
35/39	4		1	5	36
30/34	0		0	0	32
25/29	0			0	28

JUNE

Temperature Range	01–08	09–16	17–24	Total Obsn	MCWB
90/94		1	0	1	78
85/89		10	2	12	76
80/84	0	33	9	42	75
75/79	3	51	21	75	73
70/74	12	55	40	107	71
65/69	36	46	49	131	69
60/64	63	27	54	144	67
55/59	52	9	34	95	64
50/54	39	6	21	66	59
45/49	25	1	9	35	55
40/44	7	0	1	8	51
35/39	2		0	2	46
30/34	0			0	42

JULY

Temperature Range	01–08	09–16	17–24	Total Obsn	MCWB
100/104		2	0	2	77
95/99		9	2	11	77
90/94	0	40	9	49	76
85/89	3	79	30	112	74
80/84	17	70	51	138	72
75/79	54	34	69	157	71
70/74	93	12	60	165	69
65/69	47	2	20	69	64
60/64	25	0	6	31	60
55/59	8		1	9	56
50/54	1		0	1	51
45/49	0			0	48

AUGUST

Temperature Range	01–08	09–16	17–24	Total Obsn	MCWB
100/104			0	0	80
95/99		9	1	10	76
90/94	0	39	8	47	75
85/89	1	72	23	96	73
80/84	12	65	44	121	72
75/79	42	40	60	142	71
70/74	75	18	59	152	68
65/69	57	1	33	91	64
60/64	41		15	56	60
55/59	16		4	20	55
50/54	5		1	6	51
45/49	1			1	47

SEPTEMBER

Temperature Range	01–08	09–16	17–24	Total Obsn	MCWB
90/94		1		1	71
85/89		5	0	5	72
80/84		16	2	18	72
75/79		37	7	44	71
70/74	2	43	17	62	69
65/69	11	48	31	90	67
60/64	41	48	48	137	66
55/59	28	45	45	118	62
50/54	45	12	39	96	58
45/49	37	3	27	67	54
40/44	29	1	16	46	50
35/39	19		7	26	46
30/34	7		1	8	42
25/29	1			1	37

OCTOBER

Temperature Range	01–08	09–16	17–24	Total Obsn	MCWB
90/94		1		1	70
85/89		8	0	8	69
80/84	0	25	2	27	66
75/79	1	36	8	45	64
70/74	7	41	20	68	62
65/69	14	34	31	79	59
60/64	29	37	35	101	56
55/59	35	28	39	102	52
50/54	39	21	42	102	48
45/49	45	12	32	89	44
40/44	37	5	22	64	40
35/39	26	1	11	38	35
30/34	11		4	15	31
25/29	4		1	5	26
20/24	0			0	22

COINCIDENT WET BULB TEMPERATURE FOR EACH DRY BULB TEMPERATURE RANGE

EVANSVILLE/DRESS RGNL APRT INDIANA

Hour Group columns: 01 to 08 | 09 to 16 | 17 to 24 | Total Obsn | MCWB

Temperature Range	NOV 01–08	NOV 09–16	NOV 17–24	NOV Total	NOV MCWB	DEC 01–08	DEC 09–16	DEC 17–24	DEC Total	DEC MCWB	JAN 01–08	JAN 09–16	JAN 17–24	JAN Total	JAN MCWB	FEB 01–08	FEB 09–16	FEB 17–24	FEB Total	FEB MCWB	MAR 01–08	MAR 09–16	MAR 17–24	MAR Total	MAR MCWB	APR 01–08	APR 09–16	APR 17–24	APR Total	APR MCWB	ANN 01–08	ANN 09–16	ANN 17–24	ANN Total	ANN MCWB
100/104																																			77
95/99																																4	0	4	76
90/94																															0	33	5	38	75
85/89																											3	0	3	68	0	135	28	163	73
80/84		1		1	67																						19	4	23	66	7	273	87	367	70
75/79	0	5	1	6	64	0	0	0	0	65							0		0	62						1	24	11	36	64	45	320	174	539	68
70/74	0	12	2	14	60	0	1	0	1	63		1	1	2	64		1	0	1	61				0	61	9	29	22	60	62	154	289	261	704	66
65/69	3	17	8	28	58	0	3	2	5	61	1	4	1	6	61	1	4	2	7	58	0	4	1	5	60	21	35	30	86	58	314	242	311	867	61
60/64	9	28	17	54	55	3	8	3	14	57	4	7	5	16	58	2	10	4	16	55	1	9	3	13	58	28	34	33	95	55	294	188	265	747	57
55/59	16	27	21	64	51	5	13	9	27	52	7	12	10	29	53	6	17	9	32	51	2	15	9	26	54	31	29	33	93	51	279	189	236	704	52
50/54	21	36	26	83	46	10	20	15	45	48	6	16	12	34	48	8	23	17	48	46	7	24	15	46	50	35	28	33	96	46	241	171	212	624	47
45/49	26	34	32	92	42	16	26	19	61	43	12	23	13	48	42	14	29	26	69	42	13	27	22	62	46	30	22	31	83	42	220	184	211	615	43
40/44	31	31	34	96	38	22	37	29	88	38	22	30	24	76	38	25	36	32	93	38	22	31	30	83	42	39	14	27	80	39	210	190	208	608	39
35/39	37	22	37	96	34	32	48	41	121	34	30	43	38	111	34	40	44	43	127	34	26	41	39	106	38	31	4	12	47	35	234	191	214	639	34
30/34	43	16	34	93	30	55	40	52	147	30	49	48	55	152	30	50	29	41	120	30	41	37	40	118	34	12	1	3	16	30	245	194	224	663	30
25/29	30	8	19	57	25	39	26	38	103	25	41	27	36	104	25	34	12	23	69	25	44	32	41	117	30	3		0	3	26	268	151	220	639	25
20/24	15	2	4	21	21	26	13	17	56	20	29	17	25	71	20	18	9	11	38	20	48	17	31	96	25	0			0	23	176	78	128	382	21
15/19	4	2	4	10	16	17	6	11	34	16	21	8	14	43	16	10	5	7	22	15	25	5	11	41	20						100	44	61	205	16
10/14	3	1	1	5	11	11	5	7	23	11	10	6	6	22	11	3	3	5	11	10	12	3	4	19	16						55	22	37	114	11
5/9	1	0	0	1	7	7	2	3	12	6	9	2	4	15	6	4	2	1	7	6	3	1	1	5	11						35	15	19	69	6
0/4	0	0	0	0	1	3	0	2	5	2	4	1	2	7	2	2	0	1	3	2	2	0	0	2	6						22	6	9	37	2
-5/-1	0	0	0	0	-2	1	0	0	1	-3	1	1	1	3	-3	1		0	1	-3	1	0	1	2	3						10	1	5	16	-3
-10/-6						0	0	0	0	-7	1	1	1	3	-8	0	0	0	0	-9	1	0	0	1	-2						3	1	1	5	-8
-15/-11											1	0	0	1	-13	0	0		0	-13				0	-8						1	1	1	3	-13
-20/-16											0	0	0	0	-17	0	0		0	-19				0							1	0	0	1	-18
-25/-21																0			0	-21													0	0	-21

INDIANAPOLIS, INDIANA*
READINGS TAKEN AT TERRE HAUTE, IN

LAT 39 27N   LONG 87 18W   ELEV 585 FT

MEAN FREQUENCY OF OCCURRENCE OF DRY BULB TEMPERATURE (DEGREES F) WITH MEAN COINCIDENT WET BULB TEMPERATURE (DEGREES F) FOR EACH DRY BULB TEMPERATURE RANGE

Temperature Range	MAY 01–08	MAY 09–16	MAY 17–24	MAY Total	MAY MCWB	JUNE 01–08	JUNE 09–16	JUNE 17–24	JUNE Total	JUNE MCWB	JULY 01–08	JULY 09–16	JULY 17–24	JULY Total	JULY MCWB	AUG 01–08	AUG 09–16	AUG 17–24	AUG Total	AUG MCWB	SEPT 01–08	SEPT 09–16	SEPT 17–24	SEPT Total	SEPT MCWB	OCT 01–08	OCT 09–16	OCT 17–24	OCT Total	OCT MCWB
105/109												1		1	77															
100/104												2	0	2	77															
95/99							1	0	1	74		7	2	9	76															
90/94		1		1	70		5	1	6	77	0	27	5	32	75		4		4	75		0		0	71		1		1	72
85/89		14	2	16	69		31	6	37	74	2	73	19	94	74	1	20	2	23	74		2		2	70		5	0	5	67
80/84	0	26	5	31	67	1	49	15	65	73	13	76	41	130	72	4	51	9	64	72	0	7	0	7	71		19	1	20	67
75/79	3	50	17	70	64	12	54	32	98	71	46	46	69	161	70	18	60	27	105	70	1	16	1	18	69	2	25	5	32	64
70/74	11	47	31	89	62	34	50	47	131	69	82	13	67	162	69	62	14	49	125	68	4	29	5	38	68	6	33	12	51	62
65/69	29	46	47	122	59	57	26	58	141	67	56	2	31	89	64	70	21	68	159	68	19	36	17	72	66	17	42	29	88	60
60/64	47	30	50	127	57	62	17	46	125	63	32	0	12	44	60	49	30	55	134	64	47	30	38	115	64	19	39	31	89	55
55/59	53	18	49	120	53	38	5	22	65	59	13	0	3	16	56	29	21	27	77	60	44	46	51	141	61	33	35	38	106	51
50/54	53	9	30	92	49	23	1	10	34	54	3			3	52	13	16	10	39	55	39	27	47	113	58	41	24	42	107	48
45/49	31	6	10	47	45	12	0	2	14	50						1	12	1	14	51	41	6	40	87	54	40	15	40	95	44
40/44	15	1	5	21	41	2		1	3	46						1	0	0	1	46	28	14	26	68	50	39	5	28	72	40
35/39	5	1		6	36	0			0	43											12	16	10	38	46	30	5	14	49	35
30/34	0			0	30																6	6	3	15	41	14	5	5	19	31
25/29																								6	37	5	2	2	7	26
20/24																										1	1	0	1	21
15/19																										0	0	0	0	18

* Comparative design data note:

	Elevation	WINTER 97 1/2%	SUMMER DB 2 1/2%	SUMMER WB 2 1/2%
Indianapolis, IN.	793 ft.	4° F	91° F	77° F
Terre Haute AP	585 ft.	7° F	93° F	78° F

INDIANAPOLIS, INDIANA*
READINGS TAKEN AT TERRE HAUTE, IN

Temperature Range	NOVEMBER Obsn Hour Gp 01 to 08	NOVEMBER 09 to 16	NOVEMBER 17 to 24	NOVEMBER Total Obsn	NOVEMBER MCWB	DECEMBER Obsn Hour Gp 01 to 08	DECEMBER 09 to 16	DECEMBER 17 to 24	DECEMBER Total Obsn	DECEMBER MCWB	JANUARY Obsn Hour Gp 01 to 08	JANUARY 09 to 16	JANUARY 17 to 24	JANUARY Total Obsn	JANUARY MCWB
105/109															
100/104															
95/99															
90/94															
85/89															
80/84		0		0	66										
75/79		1	0	1	65										
70/74		8	0	8	61		0		0	66		0		0	64
65/69	0	14	3	17	57	0	2	2	4	63		2	2	4	62
60/64	5	21	8	34	55	1	8	4	13	58	4	5	2	11	59
55/59	13	22	17	52	52	5	8	5	18	52	5	9	8	22	54
50/54	14	32	26	72	46	12	14	10	36	48	10	15	10	35	49
45/49	20	36	30	86	42	10	23	17	50	43	12	19	16	47	45
40/44	38	31	41	110	38	19	33	21	73	39	13	28	14	55	39
35/39	44	32	43	119	34	32	48	45	125	34	32	38	38	108	34
30/34	52	25	34	111	30	55	47	50	152	30	55	51	60	166	30
25/29	29	13	25	67	25	42	28	42	112	25	37	35	35	107	25
20/24	14	2	8	24	21	29	20	23	72	21	27	20	21	68	20
15/19	5	1	3	9	16	17	9	11	37	16	19	12	19	50	15
10/14	1	0	0	1	11	11	4	9	24	11	12	9	13	34	11
5/9	0	1	1	2	6	8	1	5	14	7	10	3	6	19	6
0/4	1		0	1	2	6	2	2	10	2	7	0	3	10	1
-5/-1	1		1	2	-3	0	0	0	0	-4	3		0	3	-3
-10/-6						0		1	1	-10	1			1	-8
-15/-11						1			1	-12					
-20/-16															

Temperature Range	FEBRUARY Obsn Hour Gp 01 to 08	FEBRUARY 09 to 16	FEBRUARY 17 to 24	FEBRUARY Total Obsn	FEBRUARY MCWB	MARCH Obsn Hour Gp 01 to 08	MARCH 09 to 16	MARCH 17 to 24	MARCH Total Obsn	MARCH MCWB	APRIL Obsn Hour Gp 01 to 08	APRIL 09 to 16	APRIL 17 to 24	APRIL Total Obsn	APRIL MCWB
105/109															
100/104															
95/99															
90/94															
85/89												1		1	65
80/84							0		0	63		6	1	7	66
75/79							1		1	65		20	4	24	64
70/74		0		0	62		7	1	8	59	2	26	11	39	61
65/69	0	1	1	2	60	2	11	5	18	58	10	29	23	62	59
60/64	1	5	1	7	54	5	14	8	27	56	24	27	27	78	55
55/59	3	13	3	19	50	11	27	19	57	51	24	31	30	85	50
50/54	5	17	9	31	46	18	30	25	73	47	29	33	34	96	46
45/49	9	38	23	70	42	21	30	29	80	42	37	28	35	100	43
40/44	22	39	38	99	38	25	37	34	96	38	45	23	40	108	39
35/39	41	39	44	124	34	39	42	42	123	34	37	14	24	75	35
30/34	52	37	46	135	30	51	29	43	123	30	25	3	9	37	31
25/29	37	16	29	82	25	42	11	27	80	25	5	0	2	7	26
20/24	23	9	15	47	21	18	6	9	33	21	2			2	22
15/19	12	3	5	20	16	10	1	4	15	16	0			0	18
10/14	8	3	5	16	11	3	0	0	3	11					
5/9	6	2	2	10	6	1		1	2	7					
0/4	3	1	2	6	2	1			1	1					
-5/-1	1	0	1	2	-4	0			0	-2					
-10/-6	0	0	0	0	-8										
-15/-11	0			0	-14										
-20/-16	1			1	-18										

Temperature Range	ANNUAL TOTAL Obsn Hour Gp 01 to 08	ANNUAL TOTAL 09 to 16	ANNUAL TOTAL 17 to 24	ANNUAL TOTAL Total Obsn	ANNUAL TOTAL MCWB
105/109		1		1	77
100/104		3	0	3	76
95/99		18	3	21	75
90/94	0	88	13	101	74
85/89	4	213	46	263	72
80/84	30	287	112	429	70
75/79	107	302	208	617	68
70/74	239	247	286	772	65
65/69	293	218	295	806	62
60/64	269	177	239	685	57
55/59	251	172	232	655	52
50/54	251	175	215	641	48
45/49	211	195	211	617	43
40/44	228	197	224	649	39
35/39	266	218	251	735	34
30/34	304	192	247	743	30
25/29	197	103	162	462	25
20/24	114	57	76	247	21
15/19	63	26	42	131	16
10/14	35	16	27	78	11
5/9	25	7	15	47	6
0/4	18	3	7	28	2
-5/-1	5	0	2	7	-3
-10/-6	1	0	1	2	-9
-15/-11	1			1	-13
-20/-16	1			1	-18

DES MOINES MAP IOWA
LAT 41 32N LONG 93 39W ELEV 938 FT

MEAN FREQUENCY OF OCCURRENCE OF DRY BULB TEMPERATURE (DEGREES F) WITH MEAN COINCIDENT WET BULB TEMPERATURE (DEGREES F) FOR EACH DRY BULB TEMPERATURE RANGE

Temperature Range	MAY					JUNE					JULY					AUGUST					SEPTEMBER					OCTOBER				
	01 to 08	09 to 16	17 to 24	Total Obsn	MCWB	01 to 08	09 to 16	17 to 24	Total Obsn	MCWB	01 to 08	09 to 16	17 to 24	Total Obsn	MCWB	01 to 08	09 to 16	17 to 24	Total Obsn	MCWB	01 to 08	09 to 16	17 to 24	Total Obsn	MCWB	01 to 08	09 to 16	17 to 24	Total Obsn	MCWB
105/109														0	79					78										
100/104									0	76				0					0	74										
95/99		1	0	1	69		3	0	3	77		2	0	2	76		6	1	7	74		1	0	1	69				0	66
90/94		8	2	10	69		13	5	18	74		6	3	9	76		19	7	26	73		7	1	8	71		1	0	1	65
85/89	0	20	9	29	67		31	14	45	72	0	21	8	29	75	0	38	17	55	71		16	4	20	71		3	0	3	66
80/84	2	35	20	57	64	4	49	33	86	70	1	50	24	75	73	3	56	35	94	69		25	12	37	68		10	2	12	65
75/79	10	44	33	87	61	18	48	45	111	67	9	63	46	118	71	22	57	56	135	67	6	35	23	64	65	0	20	6	26	63
70/74	25	42	43	110	59	39	41	51	131	65	29	55	60	144	69	61	39	60	160	64	19	39	35	93	63	2	30	16	48	60
65/69	46	39	52	137	56	63	28	46	137	62	68	36	62	166	67	73	21	44	138	59	27	45	47	119	60	9	34	29	72	57
60/64	58	28	43	129	52	57	18	27	102	58	81	12	33	126	64	56	9	22	87	55	48	37	47	132	57	24	34	36	94	55
55/59	49	19	26	94	48	37	7	13	57	54	45	3	11	59	59	24	2	5	31	51	52	20	38	110	53	34	36	41	111	51
50/54	30	9	14	53	44	17	2	3	22	50	13	1	1	15	55	8	0	2	10	46	45	10	23	78	49	40	32	38	110	46
45/49	19	3	4	26	39	5	0	0	5	45	2	0	0	2	51	1	0	0	1	40	30	3	8	41	45	45	24	34	103	43
40/44	7	0	1	8	34	0	0	0	0	43											10	1	2	13	40	38	14	25	77	39
35/39	3	0	0	3	31																2	0	0	2	36	30	6	14	50	34
30/34																					0	0	0	0	31	17	2	5	24	30
25/29																										7	0	1	8	26
20/24																										2	0	0	2	21

OINCIDENT WET BULB TEMPERATURE FOR EACH DRY BULB TEMPERATURE RANGE

DES MOINES MAP IOWA

Temperature Range	Nov 01–08	Nov 09–16	Nov 17–24	Nov Tot	Nov MCWB	Dec 01–08	Dec 09–16	Dec 17–24	Dec Tot	Dec MCWB	Jan 01–08	Jan 09–16	Jan 17–24	Jan Tot	Jan MCWB	Feb 01–08	Feb 09–16	Feb 17–24	Feb Tot	Feb MCWB	Mar 01–08	Mar 09–16	Mar 17–24	Mar Tot	Mar MCWB	Apr 01–08	Apr 09–16	Apr 17–24	Apr Tot	Apr MCWB	Ann 01–08	Ann 09–16	Ann 17–24	Ann Tot	Ann MCWB
105/109																																		0	79
100/104																																2	0	2	76
95/99																																16	4	20	75
90/94																																62	21	83	74
85/89																											1	0	1	65	1	147	61	209	72
80/84																											5	2	7	64	16	228	139	383	70
75/79		0		0	63																	1		1	59		10	4	14	61	77	261	214	552	67
70/74		3	0	3	59																	3	1	4	55	1	16	10	27	58	199	252	268	719	64
65/69		9	2	11	56											0	0		0	57		4	2	6	53	5	21	17	43	56	283	216	263	762	61
60/64	3	15	8	26	54		1		1	54							1	0	1	53	1	6	5	12	51	11	25	24	60	53	291	188	232	711	56
55/59	6	20	13	39	50		3	2	5	51		1		1	45		2	1	3	46	2	11	8	21	48	21	32	27	80	50	247	163	192	602	52
50/54	12	26	23	61	46	3	8	5	16	46		4	1	5	44	0	8	2	10	44	5	16	10	31	44	26	35	37	98	46	210	157	170	537	47
45/49	20	31	25	76	42	3	13	6	22	41	1	6	2	9	41	2	12	7	21	41	7	21	20	48	41	36	37	37	110	42	180	154	155	489	42
40/44	27	30	38	95	38	7	23	16	46	38	3	16	9	28	37	4	21	15	40	38	20	33	28	81	37	37	27	32	96	38	165	168	169	502	38
35/39	41	32	38	111	34	22	31	33	86	34	13	25	25	63	34	19	31	30	80	34	30	41	42	113	34	41	22	29	92	34	205	188	212	605	34
30/34	47	30	38	115	30	40	40	43	123	30	31	31	36	98	30	46	40	49	135	30	65	47	58	170	30	41	11	16	68	30	290	201	245	736	30
25/29	32	17	21	70	25	41	39	37	117	26	35	34	34	103	26	36	33	35	104	26	46	27	29	102	26	15	1	3	19	26	212	151	160	523	26
20/24	25	13	16	54	21	35	27	30	92	21	32	30	35	97	21	33	28	29	90	21	27	17	22	66	21	4	0	0	4	21	158	115	132	405	21
15/19	11	6	9	26	16	29	22	26	77	16	28	24	22	74	16	22	18	20	60	16	20	11	11	42	16	1	0	0	1	17	111	81	88	280	16
10/14	8	4	5	17	11	23	17	20	60	11	28	23	25	76	11	20	12	13	45	11	12	6	8	26	11						91	62	71	224	11
5/9	4	2	2	8	6	15	9	12	36	6	20	21	24	65	6	15	9	10	34	6	8	2	3	13	7						62	43	51	156	6
0/4	3	0	1	4	1	12	8	8	28	2	22	15	17	54	2	11	6	7	24	2	3	1	1	5	2						51	30	34	115	2
-5/-1	1	0		1	-2	9	4	6	19	-3	16	10	10	36	-3	9	3	3	15	-3	1	0	0	1	-3						36	17	19	72	-3
-10/-6						8	1	2	11	-8	12	5	6	23	-8	4	1	1	6	-8	0	0	0	0	-8						24	7	9	40	-8
-15/-11						2	0	0	2	-13	5	1	2	8	-12	2	0	1	3	-13	1	0	0	1	-14						10	1	3	14	-13
-20/-16											1	0	0	1	-18	1	0	0	1	-18	0	0	0	0	-19						2	0		2	-18
-25/-21											0	0	0	0	-22																			0	-22

DODGE CITY, KANSAS
LAT 37 46N   LONG 99 58W   ELEV 2582 FT

MEAN FREQUENCY OF OCCURRENCE OF DRY BULB TEMPERATURE (DEGREES F) WITH MEAN COINCIDENT WET BULB TEMPERATURE (DEGREES F) FOR EACH DRY BULB TEMPERATURE RANGE

Tempera-ture Range	MAY 01-08	MAY 09-16	MAY 17-24	MAY Total Obsn	MAY MCWB	JUNE 01-08	JUNE 09-16	JUNE 17-24	JUNE Total Obsn	JUNE MCWB	JULY 01-08	JULY 09-16	JULY 17-24	JULY Total Obsn	JULY MCWB	AUG 01-08	AUG 09-16	AUG 17-24	AUG Total Obsn	AUG MCWB	SEP 01-08	SEP 09-16	SEP 17-24	SEP Total Obsn	SEP MCWB	OCT 01-08	OCT 09-16	OCT 17-24	OCT Total Obsn	OCT MCWB
105/109												0	0	0	70		0	0	0	69										
100/104		0		0	68							9	3	12	69		8	3	11	69		1	0	1	65					
95/99		4	1	5	64		5	1	6	68		31	12	43	70		28	12	40	69		8	1	9	66					
90/94		10	4	14	65		20	8	28	69		47	27	74	70		44	22	66	69		19	8	27	65		3	0	3	62
85/89		18	9	27	64		30	17	47	68	1	50	35	86	69	0	51	34	85	68		30	13	43	65		12	2	14	61
80/84	0	25	16	41	63	1	42	28	71	67	12	46	53	111	68	8	47	47	102	67	0	38	25	63	64		21	6	27	60
75/79	2	36	25	63	61	7	42	39	88	66	48	34	50	132	67	37	34	53	124	66	6	39	36	81	62	1	26	12	39	59
70/74	13	41	34	88	60	24	37	41	102	65	83	20	40	143	66	82	21	41	144	65	29	34	41	104	61	1	34	20	55	56
65/69	29	37	38	104	58	49	28	40	117	64	69	9	22	100	64	79	11	25	115	63	52	28	41	121	59	8	37	34	79	55
60/64	48	33	43	124	56	61	19	35	115	62	29	3	5	37	60	31	3	9	43	59	53	19	31	103	56	26	31	40	97	53
55/59	60	22	37	119	53	55	10	20	85	58	5	0	1	6	54	9	1	1	11	55	47	13	26	86	52	41	31	42	114	49
50/54	48	13	27	88	49	28	6	7	41	54	1	0	0	1	51	1	1	1	2	50	32	8	12	52	48	51	26	41	118	46
45/49	31	6	9	46	44	9	2	4	15	50	0	0		0	46	1	0	0	1	47	16	3	5	24	44	49	15	24	88	42
40/44	10	2	3	15	40	4	0	1	5	44											5	1	1	7	40	38	9	16	63	38
35/39	4	1	2	7	35	1			1	41											1		0	1	37	21	2	8	31	34
30/34	2	0	1	3	32																					8	1	1	10	30
25/29	0			0	29																					3	1	1	5	26
20/24																										1		0	1	22

DODGE CITY, KANSAS

Column groups per month: Obsn Hour Gp (01 to 08 | 09 to 16 | 17 to 24) · Total Obsn · M.C.W.B.

Temperature Range	Nov 01–08	Nov 09–16	Nov 17–24	Nov Total	Nov M.C.W.B.	Dec 01–08	Dec 09–16	Dec 17–24	Dec Total	Dec M.C.W.B.	Jan 01–08	Jan 09–16	Jan 17–24	Jan Total	Jan M.C.W.B.	Feb 01–08	Feb 09–16	Feb 17–24	Feb Total	Feb M.C.W.B.	Mar 01–08	Mar 09–16	Mar 17–24	Mar Total	Mar M.C.W.B.	Apr 01–08	Apr 09–16	Apr 17–24	Apr Total	Apr M.C.W.B.	Ann 01–08	Ann 09–16	Ann 17–24	Ann Total	Ann M.C.W.B.
105/109																																	0	0	69
100/104																																23	7	30	69
95/99																													0	58		91	34	125	69
90/94																						0	0	0	55		1	0	1	58		154	78	232	68
85/89							0		0	55							0		0	56		1	0	1	54	0	5	2	7	58	2	209	123	334	67
80/84		0		0	56		0		0	56							0		0	55		2	1	3	53	0	12	5	17	57	27	233	192	452	65
75/79		2	0	2	53		0	0	0	53				0	49		1		1	53	0	6	2	8	52	0	15	9	24	56	118	230	228	576	64
70/74	0	9	1	10	52		1	0	1	50	0	0	1	1	48	0	3	1	4	51	0	10	4	14	50	1	21	14	36	55	258	223	236	717	62
65/69	0	17	4	21	51	0	4	0	4	47	3	1	0	4	48	1	8	1	10	49	0	15	9	24	48	5	29	22	56	53	303	218	232	753	59
60/64	0	21	9	30	49	0	8	1	9	45	4	4	2	10	46	4	12	2	18	47	1	17	11	29	46	7	36	37	80	51	258	201	206	665	54
55/59	3	31	18	52	46	0	17	5	22	44	6	8	5	19	44	5	17	6	28	45	2	24	18	44	44	21	34	37	92	48	217	210	207	634	49
50/54	10	32	28	70	43	2	21	11	34	42	7	14	11	32	41	8	23	10	41	42	11	27	24	62	42	39	30	32	101	45	203	202	211	616	45
45/49	23	32	38	93	41	6	29	20	55	39	6	20	17	43	38	16	26	15	57	40	21	31	29	81	39	54	25	26	105	42	208	191	199	598	41
40/44	37	28	39	104	37	13	35	34	82	37	14	24	29	67	35	31	26	24	81	36	27	28	34	89	36	50	17	15	82	38	201	175	215	591	37
35/39	50	22	37	109	33	29	35	43	107	32	31	24	40	95	32	29	28	33	90	33	43	29	35	107	33	45	9	9	63	34	243	157	210	610	33
30/34	50	22	30	102	30	56	35	49	140	29	50	31	41	122	29	46	23	30	99	29	56	28	35	119	30	30	5	5	40	30	293	145	197	635	29
25/29	29	14	19	62	25	58	23	34	115	25	37	31	29	97	25	33	20	31	84	25	35	16	23	74	25	10	1	2	13	25	216	99	135	450	25
20/24	21	7	10	38	20	31	17	23	71	20	32	24	23	79	21	25	16	27	68	21	25	8	13	46	21	2	0	0	2	22	149	67	89	305	21
15/19	9	3	5	17	16	24	11	12	47	16	27	19	19	65	16	14	9	20	43	16	15	4	6	25	16	0	0	0	0	19	97	44	56	197	16
10/14	4	1	2	7	11	15	7	8	30	11	13	17	13	43	11	5	7	14	26	11	7	2	2	11	12						57	29	31	117	11
5/9	3	0	0	3	7	6	3	5	14	7	14	12	9	35	6	2	3	6	11	7	2	1	0	3	7						34	15	17	66	6
0/4	1	0	0	1	3	5	1	2	8	-1	4	8	7	19	1	1	1	3	5	2	1	0	1	2	3						17	7	11	35	2
-5/-1						2	0	0	2	-3	4	5	3	12	-3	1	0	1	2	-2	0			0	-3						11	2	3	16	-3
-10/-6						0			0	-7	0	2	1	3	-8				0	-8				0	-8						2	0	1	3	-8
-15/-11														0	-12				0	-13				0	-11									0	-13

WICHITA, KANSAS/MC CONNELL AFB

LAT 37 38N   LONG 97 16W   ELEV 1371 FT

MEAN FREQUENCY OF OCCURRENCE OF DRY BULB TEMPERATURE (DEGREES F) WITH MEAN COINCIDENT WET BULB TEMPERATURE (DEGREES F) FOR EACH DRY BULB TEMPERATURE RANGE

Hour Group columns: 01 to 08, 09 to 16, 17 to 24. Total Obsn. MCWB = Mean Coincident Wet Bulb.

Temperature Range	MAY 01-08	MAY 09-16	MAY 17-24	MAY Total	MAY MCWB	JUNE 01-08	JUNE 09-16	JUNE 17-24	JUNE Total	JUNE MCWB	JULY 01-08	JULY 09-16	JULY 17-24	JULY Total	JULY MCWB	AUG 01-08	AUG 09-16	AUG 17-24	AUG Total	AUG MCWB	SEP 01-08	SEP 09-16	SEP 17-24	SEP Total	SEP MCWB	OCT 01-08	OCT 09-16	OCT 17-24	OCT Total	OCT MCWB
105/109											0	0	0	0	72			1	1	74										
100/104		0		0	69		1	0	1	72		11	3	14	74		9	2	11	74		0	0	0	74					
95/99		1	0	1	70		7	3	10	73		29	13	42	74		17	9	26	73		3	1	4	74					
90/94		5	1	6	69		26	11	37	73		45	26	71	74		41	20	61	73		12	4	16	73		2		2	64
85/89		19	7	26	69		44	26	70	72	2	51	43	96	73	2	55	39	96	71		25	12	37	71		8	2	10	67
80/84		33	18	51	67	5	56	46	107	70	25	51	56	132	71	19	53	53	125	70	1	39	23	63	69		18	6	24	65
75/79	2	49	34	85	65	30	43	51	124	68	70	34	51	155	69	52	39	55	146	69	14	48	42	104	67	1	29	15	45	63
70/74	28	46	47	121	63	61	33	49	143	66	79	19	36	134	68	75	21	43	139	66	46	43	46	135	65	9	36	25	70	61
65/69	44	36	49	129	60	76	19	34	129	63	50	7	15	72	64	65	8	20	93	63	52	32	46	130	62	19	36	41	96	59
60/64	61	28	40	129	57	45	8	16	69	59	16	2	3	21	58	28	3	6	37	58	47	20	36	103	57	36	40	37	113	55
55/59	45	17	27	89	52	18	3	4	25	54	5	0	0	5	54	7		1	8	55	44	12	19	75	53	38	35	42	115	51
50/54	39	10	18	67	48	4	0	0	4	50	0			0	49	1			1	51	22	5	8	35	49	53	23	38	114	47
45/49	20	3	4	27	43																10	1	3	14	45	44	14	25	83	43
40/44	8	0	1	9	40																2		0	2	41	32	6	13	51	39
35/39	2	2		2	35																0			0	38	13	1	2	16	35
30/34	0	0		0	33																					4	1	1	6	30
25/29																										1	0	1	2	26

WICHITA, KANSAS/MC CONNELL AFB

Legend for each month: Obsn Hour Gp columns = "01 to 08", "09 to 16", "17 to 24"; "Total Obsn"; "MCWB" (Mean Coincident Wet Bulb).

Temperature Range	NOV 01–08	09–16	17–24	Total	MCWB	DEC 01–08	09–16	17–24	Total	MCWB	JAN 01–08	09–16	17–24	Total	MCWB	FEB 01–08	09–16	17–24	Total	MCWB	MAR 01–08	09–16	17–24	Total	MCWB	APR 01–08	09–16	17–24	Total	MCWB	ANN 01–08	09–16	17–24	Total	MCWB
105/109																																1	0	1	74
100/104																																21	5	26	74
95/99																																57	26	83	73
90/94																											0		0	62		131	62	193	73
85/89																											2	1	3	65	4	204	130	338	71
80/84																						0		0	62		10	4	14	63	50	262	207	519	69
75/79		1		1	62												0	0	0	57		2	1	3	58		20	11	31	61	169	268	262	699	67
70/74		10	2	12	59		0		0	55		0		0	51		1	0	1	52		5	3	8	56	3	31	22	56	59	301	252	276	829	65
65/69	2	21	10	33	57		1	0	1	52		2	0	2	53		4	2	6	53		12	6	18	53	15	38	33	86	57	324	219	261	804	61
60/64	9	25	17	51	53	1	9	3	13	52	1	3	3	7	54		7	4	11	50	1	15	11	27	51	25	41	39	105	54	273	209	220	702	56
55/59	11	30	23	64	49	4	16	7	27	49	2	8	3	13	49	3	13	9	25	48	4	23	16	43	48	36	34	43	113	50	223	192	201	616	51
50/54	22	35	34	91	46	5	22	16	43	45	3	17	9	29	45	4	20	15	39	44	10	24	23	57	44	43	27	34	104	46	215	188	200	603	46
45/49	31	36	42	109	42	11	32	25	68	41	7	23	18	48	41	10	25	22	57	41	19	29	28	76	41	44	19	27	90	42	201	183	195	579	42
40/44	44	32	40	116	38	26	35	40	101	37	13	29	30	72	37	19	33	37	89	37	24	30	29	83	37	36	12	17	65	38	211	179	215	605	38
35/39	49	27	36	112	34	37	39	44	120	34	29	35	36	100	33	34	32	34	100	33	31	32	37	100	33	22	5	7	34	33	230	168	194	592	33
30/34	38	14	23	75	29	56	36	43	135	29	41	35	39	115	29	44	32	31	107	29	44	29	35	108	29	12	1	3	16	29	246	145	171	562	29
25/29	23	6	7	36	25	43	21	28	92	25	42	31	36	109	25	34	23	30	87	25	51	26	31	108	25	3	0	1	4	25	177	94	120	391	25
20/24	7	3	4	14	20	28	17	20	65	20	38	24	28	90	20	31	18	23	72	20	31	13	17	61	20	0	0		0	22	121	68	82	271	20
15/19	3	1	2	6	15	17	8	11	36	16	25	17	18	60	16	26	11	12	49	16	17	6	7	30	16						81	39	45	165	16
10/14	2	0	0	2	10	12	7	7	26	11	23	13	14	50	11	10	4	5	19	11	10	2	2	14	11						49	25	27	101	11
5/9	0			0	7	3	3	2	8	6	13	7	8	28	6	5	1	1	7	7	2	1	1	4	6						23	11	12	46	6
0/4						4	1	1	6	2	7	3	4	14	2	2	0	0	2	2	2	0	1	3	2						14	4	5	23	2
-5/-1						1	0	0	1	-3	4	1	1	6	-3				0	-4											5	1	1	7	-3
-10/-6											1	0		1	-8																1	0		1	-8
-15/-11											0	0		0	-12																0	0		0	-12

LOUISVILLE, KENTUCKY*
READINGS TAKEN AT FT. KNOX
LAT 37 54N   LONG 85 58W   ELEV 753 FT

MEAN FREQUENCY OF OCCURRENCE OF DRY BULB TEMPERATURE (DEGREES F) WITH MEAN COINCIDENT WET BULB TEMPERATURE (DEGREES F) FOR EACH DRY BULB TEMPERATURE RANGE

Temperature Range	MAY 01–08	MAY 09–16	MAY 17–24	MAY Total Obsn	MAY MCWB	JUNE 01–08	JUNE 09–16	JUNE 17–24	JUNE Total Obsn	JUNE MCWB	JULY 01–08	JULY 09–16	JULY 17–24	JULY Total Obsn	JULY MCWB	AUGUST 01–08	AUGUST 09–16	AUGUST 17–24	AUGUST Total Obsn	AUGUST MCWB	SEPTEMBER 01–08	SEPTEMBER 09–16	SEPTEMBER 17–24	SEPTEMBER Total Obsn	SEPTEMBER MCWB	OCTOBER 01–08	OCTOBER 09–16	OCTOBER 17–24	OCTOBER Total Obsn	OCTOBER MCWB
100/104																														
95/99																			0	74										
90/94		1		1	71		1	0	1	75		1	0	1	79		3	0	3	75		0		0	77				0	73
85/89		18	2	20	70		16	3	19	75		21	4	25	76		23	3	26	75		6	1	7	74		2		2	70
80/84	0	43	14	57	68	0	44	13	57	73	1	67	18	86	74	0	62	17	79	74		28	5	33	73		17	1	18	66
75/79	4	47	24	75	66	4	65	33	102	70	7	81	44	132	72	5	70	37	112	71	1	45	14	60	70	0	29	6	35	64
70/74	18	47	47	112	63	22	56	53	131	68	37	50	71	158	70	27	50	65	142	70	8	52	36	96	68	2	38	19	59	62
65/69	52	37	58	147	61	58	35	63	156	66	98	20	75	193	68	84	30	73	187	67	49	48	55	152	66	15	41	37	93	59
60/64	56	27	48	131	57	74	15	49	138	63	68	6	28	102	64	71	9	36	116	63	47	35	46	128	62	38	41	45	124	56
55/59	47	14	25	86	52	49	5	17	71	58	27	1	7	35	59	37	2	13	52	58	48	17	42	107	58	39	32	39	110	51
50/54	32	9	16	57	48	23	2	7	32	54	8	0	2	10	54	17	0	4	21	54	38	6	25	69	53	43	25	38	106	47
45/49	21	4	9	34	43	8	0	1	9	50	2		0	2	51	5	1	0	6	50	31	3	13	47	49	40	16	33	89	43
40/44	13	1	5	19	40	1		0	1	43						1			1	45	14	1	4	19	45	35	6	20	61	39
35/39	4	0	1	5	35	0		0	0	39											3	1	1	4	41	24	1	8	33	34
30/34	1			1	29	0			0	36											1			1	37	11	0	2	13	30
25/29																										1			1	26

*Comparative design data note:

	Elevation	WINTER 97 1/2%	SUMMER DB 2 1/2%	SUMMER DB 2 1/2%	SUMMER WB 2 1/2%
Louisville AP, KY.	477 ft.	12° F	93° F		78° F
Ft. Knox/Godman AAF	753 ft.	11° F	92° F	–	78° F

COINCIDENT WET BULB TEMPERATURE FOR EACH DRY BULB TEMPERATURE RANGE

LOUISVILLE, KENTUCKY*
READINGS TAKEN AT FT. KNOX

Temperature Range	NOV 01-08	NOV 09-16	NOV 17-24	NOV Total Obsn	NOV MCWB	DEC 01-08	DEC 09-16	DEC 17-24	DEC Total Obsn	DEC MCWB	JAN 01-08	JAN 09-16	JAN 17-24	JAN Total Obsn	JAN MCWB	FEB 01-08	FEB 09-16	FEB 17-24	FEB Total Obsn	FEB MCWB	MAR 01-08	MAR 09-16	MAR 17-24	MAR Total Obsn	MAR MCWB	APR 01-08	APR 09-16	APR 17-24	APR Total Obsn	APR MCWB	ANN 01-08	ANN 09-16	ANN 17-24	ANN Total Obsn	ANN MCWB
100/104																																		0	74
95/99																																5	0	5	76
90/94																																67	11	78	75
85/89																											2	0	2	68	1	223	55	279	73
80/84		0		0	67																	0		0	62		15	3	18	65	17	336	146	499	70
75/79	0	2	1	3	64	0	0	0	0	62	0	0	0	0	60		0		0	66	0	3	1	4	61		24	10	34	62	98	313	267	678	68
70/74	0	8	1	9	60	0	3	1	4	59	0	2	0	2	59				0	61	0	10	3	13	58	6	31	23	60	60	315	267	359	941	66
65/69	2	16	5	23	58	4	10	4	18	55	2	5	4	11	56	1	2	1	4	60	1	13	7	21	55	17	34	29	80	57	348	213	297	858	61
60/64	9	26	17	52	54	8	15	12	35	52	5	10	10	25	53	1	8	4	13	54	7	21	17	45	53	35	39	44	118	54	313	202	262	777	56
55/59	18	33	26	77	51	12	26	18	56	47	9	15	11	35	47	4	13	8	25	51	15	21	21	57	50	36	34	36	106	50	258	180	215	653	52
50/54	28	42	35	105	46	17	24	25	66	42	11	23	16	50	42	8	16	13	37	46	20	30	26	76	46	33	23	32	88	45	231	189	204	624	47
45/49	34	37	38	109	42	20	32	28	80	38	18	31	25	74	38	11	20	18	49	41	22	36	34	92	41	34	19	30	83	42	206	180	207	593	42
40/44	38	28	41	107	38	34	45	38	117	34	27	32	31	90	34	21	33	30	84	38	36	40	42	118	38	38	11	20	69	38	222	182	212	616	38
35/39	40	23	37	100	34	48	46	48	142	29	41	45	47	133	29	28	37	35	100	34	42	32	38	112	33	25	7	10	42	34	225	177	198	600	34
30/34	37	15	23	75	29	41	22	39	102	25	37	33	36	106	25	46	37	42	125	29	46	25	33	104	29	13	0	2	15	30	243	168	197	608	29
25/29	18	6	10	34	25	31	12	18	61	20	33	22	27	82	20	37	26	30	93	25	32	11	18	61	25	2		0	2	25	168	98	133	399	25
20/24	10	3	3	16	20	17	6	7	30	16	30	12	15	57	16	27	14	21	62	20	18	3	6	27	21						116	54	78	248	20
15/19	2	1	3	6	15	7	4	5	16	11	17	9	8	34	11	16	8	11	35	15	6	1	2	9	16						68	28	41	137	16
10/14	2	0	0	2	11	5	2	2	9	6	10	6	5	21	6	12	4	5	21	11	2	0	0	2	11						40	17	18	75	11
5/9	0			0	9	2	0	2	4	2	5	5	2	12	1	7	2	2	11	6	1	0	0	1	7						23	10	9	42	6
0/4						2	0	0	2	-3	5	1	1	7	-3	4	1	2	7	1	0			0	1						11	3	9	23	1
-5/-1											2	0	0	2	-8	2	0	0	2	-3	0			0	-3						9	1	1	11	-3
-10/-6											1	0	0	1	-13																2	0	0	2	-8
-15/-11											0			0	-17																1	0	0	1	-13
-20/-16																																		0	-17

(Column groups per month: 01 to 08 / 09 to 16 / 17 to 24 = Obsn Hour Gp; Total Obsn; M C W B)

BATON ROUGE, LOUISIANA*
READINGS TAKEN AT ALEXANDRIA/ENGLAND AFB
LAT 31 20N   LONG 92 33W   ELEV 89 FT

MEAN FREQUENCY OF OCCURRENCE OF DRY BULB TEMPERATURE (DEGREES F) WITH MEAN COINCIDENT WET BULB TEMPERATURE (DEGREES F) FOR EACH DRY BULB TEMPERATURE RANGE

Temperature Range	MAY 01–08	MAY 09–16	MAY 17–24	MAY Total Obsn	MAY MC WB	JUNE 01–08	JUNE 09–16	JUNE 17–24	JUNE Total Obsn	JUNE MC WB	JULY 01–08	JULY 09–16	JULY 17–24	JULY Total Obsn	JULY MC WB	AUGUST 01–08	AUGUST 09–16	AUGUST 17–24	AUGUST Total Obsn	AUGUST MC WB	SEPTEMBER 01–08	SEPTEMBER 09–16	SEPTEMBER 17–24	SEPTEMBER Total Obsn	SEPTEMBER MC WB	OCTOBER 01–08	OCTOBER 09–16	OCTOBER 17–24	OCTOBER Total Obsn	OCTOBER MC WB
100/104														0	80				0	77										
95/99												17	4	21	78		12	3	15	77		3		3	77				0	69
90/94		11	1	12	73		6	1	7	78		81	25	106	77		81	20	101	77	0	36	6	42	76		3	0	3	71
85/89		57	17	74	72		60	19	79	76		82	35	118	77		80	32	112	76		66	17	83	75		22	3	25	71
80/84	2	76	35	113	71		87	35	122	75	25	45	66	136	75	17	52	65	134	75	4	60	38	102	73		52	12	64	69
75/79	22	55	59	136	69	16	55	59	130	74	121	19	84	224	73	109	20	92	221	73	56	43	80	179	72	6	55	29	90	67
70/74	68	32	71	171	67	75	21	75	171	72	91	4	31	126	70	98	3	34	135	70	92	22	58	172	69	26	49	51	126	65
65/69	80	11	41	132	64	106	8	41	155	69	8	0	2	10	66	19	0	3	22	65	39	9	25	73	64	45	34	54	133	62
60/64	42	4	15	61	59	30	2	9	41	65	1		0	1	59	4		1	5	59	26	2	12	40	59	51	20	39	110	58
55/59	21	2	7	30	54	11	0	2	13	60	0			0	56	0		0	0	57	16	0	3	19	55	42	11	29	82	53
50/54	12	0	1	13	50	2		0	2	56											4	0	1	5	51	34	2	19	55	49
45/49	3	0	0	3	46																1	0	0	1	44	24	1	9	34	45
40/44	0			0	43																0			0	40	15	0	3	18	40
35/39																					0			0	36	5	0	0	5	36
30/34																										1		0	1	33

*Comparative design data note:

	Elevation	WINTER 97 1/2%	SUMMER DB 2 1/2%	SUMMER WB 2 1/2%
Alexandria/England AFB, LA.	89 ft.	29° F	95° F	80° F
Baton Rouge AP	64 ft.	30° F	94° F	80° F

COINCIDENT WET BULB TEMPERATURE FOR EACH DRY BULB TEMPERATURE RANGE

BATON ROUGE, LOUISIANA*
READINGS TAKEN AT ALEXANDRIA/ENGLAND AFB

Column key per month — Obsn Hour Gp: 01 to 08 | 09 to 16 | 17 to 24 | Total Obsn | MCWB

Temp Range	Nov 01–08	Nov 09–16	Nov 17–24	Nov Total	Nov MCWB	Dec 01–08	Dec 09–16	Dec 17–24	Dec Total	Dec MCWB	Jan 01–08	Jan 09–16	Jan 17–24	Jan Total	Jan MCWB	Feb 01–08	Feb 09–16	Feb 17–24	Feb Total	Feb MCWB	Mar 01–08	Mar 09–16	Mar 17–24	Mar Total	Mar MCWB	Apr 01–08	Apr 09–16	Apr 17–24	Apr Total	Apr MCWB	Ann 01–08	Ann 09–16	Ann 17–24	Ann Total	Ann MCWB
100/104																																0	0	0	79
95/99																																38	8	46	78
90/94																															0	272	71	343	77
85/89		1		1	71																	1		1	64		7	1	8	72	1	403	140	544	75
80/84		12	1	13	69	0	0		0	68			1	1	70	0	2	0	2	70	0	6	1	7	67	0	46	12	58	70	64	407	289	760	73
75/79	2	31	7	40	67	0	8	1	9	68	0	5	1	6	67	0	9	2	11	67	0	23	8	31	65	6	65	38	109	68	397	354	476	1227	71
70/74	9	41	24	74	64	4	22	8	34	64	2	16	7	25	65	3	16	8	27	64	10	41	25	76	63	43	51	59	153	66	552	305	417	1274	67
65/69	21	40	36	97	61	12	30	20	62	61	14	21	19	54	62	11	25	17	53	60	17	41	38	96	60	48	33	54	135	62	344	246	318	908	62
60/64	30	34	39	103	57	17	31	28	76	57	13	25	20	58	57	14	29	25	68	56	26	38	44	108	56	45	22	37	104	58	280	205	262	747	57
55/59	33	30	39	102	52	21	41	37	99	52	16	30	25	71	52	15	32	33	80	51	36	36	42	114	51	40	11	21	72	53	242	193	236	671	52
50/54	34	24	35	93	48	37	37	41	115	48	23	37	35	95	47	28	39	38	105	47	40	30	38	108	47	28	4	14	46	49	240	173	222	635	48
45/49	41	16	29	86	43	35	31	42	108	43	27	34	37	98	43	35	30	39	104	43	45	17	27	89	43	19	1	5	25	44	230	130	188	548	43
40/44	32	7	18	57	39	38	26	35	99	39	34	30	38	102	38	38	22	30	90	38	38	9	15	62	39	8	0	1	9	40	203	94	140	437	39
35/39	23	3	8	34	35	35	14	23	72	34	43	25	33	101	34	37	13	18	68	34	21	5	7	33	35	3	0	0	3	36	167	60	89	316	34
30/34	12	0	4	16	30	28	5	10	43	30	37	14	19	70	29	26	7	11	44	30	12	1	2	15	30	1			1	31	117	27	46	190	30
25/29	5	0	0	5	26	15	2	3	20	26	24	7	9	40	26	14	1	4	19	25	4	0	0	4	26						62	10	16	88	26
20/24	0			0	21	4	0	1	5	21	10	2	4	16	20	4	0	0	4	22											18	2	5	25	20
15/19						1	0	0	1	16	3	1	1	5	15	0			0	19											4	1	1	6	16
10/14						0			0	13	2	0	0	2	11																2	0	0	2	11

LAKE CHARLES MAP LOUISIANA
LAT 30 07N   LONG 93 13W   ELEV   9 FT

MEAN FREQUENCY OF OCCURRENCE OF DRY BULB TEMPERATURE (DEGREES F) WITH MEAN COINCIDENT WET BULB TEMPERATURE (DEGREES F) FOR EACH DRY BULB TEMPERATURE RANGE

Temperature Range	MAY 01-08	MAY 09-16	MAY 17-24	MAY Total	MAY MCWB	JUNE 01-08	JUNE 09-16	JUNE 17-24	JUNE Total	JUNE MCWB	JULY 01-08	JULY 09-16	JULY 17-24	JULY Total	JULY MCWB	AUG 01-08	AUG 09-16	AUG 17-24	AUG Total	AUG MCWB	SEP 01-08	SEP 09-16	SEP 17-24	SEP Total	SEP MCWB	OCT 01-08	OCT 09-16	OCT 17-24	OCT Total	OCT MCWB
100/104													0	0	79															
95/99		0	0	0	79							9	1	10	77			1	1	78										
90/94		6	0	6	74		3	0	3	77		74	11	85	77		13	1	14	78		2		2	75		3	0	3	74
85/89	0	65	9	74	73		52	6	58	77	6	98	38	142	77		75	13	88	77		37	3	40	75		36	2	38	72
80/84	7	99	35	141	72	3	109	32	144	75	44	42	82	168	77	4	96	37	137	77		86	18	104	75	0	66	12	78	70
75/79	43	45	76	164	71	97	19	102	218	74	148	20	102	270	75	38	40	89	167	76	10	66	47	123	74	12	59	40	111	69
70/74	91	22	81	194	69	89	7	36	132	71	49	5	15	69	72	150	20	93	263	75	73	32	96	201	73	38	40	62	140	67
65/69	66	9	36	111	65	17	1	4	22	66	1		0	1	66	53	3	14	70	71	94	14	56	164	70	54	24	56	134	63
60/64	27	2	9	38	59	3	0	0	3	59						3		0	3	65	41	3	17	61	64	57	12	38	107	58
55/59	12	1	2	15	54	0		0	0	58						0			0	62	19	0	2	21	59	40	7	23	70	53
50/54	3		0	3	50																3	0	0	3	54	29	1	11	41	49
45/49	0		0	0	46																					13	1	3	17	44
40/44																										3		1	4	39
35/39																										1			1	36

COINCIDENT WET BULB TEMPERATURE FOR EACH DRY BULB TEMPERATURE RANGE

LAKE CHARLES MAP LOUISIANA

Each month column group shows Observations by Hour Group (01 to 08, 09 to 16, 17 to 24), Total Obsn, and MCWB (Mean Coincident Wet Bulb).

Temperature Range	NOV 01–08	NOV 09–16	NOV 17–24	NOV Total	NOV MCWB	DEC 01–08	DEC 09–16	DEC 17–24	DEC Total	DEC MCWB	JAN 01–08	JAN 09–16	JAN 17–24	JAN Total	JAN MCWB	FEB 01–08	FEB 09–16	FEB 17–24	FEB Total	FEB MCWB	MAR 01–08	MAR 09–16	MAR 17–24	MAR Total	MAR MCWB	APR 01–08	APR 09–16	APR 17–24	APR Total	APR MCWB	ANN 01–08	ANN 09–16	ANN 17–24	ANN Total	ANN MCWB
100/104																																1		1	78
95/99																																27	2	29	77
90/94																																247	33	280	77
85/89		0	0	0	62																	0	0	0	71		6	0	6	69	13	496	136	645	75
80/84			14	14	71		0	0	0	75		0	0	0	70		0	0	0	65		6	0	6	68		42	4	46	70	130	425	329	884	74
75/79	1	38	7	46	69		11	0	11	69		11	0	11	69		16	1	17	68		36	4	40	67	6	72	26	104	68	530	379	547	1456	72
70/74	18	39	26	83	66	3	29	6	38	66	2	30	8	40	67	2	35	12	49	65	13	56	32	101	65	48	56	71	175	67	500	336	419	1255	68
65/69	22	41	38	101	62	18	37	27	82	63	21	32	28	81	64	23	37	31	91	63	40	49	55	144	62	51	33	60	144	63	357	266	352	975	63
60/64	33	36	43	112	57	20	40	33	93	58	24	31	35	90	59	24	32	36	92	58	36	37	49	122	57	48	19	42	109	58	291	209	287	787	58
55/59	38	29	41	108	52	35	42	46	123	53	29	36	36	101	53	29	31	43	103	53	38	31	44	113	52	45	9	24	78	53	269	186	259	714	53
50/54	39	20	35	94	48	38	37	44	119	48	30	37	41	108	48	40	29	39	108	48	47	17	34	98	48	25	2	10	37	49	251	143	214	608	48
45/49	39	13	29	81	43	40	25	44	109	44	37	30	41	108	43	39	20	31	90	44	35	9	18	62	43	14	0	2	16	44	217	98	168	483	43
40/44	30	7	16	53	39	41	16	27	84	39	41	18	30	89	39	36	15	18	69	39	25	5	9	39	39	4		0	4	41	180	61	101	342	39
35/39	13	1	5	19	34	28	7	14	49	34	30	9	16	55	34	18	5	9	32	35	12	2	3	17	35	0			0	36	102	24	47	173	34
30/34	7	0	1	8	30	18	4	5	27	30	22	8	7	37	30	9	1	3	13	30	3	0	0	3	30						59	13	16	88	30
25/29	1			1	25	5	1	2	8	25	7	3	5	15	25	3	0	0	3	26	0			0	28						16	4	7	27	26
20/24						2	0	0	2	21	3	1	1	5	20	0	1	1	2	20											5	2	2	9	20
15/19						0	0		0	18	2	1	0	3	15	1	0	0	1	16											3	1	0	4	16
10/14																0			0	13											0			0	13

SHREVEPORT, LOUISIANA/BARKSDALE AFB

LAT 32 30N   LONG 93 40W   ELEV   167 FT

MEAN FREQUENCY OF OCCURRENCE OF DRY BULB TEMPERATURE (DEGREES F) WITH MEAN COINCIDENT WET BULB TEMPERATURE (DEGREES F) FOR EACH DRY BULB TEMPERATURE RANGE

Temperature Range	MAY 01–08	MAY 09–16	MAY 17–24	MAY Total	MAY MWB	JUNE 01–08	JUNE 09–16	JUNE 17–24	JUNE Total	JUNE MWB	JULY 01–08	JULY 09–16	JULY 17–24	JULY Total	JULY MWB	AUG 01–08	AUG 09–16	AUG 17–24	AUG Total	AUG MWB	SEP 01–08	SEP 09–16	SEP 17–24	SEP Total	SEP MWB	OCT 01–08	OCT 09–16	OCT 17–24	OCT Total	OCT MWB
105/109																	0		0	79										
100/104												1	0	1	79		2	1	3	77										
95/99		5	1	6	75		3	1	4	77		21	7	28	77		22	7	29	76		3	1	4	75					
90/94		41	13	54	73		44	16	60	76		81	30	111	77		73	22	95	76		32	6	38	76		3	0	3	68
85/89	1	73	34	108	70	0	83	34	117	74	2	80	40	122	76	2	73	35	110	75		57	17	74	74		17	3	20	71
80/84						15	62	49	126	73	36	41	60	137	75	23	48	60	131	74	2	55	33	90	72		46	9	55	68
75/79	16	62	52	130	69	62	31	67	160	72	97	18	72	187	73	91	21	77	189	73	40	46	60	146	71	3	49	22	74	66
70/74	53	37	66	156	66	88	12	51	151	69	92	5	35	132	70	90	6	39	135	70	83	31	69	183	69	18	44	40	102	64
65/69	83	22	47	152	63	54	4	16	74	65	18	1	4	23	65	31	1	7	39	65	55	12	32	99	64	35	40	52	127	61
60/64	47	7	21	75	59	15	1	5	21	60	3		1	4	60	9		1	10	61	30	3	17	50	59	52	26	42	120	58
55/59	26	2	10	38	54	5		0	5	56	1			1	56	1			1	55	22	1	4	27	55	44	15	38	97	53
50/54	16	0	4	20	49	1			1	52						0			0	51	7		1	8	50	38	6	26	70	49
45/49	6	1		7	46																1		0	1	45	31	1	12	44	44
40/44	1			1	41																1			1	40	19	0	4	23	40
35/39																					0			0	37	6		0	6	36
30/34																										1			1	32

COINCIDENT WET BULB TEMPERATURE FOR EACH DRY BULB TEMPERATURE RANGE

SHREVEPORT, LOUISIANA/BARKSDALE AFB

Obsn Hour Gp columns: 01 to 08, 09 to 16, 17 to 24; Total Obsn; MCWB (Mean Coincident Wet Bulb).

Temperature Range	Nov 01–08	Nov 09–16	Nov 17–24	Nov Total	Nov MCWB	Dec 01–08	Dec 09–16	Dec 17–24	Dec Total	Dec MCWB	Jan 01–08	Jan 09–16	Jan 17–24	Jan Total	Jan MCWB	Feb 01–08	Feb 09–16	Feb 17–24	Feb Total	Feb MCWB	Mar 01–08	Mar 09–16	Mar 17–24	Mar Total	Mar MCWB	Apr 01–08	Apr 09–16	Apr 17–24	Apr Total	Apr MCWB	Ann 01–08	Ann 09–16	Ann 17–24	Ann Total	Ann MCWB
105/109																																		0	79
100/104																																3	1	4	78
95/99																																49	16	65	77
90/94																																238	75	313	76
85/89		0		0	72																0	1	0	1	66	0	3	1	4	70	4	355	143	502	74
80/84		7	0	7	67		0	0	0	67		0	0	0	67			0	0	67	0	6	2	8	65	0	34	11	45	69	77	374	258	709	72
75/79	1	26	6	33	65	0	5	1	6	66	0	4	0	4	64	0	2	0	2	64	0	16	7	23	64	2	53	30	85	66	312	335	395	1042	70
70/74	5	33	14	52	63	1	13	5	19	63	0	10	5	15	63	1	3	1	5	61	2	29	17	48	61	27	54	50	131	64	460	285	396	1141	67
65/69	14	39	28	81	60	8	23	13	44	61	8	19	13	40	60	4	8	5	17	59	13	37	31	81	59	46	42	50	138	62	369	261	304	934	62
60/64	29	36	37	102	56	12	27	21	60	57	14	21	17	52	57	11	14	11	36	55	22	37	38	97	55	46	28	43	117	57	290	215	266	771	57
55/59	31	33	39	103	52	19	37	27	83	52	12	27	22	61	52	16	18	29	63	51	30	38	39	107	51	43	17	30	90	53	250	199	238	687	52
50/54	30	27	34	91	47	27	37	39	103	47	19	33	29	81	47	22	19	33	74	46	35	34	39	108	46	36	8	16	60	48	231	179	221	631	47
45/49	33	21	37	91	43	33	40	41	114	43	28	35	35	98	43	30	18	41	89	42	44	23	34	101	42	23	1	7	31	44	229	156	208	593	43
40/44	40	11	25	76	39	39	32	44	115	39	30	32	42	104	38	39	32	35	106	38	47	16	24	87	38	13	0	3	16	39	229	118	177	524	38
35/39	32	6	12	50	35	37	19	28	84	34	39	28	33	100	34	41	34	26	101	34	31	7	12	50	34	5	0	0	5	35	191	79	111	381	34
30/34	16	1	5	22	30	34	10	20	64	30	39	19	26	84	29	32	39	15	86	30	17	3	5	25	30	1			1	32	140	43	71	254	30
25/29	7	0	3	10	26	24	2	7	33	25	31	11	16	58	25	21	33	3	57	25	8	1	0	9	26						91	16	29	136	25
20/24	3	0	0	3	21	9	1	2	12	21	16	5	6	27	20	7	19	0	26	20	1		0	1	22						36	7	8	51	21
15/19	1	0	0	1	17	3	0	0	3	16	10	1	2	13	16	1	7		8	18	0			0	18						15	1	2	18	16
10/14						1	0	0	1	11	2	1	1	4	11		1		1												3	1	1	5	11
5/9						0	0		0	9	1	0	0	1	7																0	0	0	1	7
0/4											0		0	0	3																0	0	0	3	3

BOSTON, MASSACHUSETTS
READINGS TAKEN AT HANSCOM AFB/BEDFORD

LAT 42 28N   LONG 71 17W   ELEV 133 FT

MEAN FREQUENCY OF OCCURRENCE OF DRY BULB TEMPERATURE (DEGREES F) WITH MEAN COINCIDENT WET BULB TEMPERATURE (DEGREES F) FOR EACH DRY BULB TEMPERATURE RANGE

Temperature Range	MAY					JUNE					JULY					AUGUST					SEPTEMBER					OCTOBER				
	01 to 08	09 to 16	17 to 24	Total Obsn	MCWB	01 to 08	09 to 16	17 to 24	Total Obsn	MCWB	01 to 08	09 to 16	17 to 24	Total Obsn	MCWB	01 to 08	09 to 16	17 to 24	Total Obsn	MCWB	01 to 08	09 to 16	17 to 24	Total Obsn	MCWB	01 to 08	09 to 16	17 to 24	Total Obsn	MCWB
95/99																														
90/94												2	0	2	74			1	1	74										
85/89		1	0	1	71				0	74		10	2	12	74		7	1	8	74				0	73				0	63
80/84		5	1	6	68		6	1	7	73		31	6	37	72		24	4	28	72		2		2	75		3		3	65
75/79		10	3	13	65		20	5	25	71	2	57	21	80	69		57	17	74	69		8	1	9	74		13	1	14	64
70/74	1	21	7	29	62	1	40	14	55	68	11	69	43	123	67	9	61	39	109	67		22	5	27	70		17	5	22	61
65/69	3	32	15	50	59	4	44	25	73	65	44	48	65	157	66	35	52	56	143	65	2	37	13	52	67	3	32	15	50	59
60/64	12	46	28	86	56	19	52	40	111	63	71	22	60	153	63	62	30	59	151	62	18	48	30	96	64	17	43	27	87	56
55/59	31	40	37	108	53	46	36	51	133	61	62	8	35	105	59	64	12	44	120	59	26	42	38	106	61	29	54	42	125	52
50/54	37	40	48	125	50	50	19	42	111	57	37	1	13	51	55	41	4	19	64	55	40	43	46	129	57	43	45	45	133	48
45/49	55	26	51	132	47	59	17	37	113	54	15		2	17	50	21		8	29	50	47	27	46	120	54	40	24	48	112	44
40/44	57	10	37	104	43	36	4	20	60	50	4		0	4	46	13		2	15	46	41	10	35	86	50	41	13	33	87	39
35/39	39	6	18	63	40	18		5	23	45	1			1	42	3		0	3	41	33	2	16	51	45	38	4	20	62	35
30/34	17		3	20	35	6		0	6	41								0	0	37	19	0	8	27	41	25	1	10	36	31
25/29	5		0	5	31	1			1	37									0	33	11		2	13	36	10	0	2	12	26
20/24	1			1	28																4		0	4	31	2		0	2	22
15/19																								0	28				0	18

COINCIDENT WET BULB TEMPERATURE FOR EACH DRY BULB TEMPERATURE RANGE

BOSTON, MASSACHUSETTS
READINGS TAKEN AT HANSCOM AFB/BEDFORD

Each month group shows: Obsn Hour Gp (01 to 08 / 09 to 16 / 17 to 24), Total Obsn, and MCWB (Mean Coincident Wet Bulb).

Temperature Range	Nov 01–08	Nov 09–16	Nov 17–24	Nov Total	Nov MCWB	Dec 01–08	Dec 09–16	Dec 17–24	Dec Total	Dec MCWB	Jan 01–08	Jan 09–16	Jan 17–24	Jan Total	Jan MCWB	Feb 01–08	Feb 09–16	Feb 17–24	Feb Total	Feb MCWB	Mar 01–08	Mar 09–16	Mar 17–24	Mar Total	Mar MCWB	Apr 01–08	Apr 09–16	Apr 17–24	Apr Total	Apr MCWB	Ann 01–08	Ann 09–16	Ann 17–24	Ann Total	Ann MCWB
95/99																																3	0	3	74
90/94																																26	4	30	74
85/89																											1		1	63		89	17	106	71
80/84																											1		1	61	3	190	60	253	69
75/79		0	0	0	65																	0	0	0	57		4	1	5	60	27	249	129	405	66
70/74		2	0	2	63																	0	0	0	55	0	9	2	11	57	119	260	213	592	64
65/69	0	5	3	8	61		0	0	0	61							0	0	0	57		2	0	2	52	1	15	6	22	53	221	230	260	711	61
60/64	4	11	6	21	57	1	3	1	5	56		0	0	0	56		0	1	1	54		3	2	5	50	3	29	13	45	51	262	222	253	737	57
55/59	9	24	12	45	52	2	5	2	9	53	0	2	0	2	51	0	1	1	2	53	0	7	4	11	49	10	36	23	69	48	271	218	247	736	52
50/54	20	43	25	88	48	3	8	4	15	48	1	2	1	4	48	1	3	2	6	47	2	15	7	24	44	16	42	31	89	44	254	198	231	683	48
45/49	30	44	35	109	43	7	15	9	31	42	2	7	2	11	43	2	7	4	13	42	4	32	13	49	39	32	44	47	123	41	242	185	218	645	43
40/44	34	48	42	124	38	14	31	22	67	38	7	20	10	37	38	5	23	9	37	37	13	57	39	109	36	58	39	57	154	38	240	237	238	715	38
35/39	42	36	50	128	34	24	36	30	90	33	17	41	29	87	33	18	44	31	93	33	51	58	69	178	33	55	15	41	111	34	274	234	275	783	34
30/34	42	21	40	103	29	42	51	49	142	29	39	44	47	130	30	38	48	52	138	29	72	45	62	179	29	43	4	16	63	30	310	214	276	800	29
25/29	32	4	20	56	25	43	42	46	131	25	30	45	40	115	24	36	38	43	117	24	50	19	32	101	24	17	0	2	19	25	219	148	185	552	25
20/24	19	1	7	27	21	35	30	35	100	20	34	31	40	105	20	36	27	35	98	20	32	5	12	49	20	3		0	3	21	161	94	129	384	20
15/19	6	0	1	7	17	27	15	27	69	15	32	28	34	94	15	28	17	20	65	15	14	3	4	21	15	1			1	15	108	63	86	257	15
10/14	1	0	0	1	11	22	7	14	43	11	33	16	22	71	11	20	8	15	43	10	7	1	3	11	11						83	32	54	169	11
5/9						17	3	6	26	6	25	8	15	48	6	19	5	9	33	6	3	0	1	4	5						64	16	31	111	6
0/4						7	1	2	10	2	14	3	5	22	1	14	2	2	18	1	1	0	0	1	1						36	6	9	51	1
-5/-1						2	0	1	3	-4	6	1	2	9	-3	5	1	1	7	-3	0	0	0	0	-4						13	2	4	19	-3
-10/-6						1	0	0	1	-7	4	0	1	5	-8	2	0	0	2	-8	0	0	0	0	-8						7	0	1	8	-8
-15/-11						0	0	0	0	-13	2	0	0	2	-13	1	0	0	1	-12											3	0	0	3	-13
-20/-16											1	0	0	1	-18																1	0	0	1	-18

DETROIT, MICHIGAN
READINGS TAKEN AT SELFRIDGE ANGB/MT. CLEMENS
LAT 42 36N   LONG 82 50W   ELEV   583 FT

MEAN FREQUENCY OF OCCURRENCE OF DRY BULB TEMPERATURE (DEGREES F) WITH MEAN COINCIDENT WET BULB TEMPERATURE (DEGREES F) FOR EACH DRY BULB TEMPERATURE RANGE

Temperature Range	MAY 01–08	MAY 09–16	MAY 17–24	MAY Total Obsn	MAY MCWB	JUNE 01–08	JUNE 09–16	JUNE 17–24	JUNE Total Obsn	JUNE MCWB	JULY 01–08	JULY 09–16	JULY 17–24	JULY Total Obsn	JULY MCWB	AUG 01–08	AUG 09–16	AUG 17–24	AUG Total Obsn	AUG MCWB	SEP 01–08	SEP 09–16	SEP 17–24	SEP Total Obsn	SEP MCWB	OCT 01–08	OCT 09–16	OCT 17–24	OCT Total Obsn	OCT MCWB
95/99									0	77		1	0	1	74				0	75										
90/94		1	0	1	72		7	2	9	74		5	2	7	74		5	1	6	76										
85/89		4	1	5	69	0	18	7	25	72	0	30	10	40	72		22	7	29	73		0		0	75		1	0	1	64
80/84		10	3	13	67	2	34	18	54	69	1	57	28	86	70	1	48	23	72	70		8	1	9	74		3	0	3	68
75/79	1	19	10	30	64	7	43	29	79	67	14	69	55	138	67	9	61	40	110	68		20	7	27	71		8	2	10	65
70/74	5	26	17	48	62	24	49	43	116	64	52	54	70	176	65	37	59	65	161	65	5	36	18	59	68	1	20	8	29	62
65/69	15	41	29	85	58	48	42	52	142	61	73	23	47	143	62	69	37	60	166	62	23	52	40	115	65	6	27	18	51	60
60/64	22	44	37	103	55	53	31	42	126	57	56	7	25	88	58	62	14	31	107	59	40	47	51	138	62	20	44	33	97	57
55/59	38	38	47	123	51	45	13	28	86	53	32	2	9	43	54	40	2	16	58	54	42	38	48	128	57	29	46	43	118	52
50/54	48	34	41	123	47	34	4	15	53	48	18		2	20	50	22	1	4	27	50	37	22	37	96	53	45	44	52	141	48
45/49	44	21	32	97	43	20		4	24	44	3		0	3	45	7		1	8	46	44	13	23	80	49	44	32	41	117	43
40/44	43	9	23	75	39	6		1	7	40	1			1	40	1		0	1	41	31	3	9	43	45	45	17	30	92	39
35/39	24	1	6	31	34	1			1	35											12	1	6	19	41	33	6	14	53	35
30/34	5		1	6	30																6	0	0	6	36	15	1	5	21	30
25/29	1		0	1	26																0			0	31	8	0	2	10	26
20/24	0			0	22																			0	28	1		0	1	22
15/19																										0			0	17

COINCIDENT WET BULB TEMPERATURE FOR EACH DRY BULB TEMPERATURE RANGE

DETROIT, MICHIGAN
READINGS TAKEN AT SELFRIDGE ANGB/MT. CLEMENS

Obsn Hour Gp columns: **01 to 08**, **09 to 16**, **17 to 24** · **Total Obsn** · **MCWB** (Mean Coincident Wet Bulb)

Temperature Range	NOV 01-08	NOV 09-16	NOV 17-24	NOV Total	NOV MCWB	DEC 01-08	DEC 09-16	DEC 17-24	DEC Total	DEC MCWB	JAN 01-08	JAN 09-16	JAN 17-24	JAN Total	JAN MCWB	FEB 01-08	FEB 09-16	FEB 17-24	FEB Total	FEB MCWB	MAR 01-08	MAR 09-16	MAR 17-24	MAR Total	MAR MCWB	APR 01-08	APR 09-16	APR 17-24	APR Total	APR MCWB	ANN 01-08	ANN 09-16	ANN 17-24	ANN Total	ANN MCWB
95/99																																1	0	1	75
90/94																																18	5	23	74
85/89																											0	0	0	66	0	83	26	109	72
80/84																										0	2	1	3	64	4	174	80	258	70
75/79		0	0	0	66																					0	5	2	7	64	36	241	156	433	67
70/74		0	0	0	62																	1	0	1	57	0	8	4	12	60	142	269	247	658	65
65/69	0	2	1	3	57																0	3	1	4	54	2	15	8	25	57	253	237	267	757	61
60/64	2	7	3	12	56	0	0	1	1	57	0	1	0	1	56	0	0	0	0	54	0	4	2	6	51	6	22	14	42	54	263	212	236	711	57
55/59	6	19	11	36	52	1	2	2	5	54	0	0	1	1	54	0	0	0	0	51	2	6	4	12	49	13	31	22	66	50	244	181	219	644	52
50/54	16	32	25	73	48	2	5	3	10	48	1	1	0	2	48	0	1	1	2	47	3	10	5	18	46	21	39	34	94	46	254	184	205	643	48
45/49	29	45	38	112	43	6	9	6	21	43	1	2	2	5	44	1	5	2	8	42	5	20	14	39	41	35	40	46	121	42	226	177	195	598	43
40/44	43	52	51	146	39	13	25	21	59	39	3	10	6	19	39	4	15	9	28	38	10	35	24	69	37	41	40	44	125	38	222	204	215	641	39
35/39	50	38	45	133	34	27	39	39	105	34	14	27	22	63	34	17	31	27	75	34	39	60	56	155	34	54	28	40	122	34	265	230	249	744	34
30/34	43	29	37	109	30	45	53	47	145	30	41	45	48	134	30	34	46	43	123	30	73	53	69	195	30	43	10	19	72	30	299	237	269	805	30
25/29	29	11	19	59	25	50	53	50	153	25	42	42	38	122	25	36	45	43	124	25	45	32	36	113	25	20	2	6	28	25	231	185	194	610	25
20/24	15	4	7	26	21	40	31	37	108	21	34	40	36	110	20	39	31	37	107	20	32	15	22	69	20	4	0	1	5	21	165	121	140	426	21
15/19	5	1	3	9	16	28	17	21	66	16	32	32	35	99	16	32	29	27	88	16	20	6	11	37	16	1	0	0	1	17	125	76	99	300	16
10/14	1	0	1	2	12	17	10	15	42	11	30	26	32	88	11	22	16	17	55	11	13	2	4	19	11						83	54	69	206	11
5/9	0	0	0	0	7	13	4	5	22	7	26	15	19	60	6	15	9	11	35	6	5	1	1	7	6						59	29	36	124	6
0/4	0			0	4	5	1	2	8	2	14	5	8	27	2	10	3	5	18	1	1	0	0	1	2						30	9	15	54	2
-5/-1						1	0	0	1	-3	10	1	2	13	-3	6	1	1	8	-3											17	2	3	22	-3
-10/-6											1	0	0	1	-8	1	0	0	1	-7											2	0	0	2	-7
-15/-11											1	0	0	1	-12																1	0	0	1	-12

GRAND RAPIDS, MICHIGAN*
READINGS TAKEN AT LANSING, MI
LAT 42 47N   LONG 84 36W   ELEV 841 FT

MEAN FREQUENCY OF OCCURRENCE OF DRY BULB TEMPERATURE (DEGREES F) WITH MEAN COINCIDENT WET BULB TEMPERATURE (DEGREES F) FOR EACH DRY BULB TEMPERATURE RANGE

Temperature Range	MAY 01-08	MAY 09-16	MAY 17-24	MAY Total	MAY MCWB	JUNE 01-08	JUNE 09-16	JUNE 17-24	JUNE Total	JUNE MCWB	JULY 01-08	JULY 09-16	JULY 17-24	JULY Total	JULY MCWB	AUG 01-08	AUG 09-16	AUG 17-24	AUG Total	AUG MCWB	SEP 01-08	SEP 09-16	SEP 17-24	SEP Total	SEP MCWB	OCT 01-08	OCT 09-16	OCT 17-24	OCT Total	OCT MCWB
100/104																	0		0	79										
95/99																	1	0	1	76		0		0	75					
90/94							1	0	1	75		7	2	9	74		5	1	6	71		3	1	4	73					
85/89		4	1	5	71		6	2	8	74		33	12	45	71		16	5	21	71		7	3	10	72		1		1	67
80/84		13	4	17	67		24	9	33	72	1	62	31	94	69	1	44	17	62	69		16	6	22	70		6	0	6	64
75/79	1	25	13	39	64	1	36	19	56	69	10	59	48	117	66	3	57	36	96	66	3	27	16	46	66		14	3	17	62
70/74	6	33	22	61	61	7	47	32	86	66	43	50	61	154	65	22	62	58	142	64	18	46	28	92	64	2	23	9	34	60
65/69	15	43	32	90	57	24	48	50	122	63	60	27	46	133	62	55	42	60	157	62	25	48	40	113	60	7	30	20	57	58
60/64	24	43	43	110	54	53	38	50	141	61	64	10	31	105	61	73	18	43	134	59	39	42	46	127	59	18	33	29	80	55
55/59	38	35	45	118	51	50	23	35	108	57	42	1	14	57	57	52	3	20	75	55	43	32	44	119	53	25	35	32	92	51
50/54	48	24	39	111	47	44	10	25	79	53	21		2	23	50	26		7	33	50	41	13	29	83	49	34	35	38	107	47
45/49	50	15	24	89	43	34	6	15	55	49	7			7	46	13		1	14	46	40	4	18	62	45	45	36	47	128	44
40/44	35	10	17	62	39	20	1	2	23	45						3			3	42	19	0	7	26	41	40	23	34	97	39
35/39	20	2	6	28	35	6		0	6	41						0			0	38	8	0	2	10	37	40	9	22	71	35
30/34	9	0	1	10	31	0			0	37											4		0	4	33	25	2	9	36	31
25/29	2			2	27																					10		4	14	26
20/24																										2			2	22

*Comparative design data note:

	Elevation	WINTER 97 1/2%	SUMMER DB 2 1/2%	SUMMER WB 2 1/2%
Grand Rapids, MI.	681 ft.	6° F	89° F	74° F
Lansing AP	841 ft.	6° F	87° F	75° F

GRAND RAPIDS, MICHIGAN*
READINGS TAKEN AT LANSING, MI

Temperature Range	Nov 01-08	Nov 09-16	Nov 17-24	Nov Total	Nov MCWB	Dec 01-08	Dec 09-16	Dec 17-24	Dec Total	Dec MCWB	Jan 01-08	Jan 09-16	Jan 17-24	Jan Total	Jan MCWB	Feb 01-08	Feb 09-16	Feb 17-24	Feb Total	Feb MCWB	Mar 01-08	Mar 09-16	Mar 17-24	Mar Total	Mar MCWB	Apr 01-08	Apr 09-16	Apr 17-24	Apr Total	Apr MCWB	Ann 01-08	Ann 09-16	Ann 17-24	Ann Total	Ann MCWB
100/104																																		0	79
95/99																																2	0	2	75
90/94																																21	6	27	73
85/89																													0	69		85	30	115	71
80/84																											3	1	4	64	3	180	78	261	69
75/79		1		1	64																	0	0	0	58		6	3	9	62	24	236	151	411	66
70/74	1	2	1	4	62																	1	1	2	55		9	6	15	59	116	274	236	626	63
65/69	0	7	1	8	57									0	60							1	1	3	53	2	16	11	29	56	217	253	261	731	60
60/64	2	10	5	17	55	0		0	0	56	0	0	0	0	60	0			0	57		5	2	7	52	9	19	18	46	54	279	203	252	734	57
55/59	11	19	15	45	52	1	4	1	6	50	1	2	1	4	54		1	1	2	55	2	8	5	15	50	13	29	21	63	50	272	179	224	675	52
50/54	12	23	16	51	47	3	5	6	14	47	1	2	3	6	49	1	2	2	5	48	6	12	10	28	46	22	29	34	85	46	249	151	201	601	48
45/49	19	34	25	78	43	4	8	6	18	43	3	4	3	10	44	1	8	3	12	43	6	17	13	36	41	31	37	33	101	42	239	164	175	578	43
40/44	32	49	46	127	39	10	14	11	35	39	6	10	8	24	40	6	12	9	27	38	14	29	21	64	38	30	33	40	103	38	201	180	193	574	39
35/39	47	40	50	137	35	21	27	26	74	35	20	29	21	70	34	12	30	23	65	34	30	52	44	126	34	48	33	39	120	34	246	222	233	701	34
30/34	52	28	38	118	30	46	54	45	145	30	38	48	47	133	30	40	58	51	149	30	59	53	61	173	30	48	18	25	91	30	321	261	277	859	30
25/29	35	19	24	78	26	47	48	53	148	26	49	47	49	145	26	45	46	48	139	25	47	35	42	124	25	25	4	8	37	25	260	199	228	687	25
20/24	18	7	12	37	21	40	41	34	115	21	33	39	36	108	20	39	29	31	99	21	33	22	24	79	20	8	1	3	12	21	173	139	140	452	21
15/19	6	2	5	13	17	29	24	28	81	17	35	28	31	94	16	31	17	28	76	16	24	9	14	47	16	3	0	0	3	16	128	80	106	314	16
10/14	2	0	1	3	13	22	14	20	56	11	22	19	22	63	11	19	12	14	45	11	14	2	7	23	11	0			0	11	79	47	64	190	11
5/9	1	1	0	2	7	13	6	9	28	7	19	11	15	45	6	14	6	8	28	6	7	2	3	12	7						54	26	35	115	6
0/4	1	0	1	2	2	7	2	6	15	1	10	5	7	22	1	9	3	5	17	1	4	4	1	9	2						31	10	20	61	1
-5/-1			0	0	-1	6	1	2	9	-3	6	2	3	11	-3	7	1	1	9	-3	2	0	0	2	-3						21	4	6	31	-3
-10/-6						1	0	0	1	-7	4	1	1	6	-8	2	0		2	-8											7	1	1	9	-8
-15/-11						0			0	-13	1	0	0	1	-12																1	0	0	1	-12

SAULT STE. MARIE, MICHIGAN*
READINGS TAKEN AT KINCHELOE AFB, MI

LAT 46 15N   LONG 84 28W   ELEV 799 FT

MEAN FREQUENCY OF OCCURRENCE OF DRY BULB TEMPERATURE (DEGREES F) WITH MEAN COINCIDENT WET BULB TEMPERATURE (DEGREES F) FOR EACH DRY BULB TEMPERATURE RANGE

Temperature Range	MAY 01–08	MAY 09–16	MAY 17–24	MAY Total Obsn	MAY MCWB	JUNE 01–08	JUNE 09–16	JUNE 17–24	JUNE Total Obsn	JUNE MCWB	JULY 01–08	JULY 09–16	JULY 17–24	JULY Total Obsn	JULY MCWB	AUG 01–08	AUG 09–16	AUG 17–24	AUG Total Obsn	AUG MCWB	SEP 01–08	SEP 09–16	SEP 17–24	SEP Total Obsn	SEP MCWB	OCT 01–08	OCT 09–16	OCT 17–24	OCT Total Obsn	OCT MCWB
90/94												1		1	72															
85/89		1		1	70		0	0	0	76		8	1	9	71		2	0	2	71										
80/84		2	1	3	66		5	1	6	71		27	8	35	68		22	4	26	69				0	72		1	0	1	71
75/79		6	2	8	63		14	5	19	68	1	49	20	70	65	0	41	14	55	66	0	4	1	5	73		2	0	2	66
70/74	0	16	6	22	59	0	27	10	37	65	6	64	35	105	63	5	57	29	91	63	0	14	4	18	67		7	1	8	62
65/69	1	27	12	40	55	2	40	19	61	61	29	48	52	129	61	29	54	50	133	61	4	26	11	41	64	1	15	5	21	59
60/64	7	36	22	65	53	10	45	32	87	59	59	34	58	152	58	59	46	60	165	58	11	40	22	73	61	6	22	11	39	56
55/59	16	38	31	85	50	27	44	44	115	56	64	13	40	117	54	64	21	49	134	54	25	48	37	110	58	17	33	26	76	53
50/54	31	47	39	117	46	50	38	49	137	53	46	3	24	73	50	43	5	27	75	50	44	45	45	134	54	37	50	41	128	48
45/49	50	38	48	136	42	60	23	41	124	49	29	0	8	37	45	29	1	10	40	46	51	36	53	140	49	45	41	45	131	44
40/44	53	23	42	118	38	50	5	26	81	44	11		2	13	41	15		3	18	41	44	17	33	94	45	40	38	48	126	39
35/39	45	10	26	81	34	25	0	10	35	40	1		0	1	37	3		0	3	37	30	7	22	59	40	42	25	37	104	35
30/34	30	4	14	48	30	12		3	15	36						0			0	33	19	2	8	28	36	42	12	24	78	30
25/29	12	0	4	16	26	4		0	4	32											9	0	3	12	31	14	3	8	25	26
20/24	4	0	1	5	21	0			0	27											1		0	1	27	3	0	1	4	21
15/19	0			0	18																0			0	23	1		0	1	18
10/14																												0	0	13

*Comparative design data note:

	Elevation	WINTER 97 1/2%	SUMMER DB 2 1/2%	SUMMER DB 2 1/2%	SUMMER WB 2 1/2%
Sault Ste. Marie, MI.	721 ft.	-8° F	81° F	81° F	71° F
Kincheloe AFB	799 ft.	-10° F	81° F	81° F	70° F

COINCIDENT WET BULB TEMPERATURE FOR EACH DRY BULB TEMPERATURE RANGE

SAULT STE. MARIE, MICHIGAN*
READINGS TAKEN AT KINCHELOE AFB, MI

Each month group shows: Obsn Hour Gp (01 to 08 | 09 to 16 | 17 to 24), Total Obsn, and MCWB.

Temperature Range	Nov 01–08	Nov 09–16	Nov 17–24	Nov Total	Nov MCWB	Dec 01–08	Dec 09–16	Dec 17–24	Dec Total	Dec MCWB	Jan 01–08	Jan 09–16	Jan 17–24	Jan Total	Jan MCWB	Feb 01–08	Feb 09–16	Feb 17–24	Feb Total	Feb MCWB	Mar 01–08	Mar 09–16	Mar 17–24	Mar Total	Mar MCWB	Apr 01–08	Apr 09–16	Apr 17–24	Apr Total	Apr MCWB	Ann 01–08	Ann 09–16	Ann 17–24	Ann Total	Ann MCWB
90/94																																1		1	73
85/89																															0	16	2	18	71
80/84																															0	70	19	89	69
75/79																										0	1	0	1	60	1	140	50	191	65
70/74																										0	1	0	1	58	17	211	101	329	63
65/69																										5	5	2	7	55	81	234	175	490	60
60/64	0	1		1	57		0		0	52																9	9	3	12	52	184	240	235	659	57
55/59	1	4	2	7	52		0		0	52											0	0	0	0	50	16	1	16	7	24	47	257	208	249	714	53
50/54	2	9	5	16	48		1	0	1	47											0	2	0	2	43	5	29	15	49	44	275	205	245	725	48
45/49	11	24	13	48	44	1	2	2	5	44											1	7	3	11	39	11	36	28	75	41	271	171	216	658	44
40/44	27	38	31	96	40	3	4	3	10	39		0	0	0	39	1	2	1	4	38	3	19	8	30	37	31	46	38	115	38	239	177	208	624	39
35/39	40	47	47	134	35	15	20	17	52	34	3	8	4	15	34	2	7	4	13	34	9	37	24	70	33	48	50	54	152	34	239	205	224	668	34
30/34	65	55	62	182	30	36	41	40	117	30	17	24	20	61	30	11	23	16	50	30	35	54	54	143	29	63	31	53	147	30	312	244	286	842	30
25/29	43	35	39	117	25	34	41	36	111	25	26	35	33	94	26	23	33	29	85	25	47	47	55	149	25	44	12	29	85	25	244	206	233	683	25
20/24	24	17	22	63	21	33	41	42	116	21	29	32	38	93	21	27	34	36	97	20	41	31	39	111	20	23	3	8	34	21	184	158	181	523	21
15/19	15	6	10	31	17	33	34	36	103	16	29	35	35	100	16	28	35	37	100	16	30	26	28	84	16	9	1	2	12	16	143	137	151	431	16
10/14	7	2	5	14	11	27	29	29	85	11	37	37	32	109	11	28	30	30	88	11	28	16	23	67	11	4	0	1	5	11	131	114	123	368	11
5/9	3	1	2	6	7	23	17	21	61	7	30	29	26	91	6	32	24	27	83	6	26	5	8	39	6	1	0	0	1	6	115	76	90	281	6
0/4	1	1	1	3	2	17	10	14	41	2	27	22	15	75	1	24	17	18	59	1	18	2	3	23	2				0	2	87	52	62	201	1
-5/-1	0		0	0	-3	15	4	5	24	-3	23	15	9	53	-4	19	10	13	42	-4	6	0	1	7	-3				0	-5	63	29	34	126	-3
-10/-6			0	0	-7	6	2	2	10	-8	16	8	4	33	-8	14	7	9	30	-8	3	1	0	4	-8						38	18	21	77	-8
-15/-11						1	0	0	1	-12	8	3	1	15	-13	9	3	3	15	-13	1	0	0	1	-14						19	6	7	32	-13
-20/-16						0	0	0	0	-18	3	1	1	5	-18	5	1	1	7	-17	1	0		1	-18						3	2	8	13	-18
-25/-21						0			0	-22	1	0	0	1	-22	2	0	0	2	-22		0		0	-23						3	0	0	3	-22
-30/-26														0	-27	0	0		0	-27											0	0	0	0	-27
-35/-31														0	-33																0	0	0	0	-33

MINNEAPOLIS-ST PAUL IAP MINNESOTA

LAT 44 53N · LONG 93 13W   ELEV 834 FT

MEAN FREQUENCY OF OCCURRENCE OF DRY BULB TEMPERATURE (DEGREES F) WITH MEAN COINCIDENT WET BULB TEMPERATURE (DEGREES F) FOR EACH DRY BULB TEMPERATURE RANGE

Temperature Range	MAY 01 to 08	MAY 09 to 16	MAY 17 to 24	MAY Total Obsn	MAY MCWB	JUNE 01 to 08	JUNE 09 to 16	JUNE 17 to 24	JUNE Total Obsn	JUNE MCWB	JULY 01 to 08	JULY 09 to 16	JULY 17 to 24	JULY Total Obsn	JULY MCWB	AUGUST 01 to 08	AUGUST 09 to 16	AUGUST 17 to 24	AUGUST Total Obsn	AUGUST MCWB	SEPTEMBER 01 to 08	SEPTEMBER 09 to 16	SEPTEMBER 17 to 24	SEPTEMBER Total Obsn	SEPTEMBER MCWB	OCTOBER 01 to 08	OCTOBER 09 to 16	OCTOBER 17 to 24	OCTOBER Total Obsn	OCTOBER MCWB
100/104												0	0	0	80															
95/99												3	1	4	77									0	76					
90/94		1	0	1	67		2	1	3	74		11	5	16	75		1	0	1	75		4	1	5	75					
85/89		5	2	7	66		9	4	13	72	0	37	15	52	71		12	3	15	74		7	2	9	73		1	0	1	65
80/84		14	6	20	64	0	17	10	27	71	4	58	36	98	69	0	27	11	38	72	1	13	7	21	69		7	0	7	63
75/79	1	25	14	40	62	2	37	20	59	68	16	60	52	128	67	3	46	27	76	69	6	26	13	45	65	0	11	3	14	62
70/74	5	35	24	64	59	10	48	34	92	65	53	48	63	164	65	12	59	43	114	67	8	40	24	72	62	1	17	7	25	59
65/69	16	39	34	89	57	28	49	47	124	63	78	23	48	149	63	41	48	61	150	65	16	41	35	92	59	3	28	16	47	56
60/64	35	42	46	123	54	50	36	50	136	60	61	8	23	92	59	69	33	57	159	63	34	41	47	122	56	12	34	28	74	54
55/59	48	34	47	129	51	62	25	41	128	57	29	1	5	35	55	67	16	29	112	59	51	36	47	134	53	27	37	36	100	51
50/54	51	24	36	111	47	43	10	22	75	53	7		1	8	51	37	5	13	55	54	56	23	35	114	49	37	37	45	119	47
45/49	45	18	22	85	43	29	5	10	44	49	0			0	47	16	0	3	19	50	35	8	22	65	44	50	33	40	123	43
40/44	29	8	12	49	39	13	0	2	15	45						4		0	4	46	25	2	7	34	40	43	26	36	105	39
35/39	13	2	3	18	34	2			2	42						0			0	41	6	0	1	7	36	38	11	22	71	34
30/34	5	0	2	7	30																1	0		1	32	23	6	11	40	30
25/29	1	0	0	1	27																0			0	28	9	1	3	13	25
20/24																										4	0	1	5	21
15/19																										0	0	0	0	18

COINCIDENT WET BULB TEMPERATURE FOR EACH DRY BULB TEMPERATURE RANGE

MINNEAPOLIS-ST PAUL IAP MINNESOTA

Obsn Hour Gp / Total Obsn / MCWB

Temperature Range	NOVEMBER					DECEMBER					JANUARY					FEBRUARY					MARCH					APRIL					ANNUAL TOTAL				
	01-08	09-16	17-24	Tot Obsn	MCWB	01-08	09-16	17-24	Tot Obsn	MCWB	01-08	09-16	17-24	Tot Obsn	MCWB	01-08	09-16	17-24	Tot Obsn	MCWB	01-08	09-16	17-24	Tot Obsn	MCWB	01-08	09-16	17-24	Tot Obsn	MCWB	01-08	09-16	17-24	Tot Obsn	MCWB
100/104																																		0	80
95/99																															0	6	2	8	76
90/94																										0	0	0	0	63	0	37	13	50	74
85/89																										0	2	0	2	61	0	96	40	136	71
80/84																										0	3	1	4	61	10	178	97	285	68
75/79	0	0		0	55																0	0	0	0	54	0	6	3	9	59	45	235	162	442	66
70/74	0	0	2	2	54																0	0	0	0	58	0	9	5	14	57	136	246	231	613	63
65/69	0	6	2	8	53	0			0	53											0	1	0	1	54	1	15	11	27	54	233	218	251	702	60
60/64	2	12	7	21	50	0	0	1	1	50											0	1	1	2	52	5	21	17	43	51	276	194	234	704	56
55/59																0	1	0	1	47	0	4	2	6	48	12	22	23	57	48	249	162	203	614	52
50/54	7	18	11	36	47	2	1	0	3	49	0	0		0	38	1	0	0	1	43	1	10	5	16	44	20	33	28	81	45	226	152	174	552	47
45/49	11	28	19	58	42	1	2	2	5	44	0	3	1	4	36	0	3	1	4	40	1	13	9	23	40	28	35	33	96	41	188	140	150	478	43
40/44	23	32	32	87	38	3	11	4	18	38	4	12	9	25	33	1	10	4	15	37	10	24	20	54	37	39	39	41	119	38	175	155	157	487	38
35/39	39	37	42	118	34	11	20	18	49	34	14	20	18	52	30	8	20	16	44	34	24	41	37	102	34	50	29	39	118	34	193	172	187	552	34
30/34	48	36	42	126	30	24	33	34	91	30	22	38	33	93	25	23	36	37	96	30	40	54	58	152	29	45	18	25	88	30	223	203	227	653	30
25/29	39	25	30	94	25	38	43	39	120	26	31	33	35	99	21	30	32	32	94	25	52	38	43	133	25	26	6	11	43	25	217	183	191	591	25
20/24	29	18	22	69	21	36	36	34	106	21	31	27	28	86	16	25	32	30	87	21	41	25	29	95	20	10	1	3	14	20	176	145	154	475	21
15/19	15	14	17	46	16	31	27	30	88	16	29	29	30	88	11	30	31	33	94	16	27	16	20	63	16	2	0	0	2	16	136	115	128	379	16
10/14	13	6	11	30	11	28	21	25	74	11	29	25	27	81	6	33	22	25	80	11	18	10	12	40	11	1	0	0	1	11	122	88	103	313	11
5/9	7	3	2	12	7	22	21	21	64	6	24	24	23	71	1	21	16	19	56	6	15	7	7	29	6	0	0	0	0		94	72	76	242	6
0/4	4	2	2	8	1	19	17	18	54	1	21	16	20	57	-3	19	10	12	41	1	10	3	3	16	1						76	56	58	190	1
-5/-1	2	1	1	4	-3	14	8	11	33	-3	17	11	13	41	-8	16	7	7	30	-4	5	0	2	7	-3						58	32	41	131	-3
-10/-6	0	0	0	0	-8	11	4	6	21	-8	15	7	7	29	-13	10	3	4	17	-8	2	0	0	2	-8						40	18	23	81	-8
-15/-11	0			0	-13	5	1	2	8	-12	6	2	3	11	-18	4	2	1	7	-13	1	0	0	1	-13						25	9	11	45	-13
-20/-16						2	0	0	2	-18						2	0	1	3	-17	0	0	0	0	-18						10	2	4	16	-18
-25/-21											4	0	2	6	-23	0	0	0	0	-23	0	0	0	0	-24						4	0	2	6	-23
-30/-26											1	0	0	1	-27	0	0	0	0	-26	0	0	0	0	-27						1	0	1	1	-27

JACKSON/ALLEN THOMPSON FLD MISSISSIPPI
LAT 32 19N   LONG 90 05W   ELEV 310 FT

MEAN FREQUENCY OF OCCURRENCE OF DRY BULB TEMPERATURE (DEGREES F) WITH MEAN COINCIDENT WET BULB TEMPERATURE (DEGREES F) FOR EACH DRY BULB TEMPERATURE RANGE

For each month the columns are the Observation Hour Group (01 to 08, 09 to 16, 17 to 24), Total Obsn, and MWB (Mean Coincident Wet Bulb).

Temperature Range	MAY 01–08	MAY 09–16	MAY 17–24	MAY Total	MAY MWB	JUN 01–08	JUN 09–16	JUN 17–24	JUN Total	JUN MWB	JUL 01–08	JUL 09–16	JUL 17–24	JUL Total	JUL MWB	AUG 01–08	AUG 09–16	AUG 17–24	AUG Total	AUG MWB	SEP 01–08	SEP 09–16	SEP 17–24	SEP Total	SEP MWB	OCT 01–08	OCT 09–16	OCT 17–24	OCT Total	OCT MWB
100/104																														
95/99		1	0	1	73		2	0	2	78		2	0	2	77		5	0	5	76		1	0	1	75				0	75
90/94		17	2	19	72		17	3	20	77		22	4	26	77		25	4	29	76		7		7	73		6		6	73
85/89	0	68	18	86	71	0	53	14	67	75	0	80	20	100	76		76	17	93	76		38	4	42	73		28	3	31	70
80/84	3	65	27	95	70	2	79	29	110	74	2	83	31	116	76	3	83	33	119	75	0	69	15	84	72		45	8	53	67
75/79	21	44	52	117	68	20	53	48	121	73	28	42	58	128	75	22	39	57	118	74	4	60	31	95	71	5	50	24	79	66
70/74	59	27	65	151	67	66	24	75	165	72	103	15	89	207	73	84	16	87	187	73	31	35	69	135	70	28	45	42	115	65
65/69	88	16	51	155	64	97	9	53	159	69	103	5	45	153	71	109	4	45	158	70	92	19	73	184	69	45	37	54	136	62
60/64	40	7	19	66	59	39	3	14	56	65	10	0	1	11	66	24	0	4	28	65	56	7	30	93	64	45	19	42	106	57
55/59	20	3	8	31	54	11	1	4	16	60	1			1	61	4		1	5	60	35	3	15	53	59	38	11	34	83	52
50/54	11	1	5	17	49	4		0	4	55						2			2	57	16	0	3	19	54	36	5	22	63	48
45/49	6	1	1	7	45	0			0	51											6			6	50	30	2	11	43	44
40/44	1			1	43	0			0	48											1			1	45	14	0	6	20	40
35/39																										6		1	7	35
30/34																										2		0	2	31
25/29																										0			0	29

COINCIDENT WET BULB TEMPERATURE FOR EACH DRY BULB TEMPERATURE RANGE

JACKSON/ALLEN THOMPSON FLD MISSISSIPPI

Temperature Range	NOV 01-08	NOV 09-16	NOV 17-24	NOV Total Obsn	NOV MCWB	DEC 01-08	DEC 09-16	DEC 17-24	DEC Total Obsn	DEC MCWB	JAN 01-08	JAN 09-16	JAN 17-24	JAN Total Obsn	JAN MCWB	FEB 01-08	FEB 09-16	FEB 17-24	FEB Total Obsn	FEB MCWB	MAR 01-08	MAR 09-16	MAR 17-24	MAR Total Obsn	MAR MCWB	APR 01-08	APR 09-16	APR 17-24	APR Total Obsn	APR MCWB	ANNUAL 01-08	ANNUAL 09-16	ANNUAL 17-24	ANNUAL Total Obsn	ANNUAL MCWB
100/104																																10	0	10	76
95/99																																72	11	83	76
90/94		0	0	0	72																											270	57	327	75
85/89		7	0	7	68							0		0	64							0	0	0	69		11	1	12	69	7	421	130	558	73
80/84							1		1	67		1		1	67	2	0	0	2	67		10	1	11	67		37	10	47	67	77	362	240	679	72
75/79		22	3	25	65		6	0	6	67		7	1	8	67		13	2	15	65		23	9	32	65	2	51	22	75	65	312	306	433	1051	70
70/74	7	36	15	58	63	2	15	4	21	63	2	23	7	32	64	2	24	12	38	63	5	33	21	59	62	18	41	42	101	63	524	281	424	1229	67
65/69	12	34	25	71	59	6	26	15	47	60	17	25	24	66	62	12	29	19	60	60	23	37	30	90	59	40	34	49	123	61	372	248	316	936	62
60/64	20	33	28	81	55	18	35	26	79	57	18	24	23	65	57	20	36	31	87	56	24	41	39	104	55	49	31	43	123	57	285	230	271	786	57
55/59	27	37	35	99	51	21	35	27	83	52	19	27	24	70	52	24	29	35	88	52	34	35	39	108	51	45	22	32	99	52	250	199	237	686	52
50/54	34	28	37	99	47	27	41	36	104	47	21	33	29	83	47	35	28	32	95	47	33	29	39	101	47	37	9	21	67	48	240	174	221	635	47
45/49	33	21	36	90	43	36	37	41	114	43	30	35	38	103	43	37	26	35	98	43	42	19	31	92	43	25	3	16	44	43	240	143	209	592	43
40/44	39	14	31	84	38	38	25	40	103	38	33	31	35	99	39	32	15	26	73	39	36	12	21	69	39	19	0	5	24	40	212	97	164	473	39
35/39	34	7	17	58	34	37	16	31	84	34	38	21	31	90	34	28	12	14	54	35	31	6	14	51	34	6	0	0	6	36	180	62	108	350	34
30/34	21	2	9	32	30	34	7	18	59	30	33	12	20	65	30	17	5	10	32	30	16	2	3	21	30	0			0	33	123	28	60	211	30
25/29	9	0	4	13	25	19	2	7	28	25	22	5	10	37	25	10	3	3	16	25	3	0	1	4	24						63	10	25	98	25
20/24	4	0	0	4	21	8	1	2	11	21	11	3	5	19	21	5	0	2	7	20	1			1	22						29	4	9	42	21
15/19	0			0	18	2	0	0	2	16	1	1	1	3	15	1	1	0	2	16											3	1	2	6	16
10/14						1		0	1	10	1	1	1	3	10		0	1	1	12											2	2	1	5	11
5/9						0			0	8	1	0	1	2	5	1	0	0	1	7											2	0	1	3	6
0/4											1			1	2				0	3												1	0	1	2

KANSAS CITY, MISSOURI
READINGS TAKEN AT RICHARDS-GEBAUR AFB/GRANDVIEW
LAT 38 51N   LONG 94 33W   ELEV 1090 FT

MEAN FREQUENCY OF OCCURRENCE OF DRY BULB TEMPERATURE (DEGREES F) WITH MEAN COINCIDENT WET BULB TEMPERATURE (DEGREES F) FOR EACH DRY BULB TEMPERATURE RANGE

Subcolumn key for each month — Obsn Hour Gp: (01 to 08), (09 to 16), (17 to 24); Total Obsn; MCWB (Mean Coincident Wet Bulb).

Temperature Range	MAY 01–08	MAY 09–16	MAY 17–24	MAY Total	MAY MCWB	JUNE 01–08	JUNE 09–16	JUNE 17–24	JUNE Total	JUNE MCWB	JULY 01–08	JULY 09–16	JULY 17–24	JULY Total	JULY MCWB	AUG 01–08	AUG 09–16	AUG 17–24	AUG Total	AUG MCWB	SEP 01–08	SEP 09–16	SEP 17–24	SEP Total	SEP MCWB	OCT 01–08	OCT 09–16	OCT 17–24	OCT Total	OCT MCWB
100/104																														
95/99																	1	0	1	77										
90/94		1		1	70		0	0	0	78		0	0	0	77		7	2	9	75		0		0	72		1		1	64
85/89		12	3	15	70		7	2	9	75		4	2	6	77		26	9	35	75		6	2	8	74		4	1	5	66
80/84	1	33	13	46	68		34	13	47	73		31	10	41	75	0	55	24	79	73		22	5	27	72		12	2	14	66
75/79	1	46	29	76	65	1	60	34	95	71	0	54	26	80	73	5	61	44	110	71	0	30	14	44	70		24	7	31	63
70/74	19	47	43	109	63	18	56	55	129	69	10	66	52	128	72	37	50	62	149	69	6	49	32	87	67	3	35	21	59	61
65/69	43	36	50	129	60	55	43	59	157	66	49	54	66	169	70	78	32	54	164	67	31	48	47	126	65	14	43	34	83	59
60/64	58	31	47	136	56	76	24	45	145	63	85	27	58	170	67	62	11	34	107	63	53	39	50	142	62	34	37	39	116	55
55/59	49	24	31	104	52	55	11	23	89	59	68	8	25	101	63	46	5	15	66	59	49	13	28	90	57	43	29	42	122	51
50/54	40	12	21	73	48	25	4	8	37	54	27	2	7	36	59	14	0	4	18	55	32	6	16	54	53	41	19	40	110	46
45/49	22	6	10	38	43	8	1	2	11	50	6	0	2	8	54	5		1	6	50	16	3	5	24	49	44	8	32	95	42
40/44	13	0	3	16	39	2	0	0	2	46	3	0	0	3	50	0			0	47	4		1	5	45	35	2	20	63	38
35/39	3	3	0	3	34						0			0	47						1		0	1	40	23	0	7	32	34
30/34																					0			0	36	9		3	12	30
25/29																					2			2	33	2		0	2	26
20/24																					0			0		0			0	22

COINCIDENT WET BULB TEMPERATURE FOR EACH DRY BULB TEMPERATURE RANGE

KANSAS CITY, MISSOURI
READINGS TAKEN AT RICHARDS-GEBAUR AFB/GRANDVIEW

Temperature Range	NOV 01–08	NOV 09–16	NOV 17–24	NOV Total Obsn	NOV MCWB	DEC 01–08	DEC 09–16	DEC 17–24	DEC Total Obsn	DEC MCWB	JAN 01–08	JAN 09–16	JAN 17–24	JAN Total Obsn	JAN MCWB	FEB 01–08	FEB 09–16	FEB 17–24	FEB Total Obsn	FEB MCWB	MAR 01–08	MAR 09–16	MAR 17–24	MAR Total Obsn	MAR MCWB	APR 01–08	APR 09–16	APR 17–24	APR Total Obsn	APR MCWB	ANN 01–08	ANN 09–16	ANN 17–24	ANN Total Obsn	ANN MCWB
100/104																																1	0	1	77
95/99																																11	4	15	76
90/94																																72	23	95	75
85/89																											2	0	2	65	0	183	72	255	73
80/84				0	65																	1	0	1	60		7	2	9	64	16	270	161	447	70
75/79	0	1	0	1	62		0	0	0	60						0	0	0	0	56	0	5	1	6	59	0	18	7	25	62	111	303	259	673	68
70/74	0	9	1	10	61		2	0	2	57		0	0	0	59	0	2	1	3	53	0	8	5	13	57	3	26	16	45	60	274	275	304	853	65
65/69	2	16	7	25	58	3	6	3	12	55	0	2	0	2	56	0	4	1	5	50	2	12	7	21	54	10	35	30	75	57	330	222	283	835	61
60/64	7	24	13	44	54	3	11	6	20	50	1	2	2	5	55	1	6	5	12	49	4	16	13	33	52	21	38	34	93	54	304	206	237	747	56
55/59	10	28	21	59	50	6	16	9	31	46	2	6	3	11	51	4	17	9	30	45	10	18	16	44	48	35	34	44	113	50	247	181	210	638	51
50/54	19	32	31	82	45	9	26	17	52	41	2	10	5	17	46	6	23	16	45	41	12	23	21	56	44	38	31	34	103	46	210	177	189	576	46
45/49	28	35	35	98	42	23	33	33	89	38	5	17	11	33	41	17	27	30	74	38	19	33	29	81	41	43	22	34	99	42	194	184	189	567	42
40/44	41	32	41	114	38	35	37	42	114	33	9	25	25	59	37	32	33	38	103	33	28	31	34	93	37	42	17	21	80	38	212	173	208	593	38
35/39	49	33	37	119	34	47	40	48	135	29	24	30	32	86	33	43	36	39	118	29	39	37	44	120	33	25	7	13	45	34	231	179	213	623	33
30/34	39	18	28	85	29	41	31	33	105	25	39	33	38	110	29	37	28	28	93	25	55	32	37	124	29	17	3	4	24	30	249	162	197	608	29
25/29	22	8	14	44	25	34	22	24	80	20	37	33	33	103	25	25	23	24	72	20	34	17	21	72	25	4	0	1	5	25	177	117	130	424	25
20/24	12	4	7	23	20	21	10	15	46	16	32	27	30	89	20	24	14	20	58	15	22	9	12	43	20	1	0	0	1	22	126	85	97	308	20
15/19	7	2	3	12	15	12	7	9	28	11	27	23	26	76	15	20	8	8	36	11	12	4	5	21	16						91	53	69	213	16
10/14	2	0	1	3	11	7	5	4	16	6	23	17	18	58	11	10	3	3	16	6	7	1	1	9	11						64	33	37	134	11
5/9	1	0	0	1	6	4	4	2	10	2	21	11	13	45	6	4	0	3	7	2	2	1	1	4	7						41	20	21	82	6
0/4	0			0	3	3	1	1	5	-3	13	7	7	27	1	1	0	0	1	-3	1	0	0	1	1						22	10	13	45	2
-5/-1						1	0	0	1	-7	6	3	5	14	-4				0	-6	1	0	0	1	-3						11	4	6	21	-3
-10/-6											5	1	1	7	-8																6	1	1	8	-8
-15/-11											0	0	0	0	-13																0	0	0	0	-13

ST LOUIS/LAMBERT IAP MISSOURI
LAT 38 45N   LONG 90 23W   ELEV   535 FT

MEAN FREQUENCY OF OCCURRENCE OF DRY BULB TEMPERATURE (DEGREES F) WITH MEAN COINCIDENT WET BULB TEMPERATURE (DEGREES F) FOR EACH DRY BULB TEMPERATURE RANGE

(Obsn Hour Gp columns are 01 to 08, 09 to 16, 17 to 24; Total = Total Obsn; MCWB = Mean Coincident Wet Bulb.)

Temperature Range	MAY 01-08	MAY 09-16	MAY 17-24	MAY Total	MAY MCWB	JUNE 01-08	JUNE 09-16	JUNE 17-24	JUNE Total	JUNE MCWB	JULY 01-08	JULY 09-16	JULY 17-24	JULY Total	JULY MCWB	AUG 01-08	AUG 09-16	AUG 17-24	AUG Total	AUG MCWB	SEP 01-08	SEP 09-16	SEP 17-24	SEP Total	SEP MCWB	OCT 01-08	OCT 09-16	OCT 17-24	OCT Total	OCT MCWB
110/114												0	0	0	76															
105/109												0	1	1	76															
100/104		0		0	72		2	1	3	75		3	1	4	76		2	0	2	76		1	0	1	68					
95/99		4	1	5	71		8	3	11	75		12	4	16	75		12	2	14	75		5	1	6	71					
90/94		21	6	27	70	0	29	10	39	74	0	37	14	51	75		36	12	48	74		16	4	20	71		2		2	68
85/89		37	18	55	67	2	46	25	73	73	3	64	37	104	73	1	59	30	90	73	0	28	11	39	70		7	0	7	67
80/84	0					15	57	45	117	70	23	67	63	153	71	15	66	55	136	71	4	40	24	68	68	0	24	4	28	65
75/79	7	46	33	86	65	38	43	49	130	68	61	40	67	168	70	55	42	64	161	69	18	45	37	100	66	1	31	12	44	63
70/74	28	45	41	114	63	59	28	53	140	66	93	18	44	155	68	78	22	50	150	67	41	48	47	136	64	8	36	25	69	61
65/69	46	39	52	137	60	64	16	35	115	62	45	4	15	64	63	56	8	24	88	63	46	34	51	131	60	19	35	40	94	58
60/64	59	27	43	129	57	36	7	14	57	58	19	1	3	23	59	31	1	9	41	59	49	15	34	98	56	40	36	44	120	55
55/59	43	16	27	86	52	18	2	5	25	54	4		0	4	54	10	1	1	12	55	41	6	21	68	53	42	34	39	115	50
50/54	31	9	16	56	48	6	0	1	7	50	0			0	51	2			2	51	28	1	8	37	49	42	24	37	103	47
45/49	19	3	7	29	43	1			1	46											12	0	2	14	44	43	12	28	83	43
40/44	12	1	2	15	39																3		0	3	41	32	7	13	52	39
35/39	2	0	0	2	34																					15	2	6	23	34
30/34	0	0	0	0	31																					6	0	1	7	30
25/29																										1			1	26

COINCIDENT WET BULB TEMPERATURE FOR EACH DRY BULB TEMPERATURE RANGE

ST LOUIS/LAMBERT IAP MISSOURI

Temperature Range	NOVEMBER					DECEMBER					JANUARY					FEBRUARY					MARCH					APRIL					ANNUAL TOTAL				
	01 to 08	09 to 16	17 to 24	Total Obsn	MCWB	01 to 08	09 to 16	17 to 24	Total Obsn	MCWB	01 to 08	09 to 16	17 to 24	Total Obsn	MCWB	01 to 08	09 to 16	17 to 24	Total Obsn	MCWB	01 to 08	09 to 16	17 to 24	Total Obsn	MCWB	01 to 08	09 to 16	17 to 24	Total Obsn	MCWB	01 to 08	09 to 16	17 to 24	Total Obsn	MCWB
110/114																																0	0	0	76
105/109																																1	0	1	76
100/104																																8	2	10	74
95/99																																37	10	47	75
90/94																										0	0	0	0	68	0	124	41	165	74
85/89																										0	5	1	6	66	6	230	110	346	72
80/84		1		1	65		1		1	61				0	64				0	61				0	64	0	15	4	19	65	57	308	213	578	70
75/79	0	4	0	4	63	0	3	1	4	57	0	1	1	2	62				0	59	0	1	0	1	62	0	21	12	33	62	180	276	275	731	67
70/74	0	12	2	14	59	2	8	2	12	54	1	3	0	4	56	0	1	1	2	59	0	4	1	5	61	8	26	21	55	60	315	246	289	850	65
65/69	3	15	10	28	58	3	12	7	22	50	3	7	4	14	56	0	3	1	4	55	0	8	4	12	58	17	29	29	75	58	298	201	265	764	60
60/64	9	24	16	49	54	9	19	16	44	46	4	10	7	21	51	1	7	3	11	51	1	12	7	20	54	28	27	32	87	54	282	177	217	676	56
55/59	14	26	24	64	50	10	21	17	48	42	5	14	9	28	46	3	12	7	22	49	5	17	13	35	52	31	32	31	94	50	224	173	189	586	51
50/54	23	31	32	86	45	24	31	30	85	38	10	17	15	42	42	8	21	15	44	46	11	22	20	53	49	34	33	31	98	45	204	180	192	576	46
45/49	32	33	31	96	42	40	45	42	127	33	14	26	23	63	37	12	27	23	62	42	16	28	27	71	45	34	22	32	88	42	194	166	185	545	42
40/44	37	35	36	108	38	50	44	49	143	29	26	36	36	98	34	21	34	31	86	38	21	31	30	82	41	39	20	27	86	38	220	195	202	617	38
35/39	36	26	37	99	33	41	26	38	105	25	49	46	47	142	30	37	39	44	120	33	38	41	40	119	37	34	8	15	57	34	243	198	229	670	34
30/34	42	17	27	86	29	28	16	17	61	20	44	32	37	113	25	56	37	45	138	30	53	42	49	144	34	12	1	3	16	30	266	168	203	637	30
25/29	24	12	15	51	25	15	8	11	34	15	27	21	29	77	20	35	18	24	77	25	51	23	31	105	30	3	0	0	3	25	175	98	131	404	25
20/24	12	3	6	21	20	11	7	9	27	11	25	17	18	60	15	20	11	12	43	20	27	10	17	54	25	0	0	0	0	22	102	56	70	228	20
15/19	4	1	3	8	15	8	4	5	17	6	19	11	12	42	11	11	7	8	26	15	15	5	6	26	20						62	34	42	138	15
10/14	3	1	1	5	11	5	1	2	8	2	10	5	6	21	6	9	4	6	19	11	7	1	2	10	16						44	24	29	97	11
5/9	2	0	0	2	6	2	0	0	2	-3	6	3	3	12	1	6	1	2	9	6	2	1	1	4	11						27	10	13	50	6
0/4	0			0	3	0	0	0	0	-6	4	1	2	7	-3	1	2	1	4	1	1	0	0	1	6						13	5	6	24	2
-5/-1	0			0							1	0	0	1	-7	1	1	0	2	-3	0	0	0	0	1						8	1	2	11	-3
-10/-6																0	0	0	0	-7	0	0	0	0	-3						1	0	0	1	-7

SPRINGFIELD MAP MISSOURI

LAT 37 14N   LONG 93 23W   ELEV 1268 FT

MEAN FREQUENCY OF OCCURRENCE OF DRY BULB TEMPERATURE (DEGREES F) WITH MEAN COINCIDENT WET BULB TEMPERATURE (DEGREES F) FOR EACH DRY BULB TEMPERATURE RANGE

Temperature Range	MAY					JUNE					JULY					AUGUST					SEPTEMBER					OCTOBER				
	01 to 08	09 to 16	17 to 24	Total Obsn	MCWB	01 to 08	09 to 16	17 to 24	Total Obsn	MCWB	01 to 08	09 to 16	17 to 24	Total Obsn	MCWB	01 to 08	09 to 16	17 to 24	Total Obsn	MCWB	01 to 08	09 to 16	17 to 24	Total Obsn	MCWB	01 to 08	09 to 16	17 to 24	Total Obsn	MCWB
110/114												0	0	0	77															
105/109												1	0	1	74															
100/104												2	0	2	74		2	0	2	74										
95/99							0	0	0	73	0	10	3	13	75	0	15	4	19	74	0	0	0	0	70					
90/94		1	0	1	76		9	2	11	74	0	42	13	55	74		40	10	50	74		5	0	5	70		1	0	1	66
85/89		17	3	20	70		23	6	29	74	2	63	26	91	74	1	64	25	90	72		14	3	17	70		7		7	67
80/84	0	41	14	55	69	8	45	15	61	73	12	59	42	113	72	7	56	42	105	71	0	33	9	42	70	0	24	3	27	66
75/79	3	46	24	73	66	24	57	31	96	71	41	39	65	145	71	31	39	63	133	70	2	42	16	60	68	0	32	8	40	63
70/74	18	46	46	110	64	58	42	50	116	69	96	23	63	182	69	92	21	59	172	68	6	46	32	84	66	4	41	19	64	61
65/69	47	41	54	142	61	74	32	59	149	67	69	7	29	105	65	67	8	30	105	64	32	45	53	130	65	18	36	39	93	60
60/64	71	30	49	150	58	42	20	44	138	64	21	1	6	28	60	35	2	11	48	60	64	30	55	149	62	45	35	39	122	56
55/59	47	16	29	92	53	21	8	22	72	60	7		1	8	56	10	0	3	13	55	54	16	35	105	58	43	31	39	115	52
50/54	30	7	18	55	49	10	3	7	31	55	1			1	51	4		0	4	51	38	6	22	66	53	43	22	37	102	48
45/49	21	3	8	32	44	10	1	3	14	51						1			1	47	27	2	12	41	49	36	11	28	75	43
40/44	8	1	1	10	40	2		0	2	46											13	0	3	16	45	32	5	18	55	39
35/39	3	0	1	4	36	0			0	43											3		0	3	41	17	2	6	25	35
30/34	1		0	1	32																0			0	38	10	1	3	14	30
25/29																										2			2	25
20/24																													0	22

SPRINGFIELD MAP MISSOURI

Temperature Range	NOV 01–08	NOV 09–16	NOV 17–24	NOV Total Obsn	NOV MCWB	DEC 01–08	DEC 09–16	DEC 17–24	DEC Total Obsn	DEC MCWB	JAN 01–08	JAN 09–16	JAN 17–24	JAN Total Obsn	JAN MCWB	FEB 01–08	FEB 09–16	FEB 17–24	FEB Total Obsn	FEB MCWB	MAR 01–08	MAR 09–16	MAR 17–24	MAR Total Obsn	MAR MCWB	APR 01–08	APR 09–16	APR 17–24	APR Total Obsn	APR MCWB	ANN 01–08	ANN 09–16	ANN 17–24	ANN Total Obsn	ANN MCWB
110/114																																0	0	0	77
105/109																																1	0	1	74
100/104																															0	4	0	4	74
95/99																										0	0	0	0	72	0	39	9	48	74
90/94																										0	3	0	3	66	0	121	32	153	74
85/89																					0	0	0	0	58	0	14	3	17	65	4	232	78	314	72
80/84	0	0	0	0	63						0	0	0	0	64	0	0	0	0	63	0	2	0	2	63	0	25	9	34	63	29	295	151	475	70
75/79	0	4	0	4	64	0	0	0	0	63	0	2	0	2	59	0	1	0	1	59	0	5	1	6	61	4	33	21	58	61	105	279	252	636	68
70/74	0	14	1	15	61	0	1	0	1	56	1	6	1	8	56	0	3	1	4	58	0	11	3	14	58	15	32	30	77	58	304	272	325	901	66
65/69	4	22	7	33	58	0	4	0	4	53	3	10	4	17	55	0	5	2	7	55	3	17	9	29	56	33	33	34	100	55	362	228	300	890	62
60/64	7	24	15	46	55	2	11	3	16	53	4	14	8	26	51	2	12	5	19	52	6	22	17	45	52	34	27	38	99	51	315	204	249	768	57
55/59	13	25	21	59	50	3	16	7	26	50	7	16	11	34	46	3	18	9	30	49	10	25	19	54	49	32	25	33	90	46	235	181	203	619	52
50/54	20	33	31	84	46	9	23	15	47	46	9	25	17	51	42	8	26	19	53	46	17	27	29	73	45	38	24	29	91	42	208	182	208	598	47
45/49	30	32	39	101	42	14	33	23	70	42	17	26	29	72	37	18	30	28	76	42	24	33	36	93	41	32	15	23	70	38	206	191	211	608	42
40/44	41	32	33	106	38	24	34	34	92	38	26	32	36	94	34	25	29	34	88	38	37	31	39	107	38	28	8	15	51	35	219	173	211	603	38
35/39	34	21	34	89	34	33	33	43	109	34	45	39	42	126	30	38	31	37	106	34	56	33	39	128	34	17	2	5	24	30	235	160	211	606	34
30/34	32	14	27	73	30	50	41	47	138	30	46	30	36	112	25	45	29	38	112	30	37	23	29	89	30	6	0	0	6	26	237	149	191	577	30
25/29	30	10	17	57	25	42	23	32	97	25	28	21	28	77	21	35	18	23	76	25	34	11	17	62	26	0	0	0	0	21	195	92	125	412	25
20/24	16	5	8	29	21	31	13	22	66	21	22	17	8	47	16	20	11	15	46	20	12	4	6	22	21	0	0	0	0	19	107	54	79	240	21
15/19	8	2	5	15	16	19	6	9	34	16	20	8	10	38	11	15	7	8	30	16	10	2	3	15	16						74	28	39	141	16
10/14	4	1	1	6	11	10	6	6	22	11	8	5	5	18	6	6	2	3	11	11	2	1	1	4	11						46	18	21	85	11
5/9	1	0	0	1	6	6	2	5	13	6	6	2	3	11	1	3	1	1	5	6	1	0	1	2	6						19	8	12	39	6
0/4						4	1	1	6	2	3	1	1	5	-4	2	1	0	3	1	1	0	0	1	2						13	4	4	21	2
-5/-1						1	0	0	1	-3	1	0	0	1	-7	0	0	0	0	-4											4	1	1	6	-4
-10/-6																0	0	0	0	-8											1	0	0	1	-7

BILLINGS/LOGAN IAP MONTANA
LAT 45 48N   LONG 108 32W   ELEV 3567 FT

MEAN FREQUENCY OF OCCURRENCE OF DRY BULB TEMPERATURE (DEGREES F) WITH MEAN COINCIDENT WET BULB TEMPERATURE (DEGREES F) FOR EACH DRY BULB TEMPERATURE RANGE

Temperature Range	MAY 01 to 08	MAY 09 to 16	MAY 17 to 24	MAY Total Obsn	MAY MCWB	JUNE 01 to 08	JUNE 09 to 16	JUNE 17 to 24	JUNE Total Obsn	JUNE MCWB	JULY 01 to 08	JULY 09 to 16	JULY 17 to 24	JULY Total Obsn	JULY MCWB	AUGUST 01 to 08	AUGUST 09 to 16	AUGUST 17 to 24	AUGUST Total Obsn	AUGUST MCWB	SEPTEMBER 01 to 08	SEPTEMBER 09 to 16	SEPTEMBER 17 to 24	SEPTEMBER Total Obsn	SEPTEMBER MCWB	OCTOBER 01 to 08	OCTOBER 09 to 16	OCTOBER 17 to 24	OCTOBER Total Obsn	OCTOBER MCWB
105/109																			0	68										
100/104																	1		1	67										
95/99												2	0	2	68		5	2	7	65										
90/94		1		1	61		1	1	2	64		9	3	12	66		23	10	33	63				0	63					
85/89		3	1	4	60		5	2	7	63		29	13	42	64		35	20	55	62		1		1	63		1		1	58
80/84		10	3	13	59		15	7	22	63		42	26	68	63	1	44	33	78	61		4	1	5	62		7	1	8	56
75/79		19	10	29	57		25	15	40	61	1	45	41	87	62	7	46	44	97	59		11	4	15	60		13	3	16	54
70/74	1	27	15	43	55	1	37	22	60	59	8	45	44	97	60	20	39	45	104	57		21	9	30	59		23	9	32	52
65/69	4	39	27	70	52	6	44	34	84	57	33	37	44	114	58	50	26	40	116	56	0	26	17	43	57	1	25	19	45	50
60/64	12	42	39	93	50	19	41	42	102	52	61	23	35	119	56	75	17	28	120	54	1	35	29	67	55	7	34	29	70	48
55/59	32	37	44	113	48	51	34	44	129	53	71	9	25	105	54	61	8	17	86	51	12	35	33	80	53	20	33	37	90	45
50/54	55	31	42	128	46	64	20	36	120	51	50	5	11	66	51	27	3	7	37	48	28	34	39	101	50	34	32	40	106	43
45/49	64	21	36	121	43	58	13	26	97	48	18	1	4	23	48	7	0	1	8	44	45	27	38	110	48	54	30	35	119	40
40/44	51	11	21	83	39	30	4	8	42	44	3	0	1	4	45	1			1	39	58	19	28	105	45	51	19	30	100	37
35/39	19	5	5	29	35	8	1	2	11	40	1			1	41						46	13	19	78	42	35	16	22	73	33
30/34	5	2	3	10	31	1	1	1	3	36											28	11	14	53	39	29	12	16	57	30
25/29	3	1	1	5	27	1	1	1	3	33											13	3	5	21	35	13	4	5	22	26
20/24	1	0	1	2	21																6	2	3	11	31	3	1	1	5	22
15/19	1			1	17																			0	26				0	16
10/14	0			0	14																									

COINCIDENT WET BULB TEMPERATURE FOR EACH DRY BULB TEMPERATURE RANGE

BILLINGS/LOGAN IAP MONTANA

Within each month block the columns are: Obsn Hour Gp "01 to 08", "09 to 16", "17 to 24"; Total Obsn; MCWB.

Temperature Range	NOV 01-08	NOV 09-16	NOV 17-24	NOV Total	NOV MCWB	DEC 01-08	DEC 09-16	DEC 17-24	DEC Total	DEC MCWB	JAN 01-08	JAN 09-16	JAN 17-24	JAN Total	JAN MCWB	FEB 01-08	FEB 09-16	FEB 17-24	FEB Total	FEB MCWB	MAR 01-08	MAR 09-16	MAR 17-24	MAR Total	MAR MCWB	APR 01-08	APR 09-16	APR 17-24	APR Total	APR MCWB	ANN 01-08	ANN 09-16	ANN 17-24	ANN Total	ANN MCWB
105/109																																		0	68
100/104																																3	0	3	67
95/99																																16	6	22	65
90/94																																62	26	88	64
85/89																											0	0	0	55		107	58	165	62
80/84																										0	2	1	3	55	2	154	103	259	60
75/79																										0	4	2	6	53	16	190	142	348	58
70/74																											11	5	16	51	63	218	181	462	56
65/69		3		3	49				0	47				0	48				0	50				0	51	0	14	8	22	49	147	212	206	565	54
60/64	0	9	2	11	46			1	1	45		1		1	45		1		1	49		2		2	50	2	23	17	42	47	246	216	227	689	51
55/59	2	19	8	29	44		4	1	5	42		3	1	4	42		2		2	47	0	5	2	7	48	5	29	22	56	45	279	208	227	714	48
50/54	8	26	18	52	41	1	13	4	18	40	1	7	3	11	40	0	8	3	11	44	0	10	4	14	46	15	33	29	77	42	280	212	226	718	44
45/49	17	35	28	80	38	5	22	11	38	37	5	19	12	36	37	2	14	8	24	41	0	15	9	24	43	29	37	40	106	39	275	231	229	735	40
40/44	34	37	42	113	35	24	38	33	95	34	16	28	24	68	34	6	23	16	45	38	3	20	17	40	41	43	31	39	113	37	299	247	264	810	36
35/39	44	31	43	118	32	37	42	48	127	31	26	30	32	88	31	20	33	27	80	34	9	27	22	58	38	50	24	32	106	33	296	220	266	782	32
30/34	48	29	34	111	29	46	37	43	126	28	33	30	34	97	28	32	33	37	102	32	22	38	32	92	35	48	19	27	94	30	304	192	242	738	29
25/29	29	17	21	67	25	38	23	34	95	24	32	26	28	86	24	37	22	27	86	28	39	35	41	115	32	33	10	14	57	26	229	124	157	510	25
20/24	21	10	15	46	20	33	18	23	74	20	26	20	22	68	20	23	15	18	56	25	50	31	41	122	29	12	2	4	18	21	147	79	99	325	20
15/19	14	8	10	32	16	18	13	11	42	16	22	16	20	58	16	16	13	12	41	20	44	21	27	92	25	3	0	1	4	17	91	61	67	219	16
10/14	9	6	7	22	11	14	12	15	41	11	17	17	14	48	11	16	13	12	41	16	28	13	15	56	20	1	0		1	12	66	53	57	176	11
5/9	6	3	4	13	7	11	8	8	27	7	17	11	14	42	6	14	11	13	38	11	17	11	13	41	16						54	36	41	131	6
0/4	4	3	4	11	2	7	7	7	21	1	13	11	13	37	2	12	9	10	31	6	11	7	8	26	11						39	31	36	106	2
-5/-1	2	2	2	6	-3	7	4	5	16	-3	9	10	9	28	-4	10	6	8	24	2	8	5	5	18	7						29	22	23	74	-3
-10/-6	1	1	1	3	-8	3	2	3	8	-8	10	13	11	34	-8	6	3	4	13	-3	5	4	4	13	2						24	16	20	60	-8
-15/-11	1			1	-13	2	1	1	4	-12	7	9	7	23	-13	4	1	2	7	-8	5	3	3	11	-3						17	8	9	34	-13
-20/-16	0			0	-18	1	0	1	2	-18	2	7	5	14	-18	2	0	0	2	-13	1	2	1	4	-8						10	2	6	18	-18
-25/-21						1	0	1	2	-23	0	2	0	2	-22	1	0	0	1	-18	1	0	0	1	-17						2	1	1	4	-23
-30/-26									0	-26	0	0	0	0	-27	0			0	-21											0	0	0	0	-26

GREAT FALLS, MONTANA
READINGS TAKEN AT MALMSTROM AFB

LAT 47 30N   LONG 111 11W   ELEV 3525 FT

MEAN FREQUENCY OF OCCURRENCE OF DRY BULB TEMPERATURE (DEGREES F) WITH MEAN COINCIDENT WET BULB TEMPERATURE (DEGREES F) FOR EACH DRY BULB TEMPERATURE RANGE

Temperature Range	MAY 01-08	MAY 09-16	MAY 17-24	MAY Total Obsn	MAY MCWB	JUNE 01-08	JUNE 09-16	JUNE 17-24	JUNE Total Obsn	JUNE MCWB	JULY 01-08	JULY 09-16	JULY 17-24	JULY Total Obsn	JULY MCWB	AUG 01-08	AUG 09-16	AUG 17-24	AUG Total Obsn	AUG MCWB	SEP 01-08	SEP 09-16	SEP 17-24	SEP Total Obsn	SEP MCWB	OCT 01-08	OCT 09-16	OCT 17-24	OCT Total Obsn	OCT MCWB
105/109																		0	0	65										
100/104		0		0	60				0	58			0	0	62		1	0	1	64										
95/99		2	0	2	58		3	1	4	60		2	1	3	62		4	2	6	62		1	0	1	61					
90/94		8	3	11	57		8	4	12	61		13	7	20	61		20	9	29	61		3	1	4	59					
85/89		15	7	22	55		19	8	27	59		33	18	51	61		35	18	53	60		10	3	13	59		1	0	1	56
80/84		26	14	40	53	1	32	17	50	57		49	29	78	60	0	36	22	58	58		17	6	23	57		4	0	4	55
75/79	3	34	23	60	51	3	39	27	69	55	4	50	35	89	58	3	40	30	73	57		21	11	32	56		11	2	13	53
70/74	12	35	28	75	49	13	40	34	87	54	14	47	41	102	56	12	41	42	95	55	4	31	19	54	54		19	4	23	52
65/69	22	39	38	99	46	29	41	41	111	52	35	29	45	109	55	33	33	43	109	53	6	35	26	67	52	1	23	9	33	49
60/64	37	36	46	119	44	55	30	45	130	50	60	15	36	111	53	56	19	37	112	51	24	37	36	97	49	7	30	19	56	47
55/59	61	29	39	129	42	69	20	40	129	47	70	6	24	100	50	63	11	26	100	49	36	26	38	100	47	20	35	30	85	45
50/54	60	15	31	106	38	48	7	16	71	44	47	3	10	60	47	51	5	14	70	46	50	22	34	106	44	34	38	43	115	42
45/49	36	6	12	54	34	15	1	4	20	39	14	0	2	16	43	23	1	5	29	43	47	16	30	93	42	42	31	39	112	39
40/44	13	2	3	18	30	5	0	1	6	35	5	0	0	5	38	5	0	1	6	38	35	11	18	64	38	46	21	37	104	36
35/39						1	0	0	1	31	0	0	0	0	33	1	0	0	1	36	21	6	9	36	34	38	13	27	78	33
30/34						0			0	28									0	25	11	5	7	23	30	29	10	18	57	29
25/29	3	0	1	4	26																4	1	1	6	26	18	9	11	38	26
20/24	1	0	0	1	22																0	0	0	0	22	10	2	5	17	22
15/19	0			0	19																					2	2	1	5	17
10/14																										1	1	0	2	12
5/9																										0	0	0	0	7
0/4																										0	0	0	0	2

COINCIDENT WET BULB TEMPERATURE FOR EACH DRY BULB TEMPERATURE RANGE

GREAT FALLS, MONTANA
READINGS TAKEN AT MALMSTROM AFB

Temperature Range	Nov 01–08	Nov 09–16	Nov 17–24	Nov Total Obsn	Nov MCWB	Dec 01–08	Dec 09–16	Dec 17–24	Dec Total Obsn	Dec MCWB	Jan 01–08	Jan 09–16	Jan 17–24	Jan Total Obsn	Jan MCWB	Feb 01–08	Feb 09–16	Feb 17–24	Feb Total Obsn	Feb MCWB	Mar 01–08	Mar 09–16	Mar 17–24	Mar Total Obsn	Mar MCWB	Apr 01–08	Apr 09–16	Apr 17–24	Apr Total Obsn	Apr MCWB	Ann 01–08	Ann 09–16	Ann 17–24	Ann Total Obsn	Ann MCWB
105/109																																		0	65
100/104																																1	0	1	63
95/99																																7	3	10	62
90/94																													0	57		39	18	57	61
85/89																											1	0	1	55		89	43	132	60
80/84																															0	134	68	202	59
75/79		0		0	53																	0		0	52	0	2	1	3	53	8	171	103	282	57
70/74		1		1	51																	1	0	1	49	0	6	2	8	51	33	211	149	393	55
65/69		2		2	47														0	48		3	1	4	47	0	9	4	13	49	91	208	185	484	53
60/64		7	1	8	46		1		1	44		1		1	46		3		3	47		9	3	12	46	1	19	10	30	46	189	217	211	617	50
55/59	2	16	5	23	44	1	5	1	7	42	3			3	43		7	2	9	44	2	13	5	20	43	3	33	18	54	44	274	224	232	730	47
50/54	12	30	17	59	41	3	17	5	25	40	2	10	4	16	41	3	16	6	25	41	2	22	12	36	40	13	37	29	79	41	323	256	260	839	44
45/49	20	33	27	80	38	13	23	19	55	37	10	19	12	41	38	7	21	14	42	38	9	33	23	65	38	24	39	37	100	38	318	252	263	833	40
40/44	34	40	37	111	35	26	31	27	84	35	20	30	27	77	35	17	31	24	72	35	24	37	33	94	35	38	32	44	114	36	325	249	283	857	36
35/39	40	34	40	114	32	31	35	32	98	31	30	28	33	91	32	28	30	34	92	32	34	31	41	106	32	49	24	38	111	33	313	207	267	787	32
30/34	37	24	38	99	29	29	32	31	92	28	29	23	26	78	28	35	22	34	91	28	47	27	36	110	29	58	21	31	110	30	289	166	224	679	29
25/29	33	15	27	75	25	28	22	31	81	24	20	18	19	57	24	31	19	25	75	24	39	17	29	85	25	29	10	16	55	25	205	111	160	476	25
20/24	22	11	13	46	21	31	16	27	74	20	21	16	20	57	20	26	17	19	62	21	30	14	19	63	21	16	5	8	29	21	157	81	111	349	21
15/19	13	7	11	31	16	17	12	17	46	16	15	14	14	43	16	19	14	16	49	16	14	9	11	34	16	6	1	1	8	17	86	59	71	216	16
10/14	8	8	11	27	11	13	9	9	31	11	16	14	14	44	11	15	14	13	42	11	11	12	9	32	11	2			2	12	65	57	57	179	11
5/9	8	4	5	17	6	11	12	11	34	6	15	13	11	39	6	12	12	13	37	6	11	9	11	31	7	1			1	7	58	50	51	159	6
0/4	6	4	5	15	2	13	13	13	39	1	13	13	15	41	1	16	11	11	38	2	8	5	5	18	2				0		56	46	49	151	2
-5/-1	3	3	3	9	-3	12	11	13	36	-3	14	14	14	42	-3	6	4	6	16	-3	7	4	5	16	-3						42	36	41	119	-3
-10/-6	2	1	1	4	-8	10	6	6	22	-8	17	13	13	43	-8	5	2	5	12	-8	5	2	3	10	-8						39	24	28	91	-8
-15/-11	1	1		2	-13	3	1	3	7	-13	12	10	12	34	-13	5	1	2	8	-13	4	1	1	6	-13						25	14	18	57	-13
-20/-16	1			1	-17	1	1	1	3	-18	7	5	6	18	-18				0	-17	1	0	0	1	-17						10	6	7	23	-18
-25/-21						1	1	1	3	-23	4	3	4	11	-23						0			0	-22						5	4	5	14	-23
-30/-26						1	0	0	1	-27	2	0	1	3	-28																3	0	1	4	-28
-35/-31						0	0	0	0	-33	1	0	0	1	-32																1	0	0	1	-32
-40/-36						0	0	0	0																						0	0	0	0	
-45/-41						0	0	0	0																						0	0	0	0	

(Obsn Hour Gp = 01 to 08, 09 to 16, 17 to 24; MCWB = M C W B)

NORTH PLATTE/LEE BIRD FLD NEBRASKA
LAT 41 08N   LONG 100 41W   ELEV 2775 FT

MEAN FREQUENCY OF OCCURRENCE OF DRY BULB TEMPERATURE (DEGREES F) WITH MEAN COINCIDENT WET BULB TEMPERATURE (DEGREES F) FOR EACH DRY BULB TEMPERATURE RANGE

Temperature Range	MAY 01-08	MAY 09-16	MAY 17-24	MAY Total	MAY MCWB	JUNE 01-08	JUNE 09-16	JUNE 17-24	JUNE Total	JUNE MCWB	JULY 01-08	JULY 09-16	JULY 17-24	JULY Total	JULY MCWB	AUG 01-08	AUG 09-16	AUG 17-24	AUG Total	AUG MCWB	SEP 01-08	SEP 09-16	SEP 17-24	SEP Total	SEP MCWB	OCT 01-08	OCT 09-16	OCT 17-24	OCT Total	OCT MCWB
110/114								0	0	71		0	0	0	70															
105/109?												1		1	69															
100/104							2	1	3	70		3	1	4	70		2	1	3	69										
95/99				0	61		7	3	10	69		12	6	18	70		10	4	14	69				0	65					
90/94		1	1	2	63		14	7	21	69		29	15	44	69		28	11	39	69		3	1	4	66				0	60
85/89		7	3	10	63		26	15	41	68		44	27	71	68		43	22	65	68		10	2	12	66		6	1	7	59
80/84		15	8	23	62	2	41	29	72	66	4	57	42	103	66	2	49	34	85	67		18	7	25	65		12	2	14	58
75/79		26	14	40	61	7	43	33	83	64	18	47	46	111	64	11	49	48	108	66		28	14	42	63		21	6	27	57
70/74	2	38	25	65	58	22	41	41	104	63	49	33	46	128	63	41	36	52	129	65	3	35	22	60	61		25	10	35	55
65/69	9	46	31	86	56	47	33	40	120	60	74	14	38	126	60	71	21	40	132	62	9	38	28	75	60	1	32	18	51	53
60/64	23	44	46	113	54	61	19	34	114	58	63	6	22	91	58	70	8	26	104	59	21	33	36	90	58	8	36	28	72	51
55/59	52	33	45	130	52	53	9	23	85	54	30	1	5	36	54	33	2	8	43	55	36	30	39	105	55	17	34	35	86	48
50/54	62	18	37	117	48	31	5	9	45	50	8	0	1	9	51	13	0	2	15	50	44	21	37	102	52	28	29	38	95	46
45/49	44	12	20	76	44	12	1	3	16	45	1			1	46	3	0	1	4	46	46	14	25	85	48	37	20	36	93	42
40/44	30	6	13	49	40	4	0	1	5	40	1			1	42	2			2	42	39	8	17	64	44	47	18	34	99	39
35/39	17	2	3	22	36	2	0	0	2	37						0			0	37	25	3	9	37	40	47	10	22	79	35
30/34	7	1	1	9	31																13	0	2	15	36	31	4	11	46	31
25/29	1	0	0	1	26																3	0	0	3	31	21	1	6	28	26
20/24	0	0	0	0	22																1	0	0	1	27	8	0	1	9	22
15/19																					0			0	23	2	0	0	2	16
10/14																										0			0	12

COINCIDENT WET BULB TEMPERATURE FOR EACH DRY BULB TEMPERATURE RANGE

NORTH PLATTE/LEE BIRD FLD NEBRASKA

Temperature Range	NOVEMBER Obsn Hour Gp 01 to 08	NOVEMBER 09 to 16	NOVEMBER 17 to 24	NOVEMBER Total Obsn	NOVEMBER MCWB	DECEMBER Obsn Hour Gp 01 to 08	DECEMBER 09 to 16	DECEMBER 17 to 24	DECEMBER Total Obsn	DECEMBER MCWB	JANUARY Obsn Hour Gp 01 to 08	JANUARY 09 to 16	JANUARY 17 to 24	JANUARY Total Obsn	JANUARY MCWB
110/114															
105/109															
100/104															
95/99															
90/94															
85/89															
80/84															
75/79		0		0	53										
70/74		5	0	5	51		0		0	51		0		0	50
65/69		8	1	9	49		1	0	1	49		1	0	1	47
60/64		13	3	16	47	0	4	0	4	45		3	0	3	45
55/59	0	22	6	28	44	0	9	1	10	43		6	1	7	43
50/54	1	29	13	43	42	0	14	3	17	41		12	3	15	40
45/49	6	30	23	59	39	1	21	8	30	38	0	17	6	23	38
40/44	15	28	33	76	36	2	31	14	47	35	1	26	12	39	35
35/39	30	30	44	104	33	12	33	30	75	32	5	27	24	56	32
30/34	44	29	44	117	29	28	34	42	104	29	17	31	38	86	29
25/29	55	19	33	107	25	42	32	50	124	25	35	26	42	103	25
20/24	42	12	18	72	21	57	23	38	118	21	50	26	29	105	21
15/19	22	7	10	39	16	41	16	20	77	16	39	23	28	90	16
10/14	10	4	5	19	11	23	15	18	56	11	26	17	19	62	11
5/9	8	2	3	13	6	20	8	13	41	6	26	10	17	53	6
0/4	4	0	2	6	1	11	4	6	21	2	18	13	13	44	1
-5/-1	2	0	1	3	-3	8	2	3	13	-3	16	7	9	32	-4
-10/-6	1			1	-8	4	0	2	6	-8	9	3	4	16	-8
-15/-11						1	0	0	1	-13	3	1	2	6	-13
-20/-16						0			0	-17	2	0	0	2	-17
-25/-21											1			1	-22

Temperature Range	FEBRUARY Obsn Hour Gp 01 to 08	FEBRUARY 09 to 16	FEBRUARY 17 to 24	FEBRUARY Total Obsn	FEBRUARY MCWB	MARCH Obsn Hour Gp 01 to 08	MARCH 09 to 16	MARCH 17 to 24	MARCH Total Obsn	MARCH MCWB	APRIL Obsn Hour Gp 01 to 08	APRIL 09 to 16	APRIL 17 to 24	APRIL Total Obsn	APRIL MCWB
110/114															
105/109															
100/104															
95/99															
90/94															
85/89												2	1	3	57
80/84							0	0	0	54		6	2	8	57
75/79		0	0	0	53		2	1	3	52		8	4	12	55
70/74		1	0	1	51		5	2	7	50	0	14	8	22	54
65/69		3	1	4	49		7	3	10	49	0	22	15	37	51
60/64		5	2	7	46	0	9	6	15	47	3	27	20	50	49
55/59		11	3	14	44	0	15	9	24	44	10	34	27	71	47
50/54	0	15	7	22	41	2	22	15	39	42	20	33	32	85	44
45/49	1	21	12	34	39	7	27	22	56	39	29	28	34	91	41
40/44	4	20	18	42	36	11	29	26	66	36	43	26	34	103	38
35/39	12	30	30	72	33	28	34	34	96	33	47	21	26	94	34
30/34	30	31	40	101	30	57	34	42	133	30	43	15	25	83	30
25/29	49	26	35	110	25	48	28	37	113	25	29	4	11	44	26
20/24	40	19	24	83	21	36	18	23	77	21	12	0	2	14	21
15/19	29	18	19	66	16	23	8	13	44	16	3		0	3	17
10/14	23	13	16	52	11	17	5	9	31	11	0		0	0	14
5/9	15	6	9	30	7	11	3	4	18	6					
0/4	8	3	5	16	2	5	1	2	8	2					
-5/-1	5	1	2	8	-3	1	0	0	1	-3					
-10/-6	3	0	0	3	-8	0	0	0	0	-8					
-15/-11	2	0	0	2	-13	0	0	0	0	-13					
-20/-16	1		0	1	-18	1		0	1	-18					
-25/-21	0			0	-22	0			0	-21					

Temperature Range	ANNUAL TOTAL Obsn Hour Gp 01 to 08	ANNUAL TOTAL 09 to 16	ANNUAL TOTAL 17 to 24	ANNUAL TOTAL Total Obsn	ANNUAL TOTAL MCWB
110/114		0	0	0	70
105/109		1	0	1	69
100/104		7	3	10	70
95/99		32	14	46	69
90/94		82	36	118	69
85/89	0	146	76	222	67
80/84	8	208	131	347	65
75/79	39	231	174	444	64
70/74	123	236	212	571	61
65/69	223	221	223	667	59
60/64	264	204	226	694	55
55/59	239	197	200	636	50
50/54	211	191	185	587	46
45/49	180	185	182	547	41
40/44	185	187	194	566	37
35/39	213	187	215	615	33
30/34	260	179	243	682	30
25/29	281	136	214	631	25
20/24	245	98	135	478	21
15/19	159	72	90	321	16
10/14	99	54	67	220	11
5/9	80	29	46	155	6
0/4	46	21	28	95	1
-5/-1	32	10	15	57	-3
-10/-6	17	3	6	26	-8
-15/-11	6	1	2	9	-13
-20/-16	4	0	0	4	-17
-25/-21	1			1	-22

OMAHA, NEBRASKA
READINGS TAKEN AT OFFUTT AFB

LAT 41 07N   LONG 95 55W   ELEV 1048 FT

MEAN FREQUENCY OF OCCURRENCE OF DRY BULB TEMPERATURE (DEGREES F) WITH MEAN COINCIDENT WET BULB TEMPERATURE (DEGREES F) FOR EACH DRY BULB TEMPERATURE RANGE

Temperature Range	MAY					JUNE					JULY					AUGUST					SEPTEMBER					OCTOBER				
	01 to 08	09 to 16	17 to 24	Total Obsn	MCWB	01 to 08	09 to 16	17 to 24	Total Obsn	MCWB	01 to 08	09 to 16	17 to 24	Total Obsn	MCWB	01 to 08	09 to 16	17 to 24	Total Obsn	MCWB	01 to 08	09 to 16	17 to 24	Total Obsn	MCWB	01 to 08	09 to 16	17 to 24	Total Obsn	MCWB
105/109													0	0	78															
100/104												1	1	2	78															
95/99		0	0	0	67		0		0	75		7	3	10	77				0	77										
90/94		2	1	3	66		3	1	4	74		24	11	35	76		3	1	4	76				0	72		1		1	64
85/89		12	4	16	68		12	5	17	73		49	30	79	73		19	6	25	75		5	1	6	74		2		2	66
80/84		25	14	39	67		31	17	48	71	8	63	52	123	71		45	23	68	73		12	5	17	73		8	2	10	66
75/79	1	35	26	62	64	2	45	32	79	70	37	55	61	153	69	5	59	44	108	71		23	13	36	70	0	19	7	26	63
70/74	14	41	35	90	61	14	53	51	118	67	78	37	57	172	67	25	53	57	135	69	7	35	25	67	67	3	26	15	44	60
65/69	28	40	43	111	58	42	46	54	142	64	74	11	27	112	63	63	40	57	160	66	17	44	33	94	64	8	33	27	68	58
60/64	51	36	45	132	55	69	31	42	142	61	36	2	7	45	59	73	19	39	131	63	30	43	47	120	61	17	37	36	90	54
55/59	48	28	39	115	51	62	13	26	101	58	11		1	12	54	52	8	16	76	59	45	35	47	127	57	34	39	38	111	51
50/54	46	18	25	89	47	31	6	9	46	54	3	0		3	50	23	1	5	29	55	53	26	36	115	53	38	31	39	108	46
45/49	31	8	12	51	43	15	0	2	17	49				0	42	6	0	0	6	50	45	11	22	78	49	44	24	37	105	43
40/44	19	2	4	25	39	4	0	0	4	45						1			1	45	30	5	10	45	44	42	18	25	85	38
35/39	7	1		8	34	0			0	41						0			0	42	9	1	2	12	40	35	7	15	57	34
30/34	2	1		3	30																3	0	0	3	36	19	2	4	25	30
25/29	0			0	25																1		0	1	31	5		1	6	26
20/24																								0	28	2			2	22

OMAHA, NEBRASKA
READINGS TAKEN AT OFFUTT AFB

Temperature Range	NOVEMBER Obsn Hour Gp 01 to 08	NOVEMBER 09 to 16	NOVEMBER 17 to 24	NOVEMBER Total Obsn	NOVEMBER MCWB	DECEMBER Obsn Hour Gp 01 to 08	DECEMBER 09 to 16	DECEMBER 17 to 24	DECEMBER Total Obsn	DECEMBER MCWB	JANUARY Obsn Hour Gp 01 to 08	JANUARY 09 to 16	JANUARY 17 to 24	JANUARY Total Obsn	JANUARY MCWB	FEBRUARY Obsn Hour Gp 01 to 08	FEBRUARY 09 to 16	FEBRUARY 17 to 24	FEBRUARY Total Obsn	FEBRUARY MCWB
105/109																				
100/104																				
95/99																				
90/94																				
85/89																				
80/84		0		0	63															
75/79		1		1	61															
70/74		1	0	1	59												0		0	52
65/69	0	8	3	11	55		0		0	51							0		0	51
60/64	1	14	7	22	52		2	0	2	51		0		0	47		1	0	1	49
55/59	2	20	11	33	49	1	6	3	10	49		2	0	2	45		3	1	4	48
50/54	8	30	24	62	46	3	13	5	21	44		3	1	4	42	1	10	4	15	44
45/49	21	35	31	87	42	3	15	10	28	41	0	9	5	14	39	2	17	9	28	41
40/44	34	34	42	110	38	5	20	19	44	37	3	16	10	29	37	3	21	19	43	37
35/39	44	38	43	125	34	23	35	35	93	33	12	26	28	66	34	19	27	32	78	33
30/34	55	30	39	124	29	42	41	48	131	29	29	28	37	94	30	41	33	40	114	30
25/29	35	15	21	71	25	46	34	38	118	25	36	30	32	98	25	36	31	32	99	25
20/24	19	9	9	37	20	39	29	28	96	20	33	31	29	93	21	31	26	24	81	20
15/19	12	3	7	22	16	33	24	27	84	16	25	26	24	75	16	21	22	24	67	15
10/14	5	1	2	8	11	22	12	14	48	11	29	25	28	82	11	23	18	20	61	11
5/9	3	1	1	5	6	12	9	9	30	6	27	23	22	72	6	21	10	11	42	6
0/4	0	0	1	1	2	9	4	5	18	1	22	15	18	55	1	15	5	5	25	1
-5/-1		0	0	0	-3	4	2	4	10	-3	16	9	11	36	-3	6	1	2	9	-3
-10/-6	0	0		0	-8	4	1	1	6	-8	9	4	4	17	-8	2	0	1	3	-8
-15/-11	0			0	-11	1	0	0	1	-12	6	1	1	8	-13	1	0	0	1	-13
-20/-16											1	0		1	-17	0			0	-17

Temperature Range	MARCH Obsn Hour Gp 01 to 08	MARCH 09 to 16	MARCH 17 to 24	MARCH Total Obsn	MARCH MCWB	APRIL Obsn Hour Gp 01 to 08	APRIL 09 to 16	APRIL 17 to 24	APRIL Total Obsn	APRIL MCWB	ANNUAL TOTAL Obsn Hour Gp 01 to 08	ANNUAL TOTAL 09 to 16	ANNUAL TOTAL 17 to 24	ANNUAL TOTAL Total Obsn	ANNUAL TOTAL MCWB
105/109													0	0	78
100/104												1	1	2	77
95/99												13	5	18	76
90/94							0		0	70		63	24	87	75
85/89		0	0	0	64		2	1	3	63	0	153	80	233	72
80/84		1	0	1	60		7	3	10	62	15	231	160	406	70
75/79		2	1	3	57		10	6	16	60	84	263	234	581	67
70/74	1	7	3	11	55	1	19	12	32	58	219	261	266	746	64
65/69	1	7	5	13	53	5	24	20	49	55	288	216	253	757	60
60/64	1	10	7	18	50	11	30	26	67	52	276	188	217	681	56
55/59	3	13	11	27	47	19	38	36	93	48	225	182	190	597	51
50/54	8	17	16	41	44	39	35	40	114	45	212	168	178	558	46
45/49	10	25	22	57	40	40	32	38	110	42	186	170	174	530	42
40/44	20	31	31	82	37	44	25	31	100	38	179	168	183	530	38
35/39	37	44	42	123	34	40	13	17	70	34	220	190	213	623	34
30/34	57	36	47	140	30	28	5	8	41	30	274	176	223	673	30
25/29	45	24	25	94	25	10	0	1	11	25	213	134	150	497	25
20/24	27	14	19	60	20	3		0	3	21	154	109	109	372	20
15/19	18	8	10	36	16	0			0	16	109	83	92	284	16
10/14	10	6	5	21	11						89	62	69	220	11
5/9	7	2	2	11	6						70	45	45	160	6
0/4	1	1	1	3	2						47	25	30	102	1
-5/-1	1	0	0	1	-3						27	12	17	56	-3
-10/-6	1	0	0	1	-8						16	5	6	27	-8
-15/-11	1			1	-13						9	1	1	11	-13
-20/-16											1	0		1	-17

LAS VEGAS, NEVADA/NELLIS AFB

LAT 36 15N   LONG 115 02W   ELEV 1868 FT

MEAN FREQUENCY OF OCCURRENCE OF DRY BULB TEMPERATURE (DEGREES F) WITH MEAN COINCIDENT WET BULB TEMPERATURE (DEGREES F) FOR EACH DRY BULB TEMPERATURE RANGE

Temperature Range	MAY 01–08	MAY 09–16	MAY 17–24	MAY Total Obsn	MAY MCWB	JUNE 01–08	JUNE 09–16	JUNE 17–24	JUNE Total Obsn	JUNE MCWB	JULY 01–08	JULY 09–16	JULY 17–24	JULY Total Obsn	JULY MCWB	AUGUST 01–08	AUGUST 09–16	AUGUST 17–24	AUGUST Total Obsn	AUGUST MCWB	SEPTEMBER 01–08	SEPTEMBER 09–16	SEPTEMBER 17–24	SEPTEMBER Total Obsn	SEPTEMBER MCWB	OCTOBER 01–08	OCTOBER 09–16	OCTOBER 17–24	OCTOBER Total Obsn	OCTOBER MCWB
115/119																														
110/114														0	66				0	71										
105/109		0		0	65				0	71		13	4	17	68		5	1	6	70		4		4	67					
100/104		6	2	8	63		6	2	8	67		44	19	63	68		29	11	40	69		23	6	29	65				0	64
95/99		22	8	30	61		20	8	28	66	0	77	41	118	66		65	31	96	68		43	14	57	64		4		4	62
90/94	0	44	19	63	59	0	43	21	64	64	5	64	51	120	65	2	67	46	115	67	1	52	27	80	62		19	3	22	60
85/89	2	51	31	84	57	2	48	29	79	62	27	35	56	118	64	16	49	52	121	66	7	48	41	96	61		35	9	44	58
80/84	10	41	40	91	55	8	45	39	92	60	58	11	44	113	62	51	24	32	127	64	18	35	44	97	59	1	46	18	65	56
75/79	27	28	45	100	53	22	34	45	101	58	68	3	24	95	60	79	6	14	117	63	40	21	45	106	57	4	45	30	79	54
70/74	41	24	38	103	51	43	22	41	106	56	51	1	8	60	57	56	2	4	72	60	58	10	34	102	54	12	38	40	90	52
65/69	54	16	30	100	49	47	15	28	90	54	27	1	2	30	53	29	1	1	34	56	59	2	19	80	51	30	31	48	109	50
60/64	53	10	19	82	47	53	6	16	75	52	10		0	10	48	12		1	13	52	35		7	43	47	52	18	44	114	48
55/59	38	3	12	53	45	36	2	8	46	50	2			2	44	2			2	46	16		2	18	43	62	8	33	103	45
50/54	18	1	3	22	42	20		2	22	48				0	42				1	44	4			4	39	48	3	16	67	42
45/49	4			4	39	6		1	7	46									0	39	1			1	36	27	1	4	32	38
40/44	1			1	38				1	44																8	2	1	11	34
35/39																										3	1		4	28
30/34																										1			1	24
25/29																													0	21

COINCIDENT WET BULB TEMPERATURE FOR EACH DRY BULB TEMPERATURE RANGE

LAS VEGAS, NEVADA/NELLIS AFB

Obsn Hour Gp columns shown as 01 to 08, 09 to 16, 17 to 24; then Total Obsn and MCWB.

Temperature Range	NOVEMBER					DECEMBER					JANUARY					FEBRUARY					MARCH					APRIL					ANNUAL TOTAL				
	01 to 08	09 to 16	17 to 24	Total Obsn	MCWB	01 to 08	09 to 16	17 to 24	Total Obsn	MCWB	01 to 08	09 to 16	17 to 24	Total Obsn	MCWB	01 to 08	09 to 16	17 to 24	Total Obsn	MCWB	01 to 08	09 to 16	17 to 24	Total Obsn	MCWB	01 to 08	09 to 16	17 to 24	Total Obsn	MCWB	01 to 08	09 to 16	17 to 24	Total Obsn	MCWB
115/119																																	0	0	69
110/114																																24	7	31	68
105/109																																97	38	135	68
100/104																											1		1	60	0	214	101	315	66
95/99																										0	10	2	12	58	9	249	148	406	65
90/94																						0	0	0	58		19	7	26	56	52	254	202	508	63
85/89																						2		2	56		34	15	49	54	140	224	229	593	60
80/84		3		3	55												1		1	56		9	3	12	54						219	200	217	636	58
75/79		16	1	17	53		0		0	51		1		1	56		7	1	8	54		23	8	31	52	2	44	28	74	52	227	203	208	638	55
70/74	0	31	5	36	51		3		3	49		3	1	4	52		16	5	21	51		39	18	57	50	9	42	39	90	50	229	214	202	645	52
65/69	1	48	17	66	49		14	1	15	48	0	15	2	17	49	1	28	11	40	49	3	46	31	80	48	25	36	41	102	47	231	238	209	678	49
60/64	6	47	32	85	47	2	34	6	42	47	1	38	10	49	46	3	46	24	73	46	12	48	43	103	45	41	27	39	107	45	229	269	226	724	47
55/59	21	45	50	116	45	3	54	18	75	44	4	48	23	75	44	14	51	42	107	44	31	40	51	122	43	54	18	32	104	43	250	267	264	781	44
50/54	44	29	58	131	42	11	52	41	104	42	15	50	42	107	41	30	39	53	122	41	54	25	44	123	40	52	8	24	84	41	277	207	281	765	41
45/49	59	14	42	115	39	25	43	57	125	38	28	41	53	122	38	47	24	45	116	38	61	11	30	102	37	39	0	11	52	38	291	136	242	669	38
40/44	52	5	24	81	35	41	29	61	131	35	36	29	49	114	34	51	10	29	90	35	50	4	14	68	34	16	0	2	18	35	255	78	181	514	35
35/39	36	1	8	45	32	60	14	42	116	31	53	14	36	104	31	45	3	12	60	31	25	0	4	29	30	3			3	31	225	33	103	361	31
30/34	16		2	18	27	71	5	19	95	28	55	6	22	83	27	24	0	3	27	27	9	2	1	12	26	0			0	27	176	11	47	234	27
25/29	3		0	3	24	27	0	4	31	24	39	1	8	48	23	9		1	10	23	2	1		3	21						80	1	13	94	23
20/24	0			0	19	7	0	0	7	19	13	1	2	16	18	1			1	18	1			1	17						22	1	2	25	18
15/19						1		0	1	10	3		0	3	14																4			4	14
10/14						0			0		0			0	9																0			0	9

WINNEMUCCA MAP NEVADA
LAT 40 54N   LONG 117 48W   ELEV 4301 FT

MEAN FREQUENCY OF OCCURRENCE OF DRY BULB TEMPERATURE (DEGREES F) WITH MEAN COINCIDENT WET BULB TEMPERATURE (DEGREES F) FOR EACH DRY BULB TEMPERATURE RANGE

Hour groups: 01 to 08 / 09 to 16 / 17 to 24. MWCB = Mean Coincident Wet Bulb.

Temperature Range	MAY 01-08	MAY 09-16	MAY 17-24	MAY Total	MAY MWCB	JUNE 01-08	JUNE 09-16	JUNE 17-24	JUNE Total	JUNE MWCB	JULY 01-08	JULY 09-16	JULY 17-24	JULY Total	JULY MWCB	AUG 01-08	AUG 09-16	AUG 17-24	AUG Total	AUG MWCB	SEP 01-08	SEP 09-16	SEP 17-24	SEP Total	SEP MWCB	OCT 01-08	OCT 09-16	OCT 17-24	OCT Total	OCT MWCB
100/104																														
95/99														0	63				0	60										
90/94		2	0	2	59		1	0	1	63		28	7	35	61		12	2	14	60		5	1	6	60					
85/89		7	2	9	57		6	1	7	61		71	30	101	59		48	15	63	58		18	1	19	60				0	56
80/84		20	6	26	56		10	5	15	59	2	64	29	95	58		67	28	95	57		42	7	49	57		14		14	54
75/79	1	33	13	47	53		25	11	36	57	10	42	35	87	57	2	56	24	82	55		49	14	63	55		33	2	35	52
70/74	3	40	18	61	51	1	38	19	58	55	25	24	37	86	55	16	34	32	82	54	2	44	20	66	53		33	5	38	50
65/69	10	31	25	66	49	5	39	21	65	53	33	12	45	90	53	24	17	37	78	51	7	32	29	68	51		43	10	53	48
60/64	16	35	37	88	48	11	33	27	71	52	40	4	31	78	51	30	9	38	77	50	16	24	34	74	49	6	34	21	61	46
55/59	27	30	38	95	45	24	34	36	94	50	46	2	23	71	49	29	4	32	65	47	21	13	37	71	46	13	32	27	72	44
50/54	39	21	38	98	43	29	27	38	94	48	36	3	8	44	46	35	1	26	62	45	23	9	35	67	44	20	27	38	85	42
45/49	48	17	33	98	41	36	17	31	84	46	30	0	3	33	42	43		9	52	41	30	3	27	60	41	28	17	47	92	39
40/44	41	11	23	75	38	47	9	29	85	44	18		0	18	38	38		3	41	38	36	1	18	55	39	33	9	47	89	36
35/39	38	2	11	51	34	40	2	12	54	41	8			8	35	21			21	34	42	1	11	54	35	38	6	26	70	32
30/34	16		3	19	30	26	1	7	34	37	1			1	32	10			10	31	38	1	4	43	32	41	2	17	60	29
25/29	6		0	6	25	12		2	14	33	0			0	29	1			1	27	17		0	17	27	42		5	47	24
20/24	1			1	20	6		0	6	29											6			6	23	17		2	19	20
15/19	1			1	16	2			2	24											1			1	19	6		1	7	15
10/14																										3			3	12
5/9																										0			0	9

COINCIDENT WET BULB TEMPERATURE FOR EACH DRY BULB TEMPERATURE RANGE

WINNEMUCCA MAP NEVADA

Temperature Range	NOV 01–08	NOV 09–16	NOV 17–24	NOV Total Obsn	NOV MCWB	DEC 01–08	DEC 09–16	DEC 17–24	DEC Total Obsn	DEC MCWB	JAN 01–08	JAN 09–16	JAN 17–24	JAN Total Obsn	JAN MCWB	FEB 01–08	FEB 09–16	FEB 17–24	FEB Total Obsn	FEB MCWB	MAR 01–08	MAR 09–16	MAR 17–24	MAR Total Obsn	MAR MCWB	APR 01–08	APR 09–16	APR 17–24	APR Total Obsn	APR MCWB	ANNUAL 01–08	ANNUAL 09–16	ANNUAL 17–24	ANNUAL Total Obsn	ANNUAL MCWB
100/104																																1	0	1	63
95/99																																51	11	62	60
90/94																																149	51	200	59
85/89																															2	205	77	284	57
80/84																											1		1	54	13	220	98	331	56
75/79		1		1	49																						11	2	13	51	49	218	127	394	54
70/74		9		9	47																	3	0	3	48		26	6	32	50	78	197	167	442	51
65/69	0	32		32	45												2		2	47		8	1	9	46	1	37	14	52	47	121	204	189	514	49
60/64	1	35	3	39	44							3		3	48		8	1	9	45		17	4	21	44	5	42	21	68	45	152	217	214	583	47
55/59						1	4	1	6	46		8	1	9	45		17	1	18	43	1	34	12	47	42	10	39	30	79	44	183	226	213	622	44
50/54	1	38	13	52	41	2	16	3	21	43	1	18	3	22	42	1	24	10	35	41	1	42	22	65	40	23	34	47	104	41	238	232	242	712	42
45/49	8	31	31	70	39	7	34	8	49	39	11	28	17	56	40	4	31	16	51	38	11	36	31	78	38	35	21	40	96	39	284	218	256	758	39
40/44	20	32	38	90	36	10	45	19	74	36	17	46	31	94	36	15	41	25	81	35	28	37	41	106	35	46	15	39	100	36	307	238	281	826	36
35/39	28	33	40	101	32	20	57	34	111	33	32	54	46	132	33	22	40	43	105	32	34	30	46	110	32	39	12	20	71	32	312	235	272	819	32
30/34	32	18	47	97	29	41	51	58	150	30	49	40	56	145	30	43	35	51	129	29	55	28	38	121	29	35	4	13	52	28	336	178	283	797	29
25/29	43	6	30	79	25	34	24	48	106	25	42	27	31	100	25	45	19	45	109	25	40	13	30	83	24	24	1	5	30	25	284	90	194	568	25
20/24	40	2	17	59	20	34	11	34	79	21	26	14	26	66	21	34	5	19	58	20	35	2	17	54	21	12		1	13	21	200	34	116	350	21
15/19	29	2	12	43	16	26	5	22	53	16	21	8	19	48	16	30	2	9	41	16	25		4	29	16	5			5	16	143	17	67	227	16
10/14	20	0	7	27	11	24	1	12	37	11	18	2	10	30	11	17	1	2	20	11	11		1	12	11	3			3	12	96	4	32	132	11
5/9	11		4	15	7	30	0	5	35	7	13	1	6	20	7	6	0	2	8	7	5		0	5	7						65	1	17	83	7
0/4	5		0	5	2	12	0	2	14	2	9		1	10	2	4			4	2	1			1	2						31	0	3	34	2
-5/-1	1			1	-2	3		1	4	-4	6		1	7	-3	2			2	-2	1			1	-2						13		2	15	-3
-10/-6						3		0	3	-8	2		0	2	-7	1			1	-7											6		0	6	-7
-15/-11						1			1	-13	0			0	-12																1			1	-13

ATLANTIC CITY, NEW JERSEY*
READINGS TAKEN AT MC GUIRE AFB, NJ

LAT 40 01N LONG 74 36W ELEV 133 FT

MEAN FREQUENCY OF OCCURRENCE OF DRY BULB TEMPERATURE (DEGREES F) WITH MEAN COINCIDENT WET BULB TEMPERATURE (DEGREES F) FOR EACH DRY BULB TEMPERATURE RANGE

Temperature Range	MAY 01-08	MAY 09-16	MAY 17-24	MAY Total Obsn	MAY MCWB	JUNE 01-08	JUNE 09-16	JUNE 17-24	JUNE Total Obsn	JUNE MCWB	JULY 01-08	JULY 09-16	JULY 17-24	JULY Total Obsn	JULY MCWB	AUG 01-08	AUG 09-16	AUG 17-24	AUG Total Obsn	AUG MCWB	SEP 01-08	SEP 09-16	SEP 17-24	SEP Total Obsn	SEP MCWB	OCT 01-08	OCT 09-16	OCT 17-24	OCT Total Obsn	OCT MCWB
100/104																														
95/99			0	0	70							0		0	74															
90/94		2	0	2	72		2	0	2	77		2	0	2	74		8	1	9	75										
85/89		8	2	10	69		11	2	13	75	0	16	2	18	74		43	8	51	74		5	0	5	74		1		1	72
80/84		17	6	23	66	0	32	10	42	72	0	47	14	61	73	1	68	26	95	71		20	3	23	73	1	6		7	69
75/79	1	32	13	46	64	2	51	22	75	69	4	76	34	114	70	22	68	57	147	69	0	35	10	45	70	1	18	3	22	65
70/74	7	41	24	72	61	10	51	39	100	67	28	64	60	152	69	71	41	74	186	67	6	49	26	81	68	3	35	10	48	63
65/69	19	50	37	106	58	44	48	52	144	65	82	32	74	188	67	75	16	52	143	63	36	49	49	134	66	11	45	25	81	60
60/64	37	44	47	128	55	60	27	54	141	62	76	10	47	133	63	49	3	22	74	59	47	40	50	137	62	29	50	45	124	56
55/59	55	29	52	136	52	60	14	37	111	58	44	1	15	60	59	22	0	7	29	54	52	28	48	128	58	39	42	46	127	52
50/54	56	17	42	115	48	42	3	19	64	54	13		1	14	54	7		0	7	49	45	11	33	89	53	50	30	51	131	47
45/49	50	6	20	76	44	18	0	4	22	49	1			1	50	0			0	45	33	3	16	52	49	48	14	37	99	43
40/44	19	1	5	25	39	4		0	4	45											13	0	4	17	44	35	5	19	59	39
35/39	4		1	5	34	0			0	42											6		1	7	40	22	2	8	32	34
30/34	1			1	30																2		0	2	36	9	0	2	11	30
25/29																										2	0		2	25

*Comparative design data note:

	Elevation	WINTER 97 1/2%	SUMMER DB 2 1/2%	SUMMER WB 2 1/2%
McGuire AFB, NJ	133 ft.	14° F	90° F	77° F
Atlantic City	11 ft.	18° F	88° F	77° F

COINCIDENT WET BULB TEMPERATURE FOR EACH DRY BULB TEMPERATURE RANGE

ATLANTIC CITY, NEW JERSEY*
READINGS TAKEN AT MC GUIRE AFB, NJ

(Obsn Hour Gp columns: 01 to 08, 09 to 16, 17 to 24; Total Obsn; MCWB = Mean Coincident Wet Bulb)

NOVEMBER

Temperature Range	01 to 08	09 to 16	17 to 24	Total Obsn	MCWB
100/104					
95/99					
90/94					
85/89					
80/84		0		0	69
75/79		1	0	1	69
70/74	1	4	1	6	64
65/69	2	10	3	15	59
60/64	6	24	12	42	56
55/59	18	38	22	78	52
50/54	26	52	36	114	47
45/49	37	47	46	130	42
40/44	45	34	50	129	38
35/39	45	20	39	104	33
30/34	41	7	23	71	29
25/29	14	1	6	21	25
20/24	5	0	1	6	20
15/19	1			1	16
10/14					
5/9					
0/4					
-5/-1					

DECEMBER

Temperature Range	01 to 08	09 to 16	17 to 24	Total Obsn	MCWB
75/79		0		0	62
70/74		1	0	1	62
65/69		2	1	3	58
60/64	1	3	1	5	56
55/59	5	10	5	20	52
50/54	8	19	9	36	47
45/49	13	27	24	64	43
40/44	23	39	30	92	38
35/39	38	50	45	133	33
30/34	55	48	56	159	29
25/29	39	27	40	106	24
20/24	31	16	21	68	20
15/19	24	6	13	43	15
10/14	8	1	2	11	11
5/9	2	0	1	3	7
0/4	1			1	1

JANUARY

Temperature Range	01 to 08	09 to 16	17 to 24	Total Obsn	MCWB
70/74		0		0	59
65/69			1	1	56
60/64	1	1	1	3	58
55/59	2	3	2	7	53
50/54	4	7	4	15	48
45/49	6	20	8	34	42
40/44	16	34	22	72	38
35/39	30	51	44	125	34
30/34	43	44	57	144	29
25/29	46	34	38	118	24
20/24	35	28	34	97	19
15/19	30	16	22	68	15
10/14	22	7	11	40	11
5/9	10	3	4	17	6
0/4	3			3	2

FEBRUARY

Temperature Range	01 to 08	09 to 16	17 to 24	Total Obsn	MCWB
75/79		1		1	57
70/74		3	1	4	56
65/69	2	5	5	12	52
60/64	4	11	5	20	46
55/59	4	18	10	32	42
50/54	14	35	21	70	38
45/49	36	50	47	133	33
40/44	45	44	59	148	29
35/39	48	27	39	114	24
30/34	29	16	19	64	19
25/29	23	9	12	44	15
20/24	12	5	5	22	10
15/19	7	1	2	10	6
10/14	1			1	1
5/9				0	-4

MARCH

Temperature Range	01 to 08	09 to 16	17 to 24	Total Obsn	MCWB
80/84		0		0	60
75/79		2	0	2	58
70/74		4	1	5	57
65/69		7	2	9	54
60/64	1	10	5	16	53
55/59	3	15	9	27	49
50/54	5	28	16	49	44
45/49	13	41	29	83	41
40/44	37	49	52	138	37
35/39	62	51	65	178	34
30/34	66	27	44	137	29
25/29	36	9	16	61	24
20/24	15	3	6	24	20
15/19	6	2	1	9	15
10/14	2			2	11
5/9				0	6

APRIL

Temperature Range	01 to 08	09 to 16	17 to 24	Total Obsn	MCWB
85/89		0		0	67
80/84		2	0	2	66
75/79		6	1	7	64
70/74		10	3	13	61
65/69		15	7	22	59
60/64	2	23	13	38	55
55/59	12	33	21	66	53
50/54	23	44	31	98	50
45/49	30	42	42	114	46
40/44	46	35	54	135	42
35/39	54	22	45	121	38
30/34	46	6	20	72	34
25/29	21	1	4	26	30
20/24	4			4	25
15/19	1			1	20
10/14				0	17

ANNUAL TOTAL

Temperature Range	01 to 08	09 to 16	17 to 24	Total Obsn	MCWB
100/104				0	74
95/99				4	76
90/94		42	5	47	74
85/89	0	153	37	190	73
80/84	7	259	100	366	70
75/79	68	295	201	564	68
70/74	244	270	292	806	65
65/69	292	232	284	808	61
60/64	292	214	255	761	57
55/59	269	200	232	701	52
50/54	242	209	225	676	47
45/49	234	208	232	674	42
40/44	249	219	245	713	38
35/39	285	230	269	784	34
30/34	281	171	245	697	29
25/29	189	98	139	426	24
20/24	116	63	81	260	20
15/19	84	33	48	165	15
10/14	44	11	18	73	11
5/9	19	4	7	30	6
0/4	5	0	0	5	2
-5/-1	0	0	0	0	-4

ALBUQUERQUE IAP/KIRTLAND AFB NEW MEXICO
LAT 35 03N   LONG 106 37W   ELEV 5311 FT

MEAN FREQUENCY OF OCCURRENCE OF DRY BULB TEMPERATURE (DEGREES F) WITH MEAN COINCIDENT WET BULB TEMPERATURE (DEGREES F) FOR EACH DRY BULB TEMPERATURE RANGE

Temperature Range	MAY 01–08	MAY 09–16	MAY 17–24	MAY Total Obsn	MAY MCWB	JUNE 01–08	JUNE 09–16	JUNE 17–24	JUNE Total Obsn	JUNE MCWB	JULY 01–08	JULY 09–16	JULY 17–24	JULY Total Obsn	JULY MCWB	AUG 01–08	AUG 09–16	AUG 17–24	AUG Total Obsn	AUG MCWB	SEP 01–08	SEP 09–16	SEP 17–24	SEP Total Obsn	SEP MCWB	OCT 01–08	OCT 09–16	OCT 17–24	OCT Total Obsn	OCT MCWB
100/104												2	0	2	63															
95/99		1	0	1	57		0		0	59		20	6	26	62		6	1	7	62		0		0	61					
90/94		5	1	6	57		16	5	21	60	0	52	19	71	62		40	12	52	62		13	1	14	59					
85/89		22	5	27	55	0	47	20	67	59		65	34	99	62		65	24	89	62		40	11	51	58		2	0	2	57
80/84		46	20	66	53		57	34	91	57	6	57	49	112	61	1	66	45	112	62		57	26	83	57		15	1	16	55
75/79	0	52	31	83	52	3	55	46	104	56	35	35	59	129	60	13	45	64	122	60	1	52	44	97	56	0	40	10	50	53
70/74	7	48	44	99	50	18	36	54	108	55	80	13	49	142	60	68	20	62	150	60	18	38	61	117	55		48	21	69	52
65/69	24	35	52	111	48	54	18	43	115	53	93	3	24	120	59	109	4	35	148	59	59	22	51	132	54	2	45	42	89	50
60/64	56	20	44	120	47	76	8	23	107	52	31	1	7	39	58	53	0	6	59	57	79	13	31	123	52	20	39	58	117	48
55/59	66	12	26	104	45	52	2	11	65	49	2		0	2	53	4			4	53	54	5	11	70	49	50	29	52	131	46
50/54	48	6	14	68	42	26	0	3	29	46	0			0	53						25	1	3	29	46	68	18	35	121	43
45/49	29	1	8	38	40	9		1	10	43											3	0	1	4	44	59	8	21	88	40
40/44	13	0	3	16	35	1			1	41											0			0	40	36	4	7	47	37
35/39	5		0	5	32	0			0	42																11	0	1	12	33
30/34	0			0	28																					2			2	29

ALBUQUERQUE IAP/KIRTLAND AFB NEW MEXICO

Temperature Range	NOV 01-08	NOV 09-16	NOV 17-24	NOV Total	NOV MCWB	DEC 01-08	DEC 09-16	DEC 17-24	DEC Total	DEC MCWB	JAN 01-08	JAN 09-16	JAN 17-24	JAN Total	JAN MCWB	FEB 01-08	FEB 09-16	FEB 17-24	FEB Total	FEB MCWB	MAR 01-08	MAR 09-16	MAR 17-24	MAR Total	MAR MCWB	APR 01-08	APR 09-16	APR 17-24	APR Total	APR MCWB	ANN 01-08	ANN 09-16	ANN 17-24	ANN Total	ANN MCWB
100/104																																2	0	2	63
95/99																																43	12	55	61
90/94																																157	53	210	61
85/89																															0	251	108	359	60
80/84																															10	305	189	504	58
75/79		2		2	48		0		0	47							0		0	49		2		2	49						67	285	270	622	56
70/74		14	2	16	47		0		0	44		1		1	47		6	1	7	46		8	2	10	47						227	238	302	767	55
65/69		29	8	37	45		6	1	7	44		5	0	5	44		18	5	23	44		23	8	31	45		0		0	55	364	205	270	839	53
60/64		43	21	64	43		16	3	19	42		15	4	19	42		26	12	38	42	0	36	19	55	43		9	2	11	52	300	210	235	745	49
55/59	0																				3	42	31	76	41		23	8	31	50	235	219	207	661	44
50/54	7	45	42	94	40	1	33	12	46	39	0	30	14	44	39	1	34	26	61	39	14	39	44	97	39	0	43	20	63	48	224	230	229	683	41
45/49	29	40	55	124	38	5	39	30	74	37	4	44	27	75	37	9	39	41	89	37	33	40	47	120	36	1	44	32	77	46	228	226	258	712	38
40/44	55	30	49	134	35	16	51	49	116	34	15	46	47	108	34	30	34	45	109	34	50	28	38	116	34	9	41	45	95	44	266	199	253	718	35
35/39	59	20	31	110	32	38	44	57	139	31	39	42	58	139	31	47	30	38	115	31	59	19	33	111	31	30	31	44	105	42	288	156	225	669	31
30/34	45	11	21	77	28	64	34	54	152	28	60	32	49	141	28	54	18	28	100	27	45	9	19	73	27	51	24	38	113	40	280	104	172	556	28
25/29	31	4	8	43	24	67	17	29	113	24	58	18	26	102	24	43	11	14	68	24	30	2	8	40	23	56	15	28	99	37	230	52	85	367	24
20/24	10	1	3	14	19	35	5	9	49	20	38	8	12	58	19	20	4	8	32	20	13	0	1	14	19	51	6	15	72	35	116	18	33	167	19
15/19	4	0	0	4	15	17	2	3	22	15	16	4	6	26	15	10	2	4	16	15	2	0	0	2	15	30	1	7	38	32	49	8	13	70	15
10/14	1			1	11	3	0	1	4	10	12	2	3	17	10	6	0	1	7	11	0			0	11	10	0	1	11	28	22	2	5	29	10
5/9	0					1	0	0	1	6	4	1	1	6	6	1	0	1	2	6						1	0	0	1	23	6	1	2	9	5
0/4											1	0	1	2	1	0	0		0	1											1	0	1	2	1
-5/-1											1	0	0	1	-4	0	0		0	-4											1	0	0	1	-4
-10/-6											0			0	-6																0			0	-6

FARMINGTON MAP NEW MEXICO
LAT 36 44N   LONG 108 14W   ELEV 5503 FT

MEAN FREQUENCY OF OCCURRENCE OF DRY BULB TEMPERATURE (DEGREES F) WITH MEAN COINCIDENT WET BULB TEMPERATURE (DEGREES F) FOR EACH DRY BULB TEMPERATURE RANGE

Temperature Range	MAY 01-08	MAY 09-16	MAY 17-24	MAY Total	MAY MCWB	JUNE 01-08	JUNE 09-16	JUNE 17-24	JUNE Total	JUNE MCWB	JULY 01-08	JULY 09-16	JULY 17-24	JULY Total	JULY MCWB	AUGUST 01-08	AUGUST 09-16	AUGUST 17-24	AUGUST Total	AUGUST MCWB	SEPTEMBER 01-08	SEPTEMBER 09-16	SEPTEMBER 17-24	SEPTEMBER Total	SEPTEMBER MCWB	OCTOBER 01-08	OCTOBER 09-16	OCTOBER 17-24	OCTOBER Total	OCTOBER MCWB
100/104																														
95/99							0		0	62		0		0	66		0		0	65										
90/94		1	0	1	57		6	2	8	61		15	3	18	63		5	1	6	64							0		0	57
85/89		13	3	16	56		35	14	49	60		56	22	78	62		30	9	39	63		5	0	5	60		7	0	7	56
80/84		36	14	50	54		51	28	79	58		68	36	104	61		62	25	87	62		32	7	39	59		28	4	32	53
75/79	1	54	25	79	52	0	55	37	92	56	1	52	45	98	60		60	37	97	61		50	19	69	58		41	14	55	51
70/74	7	47	33	81	51	4	43	43	90	54	10	35	52	97	59	4	49	53	106	60	0	48	32	80	56	0	44	27	71	49
65/69	7	37	43	87	49	20	30	42	92	53	50	15	47	112	58	30	29	57	116	59	3	45	45	93	55	4	38	40	82	48
60/64	24	28	43	95	47	44	14	38	96	51	96	5	30	131	56	82	9	45	136	58	19	30	49	98	53	17	32	43	92	46
55/59	46	18	38	102	45	62	4	23	89	48	72	1	12	85	54	88	2	12	110	56	51	18	43	112	51	37	30	46	113	43
50/54	68	10	25	103	42	63	1	9	73	45	18		1	19	48	35	0	2	37	50	73	8	28	109	48	65	18	43	126	40
45/49	56	4	16	76	39	34	0	3	37	42	2		0	2	43	8			8	43	56	3	12	71	44	71	8	22	101	37
40/44	32	1	6	39	36	11		1	12	39						1			1	40	29	1	4	34	41	34	2	8	44	32
35/39	13	0	1	14	34	2		0	2	35											10	0	1	11	38	14	0	2	16	28
30/34	1			1	28	1			1	31											1			1	35					
25/29																										5			5	24
20/24																										0			0	20

COINCIDENT WET BULB TEMPERATURE FOR EACH DRY BULB TEMPERATURE RANGE

FARMINGTON MAP NEW MEXICO

Temp. Range	NOV 01–08	NOV 09–16	NOV 17–24	NOV Total Obsn	NOV MCWB	DEC 01–08	DEC 09–16	DEC 17–24	DEC Total Obsn	DEC MCWB	JAN 01–08	JAN 09–16	JAN 17–24	JAN Total Obsn	JAN MCWB	FEB 01–08	FEB 09–16	FEB 17–24	FEB Total Obsn	FEB MCWB	MAR 01–08	MAR 09–16	MAR 17–24	MAR Total Obsn	MAR MCWB	APR 01–08	APR 09–16	APR 17–24	APR Total Obsn	APR MCWB	ANN 01–08	ANN 09–16	ANN 17–24	ANN Total Obsn	ANN MCWB
100/104																																0	0	0	63
95/99																																26	6	32	63
90/94																																127	45	172	61
85/89																																226	99	325	60
80/84																										0	0	0	0	54	1	263	152	416	58
75/79		0		0	48																						3		3	51	18	273	213	504	56
70/74		5		5	47												1		1	49		0		0	49	0	16	4	20	50	104	241	251	596	54
65/69		16	3	19	46				0	42		1		1	43		6	1	7	47		5	1	6	47		29	12	41	49	248	198	257	703	53
60/64		32	9	41	43		6		6	42		4		4	42		13	4	17	44		11	4	15	46		42	21	63	46	303	175	222	700	50
55/59	2	42	22	66	41		15	2	17	40		8	1	9	41	0	26	10	36	41		22	8	30	44	2	39	29	70	44	260	187	190	637	45
50/54	11	42	38	91	39		34	8	42	37		19	5	24	37	2	34	22	58	38		37	19	56	42	8	36	37	81	42	235	209	191	635	42
45/49	22	42	43	107	36	4	40	24	68	35	2	37	16	55	35	9	47	37	93	35	3	41	28	72	39	25	34	42	101	40	230	215	214	659	39
40/44	37	33	45	115	32	18	41	40	99	32	13	49	35	97	32	30	41	45	116	33	11	40	39	90	37	44	23	38	105	38	236	230	224	690	36
35/39	63	20	47	130	29	35	42	49	126	29	36	52	59	147	29	44	27	51	122	29	26	42	45	113	35	58	13	30	101	35	247	201	242	690	32
30/34	64	7	22	93	25	48	33	52	133	25	46	35	53	134	25	60	15	33	108	25	48	30	49	127	33	52	5	19	76	32	296	156	249	701	29
25/29	23	1	8	32	20	60	20	35	115	21	45	21	35	101	21	42	9	11	62	21	67	15	35	117	29	36	0	6	42	29	285	94	178	557	25
20/24	13	0	2	15	16	43	9	21	73	16	42	13	20	75	16	21	4	6	31	16	51	4	17	72	24	11	0	1	12	24	205	51	93	349	20
15/19	4		0	4	11	22	4	8	34	12	26	6	10	42	11	9	1	3	13	12	32	0	4	36	20	3			3	20	129	26	49	204	16
10/14	1			1	8	9	1	5	15	7	18	4	8	30	6	5	0	1	6	7	10			10	15	0			0	16	62	11	21	94	11
5/9						6	1	2	9	2	10	2	3	15	2	3			3	2	1			1	11						33	5	14	52	7
0/4						2	0	0	2	-2	6	0	2	8	-3	1			1	-2											19	3	5	27	2
-5/-1						0	0	0	0	-9	2	0	0	2																	9	0	2	11	-3
-10/-6						0		1	1	-12	1			1	-14																2	0	0	2	-8
-15/-11						1		0	1	-18																					1	0	1	2	-13
-20/-16																															2	0	0	2	-18

ALBANY, NEW YORK

LAT 42 45N   LONG 73 48W   ELEV 275 FT

MEAN FREQUENCY OF OCCURRENCE OF DRY BULB TEMPERATURE (DEGREES F) WITH MEAN COINCIDENT WET BULB TEMPERATURE (DEGREES F) FOR EACH DRY BULB TEMPERATURE RANGE

Temperature Range	MAY 01-08	MAY 09-16	MAY 17-24	MAY Total	MAY MC WB	JUNE 01-08	JUNE 09-16	JUNE 17-24	JUNE Total	JUNE MC WB	JULY 01-08	JULY 09-16	JULY 17-24	JULY Total	JULY MC WB	AUG 01-08	AUG 09-16	AUG 17-24	AUG Total	AUG MC WB	SEP 01-08	SEP 09-16	SEP 17-24	SEP Total	SEP MC WB	OCT 01-08	OCT 09-16	OCT 17-24	OCT Total	OCT MC WB
95/99																														
90/94							1	0	1	76												1	0	1	76					
85/89		1	0	1	70		6	1	7	73		4	0	4	74		1	0	1	75		1	0	1	76		0	0	0	62
80/84		4	1	5	67	0	23	8	31	70		14	4	18	73		6	1	7	73		9	2	11	73		2	0	2	67
75/79		13	5	18	65	1	39	17	57	68		37	12	49	71		21	5	26	71	0	18	5	23	71		11	1	12	64
70/74	1	25	10	36	63	6	49	31	86	65	2	55	27	84	68	1	48	18	67	69	2	30	14	46	67	1	18	7	26	62
65/69	3	35	21	59	60	23	45	42	110	63	12	64	44	120	67	6	64	38	108	66	15	40	28	83	64	4	28	13	45	58
60/64	12	45	37	94	57	49	39	52	140	61	44	47	62	153	65	29	60	57	146	65	24	48	34	106	60	11	44	27	82	55
55/59	29	42	42	113	54	56	24	45	125	57	80	21	59	160	63	62	32	63	157	63	37	47	47	131	57	30	47	43	120	52
50/54	44	38	46	128	51	53	12	30	95	53	58	28	4	90	59	65	12	42	119	59	46	28	46	120	53	38	43	48	129	47
45/49	52	37	37	115	47	36	3	12	51	49	32	1	10	43	55	47	3	18	68	55	45	13	34	92	49	50	33	47	130	44
40/44	52	14	32	98	43	12	2	0	14	45	16	2	0	18	51	27	6	0	33	51	38	4	20	62	45	43	14	34	91	39
35/39	34	5	14	53	39	4	0		4	41	3			3	46	11	0		11	47	19	0	7	26	41	36	7	17	60	35
30/34	14	0	3	17	35	1			1	37	0			0	41	1			1	43	10	2		12	36	24	1	10	35	31
25/29	7			7	31																4	0		4	32	9	1		10	27
20/24	1			1	28																0			0	28	2			2	22

ALBANY, NEW YORK

Temperature Range	NOVEMBER					DECEMBER					JANUARY					FEBRUARY					MARCH					APRIL					ANNUAL TOTAL				
	01 to 08	09 to 16	17 to 24	Total Obsn	MCWB	01 to 08	09 to 16	17 to 24	Total Obsn	MCWB	01 to 08	09 to 16	17 to 24	Total Obsn	MCWB	01 to 08	09 to 16	17 to 24	Total Obsn	MCWB	01 to 08	09 to 16	17 to 24	Total Obsn	MCWB	01 to 08	09 to 16	17 to 24	Total Obsn	MCWB	01 to 08	09 to 16	17 to 24	Total Obsn	MCWB
95/99																																7	0	7	75
90/94																											0	0	0	63		28	6	34	73
85/89																											1	0	1	65	0	95	28	123	71
80/84		0		0	64																						2	1	3	63	4	177	73	254	68
75/79		0		0	65																	0	0	0	57		5	2	7	60	27	248	140	415	66
70/74		0		0	64																	1	0	1	55	0	11	5	16	57	115	257	222	594	64
65/69	1	3	1	5	59																	1	1	2	54	2	18	11	31	55	234	235	271	740	61
60/64	2	11	4	17	56	0	0	0	0	57	0	0	0	0	56	0	0	0	0	56		3	1	4	51	5	25	16	46	51	263	212	252	727	57
55/59	7	18	13	38	52	2	3	2	7	54	1	1	0	2	54		1	0	1	50	1	6	3	10	49	11	32	25	68	49	274	190	236	700	52
50/54	17	34	23	74	48	3	5	5	13	48	1	2	1	4	49	1	3	2	6	47	3	12	8	23	45	24	42	36	102	45	263	183	214	660	48
45/49	26	42	32	100	43	5	11	7	23	43	2	3	3	8	45	1	7	4	12	42	5	27	15	47	41	37	42	43	122	42	242	183	205	630	43
40/44	38	46	43	127	38	10	20	12	42	38	8	15	8	31	39	6	18	11	35	38	14	45	31	90	37	52	39	45	136	38	229	202	205	636	38
35/39	40	43	45	128	34	27	43	33	103	34	21	33	29	83	34	21	42	32	95	34	36	55	54	145	33	55	18	36	109	34	261	241	251	753	34
30/34	45	28	43	116	30	45	51	50	146	30	34	43	38	115	30	36	46	46	128	30	67	46	59	172	30	33	5	16	54	30	295	220	262	777	30
25/29	35	11	25	71	25	41	39	46	126	25	33	43	39	115	25	35	36	39	110	25	47	27	38	112	25	15	0	3	18	25	216	156	191	563	25
20/24	20	2	8	30	21	35	32	32	99	21	31	37	38	106	20	34	26	30	90	20	37	14	22	73	20	4	1	0	5	20	163	112	130	405	20
15/19	6	1	3	10	17	28	22	23	73	16	32	30	35	97	16	24	19	24	67	15	18	7	10	35	15	2	0	1	3	16	110	79	96	285	16
10/14	2	0	1	3	12	21	10	19	50	11	29	19	25	73	11	21	12	16	49	11	11	2	4	17	11						84	43	65	192	11
5/9	1			1	8	15	6	9	30	7	22	13	16	51	6	17	7	11	35	6	5	1	2	8	6						60	27	38	125	6
0/4						8	4	5	17	2	18	7	10	35	2	8	5	6	19	1	3	0	1	4	2						37	16	22	75	2
-5/-1						5	1	2	8	-3	10	1	3	14	-3	11	1	4	16	-3	1	0	0	1	-4						27	3	9	39	-3
-10/-6						2	0	1	3	-8	3	0	2	5	-8	5	0	1	6	-8	0			0	-8						10	0	4	14	-8
-15/-11						1		0	1	-12	2	0	0	2	-13	2	0		2	-13	0			0	-14						5	0	0	5	-13
-20/-16						1			1	-17	1		0	1	-17	1			1	-17	0			0	-17						3	0	0	3	-17
-25/-21											0	0	0	0	-23																0	0	0	0	-23

BUFFALO, NEW YORK*
READINGS TAKEN AT NIAGARA FALLS IAP
LAT 43 06N   LONG 78 57W   ELEV 590 FT

MEAN FREQUENCY OF OCCURRENCE OF DRY BULB TEMPERATURE (DEGREES F) WITH MEAN COINCIDENT WET BULB TEMPERATURE (DEGREES F) FOR EACH DRY BULB TEMPERATURE RANGE

WB = Mean Coincident Wet Bulb. Hour groups: 01–08, 09–16, 17–24. Tot = Total Obsn.

Temp. Range	MAY 01–08	09–16	17–24	Tot	WB	JUNE 01–08	09–16	17–24	Tot	WB	JULY 01–08	09–16	17–24	Tot	WB	AUGUST 01–08	09–16	17–24	Tot	WB	SEPT 01–08	09–16	17–24	Tot	WB	OCT 01–08	09–16	17–24	Tot	WB
95/99																														
90/94																														
85/89		1		1	70		3	0	3	77		7	1	8	74		5	0	5	73		1		1	76					
80/84	6		2	8	68		17	3	20	72		35	9	44	72		19	3	22	73		3		3	76		1		1	66
75/79	0	22	5	27	66	1	36	13	50	69	2	62	26	90	70	1	49	15	65	70	2	9		11	73		7	1	8	66
70/74	3	34	11	48	62	8	47	23	78	67	14	67	46	127	67	14	68	41	123	68	5	17		22	70	1	17	3	21	63
65/69	13	38	27	78	59	22	55	46	123	64	52	47	66	165	65	39	62	66	167	65	3	29	15	47	67	11	31	15	57	60
60/64	23	42	34	99	56	46	42	56	144	61	74	23	59	156	62	72	31	65	168	63	22	40	27	89	65	16	44	26	86	56
55/59	35	35	42	112	52	59	24	48	131	57	61	7	31	99	58	55	12	38	105	58	31	52	37	120	61	24	42	34	100	52
50/54	43	36	45	124	48	46	12	31	89	54	33	0	9	42	55	47	3	18	68	54	35	44	44	123	57	43	47	50	140	48
45/49	55	23	47	125	44	41	5	15	61	49	12	1		13	51	16	3		19	50	47	32	50	129	53	51	38	56	145	44
40/44	46	10	27	83	40	15	1	5	21	45	1			1	47	5		0	5	46	45	12	36	93	49	48	15	38	101	40
35/39	25	2	8	35	35	2			2	41											32	2	19	53	44	35	7	21	63	35
30/34	7		1	8	31	0			0	37											18	0	5	23	40	17	1	4	22	31
25/29																					5		1	6	36		2	1	3	26
20/24																					1			1	31		0		0	22

*Comparative design data note:

	Elevation	WINTER 97 1/2%	SUMMER DB 2 1/2%	DB 2 1/2%	WB 2 1/2%
Niagara Falls AP, NY	590 ft.	7° F	86° F	86° F	74° F
Buffalo AP	705 ft.	6° F	86° F	86° F	73° F

BUFFALO, NEW YORK*
READINGS TAKEN AT NIAGARA FALLS IAP

Temperature Range	NOV 01–08	NOV 09–16	NOV 17–24	NOV Total Obsn	NOV MCWB	DEC 01–08	DEC 09–16	DEC 17–24	DEC Total Obsn	DEC MCWB	JAN 01–08	JAN 09–16	JAN 17–24	JAN Total Obsn	JAN MCWB	FEB 01–08	FEB 09–16	FEB 17–24	FEB Total Obsn	FEB MCWB	MAR 01–08	MAR 09–16	MAR 17–24	MAR Total Obsn	MAR MCWB	APR 01–08	APR 09–16	APR 17–24	APR Total Obsn	APR MCWB	ANN 01–08	ANN 09–16	ANN 17–24	ANN Total Obsn	ANN MCWB
95/99																																	1	1	76
90/94																																18	1	19	75
85/89																																81	17	98	72
80/84																											1		1	68	4	172	61	237	70
75/79																											4	0	4	65	39	244	131	414	67
70/74		2		2	64																	0		0	54		9	3	12	61	139	266	222	627	65
65/69	0	5	2	7	58																	1		1	56	1	17	6	24	58	248	240	267	755	61
60/64	4	13	5	22	56			1	1	56								1	1	53		3	1	4	54	5	26	16	47	54	258	217	243	718	57
55/59	10	21	12	43	53		5	1	6	52	0	0	0	0	50		1		1	50	2	4	4	10	50	13	38	24	75	51	257	193	225	675	53
50/54	18	26	26	70	48	4	5	4	13	48	2	2	2	6	49	1	4	4	9	47	2	12	3	17	46	22	35	34	91	48	249	184	223	656	48
45/49	28	34	34	96	43	6	8	10	24	44	4	6	3	13	44	3	7	2	12	42	5	23	11	39	42	38	39	44	121	43	243	181	231	655	44
40/44	41	45	42	128	39	20	29	19	68	39	6	7	7	20	39	7	14	10	31	38	13	36	22	71	38	44	35	45	124	39	245	191	215	651	39
35/39	52	43	48	143	34	37	49	46	132	35	16	24	24	64	34	18	33	27	78	34	32	56	49	137	34	59	26	37	122	35	279	240	261	780	35
30/34	48	35	40	123	30	62	65	63	190	30	45	51	46	142	31	52	64	58	174	30	78	53	72	203	30	42	8	24	74	30	352	277	308	937	30
25/29	26	8	21	55	26	47	34	42	123	25	40	58	50	148	25	44	43	47	134	25	54	41	47	142	25	14	1	5	20	26	227	185	213	625	25
20/24	8	6	6	20	20	28	25	25	78	20	42	46	38	126	21	37	26	33	96	21	35	13	29	77	21	2	1	2	5	20	152	117	133	402	21
15/19	3	1	3	7	16	21	19	21	61	16	39	24	33	96	16	23	11	15	49	16	18	5	9	32	16	2	0	0	2	14	106	60	81	247	16
10/14	2	0	1	3	12	15	7	14	36	11	28	20	28	76	11	20	12	17	49	11	6	1	1	8	11	0	0	0	0	11	71	40	61	172	11
5/9	0	0	0	0	6	7	2	2	11	7	19	7	12	38	7	12	4	6	22	7	1	0	0	1	8						39	13	20	72	7
0/4						1		1	2	3	6	2	2	10	2	5	3	3	11	2											12	5	6	23	2
-5/-1						0		0	0	-2	1	0	1	2	-3	2	0	0	2	-2											3	0	1	4	-2
-10/-6												0	1	1	-8																	0	1	1	-8
-15/-11											1			1	-13																1			1	-13
-20/-16														0	-16																			0	-16

MEAN FREQUENCY OF OCCURRENCE OF DRY BULB TEMPERATURE (DEGREES F) WITH MEAN COINCIDENT WET BULB TEMPERATURE (DEGREES F) FOR EACH DRY BULB TEMPERATURE RANGE

CHARLOTTE, NORTH CAROLINA*
READINGS TAKEN AT FT. BRAGG, NC
LAT 35 08N   LONG 78 56W   ELEV 242 FT

Temperature Range	MAY 01-08	MAY 09-16	MAY 17-24	MAY Total Obsn	MAY MCWB	JUNE 01-08	JUNE 09-16	JUNE 17-24	JUNE Total Obsn	JUNE MCWB	JULY 01-08	JULY 09-16	JULY 17-24	JULY Total Obsn	JULY MCWB	AUG 01-08	AUG 09-16	AUG 17-24	AUG Total Obsn	AUG MCWB	SEP 01-08	SEP 09-16	SEP 17-24	SEP Total Obsn	SEP MCWB	OCT 01-08	OCT 09-16	OCT 17-24	OCT Total Obsn	OCT MCWB
100/104																														
95/99		3	0	3	73		2	1	3	76							0	0	0	75										
90/94		13	4	17	70		7	1	8	74		8	2	10	77		13	3	16	76		4	0	4	76			1	1	
85/89		25	9	34	68		26	7	33	74		34	11	45	76		30	9	39	76		16	2	18	75		9	1	10	67
80/84	1	44	18	63	66	1	62	24	87	72	0	84	30	114	74	1	61	23	85	75		42	11	53	72		29	5	34	68
75/79	3	50	40	93	64	6	71	43	120	70	8	68	53	129	73	9	67	48	124	72	1	63	30	94	70	1	46	18	65	65
70/74	25	50	57	132	62	31	41	58	130	69	59	37	77	173	72	53	47	73	173	71	14	50	51	115	69	11	58	46	115	64
65/69	64	32	48	144	60	83	22	76	181	68	138	16	67	221	70	111	24	69	204	69	60	35	64	159	67	52	48	66	166	62
60/64	55	17	33	105	57	81	5	24	110	63	37	1	9	47	66	50	5	19	74	65	65	21	46	132	63	63	33	48	144	57
55/59	47	11	26	84	53	28	1	3	32	58	5		0	5	61	19		4	23	59	54	7	27	88	59	45	16	29	90	52
50/54	40	4	12	56	49	10	2	2	14	54	0		0	0	58	5		0	5	55	33	1	6	40	54	27	6	18	51	47
45/49	11		1	12	44	1	0	2	3	51											9	0	1	10	50	22	2	11	35	43
40/44	2			2	40																3			3	46	19	0	5	24	38
35/39																										7		2	9	34
30/34																										2			2	31

*Comparative design data note:

	Elevation	WINTER 97 1/2%	SUMMER DB 2 1/2%	SUMMER WB 2 1/2%
Charlotte, NC	736 ft.	22° F	94° F	77° F
Ft. Bragg	242 ft.	20° F	94° F	79° F

COINCIDENT WET BULB TEMPERATURE FOR EACH DRY BULB TEMPERATURE RANGE

CHARLOTTE, NORTH CAROLINA*
READINGS TAKEN AT FT. BRAGG, NC

The hour groups under each month are: "01 to 08", "09 to 16", "17 to 24"; followed by "Total Obsn" and "MCWB" (M C W B).

Temp Range	Nov 01–08	Nov 09–16	Nov 17–24	Nov Total	Nov MCWB	Dec 01–08	Dec 09–16	Dec 17–24	Dec Total	Dec MCWB	Jan 01–08	Jan 09–16	Jan 17–24	Jan Total	Jan MCWB	Feb 01–08	Feb 09–16	Feb 17–24	Feb Total	Feb MCWB	Mar 01–08	Mar 09–16	Mar 17–24	Mar Total	Mar MCWB	Apr 01–08	Apr 09–16	Apr 17–24	Apr Total	Apr MCWB	Ann 01–08	Ann 09–16	Ann 17–24	Ann Total	Ann MCWB
100/104																																			76
95/99																																2	1	3	76
90/94																											1		1	64		35	6	41	75
85/89																						1	0	1	64	0	13	5	18	65		120	33	153	72
80/84		2		2	71		1		1	70											0	5	2	7	62	0	26	11	37	63	2	297	103	402	70
75/79		11	1	12	64		5	1	6	67		2	0	2	63						0	12	5	17	61	0	38	19	57	61	25	376	210	611	68
70/74	2	22	7	31	61	1	18	8	27	63		8	1	9	59	0	5	1	6	60	1	21	12	34	59	7	45	36	88	58	161	339	343	843	66
65/69	5	40	15	60	57	9	19	12	40	59	2	11	4	17	57	0	12	6	18	56	3	24	22	49	56	26	44	50	120	57	439	324	444	1207	61
60/64	15	43	32	90	55	13	26	24	63	56	3	15	12	30	54	3	18	15	36	52	11	35	33	79	53	44	34	39	117	54	394	262	321	977	56
55/59	27	35	35	97	50	20	25	25	70	51	13	21	19	53	51	11	23	17	51	48	25	39	38	102	49	40	21	37	98	50	313	229	270	812	51
50/54	34	35	43	112	46	22	38	32	92	46	13	22	21	56	46	12	38	25	75	43	43	43	45	131	45	48	13	26	87	47	276	194	234	704	46
45/49	38	24	40	102	41	25	44	37	106	41	18	36	31	85	42	16	35	34	85	40	40	34	31	105	40	46	3	12	61	42	249	199	225	673	41
40/44	44	18	37	99	37	31	32	36	99	37	29	44	43	116	37	28	33	43	104	36	41	19	31	91	36	23	2	6	31	39	219	178	197	594	37
35/39	30	7	18	55	33	31	23	30	84	32	40	32	38	110	33	44	28	38	110	32	30	9	17	56	32	6			6	35	217	148	201	566	33
30/34	24	3	8	35	28	49	14	26	89	28	52	31	34	117	29	53	21	30	104	28	41	4	11	56	28						188	99	143	430	28
25/29	15	1	4	20	25	28	3	15	46	25	38	20	32	90	24	33	8	12	53	24	11	0	1	12	24						221	73	109	403	24
20/24	4	0	0	4	21	16	0	1	17	21	24	5	10	39	19	13	2	3	18	20	2			2	21						125	32	64	221	20
15/19	1		0	1	16	2			2	17	14	2	2	18	15	7	0	1	8	15											59	7	14	80	15
10/14											3			3	11	2	0	0	2	11											2	0	3	5	11

RALEIGH, NORTH CAROLINA*
READINGS TAKEN AT SEYMOUR JOHNSON AFB

LAT 35 20N   LONG 77 58W   ELEV 109 FT

MEAN FREQUENCY OF OCCURRENCE OF DRY BULB TEMPERATURE (DEGREES F) WITH MEAN COINCIDENT WET BULB TEMPERATURE (DEGREES F) FOR EACH DRY BULB TEMPERATURE RANGE

Temperature Range	MAY					JUNE					JULY					AUGUST					SEPTEMBER					OCTOBER				
	01 to 08	09 to 16	17 to 24	Total Obsn	MCWB	01 to 08	09 to 16	17 to 24	Total Obsn	MCWB	01 to 08	09 to 16	17 to 24	Total Obsn	MCWB	01 to 08	09 to 16	17 to 24	Total Obsn	MCWB	01 to 08	09 to 16	17 to 24	Total Obsn	MCWB	01 to 08	09 to 16	17 to 24	Total Obsn	MCWB
100/104																														
95/99		0		0	71		0		0	77		0		0	77		0		0	76		0		0	77					
90/94		10	3	13	70		7	2	9	76		5	1	6	76		4	1	5	77		8	1	9	76				0	72
85/89		30	11	41	69		25	6	31	75		33	8	41	75		30	7	37	77		46	8	54	74		6	0	6	70
80/84	0	45	19	64	68		54	21	75	73		77	27	104	73		70	24	94	75	0	63	23	86	71		21	3	24	69
75/79	4	60	38	102	66	5	63	38	106	71	8	75	51	134	71	6	75	49	130	73	17	56	55	128	70	2	45	13	60	67
70/74	35	45	61	141	65	36	50	62	148	70	74	42	88	204	70	69	45	86	200	72	70	37	70	177	68	15	52	35	102	65
65/69	71	28	53	152	62	86	27	67	180	68	123	14	64	201	68	109	19	61	189	70	62	19	46	127	63	30	51	51	132	61
60/64	57	17	33	107	57	64	11	33	108	64	34	1	8	43	64	46	4	17	67	65	47	10	26	83	59	52	37	50	139	57
55/59	42	10	19	71	53	34	3	7	44	59	8	0	2	10	59	15	1	3	19	60	29	1	9	39	55	43	23	41	107	53
50/54	26	2	9	37	49	11	1	3	15	54	1		0	1	57	2		0	2	55	11	0	3	14	50	38	10	28	76	48
45/49	9	1	2	12	45	3	0	0	3	50						0			0	48	3		0	3	46	31	4	15	50	44
40/44	2	0	2	4	40	1			1	45						0			0	47	0			0	43	21	1	7	29	39
35/39	1		0	1	36																					13	0	3	16	35
30/34																										3		0	3	31
25/29																										1			1	26

*Comparative design data note:

	Elevation	WINTER 97 1/2%	SUMMER DB 2 1/2%	SUMMER WB 2 1/2%
Raleigh/Durham	434 ft.	20° F	92° F	78° F
Seymore-Johnson AFB/Goldsboro	109 ft.	21° F	92° F	79° F

COINCIDENT WET BULB TEMPERATURE FOR EACH DRY BULB TEMPERATURE RANGE

RALEIGH, NORTH CAROLINA*
READINGS TAKEN AT SEYMOUR JOHNSON AFB

Temperature Range	NOV 01–08	NOV 09–16	NOV 17–24	NOV Total Obsn	NOV MCWB	DEC 01–08	DEC 09–16	DEC 17–24	DEC Total Obsn	DEC MCWB	JAN 01–08	JAN 09–16	JAN 17–24	JAN Total Obsn	JAN MCWB	FEB 01–08	FEB 09–16	FEB 17–24	FEB Total Obsn	FEB MCWB	MAR 01–08	MAR 09–16	MAR 17–24	MAR Total Obsn	MAR MCWB	APR 01–08	APR 09–16	APR 17–24	APR Total Obsn	APR MCWB	ANN 01–08	ANN 09–16	ANN 17–24	ANN Total Obsn	ANN MCWB
100/104																																		0	76
95/99																																16	4	20	77
90/94																																109	26	135	76
85/89																							0		0	64		0	0	0	73	0	296	95	391	73
80/84		4	0	4	69		0	0	0	72		0		0	65		0		0	65	0	3	0	3	63		3	1	4	68	19	371	193	583	71
75/79	0	13	1	14	65	0	2	0	2	67	0	1	0	1	66	0	2	0	2	65	0	11	3	14	61	0	13	4	17	66	203	360	361	924	70
70/74	2	25	8	35	62	0	11	2	13	63	0	7	2	9	62	1	8	2	11	61	1	18	8	27	60	0	22	10	32	65	448	302	411	1161	67
65/69	9	37	22	68	59	6	15	9	30	60	3	11	5	19	59	2	13	7	22	59	7	26	20	53	57	1	33	15	49	63	365	255	319	939	61
60/64	19	44	33	96	56	11	23	18	52	56	6	16	11	33	55	9	16	17	42	55	14	34	31	79	54	6	39	31	76	61	316	238	275	829	57
55/59	26	41	39	106	51	14	27	21	62	51	12	23	20	55	51	11	23	18	52	50	20	38	37	95	49	31	39	48	118	59	249	216	242	707	51
50/54	40	32	43	115	47	21	36	28	85	46	12	27	23	62	46	13	33	27	73	45	32	41	42	115	45	44	37	44	125	55	234	198	232	664	47
45/49	39	24	38	101	43	20	39	38	97	42	19	37	33	89	42	23	34	37	94	42	43	35	42	120	42	38	29	35	102	51	231	179	222	632	42
40/44	39	14	30	83	38	28	38	40	106	37	37	41	42	120	38	34	36	35	105	37	48	22	35	105	38	38	17	29	84	47	239	155	196	590	38
35/39	37	5	16	58	34	42	31	39	112	33	40	33	38	111	33	40	32	41	113	33	42	12	18	72	33	43	5	17	65	43	225	113	156	494	33
30/34	19	1	7	27	29	51	17	31	99	29	41	28	36	105	29	46	18	27	91	29	28	5	7	40	29	30	3	7	40	39	188	69	108	365	29
25/29	8	0	2	10	25	32	7	16	55	25	39	16	24	79	25	29	7	9	45	24	10	1	3	14	25	10	0	1	11	35	119	31	54	204	25
20/24	2			2	20	18	2	5	25	20	26	5	10	41	20	11	2	3	16	20	2	0	0	2	21	0			0	32	59	9	18	86	20
15/19						4	1	1	6	16	9	2	2	13	16	4	1	1	6	15											17	4	4	25	16
10/14						1	0	0	1	11	3	0	0	3	11	1	0	0	1	12											5	0	0	5	11
5/9						0	0	0	0	5	0	0		0	6																0	0	0	0	5
0/4														0	1																			0	1

BISMARCK MAP NORTH DAKOTA
LAT 46 46N   LONG 100 45W   ELEV 1647 FT

MEAN FREQUENCY OF OCCURRENCE OF DRY BULB TEMPERATURE (DEGREES F) WITH MEAN COINCIDENT WET BULB TEMPERATURE (DEGREES F) FOR EACH DRY BULB TEMPERATURE RANGE

Temperature Range	MAY 01–08	MAY 09–16	MAY 17–24	MAY Total Obsn	MAY MCWB	JUNE 01–08	JUNE 09–16	JUNE 17–24	JUNE Total Obsn	JUNE MCWB	JULY 01–08	JULY 09–16	JULY 17–24	JULY Total Obsn	JULY MCWB	AUG 01–08	AUG 09–16	AUG 17–24	AUG Total Obsn	AUG MCWB	SEP 01–08	SEP 09–16	SEP 17–24	SEP Total Obsn	SEP MCWB	OCT 01–08	OCT 09–16	OCT 17–24	OCT Total Obsn	OCT MCWB
105/109												0	0	0	71			0	0	69		0		0	65					
100/104		1	0	1	63		0	0	0	67		1	0	1	72		2	1	3	69				0	67					
95/99		4	2	6	63		2	1	3	68		5	2	7	70		8	4	12	68		2		2	66				0	60
90/94		11	6	17	61		6	3	9	69		20	11	31	69		17	9	26	67		4	1	5	67				0	62
85/89							15	8	23	67	0	33	19	52	69		31	18	49	66		8	4	12	64		2		2	58
80/84							30	18	48	66	1	51	33	85	66		46	26	72	64		17	7	24	62		6	1	7	58
75/79	0	22	11	33	59	2	43	28	73	63	7	53	42	102	65	5	47	36	88	63	0	24	13	37	59		11	3	14	57
70/74	1	31	19	51	56	10	44	37	91	61	26	43	44	113	63	19	43	42	104	62	3	32	18	53	58		16	5	21	55
65/69	5	38	27	70	54	30	37	42	109	59	53	26	42	121	61	48	26	45	119	60	8	36	25	69	55	1	24	10	35	53
60/64	15	43	37	95	52	47	29	44	120	57	66	12	35	113	58	62	15	34	111	57	14	35	34	83	53	3	28	17	48	50
55/59	29	35	42	106	49	59	22	35	116	53	61	2	16	79	54	53	9	22	84	53	34	32	40	106	51	8	34	28	70	47
50/54	47	25	41	113	47	52	8	18	78	49	27	1	3	31	50	38	3	9	50	49	49	25	42	116	47	18	32	38	88	45
45/49	60	20	32	112	43	25	2	5	32	45	7	0	0	7	46	16	0	2	18	45	56	15	30	101	43	33	34	41	108	41
40/44	43	8	16	67	39	11	1	2	14	40	0			0	42	5		0	5	40	38	8	16	62	39	53	26	38	117	38
35/39	26	6	8	40	34	2	0	0	2	37						1			1	36	27	2	7	36	35	49	20	33	102	34
30/34	15	3	6	24	31	0			0	33						0			0	32	9	0	1	10	30	47	11	22	80	30
25/29	5	1		6	26																3			3	27	23	3	9	35	26
20/24	1			1	22																1			1	22	9	1	2	12	21
15/19																										2		1	3	16
10/14																										1			1	11
5/9																										0			0	6

BISMARCK MAP NORTH DAKOTA

Temp. Range	Nov 01-08	Nov 09-16	Nov 17-24	Nov Tot	Nov MCWB	Dec 01-08	Dec 09-16	Dec 17-24	Dec Tot	Dec MCWB	Jan 01-08	Jan 09-16	Jan 17-24	Jan Tot	Jan MCWB	Feb 01-08	Feb 09-16	Feb 17-24	Feb Tot	Feb MCWB	Mar 01-08	Mar 09-16	Mar 17-24	Mar Tot	Mar MCWB	Apr 01-08	Apr 09-16	Apr 17-24	Apr Tot	Apr MCWB	Ann 01-08	Ann 09-16	Ann 17-24	Ann Tot	Ann MCWB
105/109																																		0	70
100/104																																3	1	4	70
95/99																																17	7	24	68
90/94																											1	0	1	60		49	24	73	68
85/89																											1	1	2	60		94	52	146	67
80/84																										0	3	1	4	58	1	164	92	257	64
75/79																											5	2	7	56	14	205	135	354	62
70/74																											8	5	13	54	59	218	171	448	60
65/69		0		0	53																					1	15	8	24	51	146	206	200	552	58
60/64		2		2	49																					1	19	13	33	48	208	187	216	611	54
55/59		4	1	5	48		1		1	45							2		2	46				0	55	4	24	17	45	46	248	175	204	627	51
50/54	1	16	6	23	45		2		2	41		1		1	41		2	1	3	43		8	4	12	42	11	31	25	67	43	243	154	187	584	46
45/49	3	23	11	37	42		7	1	8	39		3		3	38		4	2	6	40	1	14	8	23	39	21	30	33	84	40	222	152	165	539	42
40/44	11	27	24	62	36	2	14	4	20	36	2	8	3	13	36	2	10	7	19	37	4	22	17	43	36	32	34	36	102	37	203	158	163	524	38
35/39	25	37	42	104	33	8	24	17	49	33	4	10	10	24	33	6	16	14	36	33	18	36	31	85	33	43	32	38	113	33	209	183	200	592	34
30/34	48	34	46	128	30	21	26	28	75	29	7	13	11	31	29	15	24	22	61	30	41	40	48	129	30	55	26	33	114	30	258	177	217	652	30
25/29	43	25	34	102	25	27	28	33	88	25	14	20	19	53	25	25	28	26	79	25	40	32	36	108	25	40	7	19	66	25	220	143	177	540	25
20/24	36	22	26	84	21	30	30	34	94	21	17	26	22	65	21	22	24	27	73	21	36	26	27	89	21	24	2	5	31	21	176	131	143	450	21
15/19	26	14	15	55	16	32	26	29	87	16	25	24	23	72	16	20	23	23	66	16	27	19	22	68	16	5	2	1	8	16	137	108	114	359	16
10/14	17	10	14	41	11	30	19	22	71	11	28	29	26	83	11	23	25	27	75	11	21	15	15	51	11	3	1	1	5	11	123	99	105	327	11
5/9	9	7	5	21	6	24	21	20	65	6	26	25	28	79	6	28	24	23	75	6	19	12	11	42	6	1	0	0	1	7	107	89	87	283	6
0/4	8	5	6	19	2	23	22	23	68	1	33	24	28	85	1	26	18	21	65	2	15	6	9	30	2	0			0	3	105	75	87	267	1
-5/-1	7	3	7	17	-3	21	14	19	54	-3	24	23	25	72	-3	22	14	15	51	-3	9	4	5	18	-3	0			0	-2	83	58	71	212	-3
-10/-6	6	1	2	9	-8	12	8	10	30	-8	20	18	21	59	-8	14	7	9	30	-8	6	2	4	12	-8						58	36	46	140	-8
-15/-11	2	0	1	3	-13	10	4	6	20	-13	19	12	16	47	-13	10	2	4	16	-13	5	1	1	7	-13						46	19	28	93	-13
-20/-16	1	0	0	1	-17	4	2	3	9	-18	14	7	10	31	-18	5	1	3	9	-18	3	0	1	4	-18						27	10	17	54	-18
-25/-21	0			0	-23	3	1	1	5	-23	8	2	4	14	-23	3		1	4	-23	1		0	1	-23						15	3	6	24	-23
-30/-26	0			0	-27	1	0		1	-27	4	1	2	7	-28	2	0		2	-27				0	-26						7	1	2	10	-28
-35/-31						0	0		0	-33	2	0	0	2	-33	0			0	-32											2	0	0	2	-33
-40/-36											1	0	0	1																	1	0	0	1	
-45/-41											0			0																	0			0	

GRAND FORKS AFB NORTH DAKOTA

LAT 47 57N   LONG 97 24W   ELEV 911 FT

MEAN FREQUENCY OF OCCURRENCE OF DRY BULB TEMPERATURE (DEGREES F) WITH MEAN COINCIDENT WET BULB TEMPERATURE (DEGREES F) FOR EACH DRY BULB TEMPERATURE RANGE

Column key for each month — Obsn Hour Gp: 01 to 08 | 09 to 16 | 17 to 24 | Total Obsn | MWB (Mean Wet Bulb)

MAY

Temperature Range	01–08	09–16	17–24	Total Obsn	MWB
100/104				0	65
95/99				0	66
90/94		1	0	1	71
85/89		3	1	4	66
80/84		8	4	12	62
75/79	1	15	8	24	59
70/74	1	26	16	43	56
65/69	3	34	22	59	54
60/64	12	36	30	78	52
55/59	24	34	36	94	50
50/54	41	39	44	124	46
45/49	49	24	39	112	42
40/44	49	17	26	92	39
35/39	36	7	15	58	34
30/34	23	3	5	31	30
25/29	7	1	1	9	26
20/24	2	1	1	4	21
15/19	0	0	0	0	17
10/14	0	0	0	0	14
5/9	0			0	7
0/4	0			0	3

JUNE

Temperature Range	01–08	09–16	17–24	Total Obsn	MWB
95/99		1	0	1	72
90/94		5	2	7	70
85/89		11	5	16	70
80/84	0	22	13	35	67
75/79	3	38	24	65	64
70/74	10	49	36	95	61
65/69	27	47	46	120	59
60/64	51	37	50	138	57
55/59	62	22	36	120	53
50/54	44	7	18	69	49
45/49	26	2	8	36	44
40/44	11	1	3	15	40
35/39	5	0	0	5	36
30/34	1			1	28
25/29	0			0	24

JULY

Temperature Range	01–08	09–16	17–24	Total Obsn	MWB
95/99		1	1	2	74
90/94		7	3	10	72
85/89		21	10	31	71
80/84	0	50	23	73	68
75/79	4	65	40	109	66
70/74	20	57	53	130	64
65/69	54	30	51	135	62
60/64	72	12	40	124	58
55/59	57	4	19	80	54
50/54	29	1	8	38	50
45/49	9	0	2	11	45
40/44	2	0	0	2	41
35/39	0			0	38

AUGUST

Temperature Range	01–08	09–16	17–24	Total Obsn	MWB
90/94		0		0	69
85/89		2	1	3	70
80/84	0	14	5	19	70
75/79		26	12	38	67
70/74	4	49	33	86	64
65/69	16	49	39	104	62
60/64	37	37	47	121	60
55/59	65	21	43	129	57
50/54	54	11	27	92	53
45/49	43	2	14	59	49
40/44	20	0	4	24	45
35/39	6		1	7	41
30/34	2		0	2	35
25/29	1			1	32

SEPTEMBER

Temperature Range	01–08	09–16	17–24	Total Obsn	MWB
90/94		0	0	0	76
85/89		1	1	2	71
80/84		6	2	8	68
75/79		13	5	18	66
70/74	1	20	10	31	63
65/69	3	26	17	46	60
60/64	10	37	25	72	58
55/59	21	41	34	96	55
50/54	36	38	40	114	51
45/49	41	31	38	110	47
40/44	49	16	37	102	44
35/39	43	8	22	73	40
30/34	26	3	7	36	35
25/29	7	1	1	9	30
20/24	2		0	2	26
15/19	1			1	23

OCTOBER

Temperature Range	01–08	09–16	17–24	Total Obsn	MWB
85/89		1	0	1	63
80/84		2	0	2	61
75/79		6	1	7	60
70/74		10	3	13	57
65/69		15	6	21	55
60/64	3	25	14	42	52
55/59	10	38	26	74	49
50/54	22	40	32	94	46
45/49	39	37	47	123	42
40/44	43	34	43	120	38
35/39	55	26	37	118	34
30/34	46	12	23	81	30
25/29	21	3	11	35	26
20/24	8	0	3	11	21
15/19	2		0	2	17

COINCIDENT WET BULB TEMPERATURE FOR EACH DRY BULB TEMPERATURE RANGE

GRAND FORKS AFB NORTH DAKOTA

Temperature Range	NOV 01–08	NOV 09–16	NOV 17–24	NOV Total	NOV MCWB	DEC 01–08	DEC 09–16	DEC 17–24	DEC Total	DEC MCWB	JAN 01–08	JAN 09–16	JAN 17–24	JAN Total	JAN MCWB	FEB 01–08	FEB 09–16	FEB 17–24	FEB Total	FEB MCWB	MAR 01–08	MAR 09–16	MAR 17–24	MAR Total	MAR MCWB	APR 01–08	APR 09–16	APR 17–24	APR Total	APR MCWB	ANN 01–08	ANN 09–16	ANN 17–24	ANN Total	ANN MCWB
100/104																																		0	67
95/99																																4	2	6	71
90/94																																28	11	39	71
85/89																																68	30	98	70
80/84																													0	57		131	66	197	67
75/79																								0	54		2		2	56	13	195	116	324	64
70/74		0		0	52																			0	55		3	1	4	55	50	220	165	435	61
65/69		0	1	1	47																	1		1	52		7	4	11	54	131	208	201	540	59
60/64	0	1	4	5	46																	2	1	3	50	1	14	7	22	50	225	189	219	633	56
55/59									0	42									0	48		3	2	5	49	3	21	14	38	48	246	175	201	622	52
50/54	0	8	2	10	44		0	0	0	43	0	2	1	3	36				0	45	0	5	4	9	45	7	27	23	57	45	227	160	183	570	47
45/49	4	15	7	26	41		2	1	3	41	4	8	6	18	33				0	42	1	7	4	12	41	16	35	34	85	42	213	138	183	534	43
40/44	9	22	17	48	38		3	2	5	36	6	7	7	20	29		1	1	2	37	4	11	9	24	38	32	37	38	107	38	199	136	163	498	38
35/39	20	36	37	93	34	3	8	4	15	33	11	12	10	33	25	2	7	6	15	34	14	26	25	65	34	52	39	45	136	34	219	160	182	561	34
30/34	52	47	52	151	30	12	20	14	46	30	13	11	12	36	21	9	16	16	41	30	35	39	40	114	30	63	33	42	138	30	255	178	200	633	30
25/29	48	40	39	127	25	22	23	23	68	26	15	18	19	52	16	18	23	22	63	26	32	36	35	103	25	37	15	19	71	25	198	153	160	511	25
20/24	38	27	33	98	21	26	23	27	76	21	18	23	20	61	11	22	26	19	67	21	28	35	31	94	21	18	7	10	35	21	156	130	136	422	21
15/19	27	17	19	63	16	25	29	26	80	16	22	27	28	77	6	19	23	22	64	16	32	26	28	86	16	7	2	1	10	16	127	114	116	357	16
10/14	18	11	15	44	11	27	30	31	88	11	25	32	25	82	-1	20	24	25	69	11	25	22	25	72	11	4	1		5	12	112	110	117	339	11
5/9	11	6	10	27	6	29	33	31	93	6	28	36	34	98	-4	22	25	27	74	6	25	19	19	63	6	1			1	8	110	110	115	335	6
0/4	8	3	6	17	2	29	26	27	82	-1	37	30	32	99	-8	24	23	23	70	-1	19	9	14	42	1	1			1	1	106	93	95	294	1
-5/-1	3	1	2	6	-3	25	22	22	69	-3	27	20	24	71	-13	23	22	22	67	-4	18	4	6	28	-3						97	85	86	268	-4
-10/-6	1	0	1	2	-8	22	16	16	54	-8	23	13	18	54	-18	23	17	20	60	-8	9	1	3	13	-8						92	64	72	228	-8
-15/-11	1	0	0	1	-13	14	8	15	37	-13	11	5	7	23	-23	18	10	11	39	-13	3	0	1	4	-13						63	38	51	152	-13
-20/-16	0			0	-19	8	3	7	18	-18	7	2	3	12	-28	14	6	6	26	-18	1			1	-18						46	22	31	99	-18
-25/-21			0	0	-22	4	1	2	7	-23	3	0	0	3	-32	6	2	3	11	-23				0	-23						21	8	12	41	-23
-30/-26						1	0	1	2	-28						3	1	1	5	-28				0	-28						11	3	5	19	-28
-35/-31						1			1	-33						2			2	-32				0	-31						6			6	-32
-40/-36																			0															0	

CINCINNATI APRT/COVINGTON OHIO   LAT 39 03N   LONG 84 40W   ELEV 869 FT

MEAN FREQUENCY OF OCCURRENCE OF DRY BULB TEMPERATURE (DEGREES F) WITH MEAN COINCIDENT WET BULB TEMPERATURE (DEGREES F) FOR EACH DRY BULB TEMPERATURE RANGE

Temperature Range	MAY 01 to 08	09 to 16	17 to 24	Total Obsn	MCWB	JUNE 01 to 08	09 to 16	17 to 24	Total Obsn	MCWB	JULY 01 to 08	09 to 16	17 to 24	Total Obsn	MCWB	AUGUST 01 to 08	09 to 16	17 to 24	Total Obsn	MCWB	SEPTEMBER 01 to 08	09 to 16	17 to 24	Total Obsn	MCWB	OCTOBER 01 to 08	09 to 16	17 to 24	Total Obsn	MCWB
100/104																														
95/99											0	0	0	0	78	0	0	0	0	74	0	0	0	0	69					
90/94		1	0	1	70		1	0	1	76		2	1	3	74		3	0	3	72		1	0	1	67					
85/89		11	4	15	69		12	3	15	73		21	7	28	73		19	5	24	72		8	2	10	70		3	0	3	69
80/84		26	11	37	67	0	34	14	48	71	0	53	24	77	72		48	20	68	71		21	8	29	70		13	3	16	64
75/79	1	41	25	67	64	2	57	34	93	69	3	71	45	119	70	1	70	40	111	69		30	16	46	67		27	8	35	62
70/74	10	45	40	95	62	13	55	46	114	67	25	61	67	153	69	17	56	65	138	68	5	46	33	84	66	5	35	23	63	61
65/69	40	46	50	136	60	51	42	62	155	66	91	30	69	190	68	72	37	64	173	67	32	50	48	130	64	14	36	35	85	59
60/64	53	34	49	136	57	72	24	45	141	63	77	9	28	114	64	79	15	37	131	63	46	45	49	140	60	30	39	46	115	55
55/59	50	21	31	102	52	50	11	24	85	58	38	1	6	45	59	49	2	13	64	59	46	25	40	111	57	38	35	42	115	51
50/54	45	13	21	79	48	34	3	8	45	54	12		1	13	55	23	0	3	26	55	41	10	26	77	53	49	29	37	115	47
45/49	27	7	9	43	43	14	1	2	17	50	2			2	50	6	0	0	6	51	36	4	12	52	49	46	18	30	94	43
40/44	15	3	6	24	39	3		1	4	45	0	0	0	0	48	0			0	48	23	1	4	28	44	34	8	15	57	39
35/39	7	0	2	9	35																8	0	1	9	40	20	4	5	29	35
30/34	1	0	0	1	31																2	0	0	2	36	8	1	3	12	30
25/29	0			0	28																					3	0	1	4	26
20/24																										1	0	0	1	20
15/19																										0	0	0	0	17

CINCINNATI APRT/COVINGTON OHIO

Temperature Range	NOV 01–08	NOV 09–16	NOV 17–24	NOV Total Obsn	NOV MCWB	DEC 01–08	DEC 09–16	DEC 17–24	DEC Total Obsn	DEC MCWB	JAN 01–08	JAN 09–16	JAN 17–24	JAN Total Obsn	JAN MCWB	FEB 01–08	FEB 09–16	FEB 17–24	FEB Total Obsn	FEB MCWB	MAR 01–08	MAR 09–16	MAR 17–24	MAR Total Obsn	MAR MCWB	APR 01–08	APR 09–16	APR 17–24	APR Total Obsn	APR MCWB	ANN 01–08	ANN 09–16	ANN 17–24	ANN Total Obsn	ANN MCWB
100/104																																0	0	0	74
95/99																															0	7	1	8	73
90/94																															0	61	17	78	73
85/89																											1	0	1	65	0	171	70	241	71
80/84		0		0	67																						9	3	12	64	6	276	152	434	69
75/79	0	1	0	1	64				0	61				0	62				0	56	0	1	0	1	58		18	9	27	62	61	306	253	620	67
70/74	1	5	2	8	60	0	2	1	3	59	0	1	1	2	60	1	1	1	3	58	0	5	3	8	57	2	24	18	44	60	264	273	329	866	65
65/69	2	11	6	19	57	1	6	4	11	55	3	6	4	13	58	1	7	5	13	55	1	10	6	17	55	15	23	26	64	57	347	223	285	855	61
60/64	5	20	14	39	54	5	12	8	25	51	7	8	7	22	54	4	11	8	23	51	7	19	15	41	54	25	30	31	86	54	308	200	251	759	56
55/59	16	28	23	67	51	13	14	15	42	47	9	14	14	37	48	8	16	14	38	46	11	20	20	51	50	26	33	32	91	50	267	181	209	657	51
50/54	23	29	28	80	46	13	24	19	56	43	9	19	17	45	43	11	26	23	60	42	15	23	25	63	45	31	31	32	94	46	251	174	200	625	47
45/49	26	38	34	98	42	20	27	29	76	38	16	25	24	65	38	21	31	31	83	38	20	31	30	81	41	32	28	33	93	41	210	192	200	602	42
40/44	31	32	39	102	38	35	43	35	113	34	32	38	35	105	34	36	40	43	119	34	35	40	40	115	38	42	22	29	93	38	222	188	214	624	38
35/39	41	31	36	108	34	41	45	54	140	29	49	50	52	151	30	50	39	43	132	30	42	40	43	125	33	38	16	19	73	34	253	212	218	683	34
30/34	45	25	32	102	30	44	32	33	109	25	39	35	37	111	25	39	24	25	88	25	52	34	37	123	29	21	5	6	32	30	267	199	227	693	30
25/29	30	12	15	57	25	30	19	25	74	20	32	22	27	81	20	21	11	14	46	20	35	15	18	68	25	7	1	1	9	25	197	119	130	446	25
20/24	13	4	6	23	21	21	10	11	42	16	21	13	15	49	16	14	7	8	29	15	18	5	7	30	21	0			0	21	115	61	79	255	20
15/19	3	1	2	6	16	10	7	7	24	11	14	9	7	30	11	6	5	5	16	11	8	3	3	14	16						67	34	39	140	16
10/14	1	1	2	4	11	6	4	5	15	6	9	5	4	18	6	5	4	2	11	6	3	1	1	5	11						34	23	22	79	11
5/9	1	0	0	1	6	5	1	2	8	2	4	2	2	8	6	5	2	2	9	2	2	0	0	2	6						23	13	11	47	6
0/4	1	0	0	1	2	3	0	0	3	-3	3	1	2	6	-3	1	0	1	2	-3	0			0	3						15	5	6	26	2
-5/-1						0	0	0	0	-7				0	-7	1	0	0	1	-8											7	1	3	11	-3
-10/-6														1	-13	0	0	0	0	-13											2	0	0	2	-7
-15/-11															-16																1	0	0	1	-13
-20/-16																																			-16

CLEVELAND, OHIO*
READINGS TAKEN AT AKRON/CANTON AP

LAT 40 55N   LONG 81 26W   ELEV 1208 FT

MEAN FREQUENCY OF OCCURRENCE OF DRY BULB TEMPERATURE (DEGREES F) WITH MEAN COINCIDENT WET BULB TEMPERATURE (DEGREES F) FOR EACH DRY BULB TEMPERATURE RANGE

Temperature Range	MAY 01–08	MAY 09–16	MAY 17–24	MAY Total Obsn	MAY MCWB	JUNE 01–08	JUNE 09–16	JUNE 17–24	JUNE Total Obsn	JUNE MCWB	JULY 01–08	JULY 09–16	JULY 17–24	JULY Total Obsn	JULY MCWB	AUG 01–08	AUG 09–16	AUG 17–24	AUG Total Obsn	AUG MCWB	SEP 01–08	SEP 09–16	SEP 17–24	SEP Total Obsn	SEP MCWB	OCT 01–08	OCT 09–16	OCT 17–24	OCT Total Obsn	OCT MCWB
100/104																														
95/99								0	0	74		0		0	74															
90/94							1	0	1	74		5	1	6	72		0		0	68										
85/89		1	0	1	69		3	1	4	74		33	8	41	71		7	1	8	71		1		1	71		1		1	68
80/84		12	2	14	67	0	19	4	23	72	1	59	23	83	69	0	21	4	25	71		4	0	4	70		4		4	66
75/79	0	30	11	41	64	1	41	16	58	69	8	68	44	120	67	1	56	19	76	69		12	3	15	71		16	1	17	62
70/74	4	41	24	69	61	5	47	28	80	66	44	56	72	172	66	4	73	38	115	67	0	25	7	32	68	0	25	6	31	60
65/69	15	38	35	88	59	21	51	49	121	64	85	21	59	165	63	35	53	66	154	66	1	34	18	53	66	8	29	20	57	59
60/64	42	43	45	130	56	59	43	55	157	62	64	5	27	96	59	80	29	63	172	63	16	45	34	95	64	13	38	31	82	55
55/59	44	37	39	120	51	54	21	39	114	58	32	1	12	45	54	69	8	37	114	59	39	50	43	132	61	33	39	40	112	52
50/54	41	23	38	102	48	45	9	27	81	54	13	0	2	15	51	38	0	15	53	55	44	40	47	131	57	39	40	42	121	48
45/49	42	13	28	83	44	36	4	16	56	50	1	0	0	1	48	17	0	5	22	50	47	21	41	109	53	46	34	46	126	44
40/44	37	9	17	63	40	17	2	5	24	46						4	0	0	4	47	44	6	29	79	49	58	15	40	113	40
35/39	17	1	7	25	36	2	0	0	2	42											29	2	12	43	45	33	6	17	56	35
30/34	6	0	1	7	31	0	0	0	0	39											15	1	5	21	40	15	3	4	22	31
25/29	0	0	0	0	27																4	0	1	5	36	2	0	1	3	27
20/24																					1	0	0	1	32	1	0	0	1	23

*Comparative design data note:

	Elevation	WINTER 97 1/2%	SUMMER DB 2 1/2%	SUMMER DB 1%	SUMMER WB 2 1/2%	SUMMER WB 1%
Cleveland, OH	777 ft.	7° F	89° F		75° F	
Akron/Canton AP	1208 ft.	6° F	87° F		73° F	

INCIDENT WET BULB TEMPERATURE FOR EACH DRY BULB TEMPERATURE RANGE

CLEVELAND, OHIO*
READINGS TAKEN AT AKRON/CANTON AP

Temperature Range	Nov 01–08	Nov 09–16	Nov 17–24	Nov Total Obsn	Nov MCWB	Dec 01–08	Dec 09–16	Dec 17–24	Dec Total Obsn	Dec MCWB	Jan 01–08	Jan 09–16	Jan 17–24	Jan Total Obsn	Jan MCWB	Feb 01–08	Feb 09–16	Feb 17–24	Feb Total Obsn	Feb MCWB	Mar 01–08	Mar 09–16	Mar 17–24	Mar Total Obsn	Mar MCWB	Apr 01–08	Apr 09–16	Apr 17–24	Apr Total Obsn	Apr MCWB	Ann 01–08	Ann 09–16	Ann 17–24	Ann Total Obsn	Ann MCWB
100/104																																		0	74
95/99																																2		2	72
90/94																																19	3	22	72
85/89																																87	19	106	71
80/84																											3		3	65	3	200	67	270	69
75/79		1		1	64																0			0	58	0	10	2	12	63	18	279	142	439	66
70/74		1	0	1	62																1	0	0	1	56	0	18	7	25	59	120	291	258	669	64
65/69	1	10	3	14	57				0	57		0		0	61						3	1	1	5	54	3	24	14	41	56	290	248	294	832	61
60/64	3	14	8	25	55	0	2	1	3	54	0	0	1	1	58		0	0	0	54	5	4	4	13	54	13	24	24	61	54	304	205	264	773	57
55/59	12	21	14	47	51	2	7	3	12	52	1	1	0	2	57	0	1	1	2	54	8	8	9	25	51	22	25	24	73	51	284	180	233	697	52
50/54	15	24	23	62	47	6	12	8	26	48	3	4	4	11	55	2	4	3	9	51	16	12	12	40	46	28	27	30	85	47	255	172	216	643	48
45/49	25	30	29	84	43	9	15	10	34	44	4	8	5	17	50	3	9	6	18	48	17	19	23	59	42	34	33	36	103	43	232	177	208	617	43
40/44	30	38	31	99	39	15	21	21	57	39	9	9	8	26	45	5	14	11	30	42	27	25	25	77	38	33	30	29	92	39	235	185	205	625	39
35/39	36	35	42	113	34	27	37	31	95	35	9	16	15	40	39	15	24	22	61	39	39	31	42	112	34	41	27	35	103	34	221	213	231	665	35
30/34	50	36	45	131	30	46	52	48	146	30	15	31	26	72	35	20	34	30	84	34	62	42	51	155	30	41	15	35	83	31	298	257	270	825	30
25/29	38	18	23	79	26	43	42	47	132	26	44	49	42	135	30	41	52	52	145	30	36	50	41	127	26	18	3	7	28	26	247	188	206	641	26
20/24	18	8	13	39	21	39	27	34	100	21	47	49	49	145	25	48	41	38	127	26	16	35	26	77	21	5	1	2	8	21	178	111	142	431	21
15/19	7	3	4	14	16	23	20	22	65	16	44	40	40	124	21	35	20	27	82	21	5	15	10	30	16	1		1	2	17	97	60	79	236	16
10/14	4	1	4	9	11	22	9	14	45	11	27	21	28	76	16	24	11	14	49	16	11	5	1	17	12						75	34	51	160	11
5/9	1	1	2	4	7	9	3	6	18	7	25	14	18	57	11	13	8	11	32	11	4	0	1	5	8						32	12	23	67	7
0/4	0	0		0	3	3	2	2	7	1	13	5	8	26	7	5	3	6	14	2	1			1	2						17	5	7	29	2
-5/-1	0	0		0	-1	2	1	1	4	-3	5	1	3	9	2	8	2	2	12	-3											5	2	1	8	-3
-10/-6						2	0	0	2	-7	2	0	0	2	-3	1	1	0	2	-8											3	0	1	4	-8
-15/-11						0			0	-12				0	-7	1	0	1	2	-8											0			0	-12

COLUMBUS, OHIO*
READINGS TAKEN AT WRIGHT-PATTERSON AFB/DAYTON

LAT 39 49N   LONG 84 03W   ELEV   824 FT

MEAN FREQUENCY OF OCCURRENCE OF DRY BULB TEMPERATURE (DEGREES F) WITH MEAN COINCIDENT WET BULB TEMPERATURE (DEGREES F) FOR EACH DRY BULB TEMPERATURE RANGE

Temperature Range	May 01–08	May 09–16	May 17–24	May Total Obsn	May MCWB	Jun 01–08	Jun 09–16	Jun 17–24	Jun Total Obsn	Jun MCWB	Jul 01–08	Jul 09–16	Jul 17–24	Jul Total Obsn	Jul MCWB	Aug 01–08	Aug 09–16	Aug 17–24	Aug Total Obsn	Aug MCWB	Sep 01–08	Sep 09–16	Sep 17–24	Sep Total Obsn	Sep MCWB	Oct 01–08	Oct 09–16	Oct 17–24	Oct Total Obsn	Oct MCWB
100/104							0	0	0	81		1	0	1	75		0	0	0	80										
95/99							0	0	0	80		11	3	14	75		1	0	1	76										
90/94		1	0	1	70		12	4	16	73		50	23	73	72		12	3	15	75		1	0	1	71					
85/89		9	3	12	69		32	15	47	71	2	70	46	118	70		43	17	60	73		5	1	6	73		1		1	67
80/84	0	25	9	34	67	1	53	34	88	69	22	62	68	152	68	1	66	39	106	70		20	7	27	72		8	1	9	65
75/79	1	34	23	58	65	13	55	49	117	67	75	37	62	174	66	16	61	62	139	68		35	16	51	69		20	6	26	63
70/74	9	42	40	91	62	44	43	56	143	64	77	14	35	126	63	58	39	62	159	66	6	43	33	82	67	1	25	16	42	61
65/69	37	45	52	134	60	69	27	44	140	62	46	3	9	58	58	66	20	39	125	63	34	45	52	131	65	10	36	27	73	59
60/64	46	35	44	125	56	44	12	25	81	58	20	0	1	21	54	61	6	20	87	59	46	39	40	125	61	24	43	42	109	55
55/59	41	25	32	98	51	42	3	11	56	54	5	0	0	5	50	34	1	5	40	54	38	30	39	107	57	35	38	43	116	51
50/54	45	17	21	83	48	23	1	2	26	49	0			0	48	10	1	1	11	50	37	13	26	76	53	39	33	41	113	47
45/49	34	10	15	59	43	3	0	0	3	45						2	0	0	2	46	40	7	16	63	49	43	25	33	101	43
40/44	24	4	8	36	39	1			1	41						0			0	41	25	2	7	34	45	44	13	24	81	39
35/39	9	0	1	10	35																11	0	1	12	41	32	5	10	47	35
30/34	2	0	0	2	30																3	0	0	3	33	14	1	4	19	31
25/29	0			0	27																					5	1	0	6	26
20/24																										1			1	22

*Comparative design data note:

	WINTER 97 1/2%	SUMMER DB 2 1/2%	SUMMER WB 2 1/2%	Elevation
Columbus, OH	7° F	88° F	76° F	812 ft.
Wright/Patterson AFB/Dayton	8° F	90° F	76° F	824 ft.

COINCIDENT WET BULB TEMPERATURE FOR EACH DRY BULB TEMPERATURE RANGE

COLUMBUS, OHIO*
READINGS TAKEN AT WRIGHT-PATTERSON AFB/DAYTON

Column groups: each month reports **Obsn Hour Gp** (01 to 08 / 09 to 16 / 17 to 24), **Total Obsn**, and **MCWB**.

Temperature Range	NOV 01–08	NOV 09–16	NOV 17–24	NOV Total	NOV MCWB	DEC 01–08	DEC 09–16	DEC 17–24	DEC Total	DEC MCWB	JAN 01–08	JAN 09–16	JAN 17–24	JAN Total	JAN MCWB	FEB 01–08	FEB 09–16	FEB 17–24	FEB Total	FEB MCWB	MAR 01–08	MAR 09–16	MAR 17–24	MAR Total	MAR MCWB	APR 01–08	APR 09–16	APR 17–24	APR Total	APR MCWB	ANN 01–08	ANN 09–16	ANN 17–24	ANN Total	ANN MCWB
100/104																																		0	80
95/99																																0	3	3	75
90/94																																41	11	52	74
85/89																											1	0	1	69		156	65	221	72
80/84																											7	2	9	66	4	264	147	415	69
75/79		1	0	1	64																	2	0	2	58		15	8	23	63	58	293	249	600	67
70/74	1	4	1	6	60								0	0	59			0	0	63		6	3	9	57	2	19	16	37	60	224	260	308	792	65
65/69	1	8	5	14	59		1	1	2	59			0	0	58		1	0	1	57	1	8	5	14	54	11	26	20	57	57	318	225	268	811	61
60/64	5	18	12	35	55	2	6	3	11	55	1	2	2	5	56	1	3	2	6	54	5	13	10	28	53	22	37	34	93	54	295	208	242	745	56
55/59	13	26	19	58	51	4	9	7	20	52	2	4	3	9	53	2	5	4	11	52	9	15	16	40	50	26	34	37	97	50	265	173	204	642	52
50/54	21	33	33	87	47	9	12	12	33	48	5	7	5	17	49	4	8	6	18	47	8	21	19	48	45	31	35	36	102	46	240	174	192	606	47
45/49	32	43	37	112	43	13	20	18	51	43	7	13	10	30	43	6	14	12	32	42	19	30	28	77	42	35	29	33	97	42	219	186	193	598	43
40/44	39	39	39	117	38	19	27	25	71	38	13	23	21	57	38	11	22	22	55	38	29	40	35	104	38	38	21	30	89	38	229	189	205	623	38
35/39	40	29	43	112	34	28	39	32	99	34	23	33	31	87	34	24	41	35	100	34	42	46	51	139	33	41	14	17	72	34	242	207	220	669	34
30/34	43	24	29	96	30	44	48	51	143	30	38	41	43	122	29	40	44	47	131	30	54	38	41	133	29	27	3	6	36	30	262	199	221	682	30
25/29	27	11	14	52	25	46	38	42	126	25	41	35	39	115	25	42	35	35	112	25	40	19	24	83	25	6	0	0	6	26	207	138	155	500	25
20/24	12	3	5	20	21	35	21	25	81	21	27	32	29	88	20	34	20	26	80	20	24	8	11	43	21	1			1	22	134	84	96	314	20
15/19	4	2	2	8	16	20	11	14	45	16	29	23	30	82	16	24	15	17	56	16	12	3	3	18	16	0			0	18	89	54	66	209	16
10/14	1	0	1	2	12	12	7	9	28	11	28	16	17	61	11	15	7	8	30	11	4	1	1	6	12						60	31	36	127	11
5/9	0	0	0	0	6	6	4	4	14	7	15	9	9	33	6	10	6	5	21	6	2	0	0	2	7						33	19	18	70	6
0/4	0	0		0	2	6	2	3	11	2	9	5	5	19	2	7	2	2	11	2	0			0	2						22	9	10	41	2
-5/-1						3	0	0	3	-3	7	2	3	12	-3	3	0	1	4	-3											13	2	4	19	-3
-10/-6						1			1	-7	3	1	0	4	-7	0			0	-6											4	1	0	5	-7
-15/-11											1	0	0	1	-13																1	0	0	1	-13
-20/-16											0	0	0	0	-16																0	0	0	0	-16

OKLAHOMA CITY, OKLAHOMA/TINKER AFB

LAT 35 25N   LONG 97 23W   ELEV 1291 FT

MEAN FREQUENCY OF OCCURRENCE OF DRY BULB TEMPERATURE (DEGREES F) WITH COINCIDENT WET BULB TEMPERATURE (DEGREES F) FOR EACH DRY BULB TEMPERATURE RANGE

MAY

Temperature Range	01 to 08	09 to 16	17 to 24	Total Obsn	MCWB
100/104		0		0	72
95/99		3	1	4	72
90/94		21	7	28	70
85/89	0	46	25	71	68
75/79	5	54	45	104	66
70/74	38	49	57	144	64
65/69	66	32	50	148	61
60/64	60	22	33	115	57
55/59	40	14	20	74	53
50/54	24	5	8	37	48
45/49	11	1	2	14	44
40/44	3	0	0	3	40
35/39	0			0	35

JUNE

Temperature Range	01 to 08	09 to 16	17 to 24	Total Obsn	MCWB
100/104		0	0	0	72
95/99		3	1	4	74
90/94		30	12	42	74
85/89		57	31	88	73
80/84	7	63	57	127	71
75/79	43	42	66	151	69
70/74	91	23	42	156	67
65/69	64	14	20	98	63
60/64	25	6	8	39	59
55/59	9	1	2	12	54
50/54	1	0	0	1	50

JULY

Temperature Range	01 to 08	09 to 16	17 to 24	Total Obsn	MCWB
105/109		0		0	72
100/104		7	2	9	73
95/99		36	15	51	74
90/94		59	32	91	74
85/89	3	53	47	103	73
80/84	30	44	68	142	71
75/79	95	30	46	171	70
70/74	81	14	28	123	68
65/69	31	3	8	42	64
60/64	6	1	1	8	59
55/59	1		0	1	55
50/54	0			0	51

AUGUST

Temperature Range	01 to 08	09 to 16	17 to 24	Total Obsn	MCWB
105/109		1	0	1	73
100/104		6	2	8	74
95/99		23	9	32	73
90/94		50	24	74	73
85/89	1	63	42	106	72
80/84	17	49	64	130	70
75/79	72	33	59	164	69
70/74	99	16	37	152	67
65/69	46	4	10	60	63
60/64	11	1	1	13	58
55/59	3	0	0	3	56

SEPTEMBER

Temperature Range	01 to 08	09 to 16	17 to 24	Total Obsn	MCWB
95/99		1	0	1	75
90/94		6	1	7	73
85/89		19	6	25	72
80/84		33	16	49	71
75/79	3	43	31	77	69
70/74	23	49	51	123	67
65/69	57	39	49	145	65
60/64	56	24	42	122	62
55/59	52	16	28	96	58
50/54	32	7	10	49	53
45/49	11	3	5	19	49
40/44	4	0	0	4	45
35/39	1			1	41

OCTOBER

Temperature Range	01 to 08	09 to 16	17 to 24	Total Obsn	MCWB
90/94		0		0	61
85/89		3	0	3	64
80/84		9	2	11	67
75/79		23	7	30	66
70/74	0	32	17	49	64
65/69	10	38	36	84	62
60/64	32	42	41	115	59
55/59	43	39	46	128	55
50/54	43	32	45	120	51
45/49	53	17	29	99	47
40/44	37	8	17	62	43
35/39	21	4	6	31	39
30/34	7	1	1	9	35
25/29 (1)	1	0	1	2	30
25/29 (2)	1			1	26

OKLAHOMA CITY, OKLAHOMA/TINKER AFB

NOVEMBER

Temperature Range	Obsn Hour Gp 01 to 08	Obsn Hour Gp 09 to 16	Obsn Hour Gp 17 to 24	Total Obsn	MCWB
80/84	0	0	0	0	63
75/79	1	6	0	7	61
70/74	5	21	3	29	60
65/69	5	27	20	52	57
60/64	15	30	26	71	54
55/59	20	35	32	87	50
50/54	28	34	39	101	45
45/49	42	30	39	111	42
40/44	39	28	33	100	37
35/39	46	18	27	91	34
30/34	27	7	11	45	29
25/29	10	3	6	19	24
20/24	6	1	1	8	20
15/19	1	0	0	1	15
10/14	0	0	0	0	10

DECEMBER

Temperature Range	Obsn Hour Gp 01 to 08	Obsn Hour Gp 09 to 16	Obsn Hour Gp 17 to 24	Total Obsn	MCWB
80/84	0	0	0	0	58
75/79	0	0	1	1	55
70/74	0	8	1	9	53
65/69	3	16	8	27	53
60/64	9	23	17	49	50
55/59	10	35	26	71	45
50/54	23	37	41	101	41
45/49	37	35	42	114	37
40/44	49	35	42	126	33
35/39	51	26	30	107	29
30/34	29	15	18	62	25
25/29	22	10	12	44	20
20/24	7	5	7	19	16
15/19	6	2	2	10	11
10/14	2	0	0	2	7
5/9	1	0	0	1	2

JANUARY

Temperature Range	Obsn Hour Gp 01 to 08	Obsn Hour Gp 09 to 16	Obsn Hour Gp 17 to 24	Total Obsn	MCWB
75/79	0	0	0	0	54
70/74	0	1	0	1	55
65/69	0	5	2	7	53
60/64	3	12	7	22	53
55/59	5	15	12	32	49
50/54	8	26	21	55	45
45/49	15	29	25	69	41
40/44	25	33	36	94	37
35/39	34	32	37	103	33
30/34	48	34	37	119	29
25/29	40	24	27	91	25
20/24	25	15	21	61	20
15/19	19	11	12	42	16
10/14	15	8	7	30	11
5/9	5	3	4	12	6
0/4	6	1	1	8	2
-5/-1	1	0	0	1	-2

FEBRUARY

Temperature Range	Obsn Hour Gp 01 to 08	Obsn Hour Gp 09 to 16	Obsn Hour Gp 17 to 24	Total Obsn	MCWB
80/84	0	0	0	0	62
75/79	0	1	0	1	60
70/74	0	0	1	1	56
65/69	0	4	1	5	55
60/64	0	8	5	13	53
55/59	2	12	8	22	51
50/54	6	20	16	42	49
45/49	11	27	24	62	45
40/44	21	30	32	83	41
35/39	31	34	40	105	37
30/34	37	31	34	102	33
25/29	40	23	29	92	29
20/24	37	13	20	70	25
15/19	35	4	10	49	20
10/14	14	1	4	19	16
5/9	4	0	1	5	12
0/4	1	0	0	1	7
-5/-1	0	0	0	0	3

MARCH

Temperature Range	Obsn Hour Gp 01 to 08	Obsn Hour Gp 09 to 16	Obsn Hour Gp 17 to 24	Total Obsn	MCWB
90/94	0	0	0	0	62
85/89	0	1	0	1	60
80/84	0	3	1	4	62
75/79	0	8	4	12	60
70/74	3	15	6	24	57
65/69	9	22	10	41	55
60/64	11	28	26	65	52
55/59	19	28	27	74	48
50/54	26	31	36	93	45
45/49	34	31	34	99	41
40/44	42	37	28	107	37
35/39	41	34	15	90	33
30/34	39	25	13	77	29
25/29	21	8	7	36	25
20/24	8	2	2	12	20
15/19	2	1	1	4	16
10/14	1	1	2	4	11
5/9	0	0	1	1	8
0/4	0	0	0	0	4

APRIL

Temperature Range	Obsn Hour Gp 01 to 08	Obsn Hour Gp 09 to 16	Obsn Hour Gp 17 to 24	Total Obsn	MCWB
85/89	0	1	0	1	66
80/84	0	5	2	7	66
75/79	0	15	6	21	64
70/74	0	30	17	47	62
65/69	8	40	36	84	61
60/64	27	43	42	112	58
55/59	41	37	45	123	54
50/54	47	27	37	111	50
45/49	43	20	26	89	46
40/44	34	14	17	65	42
35/39	23	5	9	37	38
30/34	11	2	3	16	34
25/29	3	0	1	4	30
20/24	1	1	1	3	26

ANNUAL TOTAL

Temperature Range	Obsn Hour Gp 01 to 08	Obsn Hour Gp 09 to 16	Obsn Hour Gp 17 to 24	Total Obsn	MCWB
105/109		1	0	1	73
100/104		14	4	18	74
95/99		68	26	94	74
90/94		165	75	240	73
85/89	4	242	147	393	72
80/84	57	287	259	603	70
75/79	238	285	306	829	67
70/74	385	261	302	948	65
65/69	330	232	257	819	60
60/64	272	220	237	729	55
55/59	234	202	218	654	50
50/54	215	198	214	627	46
45/49	221	180	207	608	41
40/44	222	167	203	592	37
35/39	225	143	169	537	33
30/34	210	108	128	446	29
25/29	137	66	79	282	25
20/24	87	41	46	174	20
15/19	40	21	24	85	16
10/14	26	12	11	49	11
5/9	9	3	4	16	6
0/4	7	1	1	9	2
-5/-1	1	0		1	-2

TULSA IAP OKLAHOMA
LAT 36 12N LONG 95 54W ELEV 650 FT

MEAN FREQUENCY OF OCCURRENCE OF DRY BULB TEMPERATURE (DEGREES F) WITH MEAN COINCIDENT WET BULB TEMPERATURE (DEGREES F) FOR EACH DRY BULB TEMPERATURE RANGE

Each month block: Obsn Hour Gp = (01 to 08 | 09 to 16 | 17 to 24); Total Obsn; MCWB = Mean Coincident Wet Bulb.

Temperature Range	May 01–08	May 09–16	May 17–24	May Total	May MCWB	Jun 01–08	Jun 09–16	Jun 17–24	Jun Total	Jun MCWB	Jul 01–08	Jul 09–16	Jul 17–24	Jul Total	Jul MCWB	Aug 01–08	Aug 09–16	Aug 17–24	Aug Total	Aug MCWB	Sep 01–08	Sep 09–16	Sep 17–24	Sep Total	Sep MCWB	Oct 01–08	Oct 09–16	Oct 17–24	Oct Total	Oct MCWB
110/114												1	0	1	76															
105/109												3	2	5	75		5	1	6	73										
100/104												11	4	15	75		19	6	25	74										
95/99		0		0	75		2	1	3	75		41	17	58	75		33	14	47	74		3	0	3	71					
90/94		6	1	7	73		15	5	20	75	1	62	33	96	75	0	57	34	91	74		14	3	17	70		0		0	67
85/89		27	10	37	72		46	18	64	74	11	56	49	116	74	12	60	46	118	72		36	11	47	69		5	1	6	69
80/84	1	49	25	75	69	2	60	39	101	74	52	33	61	146	73	36	43	58	137	72	1	40	24	65	69		16	3	19	67
75/79	15	51	45	111	67	24	49	56	129	72	84	24	44	152	72	82	21	54	157	71	6	47	34	87	68		30	9	39	65
70/74	36	43	48	127	64	64	31	53	148	70	70	12	29	111	69	76	8	25	109	68	28	41	52	121	66	0	32	20	56	64
65/69	60	34	51	145	62	66	23	38	127	67	24	4	8	36	65	30	3	8	41	64	57	32	50	139	65	4	40	33	87	61
60/64	58	21	37	116	58	51	11	20	82	64	6	1	2	9	61	10	1	2	13	59	59	19	35	113	62	14	42	44	110	58
55/59	41	11	21	73	54	22	4	8	34	59	1			1	58	3	0	0	3	54	44	5	22	71	57	24	35	46	125	55
50/54	24	4	8	36	49	9	1	2	12	54											31	1	7	39	53	49	25	38	112	51
45/49	8	1	2	11	44	2			2	51											14	1	1	16	50	44	13	30	87	47
40/44	3		1	4	40																2		0	2	46	34	6	15	55	43
35/39	1			1	35																					23	2	5	30	39
30/34																										8	1	2	11	34
																										3		1	4	29
25/29																										1			1	27

COINCIDENT WET BULB TEMPERATURE FOR EACH DRY BULB TEMPERATURE RANGE

TULSA IAP OKLAHOMA

In each monthly block the observation hour groups are "01 to 08", "09 to 16", "17 to 24"; "Total Obsn" = total observations; "MCWB" = mean coincident wet bulb.

Temp. Range	NOV 01–08	NOV 09–16	NOV 17–24	NOV Total	NOV MCWB	DEC 01–08	DEC 09–16	DEC 17–24	DEC Total	DEC MCWB	JAN 01–08	JAN 09–16	JAN 17–24	JAN Total	JAN MCWB	FEB 01–08	FEB 09–16	FEB 17–24	FEB Total	FEB MCWB	MAR 01–08	MAR 09–16	MAR 17–24	MAR Total	MAR MCWB	APR 01–08	APR 09–16	APR 17–24	APR Total	APR MCWB	ANN 01–08	ANN 09–16	ANN 17–24	ANN Total	ANN MCWB
110/114																																1	0	1	76
105/109																																8	3	11	74
100/104																																35	11	46	74
95/99																															0	103	39	142	74
90/94																						0	0	0	59						1	213	98	312	74
85/89																						1	0	1	61		1	0	1	68	26	265	173	464	72
80/84		1		1	64												1	0	1	61		4	1	5	61		5	2	7	65	119	276	251	646	70
75/79		9	1	10	61		2		2	59		0	0	0	64		2	0	2	57		8	4	12	60		19	7	26	66	277	253	290	820	68
70/74	3	23	7	33	60		3	2	5	57		5	1	6	59		5	2	7	58	2	15	12	29	58	0	32	17	49	63	333	242	279	854	65
65/69	8	26	13	47	56	1	7	3	11	54	3	10	6	19	58	1	13	6	20	55	6	23	11	40	54	9	33	32	74	62	295	228	241	764	60
60/64	7	25	20	52	52	4	16	6	26	51	6	12	8	26	55	4	22	11	37	52	9	26	19	54	51	28	36	36	100	58	251	204	217	672	55
55/59	11	35	31	77	48	7	29	17	53	49	9	18	12	39	49	9	25	21	55	49	14	31	31	76	48	37	36	36	109	54	218	210	218	646	50
50/54	25	35	39	99	45	11	35	27	73	45	9	24	20	53	46	14	30	33	77	46	24	33	37	94	45	34	34	38	106	50	205	199	226	630	46
45/49	47	27	37	111	42	20	40	40	100	41	10	31	28	69	41	24	30	33	87	42	39	37	42	118	42	38	24	31	93	46	225	187	222	634	42
40/44	37	22	33	92	37	37	42	50	129	37	24	32	34	90	38	36	26	37	99	38	46	26	35	107	38	41	15	25	81	42	237	155	208	600	38
35/39	36	20	26	82	33	49	30	39	118	33	41	35	41	117	34	42	25	29	96	34	40	20	23	83	34	31	5	13	49	38	233	132	163	528	34
30/34	32	12	18	62	29	51	20	30	101	29	47	31	38	116	30	35	18	23	76	30	37	14	20	71	30	16	1	3	20	34	210	95	130	435	30
25/29	19	5	12	36	25	34	13	21	68	25	37	19	26	82	25	25	13	17	55	25	16	4	6	26	26	5	0	0	5	30	133	55	83	271	25
20/24	11	1	4	16	20	21	6	7	34	20	30	15	20	65	21	20	8	7	35	21	9	3	3	15	21	1	1	1	3	26	91	33	41	165	21
15/19	4	0	0	4	16	7	4	4	15	15	19	9	8	36	16	9	4	4	17	17	3	1	1	5	16	0	0	0	0	22	42	18	17	77	16
10/14	1	0		1	10	4	1	3	8	11	8	4	4	16	11	3	1	1	5	12	1	1	1	3	11						17	7	9	33	11
5/9						3	0	0	3	6	3	1	2	6	6	2	0	0	2	6	2		0	2	7						10	1	2	13	6
0/4						0			0	3	0	0	1	1	1	0			0	1											0	0	1	1	1
-5/-1											1	0		1	-3																1	0		1	-3

PORTLAND IAP OREGON
LAT 45 36N   LONG 122 36W   ELEV   21 FT

MEAN FREQUENCY OF OCCURRENCE OF DRY BULB TEMPERATURE (DEGREES F) WITH MEAN COINCIDENT WET BULB TEMPERATURE (DEGREES F) FOR EACH DRY BULB TEMPERATURE RANGE

Temperature Range	MAY 01-08	MAY 09-16	MAY 17-24	MAY Total	MAY MCWB	JUNE 01-08	JUNE 09-16	JUNE 17-24	JUNE Total	JUNE MCWB	JULY 01-08	JULY 09-16	JULY 17-24	JULY Total	JULY MCWB	AUG 01-08	AUG 09-16	AUG 17-24	AUG Total	AUG MCWB	SEP 01-08	SEP 09-16	SEP 17-24	SEP Total	SEP MCWB	OCT 01-08	OCT 09-16	OCT 17-24	OCT Total	OCT MCWB
100/104												1	0	1	72															
95/99												2	1	3	70															
90/94		0		0	62		0	0	0	64		6	3	9	68		1	1	2	68		0	0	0	65					
85/89		2	1	3	63		3	1	4	67		13	6	19	67		5	1	6	69		3	0	3	65		0	0	0	64
80/84		8	3	11	63		4	2	6	67	0	29	15	44	66		11	5	16	67		8	2	10	64		2	0	2	63
75/79		10	6	16	61	0	11	5	16	64	0	37	26	63	64		24	12	36	65		16	6	22	63		6	1	7	60
70/74		18	10	28	59	0	18	11	29	62	4	50	41	95	61		35	22	57	63		25	10	35	62		13	3	16	59
65/69	1	33	20	54	56	1	34	21	56	60	13	58	55	126	59	2	56	39	97	61	0	37	20	57	60	0	29	10	39	57
60/64	8	50	35	93	54	5	49	35	89	58	75	45	63	183	57	13	63	60	136	60	4	52	41	97	58	7	51	30	88	56
55/59	38	70	64	172	51	31	69	60	160	56	120	9	36	165	54	84	44	74	202	57	37	63	72	172	57	40	65	69	174	53
50/54	90	45	69	204	49	95	44	75	214	53	33	0	2	35	50	113	9	31	153	54	91	29	65	185	54	79	55	72	206	50
45/49	77	12	34	123	45	88	8	29	125	50	2	0	0	2	47	32	0	2	34	51	69	5	20	94	51	62	19	44	125	46
40/44	29	1	6	36	41	20	1	2	23	46	0			0	44	3			3	47	29	1	4	34	46	43	7	17	67	41
35/39	4		0	4	36	1	0	0	1	43											8	0	0	8	42	15	1	2	18	37
30/34	1		0	1	33																1	0		1	38	2	0	0	2	33

PORTLAND IAP OREGON

Temperature Range	NOV 01-08	NOV 09-16	NOV 17-24	NOV Total Obsn	NOV MCWB	DEC 01-08	DEC 09-16	DEC 17-24	DEC Total Obsn	DEC MCWB	JAN 01-08	JAN 09-16	JAN 17-24	JAN Total Obsn	JAN MCWB	FEB 01-08	FEB 09-16	FEB 17-24	FEB Total Obsn	FEB MCWB	MAR 01-08	MAR 09-16	MAR 17-24	MAR Total Obsn	MAR MCWB	APR 01-08	APR 09-16	APR 17-24	APR Total Obsn	APR MCWB	ANN 01-08	ANN 09-16	ANN 17-24	ANN Total Obsn	ANN MCWB
100/104																																1	0	1	72
95/99																																3	2	5	68
90/94																																17	5	22	68
85/89																											0		0	68	0	38	16	54	67
80/84																											1	0	1	64	0	91	41	132	65
75/79																						1	0	1	56		3	0	3	58	0	134	76	210	63
70/74																						3	1	4	54		9	4	13	56	7	218	138	363	61
65/69		1	1	1	54												0		0	51		9	4	13	51	0	17	8	25	53	36	305	230	571	58
60/64	0	5	1	6	54		1	0	1	57		0		0	55		4	1	5	52	1	26	12	39	48	1	31	17	49	51	243	372	357	972	56
55/59	6	33	11	50	51	2	8	4	14	53	2	9	3	14	51	3	13	5	21	50	9	58	39	106	46	8	53	37	98	50	519	368	412	1299	53
50/54	30	69	48	147	49	11	27	14	52	49	10	21	15	46	48	14	41	25	80	47	52	80	73	205	43	38	69	64	171	47	503	398	399	1300	49
45/49	59	63	70	192	45	36	61	44	141	44	29	47	36	112	44	30	68	56	154	43	88	50	78	216	40	77	43	68	188	44	476	395	431	1302	44
40/44	67	43	58	168	40	77	85	91	253	40	53	67	68	188	40	67	59	74	200	40	62	16	33	111	36	84	12	37	133	40	517	324	429	1270	40
35/39	39	18	33	90	36	67	45	61	173	36	70	48	60	178	36	59	25	43	127	36	30	4	7	41	32	28	1	4	33	36	345	154	236	735	36
30/34	25	6	13	44	31	38	16	27	81	31	41	28	31	100	31	35	8	15	58	31	7	1	1	9	26	5	0	0	5	33	177	62	93	332	31
25/29	11	2	3	16	26	14	3	4	21	26	21	15	16	52	25	10	3	3	16	26	0			0	21	0			0	28	63	24	27	114	26
20/24	2	1	2	5	20	1	0	0	1	21	11	9	11	31	20	3	1	1	5	20											17	11	14	42	20
15/19	1	1	0	1	16	0	1	1	2	14	7	3	5	15	15	1	1	1	3	16											9	5	7	21	15
10/14	0			0	13	1	1	1	3	10	3	1	2	6	11	0	0	1	1	10											4	2	4	10	10
5/9						0		0	0	6	1	0	0	1	7	1	0	0	1	7											2	0	0	2	7
0/4											0	0		0	2	0	0		0	2											0	0		0	2
-5/-1											0			0	-1	0			0	-1											0			0	-1

HARRISBURG IAP/OLMSTED PENNSYLVANIA
LAT 40 12N   LONG 76 46W   ELEV 308 FT

MEAN FREQUENCY OF OCCURRENCE OF DRY BULB TEMPERATURE (DEGREES F) WITH MEAN COINCIDENT WET BULB TEMPERATURE (DEGREES F) FOR EACH DRY BULB TEMPERATURE RANGE

Temperature Range	MAY 01-08	MAY 09-16	MAY 17-24	MAY Total Obsn	MAY MCWB	JUNE 01-08	JUNE 09-16	JUNE 17-24	JUNE Total Obsn	JUNE MCWB	JULY 01-08	JULY 09-16	JULY 17-24	JULY Total Obsn	JULY MCWB	AUG 01-08	AUG 09-16	AUG 17-24	AUG Total Obsn	AUG MCWB	SEP 01-08	SEP 09-16	SEP 17-24	SEP Total Obsn	SEP MCWB	OCT 01-08	OCT 09-16	OCT 17-24	OCT Total Obsn	OCT MCWB
100/104												1	0	1	74		1	0	1	76		0	0	0	76					
95/99		0	0	0	74		0	0	0	78		7	1	8	75		4	0	4	75		1	0	1	75					
90/94		2	0	2	72		4	1	5	77		28	9	37	74		14	3	17	75		7	0	7	75		0		0	74
85/89		12	3	15	69	0	15	5	20	74		53	22	75	72		38	12	50	73		17	5	22	73		2	0	2	71
80/84	0	20	9	29	67	3	49	30	82	71	5	68	49	122	70	2	61	35	98	70	0	30	14	44	70		6	1	7	68
75/79	1	35	21	57	63	15	46	45	106	67	35	53	66	154	68	21	64	63	148	69	7	42	30	79	68	0	17	5	22	65
70/74	9	42	34	85	61	47	39	55	141	65	83	27	61	171	67	65	42	71	178	67	31	47	44	122	65	5	25	12	42	63
65/69	25	47	49	121	59	59	28	46	133	61	73	9	29	111	63	84	20	44	148	63	42	43	51	136	61	7	39	23	69	59
60/64	48	40	51	139	56	59	15	28	102	58	37	2	10	49	59	46	4	16	66	59	51	34	42	127	57	16	45	38	99	56
55/59	58	30	40	128	52	42	6	14	62	53	13	0	0	13	55	22	0	4	26	54	45	14	31	90	53	36	50	49	135	52
50/54	53	15	25	93	48	13	2	3	18	50	1			1	51	8	0	0	8	50	32	5	16	53	49	49	38	52	139	47
45/49	36	5	12	53	44	1	0	0	1	45						0			0	48	20	0	5	25	45	56	19	39	114	43
40/44	14	0	2	16	39																7	0	1	8	40	43	6	21	70	39
35/39	3	1	0	4	34																3	0	0	3	36	26	2	7	35	35
30/34	0	0	0	0	32																0	0	0	0	32	9	0	1	10	31
25/29																										1			1	26

COINCIDENT WET BULB TEMPERATURE FOR EACH DRY BULB TEMPERATURE RANGE

HARRISBURG IAP/OLMSTED PENNSYLVANIA

Temperature Range	NOV Obsn 01-08	NOV 09-16	NOV 17-24	NOV Total Obsn	NOV MCWB	DEC Obsn 01-08	DEC 09-16	DEC 17-24	DEC Total Obsn	DEC MCWB	JAN Obsn 01-08	JAN 09-16	JAN 17-24	JAN Total Obsn	JAN MCWB	FEB Obsn 01-08	FEB 09-16	FEB 17-24	FEB Total Obsn	FEB MCWB	MAR Obsn 01-08	MAR 09-16	MAR 17-24	MAR Total Obsn	MAR MCWB	APR Obsn 01-08	APR 09-16	APR 17-24	APR Total Obsn	APR MCWB	ANN Obsn 01-08	ANN 09-16	ANN 17-24	ANN Total Obsn	ANN MCWB
100/104																															0	2	0	2	76
95/99																															0	16	2	18	75
90/94																										0	1	0	1	69	0	67	17	84	74
85/89																										0	3	0	3	67	0	160	56	216	72
80/84																										0	8	3	11	65	10	242	141	393	69
75/79																					0	1	0	1	58	0	12	6	18	62	79	270	236	585	67
70/74	0	3	0	3	62											0	0	0	0	58	0	3	1	4	56	2	15	12	29	59	242	243	290	775	65
65/69	2	7	4	13	59	0	0	0	0	61	0	0	0	0	55	0	0	1	1	58	0	4	2	6	54	6	21	19	46	57	298	218	268	784	61
60/64	4	15	6	25	55	0	2	2	4	55	1	1	1	3	56	0	2	1	3	54	1	11	6	18	52	15	31	25	71	54	278	202	226	706	56
55/59	10	31	20	61	51	4	5	4	13	53	0	1	1	2	53	2	4	3	9	51	4	16	11	31	50	23	40	37	100	50	259	197	214	670	52
50/54	22	42	28	92	47	4	13	6	23	47	2	4	2	8	47	2	10	6	18	46	6	29	18	53	45	39	42	45	126	46	231	200	201	632	47
45/49	30	50	43	123	42	7	22	14	43	43	2	14	6	22	42	5	20	13	38	41	14	38	36	88	41	50	38	45	133	42	221	206	213	640	43
40/44	41	47	51	139	38	22	42	35	99	38	14	33	20	67	37	14	41	29	84	38	36	55	55	146	37	54	20	33	107	38	245	244	247	736	38
35/39	54	28	49	131	34	43	54	55	152	34	35	59	55	149	34	37	53	51	141	34	68	50	61	179	34	34	7	12	53	34	303	254	290	847	34
30/34	43	14	28	85	30	59	48	52	159	29	58	60	67	185	29	61	42	59	162	29	64	27	38	129	29	13	1	3	17	30	307	192	248	747	29
25/29	26	2	8	36	26	37	29	37	103	24	51	35	46	132	25	45	21	29	95	25	33	10	14	57	24	3	0	0	3	24	196	97	134	427	25
20/24	5	1	2	8	20	33	20	25	78	20	35	23	23	81	20	24	15	15	54	20	16	3	5	24	16	0	0	0	0	20	113	62	70	245	20
15/19	2	0	0	2	15	21	9	14	44	15	24	11	16	51	15	13	9	12	34	15	4	0	1	5	11						64	29	43	136	15
10/14						12	3	4	19	11	15	5	8	28	11	14	4	5	23	11	2	0	0	2							43	12	17	72	11
5/9						3	0	1	4	7	6	2	3	11	6	6	1	2	9	7											15	3	6	24	6
0/4						2	0	0	2	2	3	1	1	5	1	0	2	0	2	2											7	1	1	9	1
-5/-1						0	0	0	0	-3	1	0	0	1	-3	0	0	0	0	-3											1	0	0	1	-3
-10/-6						0	0	0	0	-7	0	0	0	0	-6	0	0	0	0	-6											0	0	0	0	-7

PHILADELPHIA, PENNSYLVANIA*
READINGS TAKEN AT MC GUIRE AFB, NJ

LAT 40 01N   LONG 74 36W   ELEV 133 FT

MEAN FREQUENCY OF OCCURRENCE OF DRY BULB TEMPERATURE (DEGREES F) WITH MEAN COINCIDENT WET BULB TEMPERATURE (DEGREES F) FOR EACH DRY BULB TEMPERATURE RANGE

Temperature Range	MAY 01–08	MAY 09–16	MAY 17–24	MAY Total Obsn	MAY MCWB	JUNE 01–08	JUNE 09–16	JUNE 17–24	JUNE Total Obsn	JUNE MCWB	JULY 01–08	JULY 09–16	JULY 17–24	JULY Total Obsn	JULY MCWB	AUG 01–08	AUG 09–16	AUG 17–24	AUG Total Obsn	AUG MCWB	SEP 01–08	SEP 09–16	SEP 17–24	SEP Total Obsn	SEP MCWB	OCT 01–08	OCT 09–16	OCT 17–24	OCT Total Obsn	OCT MCWB
100/104																														
95/99		0	0	0	70							0	0	0	74															
90/94		2	0	2	72		2	0	2	77		2	0	2	74															
85/89		8	2	10	69		11	2	13	75		16	2	18	74		8	1	9	75	0	5	0	5	74		1		1	72
80/84		17	6	23	66	0	32	10	42	72	0	47	14	61	73		43	8	51	74		20	3	23	73		6	1	7	69
75/79	1	32	13	46	64	2	51	22	75	69	4	76	34	114	70	1	68	26	95	71	0	35	10	45	70	1	18	3	22	65
70/74	7	41	24	72	61	10	51	39	100	67	28	64	60	152	69	22	68	57	147	69	6	49	26	81	68	3	35	10	48	63
65/69	19	50	37	106	58	44	48	52	144	65	82	32	74	188	67	71	41	74	186	67	36	49	49	134	66	11	45	25	81	60
60/64	37	44	47	128	55	60	27	54	141	62	76	10	47	133	63	75	16	52	143	63	47	40	50	137	62	29	50	45	124	56
55/59	55	29	52	136	52	60	14	37	111	58	44	1	15	60	59	49	3	22	74	59	52	28	48	128	58	39	42	46	127	52
50/54	56	17	42	115	48	42	3	19	64	54	13		1	14	54	22	0	7	29	54	45	11	33	89	53	50	30	51	131	47
45/49	50	6	20	76	44	18	0	4	22	49	1			1	50	7		0	7	49	33	3	16	52	49	48	14	37	99	43
40/44	19	1	5	25	39	4		0	4	45						0		0	0	45	13	0	4	17	44	35	5	19	59	39
35/39	4		1	5	34	0			0	42											6		1	7	40	22	2	8	32	34
30/34	1			1	30																2		0	2	36	9	0	2	11	30
25/29																										2		0	2	25

*Comparative design data note:

	Elevation	WINTER 97 1/2%	SUMMER DB 2 1/2%	SUMMER WB 2 1/2%
Philadelphia, PA	7 ft.	15° F	90° F	77° F
McGuire AFB/NJ	133 ft.	14° F	90° F	77° F

COINCIDENT WET BULB TEMPERATURE FOR EACH DRY BULB TEMPERATURE RANGE

PHILADELPHIA, PENNSYLVANIA*
READINGS TAKEN AT MC GUIRE AFB, NJ

For each month the sub-columns are the Observation Hour Group (01 to 08, 09 to 16, 17 to 24), Total Obsn, and MCWB (Mean Coincident Wet Bulb).

Temperature Range	Nov 01-08	Nov 09-16	Nov 17-24	Nov Total	Nov MCWB	Dec 01-08	Dec 09-16	Dec 17-24	Dec Total	Dec MCWB	Jan 01-08	Jan 09-16	Jan 17-24	Jan Total	Jan MCWB	Feb 01-08	Feb 09-16	Feb 17-24	Feb Total	Feb MCWB	Mar 01-08	Mar 09-16	Mar 17-24	Mar Total	Mar MCWB	Apr 01-08	Apr 09-16	Apr 17-24	Apr Total	Apr MCWB	Ann 01-08	Ann 09-16	Ann 17-24	Ann Total	Ann MCWB
100/104																																		0	74
95/99																																		4	76
90/94																															0	42	5	47	74
85/89																													0	67	0	153	37	190	73
80/84		0		0	69																			0	60	0	2	0	2	66	7	259	100	366	70
75/79		1	0	1	69		0	0	0	62											0	2	0	2	58	0	6	1	7	64	68	295	201	564	68
70/74	1	4	1	6	64		1		1	62											0	4	1	5	57	0	10	3	13	61	244	270	292	806	65
65/69	2	10	3	15	59	0	2	1	3	58		1		1	59		1		1	57	0	7	2	9	54	0	15	7	22	59	292	232	284	808	61
60/64	6	24	12	42	56	1	3	1	5	56		1	2	3	56		3	1	4	56	1	10	5	16	53	2	23	13	38	55	292	214	255	761	57
55/59	18	38	22	78	52	5	10	5	20	52	2	3	2	7	53	2	5	5	12	52	3	15	9	27	49	12	33	21	66	53	269	200	232	701	52
50/54	26	52	36	114	47	8	19	9	36	47	4	7	4	15	48	4	11	5	20	46	5	28	16	49	44	23	44	31	98	50	242	209	225	676	47
45/49	37	47	46	130	42	13	27	24	64	43	6	20	8	34	42	6	18	8	32	42	13	41	29	83	41	30	42	42	114	46	234	208	232	674	42
40/44	45	34	50	129	38	23	39	30	92	38	16	34	22	72	38	14	35	21	70	38	37	49	52	138	37	46	35	54	135	42	249	219	245	713	38
35/39	45	20	39	104	33	38	50	45	133	33	30	51	44	125	34	36	50	47	133	33	62	51	65	178	34	54	22	45	121	38	285	230	269	784	34
30/34	41	7	23	71	29	55	48	56	159	29	43	44	57	144	29	45	44	59	148	29	66	27	44	137	29	46	6	20	72	34	281	171	245	697	29
25/29	14	1	6	21	25	39	27	40	106	24	46	34	38	118	24	48	27	39	114	24	36	9	16	61	24	21	1	4	26	30	189	98	139	426	24
20/24	5	0	1	6	20	31	16	21	68	20	35	28	34	97	19	29	16	19	64	19	15	3	6	24	20	4			4	25	116	63	81	260	20
15/19	1			1	16	24	6	13	43	15	30	16	22	68	15	23	9	12	44	15	6	2	1	9	15	1			1	20	84	33	48	165	15
10/14						8	1	2	11	11	22	7	11	40	11	12	3	5	20	10	2	0	0	2	11				0	17	44	11	18	73	11
5/9						2	0	1	3	7	10	3	4	17	6	7	1	2	10	6				0	6						19	4	7	30	6
0/4						1			1	1	3	0	0	3	2	1	0	0	1	1											5	0	0	5	2
-5/-1																			0	-4														0	-4

PITTSBURGH/GTR PITTSBURGH IAP PA
LAT 40 30N   LONG 80 13W   ELEV 1137 FT

MEAN FREQUENCY OF OCCURRENCE OF DRY BULB TEMPERATURE (DEGREES F) WITH MEAN COINCIDENT WET BULB TEMPERATURE (DEGREES F) FOR EACH DRY BULB TEMPERATURE RANGE

Temperature Range	MAY 01-08	MAY 09-16	MAY 17-24	MAY Total	MAY MCWB	JUNE 01-08	JUNE 09-16	JUNE 17-24	JUNE Total	JUNE MCWB	JULY 01-08	JULY 09-16	JULY 17-24	JULY Total	JULY MCWB	AUG 01-08	AUG 09-16	AUG 17-24	AUG Total	AUG MCWB	SEP 01-08	SEP 09-16	SEP 17-24	SEP Total	SEP MCWB	OCT 01-08	OCT 09-16	OCT 17-24	OCT Total	OCT MCWB
95/99								0	0	72			0	0	72		1		1	69		1		1	73					
90/94							4	0	4	72		4	1	5	72		6	1	7	71		3	1	4	70					
85/89		0	0	0	71		23	6	29	71		35	10	45	71		20	5	25	71		14	2	16	71			0	0	72
80/84		4	1	5	69		47	22	69	68	0	66	30	96	69		62	22	84	69	0	27	10	37	69		6		6	65
75/79		19	6	25	66	4	50	33	87	66	7	65	52	124	67	4	67	48	119	67	1	42	20	63	66		19	3	22	62
70/74	0	35	17	52	63	26	52	54	132	64	49	48	72	169	66	32	53	71	156	66	14	45	39	98	64	1	27	12	40	60
65/69	6	42	30	78	60	56	33	52	141	61	82	23	54	159	63	82	29	61	172	63	40	41	50	131	61	8	34	23	65	58
60/64	21	43	44	108	59	59	19	41	119	58	66	6	24	96	59	67	9	28	104	59	49	37	47	133	57	15	40	39	94	54
55/59	47	39	48	134	55	46	9	21	76	53	29	0	6	35	54	41	1	9	51	54	44	19	33	96	53	31	37	43	111	51
50/54	40	27	37	104	51	33	3	9	45	49	13		1	14	50	19	0	2	21	50	44	8	25	77	48	44	37	44	125	47
45/49	46	19	29	94	47	14	2	1	17	45	2			2	45	3			3	45	29	3	10	42	45	52	28	37	117	43
40/44	39	12	20	71	43	2			2	41	0			0	41	0			0	41	13	0	2	15	40	46	15	30	91	39
35/39	30	7	13	50	39	0			0	38											6	0		6	36	33	5	12	50	35
30/34	15	0	3	18	35																0			0	33	16	2	4	22	31
25/29	4	0	0	4	30																					4	0	0	4	26
20/24	1			1	27																					0	0	0	0	22
15/19																										0	0	0	0	17

COINCIDENT WET BULB TEMPERATURE FOR EACH DRY BULB TEMPERATURE RANGE

PITTSBURGH/GTR PITTSBURGH IAP PA

Temperature Range	NOV 01–08	NOV 09–16	NOV 17–24	NOV Total	NOV MCWB	DEC 01–08	DEC 09–16	DEC 17–24	DEC Total	DEC MCWB	JAN 01–08	JAN 09–16	JAN 17–24	JAN Total	JAN MCWB	FEB 01–08	FEB 09–16	FEB 17–24	FEB Total	FEB MCWB	MAR 01–08	MAR 09–16	MAR 17–24	MAR Total	MAR MCWB	APR 01–08	APR 09–16	APR 17–24	APR Total	APR MCWB	ANN 01–08	ANN 09–16	ANN 17–24	ANN Total	ANN MCWB
95/99																																	2	2	71
90/94																																17	3	20	72
85/89		0		0	66																						1		1	67		97	24	121	71
80/84																											6	2	8	63		233	92	325	68
75/79	0	0	0	0	64	0	1	0	1	57												1	0	1	57		13	5	18	62	16	292	178	486	66
70/74	0	3	1	4	60	1	4	3	8	54											0	3	1	4	56	1	22	11	34	59	129	295	291	715	64
65/69	0	11	2	13	55	2	8	5	15	51		0	0	0	58		1	0	1	55	0	6	2	8	54	5	22	19	46	56	294	244	307	845	61
60/64	4	18	12	34	54	8	13	8	29	47	0	1	1	2	56	1	2	1	4	53	2	11	6	19	52	18	27	29	74	54	329	213	279	821	56
55/59	14	22	19	55	50	13	14	16	43	42	2	3	3	8	52	2	5	4	11	51	6	17	15	38	49	29	32	34	95	50	286	180	229	695	52
50/54	20	31	27	78	46	17	28	24	69	38	4	7	5	16	47	4	10	8	22	45	11	20	20	51	45	31	32	35	98	46	277	180	213	670	47
45/49	31	34	36	101	42	31	33	33	97	34	5	11	9	25	42	7	14	15	36	41	13	28	25	66	41	31	28	32	91	42	239	173	202	614	42
40/44	33	39	38	110	38	45	48	51	144	30	15	21	22	58	38	13	23	21	57	38	28	35	35	98	38	37	25	29	91	37	234	193	214	641	38
35/39	40	38	40	118	34	44	43	41	128	25	24	36	29	89	34	26	37	32	95	33	40	44	45	129	33	38	22	24	84	34	253	215	218	686	34
30/34	52	26	42	120	30	33	25	26	84	20	38	42	47	127	30	44	46	51	141	29	54	43	48	145	29	32	7	18	57	30	285	214	261	760	30
25/29	28	10	15	53	25	21	16	22	59	15	44	45	41	130	25	36	32	33	101	25	44	24	29	97	25	15	2	4	21	25	216	156	163	535	25
20/24	12	4	5	21	21	18	9	12	39	11	36	32	34	102	20	32	22	24	78	20	25	10	15	50	20	4	0	0	4	21	142	93	104	339	20
15/19	3	2	2	7	16	10	4	6	20	6	29	24	25	78	15	21	13	16	50	15	15	4	6	25	16	0			0	18	89	59	71	219	15
10/14	2	1	2	5	11	3	1	2	6	1	25	16	18	59	11	18	9	10	37	11	7	1	2	10	11						70	36	44	150	11
5/9	0	0	0	0	7	2	1	0	3	-3	13	6	10	29	6	8	5	7	20	6	3	0	0	3	7						34	15	23	72	6
0/4	1	0	0	1	1						8	3	4	15	1	7	2	2	11	2	0			0	4						19	6	8	33	1
-5/-1											4	1	1	6	-3	3	1	0	4	-3											9	3	1	13	-3
-10/-6											2	0	0	2	-7	2	0		2	-7											4	0	0	4	-7
-15/-11											0	0	0	0	-13																0			0	-13
-20/-16											0	0	0	0	-17																0			0	-17

Column groups within each month: Obsn Hour Gp (01 to 08 | 09 to 16 | 17 to 24), Total Obsn, MCWB.

COLUMBIA, SOUTH CAROLINA*
READINGS TAKEN AT SHAW AFB/SUMPTER
LAT 33 58N   LONG 80 28W   ELEV   252 FT

MEAN FREQUENCY OF OCCURRENCE OF DRY BULB TEMPERATURE (DEGREES F) WITH MEAN COINCIDENT WET BULB TEMPERATURE (DEGREES F) FOR EACH DRY BULB TEMPERATURE RANGE

Temperature Range	MAY 01–08	MAY 09–16	MAY 17–24	MAY Total Obsn	MAY MCWB	JUNE 01–08	JUNE 09–16	JUNE 17–24	JUNE Total Obsn	JUNE MCWB	JULY 01–08	JULY 09–16	JULY 17–24	JULY Total Obsn	JULY MCWB	AUG 01–08	AUG 09–16	AUG 17–24	AUG Total Obsn	AUG MCWB	SEP 01–08	SEP 09–16	SEP 17–24	SEP Total Obsn	SEP MCWB	OCT 01–08	OCT 09–16	OCT 17–24	OCT Total Obsn	OCT MCWB
105/109							0	0	0	78			0	0	80			0	0	79										
100/104							2	0	2	77		7	1	8	78		7	1	8	78										
95/99		2	0	2	72		6	2	8	76		46	12	58	76		41	11	52	77		1		1	78					
90/94		13	4	17	71		34	12	46	75		79	33	112	75	0	80	31	111	75		15	2	17	75				0	70
85/89		41	14	55	69	1	60	26	87	73	10	70	57	137	74	8	64	54	126	74		56	14	70	73		8	1	9	70
80/84	0	57	29	86	68	6	64	45	115	71	82	36	91	209	72	77	38	91	206	72	1	62	32	95	71		31	5	36	68
75/79	7	54	46	107	66	39	44	64	147	70	136	9	52	197	70	124	14	49	187	70	20	50	66	136	70	2	48	19	69	66
70/74	50	43	67	160	65	111	22	67	200	68	18		2	20	64	31	2	10	43	64	91	32	70	193	68	19	55	44	118	64
65/69	87	21	48	156	63	62	5	20	87	64	2			2	60	7	0	1	8	59	63	16	32	111	63	37	47	58	142	61
60/64	49	9	24	82	57	18	1	3	22	59						0			0	55	40	6	18	64	58	58	31	50	139	57
55/59	34	5	12	51	53	4	0	1	5	54											17	1	6	24	54	47	19	37	103	52
50/54	17	2	3	22	49	0			0	50											7	0	1	8	49	40	8	20	68	48
45/49	3	1	1	5	44																1		0	1	45	25	1	9	35	43
40/44	1			1	40																					14	0	4	18	38
35/39																										5		1	6	34
30/34																										1		0	1	30

*Comparative design data note:

	WINTER 97 1/2%	SUMMER DB 2 1/2%	SUMMER WB 2 1/2%	Elevation
Columbia, SC	23° F	96° F	79° F	217 ft.
Shaw AFB/Sumter	26° F	94° F	79° F	252 ft.

COINCIDENT WET BULB TEMPERATURE FOR EACH DRY BULB TEMPERATURE RANGE

COLUMBIA, SOUTH CAROLINA*
READINGS TAKEN AT SHAW AFB/SUMPTER

NOVEMBER

Temperature Range	Obsn Hour Gp 01 to 08	09 to 16	17 to 24	Total Obsn	MCWB
105/109					
100/104					
95/99					
90/94					
85/89		1		1	69
80/84		3	0	3	69
75/79		18	2	20	64
70/74	3	32	11	46	61
65/69	10	45	27	82	59
60/64	22	41	40	103	55
55/59	35	36	47	118	51
50/54	44	32	44	120	46
45/49	46	20	34	100	42
40/44	35	9	21	65	38
35/39	26	3	10	39	33
30/34	15	1	3	19	29
25/29	2	0	1	3	24
20/24	1	1		1	19
15/19		0		0	16
10/14					
5/9					

DECEMBER

Temperature Range	Obsn Hour Gp 01 to 08	09 to 16	17 to 24	Total Obsn	MCWB
105/109					
100/104					
95/99					
90/94					
85/89					
80/84		0		0	69
75/79		4	1	5	65
70/74	1	13	3	17	62
65/69	5	21	11	37	59
60/64	12	27	22	61	56
55/59	15	33	26	74	50
50/54	25	41	42	108	46
45/49	34	40	40	114	41
40/44	36	30	41	107	37
35/39	44	22	35	101	33
30/34	43	12	18	73	29
25/29	24	4	8	36	24
20/24	8	1	2	11	20
15/19	2	0	0	2	15
10/14	1	0		1	10
5/9	0			0	7

JANUARY

Temperature Range	Obsn Hour Gp 01 to 08	09 to 16	17 to 24	Total Obsn	MCWB
105/109					
100/104					
95/99					
90/94					
85/89					
80/84					
75/79		3	0	3	63
70/74		9	2	11	61
65/69	3	14	8	25	59
60/64	7	20	15	42	55
55/59	12	29	22	63	50
50/54	20	32	33	85	46
45/49	29	38	41	108	42
40/44	38	37	40	115	37
35/39	44	33	39	116	33
30/34	46	20	29	95	29
25/29	31	8	14	53	24
20/24	12	3	3	18	20
15/19	5	1	1	7	15
10/14	1	0		1	10
5/9	0			0	7

FEBRUARY

Temperature Range	Obsn Hour Gp 01 to 08	09 to 16	17 to 24	Total Obsn	MCWB
105/109					
100/104					
95/99					
90/94					
85/89					
80/84		0		0	65
75/79		4	1	5	64
70/74	0	10	4	14	60
65/69	3	16	11	30	58
60/64	12	25	19	56	55
55/59	15	27	26	68	50
50/54	18	38	37	93	45
45/49	33	37	39	109	41
40/44	34	29	39	102	37
35/39	47	21	27	95	33
30/34	35	11	15	61	29
25/29	20	3	4	27	24
20/24	5	1	1	7	19
15/19	2	0	0	2	15
10/14	1			1	10
5/9	0			0	7

MARCH

Temperature Range	Obsn Hour Gp 01 to 08	09 to 16	17 to 24	Total Obsn	MCWB
105/109					
100/104					
95/99					
90/94					
85/89		1	0	1	65
80/84		5	2	7	63
75/79		16	5	21	61
70/74	1	23	14	38	59
65/69	7	31	25	63	57
60/64	22	41	41	104	54
55/59	32	42	44	118	50
50/54	39	36	43	118	46
45/49	51	26	35	112	42
40/44	42	16	24	82	37
35/39	32	6	10	48	33
30/34	16	4	3	23	28
25/29	6	1	1	8	25
20/24	1			1	19
15/19					
10/14					
5/9					

APRIL

Temperature Range	Obsn Hour Gp 01 to 08	09 to 16	17 to 24	Total Obsn	MCWB
105/109					
100/104					
95/99		0		0	75
90/94		2	0	2	70
85/89		14	4	18	67
80/84		30	13	43	66
75/79	1	39	24	64	63
70/74	9	44	40	93	61
65/69	35	41	53	129	59
60/64	59	34	44	137	56
55/59	46	21	31	98	51
50/54	43	10	22	75	47
45/49	30	3	7	40	43
40/44	16	1	2	19	39
35/39	2			2	34
30/34	0			0	29
25/29					
20/24					
15/19					
10/14					
5/9					

ANNUAL TOTAL

Temperature Range	Obsn Hour Gp 01 to 08	09 to 16	17 to 24	Total Obsn	MCWB
105/109		0	0	0	78
100/104		2	0	2	77
95/99		23	4	27	77
90/94	0	151	41	192	75
85/89	1	340	123	464	73
80/84	25	386	237	648	71
75/79	228	354	410	992	69
70/74	545	306	423	1274	67
65/69	361	259	305	925	61
60/64	308	235	277	820	56
55/59	257	213	252	722	51
50/54	253	199	245	697	46
45/49	252	166	206	624	42
40/44	216	122	171	509	37
35/39	200	85	122	407	33
30/34	156	48	68	272	29
25/29	83	16	28	127	24
20/24	27	5	6	38	20
15/19	9	1	1	11	15
10/14	3	0	0	3	10
5/9	0			0	7

RAPID CITY, SOUTH DAKOTA/ELLSWORTH AFB

LAT 44 08N   LONG 103 06W   ELEV 3276 FT

MEAN FREQUENCY OF OCCURRENCE OF DRY BULB TEMPERATURE (DEGREES F) WITH MEAN COINCIDENT WET BULB TEMPERATURE (DEGREES F) FOR EACH DRY BULB TEMPERATURE RANGE

Temperature Range	MAY 01–08	MAY 09–16	MAY 17–24	MAY Total Obsn	MAY MCWB	JUNE 01–08	JUNE 09–16	JUNE 17–24	JUNE Total Obsn	JUNE MCWB	JULY 01–08	JULY 09–16	JULY 17–24	JULY Total Obsn	JULY MCWB	AUG 01–08	AUG 09–16	AUG 17–24	AUG Total Obsn	AUG MCWB	SEP 01–08	SEP 09–16	SEP 17–24	SEP Total Obsn	SEP MCWB	OCT 01–08	OCT 09–16	OCT 17–24	OCT Total Obsn	OCT MCWB
105/109									0	67				0	71				0	65				0	67					
100/104		0	0	0	66		1		1	67		1	0	1	67		2	0	2	66		1	0	1	66					
95/99		0	0	0	66		2	1	3	66		8	2	10	67		12	3	15	65		1	0	1	66					
90/94		4	1	5	61		6	2	8	65		23	7	30	67		34	10	44	65		8	1	9	62		1		1	59
85/89		12	3	15	60		15	5	20	65	1	43	17	61	67	0	43	18	61	64		16	4	20	61		2		2	58
80/84						2	25	12	39	64	4	58	33	95	65	4	47	30	81	63	1	25	9	35	60		10	1	11	56
75/79	0	19	7	26	59	5	39	21	65	63	18	53	46	117	63	17	40	43	100	61	2	29	14	45	58		13	2	15	54
70/74	1	28	15	44	56	14	52	35	101	60	45	35	55	135	61	46	32	52	130	59	7	37	25	69	56	1	19	5	25	53
65/69	9	36	26	71	54	31	42	48	121	58	73	18	48	139	59	58	20	40	118	57	20	32	35	87	54	4	30	13	47	50
60/64	18	45	36	99	52	58	31	53	142	55	67	7	29	103	56	58	12	30	100	54	37	27	36	100	52	11	35	22	68	48
55/59	38	38	41	117	49	68	17	39	124	52	29	1	8	38	53	39	6	15	60	51	45	23	36	104	49	23	36	32	91	46
50/54	55	30	49	134	47	42	8	18	68	48	9	0	2	11	48	16	2	7	25	47	48	17	32	97	46	36	32	40	108	43
45/49	57	19	36	112	43	14	2	5	21	43	1	0	0	1	44	7	0	1	8	44	39	12	20	71	42	42	26	44	112	40
40/44	42	9	20	71	39	4	0	2	6	39	0	0	0	0	40	1	0	0	1	39	23	8	17	48	38	46	19	37	102	37
35/39	18	5	9	32	35	1	0	0	1	34											13	3	7	23	34	40	11	25	76	33
30/34	6	2	4	12	30	0	0	0	0	32											5	0	2	7	30	26	7	17	50	29
25/29	3	0	0	3	27																1	0	0	1	26	13	3	8	24	26
20/24	0	0	0	0	24																					5	1	2	8	21
15/19																										2	1	0	3	17

RAPID CITY, SOUTH DAKOTA/ELLSWORTH AFB

Columns per month: Obsn Hour Gp (01 to 08 / 09 to 16 / 17 to 24), Total Obsn, MCWB.

Temp. Range	NOV 01–08	NOV 09–16	NOV 17–24	NOV Total	NOV MCWB	DEC 01–08	DEC 09–16	DEC 17–24	DEC Total	DEC MCWB	JAN 01–08	JAN 09–16	JAN 17–24	JAN Total	JAN MCWB	FEB 01–08	FEB 09–16	FEB 17–24	FEB Total	FEB MCWB	MAR 01–08	MAR 09–16	MAR 17–24	MAR Total	MAR MCWB	APR 01–08	APR 09–16	APR 17–24	APR Total	APR MCWB	ANN 01–08	ANN 09–16	ANN 17–24	ANN Total	ANN MCWB
105/109																																	0	0	69
100/104																																5		5	66
95/99																																23	6	29	66
90/94																																72	20	92	65
85/89																													0	55	1	123	45	169	65
80/84																					0	0	0	0	55		3		3	55	11	180	88	279	63
75/79																					0	1	0	1	52		6	1	7	53	42	200	134	376	61
70/74		2	0	2	50		0		0	47							0		0	52		3	1	4	50		12	4	16	52	114	220	192	526	59
65/69		5	0	5	48		1		1	45				0	50		2		2	49		6	2	8	48	1	16	7	24	50	197	207	219	623	56
60/64	1	14	1	16	46	0	4	0	4	45		2		2	45	0	5	0	5	46	1	12	3	16	46	2	22	13	37	48	253	216	223	692	52
55/59	2	22	3	27	44	1	10	1	12	43		7		7	43	1	8	2	11	44	1	15	7	23	44	7	31	22	60	45	254	214	206	674	49
50/54	5	29	12	46	41	3	15	3	21	40	2	11	3	16	40	2	12	6	20	41	6	18	11	35	41	19	32	31	82	43	243	206	214	663	44
45/49	15	32	26	73	38	5	22	9	36	37	5	17	7	29	38	6	18	9	33	38	9	22	20	51	38	35	35	37	107	40	235	205	214	654	40
40/44	32	32	40	104	35	16	28	21	65	35	13	26	16	55	35	12	25	15	52	35	18	30	25	73	35	47	28	37	112	37	254	205	230	689	36
35/39	41	29	42	112	33	29	30	32	91	31	22	26	26	74	32	20	24	28	72	32	30	31	36	97	32	45	23	37	105	33	259	182	242	683	33
30/34	46	27	44	117	29	37	32	42	111	28	26	27	28	81	28	28	24	30	82	28	45	37	42	124	29	48	21	33	102	30	267	177	242	686	29
25/29	46	21	31	98	25	38	28	36	102	24	27	23	32	82	24	35	24	31	90	25	44	25	38	107	25	24	8	12	44	25	231	132	188	551	25
20/24	24	11	20	55	20	33	21	30	84	20	30	17	28	75	20	29	21	27	77	20	35	20	27	82	21	8	2	3	13	20	164	93	137	394	20
15/19	13	7	9	29	16	22	15	20	57	16	26	20	20	66	16	24	14	23	61	16	24	9	17	50	16	3	1	1	5	15	113	70	88	271	16
10/14	10	4	7	21	11	22	17	19	58	11	23	21	20	64	11	23	20	17	60	11	15	9	9	33	11	1	0	0	1	10	94	71	72	237	11
5/9	3	2	3	8	6	21	13	16	50	6	18	16	20	54	6	19	12	17	48	7	7	4	6	17	6	0	0	0	0	7	68	47	62	177	6
0/4	2	1	1	4	2	10	7	10	27	2	17	16	17	50	1	14	9	11	34	2	5	2	3	10	1						48	35	42	125	2
-5/-1	1	1	1	3	-3	5	2	5	12	-3	15	12	15	42	-3	9	3	6	18	-3	5	2	2	9	-3						35	20	29	84	-3
-10/-6	1	0	0	1	-9	4	1	2	7	-8	14	6	10	30	-8	2	1	1	4	-7	1	0	1	2	-8						22	8	14	44	-8
-15/-11	0		0	0	-12	1	1	1	3	-13	7	2	5	14	-13	1	0	0	1	-13	0	0	0	0	-13						9	3	6	18	-13
-20/-16						1	0	1	2	-18	1	0	1	2	-18	1	0	0	1	-17	0	0	0	0	-17						3	0	2	5	-18
-25/-21						0	0		0	-21	0	0		0	-22																0	0	0	0	-21

SIOUX FALLS/FOSS FLD SOUTH DAKOTA LAT 43 34N LONG 96 44W ELEV 1418 FT

MEAN FREQUENCY OF OCCURRENCE OF DRY BULB TEMPERATURE (DEGREES F) WITH MEAN COINCIDENT WET BULB TEMPERATURE (DEGREES F) FOR EACH DRY BULB TEMPERATURE RANGE

Temperature Range	MAY					JUNE					JULY					AUGUST					SEPTEMBER					OCTOBER				
	01 to 08	09 to 16	17 to 24	Total Obsn	M C W B	01 to 08	09 to 16	17 to 24	Total Obsn	M C W B	01 to 08	09 to 16	17 to 24	Total Obsn	M C W B	01 to 08	09 to 16	17 to 24	Total Obsn	M C W B	01 to 08	09 to 16	17 to 24	Total Obsn	M C W B	01 to 08	09 to 16	17 to 24	Total Obsn	M C W B
100/104																														
95/99							0		0	72		1	0	1	76		1	0	1	74		1	0	1	66					
90/94		1	1	2	69		3	1	4	73		5	2	7	75		6	2	8	72		7	2	9	70		1	0	1	63
85/89		7	3	10	66	0	13	6	19	72	0	23	10	33	73		20	7	27	72		10	4	14	68		2		2	63
80/84		15	8	23	63		25	13	38	70		42	23	65	70	1	34	17	52	71	1	20	9	30	65		7	1	8	61
75/79	0	28	16	44	60	1	36	24	61	67	3	57	40	100	68	3	50	30	83	69	6	31	15	52	63		15	4	19	59
70/74	6	36	23	65	59	12	45	37	94	65	23	55	50	128	67	14	53	46	113	67	12	38	25	75	61	1	23	10	34	57
65/69	12	45	35	92	56	30	48	43	121	63	51	40	50	142	65	41	44	52	137	65	16	41	36	93	58	3	31	19	53	55
60/64	29	42	44	115	54	44	33	44	121	60	68	19	39	126	62	64	26	47	137	62	32	40	42	114	55	13	33	28	74	53
55/59	52	31	42	125	51	60	20	36	116	57	57	4	26	87	59	58	12	31	101	59	42	25	42	109	52	21	36	34	91	49
50/54	47	21	34	102	47	43	8	22	73	53	33	1	6	40	55	43	3	12	58	55	50	17	35	102	48	35	30	39	104	46
45/49	45	14	26	85	43	30	6	11	47	49	11	1	1	12	51	17	0	3	20	50	44	8	20	72	44	42	29	34	105	42
40/44	31	5	10	46	39	15	1	3	19	45	1		0	1	47	6		0	6	46	23	1	8	32	40	46	24	38	108	38
35/39	15	3	5	23	34	3		0	3	41						1		0	1	41	11	0	2	13	36	36	11	22	69	34
30/34	7	0	2	9	30	1			1	36						1			1	37	3	0	1	4	31	27	5	13	45	29
25/29	3	0	0	3	26																		1	1	27	16	1	6	23	25
20/24	0			0	23																					6	0	1	7	21
15/19																										1			1	17

COINCIDENT WET BULB TEMPERATURE FOR EACH DRY BULB TEMPERATURE RANGE

SIOUX FALLS/FOSS FLD SOUTH DAKOTA

Temperature Range	NOV 01–08	NOV 09–16	NOV 17–24	NOV Total Obsn	NOV MCWB	DEC 01–08	DEC 09–16	DEC 17–24	DEC Total Obsn	DEC MCWB	JAN 01–08	JAN 09–16	JAN 17–24	JAN Total Obsn	JAN MCWB	FEB 01–08	FEB 09–16	FEB 17–24	FEB Total Obsn	FEB MCWB	MAR 01–08	MAR 09–16	MAR 17–24	MAR Total Obsn	MAR MCWB	APR 01–08	APR 09–16	APR 17–24	APR Total Obsn	APR MCWB	ANNUAL 01–08	ANNUAL 09–16	ANNUAL 17–24	ANNUAL Total Obsn	ANNUAL MCWB
100/104																																2	0	2	75
95/99																																15	5	20	73
90/94																											1		1	61	1	66	26	92	72
85/89									0	48																	1		1	60	1	121	60	182	70
80/84							0	2	2	48																3	3	2	5	59	8	188	114	310	67
75/79		1		1	52	1	4	2	7	46										55		1	0	1	55	8	8	4	12	58	55	236	172	463	65
70/74		5	0	5	52	1	7	3	11	41										53		1	0	1	53	2	15	7	22	55	141	246	211	598	62
65/69		9	2	11	49	11	16	9	28	36										51		1	1	2	51	4	18	12	32	53	209	219	233	661	59
60/64	0	15	7	22	47	25	24	9	58	33	0			0	41	3	3	2	7	49	3	3	2	5	49	12	21	16	41	50	253	184	227	664	56
55/59						34	33	21	88	29		0	0	0	46	9	5	1	9	46	6	3	0	9	46	18	29	21	62	47	246	158	189	593	51
50/54	3	21	11	35	44	45	37	26	108	25	1	1	0	1	40	29	7	4	23	42	27	2	6	19	43	29	30	30	77	44	214	145	173	532	47
45/49	11	31	22	64	41	33	37	34	116	21	4	4	1	5	38	28	13	7	60	41	50	9	12	33	40	30	35	35	95	41	199	149	160	508	42
40/44	23	32	30	85	37	24	27	41	92	16	7	7	3	10	36	29	30	21	94	37	27	26	21	56	37	42	26	32	112	37	184	159	161	504	38
35/39	36	34	41	111	33	24	21	24	69	11	15	15	11	29	32	34	31	35		33	50	42	38	107	33	48	18	30	100	33	192	185	195	572	33
30/34	48	32	43	123	29	17	18	26	61	6	27	27	19	59	29	28	31	35	94	30	50	46	54	150	30	48	18	30	96	30	250	191	227	668	29
25/29	44	24	32	100	25	13	10	17	40	1	19	29	27	75	25	28	31	33	92	25	48	31	38	117	25	27	5	12	44	25	220	158	185	563	25
20/24	29	14	21	64	20	7	7	16	30	-3	32	32	36	100	20	29	27	29	85	20	32	23	23	78	21	12	1	2	15	20	185	134	146	465	20
15/19	21	9	13	43	16	2	3	12	17	-8	35	35	35	103	16	34	25	27	86	16	28	16	21	65	16	3	0	1	4	16	155	110	129	394	16
10/14	8	6	8	22	11	0	1	11	12	-13	32	33	35	85	11	22	21	21	64	11	15	10	11	36	11	1			1	11	102	82	93	277	11
5/9	8	4	4	16	6	0	0	3	3	-18	27	24	23	74	6	20	17	20	57	6	13	8	9	30	6						92	71	75	238	6
0/4	5	1	3	9	1	0	0	0	0	-24	22	21	21	64	1	18	9	13	40	1	10	2	4	16	2						72	43	54	169	1
-5/-1	3	1	2	6	-3						20	16	19	55	-4	14	5	8	27	-4	6	1	1	8	-3						56	30	40	126	-4
-10/-6	1	0	0	1	-8						21	10	14	45	-9	11	2	3	16	-8	4	0	1	5	-8						44	15	25	84	-8
-15/-11	0	0	0	0	-13						14	4	9	27	-13	4	1	1	6	-13	1	0	0	1	-14						26	6	14	46	-13
-20/-16	0	0	0	0	-17						7	1	1	9	-18	2	0	0	2	-19	1	0	0	1	-18						12	1	2	15	-18
-25/-21											1	0	0	1	-23	1	1	0	1	-23											2	2	0	2	-23
-30/-26											0	0	0	0	-26	0	0	0	0	-29											0	0	0	0	-28

KNOXVILLE/ALCOA ANG STA TENNESSEE
LAT 35 49N   LONG 83 59W   ELEV 980 FT

MEAN FREQUENCY OF OCCURRENCE OF DRY BULB TEMPERATURE (DEGREES F) WITH MEAN COINCIDENT WET BULB TEMPERATURE (DEGREES F) FOR EACH DRY BULB TEMPERATURE RANGE

MAY

Temperature Range	01 to 08	09 to 16	17 to 24	Total Obsn	MCWB
100/104					
95/99					
90/94		3	1	4	70
85/89		22	10	32	69
80/84		51	25	76	67
75/79	3	58	42	103	65
70/74	24	46	55	125	64
65/69	66	31	54	151	61
60/64	67	21	30	118	58
55/59	41	11	18	70	53
50/54	26	3	8	37	49
45/49	13	2	4	19	44
40/44	7	0	0	7	40
35/39	0			0	39

JUNE

Temperature Range	01 to 08	09 to 16	17 to 24	Total Obsn	MCWB
90/94		0	0	0	77
85/89		3	2	5	75
80/84		18	8	26	74
75/79	0	49	24	73	72
70/74	3	66	43	112	70
65/69	26	54	61	141	69
60/64	70	31	59	160	67
55/59	83	13	31	127	64
50/54	41	3	8	52	59
45/49	14	1	2	17	55
40/44	3	0	0	3	50
35/39	0			0	45

JULY

Temperature Range	01 to 08	09 to 16	17 to 24	Total Obsn	MCWB
90/94		0	0	0	71
85/89		6	2	8	74
80/84		33	14	47	74
75/79	0	68	35	103	73
70/74	5	73	53	131	72
65/69	45	47	76	168	71
60/64	132	19	57	208	69
55/59	52	2	10	64	65
50/54	11	0	1	12	60
45/49	2		0	2	56
40/44	0			0	51

AUGUST

Temperature Range	01 to 08	09 to 16	17 to 24	Total Obsn	MCWB
85/89		4	1	5	74
80/84		29	10	39	73
75/79		63	30	93	72
70/74	2	72	50	124	71
65/69	34	50	79	163	70
60/64	113	23	58	194	69
55/59	72	6	17	95	65
50/54	24	1	2	27	60
45/49	3	0	0	3	57
40/44	0			0	51

SEPTEMBER

Temperature Range	01 to 08	09 to 16	17 to 24	Total Obsn	MCWB
90/94		1		1	71
85/89		2	1	3	71
80/84		10	3	13	70
75/79		34	14	48	70
70/74	1	53	29	83	69
65/69	7	49	46	102	67
60/64	49	48	61	158	66
55/59	70	28	49	147	63
50/54	54	12	24	90	59
45/49	36	4	9	49	54
40/44	18	1	3	22	50
35/39	5	0	0	5	45
30/34	0			0	42

OCTOBER

Temperature Range	01 to 08	09 to 16	17 to 24	Total Obsn	MCWB
90/94		0	0	0	71
85/89		4	1	5	71
80/84		17	4	21	67
75/79	0	35	15	50	64
70/74	5	48	32	85	62
65/69	24	42	46	112	60
60/64	39	39	52	130	57
55/59	46	30	39	115	53
50/54	47	19	30	96	48
45/49	44	9	18	71	44
40/44	25	4	6	35	39
35/39	11	2	4	17	35
30/34	5	0	1	6	30
25/29	2			2	26

COINCIDENT WET BULB TEMPERATURE FOR EACH DRY BULB TEMPERATURE RANGE

KNOXVILLE/ALCOA ANG STA TENNESSEE

Column groups per month: Obsn Hour Gp (01 to 08 | 09 to 16 | 17 to 24) | Total Obsn | MCWB

Temp Range	Nov 01–08	Nov 09–16	Nov 17–24	Nov Total	Nov MCWB	Dec 01–08	Dec 09–16	Dec 17–24	Dec Total	Dec MCWB	Jan 01–08	Jan 09–16	Jan 17–24	Jan Total	Jan MCWB	Feb 01–08	Feb 09–16	Feb 17–24	Feb Total	Feb MCWB	Mar 01–08	Mar 09–16	Mar 17–24	Mar Total	Mar MCWB	Apr 01–08	Apr 09–16	Apr 17–24	Apr Total	Apr MCWB	Ann 01–08	Ann 09–16	Ann 17–24	Ann Total	Ann MCWB
100/104																																1	0	1	72
95/99																															0	15	6	21	74
90/94																													0	70	0	93	36	129	73
85/89																										0	3	1	4	66	0	243	115	358	72
80/84			1	1	66				0	65												1	0	1	66	0	17	7	24	65	11	351	211	573	70
75/79	0	3	1	4	63	0	2	1	3	62				0	64	0	0	0	0	62	0	5	3	8	63	0	28	18	46	62	115	329	341	785	68
70/74	2	12	4	18	61	3	7	4	14	59	0	3	1	4	62	0	5	2	7	60	2	13	8	23	60	6	36	31	73	60	403	286	369	1058	66
65/69	4	21	12	37	57	5	12	11	28	56	3	9	7	19	60	3	11	7	21	57	7	22	16	45	57	22	36	38	96	58	409	228	291	928	61
60/64	10	29	23	62	55	9	22	14	45	52	9	13	15	37	57	6	20	17	43	54	10	30	26	66	53	36	38	43	117	55	312	218	252	782	56
55/59	17	32	31	80	51	14	28	26	68	48	11	17	15	43	52	11	28	27	66	51	17	35	35	87	50	40	32	35	107	51	247	212	225	684	52
50/54	22	38	36	96	47	23	39	33	95	43	15	27	23	65	47	23	34	37	94	47	31	39	45	115	46	41	23	29	93	47	240	212	237	689	47
45/49	34	39	43	116	43	28	47	50	125	38	20	35	31	86	43	31	38	37	106	43	42	38	40	120	42	35	17	20	72	42	247	217	226	690	43
40/44	42	30	39	111	38	47	42	47	136	34	31	39	41	111	39	34	32	34	100	38	41	28	32	101	38	29	9	14	52	38	237	189	216	642	38
35/39	45	19	29	93	34	52	28	32	112	29	41	39	44	124	34	41	26	31	98	34	43	22	25	90	33	21	2	4	27	34	249	152	184	585	34
30/34	42	11	15	68	30	39	14	19	72	25	50	36	39	125	30	34	14	15	63	29	33	11	13	57	29	8	0	1	9	30	224	100	116	440	30
25/29	16	3	5	24	25	16	5	6	27	21	30	15	18	63	25	19	7	8	34	25	17	4	4	25	25	0	0	0	0	26	123	43	54	220	25
20/24	4	1	1	6	21	7	2	2	11	16	21	8	9	38	20	11	5	4	20	20	4	1	1	6	20						56	20	21	97	20
15/19	2	0	0	2	16	3	1	1	5	11	8	4	4	16	16	4	2	2	8	16	2	0	1	3	15						23	8	9	40	16
10/14	0	0	1	1	10	1	0	0	1	6	5	2	2	9	11	2	1	2	5	10	1	0	0	1	11						11	4	6	21	11
5/9	0	0	0	0	6						2	0	1	3	6	2	0	0	2	6	0	0	0	0	8						5	0	1	6	6
0/4						1	0	0	1	2	0	0	0	0	1	1	0	0	1	1											2	0	0	2	2
-5/-1						0	0	0	0	-1	0	0	0	0		0	0	0	0	-2											0	0	0	0	-1

MEMPHIS NAS/MILLINGTON TENNESSEE
LAT 35 20N   LONG 89 53W   ELEV 322 FT

MEAN FREQUENCY OF OCCURRENCE OF DRY BULB TEMPERATURE (DEGREES F) WITH MEAN COINCIDENT WET BULB TEMPERATURE (DEGREES F) FOR EACH DRY BULB TEMPERATURE RANGE

Obsn Hour Gp columns: 01 to 08 | 09 to 16 | 17 to 24. MCWB = Mean Coincident Wet Bulb.

Temperature Range	MAY 01–08	MAY 09–16	MAY 17–24	MAY Total Obsn	MAY MCWB	JUNE 01–08	JUNE 09–16	JUNE 17–24	JUNE Total Obsn	JUNE MCWB	JULY 01–08	JULY 09–16	JULY 17–24	JULY Total Obsn	JULY MCWB	AUG 01–08	AUG 09–16	AUG 17–24	AUG Total Obsn	AUG MCWB	SEP 01–08	SEP 09–16	SEP 17–24	SEP Total Obsn	SEP MCWB	OCT 01–08	OCT 09–16	OCT 17–24	OCT Total Obsn	OCT MCWB
100/104													1	1	78				0	78		0		0	78					
95/99							0		0	74		10	2	12	78		6	1	7	78		2	0	2	76					
90/94		8	2	10	73		4	1	5	76		54	18	72	77		49	13	62	77		12	2	14	74		8	1	9	70
85/89		34	11	45	71		42	13	55	75	3	83	43	129	75	0	81	32	113	75		47	12	59	74		34	5	39	68
80/84	2	61	30	93	69	1	70	30	101	73	29	62	66	157	74	15	67	62	144	73	2	60	26	88	71	1	44	17	62	66
75/79	15	54	52	121	67	18	64	55	137	72	90	27	77	194	72	75	32	78	185	72	26	56	60	142	70	12	44	32	88	63
70/74	51	38	60	149	65	55	37	71	163	70	94	10	36	140	69	102	11	49	162	69	74	34	63	171	68	29	40	47	116	60
65/69	73	26	45	144	62	94	18	49	161	68	23	2	6	31	63	41	2	10	53	64	57	18	40	115	63	47	38	48	133	56
60/64	52	18	26	96	57	48	3	16	67	63	8	0	1	9	59	12	0	3	15	59	42	7	23	72	58	46	24	42	112	52
55/59	29	7	13	49	52	19	1	4	24	59	1			1	56	2			2	54	26	3	9	38	54	45	13	34	92	48
50/54	16	2	8	26	47	4	0	0	4	55											9	1	4	14	49	38	3	17	58	44
45/49	9	1		10	43	0			0	50											2		1	3	44	24	0	5	29	39
40/44	1			1	39																1			1	40	5	0	1	6	35
35/39																										1			1	31
30/34																														

COINCIDENT WET BULB TEMPERATURE FOR EACH DRY BULB TEMPERATURE RANGE

MEMPHIS NAS/MILLINGTON TENNESSEE

Temperature Range	NOV 01–08	NOV 09–16	NOV 17–24	NOV Total Obsn	NOV MCWB	DEC 01–08	DEC 09–16	DEC 17–24	DEC Total Obsn	DEC MCWB	JAN 01–08	JAN 09–16	JAN 17–24	JAN Total Obsn	JAN MCWB	FEB 01–08	FEB 09–16	FEB 17–24	FEB Total Obsn	FEB MCWB	MAR 01–08	MAR 09–16	MAR 17–24	MAR Total Obsn	MAR MCWB	APR 01–08	APR 09–16	APR 17–24	APR Total Obsn	APR MCWB	ANN 01–08	ANN 09–16	ANN 17–24	ANN Total Obsn	ANN MCWB
100/104																																1		1	78
95/99																																22	4	26	77
90/94																																165	48	213	76
85/89																											0		0	68	4	327	130	461	74
80/84		1	0	1	69												0	0	0	63		3	1	4	63		4	1	5	69	66	375	254	695	72
75/79		6	1	7	65											1	1	0	1	63		8	4	12	63	3	23	9	32	67	265	305	383	953	70
70/74	2	23	6	31	62	0	3	0	3	63	0	2	1	3	64	1	4	1	6	62	2	16	9	27	61	17	40	23	66	65	449	250	342	1041	66
65/69	8	27	16	51	60	2	10	5	17	61	2	7	5	14	61	5	7	4	12	59	7	22	16	45	58	37	47	36	100	62	328	204	257	789	61
60/64	16	37	31	84	56	7	19	10	36	57	8	14	9	31	58	5	16	10	31	56	16	32	26	74	54	46	40	47	124	60	278	215	235	728	56
55/59	27	40	35	102	51	17	26	20	63	53	10	18	14	42	53	9	20	19	48	52	22	32	30	84	51	38	33	44	123	56	231	196	217	644	52
50/54	36	36	41	113	47	19	31	30	80	48	9	22	18	49	47	15	29	22	66	47	26	37	40	103	46	40	26	35	99	51	215	187	222	624	47
45/49	40	30	40	110	43	24	38	29	91	43	13	30	26	69	43	25	33	36	94	43	41	38	40	119	42	33	16	25	81	47	225	181	204	610	43
40/44	40	21	37	98	38	36	45	45	126	39	28	34	34	96	38	32	38	39	109	38	43	28	39	110	38	19	9	14	56	43	224	168	204	596	38
35/39	36	10	18	64	34	45	35	44	124	34	36	40	42	118	34	38	32	34	104	34	43	19	26	88	34	7	2	5	26	39	210	137	166	513	34
30/34	20	6	9	35	29	44	22	35	101	29	50	36	47	133	30	42	24	32	98	29	33	10	14	57	30	1	1	1	9	35	191	98	137	426	29
25/29	10	2	4	16	25	29	11	17	57	25	39	19	27	85	25	30	12	17	59	25	13	3	3	19	25			0	1	32	121	47	68	236	25
20/24	3	0	2	5	20	12	5	7	24	20	25	12	12	49	20	17	5	7	29	20	2	0	1	3	21						59	22	29	110	20
15/19	2	0	0	2	17	8	3	3	14	16	13	7	8	28	16	6	2	2	10	15	0	0	0	0	14						29	12	13	54	16
10/14						2	1	1	4	11	8	3	4	15	11	2	3	1	5	11	0	0		0	10						13	5	6	24	11
5/9						1	0	1	2	6	4	1	2	7	6	2	1	0	2	6											7	1	3	11	6
0/4						0	0	0	0	3	2	1	1	4	4																2	2	1	4	2
-5/-1							0	0	0	-4	1		0	1	-2																1	1	0	1	-2
-10/-6						0	0		0	-9																					0			0	-9
-15/-11									0	-12																					0			0	-12

NASHVILLE, TENNESSEE*
READINGS TAKEN AT SEWART AFB/SMYRNA, TN

LAT 36 00N LONG 86 32W ELEV 543 FT

MEAN FREQUENCY OF OCCURRENCE OF DRY BULB TEMPERATURE (DEGREES F) WITH MEAN COINCIDENT WET BULB TEMPERATURE (DEGREES F) FOR EACH DRY BULB TEMPERATURE RANGE

Hour groups: 01–08, 09–16, 17–24 (Obsn Hour Gp); Tot = Total Obsn; WB = Mean Coincident Wet Bulb (MCWB)

Temperature Range	MAY 01–08	MAY 09–16	MAY 17–24	MAY Tot	MAY WB	JUNE 01–08	JUNE 09–16	JUNE 17–24	JUNE Tot	JUNE WB	JULY 01–08	JULY 09–16	JULY 17–24	JULY Tot	JULY WB	AUGUST 01–08	AUGUST 09–16	AUGUST 17–24	AUGUST Tot	AUGUST WB	SEPTEMBER 01–08	SEPTEMBER 09–16	SEPTEMBER 17–24	SEPTEMBER Tot	SEPTEMBER WB	OCTOBER 01–08	OCTOBER 09–16	OCTOBER 17–24	OCTOBER Tot	OCTOBER WB
100/104																														
95/99						0	0		0	77	0	1	0	1	77	0	1	0	1	73	0	1	0	1	71					
90/94		6	1	7	71	0	2	0	2	74	0	10	1	11	75	0	11	1	12	76	0	3	0	3	72		1		1	73
85/89		29	6	35	70	0	28	6	34	74	0	44	10	54	75	0	44	10	54	75	0	16	2	18	71		4	0	4	71
80/84	1	52	17	70	68	0	62	19	81	72	2	81	28	111	74	1	69	24	94	73	0	39	9	48	71		27	2	29	66
75/79	6	53	28	87	66	7	63	35	105	70	11	66	49	126	72	9	67	44	120	72	2	56	19	77	69	1	40	9	50	64
70/74	23	43	51	117	65	23	49	49	121	69	46	33	74	153	71	39	35	67	141	71	11	50	37	98	68	8	42	21	71	62
65/69	62	32	61	155	62	60	24	62	146	67	113	12	63	188	69	95	16	63	174	69	43	42	59	144	66	16	43	35	94	59
60/64	58	19	37	114	58	79	9	43	131	64	51	2	17	70	69	56	4	27	87	65	60	22	52	134	63	36	36	42	114	56
55/59	40	9	23	72	53	43	4	17	64	59	16		5	21	65	32	1	9	42	60	51	9	31	91	59	33	29	42	104	52
50/54	28	3	14	45	49	20	0	6	26	55	7		1	8	60	11		3	14	56	35	2	16	53	55	44	17	39	100	48
45/49	16	2	7	25	45	7		1	8	51	2		0	2	55	3		0	3	51	21	0	10	31	50	39	8	29	76	44
40/44	11		3	14	40	2	0		2	46	0			0	52	0			0	48	13	1	4	18	46	34	2	17	53	40
35/39	2		0	2	36	1	0		1	42											4		1	5	42	22	1	8	31	35
30/34	0			0	32	0			0	38											1		0	1	37	11		3	14	31
25/29																										4		0	4	27
20/24																										0			0	22

*Comparative design data note:

	Elevation	WINTER 97 1/2%	SUMMER DB 2 1/2%	SUMMER DB 2 1/2%	SUMMER WB 2 1/2%
Nashville, TN	577 ft.	16° F	95° F	95° F	78° F
Sewart AFB	543 ft.	17° F	95° F	95° F	77° F

COINCIDENT WET BULB TEMPERATURE FOR EACH DRY BULB TEMPERATURE RANGE

NASHVILLE, TENNESSEE*
READINGS TAKEN AT SEWART AFB/SMYRNA, TN

Note: For each month the observation hour groups are 01 to 08, 09 to 16, and 17 to 24; "Total" is the total observations and "MCWB" is the mean coincident wet bulb temperature.

Temperature Range	Nov 01-08	Nov 09-16	Nov 17-24	Nov Total	Nov MCWB	Dec 01-08	Dec 09-16	Dec 17-24	Dec Total	Dec MCWB	Jan 01-08	Jan 09-16	Jan 17-24	Jan Total	Jan MCWB	Feb 01-08	Feb 09-16	Feb 17-24	Feb Total	Feb MCWB	Mar 01-08	Mar 09-16	Mar 17-24	Mar Total	Mar MCWB	Apr 01-08	Apr 09-16	Apr 17-24	Apr Total	Apr MCWB	Ann 01-08	Ann 09-16	Ann 17-24	Ann Total	Ann MCWB
100/104																																3		3	74
95/99																																26	2	28	75
90/94																											5	1	6	67	0	139	29	168	74
85/89																											22	5	27	66	3	289	87	379	73
80/84		1		1	65				0										0	62		2		2	63	1	40	15	56	63	30	356	171	557	70
75/79		5	1	6	64		2	1	2	63		1	0	1	61	1	3	1	4	62	1	8	1	9	62	8	40	27	75	61	127	313	281	721	68
70/74	2	18	3	23	60	1	8	9	10	61	1	7	2	10	59	4	10	6	17	60	7	17	6	24	60	29	39	42	110	59	353	260	356	969	66
65/69	5	27	9	41	58	6	18	18	33	59	6	12	8	26	56	10	17	9	30	58	12	23	14	44	57	40	33	41	114	57	368	226	309	903	62
60/64	11	32	20	63	54	12	27	23	57	56	7	18	13	38	52	17	23	14	47	54	18	29	22	63	54	39	26	39	104	55	315	210	250	775	57
55/59	19	37	29	85	51	18	27	18	57	52	12	18	14	48	46	23	23	23	65	51	18	36	28	82	49	37	26	30	104	51	251	207	232	690	52
50/54	28	36	35	99	47	16	31	23	70	47	23	23	14	77	43	17	25	23	73	47	28	33	36	97	46	34	21	30	85	47	239	189	225	653	47
45/49	33	32	39	104	43	23	34	28	85	42	33	33	25	87	38	18	30	25	98	42	28	32	37	97	42	35	11	22	68	43	226	183	216	625	43
40/44	34	23	36	93	39	30	38	35	103	38	21	34	32	113	34	28	33	37	100	38	34	30	36	100	38	28	3	12	43	39	225	163	209	597	38
35/39	40	16	31	87	34	34	39	42	115	34	31	41	41	129	29	34	32	35	86	34	37	21	32	90	34	17	1	5	23	35	217	151	194	562	34
30/34	31	9	22	62	30	39	27	41	107	29	46	37	46	86	25	41	22	30	75	30	41	11	23	75	30	7		2	9	30	209	106	167	482	30
25/29	20	4	10	34	25	35	15	29	79	25	34	20	32	61	20	33	16	32	71	25	26	4	10	40	25	2		0	2	27	154	59	103	316	25
20/24	11	1	5	17	21	29	6	15	50	21	32	10	19	35	16	19	6	11	36	20	11	1	3	15	21						102	24	53	179	20
15/19	5		1	6	17	14	3	6	23	16	19	8	8	19	11	7	3	6	23	16	4	0	1	5	16						56	14	22	92	16
10/14	0			0	13	5	1	2	8	11	11	4	4	8	6	5	2	3	12	11	1	0		1	12						24	7	9	40	11
5/9						2	0	1	3	7	4	2	2	5	2	2	0	1	5	7	0			0	7						10	2	4	16	7
0/4						0	1	0	1	2	3	1	1	3	-3	2	2	0	2	2											5	1	1	7	2
-5/-1						1	1	0	1	-4	2	0	1	1	-8	0	0	0	0	-2											3	0	1	4	-3
-10/-6						1			1	-8	1	0	0	0	-12																2	0	0	2	-8
-15/-11											0	0	0	0																	0	0	0	0	-12

AMARILLO, TEXAS
LAT 35 14N   LONG 101 42W   ELEV 3604 FT

MEAN FREQUENCY OF OCCURRENCE OF DRY BULB TEMPERATURE (DEGREES F) WITH MEAN COINCIDENT WET BULB TEMPERATURE (DEGREES F) FOR EACH DRY BULB TEMPERATURE RANGE

Temperature Range	MAY 01-08	MAY 09-16	MAY 17-24	MAY Total Obsn	MAY MCWB	JUNE 01-08	JUNE 09-16	JUNE 17-24	JUNE Total Obsn	JUNE MCWB	JULY 01-08	JULY 09-16	JULY 17-24	JULY Total Obsn	JULY MCWB	AUGUST 01-08	AUGUST 09-16	AUGUST 17-24	AUGUST Total Obsn	AUGUST MCWB	SEPTEMBER 01-08	SEPTEMBER 09-16	SEPTEMBER 17-24	SEPTEMBER Total Obsn	SEPTEMBER MCWB	OCTOBER 01-08	OCTOBER 09-16	OCTOBER 17-24	OCTOBER Total Obsn	OCTOBER MCWB
105/109							0	0	0	68																				
100/104		0		0	64		4	1	5	68		2	1	3	68															
95/99		4	1	5	63		16	8	24	66		24	9	33	68		1	0	1	68		2	1	3	65					
90/94		13	6	19	61		36	19	55	66		52	28	80	68		18	5	23	68		19	6	25	65		2	0	2	63
85/89		26	13	39	60		46	28	74	66		59	36	95	68		53	23	76	67		39	15	54	64		13	2	15	59
80/84	0	35	22	57	60	4	48	39	91	65	6	51	47	104	66	0	60	33	93	67	0	45	25	70	63		26	9	35	58
75/79	1	39	29	69	58	22	38	44	104	64	37	34	56	127	65	3	51	44	98	66	2	42	36	80	62		33	13	46	57
70/74	11	39	38	88	57	52	25	41	118	63	86	18	43	147	64	23	36	58	117	65	24	35	49	108	60	1	37	22	60	56
65/69	31	32	39	102	56	66	12	31	109	61	87	7	22	116	63	82	18	52	152	63	60	24	48	132	59	8	36	37	81	54
60/64	54	24	39	117	54	58	8	19	85	58	29	2	5	36	60	100	7	25	132	62	69	18	33	120	56	26	35	46	107	52
55/59	59	19	32	110	52	27	4	7	38	54	3		1	4	55	33	3	5	41	59	45	9	16	70	52	44	25	45	114	49
50/54	50	11	18	79	48	9	1	2	12	49						6	1	1	8	55	27	5	7	39	48	63	19	35	117	46
45/49	27	5	10	42	44	2	0	1	3	44						1	0		1	52	9	1	3	13	44	53	14	25	92	42
40/44	10	1	1	12	39	0			0	42						0			0	48	3	1	1	5	41	33	5	10	48	38
35/39	3	1	1	5	35																					16	2	4	22	34
30/34	1	0	0	1	30																					4	1	1	6	30
25/29	0	0		0	28																					1			1	27

AMARILLO, TEXAS

Obsn Hour Gp columns: 01 to 08, 09 to 16, 17 to 24; Total Obsn; MCWB (mean coincident wet bulb).

Temperature Range	NOV 01–08	NOV 09–16	NOV 17–24	NOV Total	NOV MCWB	DEC 01–08	DEC 09–16	DEC 17–24	DEC Total	DEC MCWB	JAN 01–08	JAN 09–16	JAN 17–24	JAN Total	JAN MCWB	FEB 01–08	FEB 09–16	FEB 17–24	FEB Total	FEB MCWB	MAR 01–08	MAR 09–16	MAR 17–24	MAR Total	MAR MCWB	APR 01–08	APR 09–16	APR 17–24	APR Total	APR MCWB	ANN 01–08	ANN 09–16	ANN 17–24	ANN Total	ANN MCWB
105/109																																0	0	0	68
100/104																																7	2	9	68
95/99																																64	24	88	67
90/94																																176	82	258	66
85/89																										0	1	0	1	56	0	254	131	385	65
80/84		0		0	56		0		0	54		0		0	54		0		0	58		0	0	0	53	4	11	4	15	56	13	276	196	485	63
75/79		5	0	5	52		1	0	1	52		1	0	1	51		1	0	1	55		2	1	3	52	17	17	9	26	55	85	264	253	602	62
70/74		16	3	19	51		4	0	4	49		4	1	5	49	0	2	1	3	51	0	10	4	14	51	23	23	12	35	53	256	252	282	790	60
65/69	0	24	6	30	49		11	2	13	47		11	2	13	47	1	8	3	11	50	1	19	9	28	49	29	29	21	50	52	356	234	262	852	57
60/64	1	30	15	46	48	1	19	6	26	45	0	15	6	21	45	2	15	7	22	47	6	23	15	38	47	32	28	34	64	50	290	237	239	766	53
55/59	5	30	24	59	45	1	22	12	35	43	1	22	12	35	43	7	20	10	31	46	29	29	21	62	45	34	34	37	85	49	228	212	230	670	48
50/54	12	32	36	80	43	5	29	20	54	41	5	28	19	52	40	16	22	16	40	44	15	29	31	75	43	46	22	34	102	47	240	201	226	667	44
45/49	30	28	39	97	40	10	33	29	72	38	10	29	26	65	37	28	25	24	56	41	27	27	35	89	41	44	18	25	87	44	228	183	223	634	40
40/44	46	24	41	111	36	20	35	40	95	35	20	31	34	85	34	34	28	30	74	39	42	26	34	102	38	44	13	19	76	37	246	159	210	615	36
35/39	53	21	30	104	33	39	32	45	116	32	36	28	41	105	32	43	23	31	81	36	50	21	30	101	35	31	8	10	49	34	262	138	192	592	32
30/34	44	16	24	84	29	65	28	42	135	29	46	26	37	109	28	37	25	30	90	32	45	16	21	82	29	17	2	4	23	30	265	109	159	533	29
25/29	29	9	12	50	25	54	16	28	98	25	48	17	25	90	25	37	20	18	93	29	31	9	11	51	25	6	1	1	8	25	206	68	95	369	25
20/24	11	3	7	21	20	27	9	11	47	20	30	15	16	61	20	25	16	13	71	25	17	4	6	27	20	1	0		1	22	111	41	53	205	20
15/19	7	1	3	11	15	12	5	9	26	16	22	9	12	43	15	20	10	9	48	21	9	1	2	12	16						70	22	35	127	16
10/14	3	0	0	3	11	9	3	3	15	12	14	5	7	26	11	6	6	2	35	16	3	0	0	0	11						35	11	12	58	11
5/9	1			1	8	3	1	1	5	7	9	4	5	18	6	3	3	1	11	12	0	0		0	7						16	5	7	28	6
0/4						1	0	0	1	2	4	2	2	8	1	0	0		4	7	0	0		0	3						5	2	2	9	1
-5/-1							0		0	-2	2	1	1	4	-3	0	0		0	-3											2	1	1	4	-3
-10/-6											2	0	0	2	-8	0	0		0	-8											2	0	0	2	-8
-15/-11																0			0	-12											0	0	0	0	-12

CORPUS CHRISTI NAS TEXAS
LAT 27 42N   LONG 97 17W   ELEV   19 FT

MEAN FREQUENCY OF OCCURRENCE OF DRY BULB TEMPERATURE (DEGREES F) WITH MEAN COINCIDENT WET BULB TEMPERATURE (DEGREES F) FOR EACH DRY BULB TEMPERATURE RANGE

Temperature Range	MAY					JUNE					JULY					AUGUST					SEPTEMBER					OCTOBER				
	01 to 08	09 to 16	17 to 24	Total Obsn	MCWB	01 to 08	09 to 16	17 to 24	Total Obsn	MCWB	01 to 08	09 to 16	17 to 24	Total Obsn	MCWB	01 to 08	09 to 16	17 to 24	Total Obsn	MCWB	01 to 08	09 to 16	17 to 24	Total Obsn	MCWB	01 to 08	09 to 16	17 to 24	Total Obsn	MCWB
95/99														0	79		2		2	79				0	76					
90/94		1		1	76		1		1	80		65	5	70	79		63	6	69	79		26	1	27	79		1		1	78
85/89		40	4	44	76		21	1	22	78	10	154	71	235	78	6	142	67	215	78	3	115	31	149	78		39	3	42	77
80/84	16	124	57	197	75	5	147	40	192	76	180	25	164	369	77	175	30	161	366	77	110	65	152	327	76	22	85	53	160	74
75/79	134	63	137	334	73	134	60	160	354	74	57	3	8	68	75	62	9	14	85	75	92	23	41	156	73	79	61	91	231	71
70/74	72	13	38	123	69	88	10	36	134	68	1			1	69	4	1	1	6	70	25	8	11	44	68	63	34	58	155	67
65/69	16	5	9	30	63	10	2	3	15	64				0	61				0	62	8	3	3	14	63	44	16	27	87	61
60/64	10	3	2	15	60	2			2												2			2	58	27	8	11	46	58
55/59				0	54																					10	4	4	18	52
50/54																										2	1	1	4	49
45/49																										1			1	43

COINCIDENT WET BULB TEMPERATURE FOR EACH DRY BULB TEMPERATURE RANGE

CORPUS CHRISTI NAS TEXAS

Each monthly block gives the Observation Hour Group (01 to 08, 09 to 16, 17 to 24), the Total Observations, and the MCWB (Mean Coincident Wet Bulb).

NOVEMBER

Temperature Range	Obsn Hour Gp 01 to 08	Obsn Hour Gp 09 to 16	Obsn Hour Gp 17 to 24	Total Obsn	MCWB
85/89		2	0	2	71
80/84		31	2	33	73
75/79	18	57	38	113	71
70/74	54	44	62	160	68
65/69	50	34	50	134	63
60/64	38	28	38	104	57
55/59	32	22	26	80	52
50/54	25	13	16	54	47
45/49	15	4	6	25	43
40/44	6	3	2	11	38
35/39	2	1	1	4	35
30/34		0		0	32

DECEMBER

Temperature Range	Obsn Hour Gp 01 to 08	Obsn Hour Gp 09 to 16	Obsn Hour Gp 17 to 24	Total Obsn	MCWB
85/89		0		0	74
80/84		2		2	70
75/79		27	1	28	69
70/74	19	48	37	104	67
65/69	41	37	49	127	63
60/64	44	43	49	136	58
55/59	43	33	44	120	53
50/54	45	27	35	107	48
45/49	31	19	20	70	43
40/44	18	10	11	39	38
35/39	6	2	2	10	34
30/34	2	0	0	2	29

JANUARY

Temperature Range	Obsn Hour Gp 01 to 08	Obsn Hour Gp 09 to 16	Obsn Hour Gp 17 to 24	Total Obsn	MCWB
80/84				0	73
75/79		6	1	7	69
70/74	1	32	7	40	67
65/69	26	35	38	99	64
60/64	40	39	52	131	59
55/59	35	39	46	120	54
50/54	52	42	45	139	48
45/49	44	26	32	102	44
40/44	27	14	15	56	39
35/39	14	8	8	30	34
30/34	5	4	2	11	29
25/29	2	2	2	6	23
20/24	2	1	0	3	19

FEBRUARY

Temperature Range	Obsn Hour Gp 01 to 08	Obsn Hour Gp 09 to 16	Obsn Hour Gp 17 to 24	Total Obsn	MCWB
85/89				0	66
80/84			1	1	66
75/79		1	13	14	68
70/74	2	13	34	49	66
65/69	33	46	44	123	63
60/64	51	43	58	152	58
55/59	46	34	47	127	53
50/54	40	25	31	96	48
45/49	26	14	17	57	44
40/44	16	9	9	34	39
35/39	6	4	3	13	34
30/34	3	0	0	3	30

MARCH

Temperature Range	Obsn Hour Gp 01 to 08	Obsn Hour Gp 09 to 16	Obsn Hour Gp 17 to 24	Total Obsn	MCWB
85/89				0	62
80/84		3		3	65
75/79		30	4	34	68
70/74	9	73	35	117	67
65/69	75	60	89	224	63
60/64	67	37	60	164	58
55/59	46	20	33	99	52
50/54	27	14	17	58	47
45/49	14	8	8	30	43
40/44	8	2	2	12	39
35/39	1	0	0	1	33

APRIL

Temperature Range	Obsn Hour Gp 01 to 08	Obsn Hour Gp 09 to 16	Obsn Hour Gp 17 to 24	Total Obsn	MCWB
85/89				0	74
80/84		3		3	71
75/79		42	6	48	73
70/74	24	97	49	170	71
65/69	102	63	113	278	69
60/64	73	23	50	146	64
55/59	24	9	17	50	57
50/54	12	4	5	21	53
45/49	4	1		5	49

ANNUAL TOTAL

Temperature Range	Obsn Hour Gp 01 to 08	Obsn Hour Gp 09 to 16	Obsn Hour Gp 17 to 24	Total Obsn	MCWB
95/99		2		2	79
90/94		177	13	190	79
85/89	24	642	216	882	78
80/84	637	468	755	1860	76
75/79	554	399	421	1374	72
70/74	362	352	378	1092	68
65/69	368	259	359	986	63
60/64	303	210	287	800	58
55/59	224	156	205	585	53
50/54	195	123	145	463	48
45/49	131	71	83	285	43
40/44	75	38	39	152	39
35/39	29	15	14	58	34
30/34	10	4	2	16	29
25/29	2	2	2	6	23
20/24	2	1	0	3	19

DALLAS, TEXAS*
READINGS TAKEN AT CARLSWELL AFB/FT. WORTH

LAT 32 47N   LONG 97 26W   ELEV 650 FT

MEAN FREQUENCY OF OCCURRENCE OF DRY BULB TEMPERATURE (DEGREES F) WITH MEAN COINCIDENT WET BULB TEMPERATURE (DEGREES F) FOR EACH DRY BULB TEMPERATURE RANGE

Temperature Range	MAY 01–08	MAY 09–16	MAY 17–24	MAY Total Obsn	MAY MC WB	JUNE 01–08	JUNE 09–16	JUNE 17–24	JUNE Total Obsn	JUNE MC WB	JULY 01–08	JULY 09–16	JULY 17–24	JULY Total Obsn	JULY MC WB	AUGUST 01–08	AUGUST 09–16	AUGUST 17–24	AUGUST Total Obsn	AUGUST MC WB	SEPT 01–08	SEPT 09–16	SEPT 17–24	SEPT Total Obsn	SEPT MC WB	OCT 01–08	OCT 09–16	OCT 17–24	OCT Total Obsn	OCT MC WB
105/109												0	0	0	74		1	0	1	76										
100/104		0		0	75		1	0	1	76		19	8	27	75		17	7	24	74		1	0	1	74					
95/99		2	1	3	75		21	10	31	75		60	33	93	75		54	26	80	74		16	5	21	74					
90/94		11	5	16	73		58	33	91	74	0	73	49	122	74	0	68	44	112	73		37	16	53	73		7	1	8	69
85/89		43	22	65	71	1	69	53	123	73	13	50	66	129	73	11	53	60	124	72	0	50	33	83	72		18	5	23	69
80/84	1	61	43	105	69	28	49	64	141	72	81	27	52	160	72	65	33	59	157	71	12	50	50	112	70		40	17	57	68
75/79	22	56	59	137	68	93	23	46	162	70	100	12	29	141	71	101	17	39	157	70	65	38	56	159	69	7	45	33	85	66
70/74	70	39	56	165	65	78	13	25	116	68	47	5	10	62	68	59	5	11	75	68	72	28	43	143	66	32	46	50	128	63
65/69	77	22	38	137	62	30	4	6	40	64	6	0	0	6	64	10	0	1	11	63	49	13	26	88	62	44	38	47	129	60
60/64	43	9	17	69	58	8	3	2	13	59	1			1	58	2	1	1	4	59	27	5	8	40	57	46	16	30	92	56
55/59	22	3	7	32	53	2	0	0	2	54											11	2	3	16	53	42	6	15	63	51
50/54	13	0	1	14	49																2	0	1	3	49	20	3	5	28	47
45/49	1			1	44																1			1	46	5	1	1	7	43
40/44																										1	0	0	1	39
35/39																										0			0	34
30/34																													0	32

*Comparative design data note:

	WINTER 97 1/2%	SUMMER DB 2 1/2%	WB 2 1/2%
Dallas, TX	24° F	99° F	78° F
Carswell AFB/Ft. Worth	24° F	101° F	78° F

Elevation
Dallas, TX   481 ft.
Carswell AFB/Ft. Worth   650 ft.

COINCIDENT WET BULB TEMPERATURE FOR EACH DRY BULB TEMPERATURE RANGE

DALLAS, TEXAS*
READINGS TAKEN AT CARLSWELL AFB/FT. WORTH

Each month group: Obsn Hour Gp columns "01 to 08", "09 to 16", "17 to 24", then "Total Obsn", then "MCWB".

Temp. Range	NOV 01-08	NOV 09-16	NOV 17-24	NOV Total	NOV MCWB	DEC 01-08	DEC 09-16	DEC 17-24	DEC Total	DEC MCWB	JAN 01-08	JAN 09-16	JAN 17-24	JAN Total	JAN MCWB	FEB 01-08	FEB 09-16	FEB 17-24	FEB Total	FEB MCWB	MAR 01-08	MAR 09-16	MAR 17-24	MAR Total	MAR MCWB	APR 01-08	APR 09-16	APR 17-24	APR Total	APR MCWB	ANN 01-08	ANN 09-16	ANN 17-24	ANN Total	ANN MCWB
105/109																																1	0	1	75
100/104																															0	38	15	53	75
95/99																								0	69		1	0	1	65	0	154	75	229	74
90/94		1	0	1	66																	1	0	1	67		1	0	1	69	0	256	148	404	73
85/89		8	1	9	65									0	58		1	0	1	60		3	1	4	65	0	9	4	13	68	25	297	244	566	72
80/84							1		1	62				0	61		2	1	3	61		8	4	12	64	0	34	17	51	67	187	313	308	808	70
75/79	1	21	8	30	63	0	4	1	5	62	0	4	1	5	59	0	5	2	7	59	0	17	9	26	61	2	43	36	81	65	391	285	319	995	68
70/74	5	32	18	55	61	4	13	3	16	59	0	11	3	14	58	0	12	5	17	57	2	26	19	47	59	26	51	51	128	63	391	281	294	966	65
65/69	15	34	29	78	58	4	22	13	39	57	3	15	10	28	58	1	18	14	33	55	11	34	32	77	57	49	41	49	139	60	299	241	265	805	60
60/64	24	35	37	96	55	13	31	20	64	54	9	20	16	45	54	9	24	20	53	53	24	35	39	98	54	56	30	37	123	56	266	220	241	727	55
55/59	33	36	40	109	51	12	33	32	77	49	7	28	22	57	49	15	27	30	72	49	32	33	36	101	50	44	18	25	87	51	224	196	225	645	50
50/54	41	29	41	111	46	27	36	41	104	46	23	35	37	95	46	25	33	39	97	45	41	28	39	108	45	31	10	15	56	47	245	177	229	651	46
45/49	42	22	31	95	42	41	34	46	121	42	27	32	39	98	42	36	32	38	106	41	48	28	29	105	42	21	2	4	27	42	237	153	192	582	42
40/44	40	15	22	77	38	52	33	39	124	38	39	30	37	106	38	46	31	35	112	37	41	19	20	80	38	9	0	1	10	38	232	129	155	516	38
35/39	25	5	10	40	33	45	22	29	96	34	42	26	31	99	33	39	19	21	79	33	25	10	13	48	33	2	1	0	3	34	179	83	104	366	33
30/34	10	2	4	16	29	29	12	15	56	29	40	21	25	86	29	33	14	15	62	29	15	4	5	24	29	1	0	0	1	32	128	53	64	245	29
25/29	3	0	0	3	25	17	4	7	28	25	27	11	13	51	24	15	4	5	24	25	6	1	1	8	25						68	20	26	114	25
20/24	1	0		1	20	6	2	2	10	20	16	8	9	33	20	3	1	1	5	21	2	0	0	2	21						28	11	12	51	20
15/19						1	0		1	15	7	4	4	15	15	1	0	0	1	17	0			0	16						9	4	4	17	15
10/14						0			0	12	6	2	1	9	11																6	2	1	9	11
5/9											0	0	0	0	8																0	0	0	0	8

EL PASO, TEXAS
READINGS TAKEN AT BIGGS AAF/FT. BLISS

LAT 31 51N   LONG 106 23W   ELEV 3947 FT

MEAN FREQUENCY OF OCCURRENCE OF DRY BULB TEMPERATURE (DEGREES F) WITH MEAN COINCIDENT WET BULB TEMPERATURE (DEGREES F) FOR EACH DRY BULB TEMPERATURE RANGE

Temperature Range	MAY 01 to 08	MAY 09 to 16	MAY 17 to 24	MAY Total Obsn	MAY MCWB	JUNE 01 to 08	JUNE 09 to 16	JUNE 17 to 24	JUNE Total Obsn	JUNE MCWB	JULY 01 to 08	JULY 09 to 16	JULY 17 to 24	JULY Total Obsn	JULY MCWB	AUGUST 01 to 08	AUGUST 09 to 16	AUGUST 17 to 24	AUGUST Total Obsn	AUGUST MCWB	SEPTEMBER 01 to 08	SEPTEMBER 09 to 16	SEPTEMBER 17 to 24	SEPTEMBER Total Obsn	SEPTEMBER MCWB	OCTOBER 01 to 08	OCTOBER 09 to 16	OCTOBER 17 to 24	OCTOBER Total Obsn	OCTOBER MCWB
105/109		0		0	63		1		1	64	0	0	0	0	68															
100/104		1	0	1	62		12	4	16	64		9	3	12	66		1	0	1	69										
95/99		4	1	5	61		40	19	59	63	0	39	16	55	66		25	8	33	66										
90/94		26	11	37	59	1	67	44	112	61	0	66	40	106	65		68	32	100	65		6	1	7	64		1		1	62
85/89	1	52	29	82	57	9	60	54	123	60	5	65	54	124	65	1	73	53	127	65		38	9	47	63		16	2	18	60
80/84	3	62	47	112	55	29	38	51	118	59	32	40	59	131	64	16	51	68	135	64		57	26	83	62		47	13	60	58
75/79	18	49	55	122	53	66	16	40	122	58	84	18	46	148	63	73	24	59	156	63	3	59	48	110	61	2	54	30	86	56
70/74	45	30	46	121	52	68	5	18	91	57	91	7	24	122	63	108	5	22	135	62	19	45	64	128	60	9	53	45	107	55
65/69	60	15	29	104	50	43	1	7	51	54	33	3	6	42	63	48	1	5	54	61	68	24	54	146	59	27	38	54	119	53
60/64	59	8	18	85	48	20	0	2	22	50	3	0	1	4	60	3	0	0	3	60	83	9	28	120	57	47	24	51	122	51
55/59	37	2	8	47	45	4		0	4	46											50	2	7	59	54	66	10	34	110	48
50/54	17	0	2	19	41																13	1	2	16	51	56	3	12	71	44
45/49	6	1		7	37	1			1	40											3	0	0	3	46	29	1	5	35	40
40/44	2	0	0	2	35																0	0	0	0	43	11	1	1	13	37
35/39	0			0	29																					1	0		1	33
30/34																										0			0	28

EL PASO, TEXAS
READINGS TAKEN AT BIGGS AAF/FT. BLISS

For each month the three "Obsn Hour Gp" columns are 01 to 08, 09 to 16, and 17 to 24; followed by Total Obsn and MCWB (mean coincident wet bulb).

Temperature Range	Nov 01-08	Nov 09-16	Nov 17-24	Nov Total	Nov MCWB	Dec 01-08	Dec 09-16	Dec 17-24	Dec Total	Dec MCWB	Jan 01-08	Jan 09-16	Jan 17-24	Jan Total	Jan MCWB	Feb 01-08	Feb 09-16	Feb 17-24	Feb Total	Feb MCWB	Mar 01-08	Mar 09-16	Mar 17-24	Mar Total	Mar MCWB	Apr 01-08	Apr 09-16	Apr 17-24	Apr Total	Apr MCWB	Ann 01-08	Ann 09-16	Ann 17-24	Ann Total	Ann MCWB
105/109																																1	0	1	65
100/104																																23	7	30	65
95/99																										0	0	0	0	59		114	45	159	65
90/94																										0	1	0	1	57	1	267	136	404	63
85/89																										0	9	4	13	55	16	332	222	570	62
80/84	0	1	0	1	56											0	0	0	0	55	0	4	1	5	53	0	33	15	48	53	83	335	302	720	60
75/79	0	6	1	7	54	0	0	0	0	52	0	0	0	0	59	0	3	1	4	53	0	20	8	28	51	1	55	39	95	51	263	290	343	896	58
70/74	0	33	7	40	51	0	6	1	7	51	0	3	1	4	51	0	13	5	18	49	1	39	23	63	49	10	53	50	113	49	400	271	296	967	56
65/69	2	44	22	68	49	0	14	5	19	48	0	15	6	21	48	0	25	14	39	47	6	42	40	88	47	32	39	48	119	48	334	246	264	844	52
60/64	8	45	35	88	47	3	35	16	54	46	2	34	20	56	46	4	35	28	67	45	21	43	45	109	45	44	27	38	109	46	264	253	261	778	48
55/59	20	38	41	99	45	7	44	28	79	44	7	41	29	77	43	14	38	33	85	43	36	40	41	117	43	57	14	26	97	43	261	228	242	731	44
50/54	31	31	45	107	42	14	46	38	98	41	16	48	40	104	41	21	40	40	101	40	41	27	36	104	40	46	6	12	64	41	246	201	225	672	41
45/49	45	23	41	109	39	23	42	49	114	38	28	41	44	113	38	35	28	38	101	37	49	19	26	94	38	33	2	6	41	38	248	156	210	614	38
40/44	53	13	29	95	36	38	29	47	114	35	38	31	44	113	35	39	19	29	87	34	38	9	16	63	34	13	1	1	15	34	232	103	167	502	35
35/39	45	5	14	64	32	54	18	37	109	32	48	20	35	103	31	42	12	19	73	31	30	4	9	43	31	3	0	0	3	31	223	59	114	396	31
30/34	24	2	4	30	28	58	10	22	90	28	49	8	18	75	28	35	5	10	50	27	17	1	2	20	27	0	0	0	0	27	183	26	56	265	28
25/29	11	0	2	13	24	34	2	7	43	24	34	3	6	43	24	19	3	5	27	23	7	1	1	9	23						105	9	21	135	24
20/24	2	0	0	2	20	12	1	1	14	20	17	1	3	21	19	9	1	2	12	20	1	0	0	1	21						41	3	6	50	20
15/19	0	0	0	0	16	3	0	0	3	16	5	1	2	8	14	4	1	1	6	16	0	0	0	0	15						12	2	3	17	15
10/14						1	0	0	1	11	3	1	0	4	10	1	0	0	1	12					13						5	1	0	6	11
5/9						0	0	0	0	6	0	0	1	1	6	0	0	0	0	9											0	0	1	1	7
0/4											1	0	0	1	0																1	0	0	1	0
-5/-1											0	0	0	0	-4																0	0	0	0	-4
-10/-6											0	0	0	0	-8																0	0	0	0	-8

HOUSTON, TEXAS/ELLINGTON AFB

LAT 29 37N   LONG 95 10W   ELEV   40 FT

MEAN FREQUENCY OF OCCURRENCE OF DRY BULB TEMPERATURE (DEGREES F) WITH MEAN COINCIDENT WET BULB TEMPERATURE (DEGREES F) FOR EACH DRY BULB TEMPERATURE RANGE

Temperature Range	MAY Obsn Hour Gp 01–08	MAY 09–16	MAY 17–24	MAY Total Obsn	MAY MCWB	JUNE 01–08	JUNE 09–16	JUNE 17–24	JUNE Total	JUNE MCWB	JULY 01–08	JULY 09–16	JULY 17–24	JULY Total	JULY MCWB	AUG 01–08	AUG 09–16	AUG 17–24	AUG Total	AUG MCWB	SEP 01–08	SEP 09–16	SEP 17–24	SEP Total	SEP MCWB	OCT 01–08	OCT 09–16	OCT 17–24	OCT Total	OCT MCWB
100/104																														
95/99		0	0	0	78		4	0	4	78		0	0	0	80		1	0	1	77				0	77					78
90/94		4	1	5	76		56	7	63	77		16	2	18	79		15	2	17	78		2	0	2	77				0	77
85/89		52	6	58	74	4	103	36	143	76		87	19	106	78		81	16	97	78		29	2	31	76		2		2	74
80/84	4	103	32	139	72	28	48	64	140	75	5	93	44	142	77	3	90	38	131	77		89	20	109	75		34	2	36	72
75/79	50	57	82	189	71	100	19	92	211	73	39	34	80	153	74	33	41	81	155	74	14	67	54	135	73	1	65	13	79	69
70/74	95	21	79	195	69	83	9	34	126	70	148	13	89	250	70	152	17	95	264	71	92	35	94	221	70	17	65	43	125	67
65/69	55	9	33	97	64	21	1	5	27	65	51	4	13	68	65	55	3	14	72	65	79	14	50	143	64	47	39	68	154	63
60/64	27	2	13	42	59	3	0	1	4	59	4	0	1	5	59	5	1	1	7	59	35	4	16	55	59	58	25	51	134	58
55/59	15	1	2	18	54	1		1	1	54	1			1		1	0	0	1	55	14	1	3	18	56	48	12	36	96	53
50/54	3		0	3	50											0			0		5	0	1	6	49	36	5	22	63	49
45/49	0			0	48																	0	0	0	45	26	2	10	38	45
40/44																								0		11	0	2	13	40
35/39																										1			1	37

COINCIDENT WET BULB TEMPERATURE FOR EACH DRY BULB TEMPERATURE RANGE

HOUSTON, TEXAS/ELLINGTON AFB

The following table gives, for each month and for the annual total, the number of observations (grouped by hour: 01 to 08, 09 to 16, 17 to 24), the Total Observations, and the Mean Coincident Wet Bulb (MCWB) for each dry bulb temperature range.

Temperature Range	NOV 01-08	NOV 09-16	NOV 17-24	NOV Total Obsn	NOV MCWB	DEC 01-08	DEC 09-16	DEC 17-24	DEC Total Obsn	DEC MCWB	JAN 01-08	JAN 09-16	JAN 17-24	JAN Total Obsn	JAN MCWB	FEB 01-08	FEB 09-16	FEB 17-24	FEB Total Obsn	FEB MCWB	MAR 01-08	MAR 09-16	MAR 17-24	MAR Total Obsn	MAR MCWB	APR 01-08	APR 09-16	APR 17-24	APR Total Obsn	APR MCWB	ANNUAL 01-08	ANNUAL 09-16	ANNUAL 17-24	ANNUAL Total Obsn	ANNUAL MCWB
100/104																																1		1	77
95/99																																37	4	41	78
90/94		2		2	71																							0	0	74		259	45	304	78
85/89		20	1	21	71													0	0	66		0		0	70		4	0	4	73	12	467	146	625	76
80/84							1		1	69		2	0	2	70		3		3	69		7	1	8	67		50	6	56	71	119	441	332	892	74
75/79	4	48	10	62	69		19	1	20	68		12	1	13	68		10	1	11	67		30	6	36	66	10	82	36	128	70	573	407	550	1530	72
70/74	19	45	32	96	66	6	33	14	53	66	2	28	10	40	65	2	26	10	38	65	8	54	25	87	65	72	53	82	207	68	519	329	431	1279	68
65/69	38	40	47	125	63	21	38	28	87	63	21	28	26	75	63	19	34	24	77	62	34	52	50	136	62	53	31	55	139	63	364	263	337	964	63
60/64	37	30	42	109	58	31	41	40	112	58	24	32	28	84	58	19	35	30	84	57	44	42	55	141	57	41	14	35	90	58	290	209	283	782	58
55/59	32	24	35	91	53	33	38	43	114	53	26	34	36	96	53	27	38	40	105	53	45	27	44	116	52	35	5	18	58	53	255	172	241	668	53
50/54	36	18	35	89	48	35	32	42	109	48	29	36	43	108	48	41	34	44	119	48	41	17	32	90	47	17	1	6	24	48	228	140	212	580	48
45/49	35	8	22	65	44	42	25	41	108	44	33	28	37	98	43	39	21	37	97	43	34	11	23	68	43	10		1	11	44	204	93	163	460	43
40/44	22	4	10	36	39	36	13	23	72	39	42	24	32	98	39	37	14	22	73	39	24	5	9	38	39	2	0	0	2	38	165	60	96	321	39
35/39	10	1	4	15	34	26	6	12	44	35	33	14	23	70	34	22	6	11	39	35	13	1	3	17	34	0			0	37	105	28	53	186	34
30/34	5	0	0	5	30	13	2	4	19	30	24	6	9	39	29	14	2	4	20	30	4	0	0	4	30						60	10	17	87	30
25/29	0			0	26	4	0	1	5	25	10	3	3	16	25	4	0	0	4	26	0	0	0	0	26						18	3	4	25	25
20/24						1	0		1	21	3	1	2	6	20																4	1	2	7	20
15/19											2	0	0	2	15																2	0	0	2	15

SAN ANGELO, TEXAS*
READINGS TAKEN AT DYERS AFB/ABILENE, TX

LAT 32 25N   LONG 99 51W   ELEV 1789 FT

MEAN FREQUENCY OF OCCURRENCE OF DRY BULB TEMPERATURE (DEGREES F) WITH MEAN COINCIDENT WET BULB TEMPERATURE (DEGREES F) FOR EACH DRY BULB TEMPERATURE RANGE

Temperature Range	MAY 01 to 08	MAY 09 to 16	MAY 17 to 24	MAY Total Obsn	MAY MCWB	JUNE 01 to 08	JUNE 09 to 16	JUNE 17 to 24	JUNE Total Obsn	JUNE MCWB	JULY 01 to 08	JULY 09 to 16	JULY 17 to 24	JULY Total Obsn	JULY MCWB	AUGUST 01 to 08	AUGUST 09 to 16	AUGUST 17 to 24	AUGUST Total Obsn	AUGUST MCWB	SEPTEMBER 01 to 08	SEPTEMBER 09 to 16	SEPTEMBER 17 to 24	SEPTEMBER Total Obsn	SEPTEMBER MCWB	OCTOBER 01 to 08	OCTOBER 09 to 16	OCTOBER 17 to 24	OCTOBER Total Obsn	OCTOBER MCWB
105/109		0		0	64		0	0	0	70				0	71				0	72										
100/104		0	0	0	64		4	2	6	72		9	5	14	71		8	3	11	71		1		1	71		1		1	66
95/99		4	2	6	67		15	9	24	72		49	31	80	71		43	23	66	71		9	4	13	70		5	1	6	67
90/94		18	8	26	67		42	27	69	71		66	43	109	71		64	36	100	71		28	13	41	69		16	6	22	65
85/89	0	36	21	57	67	1	60	43	104	70	4	59	56	119	70	3	57	47	107	70	0	46	24	70	67		33	13	46	65
80/84	1	50	38	89	66	14	56	57	127	69	54	38	55	147	68	42	41	57	140	69	6	48	40	94	66	2	43	28	73	63
75/79	17	50	51	118	65	68	35	52	155	68	105	15	35	155	68	89	22	48	159	68	42	43	48	133	65	27	47	44	118	61
70/74	57	41	47	145	63	84	17	30	131	65	63	8	20	91	67	76	9	27	112	67	71	30	49	150	62	42	37	44	123	58
65/69	66	26	38	130	60	49	8	13	70	63	19	2	3	24	64	30	2	5	37	66	53	19	34	106	57	44	29	38	111	55
60/64	55	13	26	94	57	20	3	5	28	59	2	0	0	2	58	6	1	2	8	62	34	4	18	61	53	41	19	35	95	51
55/59	30	7	10	47	52	3	1	1	5	54	0			0	51	2	0	0	2	58	23	2	8	35	48	45	11	21	77	47
50/54	11	2	4	17	48	1		0	1	49						0			0	55	9	2	2	13	44	26	5	12	43	43
45/49	7	1	1	9	44																1		0	1	39	16	3	5	24	38
40/44	3	0	0	3	39																					4	0	1	5	35
35/39	0	0		0	30																					1			1	30
30/34																														

*Comparative design data note:

	Elevation	WINTER 97 1/2%	SUMMER DB 2 1/2%	SUMMER DB 2 1/2%	SUMMER WB 2 1/2%	SUMMER WB 2 1/2%
San Angelo, TX	1878 ft.	25° F	99° F		75° F	
Dyess AFB/Abilene	1789 ft.	21° F	99° F		74° F	

SAN ANGELO, TEXAS*
READINGS TAKEN AT DYERS AFB/ABILENE, TX

Note: This page is a single wide data table giving, for each dry-bulb Temperature Range, the number of observations by hour group (01 to 08, 09 to 16, 17 to 24), the Total Obsn, and the Mean Coincident Wet Bulb (MCWB) for each month and for the annual total. It is reproduced below as one table per month.

NOVEMBER

Temperature Range	Obsn Hour Gp 01 to 08	09 to 16	17 to 24	Total Obsn	MCWB
105/109					
100/104					
95/99					
90/94					
85/89		1		1	61
80/84		6	1	7	61
75/79		20	5	25	60
70/74	2	28	14	44	58
65/69	8	30	28	66	56
60/64	29	35	35	99	53
55/59	29	31	35	95	49
50/54	36	32	36	104	45
45/49	44	27	36	107	42
40/44	39	16	27	82	37
35/39	29	10	16	55	34
30/34	15	4	6	25	29
25/29	7	1	2	10	24
20/24	1			1	20
15/19	0			0	15
10/14					
5/9					
0/4					

DECEMBER

Temperature Range	Obsn Hour Gp 01 to 08	09 to 16	17 to 24	Total Obsn	MCWB
85/89				0	
80/84		1		1	55
75/79		3	0	3	57
70/74	1	13	3	16	56
65/69	9	22	9	32	54
60/64	16	31	21	61	53
55/59	29	35	29	80	51
50/54	33	33	36	98	48
45/49	36	31	40	104	44
40/44	54	26	35	97	40
35/39	37	24	32	110	37
30/34	19	16	25	78	33
25/29	10	8	12	39	29
20/24	6	3	3	16	25
15/19	1	1	1	8	20
10/14	0	0	0	1	16
5/9				0	12

JANUARY

Temperature Range	Obsn Hour Gp 01 to 08	09 to 16	17 to 24	Total Obsn	MCWB
90/94				0	
85/89		1	1	1	57
80/84		5	4	6	56
75/79		12	10	16	55
70/74	0	16	18	26	53
65/69	6	23	24	47	52
60/64	13	27	32	64	50
55/59	21	30	35	83	47
50/54	26	34	33	95	44
45/49	38	29	25	100	40
40/44	37	23	17	91	36
35/39	39	17	15	81	33
30/34	30	15	8	60	29
25/29	17	8	7	33	24
20/24	11	5	3	23	20
15/19	7	3	1	13	15
10/14	4	1		6	11
5/9	0			0	6
0/4				0	4

FEBRUARY

Temperature Range	Obsn Hour Gp 01 to 08	09 to 16	17 to 24	Total Obsn	MCWB
85/89				0	
80/84		3	1	4	62
75/79	1	6	3	9	57
70/74	7	10	5	15	55
65/69	15	19	12	32	54
60/64	23	23	20	50	52
55/59	29	29	27	71	50
50/54	28	30	31	84	47
45/49	42	29	38	95	44
40/44	43	26	32	100	41
35/39	29	20	25	88	37
30/34	21	13	15	57	33
25/29	12	11	10	42	29
20/24	3	5	6	23	25
15/19	1	1	1	5	21
10/14	0		0	1	16
5/9				0	11

MARCH

Temperature Range	Obsn Hour Gp 01 to 08	09 to 16	17 to 24	Total Obsn	MCWB
90/94				0	
85/89		2	1	3	65
80/84		5	3	8	62
75/79		9	4	13	59
70/74	2	14	9	23	58
65/69	8	26	20	48	57
60/64	24	34	28	70	55
55/59	32	33	33	90	53
50/54	32	31	35	98	51
45/49	38	28	33	93	48
40/44	38	24	29	91	44
35/39	33	16	22	76	41
30/34	26	12	17	62	37
25/29	9	10	10	46	33
20/24	4	3	3	15	29
15/19	1	1	1	6	25
10/14	0	0	0	1	21
5/9	0	0		0	16
0/4				0	10

APRIL

Temperature Range	Obsn Hour Gp 01 to 08	09 to 16	17 to 24	Total Obsn	MCWB
90/94		1	1	2	63
85/89		6	3	9	63
80/84	1	17	9	26	63
75/79		28	17	45	62
70/74	20	39	29	69	61
65/69	45	42	41	103	59
60/64	46	35	41	121	57
55/59	43	28	36	110	54
50/54	36	19	27	89	50
45/49	26	14	21	71	46
40/44	13	8	10	44	42
35/39	7	2	3	18	37
30/34	2	0	1	8	33
25/29		1	1	4	30
20/24	1			1	27

ANNUAL TOTAL

Temperature Range	Obsn Hour Gp 01 to 08	09 to 16	17 to 24	Total Obsn	MCWB
105/109				0	69
100/104		0		0	71
95/99	0	22	10	32	71
90/94	8	122	70	192	70
85/89	117	231	132	363	69
80/84	324	297	209	514	67
75/79	402	314	283	714	65
70/74	322	295	309	928	63
65/69	282	283	304	989	58
60/64	247	250	265	837	54
55/59	243	228	251	761	49
50/54	229	203	231	681	45
45/49	226	182	216	641	41
40/44	207	159	201	589	37
35/39	149	118	157	501	33
30/34	87	89	123	419	29
25/29	44	61	82	292	25
20/24	21	38	42	167	20
15/19	9	17	18	79	16
10/14	4	7	9	37	11
5/9	0	3	3	15	6
0/4		1	1	6	4

SALT LAKE CITY, UTAH*
READINGS TAKEN AT HILL AFB/OGDEN
LAT 41 07N   LONG 111 58W   ELEV 4785 FT

MEAN FREQUENCY OF OCCURRENCE OF DRY BULB TEMPERATURE (DEGREES F) WITH MEAN COINCIDENT WET BULB TEMPERATURE (DEGREES F) FOR EACH DRY BULB TEMPERATURE RANGE

Temperature Range	MAY 01–08	MAY 09–16	MAY 17–24	MAY Total Obsn	MAY MCWB	JUNE 01–08	JUNE 09–16	JUNE 17–24	JUNE Total Obsn	JUNE MCWB	JULY 01–08	JULY 09–16	JULY 17–24	JULY Total Obsn	JULY MCWB	AUG 01–08	AUG 09–16	AUG 17–24	AUG Total Obsn	AUG MCWB	SEP 01–08	SEP 09–16	SEP 17–24	SEP Total Obsn	SEP MCWB	OCT 01–08	OCT 09–16	OCT 17–24	OCT Total Obsn	OCT MCWB
100/104									0																					
95/99							2	1	3	64		0	0	0	64		0		0	67										
90/94		0	0	0	59		11	6	17	62		7	3	10	62		4	1	5	63		0		0	62					
85/89		3	1	4	58		23	13	36	60		41	23	64	62		31	15	46	62		2	0	2	61		0	0	0	58
80/84		14	6	20	55	1	33	22	56	59		69	41	110	60		56	30	86	61		12	4	16	59		1	0	1	56
75/79	0	25	13	38	54	5	38	33	76	58	4	61	55	120	59	1	58	45	104	59		32	14	46	57	0	10	2	12	53
70/74	2	36	25	63	52	21	37	38	96	56	25	41	58	124	57	17	45	61	123	58	2	40	25	67	55		19	8	27	51
65/69	13	40	39	92	50	40	36	38	114	54	73	21	42	136	55	64	27	48	139	56	11	42	39	92	53	3	31	17	51	50
60/64	29	40	42	111	48	50	29	35	114	52	83	6	20	109	53	87	14	26	127	54	29	31	44	104	51	11	40	29	80	47
55/59	44	33	41	118	46	50	18	27	95	50	48	2	6	56	51	44	8	13	65	51	46	32	41	119	49	25	41	39	105	45
50/54	58	28	37	123	43	48	9	21	78	48	13	0	1	14	48	19	3	7	29	47	53	22	31	106	46	40	35	49	124	42
45/49	52	16	24	92	41	21	3	5	29	46	3		0	3	44	10	2	3	15	44	44	14	22	80	43	57	32	44	133	39
40/44	32	8	12	52	37	4	0	1	5	43						5	0	1	6	40	31	9	12	52	40	55	22	32	109	36
35/39	13	4	6	23	34	1			1	38						0			0	35	15	6	2	23	36	34	17	10	61	33
30/34	5	2	2	9	30											0			0	33	9	1	1	11	31	17	5	7	29	28
25/29	1	0	0	1	25																1	1	1	3	27	4	1	2	7	24
20/24	0	0		0	21																0			0		2	1	0	3	20

*Comparative design data note:

	WINTER 97 1/2%	SUMMER DB 2 1/2%	SUMMER WB 2 1/2%	Elevation
Hill AFB/Ogden, UT	10° F	91° F	65° F	4785 ft.
Salt Lake City	9° F	94° F	66° F	4220 ft.

SALT LAKE CITY, UTAH*
READINGS TAKEN AT HILL AFB/OGDEN

Temperature Range	NOVEMBER					DECEMBER					JANUARY					FEBRUARY					MARCH					APRIL					ANNUAL TOTAL				
	01-08	09-16	17-24	Total	MCWB	01-08	09-16	17-24	Total	MCWB	01-08	09-16	17-24	Total	MCWB	01-08	09-16	17-24	Total	MCWB	01-08	09-16	17-24	Total	MCWB	01-08	09-16	17-24	Total	MCWB	01-08	09-16	17-24	Total	MCWB
100/104																																0	0	0	65
95/99																																13	5	18	62
90/94																																85	44	129	61
85/89																															0	163	89	252	60
80/84																											0	0	0	54	6	199	142	347	58
75/79		0	0	0	52																	0	0	0	50		3	1	4	52	49	202	193	444	56
70/74		1	0	1	47																	5	2	7	47		8	5	13	50	171	190	205	566	54
65/69		9	1	10	45												0	0	0	49		10	5	15	45	1	18	10	29	48	256	182	196	634	52
60/64	1	18	7	26	44												1		1	49	2	18	12	32	43	5	23	20	48	46	233	194	192	619	49
55/59							0	0	0	45		0	0	0	44		5	2	7	45						11	32	26	69	43	218	190	193	601	46
50/54	10	29	21	60	41	1	3	1	5	42	0	2	1	3	42	2	13	9	24	42	5	26	23	54	41	26	39	38	103	41	247	200	225	672	43
45/49	20	36	34	90	39	7	12	8	27	39	5	12	7	24	39	10	25	21	56	39	21	34	33	88	38	33	42	40	115	38	262	221	229	712	39
40/44	42	46	45	133	36	14	29	17	60	36	13	24	19	56	36	19	32	32	83	36	35	42	43	120	35	52	39	45	136	36	281	244	252	777	36
35/39	52	40	47	139	32	28	42	36	106	33	35	44	38	117	33	40	43	45	128	32	53	42	50	145	32	61	24	33	118	33	326	249	274	849	32
30/34	50	38	49	137	29	42	54	57	153	29	31	48	48	127	29	51	46	49	146	29	57	39	42	138	28	44	10	20	74	29	298	243	275	816	29
25/29	41	16	27	84	25	58	51	59	168	25	49	49	51	149	24	42	28	34	104	24	37	20	24	81	24	6	0	1	7	25	238	165	198	601	24
20/24	16	4	6	26	20	49	36	37	122	20	47	34	41	122	20	31	21	21	73	20	21	8	9	38	20	1			1	20	167	103	115	385	20
15/19	6	1	3	10	16	33	13	24	70	16	32	19	22	73	15	16	6	9	31	16	12	2	3	17	15						99	41	61	201	16
10/14	1	0		1	12	13	6	7	26	11	16	8	11	35	11	9	3	3	15	11	3	1	1	5	10						42	18	22	82	11
5/9						4	2	1	7	6	11	4	7	22	6	4	1	1	6	6	1	0		1	6						20	7	9	36	6
0/4						1			1	2	5	2	2	9	2	1			1	1	0			0	3						7	2	2	11	2
-5/-1							0		0	-2	1	1	1	3	-4		0		0	-1											1	1	1	3	-3
-10/-6											1	0	0	1	-8																1	0	0	1	-8
-15/-11											1	0	0	1	-13																1	0	0	1	-13

NORFOLK, VIRGINIA
READINGS TAKEN AT LANGLEY AFB/HAMPTON
LAT 37 05N   LONG 76 21W   ELEV   10 FT

MEAN FREQUENCY OF OCCURRENCE OF DRY BULB TEMPERATURE (DEGREES F) WITH COINCIDENT WET BULB TEMPERATURE (DEGREES F) FOR EACH DRY BULB TEMPERATURE RANGE

MAY

Temperature Range	Obsn Hour Gp 01 to 08	09 to 16	17 to 24	Total Obsn	MWB
95/99		0		0	76
90/94		2		2	74
85/89		13	3	16	71
80/84	0	32	10	42	69
75/79	3	40	25	68	67
70/74	30	49	44	123	65
65/69	57	46	50	153	61
60/64	57	41	53	151	57
55/59	51	18	39	108	53
50/54	33	6	19	58	49
45/49	11	1	4	16	45
40/44	5		1	6	40
35/39	1		0	1	36
30/34					
25/29					

JUNE

Temperature Range	Obsn Hour Gp 01 to 08	09 to 16	17 to 24	Total Obsn	MWB
95/99		2	0	2	78
90/94		15	3	18	77
85/89	1	39	15	55	75
80/84	5	55	33	93	73
75/79	33	58	52	143	70
70/74	87	45	70	202	68
65/69	64	19	45	128	63
60/64	32	7	18	57	59
55/59	13	1	3	17	55
50/54	3	1	0	4	50
45/49	1	0	0	1	46
40/44	0			0	43

JULY

Temperature Range	Obsn Hour Gp 01 to 08	09 to 16	17 to 24	Total Obsn	MWB
95/99		3	0	3	78
90/94		23	4	27	77
85/89	0	56	19	75	76
80/84	12	81	52	145	74
75/79	92	62	93	247	72
70/74	101	21	66	188	69
65/69	33	2	13	48	65
60/64	8	0	2	10	60
55/59	2		0	2	56

AUGUST

Temperature Range	Obsn Hour Gp 01 to 08	09 to 16	17 to 24	Total Obsn	MWB
95/99		2	0	2	79
90/94		17	3	20	78
85/89	0	49	14	63	76
80/84	11	83	44	138	74
75/79	82	65	94	241	72
70/74	97	28	69	194	69
65/69	41	4	19	64	65
60/64	12	0	4	16	60
55/59	4		1	5	55
50/54	1		0	1	51

SEPTEMBER

Temperature Range	Obsn Hour Gp 01 to 08	09 to 16	17 to 24	Total Obsn	MWB
90/94		3	0	3	77
85/89		24	3	27	75
80/84	1	49	17	67	73
75/79	28	65	51	144	71
70/74	71	52	66	189	68
65/69	58	30	54	142	63
60/64	45	15	33	93	58
55/59	26	2	12	40	54
50/54	5	4	4	13	50
45/49	1	1	1	3	46
40/44	0			0	43

OCTOBER

Temperature Range	Obsn Hour Gp 01 to 08	09 to 16	17 to 24	Total Obsn	MWB
85/89		2	0	2	73
80/84		7	1	8	71
75/79	2	20	6	28	69
70/74	12	52	21	85	66
65/69	35	62	53	150	62
60/64	59	50	58	167	58
55/59	44	34	46	124	52
50/54	40	14	35	89	48
45/49	31	5	17	53	44
40/44	16	1	8	25	39
35/39	9	0	2	11	35
30/34	1		0	1	30
25/29	0			0	26

COINCIDENT WET BULB TEMPERATURE FOR EACH DRY BULB TEMPERATURE RANGE

NORFOLK, VIRGINIA
READINGS TAKEN AT LANGLEY AFB/HAMPTON

Temperature Range	NOVEMBER					DECEMBER					JANUARY					FEBRUARY					MARCH					APRIL					ANNUAL TOTAL				
	01–08	09–16	17–24	Total	MCWB	01–08	09–16	17–24	Total	MCWB	01–08	09–16	17–24	Total	MCWB	01–08	09–16	17–24	Total	MCWB	01–08	09–16	17–24	Total	MCWB	01–08	09–16	17–24	Total	MCWB	01–08	09–16	17–24	Total	MCWB
95/99																											0	0	0	68		7	0	7	78
90/94																											2		2	68		62	10	72	77
85/89																											4	1	5	67	1	187	55	243	75
80/84		1		1	70																	3		3	63		11	3	14	66	29	322	160	511	73
75/79		5	1	6	66		1		1	67				0	62						0	6	1	7	61	0	18	10	28	64	240	340	333	913	71
70/74	2	14	3	19	63	0	4	1	5	63	0	3	0	3	60	0	3	0	3	60	0	9	3	12	59	5	26	15	46	62	405	306	358	1069	67
65/69	5	25	12	42	61	1	9	3	13	60	0	6	2	8	60	1	6	3	10	58	3	15	9	27	58	22	29	26	77	60	320	253	289	862	62
60/64	20	40	29	89	57	7	13	10	30	57	4	11	7	22	55	4	10	7	21	56	10	19	16	45	54	30	41	34	105	55	288	247	271	806	57
55/59	32	49	39	120	52	13	18	14	45	52	8	13	10	31	52	6	12	10	28	51	13	28	22	63	50	39	44	44	127	51	251	219	240	710	52
50/54	37	48	47	132	47	16	32	25	73	47	11	18	12	41	46	10	22	15	47	46	21	38	27	86	46	40	40	48	128	47	221	218	233	672	47
45/49	42	34	44	120	43	26	46	35	107	43	17	33	25	75	42	18	34	29	81	42	38	54	56	148	42	54	20	40	114	43	240	227	251	718	43
40/44	46	17	37	100	38	39	46	44	129	38	33	47	45	125	38	34	47	47	128	38	63	48	64	175	38	35	4	15	54	39	271	210	261	742	38
35/39	28	5	18	51	34	40	38	44	122	33	43	45	46	134	33	46	45	50	141	33	55	20	31	106	33	11	1	2	14	35	233	154	193	580	33
30/34	19	1	9	29	29	47	28	41	116	29	45	36	46	127	29	49	28	38	115	29	27	8	14	49	28	3	0	1	4	31	191	101	149	441	29
25/29	6	2	0	8	25	35	9	21	65	25	44	23	35	102	24	33	11	18	62	24	14	2	5	21	24						132	45	81	258	24
20/24	1			1	20	17	3	8	28	20	28	9	13	50	20	16	4	7	27	20	3	0	0	3	20						65	16	28	109	20
15/19						6	1	2	9	16	11	3	5	19	15	6	1	1	8	15											23	5	5	36	15
10/14						1		0	1	12	3	1	1	5	11	1	0	0	1	11											5	1	1	7	11
5/9											1			1	7	0			0	8											1	0	0	1	7

Note: Obsn Hour Gp = Observation Hour Group; MCWB = Mean Coincident Wet Bulb.

ROANOKE/WOODRUM APRT VIRGINIA
LAT 37 19N   LONG 79 58W   ELEV 1193 FT

MEAN FREQUENCY OF OCCURRENCE OF DRY BULB TEMPERATURE (DEGREES F) WITH MEAN COINCIDENT WET BULB TEMPERATURE (DEGREES F) FOR EACH DRY BULB TEMPERATURE RANGE

(Column groups per month — Obsn Hour Gp: "01 to 08", "09 to 16", "17 to 24"; "Total Obsn"; "MCWB" = Mean Coincident Wet Bulb)

Temperature Range	MAY 01-08	MAY 09-16	MAY 17-24	MAY Total	MAY Wb	JUNE 01-08	JUNE 09-16	JUNE 17-24	JUNE Total	JUNE Wb	JULY 01-08	JULY 09-16	JULY 17-24	JULY Total	JULY Wb	AUG 01-08	AUG 09-16	AUG 17-24	AUG Total	AUG Wb	SEP 01-08	SEP 09-16	SEP 17-24	SEP Total	SEP Wb	OCT 01-08	OCT 09-16	OCT 17-24	OCT Total	OCT Wb
100/104																			0	72										
95/99		0	0	0	73		3	1	4	74		1	0	1	75		3	1	4	71										
90/94		3	0	3	69		19	5	24	72		6	1	7	73		22	3	25	72		2	0	2	70		1	0	1	69
85/89		20	5	25	67	0	45	15	60	70		25	6	31	72		54	17	71	71		6	1	7	70		5	0	5	68
80/84	1	38	14	53	65	2	55	28	85	68	1	59	22	82	71	1	67	35	103	69		25	6	31	70		13	2	15	64
75/79	3	46	29	78	63	14	52	50	116	67	3	74	41	118	69	16	55	61	132	68		37	15	52	68		28	7	35	62
70/74	14	47	42	103	61	42	35	62	139	65	23	48	66	137	69	80	32	80	192	67	2	47	31	80	66	2	35	19	56	60
65/69	42	35	54	131	60	79	19	49	147	63	91	27	76	194	67	90	11	39	140	64	28	47	52	127	65	13	40	35	88	58
60/64	61	27	47	135	57	56	8	23	87	59	86	7	31	124	64	43	3	10	56	60	58	41	57	156	62	29	43	47	119	55
55/59	56	19	32	107	52	33	3	6	42	55	31	1	5	37	59	13		1	14	55	52	22	43	117	58	46	39	48	133	52
50/54	40	10	17	67	48	10	1	2	13	50	11		0	11	54	3		0	3	51	47	8	23	78	54	50	28	44	122	47
45/49	23	3	7	33	43	3		0	3	46	1			1	50				0	47	30	3	10	43	49	48	11	29	88	43
40/44	8	0	1	9	39	0			0	43											15	1	3	19	45	35	4	10	49	39
35/39	2		0	2	34																6		1	7	41	16	1	4	21	34
30/34																					1			1	37	8		2	10	30
25/29																										1		0	1	25

COINCIDENT WET BULB TEMPERATURE FOR EACH DRY BULB TEMPERATURE RANGE

ROANOKE/WOODRUM APRT VIRGINIA

Hour groups: 01 to 08, 09 to 16, 17 to 24 (Obsn Hour Gp); Total Obsn; MCWB

Temperature Range	NOV 01–08	NOV 09–16	NOV 17–24	NOV Total	NOV MCWB	DEC 01–08	DEC 09–16	DEC 17–24	DEC Total	DEC MCWB	JAN 01–08	JAN 09–16	JAN 17–24	JAN Total	JAN MCWB	FEB 01–08	FEB 09–16	FEB 17–24	FEB Total	FEB MCWB	MAR 01–08	MAR 09–16	MAR 17–24	MAR Total	MAR MCWB	APR 01–08	APR 09–16	APR 17–24	APR Total	APR MCWB	ANN 01–08	ANN 09–16	ANN 17–24	ANN Total	ANN MCWB
100/104																																1		1	75
95/99																																14	3	17	73
90/94																																77	15	92	72
85/89																											1		1	66	1	214	66	281	70
80/84		0		0	65																	1		1	57		6	1	7	64	7	301	140	448	68
75/79		3	0	3	62		1		1	60		1		1	63				0	57		4	1	5	57		16	5	21	62	58	308	256	622	66
70/74		11	2	13	58	1	4	1	6	57		2		2	60		1	0	1	56		8	4	12	56		24	11	35	60	260	274	358	892	65
65/69	3	19	8	30	56	2	9	4	15	53		5	2	7	57		5	2	7	54	2	17	9	28	54	3	28	21	52	58	387	234	318	939	61
60/64	9	27	19	55	53	7	19	12	38	50	2	8	5	15	54	1	13	5	19	50	5	22	17	44	51	13	31	31	75	56	318	212	263	793	56
55/59	19	35	31	85	50	8	24	21	53	45	7	17	11	35	50	5	18	13	36	48	11	29	27	67	48	27	29	38	94	53	290	219	242	751	51
50/54	27	39	38	104	46	20	30	29	79	41	11	20	17	48	45	11	25	22	58	44	24	31	32	87	44	35	32	38	105	50	257	213	237	707	46
45/49	33	35	39	107	41	27	43	37	107	37	15	29	27	71	41	19	32	30	81	41	31	39	37	107	40	42	32	34	108	46	250	204	228	682	42
40/44	40	33	38	111	37	44	44	45	133	33	31	43	39	113	37	31	37	41	109	37	38	41	41	120	37	43	24	27	94	41	255	215	232	702	37
35/39	41	21	33	95	33	53	36	44	133	29	44	47	47	138	33	44	39	45	128	33	57	33	45	135	33	39	14	24	77	37	273	188	226	687	33
30/34	40	12	20	72	29	35	22	28	85	24	50	39	48	137	29	48	29	34	111	29	47	15	24	86	29	24	3	7	34	33	257	131	175	563	29
25/29	17	9	3	29	25	25	10	17	52	20	36	20	28	84	24	31	13	16	60	24	20	4	7	31	24	11	0	3	14	29	142	62	88	292	24
20/24	8	2	1	11	20	18	4	7	29	15	27	11	15	53	19	19	6	9	34	19	6	3	3	12	19	2	0	0	2	25	85	31	46	162	19
15/19	2	0	0	2	16	4	1	1	6	10	16	5	7	28	15	8	4	4	16	15	6	0	1	7	15						50	13	19	82	15
10/14	1	0	0	1	10	3	0	0	3	8	6	1	3	10	10	5	1	2	8	10		0		0	12						16	3	6	25	10
5/9				0	8						3	0	0	3	5	3	0	0	3	5											8	1	0	9	6
0/4									0	2		0		0																		0	0	0	1
-5/-1												0		0	-4																	0		0	-4

MEAN FREQUENCY OF OCCURRENCE OF DRY BULB TEMPERATURE (DEGREES F) WITH MEAN COINCIDENT WET BULB TEMPERATURE (DEGREES F) FOR EACH DRY BULB TEMPERATURE RANGE

SEATTLE NSA WASHINGTON
LAT 47 41N   LONG 122 15W   ELEV 47 FT

Temperature Range	MAY 01–08	MAY 09–16	MAY 17–24	MAY Total	MAY MCWB	JUNE 01–08	JUNE 09–16	JUNE 17–24	JUNE Total	JUNE MCWB	JULY 01–08	JULY 09–16	JULY 17–24	JULY Total	JULY MCWB	AUG 01–08	AUG 09–16	AUG 17–24	AUG Total	AUG MCWB	SEP 01–08	SEP 09–16	SEP 17–24	SEP Total	SEP MCWB	OCT 01–08	OCT 09–16	OCT 17–24	OCT Total	OCT MCWB
95/99		0	0	0	65		0	0	0	67		0	0	0	79	0	1	0	1	69										
90/94		0	0	0	67		1	0	1	69		2	1	3	72		1	0	1	67		0	0	0	70					
85/89		1	0	1	65		2	2	4	68		9	5	14	69		5	2	7	68		1	0	1	67					
80/84		5	2	7	64		7	4	11	66		20	13	33	67		17	9	26	66		5	2	7	65		0	0	0	67
75/79		8	4	12	62		16	10	26	64		31	25	56	65		30	19	49	64	0	16	5	21	64		1	0	1	64
70/74		16	9	25	60	1	33	21	55	61	2	53	41	96	62	1	54	38	93	62	0	31	15	46	62		5	1	6	60
65/69	1	32	21	54	57	6	55	41	102	58	15	63	55	133	60	10	66	62	138	60	2	56	37	95	59	0	19	4	23	58
60/64	6	53	39	98	54	30	66	65	161	56	70	52	72	194	57	88	58	81	227	58	39	70	78	187	57	7	49	24	80	56
55/59	33	66	65	164	52	103	47	69	219	54	131	17	33	181	54	120	16	35	171	55	101	48	76	225	54	40	77	73	190	53
50/54	98	50	69	217	49	92	12	26	130	50	29	1	2	32	51	28	0	3	31	51	78	12	25	115	51	90	67	92	249	50
45/49	81	15	34	130	45	9	0	1	10	47	1	0	0	1	48	1	0	0	1	48	18	1	2	21	47	80	24	46	150	46
40/44	28	1	4	33	41																1		0	1	43	29	5	8	42	42
35/39	2	0	0	2	37																					3	0	0	3	38

COINCIDENT WET BULB TEMPERATURE FOR EACH DRY BULB TEMPERATURE RANGE

SEATTLE NSA WASHINGTON

Temperature Range	NOVEMBER					DECEMBER					JANUARY					FEBRUARY					MARCH					APRIL					ANNUAL TOTAL				
	01 to 08	09 to 16	17 to 24	Total Obsn	MCWB	01 to 08	09 to 16	17 to 24	Total Obsn	MCWB	01 to 08	09 to 16	17 to 24	Total Obsn	MCWB	01 to 08	09 to 16	17 to 24	Total Obsn	MCWB	01 to 08	09 to 16	17 to 24	Total Obsn	MCWB	01 to 08	09 to 16	17 to 24	Total Obsn	MCWB	01 to 08	09 to 16	17 to 24	Total Obsn	MCWB
95/99																															0	1	0	1	71
90/94																															0	4	1	5	70
85/89																															0	18	9	27	68
80/84																															0	54	30	84	66
75/79																										0			0		0	103	63	166	64
70/74																										0	1	0	1	59	4	196	126	326	62
65/69																0	0	0	0	56						0	4	1	5	58	34	307	225	566	59
60/64	0	0	0	0	56	0	0	0	0	52						0	1	0	1	55	0	0	0	0	55	0	12	4	16	55	240	384	376	1000	57
55/59	0	3	1	4	54	0	4	2	6	52	0	0	0	0	51	0	3	1	4	52	0	3	1	4	54	0	21	12	33	52	535	389	408	1332	53
50/54	4	24	8	36	52	18	39	24	81	49	0	4	1	5	50	1	13	5	19	50	0	9	3	12	52	2	50	32	84	50	520	454	441	1415	49
45/49	37	74	54	165	49	64	79	74	217	45	9	21	14	44	48	11	40	25	76	48	0	23	9	32	49	24	81	71	176	47	564	471	538	1573	45
40/44	77	73	86	236	45	68	68	73	209	40	42	64	57	163	45	43	73	68	184	44	6	57	36	99	47	99	56	83	238	44	530	323	405	1258	40
35/39	66	43	60	169	40	58	39	53	150	36	72	80	76	228	40	77	60	74	211	40	49	86	87	222	44	87	13	32	132	41	327	146	214	687	36
30/34	38	15	24	77	36	27	13	17	57	31	72	50	64	186	36	61	27	40	128	36	102	78	53	233	40	26	0	5	31	37	116	42	56	214	31
25/29	13	5	4	22	32	7	3	2	12	27	29	16	22	67	31	24	6	9	39	31	67	15	28	110	36	1	0	0	1	33	27	15	15	57	25
20/24	2	1	1	4	25	2	1	2	5	20	12	9	9	30	25	5	1	2	8	25	22	2	4	28	31						11	6	8	25	20
15/19	1	1	0	2	19	1	2	1	4	15	6	3	5	14	20	2	1	0	3	19	1	1	1	3	26						9	3	3	15	16
10/14	2	0	1	3	16	1	1	1	3	11	5	1	1	7	16	1	0	0	1	16	1	0	0	1	20						1	1	1	3	12
5/9	0	0	0	0	14	0	0	0	0	8	0	0	0	0	13																0	0	0	0	8

SPOKANE, WASHINGTON/FAIRCHILD AFB

LAT 47 37N   LONG 117 38W   ELEV 2462 FT

MEAN FREQUENCY OF OCCURRENCE OF DRY BULB TEMPERATURE (DEGREES F) WITH MEAN COINCIDENT WET BULB TEMPERATURE (DEGREES F) FOR EACH DRY BULB TEMPERATURE RANGE

Within each month: Obsn Hour Gp = three observation-hour groups (01 to 08, 09 to 16, 17 to 24); Total Obsn = total observations; MWB = mean coincident wet bulb temperature.

Temperature Range	MAY 01-08	MAY 09-16	MAY 17-24	MAY Total	MAY MWB	JUNE 01-08	JUNE 09-16	JUNE 17-24	JUNE Total	JUNE MWB	JULY 01-08	JULY 09-16	JULY 17-24	JULY Total	JULY MWB	AUG 01-08	AUG 09-16	AUG 17-24	AUG Total	AUG MWB	SEP 01-08	SEP 09-16	SEP 17-24	SEP Total	SEP MWB	OCT 01-08	OCT 09-16	OCT 17-24	OCT Total	OCT MWB
100/104																														
95/99																	1	0	1	65										
90/94		0		0	60		0	0	0	65		1	0	1	66		6	2	8	63										
85/89		2	1	3	62		4	2	6	64		5	2	7	64		15	7	22	62		1	0	1	61					
80/84		6	2	8	59		12	6	18	62	1	21	9	30	63		30	15	45	60		6	2	8	61				0	58
75/79	0	14	7	21	57	0	19	11	30	61	7	48	42	97	61	0	41	27	68	59		18	5	23	59		5	0	5	55
70/74	1	27	15	43	54	1	33	20	54	58	26	41	49	116	58	3	42	34	78	57	0	27	13	40	57		8	2	10	54
65/69	4	38	25	67	52	7	42	33	82	56	51	29	40	120	56	20	33	46	108	55	1	34	23	58	54		14	5	19	52
60/64	12	41	35	88	50	19	46	39	104	54	63	15	27	105	54	44	24	41	118	53	7	41	32	80	52	0	25	12	37	50
55/59	30	43	43	116	48	36	41	49	126	52	52	6	18	76	52	58	12	36	118	51	25	46	46	117	50	6	42	27	75	48
50/54	53	41	50	144	45	58	27	44	129	50	35	1	7	43	49	61	3	28	101	50	48	34	46	128	48	23	58	44	125	45
45/49	60	24	40	124	42	61	12	28	101	47	12		2	14	46	43	0	10	56	47	61	25	42	128	46	51	54	66	171	42
40/44	52	9	22	83	39	45	3	8	56	43	1		1	2	42	15		1	16	43	56	7	22	85	42	69	27	55	151	39
35/39	27	1	8	36	34	11	0	1	12	39	0		0	0	38	3			3	40	31	1	7	39	38	60	9	27	96	35
30/34	8	0	1	9	31	2		0	2	36					34				0	36	8	0	1	9	33	29	4	9	42	30
25/29	1			1	27																2		0	2	28	7	1	1	9	26
20/24																					0			0	25	1	0	0	1	20
15/19																										0	0	0	0	16

COINCIDENT WET BULB TEMPERATURE FOR EACH DRY BULB TEMPERATURE RANGE

SPOKANE, WASHINGTON/FAIRCHILD AFB

Obsn Hour Gp columns: **01 to 08**, **09 to 16**, **17 to 24**; **Total Obsn**; **MCWB**

Temperature Range	Nov 01-08	Nov 09-16	Nov 17-24	Nov Tot	Nov MCWB	Dec 01-08	Dec 09-16	Dec 17-24	Dec Tot	Dec MCWB	Jan 01-08	Jan 09-16	Jan 17-24	Jan Tot	Jan MCWB	Feb 01-08	Feb 09-16	Feb 17-24	Feb Tot	Feb MCWB	Mar 01-08	Mar 09-16	Mar 17-24	Mar Tot	Mar MCWB	Apr 01-08	Apr 09-16	Apr 17-24	Apr Tot	Apr MCWB	Ann 01-08	Ann 09-16	Ann 17-24	Ann Tot	Ann MCWB
100/104																																			
95/99																																2		2	66
90/94																																11	4	15	63
85/89																																41	18	59	62
80/84																											0	0	0	59		88	47	135	61
75/79																											1	0	1	56	1	127	75	203	59
70/74																											3	1	4	54	11	169	116	296	57
65/69		0		0	50																						8	3	11	51	55	197	169	421	55
60/64		0		0	46																					0	18	9	27	49	125	211	185	521	53
55/59		2	0	2	46		1	0	1	45	0			0	53		1	0	1	50		0	0	0	52	3	37	19	59	46	194	214	215	623	51
50/54	1	13	3	17	45	1	6	2	9	42	1	0	0	0	48	0	1	0	1	48	0	2	0	2	51	8	58	37	103	43	258	213	229	700	48
45/49	9	37	20	66	42	11	27	16	54	39	1	5	1	7	42	0	7	2	9	45	0	4	1	5	49	26	65	60	151	40	285	242	234	761	45
40/44	40	63	51	154	39	36	49	51	136	35	9	22	15	46	39	2	18	10	30	42	0	9	4	13	46	68	39	66	173	37	283	265	260	808	42
35/39	53	54	63	170	34	75	69	70	214	31	34	43	43	120	35	14	41	29	84	38	0	23	11	34	43	84	10	36	130	34	339	291	318	948	38
30/34	72	41	61	174	30	58	53	55	166	26	53	55	57	165	30	38	65	63	166	34	5	46	28	79	40	44	1	8	53	30	397	283	358	1038	34
25/29	39	21	28	88	26	36	26	30	92	21	50	46	47	143	26	80	53	69	202	30	30	62	56	148	37	7	0	0	7	26	451	254	328	1033	30
20/24	18	5	9	32	21	18	10	13	41	17	38	31	34	103	21	48	23	30	101	26	55	52	66	173	33	0	0	0	0	21	254	157	180	591	26
15/19	6	2	3	11	16	5	5	5	15	12	22	20	20	62	16	24	10	11	45	21	88	31	53	172	30						134	76	90	300	21
10/14	1	0	1	2	11	3	2	2	7	7	15	12	15	42	11	10	4	7	21	16	44	13	19	76	25						62	37	45	144	16
5/9	1	0	0	1	6	2	1	2	5	2	12	8	9	29	6	5	1	2	8	11	17	4	6	27	20						28	10	24	67	11
0/4	0			0	3	0	1	1	2	-4	7	4	4	15	1	2	0	0	2	7	7	0	2	9	15						19	5	11	40	6
-5/-1						0	1	1	2	-9	4	2	2	8	-3	1			1	3	2	0	1	3	10						10	3	6	21	-3
-10/-6						1	1	1	3	-14	1	0	1	2	-8						1		0	1	5						4	1	3	4	-9
-15/-11						1	0	0	1	-17	1		0	1	-13																1	1	2	4	-13
-20/-16											0			0	-16																1	0	1	1	-17

CHARLESTON/KANAWHA APRT WEST VIRGINIA
LAT 38 22N LONG 81 36W ELEV 939 FT

MEAN FREQUENCY OF OCCURRENCE OF DRY BULB TEMPERATURE (DEGREES F) WITH MEAN COINCIDENT WET BULB TEMPERATURE (DEGREES F) FOR EACH DRY BULB TEMPERATURE RANGE

Temperature Range	MAY 01–08	MAY 09–16	MAY 17–24	MAY Total	MAY MCWB	JUNE 01–08	JUNE 09–16	JUNE 17–24	JUNE Total	JUNE MCWB	JULY 01–08	JULY 09–16	JULY 17–24	JULY Total	JULY MCWB	AUG 01–08	AUG 09–16	AUG 17–24	AUG Total	AUG MCWB	SEP 01–08	SEP 09–16	SEP 17–24	SEP Total	SEP MCWB	OCT 01–08	OCT 09–16	OCT 17–24	OCT Total	OCT MCWB
100/104																														
95/99							1		1	76		0		0	78		0	0	0	70		1		1	72					
90/94		1	0	1	70		13	4	17	74		2	0	2	76		3	0	3	72		1	0	1	71		0		0	70
85/89		17	6	23	67		37	14	51	71		20	5	25	73		15	4	19	74		8	2	10	70		4	0	4	68
80/84	0	38	15	53	65	2	55	27	84	69		52	18	70	72		44	14	58	72		30	8	38	70		12	2	14	65
75/79	4	41	28	73	63	12	51	46	109	67	2	73	41	116	70	1	70	35	106	71	0	41	17	58	68	0	31	8	39	62
70/74	13	43	38	94	61	39	41	56	136	66	14	55	63	132	69	11	56	58	125	69	3	43	30	76	66	3	37	21	61	61
65/69	34	40	52	126	60	64	25	49	138	63	77	32	74	183	68	65	40	73	178	68	29	45	50	124	65	10	38	34	82	58
60/64	53	29	44	126	57	51	12	27	90	59	89	13	35	137	65	83	15	43	141	65	51	20	50	134	62	24	34	44	102	56
55/59	44	18	30	92	53	40	4	12	56	55	39	3	10	52	61	50	4	15	69	61	46	12	40	106	58	40	31	40	111	52
50/54	44	13	20	77	49	26	2	4	32	51	20		2	22	56	25	1	5	31	56	44	4	26	82	54	48	29	41	118	48
45/49	28	7	11	46	44	7		0	7	47	6		0	6	52	11	0	1	12	52	36	1	12	52	50	45	19	30	94	44
40/44	20	2	4	26	40	0			0	42	1			1	47	2			2	48	21	0	3	25	46	34	8	17	59	40
35/39	6		0	6	36																8		1	9	42	26	4	8	38	36
30/34	1			1	32																3		0	3	37	15	1	3	19	31
25/29	0			0	29																0			0	34	2		0	2	27
20/24																										1			1	22

COINCIDENT WET BULB TEMPERATURE FOR EACH DRY BULB TEMPERATURE RANGE

CHARLESTON/KANAWHA APRT WEST VIRGINIA

Each month's sub-columns are the Observation Hour Groups (01 to 08, 09 to 16, 17 to 24), the Total Obsn, and the MCWB (Mean Coincident Wet Bulb).

Temp Range	Nov 01–08	Nov 09–16	Nov 17–24	Nov Total	Nov MCWB	Dec 01–08	Dec 09–16	Dec 17–24	Dec Total	Dec MCWB	Jan 01–08	Jan 09–16	Jan 17–24	Jan Total	Jan MCWB	Feb 01–08	Feb 09–16	Feb 17–24	Feb Total	Feb MCWB	Mar 01–08	Mar 09–16	Mar 17–24	Mar Total	Mar MCWB	Apr 01–08	Apr 09–16	Apr 17–24	Apr Total	Apr MCWB	Ann 01–08	Ann 09–16	Ann 17–24	Ann Total	Ann MCWB
100/104																																	1	1	73
95/99																																7	0	7	74
90/94																											0		0	66		57	15	72	73
85/89		1		1	64																			0	59		6	2	8	63		190	62	252	71
80/84																						1		1	58		17	8	25	62	5	308	145	458	69
75/79		4	1	5	61		1	0	1	61		0	0	0	63		0	0	0	63		3	2	5	59	1	25	15	41	60	45	310	251	606	67
70/74	2	13	4	19	59		2	1	3	57		3	1	4	60		2	0	2	56		11	5	16	56	9	26	23	58	58	237	295	346	878	65
65/69	5	21	13	39	56	1	6	3	10	56	2	4	3	9	57	1	5	2	8	55	4	14	9	27	54	17	27	30	74	56	361	241	323	925	61
60/64	10	24	20	54	52	5	10	8	23	54	6	10	9	25	54	4	10	10	24	52	10	21	20	51	52	29	29	34	92	54	327	206	281	814	56
55/59	22	26	28	76	49	10	15	13	38	51	10	15	13	38	50	7	16	15	38	49	15	25	25	65	49	32	28	34	94	50	309	191	243	743	52
50/54	24	30	29	83	46	14	23	19	56	46	12	19	19	50	46	12	22	19	53	45	20	29	27	76	45	29	27	27	83	46	282	198	218	698	47
45/49	23	29	30	82	42	15	26	25	66	42	15	25	23	63	42	17	30	28	75	41	24	34	36	94	41	31	24	26	81	42	229	195	212	636	42
40/44	31	29	32	92	38	27	34	32	93	38	19	28	27	74	38	25	29	32	86	38	35	35	38	108	37	35	18	23	76	38	234	183	206	623	38
35/39	39	28	34	101	34	31	36	36	107	34	32	34	35	101	34	36	33	33	102	34	41	33	35	109	33	33	10	14	57	34	247	178	199	624	34
30/34	43	19	27	89	30	49	39	42	130	29	46	43	47	136	30	43	34	38	115	30	47	28	32	107	29	19	3	5	27	30	263	167	194	624	30
25/29	28	10	13	51	25	35	29	30	94	25	34	28	28	90	25	29	17	21	67	25	28	10	12	50	25	5	0	1	6	26	161	94	105	360	25
20/24	9	3	5	17	21	28	15	18	61	20	29	19	22	70	20	23	11	12	46	20	12	4	4	20	20	1	0		1	22	103	52	61	216	20
15/19	4	2	2	7	15	14	7	10	31	15	18	12	12	42	15	12	7	5	24	15	7	1	2	10	15						55	28	31	114	15
10/14	1	1	1	2	11	12	5	5	22	11	13	6	6	25	11	9	4	5	18	11	2	0	0	2	11						37	15	17	69	11
5/9	1	1	0	2	7	4	1	1	6	6	3	1	3	10	6	3	2	2	7	6	0	0	0	0	8						14	5	6	25	6
0/4						2			2	2	3	1	1	5	1	3	1	0	4	1											8	2	1	11	1
-5/-1									0	-2	1	0	0	1	-3	1	0	0	1	-2											2	0	0	2	-2
-10/-6											1	0	0	1	-8																1	0	0	1	-8
-15/-11											0	0	0	0	-12																0	0	0	0	-12

LA CROSSE MAP WISCONSIN
LAT 43 52N   LONG 91 15W   ELEV 651 FT

MEAN FREQUENCY OF OCCURRENCE OF DRY BULB TEMPERATURE (DEGREES F) WITH MEAN COINCIDENT WET BULB TEMPERATURE (DEGREES F) FOR EACH DRY BULB TEMPERATURE RANGE

(Obsn Hour Gp columns: 01 to 08 / 09 to 16 / 17 to 24; Total = Total Obsn; MCWB = Mean Coincident Wet Bulb)

Temperature Range	MAY 01-08	MAY 09-16	MAY 17-24	MAY Total	MAY MCWB	JUNE 01-08	JUNE 09-16	JUNE 17-24	JUNE Total	JUNE MCWB	JULY 01-08	JULY 09-16	JULY 17-24	JULY Total	JULY MCWB	AUG 01-08	AUG 09-16	AUG 17-24	AUG Total	AUG MCWB	SEP 01-08	SEP 09-16	SEP 17-24	SEP Total	SEP MCWB	OCT 01-08	OCT 09-16	OCT 17-24	OCT Total	OCT MCWB
100/104																														
95/99																														
90/94		0		0	71	0	1	1	1	75		0		0	78		0	0	0	72				0	71				0	63
85/89		6	2	8	69	0	8	0	10	74		2	0	2	78		2	0	2	75		0	0	4	74		0	0	0	64
80/84	0	15	6	21	65	1	20	2	29	72	0	10	3	13	77	0	10	3	13	74	0	4	2	9	74		0	0	4	64
75/79	1	30	15	46	63	11	40	9	63	69	3	35	15	50	72	3	24	10	34	72	7	7	7	18	70		0	0	14	62
70/74	9	34	26	69	60	34	52	22	103	66	13	56	34	94	70	13	48	26	77	70	12	11	14	49	67	1	4	2	31	60
65/69	19	44	39	102	58	54	49	40	130	64	51	63	53	135	68	44	59	45	117	68	19	28	23	76	63	7	12	10	56	58
60/64	34	43	46	123	55	56	36	47	137	61	76	51	63	165	66	67	52	58	154	66	36	41	37	101	60	16	20	18	79	55
55/59	53	31	43	127	52	44	21	47	116	58	62	25	49	150	63	63	35	53	155	63	53	45	48	129	57	31	31	28	108	51
50/54	49	21	35	105	47	27	10	39	77	54	28	6	26	94	60	41	15	35	113	59	51	45	49	136	53	35	38	39	116	47
45/49	42	16	22	80	43	11	3	23	39	50	8	1	5	34	56	15	3	14	58	55	38	34	35	104	49	47	37	44	120	43
40/44	27	5	9	41	39	2	0	9	12	46	0	1	1	9	52	3		3	18	51	16	18	16	60	45	46	34	39	105	39
35/39	11	1	4	16	34			1	2	42		1		0	49	1	3	0	3	47	6	6	6	22	41	34	22	37	66	34
30/34	3	0	1	4	30			0								0		0	1	42	1	0	1	7	36	23	11	21	34	30
25/29	0			0	28														0	37				1	32	5	4	7	7	25
20/24																										2	0	2	2	22
15/19																										0		0	0	19

COINCIDENT WET BULB TEMPERATURE FOR EACH DRY BULB TEMPERATURE RANGE

LA CROSSE MAP WISCONSIN

Columns per month: Obsn Hour Gp (01 to 08 / 09 to 16 / 17 to 24), Total Obsn, MCWB (Mean Coincident Wet Bulb).

Temp. Range	NOV 01–08	NOV 09–16	NOV 17–24	NOV Total	NOV MCWB	DEC 01–08	DEC 09–16	DEC 17–24	DEC Total	DEC MCWB	JAN 01–08	JAN 09–16	JAN 17–24	JAN Total	JAN MCWB	FEB 01–08	FEB 09–16	FEB 17–24	FEB Total	FEB MCWB	MAR 01–08	MAR 09–16	MAR 17–24	MAR Total	MAR MCWB	APR 01–08	APR 09–16	APR 17–24	APR Total	APR MCWB	ANN 01–08	ANN 09–16	ANN 17–24	ANN Total	ANN MCWB
100/104																																		0	76
95/99																																5		5	76
90/94																													0	62		32	8	40	75
85/89																											1		1	63		93	38	131	72
80/84																											3	1	4	61	8	177	96	281	69
75/79																								0	51		7	2	9	59	51	251	171	473	66
70/74		1		1	58																			0	56	1	10	5	16	57	152	258	232	642	64
65/69		3		3	56																	1		1	54	4	19	11	34	54	246	239	254	739	61
60/64	2	7	4	13	55				0	54									0	51	1	2	1	4	51	7	22	20	49	52	277	196	247	720	57
55/59	6	15	8	29	51	1	1	1	3	52							1		1	45		5	3	8	48	14	26	25	65	49	271	165	210	646	52
50/54	8	24	15	47	47	2	1	2	5	49				0	45		2	1	3	44	2	11	5	18	44	23	33	31	87	45	220	150	181	551	47
45/49	15	26	23	64	42	1	4	2	7	43		1		1	40	1	5	2	8	41	3	15	9	27	40	31	38	37	106	41	192	145	151	488	43
40/44	25	34	33	92	38	5	13	7	25	38		6	2	8	37	2	12	5	19	37	9	31	22	62	37	39	38	40	117	38	172	161	161	494	38
35/39	41	38	39	118	34	14	24	23	61	34	10	20	16	46	34	10	28	22	60	33	27	48	44	119	33	51	26	35	112	34	204	196	205	605	34
30/34	50	35	46	131	30	33	42	42	117	30	20	34	30	84	30	32	41	43	116	30	50	55	61	166	30	41	12	22	75	30	253	223	252	728	30
25/29	38	24	28	90	25	38	47	40	125	25	30	34	34	98	25	32	34	36	102	25	51	34	41	126	25	21	3	8	32	25	215	176	189	580	25
20/24	21	16	17	54	20	37	34	32	103	21	32	36	32	100	21	28	35	31	94	21	37	22	26	85	20	6	1	1	8	21	163	144	139	446	21
15/19	14	8	14	36	16	32	23	29	84	16	28	27	31	86	16	27	27	26	80	16	25	13	16	54	16				0	16	126	98	116	340	16
10/14	8	5	8	21	11	25	21	18	64	11	30	30	27	87	11	27	15	21	63	11	17	7	10	34	11	1			1	10	108	78	84	270	11
5/9	7	2	2	11	7	19	18	22	59	6	26	21	23	70	6	22	11	16	49	6	14	3	5	22	6						88	55	68	211	6
0/4	4	1	2	7	1	13	11	13	37	2	20	17	20	57	1	18	8	9	35	1	7	1	2	10	2						62	38	46	146	1
-5/-1	1		1	2	-3	11	5	11	27	-3	20	13	17	50	-4	10	4	7	21	-3	3		1	4	-4						45	22	37	104	-3
-10/-6				0	-7	10	3	5	18	-8	15	7	9	31	-8	7	2	3	12	-8	1			1	-8						33	12	17	62	-8
-15/-11						5		1	6	-13	8	3	5	16	-13	5	1	1	7	-13				0	-14						18	4	7	29	-13
-20/-16						1			1	-17	5	1	1	7	-18	2	1		3	-18				0	-18						8	1	2	11	-18
-25/-21									0	-22	2		1	3	-23	1			1	-22				0	-23						3		1	4	-23
-30/-26											1			1	-28									0	-27						1			1	-28
-35/-31														0	-33																			0	-33

MADISON/TRAUX FIELD WISCONSIN
LAT 43 08N   LONG 89 20W   ELEV   858 FT

MEAN FREQUENCY OF OCCURRENCE OF DRY BULB TEMPERATURE (DEGREES F) WITH MEAN COINCIDENT WET BULB TEMPERATURE (DEGREES F) FOR EACH DRY BULB TEMPERATURE RANGE

Temperature Range	MAY 01 to 08	MAY 09 to 16	MAY 17 to 24	MAY Total Obsn	MAY MC WB	JUNE 01 to 08	JUNE 09 to 16	JUNE 17 to 24	JUNE Total Obsn	JUNE MC WB	JULY 01 to 08	JULY 09 to 16	JULY 17 to 24	JULY Total Obsn	JULY MC WB	AUG 01 to 08	AUG 09 to 16	AUG 17 to 24	AUG Total Obsn	AUG MC WB	SEPT 01 to 08	SEPT 09 to 16	SEPT 17 to 24	SEPT Total Obsn	SEPT MC WB	OCT 01 to 08	OCT 09 to 16	OCT 17 to 24	OCT Total Obsn	OCT MC WB
100/104																														
95/99												0	0	0	80		0	0	0	72										
90/94		0		0	71		1		1	76		2	0	2	77		2	0	2	73										
85/89		5	1	6	68		10	2	12	73		12	2	14	74		11	2	13	74		1	0	1	71					
80/84		17	4	21	67	0	24	7	31	72	0	40	10	50	71	0	26	8	34	72		3	0	3	74					
75/79	1	31	11	43	63	2	45	17	64	69	4	66	29	99	69	2	54	19	75	70	0	12	2	14	72		1		1	65
70/74	6	39	21	66	60	12	51	32	95	66	18	62	45	125	67	11	67	38	116	68	0	15	6	21	70		3	0	3	65
65/69	18	41	32	91	58	27	43	46	116	64	46	40	59	145	66	39	48	56	143	66	4	30	13	47	66	0	15	1	16	64
60/64	36	38	44	118	55	48	34	48	130	61	63	19	56	138	63	61	27	55	143	63	14	49	21	84	63	0	24	7	31	60
55/59	40	32	43	115	51	49	20	43	112	57	64	7	33	104	59	60	11	43	114	59	18	45	33	96	60	5	33	17	55	58
50/54	45	21	37	103	47	49	8	28	85	54	35	1	12	48	55	43	1	20	64	55	40	43	47	130	57	18	37	26	81	55
45/49	41	16	28	85	43	29	4	13	46	49	15		2	17	51	21	7		28	51	45	27	49	121	53	26	38	35	99	51
40/44	34	6	18	58	40	17	0	4	21	45	3		0	3	47	10	1		11	46	47	13	36	96	49	34	36	40	110	47
35/39	18	2	8	28	35	6		1	7	41						2			2	42	36	3	19	58	45	42	31	45	118	43
30/34	9		2	11	30	1			1	37						0			0	39	19	0	10	29	41	44	17	37	98	39
25/29	1			1	26																11		3	14	36	39	11	25	75	35
20/24																					4		0	4	32	28	2	10	40	30
15/19																					0			0	28	8	0	4	12	26
10/14																										2		1	3	20
5/9																										1			1	17

COINCIDENT WET BULB TEMPERATURE FOR EACH DRY BULB TEMPERATURE RANGE

MADISON/TRAUX FIELD WISCONSIN

For each month the column groups are: **Obsn Hour Gp** (01 to 08, 09 to 16, 17 to 24), **Total Obsn**, and **M C W B** (mean coincident wet bulb).

NOVEMBER

Temperature Range	01 to 08	09 to 16	17 to 24	Total Obsn	M C W B
75/79		0	0	0	62
70/74		1	0	1	61
65/69		4	0	4	56
60/64	2	9	4	15	55
55/59	6	16	10	32	51
50/54	7	21	14	42	47
45/49	16	28	21	65	43
40/44	23	38	28	89	38
35/39	34	38	45	117	34
30/34	58	36	46	140	30
25/29	40	26	32	98	25
20/24	23	11	18	52	21
15/19	12	5	12	29	16
10/14	8	3	6	17	11
5/9	4	2	3	9	6
0/4	2	1	1	4	1
-5/-1	1	1	1	2	-3
-10/-6	0			0	-7

DECEMBER

Temperature Range	01 to 08	09 to 16	17 to 24	Total Obsn	M C W B
60/64		0	0	0	54
55/59	1	2	0	3	52
50/54	0	3	2	5	48
45/49	2	7	4	13	43
40/44	4	15	5	24	38
35/39	14	25	20	59	34
30/34	42	47	48	137	30
25/29	39	48	46	133	25
20/24	40	35	31	106	21
15/19	27	24	26	77	16
10/14	21	18	21	60	11
5/9	20	14	20	54	6
0/4	16	7	14	37	1
-5/-1	11	4	8	23	-3
-10/-6	9	1	3	13	-8
-15/-11	2	0	0	2	-13
-20/-16	1	0	0	1	-17
-25/-21	0	0		0	-21

JANUARY

Temperature Range	01 to 08	09 to 16	17 to 24	Total Obsn	M C W B
50/54		1	0	1	46
45/49	0	2	1	3	44
40/44	2	7	2	11	38
35/39	6	23	13	42	34
30/34	26	37	36	99	30
25/29	39	45	41	125	26
20/24	34	35	34	103	21
15/19	29	28	30	87	16
10/14	32	27	28	87	11
5/9	20	18	22	60	6
0/4	20	13	21	54	1
-5/-1	17	7	12	36	-3
-10/-6	14	4	6	24	-8
-15/-11	5	1	2	8	-13
-20/-16	3	0	1	4	-18
-25/-21	0	0	0	0	-22
-30/-26	1	0	0	1	-28
-35/-31	0	0		0	-33
-40/-36	0			0	

FEBRUARY

Temperature Range	01 to 08	09 to 16	17 to 24	Total Obsn	M C W B
55/59		0		0	50
50/54	1	3	0	4	46
45/49	1	5	2	8	42
40/44	4	14	5	21	37
35/39	10	30	21	61	34
30/34	35	47	43	125	30
25/29	36	45	43	124	25
20/24	36	31	39	106	20
15/19	27	18	25	70	16
10/14	24	13	18	55	11
5/9	22	8	11	41	6
0/4	11	5	9	25	1
-5/-1	9	3	5	17	-4
-10/-6	7	1	2	10	-8
-15/-11	2	0	1	3	-13
-20/-16	1		0	1	-18
-25/-21	0	0	0	0	-23
-30/-26	0			0	-26

MARCH

Temperature Range	01 to 08	09 to 16	17 to 24	Total Obsn	M C W B
60/64	0	1	0	1	55
55/59	0	1	0	1	55
50/54	1	1	2	4	52
45/49	1	3	3	7	49
40/44	4	5	7	16	45
35/39	9	10	15	34	41
30/34	24	21	11	56	37
25/29	60	29	34	123	34
20/24	56	33	94	183	30
15/19	32	20	82	134	25
10/14	26	9	44	79	20
5/9	14	3	32	49	16
0/4	10	1	16	27	11
-5/-1	4	1	10	15	7
-10/-6	3	0	3	6	2
-15/-11	2	0	1	3	-3
-20/-16	0	0	2	2	-8
-25/-21	0	0	0	0	-13
-30/-26	0	0	0	0	-19
-35/-31				0	-23
-40/-36				0	-27

APRIL

Temperature Range	01 to 08	09 to 16	17 to 24	Total Obsn	M C W B
70/74		1		1	62
65/69	0	3	1	4	62
60/64	2	7	2	9	60
55/59	7	7	4	18	57
50/54	7	14	10	31	55
45/49	14	19	17	48	53
40/44	20	24	23	65	49
35/39	30	28	30	80	45
30/34	39	30	35	104	42
25/29	47	39	42	115	38
20/24	25	34	38	111	34
15/19	7	26	29	88	30
10/14	1	12	9	36	25
5/9	1	2	2	9	20
0/4		0	0	1	16
-5/-1		0		1	11
-10/-6					9

ANNUAL TOTAL

Temperature Range	01 to 08	09 to 16	17 to 24	Total Obsn	M C W B
95/99		0	0	0	76
90/94		6	0	6	75
85/89		36	6	42	74
80/84	0	109	28	137	72
75/79	8	203	76	287	69
70/74	46	263	142	451	66
65/69	132	259	214	605	64
60/64	215	223	251	689	61
55/59	276	192	258	726	57
50/54	259	158	222	639	52
45/49	220	142	186	548	48
40/44	202	152	169	523	43
35/39	184	160	166	510	39
30/34	204	218	218	631	34
25/29	309	237	281	827	30
20/24	244	199	220	663	25
15/19	174	132	152	458	20
10/14	123	84	107	314	16
5/9	100	64	83	247	11
0/4	76	43	60	179	6
-5/-1	53	27	46	126	1
-10/-6	41	14	26	81	-3
-15/-11	32	6	11	49	-8
-20/-16	9	1	3	13	-13
-25/-21	5	0	1	6	-18
-30/-26	0	0	0	0	-23
-35/-31	1	0	0	0	-28
-40/-36	0	0	0	0	-33

MEAN FREQUENCY OF OCCURRENCE OF DRY BULB TEMPERATURE (DEGREES F) WITH MEAN COINCIDENT WET BULB TEMPERATURE (DEGREES F) FOR EACH DRY BULB TEMPERATURE RANGE

MILWAUKEE, WISCONSIN*
READINGS TAKEN AT MADISON, WI
LAT 43 08N   LONG 89 20W   ELEV 858 FT

Column key within each month: Obsn Hour Gp (01 to 08 | 09 to 16 | 17 to 24) | Total Obsn | MCWB (Mean Coincident Wet Bulb, M C W B)

Temperature Range	MAY 01‑08	MAY 09‑16	MAY 17‑24	MAY Total	MAY WB	JUNE 01‑08	JUNE 09‑16	JUNE 17‑24	JUNE Total	JUNE WB	JULY 01‑08	JULY 09‑16	JULY 17‑24	JULY Total	JULY WB	AUG 01‑08	AUG 09‑16	AUG 17‑24	AUG Total	AUG WB	SEPT 01‑08	SEPT 09‑16	SEPT 17‑24	SEPT Total	SEPT WB	OCT 01‑08	OCT 09‑16	OCT 17‑24	OCT Total	OCT WB
100/104																														
95/99											0	0	0	0	80	0	0	0	0	72										
90/94		0		0	71		1		1	76		2	0	2	77		2		2	73										
85/89		5	1	6	68		10	2	12	73		12	2	14	74		11	2	13	74		1		1	71		1		1	65
80/84		17	4	21	67		24	7	31	72		40	10	50	71	0	26	8	34	72		3		3	74		3		3	65
75/79	1	31	11	43	63	2	45	17	64	69	4	66	29	99	69	2	54	19	75	70		12	2	14	72		15	1	16	64
70/74	6	39	21	66	60	12	51	32	95	66	18	62	45	125	67	11	67	38	116	68	4	15	2	21	70		24	7	31	60
65/69	18	41	32	91	58	27	43	46	116	64	46	40	59	145	66	39	48	56	143	66	14	30	3	47	66	5	33	17	55	58
60/64	36	38	44	118	55	48	34	48	130	61	63	19	56	138	63	61	27	55	143	63	18	49	17	84	63	18	37	26	81	55
55/59	40	32	43	115	51	49	20	43	112	57	64	7	33	104	59	60	11	43	114	59	40	45	11	96	60	26	38	35	99	51
50/54	45	21	37	103	47	49	8	28	85	54	35	1	12	48	55	43	1	20	64	55	45	43	42	130	57	34	36	40	110	47
45/49	41	16	28	85	43	29	4	13	46	49	15		2	17	51	21		7	28	51	47	27	47	121	53	42	31	45	118	43
40/44	34	6	18	58	40	17	0	4	21	45	3			3	47	10		1	11	46	36	13	47	96	49	44	17	37	98	39
35/39	18	2	8	28	35	6		1	7	41						2			2	42	19	3	36	58	45	39	11	25	75	35
30/34	9	0	2	11	30	1			1	37						0			0	39	11	0	18	29	41	28	2	10	40	30
25/29	1			1	26																4		0	4	36	8	0	4	12	26
20/24																					0			0	32	2		1	3	20
15/19																								0	28	1			1	17

*Comparative design data note:

	Elevation	WINTER 97 1/2%	SUMMER DB 2 1/2%	SUMMER WB 2 1/2%
Madison, WI	858 ft.	-5° F	88° F	75° F
Milwaukee	762 ft.	-2° F	87° F	75° F

COINCIDENT WET BULB TEMPERATURE FOR EACH DRY BULB TEMPERATURE RANGE

MILWAUKEE, WISCONSIN*
READINGS TAKEN AT MADISON, WI

In each month block the three "Obsn Hour Gp" columns are hour groups 01 to 08, 09 to 16, and 17 to 24; "Total" is Total Obsn; "WB" is MCWB (mean coincident wet bulb).

Temp. Range	Nov 01–08	Nov 09–16	Nov 17–24	Nov Total	Nov WB	Dec 01–08	Dec 09–16	Dec 17–24	Dec Total	Dec WB	Jan 01–08	Jan 09–16	Jan 17–24	Jan Total	Jan WB	Feb 01–08	Feb 09–16	Feb 17–24	Feb Total	Feb WB	Mar 01–08	Mar 09–16	Mar 17–24	Mar Total	Mar WB	Apr 01–08	Apr 09–16	Apr 17–24	Apr Total	Apr WB	Ann 01–08	Ann 09–16	Ann 17–24	Ann Total	Ann WB
100/104																																		0	76
95/99																																6	0	6	75
90/94																																36	6	42	74
85/89																											1		1	62	0	109	28	137	72
80/84																											3	1	4	62	8	203	76	287	69
75/79		0		0	62																					0	7	2	9	60	46	263	142	451	66
70/74		1	0	1	61																0	1	0	1	55	0	14	4	18	57	132	259	214	605	64
65/69	0	0	4	4	56				0	54											0	1	0	1	55	2	19	10	31	55	215	223	251	689	61
60/64	2	4	9	15	55	1	2	0	3	52											0	3	1	4	52	7	24	17	48	53	276	192	258	726	57
55/59	6	16	10	32	51											0	0	0	0	50	0	5	2	7	49	14	28	23	65	49	259	158	222	639	52
50/54	7	21	14	42	47	0	3	2	5	48	0	1	0	1	46	1	3	0	4	46	1	10	5	16	45	20	30	30	80	45	220	142	186	548	48
45/49	16	28	21	65	43	2	7	4	13	43	0	3	0	3	44	1	5	2	8	42	4	21	9	34	41	30	39	35	104	42	202	152	169	523	43
40/44	23	38	28	89	38	4	15	5	24	38	2	7	2	11	38	2	14	5	21	37	9	29	18	56	37	39	34	42	115	38	184	160	166	510	39
35/39	34	38	45	117	34	14	25	20	59	34	6	23	13	42	34	10	30	21	61	34	24	54	45	123	34	47	26	38	111	34	204	209	218	631	34
30/34	58	36	46	140	30	42	47	48	137	30	26	37	36	99	30	35	47	43	125	30	60	56	67	183	30	47	12	29	88	30	309	237	281	827	30
25/29	40	26	32	98	25	39	48	46	133	25	39	45	41	125	26	36	45	43	124	25	56	33	45	134	25	25	2	9	36	25	244	199	220	663	25
20/24	23	11	18	52	21	40	35	31	106	21	34	35	34	103	21	36	31	39	106	20	32	20	27	79	20	7	0	2	9	20	174	132	152	458	20
15/19	12	5	12	29	16	27	24	26	77	16	29	28	30	87	16	27	18	25	70	16	26	9	14	49	16	1	0	0	1	16	123	84	107	314	16
10/14	8	3	6	17	11	21	18	21	60	11	32	27	28	87	11	24	13	18	55	11	14	3	10	27	11	1	0	0	1	9	100	64	83	247	11
5/9	4	2	3	9	6	20	14	20	54	6	20	18	22	60	6	22	8	11	41	6	10	1	4	15	7						76	43	60	179	6
0/4	2	1	1	4	1	16	7	14	37	1	20	13	21	54	1	11	5	9	25	1	4	1	1	6	2						53	27	46	126	1
-5/-1	1		1	2	-3	11	4	8	23	-3	17	7	12	36	-3	9	3	5	17	-4	3	0	0	3	-3						41	14	26	81	-3
-10/-6	0			0	-7	9	1	3	13	-8	14	4	6	24	-8	7	1	2	10	-8	2	0	0	2	-8						32	6	11	49	-8
-15/-11						2	0	0	2	-13	1	1	2	4	-13	2	0	1	3	-13	0	0	0	0	-13						9	1	3	13	-13
-20/-16						1	0	0	1	-17	0	0	1	1	-18	1	0	0	1	-18	0	0	0	0	-19						5	0	1	6	-18
-25/-21						0			0	-21	0	0	0	0	-22	0	0	0	0	-23	0	0		0	-23						0	0	0	0	-23
-30/-26											1	0	0	1	-28	0	0		0	-26	0	0		0	-27						1	0	0	1	-28
-35/-31											0	0	0	0	-33																0	0	0	0	-33
-40/-36											0	0	0	0																	0	0	0	0	

CASPER IAP WYOMING
LAT 42 55N   LONG 106 28W   ELEV 5338 FT

MEAN FREQUENCY OF OCCURRENCE OF DRY BULB TEMPERATURE (DEGREES F) WITH MEAN COINCIDENT WET BULB TEMPERATURE (DEGREES F) FOR EACH DRY BULB TEMPERATURE RANGE

Temperature Range	MAY 01-08	MAY 09-16	MAY 17-24	MAY Total	MAY MWB	JUNE 01-08	JUNE 09-16	JUNE 17-24	JUNE Total	JUNE MWB	JULY 01-08	JULY 09-16	JULY 17-24	JULY Total	JULY MWB	AUG 01-08	AUG 09-16	AUG 17-24	AUG Total	AUG MWB	SEP 01-08	SEP 09-16	SEP 17-24	SEP Total	SEP MWB	OCT 01-08	OCT 09-16	OCT 17-24	OCT Total	OCT MWB
100/104																														
95/99																														
90/94												1	0	1	62															
85/89		2	0	2	55		1	0	1	58		4	1	5	60		0	0	0	57										
80/84		8	2	10	54		8	2	10	56		29	9	38	58		16	4	20	58		1	0	1	58					
75/79		20	6	26	52		23	8	31	56	0	59	24	83	58		52	17	69	57		15	2	17	56		0	0	0	54
70/74	1	34	13	48	51	0	34	14	48	55	2	58	31	91	58	1	64	26	91	57		31	8	39	54		2	0	2	52
65/69	3	38	21	62	50	3	41	21	65	55	10	42	40	92	57	6	49	37	92	56	0	39	14	53	53		13	1	14	50
60/64	9	36	30	75	48	6	38	27	71	54	28	29	47	104	56	22	33	49	104	55	4	37	25	66	52		26	4	30	48
55/59	24	39	41	104	47	18	36	41	95	52	48	16	45	109	55	48	16	50	114	54	13	32	33	78	50	0	34	8	42	47
50/54	39	31	44	114	45	34	27	40	101	51	67	8	30	105	53	66	10	36	112	52	23	29	38	90	48	6	34	17	57	45
45/49	59	24	43	126	42	56	18	37	111	49	55	3	15	73	51	59	5	16	80	49	37	19	39	95	46	14	34	31	79	43
40/44	61	11	32	104	39	66	9	29	104	47	29	1	5	35	48	31	2	9	42	47	43	13	29	85	44	25	29	38	92	41
35/39	35	5	12	52	35	39	3	14	56	44	7	0	1	8	45	10	1	3	14	43	53	11	23	87	41	36	26	42	104	39
30/34	14	1	3	18	31	14	1	4	19	40	1	0	0	1	41	5		1	6	39	36	8	17	61	38	56	22	42	120	36
25/29	1	1	1	3	25	3	1	1	5	35						1			1	36	21	4	9	34	34	47	15	29	91	33
20/24	1	0	1	2	21	1	1	1	3	31											8	2	3	13	31	37	8	22	67	29
15/19	1	1	0	1	18	0			0	28											2	1	0	3	26	18	4	10	32	26
10/14																								0	23	7	1	2	10	21
																										2		1	3	16
																													0	14

COINCIDENT WET BULB TEMPERATURE FOR EACH DRY BULB TEMPERATURE RANGE

CASPER IAP WYOMING

Temperature Range	NOV 01–08	NOV 09–16	NOV 17–24	NOV Total Obsn	NOV MCWB	DEC 01–08	DEC 09–16	DEC 17–24	DEC Total Obsn	DEC MCWB	JAN 01–08	JAN 09–16	JAN 17–24	JAN Total Obsn	JAN MCWB	FEB 01–08	FEB 09–16	FEB 17–24	FEB Total Obsn	FEB MCWB	MAR 01–08	MAR 09–16	MAR 17–24	MAR Total Obsn	MAR MCWB	APR 01–08	APR 09–16	APR 17–24	APR Total Obsn	APR MCWB	ANN 01–08	ANN 09–16	ANN 17–24	ANN Total Obsn	ANN MCWB
100/104																																1	0	1	62
95/99																																5	1	6	60
90/94																																54	15	69	58
85/89																															0	151	51	202	57
80/84																													0	52	3	197	81	281	56
75/79																											3	0	3	50	19	207	119	345	55
70/74																						0		0	48		11	2	13	48	61	208	167	436	53
65/69		1		1	47																0	3	1	4	45	0	20	6	26	46	130	196	205	531	52
60/64		8	0	8	44												2		2	44	0	8	2	10	43	1	24	10	35	44	206	186	203	595	50
55/59		17	2	19	42		1		1	41		0		0	42		5	1	6	42	0	13	4	17	42	4	25	18	47	42	249	179	204	632	47
50/54	3	26	10	39	39	1	7	1	9	39		4	0	4	39	1	11	3	15	39	1	20	8	29	39	11	31	25	67	40	250	184	201	635	43
45/49	13	37	22	72	37	2	22	5	29	37	1	17	3	21	36	3	22	8	33	37	5	30	16	51	37	20	31	33	84	38	248	224	213	685	39
40/44	31	38	36	105	34	12	35	18	65	34	7	33	13	53	33	14	30	20	64	34	16	35	30	81	34	34	32	37	103	36	287	245	250	782	36
35/39	39	29	41	109	32	32	45	38	115	31	25	42	37	104	31	21	31	29	81	31	29	34	40	103	32	47	24	38	109	33	300	230	274	804	32
30/34	42	27	39	108	28	43	47	48	138	28	38	38	43	119	27	26	31	33	90	28	46	35	40	121	28	54	19	32	105	30	309	209	264	782	28
25/29	40	20	34	94	25	41	35	44	120	24	39	30	39	108	24	37	33	37	107	24	41	27	38	106	25	40	16	24	80	25	259	166	228	653	25
20/24	31	16	18	65	21	41	23	33	97	20	38	28	34	100	20	43	23	33	99	20	40	22	28	90	21	21	4	12	37	20	222	117	161	500	20
15/19	15	11	15	41	16	34	16	25	75	16	29	17	24	70	15	30	15	19	72	16	29	11	18	58	16	8	0	2	10	16	148	70	112	330	16
10/14	11	5	9	25	11	16	7	16	39	11	22	12	18	52	11	20	9	13	42	11	18	4	11	33	11	1	0	0	1	12	88	37	67	192	11
5/9	7	2	6	15	7	10	5	11	26	7	17	8	11	36	6	11	4	8	23	6	9	4	5	18	7						54	23	41	118	6
0/4	5	1	4	10	2	8	2	5	15	2	10	7	7	24	1	7	4	5	16	2	6	2	4	12	2						36	16	25	77	2
-5/-1	2	1	2	5	-4	4	2	3	9	-3	8	5	8	21	-3	4	2	4	10	-3	4	1	2	7	-3						22	11	19	52	-3
-10/-6	2	0	1	3	-8	3	1	2	6	-8	5	5	4	14	-9	4	0	1	5	-8	3	1	0	4	-8						17	6	9	32	-8
-15/-11	0			0	-12	1	0	1	2	-13	4	2	4	10	-13	2	0	1	3	-13	1	0	0	1	-13						8	2	6	16	-13
-20/-16						1	0	0	1	-17	3	1	2	6	-18	0			0	-18	0	0	0	0	-17						4	1	2	7	-18
-25/-21						0	0	0	0	-24	2	1	0	3	-23																2	0	1	3	-23
-30/-26						0	0	0	0	-27	0	0	0	0	-27																0	0	0	0	-27

ROCK SPRINGS, WYOMING
LAT 41 36N   LONG 109 04W   ELEV 6745 FT

MEAN FREQUENCY OF OCCURRENCE OF DRY BULB TEMPERATURE (DEGREES F) WITH MEAN COINCIDENT WET BULB TEMPERATURE (DEGREES F) FOR EACH DRY BULB TEMPERATURE RANGE

Temperature Range	MAY 01–08	MAY 09–16	MAY 17–24	MAY Total Obsn	MAY MC WB	JUNE 01–08	JUNE 09–16	JUNE 17–24	JUNE Total Obsn	JUNE MC WB	JULY 01–08	JULY 09–16	JULY 17–24	JULY Total Obsn	JULY MC WB	AUGUST 01–08	AUGUST 09–16	AUGUST 17–24	AUGUST Total Obsn	AUGUST MC WB	SEPTEMBER 01–08	SEPTEMBER 09–16	SEPTEMBER 17–24	SEPTEMBER Total Obsn	SEPTEMBER MC WB	OCTOBER 01–08	OCTOBER 09–16	OCTOBER 17–24	OCTOBER Total Obsn	OCTOBER MC WB
95/99																														
90/94												0	0	0	59															
85/89		0	0	0	51		1	0	1	54		2	0	2	57		0	0	0	57										
80/84		1	0	1	52		5	1	6	53		23	7	30	55		10	3	13	55										
75/79		6	2	8	51	0	24	9	33	53	0	64	29	93	55	0	48	17	65	54		2	0	2	53		1		1	51
70/74		24	7	31	48	0	39	20	59	52	1	67	37	105	54	0	61	27	88	53		10	2	12	53		13	1	14	47
65/69	0	41	18	59	47	1	46	28	75	50	7	48	51	106	52	1	56	42	99	53		31	9	40	51		27	6	33	46
60/64	3	41	28	72	45	10	39	38	87	49	36	27	55	118	51	20	39	59	118	51		45	22	67	49	0	36	16	52	44
55/59	16	37	38	91	43	31	36	44	111	47	81	11	44	136	49	64	20	53	137	50	2	39	33	74	48	4	37	29	70	42
50/54	35	32	43	110	42	52	23	35	110	45	73	4	17	94	47	88	8	30	126	48	16	37	45	98	46	15	37	44	96	40
45/49	49	29	39	117	40	53	13	30	96	44	37	1	6	44	45	47	4	12	63	45	35	29	44	108	44	35	30	48	113	37
40/44	58	20	33	111	37	47	9	20	76	41	11	0	2	13	42	19	1	4	24	41	53	19	34	106	42	57	28	38	123	35
35/39	45	11	24	80	34	30	3	10	43	38	2	0	0	2	39	7	0	2	9	37	57	12	23	92	39	58	20	27	105	32
30/34	29	4	12	45	30	11	2	4	17	34	0		0	0	38	2	0	0	2	34	41	10	15	66	37	44	14	25	83	28
25/29	9	1	3	13	26	4	0	1	5	30						0			0	32	23	5	8	36	34	24	5	8	37	25
20/24	3	0	1	4	21	0	1	0	1	26											10	1	4	15	29	8	2	4	14	21
15/19	0	0		0	19																3	0	1	4	26	3	1	1	5	17
10/14	0			0	13																0			0	22	0			0	12

ROCK, SPRINGS WYOMING

Temperature Range	NOVEMBER Obsn Hour Gp 01 to 08	09 to 16	17 to 24	Total Obsn	MCWB	DECEMBER Obsn Hour Gp 01 to 08	09 to 16	17 to 24	Total Obsn	MCWB	JANUARY Obsn Hour Gp 01 to 08	09 to 16	17 to 24	Total Obsn	MCWB
95/99															
90/94															
85/89															
80/84															
75/79															
70/74															
65/69															
60/64		1		1	44										
55/59		7	0	7	41										
50/54		17	3	20	38		0	0	0	39		0		0	38
45/49	1	26	12	39	36	1	4	0	5	37		3		3	37
40/44	10	36	29	75	34	1	21	4	26	34	0	12	2	14	34
35/39	34	42	47	123	31	9	37	23	69	31	7	25	15	47	32
30/34	48	33	45	126	28	30	49	46	125	28	19	42	33	94	28
25/29	44	28	35	107	24	46	46	51	143	24	32	44	42	118	24
20/24	39	25	27	91	20	49	40	46	135	20	41	36	45	122	20
15/19	26	14	19	59	16	43	25	36	104	16	42	33	36	111	15
10/14	19	7	13	39	11	29	13	20	62	11	36	23	27	86	11
5/9	8	3	6	17	6	18	8	12	38	6	25	14	21	60	6
0/4	5	2	2	9	2	12	4	6	22	2	21	7	12	40	2
-5/-1	3	0	1	4	-3	5	2	3	10	-3	11	4	5	20	-3
-10/-6	1		0	1	-8	3	1	1	5	-8	7	4	3	14	-8
-15/-11			0	0	-12	2	0	0	2	-13	4	2	2	8	-13
-20/-16						0			0	-16	2	1	2	5	-18
-25/-21											1	0	0	1	-23
-30/-26											0	0	0	0	-27

Temperature Range	FEBRUARY Obsn Hour Gp 01 to 08	09 to 16	17 to 24	Total Obsn	MCWB	MARCH Obsn Hour Gp 01 to 08	09 to 16	17 to 24	Total Obsn	MCWB	APRIL Obsn Hour Gp 01 to 08	09 to 16	17 to 24	Total Obsn	MCWB
95/99															
90/94															
85/89															
80/84															
75/79															
70/74												1	0	1	47
65/69							0	0	0	43		9	2	11	45
60/64							2	0	2	41		21	7	28	43
55/59		0		0	44		5	1	6	40	1	29	14	44	40
50/54		3	1	4	40		12	4	16	38	6	34	24	64	38
45/49	0	9	2	11	37	1	19	8	28	36	15	33	33	81	36
40/44	2	19	9	30	34	4	31	19	54	33	33	36	40	109	34
35/39	12	35	24	71	32	18	41	36	95	31	45	34	41	120	31
30/34	26	39	41	106	28	43	44	49	136	28	53	26	39	118	28
25/29	37	38	39	114	24	49	38	46	133	24	45	14	24	83	25
20/24	43	32	39	114	20	46	28	38	112	20	31	4	13	48	20
15/19	36	23	29	88	16	38	17	24	79	16	10	0	2	12	17
10/14	25	12	18	55	11	25	6	14	45	11	1		0	1	12
5/9	17	7	12	36	6	13	2	5	20	7					
0/4	13	4	6	23	1	6	1	2	9	1					
-5/-1	6	2	3	11	-3	4	0	0	4	-3					
-10/-6	4	1	1	6	-8	0			0	-6					
-15/-11	2	0	0	2	-13										
-20/-16	0		0	0	-16										
-25/-21															
-30/-26															

Temperature Range	ANNUAL TOTAL Obsn Hour Gp 01 to 08	09 to 16	17 to 24	Total Obsn	MCWB
95/99		0		0	59
90/94		3	0	3	57
85/89		40	11	51	55
80/84	0	147	57	204	54
75/79	1	205	95	301	53
70/74	9	233	151	393	51
65/69	68	221	211	500	49
60/64	195	205	237	637	47
55/59	269	179	208	656	45
50/54	246	172	201	619	42
45/49	236	175	191	602	38
40/44	245	216	201	662	35
35/39	264	252	249	765	32
30/34	306	252	295	853	28
25/29	290	214	249	753	24
20/24	260	167	213	640	20
15/19	198	113	147	458	16
10/14	135	61	92	288	11
5/9	81	34	56	171	6
0/4	57	18	28	103	2
-5/-1	29	8	12	49	-3
-10/-6	15	6	5	26	-8
-15/-11	8	2	2	12	-13
-20/-16	2	1	2	5	-17
-25/-21	1	0	0	1	-23
-30/-26	0	0	0	0	-27

Section 1: INTRODUCTION

The tabulations and maps in the manual present design data for more than 1000 locations throughout the United States. Even with that large set of reference material there will be need for design data at many precise locations which are not identified specifically in the tables herein. To make reliable estimates, however, consideration must be given not only to the recorded variations between the states but also to the various factors that influence these variations. Some of the additional factors would include:

• Variation in wet bulb temperature due to elevation
• Variation in dry bulb temperature due to elevation
• Solar radiation
• Influence of terrain and adjacent operations
• Influence of vegetation
• Heat Islands

Even under the best conditions, design estimates made by direct transposition from the nearest location at which data is available to the point of installation may be in error. When accuracy is imperative, such as in installations involving large expenditures of money or critical temperature balance, further detailed studies are recommended.

Section 2: VARIATION IN WET BULB TEMPERATURE DUE TO ELEVATION

The rate of decrease in wet bulb temperatures will change with elevation for different ranges of temperatures. However, since most design summer wet bulb temperatures range between 60°F and 80°F , an approximate rate is one degree wet bulb temperature decrease for each 500-foot increase in elevation, all other factors being equal.

A variation of one degree wet bulb for each 400-foot change in height is approximately correct if the change in height is directly upward, as would be the case on the top of a building at a specific location.

Thus, a cooling tower located on the roof of a building 800 feet above the ground can safely have a design wet bulb temperature of two degrees less than the same cooling tower located on the ground. The mixing of air which takes place in the upper portions of the atmosphere allows the air to be more completely mixed 800 feet above the ground than it would be in the area along the earth's surface, where considerable moisture enters the atmosphere through evaporation and transpiration.

Section 3: VARIATION IN DRY BULB TEMPERATURE DUE TO ELEVATION

During higher wet bulb temperatures it is typical that the air mass will be quite moist near the earth's surface. Due to the high moisture content, clouds will form at relatively low levels because of the small lifting necessary to cool to a point of condensation. This point of condensation is generally visible in the form of the base of the clouds. Below the cloud base during the warmer part of the day the dry bulb temperature lapse rate is approximately 5.5°F per thousand-foot elevation. Although the local surroundings and type of surface material which can absorb solar radiation are highly important, an approximate rule can be used for dry bulb temperature variation. A decrease of 1°F in the dry bulb temperature for each 200 feet of elevation is reasonable.

Section 4: SOLAR RADIATION

Variations in solar radiation develop corresponding variations in both wet bulb and dry bulb temperatures.

If the entire earth's surface had an equal and abundant moisture supply to be picked up by the atmosphere and there were no large movements of air masses from north to south or south to north, the variation in both dry bulb and wet bulb temperatures would depend only on the sun angle and daylight duration. The hotter air in the low latitudes could evaporate and hold more moisture, and thus, dry bulb and wet bulb temperatures would be highest near the Equator and lowest near the poles. Under these conditions for any given period in the year the variation in solar influence could be measured on a scale of latitude.

Actually, however, the amount of solar radiation received near the ground at various locations throughout the land-covered surface of the earth is quite variable and does not resolve itself to a simple gradation of latitude. Cloud cover modifies the amount of solar radiation. Locations at high elevations receive proportionately higher quantities of solar radiation than locations near sea level.

By examining the average solar radiation received at a number of recording stations throughout the United States, it is possible to note the gradation in wet bulb design temperatures which would be due to the influence of solar radiation. The highest values occur in the arid Southwest where clear skies prevail during hot summer days, and the lowest values are found in the higher latitudes where cloud cover is greatest.

Section 5:   INFLUENCE OF TERRAIN AND ADJACENT OPERATIONS

When a cooling tower is located at a horizontal distance of ten times the height of surrounding buildings, its exposure to the wind can be considered as open. On the other hand, when a cooling tower is located near several taller structures, there will be a modification of the air flow. Should the higher building be in the direction of the prevailing wind (upwind from the cooling tower) during high wet bulb temperatures, there will be a corresponding decrease in the velocities of air moving past the cooling tower and a greater tendency for recirculation.

Other towers and industrial processes can often raise surrounding wet bulb temperatures. Towers located in valleys between ridges 200 feet high or higher, within one mile distance, can be expected to have downslope drainage of air during nighttime hours and upslope air motion during daylight hours. Since higher wet bulb temperatures occur during daylight hours, open exposure to upslope motion of air is desirable.

Section 6:   INFLUENCE OF VEGETATION

When a cooling tower is surrounded by dense vegetation it is to be expected that this will furnish a modifying influence in increasing the amount of moisture in the lower layers of the atmosphere. Although it is very difficult to estimate the variation in influence of this type of exposure, the contrast between a cooling tower located in a surrounding of dense foliage as compared to one located near the center of a one-mile square of non-evaporating surface is probably on the order of two degrees wet bulb temperature.

When a choice can be made it is preferred that the area immediately upwind from a cooling tower be a dry surface. If this is a dry surface area extending for approximately one-half mile it will be an area where greater reception of solar radiation will bring about vertical motion and a mixing of the lower layers of the atmosphere during the forenoon hours, thus reducing somewhat the ultimate peak wet bulb temperature.

Section 7:   HEAT ISLANDS

In major metropolitan areas, the quantity of heat released into and mixed with the air is sufficient to prevent minima temperatures from reaching the lower values which are recorded in nearby open terrain. This is an important factor in many major metropolitan areas throughout the United States. It has its greatest influence in modifying the design temperatures which might safely be used near the core of major metropolitan areas.

Table 19 presents comparative data for airport and city office records of monthly average minima temperatures. Most of the comparative data was taken from the 30-year period 1921 through 1950 while temperature observations were made at both city center and airport offices. Comparative data were not available for all major cities. These data give the approximate value of the "heat island" for each respective city. Using the monthly values does not portray the magnitude of the difference which can occur on extreme days. There have been many instances where variations of 10° or more were recorded.

Fig. 21 presents a hypothetical heat island pattern for the early morning hours over a hypothetical city. The city illustrated in Fig. 21 is located on a river. Under weather conditions capable of producing cold minima temperatures the winds would tend to be light or very light. Most of the airflow would be produced by drainage of colder air near the surface downslope. This colder air would penetrate toward the core of the built-up portion of the city. As air moves toward the core, it is heated more and more by the surrounding buildings.

The higher minimum temperature in the heat island decreases the daily range between the minimum and the maximum. If the minimum temperature in the heart of the city is two degrees warmer than it is at the airport, and the maximum temperature is the same at both, the daily range between the minimum and maximum will be decreased by these same two degrees in the heart of the city.

There is some evidence that air pollution over major metropolitan areas decreases slightly the maximum temperatures which are recorded.

For each particular city careful analysis is required to determine the magnitude and location of its own heat island. If large installations are planned, detailed analysis by professional personnel may be advisable.

TABLE 19   COMPARATIVE MONTHLY AVERAGE MINIMA TEMPERATURES

City	Coldest Month			Hottest Month		
	Airport	City Office	Diff.	Airport	City Office	Diff.
Los Angeles, CA	43.0°	45.4°	2.4°	61.3°	52.1°	.8°
Sacramento, CA	36.2	38.3	2.1	57.2	58.6	1.4
San Francisco, CA	41.7	45.5	3.8	53.8	53.9	.1
Denver, CO	16.8	21.6	4.8	59.4	62.1	2.7
Jacksonville, FL	54.5	48.7	3.3	72.9	73.9	1.0
Indianapolis, IA	20.5	23.4	2.9	64.1	67.7	3.6
Chicago, IL	18.9	20.9	2.0	65.7	66.7	1.0
Topeka, KS	18.6	20.8	2.1	67.7	69.4	1.7
Louisville, KY	26.3	27.9	1.7	66.6	69.3	2.7
New Orleans, LA	43.8	48.2	4.4	72.0	76.4	4.4
Baltimore, MD	25.3	30.4	5.1	66.4	70.7	4.3
Grand Rapids, MI	16.3	19.7	3.4	59.4	63.2	3.8
St. Louis, MO	23.5	25.8	2.3	68.9	71.6	2.7
Lincoln, NB	13.6	15.7	2.1	66.1	67.8	1.7
Albany, NY	14.4	18.0	3.6	60.5	63.9	3.4
Raleigh, NC	32.0	34.0	2.0	68.0	69.6	1.6
Cincinnati, OH	23.8	26.9	3.1	64.3	68.1	3.8
Cleveland, OH	20.9	23.0	2.1	62.6	66.5	3.9
Columbus, OH	21.6	23.9	2.3	62.6	65.8	3.2
Portland, OR	33.0	35.5	2.5	55.7	57.9	2.2
Erie, PA	20.1	22.3	2.2	60.1	64.9	4.8
Philadelphia, PA	25.4	28.7	3.3	66.0	69.0	3.0
Pittsburgh, PA	21.2	26.2	5.0	60.9	66.1	5.2
Providence, RI	20.6	23.0	2.4	61.9	64.4	2.5
Charleston, SC	39.3	43.6	4.3	71.0	75.0	4.0
Memphis, TN	32.9	34.5	1.6	71.3	73.2	1.9
Houston, TX	44.0	45.7	1.7	73.0	75.4	2.4
Seattle, WA	31.4	36.2	4.8	52.8	56.1	3.3
Salt Lake City, UT	17.0	21.1	4.1	60.8	64.7	3.9
Norfolk, VA	33.0	35.4	2.4	68.9	70.7	1.8

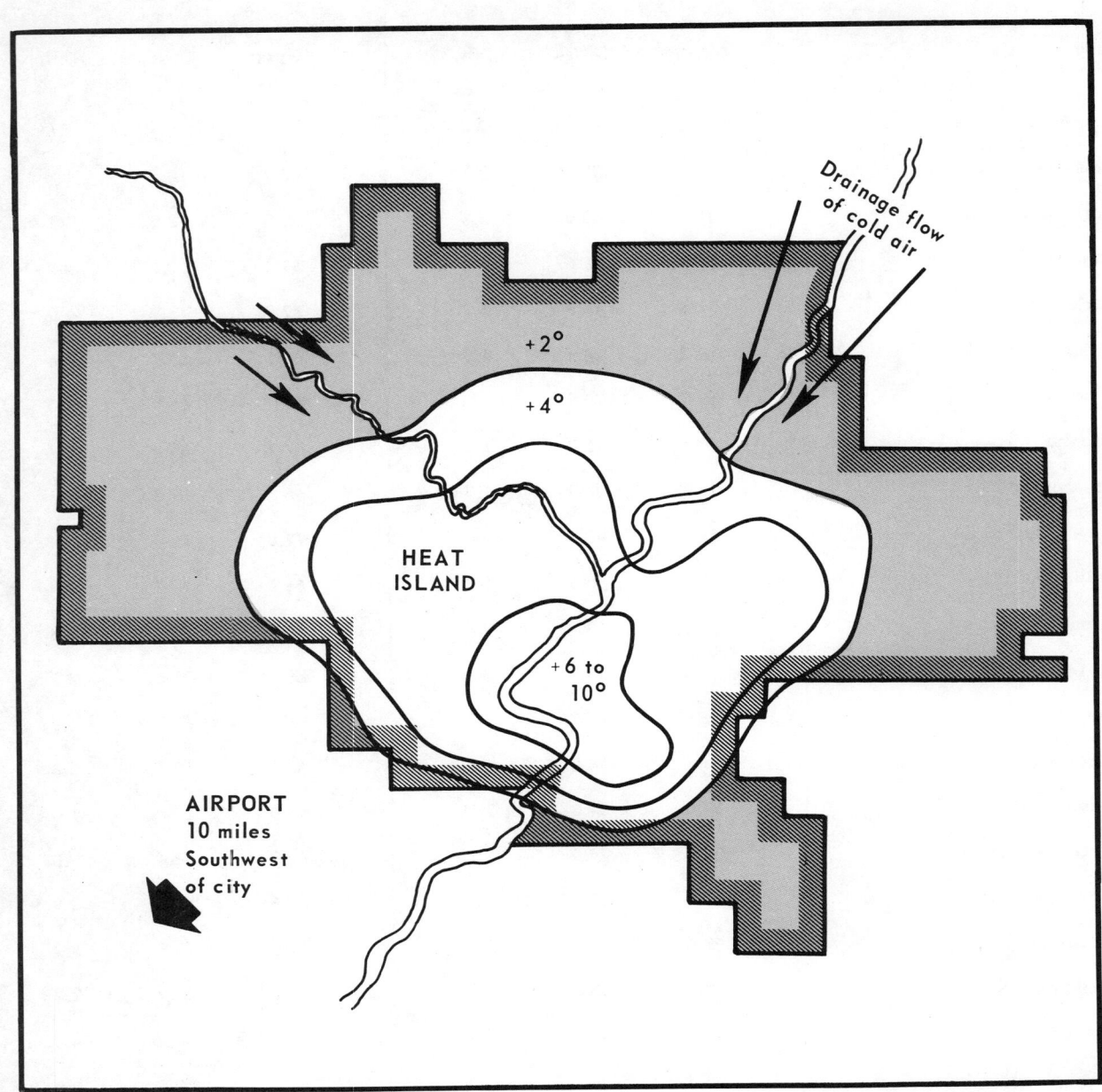

+2°
+4°
HEAT ISLAND
+6 to 10°

Drainage flow of cold air

AIRPORT 10 miles Southwest of city

Fig. 21.   A typical heat island of comparative minimum temperatures over a hypothetical city during early morning hours.